LONGER STORIES

FROM

THE LAST DECADE

ANTON CHEKHOV

LONGER STORIES FROM

FROM

THE LAST DECADE

EDITED, AND WITH AN INTRODUCTION
BY SHELBY FOOTE

TRANSLATED BY CONSTANCE GARNETT

THE MODERN LIBRARY

NEW YORK

2000 Modern Library Edition

Biographical note copyright © 1993 by Random House, Inc.
Compilation copyright © 1993 by Random House, Inc.
Introduction copyright © 1999 by Shelby Foote

All rights reserved under International and Pan-American Copyright Conventions.
Published in the United States by Random House, Inc., New York, and simultaneously
in Canada by Random House of Canada Limited, Toronto.

MODERN LIBRARY and colophon are registered trademarks of Random House, Inc.

LIBRARY OF CONGRESS CATALOGING-IN-PUBLICATION DATA
Chekhov, Anton Pavlovich, 1860–1904.
[Short stories. English. Selections]
Longer stories from the last decade/Anton Chekhov; selected, and with
an introduction, by Shelby Foote; translated by Constance Garnett
p.   cm.
ISBN 0-679-60663-7
1. Chekhov, Anton Pavlovich, 1860–1904—Translations into English.
I. Title. II. Garnett, Constance Black, 1862–1946. III. Foote, Shelby.
PG3456.A13G38 1999
891.73'3—dc21   99-45466

Modern Library website address: www.modernlibrary.com

Printed in the United States of America on acid-free paper

2 4 6 8 9 7 5 3

ANTON CHEKHOV

Anton Pavlovich Chekhov was born on January 17, 1860, in Taganrog, a small provincial port in southern Russia located on the Sea of Azov. His grandfather had been a serf who for 3,500 roubles had purchased the family's freedom. Chekhov's domineering father was a lower-middle-class bigot: a petty merchant who kept a grocery store, bullied his wife, and beat his six children. Although Anton Pavlovich's early life was monotonous and oppressive ("In my childhood there was no childhood," the writer recalled), he found his own strange way of compensating for the dismal atmosphere. Possessing a natural gift for clowning and mimicry, the boy delighted schoolmates with hilarious imitations of virtually everyone in the village. (Much as in his later stories, things for him were funny and sad at the same time, but you would not see their sadness if you did not see their fun, because both were linked up.)

Chekhov was sixteen when the family business failed and his father escaped debtors' prison by fleeing to Moscow. The young man's mother and siblings soon followed, but Anton Pavlovich remained behind to complete his education at the Taganrog Secondary School; three years later, in 1879, he joined them in Moscow and entered the medical faculty of Moscow University. During his university years Chekhov became the family's chief breadwinner: He supported them by writing stories, sketches, and parodies for humor magazines. All his early works were signed with pseudonyms, most frequently "Antosha Chekhonte." He completed medical school in 1884 and practiced medicine intermittently for several years while continuing to write. "Medicine is my lawful wife," Chekhov wrote to a friend, "and literature is my mistress. When I get fed up with one, I spend the night with the other. Though it is irregular, it is less boring this way, and besides, neither of them loses anything through my infidelity."

All the while, Chekhov's fiction continued to grow in depth and range. He published his first volume of stories, *Motley Stories*, in 1886; a year later he brought out his second collection, *In the Twilight*, for which he was awarded the Pushkin Prize for distinguished literary achievement by the Russian Academy. Fellow countryman Vladimir Nabokov perfectly explained Chekhov's appeal: "What really attracted the Russian reader was that in Chekhov's heroes he recognized the Russian idealist . . . a man who combined the deepest human decency of which man is capable with an almost ridiculous inability to put his ideals and principles into action; a man devoted to moral beauty, the welfare of his people, the welfare of the universe, but unable in his private life to do anything useful; frittering away his provincial existence in a haze of utopian dreams; knowing exactly what is good, what is worth while living for, but at the same time sinking lower and lower in the mud of a humdrum existence, unhappy in love, hopelessly inefficient in everything—a good man who cannot make good. This is the character that passes—in the guise of a doctor, a student, a village teacher, many other professional people—all through Chekhov's stories."

Despite the success of his literary career, Chekhov felt guilty about neglecting medicine. Moreover, he still owed a dissertation to obtain a full M.D. Partly to discharge this debt, partly for the sake of adventure, Chekhov in 1890 undertook an exhausting—and at times dangerous—six-thousand-mile journey (prerailroad) across Siberia to Sakhalin Island. There he made a thorough study of social, economic, and medical conditions, both of the Russian settlers (mostly convicts) and of native populations. Upon his return (by sea, via the Suez Canal) from this "descent into hell," circumstances quickly forced him back into medicine and public health service—first the terrible famine of 1891 and then the cholera epidemic that followed. In 1892 Chekhov bought a six-hundred-acre country estate near the village of Melihovo, where for the next five years he served as doctor to the local peasants and even helped build schools, while his literary output continued unabated.

The turn of the century witnessed a dramatic new phase in Chekhov's career. Between 1896 and 1903 he wrote the plays that established his reputation as one of the great dramatists of modern times: *The Sea Gull* (1896), *Uncle Vanya* (1897), *Three Sisters* (1901), and *The Cherry Orchard* (1904). However, in 1897 a massive pulmonary hemorrhage forced him finally to acknowledge that he was stricken with tuberculosis, an illness he had long concealed. For the remainder of his life, Chekhov was virtually a semi-invalid; he lived mostly in a villa at Yalta, his "warm Siberia" where he met Tolstoy and Gorky. In 1901 Chekhov married Olga Knipper, an actress with the Moscow Art Theater who had played the role of Irina in *The Sea Gull*.

Chekhov's last public appearance took place at the Moscow premiere of *The Cherry Orchard* on January 17, 1904, the playwright's forty-fourth birthday. Shaken with coughing, he was hardly able to stand and acknowledge a thunderous ovation. In June Chekhov was rushed to a health resort at Badenweiler in the Black Forest, where he died of consumption on July 2. His body was transported back to Moscow in a refrigerating car used for the transportation of oysters—a quirk of fate that no doubt he would have been amused to jot down in his notebook.

Contents

Introduction

by Shelby Foote

Anton Chekhov had a writing life of just under twenty-five years—from 1880, when he turned twenty as a medical student in Moscow, to 1904, when he died of tuberculosis in a Black Forest sanitorium. Within this span, in addition to four plays admired worldwide as modern classics, he wrote perhaps five hundred "stories," long and short—ranging from newspaper squibs and fillers to near-*Gatsby*-length novellas—which set the pattern for the short story in the century whose beginning was all he saw before his forty-four years were up.

On its eve, in 1899, under pressure from his publisher and the unrelenting need for money to sustain his generosity, he began selecting from his so-far six books of stories—together with a clutch of fugitive pieces that had appeared in various periodicals all the way back to his youth—a *Collected Works* whose ten volumes were released in the course of the next two years. They contained 240 stories in all, and another 196 were added in ten supplementary volumes after his death. Of these 436 stories, Constance Garnett* translated 188, and I have chosen 123 for inclusion in these three Modern Library volumes: volume I, seventy "early" stories, from 1883 to 1888, his breakthrough year when he received the Pushkin Prize; volume II, forty-two "later"

---

*I agree with V. S. Pritchett, who called her work "remarkable." Although he noted that "inaccuracies have been pounced on," he preferred her translations mainly, as he said, because "her voice is close to Chekhov's period." Moreover, it was she who passed his work on to Virginia Woolf, E. M. Forster, D. H. Lawrence, and H. E. Bates, as well as to practically every American short-story writer who, at one time or another, sat at his and her feet during the past eight decades.

stories, 1888 to 1903, containing most of his best-known work; and finally volume III, eleven "Longer Stories of the Last Decade," which I believe calls attention to a broader and deeper talent than has generally been recognized, either by critics or the reading public, down the years. Aside from his one full-length novel, an early experimental detective story of limited literary worth, nearly all the omitted stories are quite brief ones out of his journalistic youth. By way of summation, then, these three volumes include barely one fourth of his fiction titles, but they do contain, by page count, about three fourths of his output in that category—including all fifty-five of the great stories of his final fifteen years. All are printed here in the order in which they were written.

Few major writers have had fewer detractors regarding either their person or their work. A rare detractive exception is Ernest Hemingway, who enjoyed turning bumptious in his spare time; and in one such, in his middle twenties, referred to Chekhov as "an amateur writer" who "wrote about six good stories." Six is rather a large figure in the category of goodness, but I would put the number closer to one hundred, and so would many grateful practitioners of the art of the short story. Raymond Carver, for example: "Chekhov's stories are as wonderful (and necessary) now as when they first appeared. They present, in an extraordinarily precise manner, an unparalleled account of human activity and behavior in his time; and so they are valid for all time. Anyone who reads literature, anyone who believes, as one must, in the transcendent power of art, sooner or later has to read Chekhov." Or Elizabeth Hardwick: "The short stories of Chekhov are an inexhaustible treasury of humanity and wisdom. The naturalness of their form and the luminous simplicity of their turning away from the forced conclusion defined a large part of the modern tradition in short fiction." Or Cynthia Ozick: "Each story, no matter how allusive or broken-off, is nevertheless exhaustive—like the curve of a shard that implies not simply the form of the pitcher entire, but also the thirsts of its shattered civilization." Or John Barth: "Dr. Chekhov is a superb anatomist of the human heart and an utter master of his literary means. The details of scene and behavior, the emotions registered—seldom bravura, typically muted and complex, often as surprising to the characters themselves as to the reader, but always right—move, astonish, and delight us, line after line, story after story, volume after volume." Or William Maxwell: "It seems to be part of the human condition that a wall of glass separates one life from another. For Chekhov it did not exist. . . . The greatest of his stories are, no matter how many times reread, always an experience that strikes deep into the soul and produces an alteration there."

Little or none of this was the case at the start. "Oh, with what trash I began; my God, with what trash!" Chekhov declared later, looking back with amused dismay. Parodies, jokes, boutades, all limited to a thousand words by close-fisted editors, earned him the roubles needed to pay for his education and that of his two younger brothers and his sister, along with the support of two older brothers and his mother and bankrupt father. After half a dozen years of this, having received his license to practice medicine, he confessed to an established older novelist, who urged him to take his work seriously, that he had never spent more than a day on a story, and moreover had written them "the way reporters write notices of fires: mechanically, half-consciously, without caring a pin either about the reader or myself." Coincidentally, around this time, he combined a baleful definition with a hopeful prophecy: "The word newspaper-writer means, at the very least, a scoundrel. I am one of them; I work with them; I shake hands with them; I'm even told that I've begun to look like one. But I shan't die as one."

He didn't, of course, though in the process of transition that followed close on the heels of his confession, he underrated what he had gained from those half-dozen years of comic-writer apprenticeship. For one thing, the elderly novelist had noted his "feeling for the plastic," and, for another, the stipulated compression had encouraged him to develop what William Trevor later called "the art of the glimpse," a start-to-finish major component of his style. Moreover, there were, among those various humoristic bits and pieces, such things as "A Daughter of Albion," "The Fish," and "The Huntsman," which had drawn the elderly novelist's attention and admiration. And now there followed, with the help of Maupassant's Norman and Parisian tales and Turgenev's

Sportsman's Sketches, such things as "Anyuta," "Agafya," "The Chorus Girl," and "Vanka." Those came out in 1886. By then he had moved on to the so-called "thick journals," which paid better and, above all, gave him room to stretch his talent. The following year he produced a solid fifty stories, and "The Steppe"—at forty thousand words, the longest of his stories, called by Pritchett "a superb and sustained prose poem"—appeared in early 1888, followed by "Lights," which also broke new ground. By way of an upshot, he won the Pushkin Prize that year, along with the admiration of his fellow Russian writers, who two years before had mostly seen him, as he himself did, as a bits-and-pieces hack. He was clearly on his way.

That "way" has been marveled and wondered at by critics ever since, perhaps most successfully by his compatriot Vladimir Nabokov, who contrived to lift him to the skies by bringing him down to earth: "Chekhov managed to convey an impression of artistic beauty far surpassing that of writers who thought they knew what rich, beautiful prose was. He did it by keeping all his words in the same dim light of the same exact tint of gray, a tint between the color of an old fence and that of a low cloud. The variety of his moods, the flicker of his charming wit, the deeply artistic economy of characterization, the vivid detail, and the fade-out of human life—all peculiar Chekhovian features—are enhanced by being suffused and surrounded by a faintly iridescent verbal haziness." In simpler words Nabokov also defined a specific many Chekhov readers felt the force of down the years: "Things for him were funny and sad at the same time, but you would not see their sadness if you did not see their fun, because both were linked up." Chekhov himself pointed out something along this line, carried over from his early days, in advice to a fellow writer: "When you want to touch a reader's heart, try to be colder. It gives their grief, as it were, a background against which it stands out in greater relief." In much the same vein, he declared at another time: "Patients in a fever do not want food, but they do want something, and that vague craving they express as 'longing for something sour.' I want something sour."

For the most part, though, he kept his opinions and judgments to himself—especially in his fiction, where, as he said, he aimed not at solutions to problems but rather at their correct presentation. Walker Percy, a fellow physician-writer, called him a diagnostician, and in his choice of subjects for delineation he was guided by what Susan Sontag defined as "perfect moral pitch." As a result, there were those who, in the absence of didactic comments and summations in his work, accused him of having no philosophy of life. His friend Maxim Gorky found the charge absurd and such readers deaf and blind. "Often our ears can catch in his stories the melancholy but severe and deserved reproach that men do not know how to live. But at the same time, his sympathy with all men glows even brighter." Chekhov himself met the charge head-on, along with others by critics who fine-toothcombed his work in search of "convictions," whether political or religious: "I am afraid of those who look for a tendency between the lines and insist on seeing me as necessarily a liberal or a conservative. I am not a liberal, not a conservative, not a gradualist, not a monk, not an indifferentist. I should like to be a free artist and nothing more, and I regret that God has not given me the power to be one. . . . I regard trademarks and labels as prejudicial. My holy of holies is the human body, health, intelligence, talent, inspiration, love, and absolute freedom—freedom from force and falsehood."

His overriding subject was the Russia of his time and the failure of men of goodwill to find contentment, or even peace, from having exercised that goodwill all their lives. "We Russians of the educated class have a partiality for questions that remain unanswered," he observed. He later added: "To an educated Russian his past is always beautiful, his present a state of calamity." He seemed always to have to ponder things, turning them over and over in his mind, as if in search not of an answer but of a new phrasing of the question. Once while abroad he was asked to write "an international story" set in the region, and he replied that he couldn't do it until he got back home, if at all. "I can write only from memory," he explained; "I never write directly from life. The subject must pass through the sieve of my memory, so that only what is important or typical remains, as on a filter."

He had a habit of expressing himself obliquely, as when he said of his portrait by an artist whose work he did not admire, "It smells of horseradish." And though he could be insightful—forty-odd years before the Holocaust, in the wake of the Dreyfus affair, he wrote to a friend a definition of anti-Semitism as "a fuel that reeks of the slaughterhouse"—he still could not abide the strained delivery of a "message" in a story or a novel. After reading *Uncle Tom's Cabin*, for example, he experienced "an unpleasant sensation which mortals feel after eating too many raisins or currants." He liked to be precise in a general way, as when he described "the genial expression of a man who has just said goodbye to his relatives and has had a good drink at parting." It is important in this depiction that the people are relatives and that the drink was a good one.

Similarly in a late story, "In the Ravine," a young woman loses her infant son to a sudden and painful death by scalding, and is comforted at the funeral dinner by a priest who, "lifting his fork on which there was a salted mushroom, said to her: 'Grieve not for the babe, for of such is the Kingdom of Heaven.' " The forked mushroom is very Chekhovian, and even more so are the words spoken earlier, in a quite different tone, by an old man who gave her a lift in his wagon while she was returning from the hospital, walking along the road at night with her dead baby wrapped in a quilt in her arms. "Never mind," he told her. "Yours is not the worst of sorrows. Life is long, there will be good and bad to come, there will be everything. Great is Mother Russia." Chekhov dealt in powerful iotas, such as a sidelong glance in his last story, "Betrothed," in which a young man "took off his hat, and his hair floated in the wind."

Consequential or inconsequential, such wonderments abound in the nearly two thousand pages of these three volumes. Moreover, like most good writers, his work is even better on rereading, since then you can better appreciate how he goes about getting where he's going. Often, after a stretch of such rereading, I wax enthusiastic beyond all bounds. (Like Hemingway, I sometimes play the fool, but in the opposite direction.) Walker Percy and I shared this reaction, and once, in the course of a discussion, I asked him if he had read "In the Ravine." He said he hadn't, and I said: "I'd rather have written 'In the Ravine' than *Moby-Dick*." His eyebrows rose at this, as well they might, but he went home and read that great last long story—in which all the author's talents seem to be gathered together as naturally as a hand closing into a fist—and wound up in a state of exaltation similar to my own. Echoing Nabokov on Chekhov's near-miraculous combination of the funny and the sad, he shook his head in wonder. "I don't know how it can be so pitiful and funny," he wrote me later. "I have to laugh out loud."

We saw clearly enough what this Russian master had done, but *how* he did it we could never really figure out—until finally we happened on the answer provided by Buffon in his mid-eighteenth-century *Discourse on Style*, which pronounces that "style is the man himself." We settled for that: Chekhov did it by being Chekhov. That was as close as we could come to a solution.

LONGER STORIES
FROM
THE LAST DECADE

The Duel

I

It was eight o'clock in the morning—the time when the officers, the local officials, and the visitors usually took their morning dip in the sea after the hot, stifling night, and then went into the pavilion to drink tea or coffee. Ivan Andreitch Laevsky, a thin, fair young man of twenty-eight, wearing the cap of a clerk in the Ministry of Finance and with slippers on his feet, coming down to bathe, found a number of acquaintances on the beach, and among them his friend Samoylenko, the army doctor.

With his big cropped head, short neck, his red face, his big nose, his shaggy black eyebrows and grey whiskers, his stout puffy figure and his hoarse military bass, this Samoylenko made on every newcomer the unpleasant impression of a gruff bully; but two or three days after making his acquaintance, one began to think his face extraordinarily good-natured, kind, and even handsome. In spite of his clumsiness and rough manner, he was a peaceable man, of infinite kindliness and goodness of heart, always ready to be of use. He was on familiar terms with every one in the town, lent every one money, doctored every one, made matches, patched up quarrels, arranged picnics at which he cooked *shashlik* and an awfully good soup of grey mullets. He was always looking after other people's affairs and trying to interest some one on their behalf, and was always delighted about something. The general opinion about him was that he was without faults of character. He had only two weaknesses: he was ashamed of his own good nature, and tried to disguise it by a surly expression and an assumed gruffness; and he liked his assistants and his soldiers to call him "Your Excellency," although he was only a civil councillor.

"Answer one question for me, Alexandr Daviditch," Laevsky

began, when both he and Samoylenko were in the water up to their shoulders. "Suppose you had loved a woman and had been living with her for two or three years, and then left off caring for her, as one does, and began to feel that you had nothing in common with her. How would you behave in that case?"

"It's very simple. 'You go where you please, madam'—and that would be the end of it."

"It's easy to say that! But if she has nowhere to go? A woman with no friends or relations, without a farthing, who can't work . . ."

"Well? Five hundred roubles down or an allowance of twenty-five roubles a month—and nothing more. It's very simple."

"Even supposing you have five hundred roubles and can pay twenty-five roubles a month, the woman I am speaking of is an educated woman and proud. Could you really bring yourself to offer her money? And how would you do it?"

Samoylenko was going to answer, but at that moment a big wave covered them both, then broke on the beach and rolled back noisily over the shingle. The friends got out and began dressing.

"Of course, it is difficult to live with a woman if you don't love her," said Samoylenko, shaking the sand out of his boots. "But one must look at the thing humanely, Vanya. If it were my case, I should never show a sign that I did not love her, and I should go on living with her till I died."

He was at once ashamed of his own words; he pulled himself up and said:

"But for aught I care, there might be no females at all. Let them all go to the devil!"

The friends dressed and went into the pavilion. There Samoylenko was quite at home, and even had a special cup and saucer. Every morning they brought him on a tray a cup of coffee, a tall cut glass of iced water, and a tiny glass of brandy. He would first drink the brandy, then the hot coffee, then the iced water, and this must have been very nice, for after drinking it his eyes looked moist with pleasure, he would stroke his whiskers with both hands, and say, looking at the sea:

"A wonderfully magnificent view!"

After a long night spent in cheerless, unprofitable thoughts which prevented him from sleeping, and seemed to intensify the darkness and sultriness of the night, Laevsky felt listless and shattered. He felt no better for the bathe and the coffee.

"Let us go on with our talk, Alexandr Daviditch," he said. "I won't make a secret of it; I'll speak to you openly as to a friend. Things are in a bad way with Nadyezhda Fyodorovna and me . . . a very bad way! Forgive me for forcing my private affairs upon you, but I must speak out."

Samoylenko, who had a misgiving of what he was going to speak about, dropped his eyes and drummed with his fingers on the table.

"I've lived with her for two years and have ceased to love her," Laevsky went on; "or, rather, I realised that I never had felt any love for her. . . . These two years have been a mistake."

It was Laevsky's habit as he talked to gaze attentively at the pink palms of his hands, to bite his nails, or to pinch his cuffs. And he did so now.

"I know very well you can't help me," he said. "But I tell you, because unsuccessful and superfluous people like me find their salvation in talking. I have to generalise about everything I do. I'm bound to look for an explanation and justification of my absurd existence in somebody else's theories, in literary types—in the idea that we, upper-class Russians, are degenerating, for instance, and so on. Last night, for example, I comforted myself by thinking all the time: 'Ah, how true Tolstoy is, how mercilessly true!' And that did me good. Yes, really, brother, he is a great writer, say what you like!"

Samoylenko, who had never read Tolstoy and was intending to do so every day of his life, was a little embarrassed, and said:

"Yes, all other authors write from imagination, but he writes straight from nature."

"My God!" sighed Laevsky; "how distorted we all are by civilisation! I fell in love with a married woman and she with me. . . . To begin with, we had kisses, and calm evenings, and vows, and Spencer, and ideals, and interests in common. . . . What a deception! We really ran away from her husband, but we lied to ourselves and made out that we ran away from the emptiness of the life of the educated class. We pictured our future like this: to begin with, in the Caucasus, while we were getting to know the people and the place, I would put on the Government uniform and enter the service; then at our leisure we would pick out a plot of ground, would toil in the sweat of our brow, would have a vineyard and a field, and so on. If you were in my place, or that zoologist of yours, Von Koren, you might live with Nadyezhda Fyodorovna for thirty years, perhaps, and might leave your heirs a rich vineyard and three thousand acres of maize; but I felt like a bankrupt from the first day. In the town you have insufferable heat, boredom, and no society; if you go out into the country, you fancy poisonous spiders, scorpions, or snakes lurking under every stone and behind every bush, and beyond the fields—mountains and the desert. Alien people, an alien country, a wretched form of civilisation—all that is not so easy, brother, as walking on the Nevsky Prospect in one's fur coat, arm-in-arm with Nadyezhda Fyodorovna, dreaming of the sunny South. What is needed here is a life and death struggle, and I'm not a fighting man. A wretched neurasthenic, an idle gentleman. . . . From the first day I knew that my dreams of a life of labour and of a vineyard were worthless. As for love, I ought to tell you that living with a woman who has read Spencer and has followed you to the ends of the earth is no more interesting than living with any Anfissa or Akulina. There's the same smell of ironing, of powder, and of medicines, the same curl-papers every morning, the same self-deception."

"You can't get on in the house without an iron," said Samoylenko, blushing at Laevsky's speaking to him so openly of a lady he knew. "You are out of humour to-day, Vanya, I notice. Nadyezhda Fyodorovna is a splendid woman, highly educated, and you are a man of the highest intellect. Of course, you are not married," Samoylenko went on, glancing round at the adjacent tables, "but that's not your fault; and besides . . . one ought to be above conventional prejudices and rise to the level of modern ideas. I believe in free love myself, yes. . . . But to my thinking, once you have settled together, you ought to go on living together all your life."

"Without love?"

"I will tell you directly," said Samoylenko. "Eight years ago there was an old fellow, an agent, here—a man of very great intelligence. Well, he used to say that the great thing in married life was patience. Do you hear, Vanya? Not love, but patience. Love cannot last long. You have lived two years in love, and now evidently your married life has reached the period when, in order to preserve equilibrium, so to speak, you ought to exercise all your patience. . . ."

"You believe in your old agent; to me his words are meaningless. Your old man could be a hypocrite; he could exercise himself in the virtue of patience, and, as he did so, look upon a person he did not love as an object indispensable for his moral exercises; but I have not yet fallen so low. If I want to exercise myself in patience, I will buy dumbbells or a frisky horse, but I'll leave human beings alone."

Samoylenko asked for some white wine with ice. When they had drunk a glass each, Laevsky suddenly asked:

"Tell me, please, what is the meaning of softening of the brain?"

"How can I explain it to you? . . . It's a disease in which the brain becomes softer . . . as it were, dissolves."

"Is it curable?"

"Yes, if the disease is not neglected. Cold douches, blisters. . . . Something internal, too."

"Oh! . . . Well, you see my position; I can't live with her: it is more than I can do. While I'm with you I can be philosophical about it and smile, but at home I lose heart completely; I am so utterly miserable, that if I were told, for instance, that I should have to live another month with her, I should blow out my brains. At the same time, parting with her is out of the question. She has no friends or relations; she cannot work, and neither she nor I have any money. . . . What could become of her? To whom could she go? There is nothing one can think of. . . . Come, tell me, what am I to do?"

"H'm! . . ." growled Samoylenko, not knowing what to answer. "Does she love you?"

"Yes, she loves me in so far as at her age and with her temperament she wants a man. It would be as difficult for her to do without me as to do without her powder or her curl-papers. I am for her an indispensable, integral part of her boudoir."

Samoylenko was embarrassed.

"You are out of humour to-day, Vanya," he said. "You must have had a bad night."

"Yes, I slept badly. . . . Altogether, I feel horribly out of sorts, brother. My head feels empty; there's a sinking at my heart, a weakness. . . . I must run away."

"Run where?"

"There, to the North. To the pines and the mushrooms, to people and ideas. . . . I'd give half my life to bathe now in some little stream in the province of Moscow or Tula; to feel chilly, you know, and then to stroll for three hours even with the feeblest student, and to talk and talk endlessly. . . . And the scent of the hay! Do you remember it? And in the evening, when one walks in the garden, sounds of the piano float from the house; one hears the train passing. . . ."

Laevsky laughed with pleasure; tears came into his eyes, and to cover them, without getting up, he stretched across the next table for the matches.

"I have not been in Russia for eighteen years," said Samoylenko. "I've forgotten what it is like. To my mind, there is not a country more splendid than the Caucasus."

"Vereshtchagin has a picture in which some men condemned to death are languishing at the bottom of a very deep well. Your magnificent Caucasus strikes me as just like that well. If I were offered the choice of a chimney-sweep in Petersburg or a prince in the Caucasus, I should choose the job of chimney-sweep."

Laevsky grew pensive. Looking at his stooping figure, at his eyes fixed dreamily at one spot, at his pale, perspiring face and sunken temples, at his bitten nails, at the slipper which had dropped off his heel, displaying a badly darned sock, Samoylenko was moved to pity, and probably because Laevsky reminded him of a helpless child, he asked:

"Is your mother living?"

"Yes, but we are on bad terms. She could not forgive me for this affair."

Samoylenko was fond of his friend. He looked upon Laevsky as a good-natured fellow, a student, a man with no nonsense about him, with whom one could drink, and laugh, and talk without reserve. What he understood in him he disliked extremely. Laevsky drank a great deal and at unsuitable times; he played cards, despised his work, lived beyond his means, frequently made use of unseemly expressions in conversation, walked about the streets in his slippers, and quarrelled with Nadyezhda Fyodorovna before other people—and Samoylenko did not like this. But the fact that Laevsky had once been a student in the Faculty of Arts, subscribed to two fat reviews, often talked so cleverly that only a few people understood him, was living with a well-educated woman—all this Samoylenko did not understand, and he liked this and respected Laevsky, thinking him superior to himself.

"There is another point," said Laevsky, shaking his head. "Only it is between ourselves. I'm concealing it from Nadyezhda Fyodorovna for the time. . . . Don't let it out before her. . . . I got a letter the day before yesterday, telling me that her husband has died from softening of the brain."

"The Kingdom of Heaven be his!" sighed Samoylenko. "Why are you concealing it from her?"

"To show her that letter would be equivalent to 'Come to church to be married.' And we should first have to make our relations clear. When she understands that we can't go on living together, I will show her the letter. Then there will be no danger in it."

"Do you know what, Vanya," said Samoylenko, and a sad and imploring expression came into his face, as though he were going to ask him about something very touching and were afraid of being refused. "Marry her, my dear boy!"

"Why?"

"Do your duty to that splendid woman! Her husband is dead, and so Providence itself shows you what to do!"

"But do understand, you queer fellow, that it is impossible. To marry without love is as base and unworthy of a man as to perform mass without believing in it."

"But it's your duty to."

"Why is it my duty?" Laevsky asked irritably.

"Because you took her away from her husband and made yourself responsible for her."

"But now I tell you in plain Russian, I don't love her!"

"Well, if you've no love, show her proper respect, consider her wishes. . . ."

" 'Show her respect, consider her wishes,' " Laevsky mimicked him. "As though she were some Mother Superior! . . . You are a poor psychologist and physiologist if you think that living with a woman one can get off with nothing but respect and consideration. What a woman thinks most of is her bedroom."

"Vanya, Vanya!" said Samoylenko, overcome with confusion.

"You are an elderly child, a theorist, while I am an old man in spite of my years, and practical, and we shall never understand one another. We had better drop this conversation. Mustapha!" Laevsky shouted to the waiter. "What's our bill?"

"No, no . . ." the doctor cried in dismay, clutching Laevsky's arm. "It is for me to pay. I ordered it. Make it out to me," he cried to Mustapha.

The friends got up and walked in silence along the sea-front. When they reached the boulevard, they stopped and shook hands at parting.

"You are awfully spoilt, my friend!" Samoylenko sighed. "Fate has sent you a young, beautiful, cultured woman, and you refuse the gift, while if God were to give me a crooked old woman, how pleased I should be if only she were kind and affectionate! I would live with her in my vineyard and . . ."

Samoylenko caught himself up and said:

"And she might get the samovar ready for me there, the old hag."

After parting with Laevsky he walked along the boulevard. When, bulky and majestic, with a stern expression on his face, he walked along the boulevard in his snow-white tunic and superbly polished boots, squaring his chest, decorated with the Vladimir cross on a ribbon, he was very much pleased with himself, and it seemed as though the whole world were looking at him with pleasure. Without turning his head, he looked to each side and thought that the boulevard was extremely well laid out; that the young cypress-trees, the eucalyptuses, and the ugly, anæmic palm-trees were very handsome and would in time give abundant shade; that the Circassians were an honest and hospitable people.

"It's strange that Laevsky does not like the Caucasus," he thought, "very strange."

Five soldiers, carrying rifles, met him and saluted him. On the right side of the boulevard the wife of a local official was walking along the pavement with her son, a schoolboy.

"Good-morning, Marya Konstantinovna," Samoylenko shouted to her with a pleasant smile. "Have you been to bathe? Ha, ha, ha! . . . My respects to Nikodim Alexandritch!"

And he went on, still smiling pleasantly, but seeing an assistant of the military hospital coming towards him, he suddenly frowned, stopped him, and asked:

"Is there any one in the hospital?"

"No one, Your Excellency."

"Eh?"

"No one, Your Excellency."

"Very well, run along. . . ."

Swaying majestically, he made for the lemonade stall, where sat a full-bosomed old Jewess, who gave herself out to be a Georgian, and said to her as loudly as though he were giving the word of command to a regiment:

"Be so good as to give me some soda-water!"

II

Laevsky's not loving Nadyezhda Fyodorovna showed itself chiefly in the fact that everything she said or did seemed to him a lie, or equivalent to a lie, and everything he read against women and love seemed to him to apply perfectly to himself, to Nadyezhda Fyodorovna and her husband. When he returned home, she was sitting at the window, dressed and with her hair done, and with a preoccupied face was drinking coffee and turning over the leaves of a fat magazine; and he thought the drinking of coffee was not such a remarkable event that she need put on a preoccupied expression over it, and that she had been wasting her time doing her hair in a fashionable style, as there was no one here to attract and no need to be attractive. And in the magazine he saw nothing but falsity. He thought she had dressed and done her hair so as to look handsomer, and was reading in order to seem clever.

"Will it be all right for me to go to bathe to-day?" she said.

"Why? There won't be an earthquake whether you go or not, I suppose. . . ."

"No, I only ask in case the doctor should be vexed."

"Well, ask the doctor, then; I'm not a doctor."

On this occasion what displeased Laevsky most in Nadyezhda Fyodorovna was her white open neck and the little curls at the back of her head. And he remembered that when Anna Karenin got tired of her husband, what she disliked most of all was his ears, and thought: "How true it is, how true!"

Feeling weak and as though his head were perfectly empty, he went into his study, lay down on his sofa, and covered his face with a handkerchief that he might not be bothered by the flies. Despondent and oppressive thoughts always about the same thing trailed slowly across his brain like a long string of waggons on a gloomy autumn evening, and he sank into a state of drowsy oppression. It seemed to him that he had wronged Nadyezhda Fyodorovna and her husband, and that it was through his fault that her husband had died. It seemed to him that he had sinned against his own life, which he had ruined, against the world of lofty ideas, of learning, and of work, and he conceived that wonderful world as real and possible, not on this sea-front with hungry Turks and lazy mountaineers sauntering upon it, but there in the North, where there were operas, theatres, newspapers, and all kinds of intellectual activity. One could only there—not here—be honest, intelligent, lofty, and pure. He accused himself of having no ideal, no guiding principle in life, though he had a dim understanding now what it meant. Two years before, when he fell in love with Nadyezhda Fyodorovna, it seemed to him that he had only to go with her as his wife to the Caucasus, and he would be saved from vulgarity and emptiness; in the same way now, he was convinced that he had only to part from Nadyezhda Fyodorovna and to go to Petersburg, and he would get everything he wanted.

"Run away," he muttered to himself, sitting up and biting his nails. "Run away!"

He pictured in his imagination how he would go aboard the steamer and then would have some lunch, would drink some cold beer, would talk on deck with ladies, then would get into the train at Sevastopol and set off. Hurrah for freedom! One station after another would flash by, the air would keep growing colder and keener, then the birches and the fir-trees, then Kursk, Moscow. . . .

In the restaurants cabbage soup, mutton with kasha, sturgeon, beer, no more Asiaticism, but Russia, real Russia. The passengers in the train would talk about trade, new singers, the Franco-Russian *entente*; on all sides there would be the feeling of keen, cultured, intellectual, eager life. . . . Hasten on, on! At last Nevsky Prospect, and Great Morskaya Street, and then Kovensky Place, where he used to live at one time when he was a student, the dear grey sky, the drizzling rain, the drenched cabmen. . . .

"Ivan Andreitch!" some one called from the next room. "Are you at home?"

"I'm here," Laevsky responded. "What do you want?"

"Papers."

Laevsky got up languidly, feeling giddy, walked into the other room, yawning and shuffling with his slippers. There, at the open window that looked into the street, stood one of his young fellow-clerks, laying out some government documents on the window-sill.

"One minute, my dear fellow," Laevsky said softly, and he went to look for the ink; returning to the window, he signed the papers without looking at them, and said: "It's hot!"

"Yes. Are you coming to-day?"

"I don't think so. . . . I'm not quite well. Tell Sheshkovsky that I will come and see him after dinner."

The clerk went away. Laevsky lay down on his sofa again and began thinking:

"And so I must weigh all the circumstances and reflect on them. Before I go away from here I ought to pay up my debts. I owe about two thousand roubles. I have no money. . . . Of course, that's not important; I shall pay part now, somehow, and I shall send the rest, later, from Petersburg. The chief point is Nadyezhda Fyodorovna. . . . First of all we must define our relations. . . . Yes."

A little later he was considering whether it would not be better to go to Samoylenko for advice.

"I might go," he thought, "but what use would there be in it? I shall only say something inappropriate about boudoirs, about women, about what is honest or dishonest. What's the use of talking about what is honest or dishonest, if I must make haste to save my life, if I am suffocating in this cursed slavery and am killing myself? . . . One must realise at last that to go on leading the life I do is something so base and so cruel that everything else seems petty and trivial beside it. To run away," he muttered, sitting down, "to run away."

The deserted seashore, the insatiable heat, and the monotony of the smoky lilac mountains, ever the same and silent, everlastingly solitary, overwhelmed him with depression, and, as it were, made him drowsy and sapped his energy. He was perhaps very clever, talented, remarkably honest; perhaps if the sea and the mountains had not closed him in on all sides, he might have become an excellent Zemstvo leader, a statesman, an orator, a political writer, a saint. Who knows? If so, was it not stupid to argue whether it were honest or dishonest when a gifted and useful man—an artist or musician, for instance—to escape from prison, breaks a wall and deceives his jailers? Anything is honest when a man is in such a position.

At two o'clock Laevsky and Nadyezhda Fyodorovna sat down to dinner. When the cook gave them rice and tomato soup, Laevsky said:

"The same thing every day. Why not have cabbage soup?"

"There are no cabbages."

"It's strange. Samoylenko has cabbage soup and Marya Konstantinovna has cabbage soup, and only I am obliged to eat this mawkish mess. We can't go on like this, darling."

As is common with the vast majority of husbands and wives, not a single dinner had in earlier days passed without scenes and fault-finding between Nadyezhda Fyodorovna and Laevsky; but ever since Laevsky had made up his mind that he did not love her, he had tried to give way to Nadyezhda Fyodorovna in everything, spoke to her gently and politely, smiled, and called her "darling."

"This soup tastes like liquorice," he said, smiling; he made an effort to control himself and seem amiable, but could not refrain from saying: "Nobody looks after the housekeeping. . . . If you are too ill or busy with reading, let me look after the cooking."

In earlier days she would have said to him, "Do by all means," or, "I see you want to turn me into a cook"; but now she only looked at him timidly and flushed crimson.

"Well, how do you feel to-day?" he asked kindly.

"I am all right to-day. There is nothing but a little weakness."

"You must take care of yourself, darling. I am awfully anxious about you."

Nadyezhda Fyodorovna was ill in some way. Samoylenko said she had intermittent fever, and gave her quinine; the other doctor, Ustimovitch, a tall, lean, unsociable man, who used to sit at home in the daytime, and in the evenings walk slowly up and down on the sea-front coughing, with his hands folded behind him and a cane stretched along his back, was of the opinion that she had a female complaint, and prescribed warm compresses. In old days, when Laevsky loved her, Nadyezhda Fyodorovna's illness had excited his pity and terror; now he saw falsity even in her illness. Her yellow, sleepy face, her lustreless eyes, her apathetic expression, and the yawning that always followed her attacks of fever, and the fact that during them she lay under a shawl and looked more like a boy than a woman, and that it was close and stuffy in her room—all this, in his opinion, destroyed the illusion and was an argument against love and marriage.

The next dish given him was spinach with hard-boiled eggs, while Nadyezhda Fyodorovna, as an invalid, had jelly and milk. When with a preoccupied face she touched the jelly with a spoon and then began languidly eating it, sipping milk, and he heard her swallowing, he was possessed by such an overwhelming aversion that it made his head tingle. He recognised that such a feeling would be an insult even to a dog, but he was angry, not with himself but with Nadyezhda Fyodorovna, for arousing such a feeling, and he understood why lovers sometimes murder their mistresses. He would not murder her, of course, but if he had been on a jury now, he would have acquitted the murderer.

"Merci, darling," he said after dinner, and kissed Nadyezhda Fyodorovna on the forehead.

Going back into his study, he spent five minutes in walking to and fro, looking at his boots; then he sat down on his sofa and muttered:

"Run away, run away! We must define the position and run away!"

He lay down on the sofa and recalled again that Nadyezhda Fyodorovna's husband had died, perhaps, by his fault.

"To blame a man for loving a woman, or ceasing to love a woman, is stupid," he persuaded himself, lying down and raising his legs in order to put on his high boots. "Love and hatred are not under our control. As for her husband, maybe I was in an indirect way one of the causes of his death; but again, is it my fault that I fell in love with his wife and she with me?"

Then he got up, and finding his cap, set off to the lodgings of his colleague, Sheshkovsky, where the Government clerks met every day to play *vint* and drink beer.

"My indecision reminds me of Hamlet," thought Laevsky on the way. "How truly Shakespeare describes it! Ah, how truly!"

III

For the sake of sociability and from sympathy for the hard plight of newcomers without families, who, as there was not an hotel in the town, had nowhere to dine, Dr. Samoylenko kept a sort of table d'hôte. At this time there were only two men who habitually dined with him: a young zoologist called Von Koren, who had come for the summer to the Black Sea to study the embryology of the medusa, and a deacon called Pobyedov, who had only just left the seminary and been sent to the town to take the duty of the old deacon who had gone away for a cure. Each of them paid twelve roubles a month for their dinner and supper, and Samoylenko made them promise to turn up at two o'clock punctually.

Von Koren was usually the first to appear. He sat down in the drawing-room in silence, and taking an album from the table, began attentively scrutinising the faded photographs of unknown men in full trousers and top-hats, and ladies in crinolines and caps. Samoylenko only remembered a few of them by name, and of those whom he had forgotten he said with a sigh: "A very fine fellow, remarkably intelligent!" When he had finished with the album, Von Koren took a pistol from the whatnot, and screwing up his left eye, took deliberate aim at the portrait of Prince Vorontsov, or stood still at the looking-glass and gazed a long time at his swarthy face, his big forehead, and his black hair, which curled like a negro's, and his shirt of dull-coloured cotton with big flowers on it like a Persian rug, and the broad leather belt he wore instead of a waistcoat. The contemplation of his own image seemed to afford him almost more satisfaction than looking at photographs or playing with the pistols. He was very well satisfied with his face, and his becomingly clipped beard, and the broad shoulders, which were unmistakable evidence of his excellent health and physical strength. He was satisfied, too, with his stylish get-up, from the cravat, which matched the colour of his shirt, down to his brown boots.

While he was looking at the album and standing before the glass, at that moment, in the kitchen and in the passage near, Samoylenko, without his coat and waistcoat, with his neck bare, excited and bathed in perspiration, was bustling about the tables, mixing the salad, or making some sauce, or preparing meat, cucumbers, and onion for the cold soup, while he glared fiercely at the orderly who was helping him, and brandished first a knife and then a spoon at him.

"Give me the vinegar!" he said. "That's not the vinegar—it's the salad oil!" he shouted, stamping. "Where are you off to, you brute?"

"To get the butter, Your Excellency," answered the flustered orderly in a cracked voice.

"Make haste; it's in the cupboard! And tell Daria to put some fennel in the jar with the cucumbers! Fennel! Cover the cream up, gaping laggard, or the flies will get into it!"

And the whole house seemed resounding with his shouts. When

it was ten or fifteen minutes to two the deacon would come in; he was a lanky young man of twenty-two, with long hair, with no beard and a hardly perceptible moustache. Going into the drawing-room, he crossed himself before the ikon, smiled, and held out his hand to Von Koren.

"Good-morning," the zoologist said coldly. "Where have you been?"

"I've been catching sea-gudgeon in the harbour."

"Oh, of course. . . . Evidently, deacon, you will never be busy with work."

"Why not? Work is not like a bear; it doesn't run off into the woods," said the deacon, smiling and thrusting his hands into the very deep pockets of his white cassock.

"There's no one to whip you!" sighed the zoologist.

Another fifteen or twenty minutes passed and they were not called to dinner, and they could still hear the orderly running into the kitchen and back again, noisily treading with his boots, and Samoylenko shouting:

"Put it on the table! Where are your wits? Wash it first."

The famished deacon and Von Koren began tapping on the floor with their heels, expressing in this way their impatience like the audience at a theatre. At last the door opened and the harassed orderly announced that dinner was ready! In the dining-room they were met by Samoylenko, crimson in the face, wrathful, perspiring from the heat of the kitchen; he looked at them furiously, and with an expression of horror, took the lid off the soup tureen and helped each of them to a plateful; and only when he was convinced that they were eating it with relish and liked it, he gave a sigh of relief and settled himself in his deep arm-chair. His face looked blissful and his eyes grew moist. . . . He deliberately poured himself out a glass of vodka and said:

"To the health of the younger generation."

After his conversation with Laevsky, from early morning till dinner Samoylenko had been conscious of a load at his heart, although he was in the best of humours; he felt sorry for Laevsky and wanted to help him. After drinking a glass of vodka before the soup, he heaved a sigh and said:

"I saw Vanya Laevsky to-day. He is having a hard time of it, poor fellow! The material side of life is not encouraging for him, and the worst of it is all this psychology is too much for him. I'm sorry for the lad."

"Well, that is a person I am not sorry for," said Von Koren. "If that charming individual were drowning, I would push him under with a stick and say, 'Drown, brother, drown away.' . . ."

"That's untrue. You wouldn't do it."

"Why do you think that?" The zoologist shrugged his shoulders. "I'm just as capable of a good action as you are."

"Is drowning a man a good action?" asked the deacon, and he laughed.

"Laevsky? Yes."

"I think there is something amiss with the soup . . ." said Samoylenko, anxious to change the conversation.

"Laevsky is absolutely pernicious and is as dangerous to society as the cholera microbe," Von Koren went on. "To drown him would be a service."

"It does not do you credit to talk like that about your neighbour. Tell us: what do you hate him for?"

"Don't talk nonsense, doctor. To hate and despise a microbe is stupid, but to look upon everybody one meets without distinction as one's neighbour, whatever happens—thanks very much, that is equivalent to giving up criticism, renouncing a straightforward attitude to people, washing one's hands of responsibility, in fact! I consider your Laevsky a blackguard; I do not conceal it, and I am perfectly conscientious in treating him as such. Well, you look upon him as your neighbour—and you may kiss him if you like: you look upon him as your neighbour, and that means that your attitude to him is the same as to me and to the deacon; that is no attitude at all. You are equally indifferent to all."

"To call a man a blackguard!" muttered Samoylenko, frowning with distaste—"that is so wrong that I can't find words for it!"

"People are judged by their actions," Von Koren continued. "Now you decide, deacon. . . . I am going to talk to you, deacon. Mr. Laevsky's career lies open before you, like a long Chinese puzzle, and you can read it from beginning to end. What has he been doing these two years that he has been living here? We will reckon his doings on our fingers. First, he has taught the inhabitants of the town to play *vint:* two years ago that game was unknown here; now they all play it from morning till late at night, even the women and the boys. Secondly, he has taught the residents to drink beer, which was not known here either; the inhabitants are indebted to him for the knowledge of various sorts of spirits, so that now they can distinguish Kospelov's vodka from Smirnov's No. 21, blindfold. Thirdly, in former days, people here made love to other men's wives in secret, from the same motives as thieves steal in secret and not openly; adultery was considered something they were ashamed to make a public display of. Laevsky has come as a pioneer in that line; he lives with another man's wife openly. . . . Fourthly . . ."

Von Koren hurriedly ate up his soup and gave his plate to the orderly.

"I understood Laevsky from the first month of our acquaintance," he went on, addressing the deacon. "We arrived here at the same time. Men like him are very fond of friendship, intimacy, solidarity, and all the rest of it, because they always want company for *vint*, drinking, and eating; besides, they are talkative and must have listeners. We made friends—that is, he turned up every day, hindered me working, and indulged in confidences in regard to his mistress. From the first he struck me by his exceptional falsity, which simply made me sick. As a friend I pitched into him, asking him why he drank too much, why he lived beyond his means and got into debt, why he did nothing and read nothing, why he had so little culture and so little knowledge; and in answer to all my questions he used to smile bitterly, sigh, and say: 'I am a failure, a superfluous man'; or: 'What do you expect, my dear fellow, from us, the débris of the serf-owning class?' or: 'We are degenerate. . . .' Or he would begin a long rigmarole about Onyegin, Petchorin, Byron's Cain, and Bazarov, of whom he would say: 'They are our fathers in flesh and in spirit.' So we are to understand that it was not his fault that Government envelopes lay unopened in his office for weeks together, and that he drank and taught others to drink, but Onyegin, Petchorin, and Turgenev, who had invented the failure and the superfluous man, were responsible for it. The cause of his extreme dissoluteness and unseemliness lies, do you see, not in himself, but somewhere outside in space. And so—an ingenious idea!—it is not only he who is dissolute, false, and disgusting, but we . . . 'we men of the eighties,' 'we the spiritless, nervous offspring of the serf-owning class'; 'civilisation has crippled us' . . . in fact, we are to understand that such a great man as Laevsky is great even in his fall: that his dissoluteness, his lack of culture and of moral purity, is a phenomenon of natural history, sanctified by inevitability; that the causes of it are world-wide, elemental; and that we ought to hang up a lamp before Laevsky, since he is the fated victim of the age, of influences, of heredity, and so on. All the officials and their ladies were in ecstasies when they listened to him, and I could not make out for a long time what sort of man I had to deal with, a cynic or a clever rogue. Such types as he, on the surface intellectual with a smattering of education and a great deal of talk about their own nobility, are very clever in posing as exceptionally complex natures."

"Hold your tongue!" Samoylenko flared up. "I will not allow a splendid fellow to be spoken ill of in my presence!"

"Don't interrupt, Alexandr Daviditch," said Von Koren coldly; "I am just finishing. Laevsky is by no means a complex organism. Here is his moral skeleton: in the morning, slippers, a bathe, and coffee; then till dinner-time, slippers, a constitutional, and conversation; at two o'clock slippers, dinner, and wine; at five o'clock a bathe, tea and wine, then *vint* and lying; at ten o'clock supper and wine; and after midnight sleep and *la femme*. His existence is confined within this narrow programme like an egg within its shell. Whether he walks or sits, is angry, writes, rejoices, it may all be reduced to wine, cards, slippers, and women. Woman plays a fatal, overwhelming part in his life. He tells us himself that at thirteen he was in love; that when he was a student in his first year he was living with a lady who had a good influence over him, and to whom he was indebted for his musical education. In his second year he bought a prostitute from a brothel and raised her to his level—that is, took her as his kept mistress, and she lived with him for six months and then ran away back to the brothel-keeper, and her flight caused him much spiritual suffering. Alas! his sufferings were so great that he had to leave the university and spend two years at home doing nothing. But this was all for the best. At home he made friends with a widow who advised him to leave the Faculty of Jurisprudence and go into the Faculty of Arts. And so he did. When he had taken his degree, he fell passionately in love with his present . . . what's her name? . . . married lady, and was obliged to flee with her here to the Caucasus for the sake of his ideals, he would have us believe, seeing that . . . to-morrow, if not to-day, he will be tired of her and flee back again to Petersburg, and that, too, will be for the sake of his ideals."

"How do you know?" growled Samoylenko, looking angrily at the zoologist. "You had better eat your dinner."

The next course consisted of boiled mullet with Polish sauce. Samoylenko helped each of his companions to a whole mullet and poured out the sauce with his own hand. Two minutes passed in silence.

"Woman plays an essential part in the life of every man," said the deacon. "You can't help that."

"Yes, but to what degree? For each of us woman means mother, sister, wife, friend. To Laevsky she is everything, and at the same time nothing but a mistress. She—that is, cohabitation with her—is the happiness and object of his life; he is gay, sad, bored, disenchanted—on account of woman; his life grows disagreeable—woman is to blame; the dawn of a new life begins to glow, ideals turn up—and again look for the woman. . . . He only derives enjoyment from books and pictures in which there is woman. Our age is, to his thinking, poor and inferior to the forties and the sixties only because we do not know how to abandon ourselves obliviously to the passion and ecstasy of love. These voluptuaries must have in their brains a special growth of the nature of sarcoma, which stifles the brain and directs their whole psychology. Watch Laevsky when he is sitting anywhere in company. You notice: when one raises any general question in his presence, for instance, about the cell or instinct, he sits apart, and neither speaks nor listens; he looks languid and disillusioned; nothing has any interest for him, everything is vulgar and trivial. But as soon as you speak of male and female—for instance, of the fact that the female spider, after fertilisation, devours the male—his eyes glow with curiosity, his face brightens, and the man revives, in fact. All his thoughts, however noble, lofty, or neutral they may be, they all have one point of resemblance. You walk along the street with him and meet a donkey, for instance. . . . 'Tell me, please,' he asks, 'what would happen if you mated a donkey with a camel?' And his dreams! Has he told you of his dreams? It is magnificent! First, he dreams that he is married to the moon, then that he is summoned before the police and ordered to live with a guitar . . ."

The deacon burst into resounding laughter; Samoylenko frowned and wrinkled up his face angrily so as not to laugh, but could not restrain himself, and laughed.

"And it's all nonsense!" he said, wiping his tears. "Yes, by Jove, it's nonsense!"

IV

The deacon was very easily amused, and laughed at every trifle till he got a stitch in his side, till he was helpless. It seemed as though he only liked to be in people's company because there was a ridiculous side to them, and because they might be given ridiculous nicknames. He had nicknamed Samoylenko "the tarantula," his orderly "the drake," and was in ecstasies when on one occasion Von Koren spoke of Laevsky and Nadyezhda Fyodorovna as "Japanese monkeys." He watched people's faces greedily, listened without blinking, and it could be seen that his eyes filled with laughter and his face was tense with expectation of the moment when he could let himself go and burst into laughter.

"He is a corrupt and depraved type," the zoologist continued, while the deacon kept his eyes riveted on his face, expecting he would say something funny. "It is not often one can meet with such a nonentity. In body he is inert, feeble, prematurely old, while in intellect he differs in no respect from a fat shopkeeper's wife who does nothing but eat, drink, and sleep on a feather-bed, and who keeps her coachman as a lover."

The deacon began guffawing again.

"Don't laugh, deacon," said Von Koren. "It grows stupid, at last. I should not have paid attention to his insignificance," he went on, after waiting till the deacon had left off laughing; "I should have passed him by if he were not so noxious and dangerous. His noxiousness lies first of all in the fact that he has great success with women, and so threatens to leave descendants—that is, to present the world with a dozen Laevskys as feeble and as depraved as himself. Secondly, he is in the highest degree contaminating. I have spoken to you already of *vint* and beer. In another year or two he will dominate the whole Caucasian coast. You know how the mass, especially its middle stratum, believe in intellectuality, in a university education, in gentlemanly manners, and in literary language. Whatever filthy thing he did, they would all believe that it was as it should be, since he is an intellectual man, of liberal ideas and university education. What is more, he is a failure, a superfluous man, a neurasthenic, a victim of the age, and that means he can do anything. He is a charming fellow, a regular good sort, he is so genuinely indulgent to human weaknesses; he is compliant, accommodating, easy and not proud; one can drink with him and gossip and talk evil of people. . . . The masses, always inclined to anthropomorphism in religion and morals, like best of all the little gods who have the same weaknesses as themselves. Only think what a wide field he has for contamination! Besides, he is not a bad actor and is a clever hypocrite, and knows very well how to twist things round. Only take his little shifts and dodges, his attitude to civilisation, for instance. He has scarcely sniffed at civilisation, yet: 'Ah, how we have been crippled by civilisation! Ah, how I envy those savages, those children of nature, who know nothing of civilisation!' We are to understand, you see, that at one time, in ancient days, he has been devoted to civilisation with his whole soul, has served it, has sounded it to its depths, but it has exhausted him, disillusioned him, deceived him; he is a Faust, do you see? —a second Tolstoy. . . . As for Schopenhauer and Spencer, he treats them like small boys and slaps them on the shoulder in a fatherly way: 'Well, what do you say, old Spencer?' He has not read Spencer, of course, but how charming he is when with light, careless irony he says of his lady friend: 'She has read Spencer!' And they all listen to him, and no one cares to understand that this charlatan has not the right to kiss the sole of Spencer's foot, let alone speaking about him in that tone! Sapping the foundations of civilisation, of authority, of other people's altars, spattering them with filth, winking jocosely at them only to justify and conceal one's own rottenness and moral poverty is only possible for a very vain, base, and nasty creature."

"I don't know what it is you expect of him, Kolya," said Samoylenko, looking at the zoologist, not with anger now, but with a guilty air. "He is a man the same as every one else. Of course, he has his weaknesses, but he is abreast of modern ideas, is in the service, is of use to his country. Ten years ago there was an old fellow serving as agent here, a man of the greatest intelligence . . . and he used to say . . ."

"Nonsense, nonsense!" the zoologist interrupted. "You say he is in the service; but how does he serve? Do you mean to tell me that things have been done better because he is here, and the officials are more punctual, honest, and civil? On the contrary, he has only sanctioned their slackness by his prestige as an intellectual university man. He is only punctual on the 20th of the month, when he gets his salary;

on the other days he lounges about at home in slippers and tries to look as if he were doing the Government a great service by living in the Caucasus. No, Alexandr Daviditch, don't stick up for him. You are insincere from beginning to end. If you really loved him and considered him your neighbour, you would above all not be indifferent to his weaknesses, you would not be indulgent to them, but for his own sake would try to make him innocuous."

"That is?"

"Innocuous. Since he is incorrigible, he can only be made innocuous in one way. . . ." Von Koren passed his finger round his throat. "Or he might be drowned . . . ," he added. "In the interests of humanity and in their own interests, such people ought to be destroyed. They certainly ought."

"What are you saying?" muttered Samoylenko, getting up and looking with amazement at the zoologist's calm, cold face. "Deacon, what is he saying? Why—are you in your senses?"

"I don't insist on the death penalty," said Von Koren. "If it is proved that it is pernicious, devise something else. If we can't destroy Laevsky, why then, isolate him, make him harmless, send him to hard labour."

"What are you saying!" said Samoylenko in horror. "With pepper, with pepper," he cried in a voice of despair, seeing that the deacon was eating stuffed aubergines without pepper. "You with your great intellect, what are you saying! Send our friend, a proud intellectual man, to penal servitude!"

"Well, if he is proud and tries to resist, put him in fetters!"

Samoylenko could not utter a word, and only twiddled his fingers; the deacon looked at his flabbergasted and really absurd face, and laughed.

"Let us leave off talking of that," said the zoologist. "Only remember one thing, Alexandr Daviditch: primitive man was preserved from such as Laevsky by the struggle for existence and by natural selection; now our civilisation has considerably weakened the struggle and the selection, and we ought to look after the destruction of the rotten and worthless for ourselves; otherwise, when the Laevskys multiply, civilisation will perish and mankind will degenerate utterly. It will be our fault."

"If it depends on drowning and hanging," said Samoylenko,

"damnation take your civilisation, damnation take your humanity! Damnation take it! I tell you what: you are a very learned and intelligent man and the pride of your country, but the Germans have ruined you. Yes, the Germans! The Germans!"

Since Samoylenko had left Dorpat, where he had studied medicine, he had rarely seen a German and had not read a single German book, but, in his opinion, every harmful idea in politics or science was due to the Germans. Where he had got this notion he could not have said himself, but he held it firmly.

"Yes, the Germans!" he repeated once more. "Come and have some tea."

All three stood up, and putting on their hats, went out into the little garden, and sat there under the shade of the light green maples, the pear-trees, and a chestnut-tree. The zoologist and the deacon sat on a bench by the table, while Samoylenko sank into a deep wicker chair with a sloping back. The orderly handed them tea, jam, and a bottle of syrup.

It was very hot, thirty degrees Réaumur in the shade. The sultry air was stagnant and motionless, and a long spider-web, stretching from the chestnut-tree to the ground, hung limply and did not stir.

The deacon took up the guitar, which was constantly lying on the ground near the table, tuned it, and began singing softly in a thin voice:

" 'Gathered round the tavern were the seminary lads,' "

but instantly subsided, overcome by the heat, mopped his brow and glanced upwards at the blazing blue sky. Samoylenko grew drowsy; the sultry heat, the stillness and the delicious after-dinner languor, which quickly pervaded all his limbs, made him feel heavy and sleepy; his arms dropped at his sides, his eyes grew small, his head sank on his breast. He looked with almost tearful tenderness at Von Koren and the deacon, and muttered:

"The younger generation. . . . A scientific star and a luminary of the Church. . . . I shouldn't wonder if the long-skirted alleluia will be shooting up into a bishop; I dare say I may come to kissing his hand . . . Well . . . please God. . . ."

Soon a snore was heard. Von Koren and the deacon finished their tea and went out into the street.

"Are you going to the harbour again to catch sea-gudgeon?" asked the zoologist.

"No, it's too hot."

"Come and see me. You can pack up a parcel and copy something for me. By the way, we must have a talk about what you are to do. You must work, deacon. You can't go on like this."

"Your words are just and logical," said the deacon. "But my laziness finds an excuse in the circumstances of my present life. You know yourself that an uncertain position has a great tendency to make people apathetic. God only knows whether I have been sent here for a time or permanently. I am living here in uncertainty, while my wife is vegetating at her father's and is missing me. And I must confess my brain is melting with the heat."

"That's all nonsense," said the zoologist. "You can get used to the heat, and you can get used to being without the deaconess. You mustn't be slack; you must pull yourself together."

V

Nadyezhda Fyodorovna went to bathe in the morning, and her cook, Olga, followed her with a jug, a copper basin, towels, and a sponge. In the bay stood two unknown steamers with dirty white funnels, obviously foreign cargo vessels. Some men dressed in white and wearing white shoes were walking along the harbour, shouting loudly in French, and were answered from the steamers. The bells were ringing briskly in the little church of the town.

"To-day is Sunday!" Nadyezhda Fyodorovna remembered with pleasure.

She felt perfectly well, and was in a gay holiday humour. In a new loose-fitting dress of coarse thick tussore silk, and a big wide-brimmed straw hat which was bent down over her ears, so that her face looked out as though from a basket, she fancied she looked very charming. She thought that in the whole town there was only one young, pretty, intellectual woman, and that was herself, and that she was the only one who knew how to dress herself cheaply, elegantly, and with taste. That dress, for example, cost only twenty-two roubles, and yet how charming it was! In the whole town she was the only one who could be attractive, while there were numbers of men, so they must all, whether they would or not, be envious of Laevsky.

She was glad that of late Laevsky had been cold to her, reserved and polite, and at times even harsh and rude; in the past she had met all his outbursts, all his contemptuous, cold or strange incomprehensible glances, with tears, reproaches, and threats to leave him or to starve herself to death; now she only blushed, looked guiltily at him, and was glad he was not affectionate to her. If he had abused her, threatened her, it would have been better and pleasanter, since she felt hopelessly guilty towards him. She felt she was to blame, in the first place, for not sympathising with the dreams of a life of hard work, for the sake of which he had given up Petersburg and had come here to the Caucasus, and she was convinced that he had been angry with her of late for precisely that. When she was travelling to the Caucasus, it seemed that she would find here on the first day a cosy nook by the sea, a snug little garden with shade, with birds, with little brooks, where she could grow flowers and vegetables, rear ducks and hens, entertain her neighbours, doctor poor peasants and distribute little books amongst them. It had turned out that the Caucasus was nothing but bare mountains, forests, and huge valleys, where it took a long time and a great deal of effort to find anything and settle down; that there were no neighbours of any sort; that it was very hot and one might be robbed. Laevsky had been in no hurry to obtain a piece of land; she was glad of it, and they seemed to be in a tacit compact never to allude to a life of hard work. He was silent about it, she thought, because he was angry with her for being silent about it.

In the second place, she had without his knowledge during those two years bought various trifles to the value of three hundred roubles at Atchmianov's shop. She had bought the things by degrees, at one time materials, at another time silk or a parasol, and the debt had grown imperceptibly.

"I will tell him about it to-day . . . ," she used to decide, but at once reflected that in Laevsky's present mood it would hardly be convenient to talk to him of debts.

Thirdly, she had on two occasions in Laevsky's absence received a visit from Kirilin, the police captain: once in the morning when Laevsky had gone to bathe, and another time at midnight when he was playing cards. Remembering this, Nadyezhda Fyodorovna flushed crimson, and looked round at the cook as though she might overhear her thoughts. The long, insufferably hot, wearisome days, beautiful languorous evenings and stifling nights, and the whole manner of living, when from morning to night one is at a loss to fill up the useless hours, and the persistent thought that she was the prettiest young woman in the town, and that her youth was passing and being wasted, and Laevsky himself, though honest and idealistic, always the same, always lounging about in his slippers, biting his nails, and wearying her with his caprices, led by degrees to her becoming possessed by desire, and as though she were mad, she thought of nothing else day and night. Breathing, looking, walking, she felt nothing but desire. The sound of the sea told her she must love; the darkness of evening—the same; the mountains—the same. . . . And when Kirilin began paying her attentions, she had neither the power nor the wish to resist, and surrendered to him. . . .

Now the foreign steamers and the men in white reminded her for some reason of a huge hall; together with the shouts of French she heard the strains of a waltz, and her bosom heaved with unaccountable delight. She longed to dance and talk French.

She reflected joyfully that there was nothing terrible about her infidelity. Her soul had no part in her infidelity; she still loved Laevsky, and that was proved by the fact that she was jealous of him, was sorry for him, and missed him when he was away. Kirilin had turned out to be very mediocre, rather coarse though handsome; everything was broken off with him already and there would never be anything more. What had happened was over; it had nothing to do with any one, and if Laevsky found it out he would not believe in it.

There was only one bathing-house for ladies on the sea-front; men bathed under the open sky. Going into the bathing-house, Nadyezhda Fyodorovna found there an elderly lady, Marya Konstantinovna Bityugov, and her daughter Katya, a schoolgirl of fifteen; both of them were sitting on a bench undressing. Marya Konstantinovna was a good-natured, enthusiastic, and genteel person, who talked in a drawling and pathetic voice. She had been a governess until she was thirty-two, and then had married Bityugov, a Government official—a bald little man with his hair combed on to his temples and with a very meek disposition. She was still in love with him, was jealous, blushed at the word "love," and told every one she was very happy.

"My dear," she cried enthusiastically, on seeing Nadyezhda Fyodorovna, assuming an expression which all her acquaintances called
"almond-oily." "My dear, how delightful that you have come! We'll
bathe together—that's enchanting!"

Olga quickly flung off her dress and chemise, and began undressing her mistress.

"It's not quite so hot to-day as yesterday?" said Nadyezhda Fyodorovna, shrinking at the coarse touch of the naked cook. "Yesterday
I almost died of the heat."

"Oh, yes, my dear; I could hardly breathe myself. Would you
believe it? I bathed yesterday three times! Just imagine, my dear, three
times! Nikodim Alexandritch was quite uneasy."

"Is it possible to be so ugly?" thought Nadyezhda Fyodorovna,
looking at Olga and the official's wife; she glanced at Katya and
thought: "The little girl's not badly made."

"Your Nikodim Alexandritch is very charming!" she said. "I'm simply in love with him."

"Ha, ha, ha!" cried Marya Konstantinovna, with a forced laugh;
"that's quite enchanting."

Free from her clothes, Nadyezhda Fyodorovna felt a desire to fly.
And it seemed to her that if she were to wave her hands she would fly
upwards. When she was undressed, she noticed that Olga looked
scornfully at her white body. Olga, a young soldier's wife, was living
with her lawful husband, and so considered herself superior to her mistress. Marya Konstantinovna and Katya were afraid of her, and did not
respect her. This was disagreeable, and to raise herself in their opinion,
Nadyezhda Fyodorovna said:

"At home, in Petersburg, summer villa life is at its height now. My
husband and I have so many friends! We ought to go and see them."

"I believe your husband is an engineer?" said Marya Konstantinovna timidly.

"I am speaking of Laevsky. He has a great many acquaintances.
But unfortunately his mother is a proud aristocrat, not very intelligent. . . ."

Nadyezhda Fyodorovna threw herself into the water without finishing; Marya Konstantinovna and Katya made their way in after her.

"There are so many conventional ideas in the world," Nadyezhda
Fyodorovna went on, "and life is not so easy as it seems."

Marya Konstantinovna, who had been a governess in aristocratic families and who was an authority on social matters, said:

"Oh yes! Would you believe me, my dear, at the Garatynskys' I was expected to dress for lunch as well as for dinner, so that, like an actress, I received a special allowance for my wardrobe in addition to my salary."

She stood between Nadyezhda Fyodorovna and Katya as though to screen her daughter from the water that washed the former.

Through the open doors looking out to the sea they could see some one swimming a hundred paces from their bathing-place.

"Mother, it's our Kostya," said Katya.

"Ach, ach!" Marya Konstantinovna cackled in her dismay. "Ach, Kostya!" she shouted, "Come back! Kostya, come back!"

Kostya, a boy of fourteen, to show off his prowess before his mother and sister, dived and swam farther, but began to be exhausted and hurried back, and from his strained and serious face it could be seen that he could not trust his own strength.

"The trouble one has with these boys, my dear!" said Marya Konstantinovna, growing calmer. "Before you can turn round, he will break his neck. Ah, my dear, how sweet it is, and yet at the same time how difficult, to be a mother! One's afraid of everything."

Nadyezhda Fyodorovna put on her straw hat and dashed out into the open sea. She swam some thirty feet and then turned on her back. She could see the sea to the horizon, the steamers, the people on the sea-front, the town; and all this, together with the sultry heat and the soft, transparent waves, excited her and whispered that she must live, live. . . . A sailing-boat darted by her rapidly and vigorously, cleaving the waves and the air; the man sitting at the helm looked at her, and she liked being looked at. . . .

After bathing, the ladies dressed and went away together.

"I have fever every alternate day, and yet I don't get thin," said Nadyezhda Fyodorovna, licking her lips, which were salt from the bathe, and responding with a smile to the bows of her acquaintances. "I've always been plump, and now I believe I'm plumper than ever."

"That, my dear, is constitutional. If, like me, one has no constitutional tendency to stoutness, no diet is of any use. . . . But you've wetted your hat, my dear."

"It doesn't matter; it will dry."

Nadyezhda Fyodorovna saw again the men in white who were walking on the sea-front and talking French; and again she felt a sudden thrill of joy, and had a vague memory of some big hall in which she had once danced, or of which, perhaps, she had once dreamed. And something at the bottom of her soul dimly and obscurely whispered to her that she was a petty, common, miserable, worthless woman. . . .

Marya Konstantinovna stopped at her gate and asked her to come in and sit down for a little while.

"Come in, my dear," she said in an imploring voice, and at the same time she looked at Nadyezhda Fyodorovna with anxiety and hope; perhaps she would refuse and not come in!

"With pleasure," said Nadyezhda Fyodorovna, accepting. "You know how I love being with you!"

And she went into the house. Marya Konstantinovna sat her down and gave her coffee, regaled her with milk rolls, then showed her photographs of her former pupils, the Garatynskys, who were by now married. She showed her, too, the examination reports of Kostya and Katya. The reports were very good, but to make them seem even better, she complained, with a sigh, how difficult the lessons at school were now. . . . She made much of her visitor, and was sorry for her, though at the same time she was harassed by the thought that Nadyezhda Fyodorovna might have a corrupting influence on the morals of Kostya and Katya, and was glad that her Nikodim Alexandritch was not at home. Seeing that in her opinion all men are fond of "women like that," Nadyezhda Fyodorovna might have a bad effect on Nikodim Alexandritch too.

As she talked to her visitor, Marya Konstantinovna kept remembering that they were to have a picnic that evening, and that Von Koren had particularly begged her to say nothing about it to the "Japanese monkeys"—that is, Laevsky and Nadyezhda Fyodorovna; but she dropped a word about it unawares, crimsoned, and said in confusion:

"I hope you will come too!"

VI

It was agreed to drive about five miles out of town on the road to the south, to stop near a *duhan* at the junction of two streams—the Black

River and the Yellow River—and to cook fish soup. They started out soon after five. Foremost of the party in a char-à-banc drove Samoylenko and Laevsky; they were followed by Marya Konstanti-novna, Nadyezhda Fyodorovna, Katya and Kostya, in a coach with three horses, carrying with them the crockery and a basket with provisions. In the next carriage came the police captain, Kirilin, and the young Atchmianov, the son of the shopkeeper to whom Nadyezhda Fyodorovna owed three hundred roubles; opposite them, huddled up on the little seat with his feet tucked under him, sat Nikodim Alexandritch, a neat little man with hair combed on to his temples. Last of all came Von Koren and the deacon; at the deacon's feet stood a basket of fish.

"R-r-right!" Samoylenko shouted at the top of his voice when he met a cart or a mountaineer riding on a donkey.

"In two years' time, when I shall have the means and the people ready, I shall set off on an expedition," Von Koren was telling the deacon. "I shall go by the sea-coast from Vladivostok to the Behring Straits, and then from the Straits to the mouth of the Yenisei. We shall make the map, study the fauna and the flora, and make detailed geological, anthropological, and ethnographical researches. It depends upon you to go with me or not."

"It's impossible," said the deacon.

"Why?"

"I'm a man with ties and a family."

"Your wife will let you go; we will provide for her. Better still if you were to persuade her for the public benefit to go into a nunnery; that would make it possible for you to become a monk, too, and join the expedition as a priest. I can arrange it for you."

The deacon was silent.

"Do you know your theology well?" asked the zoologist.

"No, rather badly."

"H'm! . . . I can't give you any advice on that score, because I don't know much about theology myself. You give me a list of books you need, and I will send them to you from Petersburg in the winter. It will be necessary for you to read the notes of religious travellers, too; among them are some good ethnologists and Oriental scholars. When you are familiar with their methods, it will be easier for you to set to work. And you needn't waste your time till you get the books; come to me, and we will study the compass and go through a course of meteorology. All that's indispensable."

"To be sure . . ." muttered the deacon, and he laughed. "I was trying to get a place in Central Russia, and my uncle, the head priest, promised to help me. If I go with you I shall have troubled them for nothing."

"I don't understand your hesitation. If you go on being an ordinary deacon, who is only obliged to hold a service on holidays, and on the other days can rest from work, you will be exactly the same as you are now in ten years' time, and will have gained nothing but a beard and moustache; while on returning from this expedition in ten years' time you will be a different man, you will be enriched by the consciousness that something has been done by you."

From the ladies' carriage came shrieks of terror and delight. The carriages were driving along a road hollowed in a literally overhanging precipitous cliff, and it seemed to every one that they were galloping along a shelf on a steep wall, and that in a moment the carriages would drop into the abyss. On the right stretched the sea; on the left was a rough brown wall with black blotches and red veins and with climbing roots; while on the summit stood shaggy fir-trees bent over, as though looking down in terror and curiosity. A minute later there were shrieks and laughter again: they had to drive under a huge overhanging rock.

"I don't know why the devil I'm coming with you," said Laevsky. "How stupid and vulgar it is! I want to go to the North, to run away, to escape; but here I am, for some reason, going to this stupid picnic."

"But look, what a view!" said Samoylenko as the horses turned to the left, and the valley of the Yellow River came into sight and the stream itself gleamed in the sunlight, yellow, turbid, frantic.

"I see nothing fine in that, Sasha," answered Laevsky. "To be in continual ecstasies over nature shows poverty of imagination. In comparison with what my imagination can give me, all these streams and rocks are trash, and nothing else."

The carriages now were by the banks of the stream. The high mountain banks gradually grew closer, the valley shrank together and ended in a gorge; the rocky mountain round which they were driving had been piled together by nature out of huge rocks, pressing upon each other with such terrible weight, that Samoylenko could not help gasping every time he looked at them. The dark and beautiful mountain was cleft in places by narrow fissures and gorges from which came a breath of dewy moisture and mystery; through the gorges could be seen other mountains, brown, pink, lilac, smoky, or bathed in vivid sunlight. From time to time as they passed a gorge they caught the sound of water falling from the heights and splashing on the stones.

"Ach, the damned mountains!" sighed Laevsky. "How sick I am of them!"

At the place where the Black River falls into the Yellow, and the water black as ink stains the yellow and struggles with it, stood the Tatar Kerbalay's *duhan*, with the Russian flag on the roof and with an inscription written in chalk: "The Pleasant Duhan." Near it was a little garden, enclosed in a hurdle fence, with tables and chairs set out in it, and in the midst of a thicket of wretched thorn-bushes stood a single solitary cypress, dark and beautiful.

Kerbalay, a nimble little Tatar in a blue shirt and a white apron, was standing in the road, and, holding his stomach, he bowed low to welcome the carriages, and smiled, showing his glistening white teeth.

"Good-evening, Kerbalay," shouted Samoylenko. "We are driving on a little further, and you take along the samovar and chairs! Look sharp!"

Kerbalay nodded his shaven head and muttered something, and only those sitting in the last carriage could hear: "We've got trout, your Excellency."

"Bring them, bring them!" said Von Koren.

Five hundred paces from the *duhan* the carriages stopped. Samoylenko selected a small meadow round which there were scattered stones convenient for sitting on, and a fallen tree blown down by the storm with roots overgrown by moss and dry yellow needles. Here there was a fragile wooden bridge over the stream, and just opposite on the other bank there was a little barn for drying maize, standing on four low piles, and looking like the hut on hen's legs in the fairy tale; a little ladder sloped from its door.

The first impression in all was a feeling that they would never get out of that place again. On all sides wherever they looked, the mountains rose up and towered above them, and the shadows of evening were stealing rapidly, rapidly from the *duhan* and dark cypress, making the narrow winding valley of the Black River narrower and the mountains higher. They could hear the river murmuring and the unceasing chirrup of the grasshoppers.

"Enchanting!" said Marya Konstantinovna, heaving deep sighs of ecstasy. "Children, look how fine! What peace!"

"Yes, it really is fine," assented Laevsky, who liked the view, and for some reason felt sad as he looked at the sky and then at the blue smoke rising from the chimney of the *duhan*. "Yes, it is fine," he repeated.

"Ivan Andreitch, describe this view," Marya Konstantinovna said tearfully.

"Why?" asked Laevsky. "The impression is better than any description. The wealth of sights and sounds which every one receives from nature by direct impression is ranted about by authors in a hideous and unrecognisable way."

"Really?" Von Koren asked coldly, choosing the biggest stone by the side of the water, and trying to clamber up and sit upon it. "Really?" he repeated, looking directly at Laevsky. "What of 'Romeo and Juliet'? Or, for instance, Pushkin's 'Night in the Ukraine'? Nature ought to come and bow down at their feet."

"Perhaps," said Laevsky, who was too lazy to think and oppose him. "Though what is 'Romeo and Juliet' after all?" he added after a short pause. "The beauty of poetry and holiness of love are simply the roses under which they try to hide its rottenness. Romeo is just the same sort of animal as all the rest or us."

"Whatever one talks to you about, you always bring it round to . . ." Von Koren glanced round at Katya and broke off.

"What do I bring it round to?" asked Laevsky.

"One tells you, for instance, how beautiful a bunch of grapes is, and you answer: 'Yes, but how ugly it is when it is chewed and digested in one's stomach!' Why say that? It's not new, and . . . altogether it is a queer habit."

Laevsky knew that Von Koren did not like him, and so was afraid of him, and felt in his presence as though every one were constrained and some one were standing behind his back. He made no answer and walked away, feeling sorry he had come.

"Gentlemen, quick march for brushwood for the fire!" commanded Samoylenko.

They all wandered off in different directions, and no one was left but Kirilin, Atchmianov, and Nikodim Alexandritch. Kerbalay brought chairs, spread a rug on the ground, and set a few bottles of wine.

The police captain, Kirilin, a tall, good-looking man, who in all weathers wore his great-coat over his tunic, with his haughty deportment, stately carriage, and thick, rather hoarse voice, looked like a young provincial chief of police; his expression was mournful and sleepy, as though he had just been waked against his will.

"What have you brought this for, you brute?" he asked Kerbalay, deliberately articulating each word. "I ordered you to give us _kvarel_, and what have you brought, you ugly Tatar? Eh? What?"

"We have plenty of wine of our own, Yegor Alekseitch," Nikodim Alexandritch observed, timidly and politely.

"What? But I want us to have my wine, too; I'm taking part in the picnic and I imagine I have full right to contribute my share. I im-magine so! Bring ten bottles of _kvarel_."

"Why so many?" asked Nikodim Alexandritch, in wonder, knowing Kirilin had no money.

"Twenty bottles! Thirty!" shouted Kirilin.

"Never mind, let him," Atchmianov whispered to Nikodim Alexandritch; "I'll pay."

Nadyezhda Fyodorovna was in a light-hearted, mischievous mood; she wanted to skip and jump, to laugh, to shout, to tease, to flirt. In her cheap cotton dress with blue pansies on it, in her red shoes and the same straw hat, she seemed to herself, little, simple, light, ethereal as a butterfly. She ran over the rickety bridge and looked for a minute into the water, in order to feel giddy; then, shrieking and laughing, ran to the other side to the drying-shed, and she fancied that all the men were admiring her, even Kerbalay. When in the rapidly falling darkness the trees began to melt into the mountains and the horses into the carriages, and a light gleamed in the windows of the _duhan_, she climbed up the mountain by the little path which zigzagged between stones and thorn-bushes and sat on a stone. Down below, the camp-fire was burning. Near the fire, with his sleeves tucked up, the deacon was moving to and fro, and his long black shadow kept describing a circle round it; he put on wood, and with a spoon tied to a long stick he stirred the cauldron. Samoylenko, with a copper-red face, was fussing round the fire just as though he were in his own kitchen, shouting furiously:

"Where's the salt, gentlemen? I bet you've forgotten it. Why are you all sitting about like lords while I do the work?"

Laevsky and Nikodim Alexandritch were sitting side by side on the fallen tree looking pensively at the fire. Marya Konstantinovna, Katya, and Kostya were taking the cups, saucers, and plates out of the baskets. Von Koren, with his arms folded and one foot on a stone, was standing on a bank at the very edge of the water, thinking about something. Patches of red light from the fire moved together with the shadows over the ground near the dark human figures, and quivered on the mountain, on the trees, on the bridge, on the drying-shed; on the other side the steep, scooped-out bank was all lighted up and glimmering in the stream, and the rushing turbid water broke its reflection into little bits.

The deacon went for the fish which Kerbalay was cleaning and washing on the bank, but he stood still half-way and looked about him.

"My God, how nice it is!" he thought. "People, rocks, the fire, the twilight, a monstrous tree—nothing more, and yet how fine it is!"

On the further bank some unknown persons made their appearance near the drying-shed. The flickering light and the smoke from the camp-fire puffing in that direction made it impossible to get a full view of them all at once, but glimpses were caught now of a shaggy hat and a grey beard, now of a blue shirt, now of a figure, ragged from shoulder to knee, with a dagger across the body; then a swarthy young face with black eyebrows, as thick and bold as though they had been drawn in charcoal. Five of them sat in a circle on the ground, and the other five went into the drying-shed. One was standing at the door with his back to the fire, and with his hands behind his back was telling something, which must have been very interesting, for when Samoylenko threw on twigs and the fire flared up, and scattered sparks and threw a glaring light on the shed, two calm countenances with an expression on them of deep attention could be seen, looking out of the door, while those who were sitting in a circle turned round and began listening to the speaker. Soon after, those sitting in a circle began softly singing something slow and melodious, that sounded like Lenten Church music. . . . Listening to them, the deacon imagined how it would be with him in ten years' time, when he would come back from the expedition: he would be a young priest and monk, an author with a name and a splendid past; he would be consecrated an archimandrite, then a bishop; and he would serve mass in the cathedral; in a golden mitre he would come out into the body of the church with the ikon on his breast, and blessing the mass of the people with the triple and the double candelabra, would proclaim: "Look down from Heaven, O God, behold and visit this vineyard which Thy Hand has planted," and the children with their angel voices would sing in response: "Holy God. . . ."

"Deacon, where is that fish?" he heard Samoylenko's voice.

As he went back to the fire, the deacon imagined the Church procession going along a dusty road on a hot July day; in front the peasants carrying the banners and the women and children the ikons, then the boy choristers and the sacristan with his face tied up and a straw in his hair, then in due order himself, the deacon, and behind him the priest wearing his *calotte* and carrying a cross, and behind them, tramping in the dust, a crowd of peasants—men, women, and children; in the crowd his wife and the priest's wife with kerchiefs on their heads. The choristers sing, the babies cry, the corncrakes call, the lark carols. . . . Then they make a stand and sprinkle the herd with holy water. . . . They go on again, and then kneeling pray for rain. Then lunch and talk. . . .

"And that's nice too . . ." thought the deacon.

VII

Kirilin and Atchmianov climbed up the mountain by the path. Atchmianov dropped behind and stopped, while Kirilin went up to Nadyezhda Fyodorovna.

"Good-evening," he said, touching his cap.

"Good-evening."

"Yes!" said Kirilin, looking at the sky and pondering.

"Why 'yes'?" asked Nadyezhda Fyodorovna after a brief pause, noticing that Atchmianov was watching them both.

"And so it seems," said the officer, slowly, "that our love has withered before it has blossomed, so to speak. How do you wish me to understand it? Is it a sort of coquetry on your part, or do you look upon me as a nincompoop who can be treated as you choose."

"It was a mistake! Leave me alone!" Nadyezhda Fyodorovna said sharply, on that beautiful, marvellous evening, looking at him with terror and asking herself with bewilderment, could there really have been a moment when that man attracted her and had been near to her?

"So that's it!" said Kirilin; he thought in silence for a few minutes and said: "Well, I'll wait till you are in a better humour, and meanwhile I venture to assure you I am a gentleman, and I don't allow any one to doubt it. Adieu!"

He touched his cap again and walked off, making his way between the bushes. After a short interval Atchmianov approached hesitatingly.

"What a fine evening!" he said with a slight Armenian accent.

He was nice-looking, fashionably dressed, and behaved unaffectedly like a well-bred youth, but Nadyezhda Fyodorovna did not like him because she owed his father three hundred roubles; it was displeasing to her, too, that a shopkeeper had been asked to the picnic, and she was vexed at his coming up to her that evening when her heart felt so pure.

"The picnic is a success altogether," he said, after a pause.

"Yes," she agreed, and as though suddenly remembering her debt, she said carelessly: "Oh, tell them in your shop that Ivan Andreitch will come round in a day or two and will pay three hundred roubles. . . . I don't remember exactly what it is."

"I would give another three hundred if you would not mention that debt every day. Why be prosaic?"

Nadyezhda Fyodorovna laughed; the amusing idea occurred to her that if she had been willing and sufficiently immoral she might in one minute be free from her debt. If she, for instance, were to turn the head of this handsome young fool! How amusing, absurd, wild it would be really! And she suddenly felt a longing to make him love her, to plunder him, throw him over, and then to see what would come of it.

"Allow me to give you one piece of advice," Atchmianov said timidly. "I beg you to beware of Kirilin. He says horrible things about you everywhere."

"It doesn't interest me to know what every fool says of me," Nadyezhda Fyodorovna said coldly, and the amusing thought of playing with handsome young Atchmianov suddenly lost its charm.

"We must go down," she said; "they're calling us."

The fish soup was ready by now. They were ladling it out by platefuls, and eating it with the religious solemnity with which this is only done at a picnic; and every one thought the fish soup very good, and thought that at home they had never eaten anything so nice. As is always the case at picnics, in the mass of dinner napkins, parcels, useless greasy papers fluttering in the wind, no one knew where was his glass or where his bread. They poured the wine on the carpet and on their own knees, spilt the salt, while it was dark all round them and the fire burnt more dimly, and every one was too lazy to get up and put wood on. They all drank wine, and even gave Kostya and Katya half a glass each. Nadyezhda Fyodorovna drank one glass and then another, got a little drunk and forgot about Kirilin.

"A splendid picnic, an enchanting evening," said Laevsky, growing lively with the wine. "But I should prefer a fine winter to all this. 'His beaver collar is silver with hoar-frost.'"

"Every one to his taste," observed Von Koren.

Laevsky felt uncomfortable; the heat of the camp-fire was beating upon his back, and the hatred of Von Koren upon his breast and face: this hatred on the part of a decent, clever man, a feeling in which there probably lay hid a well-grounded reason, humiliated him and enervated him, and unable to stand up against it, he said in a propitiatory tone:

"I am passionately fond of nature, and I regret that I'm not a naturalist. I envy you."

"Well, I don't envy you, and don't regret it," said Nadyezhda Fyodorovna. "I don't understand how any one can seriously interest himself in beetles and ladybirds while the people are suffering."

Laevsky shared her opinion. He was absolutely ignorant of natural science, and so could never reconcile himself to the authoritative tone and the learned and profound air of the people who devoted themselves to the whiskers of ants and the claws of beetles, and he always felt vexed that these people, relying on these whiskers, claws, and something they called protoplasm (he always imagined it in the form of an oyster), should undertake to decide questions involving the origin and life of man. But in Nadyezhda Fyodorovna's words he heard a note of falsity, and simply to contradict her he said: "The point is not the ladybirds, but the deductions made from them."

VIII

It was late, eleven o'clock, when they began to get into the carriages to go home. They took their seats, and the only ones missing were Nadyezhda Fyodorovna and Atchmianov, who were running after one another, laughing, the other side of the stream.

"Make haste, my friends," shouted Samoylenko.

"You oughtn't to give ladies wine," said Von Koren in a low voice.

Laevsky, exhausted by the picnic, by the hatred of Von Koren, and by his own thoughts, went to meet Nadyezhda Fyodorovna, and when, gay and happy, feeling light as a feather, breathless and laughing, she took him by both hands and laid her head on his breast, he stepped back and said dryly:

"You are behaving like a . . . cocotte."

It sounded horribly coarse, so that he felt sorry for her at once. On his angry, exhausted face she read hatred, pity and vexation with himself, and her heart sank at once. She realised instantly that she had gone too far, had been too free and easy in her behaviour, and overcome with misery, feeling herself heavy, stout, coarse, and drunk, she got into the first empty carriage together with Atchmianov. Laevsky got in with Kirilin, the zoologist with Samoylenko, the deacon with the ladies, and the party set off.

"You see what the Japanese monkeys are like," Von Koren began, rolling himself up in his cloak and shutting his eyes. "You heard she doesn't care to take an interest in beetles and ladybirds because the people are suffering. That's how all the Japanese monkeys look upon people like us. They're a slavish, cunning race, terrified by the whip and the fist for ten generations; they tremble and burn incense only before violence; but let the monkey into a free state where there's no one to take it by the collar, and it relaxes at once and shows itself in its true colours. Look how bold they are in picture galleries, in museums, in theatres, or when they talk of science: they puff themselves out and get excited, they are abusive and critical . . . they are bound to criticise—it's the sign of the slave. You listen: men of the liberal professions are more often sworn at than pickpockets—that's because three-quarters of society are made up of slaves, of just such monkeys. It never happens that a slave holds out his hand to you and sincerely says 'Thank you' to you for your work."

"I don't know what you want," said Samoylenko, yawning; "the poor thing, in the simplicity of her heart, wanted to talk to you of scientific subjects, and you draw a conclusion from that. You're cross with him for something or other, and with her, too, to keep him company. She's a splendid woman."

"Ah, nonsense! An ordinary kept woman, depraved and vulgar.

Listen, Alexandr Daviditch; when you meet a simple peasant woman, who isn't living with her husband, who does nothing but giggle, you tell her to go and work. Why are you timid in this case and afraid to tell the truth? Simply because Nadyezhda Fyodorovna is kept, not by a sailor, but by an official."

"What am I to do with her?" said Samoylenko, getting angry. "Beat her or what?"

"Not flatter vice. We curse vice only behind its back, and that's like making a long nose at it round a corner. I am a zoologist or a sociologist, which is the same thing; you are a doctor; society believes in us; we ought to point out the terrible harm which threatens it and the next generation from the existence of ladies like Nadyezhda Ivanovna."

"Fyodorovna," Samoylenka corrected. "But what ought society to do?"

"Society? That's its affair. To my thinking the surest and most direct method is compulsion. *Manu militari* she ought to be returned to her husband; and if her husband won't take her in, then she ought to be sent to penal servitude or some house of correction ."

"Ouf!" sighed Samoylenko. He paused and asked quietly: "You said the other day that people like Laevsky ought to be destroyed. . . . Tell me, if you . . . if the State or society commissioned you to destroy him, could you . . . bring yourself to it?"

"My hand would not tremble."

IX

When they got home, Laevsky and Nadyezhda Fyodorovna went into their dark, stuffy, dull rooms. Both were silent. Laevsky lighted a candle, while Nadyezhda Fyodorovna sat down, and without taking off her cloak and hat, lifted her melancholy, guilty eyes to him.

He knew that she expected an explanation from him, but an explanation would be wearisome, useless and exhausting, and his heart was heavy because he had lost control over himself and been rude to her. He chanced to feel in his pocket the letter which he had been intending every day to read to her, and thought if he were to show her that letter now, it would turn her thoughts in another direction.

"It is time to define our relations," he thought. "I will give it her; what is to be will be."

He took out the letter and gave it her.

"Read it. It concerns you."

Saying this, he went into his own room and lay down on the sofa in the dark without a pillow. Nadyezhda Fyodorovna read the letter, and it seemed to her as though the ceiling were falling and the walls were closing in on her. It seemed suddenly dark and shut in and terrible. She crossed herself quickly three times and said:

"Give him peace, O Lord . . . give him peace. . . ."

And she began crying.

"Vanya," she called. "Ivan Andreitch!"

There was no answer. Thinking that Laevsky had come in and was standing behind her chair, she sobbed like a child, and said:

"Why did you not tell me before that he was dead? I wouldn't have gone to the picnic; I shouldn't have laughed so horribly. . . . The men said horrid things to me. What a sin, what a sin! Save me, Vanya, save me. . . . I have been mad. . . . I am lost. . . ."

Laevsky heard her sobs. He felt stifled and his heart was beating violently. In his misery he got up, stood in the middle of the room, groped his way in the dark to an easy-chair by the table, and sat down.

"This is a prison . . ." he thought. "I must get away. . . . I can't bear it."

It was too late to go and play cards; there were no restaurants in the town. He lay down again and covered his ears that he might not hear her sobbing, and he suddenly remembered that he could go to Samoylenko. To avoid going near Nadyezhda Fyodorovna, he got out of the window into the garden, climbed over the garden fence and went along the street. It was dark. A steamer, judging by its lights, a big passenger one, had just come in. . . . He heard the clank of the anchor chain. A red light was moving rapidly from the shore in the direction of the steamer: it was the Customs boat going out to it.

"The passengers are asleep in their cabins . . ." thought Laevsky, and he envied the peace of mind of other people.

The windows in Samoylenko's house were open. Laevsky looked in at one of them, then in at another; it was dark and still in the rooms.

"Alexandr Daviditch, are you asleep?" he called. "Alexandr Daviditch!"

He heard a cough and an uneasy shout:

"Who's there? What the devil?"

"It is I, Alexandr Daviditch; excuse me."

A little later the door opened; there was a glow of soft light from the lamp, and Samoylenka's huge figure appeared all in white, with a white nightcap on his head.

"What now?" he asked, scratching himself and breathing hard from sleepiness. "Wait a minute; I'll open the door directly."

"Don't trouble; I'll get in at the window. . . ."

Laevsky climbed in at the window, and when he reached Samoylenko, seized him by the hand.

"Alexandr Daviditch," he said in a shaking voice, "save me! I beseech you, I implore you. Understand me! My position is agonising. If it goes on for another two days I shall strangle myself like . . . like a dog."

"Wait a bit. . . . What are you talking about exactly?"

"Light a candle."

"Oh . . . oh! . . ." sighed Samoylenko, lighting a candle. "My God! My God! . . . Why, it's past one, brother."

"Excuse me, but I can't stay at home," said Laevsky, feeling great comfort from the light and the presence of Samoylenko. "You are my best, my only friend, Alexandr Daviditch. . . . You are my only hope. For God's sake, come to my rescue, whether you want to or not. I must get away from here, come what may! . . . Lend me the money!"

"Oh, my God, my God! . . . sighed Samoylenko, scratching himself. "I was dropping asleep and I hear the whistle of the steamer, and now you . . . Do you want much ?"

"Three hundred roubles at least. I must leave her a hundred, and I need two hundred for the journey. . . . I owe you about four hundred already, but I will send it you all . . . all. . . ."

Samoylenko took hold of both his whiskers in one hand, and standing with his legs wide apart, pondered.

"Yes . . ." he muttered, musing. "Three hundred. . . . Yes. . . . But I haven't got so much. I shall have to borrow it from some one."

"Borrow it, for God's sake!" said Laevsky, seeing from Samoylenka's face that he wanted to lend him the money and certainly would lend it. "Borrow it, and I'll be sure to pay you back. I will send it from Petersburg as soon as I get there. You can set your mind at rest about that. I'll tell you what, Sasha," he said, growing more animated; "let us have some wine."

"Yes . . . we can have some wine, too."

They both went into the dining-room.

"And how about Nadyezhda Fyodorovna?" asked Samoylenko, setting three bottles and a plate of peaches on the table. "Surely she's not remaining?"

"I will arrange it all, I will arrange it all," said Laevsky, feeling an unexpected rush of joy. "I will send her the money afterwards and she will join me. . . . Then we will define our relations. To your health, friend."

"Wait a bit," said Samoylenko. "Drink this first. . . . This is from my vineyard. This bottle is from Navaridze's vineyard and this one is from Ahatulov's. . . . Try all three kinds and tell me candidly. . . . There seems a little acidity about mine. Eh? Don't you taste it ?"

"Yes. You have comforted me, Alexandr Daviditch. Thank you. . . . I feel better."

"Is there any acidity ?"

"Goodness only knows, I don't know. But you are a splendid, wonderful man!"

Looking at his pale, excited, good-natured face, Samoylenko remembered Von Koren's view that men like that ought to be destroyed, and Laevsky seemed to him a weak, defenceless child, whom any one could injure and destroy.

"And when you go, make it up with your mother," he said. "It's not right."

"Yes, yes; I certainly shall."

They were silent for a while. When they had emptied the first bottle, Samoylenko said:

"You ought to make it up with Von Koren too. You are both such splendid, clever fellows, and you glare at each other like wolves."

"Yes, he's a fine, very intelligent fellow," Laevsky assented, ready now to praise and forgive every one. "He's a remarkable man, but it's impossible for me to get on with him. No! Our natures are too different. I'm an indolent, weak, submissive nature. Perhaps in a good minute I might hold out my hand to him, but he would turn away from me . . . with contempt."

Laevsky took a sip of wine, walked from corner to corner and went on, standing in the middle of the room:

"I understand Von Koren very well. His is a resolute, strong, despotic nature. You have heard him continually talking of 'the expedition,' and it's not mere talk. He wants the wilderness, the moonlit night: all around in little tents, under the open sky, lie sleeping his sick and hungry Cossacks, guides, porters, doctor, priest, all exhausted with their weary marches, while only he is awake, sitting like Stanley on a camp-stool, feeling himself the monarch of the desert and the master of these men. He goes on and on and on, his men groan and die, one after another, and he goes on and on, and in the end perishes himself, but still is monarch and ruler of the desert, since the cross upon his tomb can be seen by the caravans for thirty or forty miles over the desert. I am sorry the man is not in the army. He would have made a splendid military genius. He would not have hesitated to drown his cavalry in the river and make a bridge out of dead bodies. And such hardihood is more needed in war than any kind of fortification or strategy. Oh, I understand him perfectly! Tell me: why is he wasting his substance here? What does he want here?"

"He is studying the marine fauna."

"No, no, brother, no!" Laevsky sighed. "A scientific man who was on the steamer told me the Black Sea was poor in animal life, and that in its depths, thanks to the abundance of sulphuric hydrogen, organic life was impossible. All the serious zoologists work at the biological station at Naples or Villefranche. But Von Koren is independent and obstinate: he works on the Black Sea because nobody else is working there; he is at loggerheads with the university, does not care to know his comrades and other scientific men because he is first of all a despot and only secondly a zoologist. And you'll see he'll do something. He is already dreaming that when he comes back from his expedition he will purify our universities from intrigue and mediocrity, and will make the scientific men mind their ps and qs. Despotism is just as strong in science as in the army. And he is spending his second summer in this stinking little town because he would rather be first in a village than second in a town. Here he is a king and an eagle; he keeps all the inhabitants under his thumb and oppresses them with his authority. He has appropriated every one, he meddles in other people's affairs; everything is of use to him, and every one is afraid of him. I am slipping out of his clutches, he feels that and hates me. Hasn't he told you that I ought to be destroyed or sent to hard labour ?"

"Yes," laughed Samoylenko.

Laevsky laughed too, and drank some wine.

"His ideals are despotic too," he said, laughing, and biting a peach. "Ordinary mortals think of their neighbour—me, you, man in fact—if they work for the common weal. To Von Koren men are puppets and nonentities, too trivial to be the object of his life. He works, will go for his expedition and break his neck there, not for the sake of love for his neighbour, but for the sake of such abstractions as humanity, future generations, an ideal race of men. He exerts himself for the improvement of the human race, and we are in his eyes only slaves, food for the cannon, beasts of burden; some he would destroy or stow away in Siberia, others he would break by discipline, would, like Araktcheev, force them to get up and go to bed to the sound of the drum; would appoint eunuchs to preserve our chastity and morality, would order them to fire at any one who steps out of the circle of our narrow conservative morality; and all this in the name of the improvement of the human race. . . . And what is the human race? Illusion, mirage . . . despots have always been illusionists. I understand him very well, brother. I appreciate him and don't deny his importance; this world rests on men like him, and if the world were left only to such men as us, for all our good-nature and good intentions, we should make as great a mess of it as the flies have of that picture. Yes."

Laevsky sat down beside Samoylenko, and said with genuine feeling: "I'm a foolish, worthless, depraved man. The air I breathe, this wine, love, life in fact—for all that, I have given nothing in exchange so far but lying, idleness, and cowardice. Till now I have deceived myself and other people; I have been miserable about it, and my misery was cheap and common. I bow my back humbly before Von Koren's hatred because at times I hate and despise myself."

Laevsky began again pacing from one end of the room to the other in excitement, and said:

"I'm glad I see my faults clearly and am conscious of them. That will help me to reform and become a different man. My dear fellow, if only you knew how passionately, with what anguish, I long for such a change. And I swear to you I'll be a man! I will! I don't know whether it is the wine that is speaking in me, or whether it really is so, but it seems to me that it is long since I have spent such pure and lucid moments as I have just now with you."

"It's time to sleep, brother," said Samoylenko.

"Yes, yes. . . . Excuse me; I'll go directly."

Laevsky moved hurriedly about the furniture and windows, looking for his cap.

"Thank you," he muttered, sighing. "Thank you. . . . Kind and friendly words are better than charity. You have given me new life."

He found his cap, stopped, and looked guiltily at Samoylenko.

"Alexandr Daviditch," he said in an imploring voice.

"What is it?"

"Let me stay the night with you, my dear fellow!"

"Certainly. . . . Why not?"

Laevsky lay down on the sofa, and went on talking to the doctor for a long time.

X

Three days after the picnic, Marya Konstantinovna unexpectedly called on Nadyezhda Fyodorovna, and without greeting her or taking off her hat, seized her by both hands, pressed them to her breast and said in great excitement:

"My dear, I am deeply touched and moved: our dear kind-hearted doctor told my Nikodim Alexandritch yesterday that your husband was dead. Tell me, my dear . . . tell me, is it true?"

"Yes, it's true; he is dead," answered Nadyezhda Fyodorovna.

"That is awful, awful, my dear! But there's no evil without some compensation; your husband was no doubt a noble, wonderful, holy man, and such are more needed in Heaven than on earth."

Every line and feature in Marya Konstantinovna's face began quivering as though little needles were jumping up and down under her skin; she gave an almond-oily smile and said, breathlessly, enthusiastically:

"And so you are free, my dear. You can hold your head high now, and look people boldly in the face. Henceforth God and man will bless your union with Ivan Andreitch. It's enchanting. I am trembling with joy, I can find no words. My dear, I will give you away. . . . Nikodim Alexandritch and I have been so fond of you, you will allow us to give our blessing to your pure, lawful union. When, when do you think of being married?"

"I haven't thought of it," said Nadyezhda Fyodorovna, freeing her hands.

"That's impossible, my dear. You have thought of it, you have."

"Upon my word, I haven't," said Nadyezhda Fyodorovna, laughing. "What should we be married for? I see no necessity for it. We'll go on living as we have lived."

"What are you saying!" cried Marya Konstantinovna in horror. "For God's sake, what are you saying!"

"Our getting married won't make things any better. On the contrary, it will make them even worse. We shall lose our freedom."

"My dear, my dear, what are you saying!" exclaimed Marya Konstantinovna, stepping back and flinging up her hands. "You are talking wildly! Think what you are saying. You must settle down!"

" 'Settle down.' How do you mean? I have not lived yet, and you tell me to settle down."

Nadyezhda Fyodorovna reflected that she really had not lived. She had finished her studies in a boarding-school and had been married to a man she did not love; then she had thrown in her lot with Laevsky, and had spent all her time with him on this empty, desolate coast, always expecting something better. Was that life?

"I ought to be married though," she thought, but remembering Kirilin and Atchmianov she flushed and said:

"No, it's impossible. Even if Ivan Andreitch begged me to on his knees—even then I would refuse."

Marya Konstantinovna sat on the sofa for a minute in silence, grave and mournful, gazing fixedly into space; then she got up and said coldly:

"Good-bye, my dear! Forgive me for having troubled you. Though it's not easy for me, it's my duty to tell you that from this day all is over between us, and, in spite of my profound respect for Ivan Andreitch, the door of my house is closed to you henceforth."

She uttered these words with great solemnity and was herself overwhelmed by her solemn tone. Her face began quivering again; it assumed a soft almond-oily expression. She held out both hands to Nadyezhda Fyodorovna, who was overcome with alarm and confusion, and said in an imploring voice:

"My dear, allow me if only for a moment to be a mother or an elder sister to you! I will be as frank with you as a mother."

Nadyezhda Fyodorovna felt in her bosom warmth, gladness, and pity for herself, as though her own mother had really risen up and were standing before her. She impulsively embraced Marya Konstantinovna and pressed her face to her shoulder. Both of them shed tears. They sat down on the sofa and for a few minutes sobbed without looking at one another or being able to utter a word.

"My dear child," began Marya Konstantinovna, "I will tell you some harsh truths, without sparing you."

"For God's sake, for God's sake, do!"

"Trust me, my dear. You remember of all the ladies here, I was the only one to receive you. You horrified me from the very first day, but I had not the heart to treat you with disdain like all the rest. I grieved over dear, good Ivan Andreitch as though he were my son—a young man in a strange place, inexperienced, weak, with no mother; and I was worried, dreadfully worried. . . . My husband was opposed to our making his acquaintance, but I talked him over . . . persuaded him. . . . We began receiving Ivan Andreitch, and with him, of course, you. If we had not, he would have been insulted. I have a daughter, a son. . . . You understand the tender mind, the pure heart of childhood . . . 'whoso offendeth one of these little ones.'. . . I received you into my house and trembled for my children. Oh, when you become a mother, you will understand my fears. And every one was surprised at my receiving you, excuse my saying so, as a respectable woman, and hinted to me . . . well, of course, slanders, suppositions. . . . At the bottom of my heart I blamed you, but you were unhappy, flighty, to be pitied, and my heart was wrung with pity for you."

"But why, why?" asked Nadyezhda Fyodorovna, trembling all over. "What harm have I done any one ?"

"You are a terrible sinner. You broke the vow you made your husband at the altar. You seduced a fine young man, who perhaps had he not met you might have taken a lawful partner for life from a good family in his own circle, and would have been like every one else now. You have ruined his youth. Don't speak, don't speak, my dear! I never believe that man is to blame for our sins. It is always the woman's fault. Men are frivolous in domestic life; they are guided by their minds, and not by their hearts. There's a great deal they don't understand; woman understands it all. Everything depends on her. To her much is given and from her much will be required. Oh, my dear, if she had been more foolish or weaker than man on that side, God would not have entrusted her with the education of boys and girls. And then, my dear, you entered on the path of vice, forgetting all modesty; any other woman in your place would have hidden herself from people, would have sat shut up at home, and would only have been seen in the temple of God, pale, dressed all in black and weeping, and every one would have said in genuine compassion: 'O Lord, this erring angel is coming back again to Thee. . . .' But you, my dear, have forgotten all discretion; have lived openly, extravagantly; have seemed to be proud of your sin; you have been gay and laughing, and I, looking at you, shuddered with horror, and have been afraid that thunder from Heaven would strike our house while you were sitting with us. My dear, don't speak, don't speak," cried Marya Konstantinovna, observing that Nadyezhda Fyodorovna wanted to speak. "Trust me, I will not deceive you, I will not hide one truth from the eyes of your soul. Listen to me, my dear. . . . God marks great sinners, and you have been marked out: only think—your costumes have always been appalling."

Nadyezhda Fyodorovna, who had always had the highest opinion of her costumes, left off crying and looked at her with surprise.

"Yes, appalling," Marya Konstantinovna went on. "Any one could judge of your behaviour from the elaboration and gaudiness of your attire. People laughed and shrugged their shoulders as they looked at you, and I grieved, I grieved. . . . And forgive me, my dear; you are not nice in your person! When we met in the bathing-place, you made me tremble. Your outer clothing was decent enough, but your petticoat, your chemise. . . . My dear, I blushed! Poor Ivan Andreitch! No one ever ties his cravat properly, and from his linen and his boots, poor fellow! one can see he has no one at home to look after him. And he is always hungry, my darling, and of course, if there is no one at home to think of the samovar and the coffee, one is forced to spend half one's salary at the pavilion. And it's simply awful, awful in your home! No one else in the town has flies, but there's no getting rid of them in your rooms: all the plates and dishes are black with them. If you look at the windows and the chairs, there's nothing but dust, dead flies, and glasses. . . . What do you want glasses standing about for? And, my dear, the table's not cleared till this time in the day. And one's ashamed to go into your bedroom: underclothes flung about everywhere, india-rubber tubes hanging on the walls, pails and basins standing about. . . . My dear! A husband ought to know nothing, and his wife ought to be as neat as a little angel in his presence. I wake up every morning before

it is light, and wash my face with cold water that my Nikodim Alexandritch may not see me looking drowsy."

"That's all nonsense," Nadyezhda Fyodorovna sobbed. "If only I
were happy, but I am so unhappy!"

"Yes, yes; you are very unhappy!" Marya Konstantinovna sighed,
hardly able to restrain herself from weeping. "And there's terrible grief
in store for you in the future! A solitary old age, ill-health; and then
you will have to answer at the dread judgment seat. . . . It's awful, awful.
Now fate itself holds out to you a helping hand, and you madly thrust
it from you. Be married, make haste and be married!"

"Yes, we must, we must," said Nadyezhda Fyodorovna; "but it's
impossible!"

"Why ?"

"It's impossible. Oh, if only you knew!"

Nadyezhda Fyodorovna had an impulse to tell her about Kirilin,
and how the evening before she had met handsome young Atchmianov at the harbour, and how the mad, ridiculous idea had occurred to
her of cancelling her debt for three hundred; it had amused her very
much, and she returned home late in the evening feeling that she had
sold herself and was irrevocably lost. She did not know herself how it
had happened. And she longed to swear to Marya Konstantinovna that
she would certainly pay that debt, but sobs and shame prevented her
from speaking.

"I am going away," she said. "Ivan Andreitch may stay, but I am
going."

"Where ?"

"To Russia."

"But how will you live there? Why, you have nothing."

"I will do translation, or . . . or I will open a library. . . ."

"Don't let your fancy run away with you, my dear. You must have
money for a library. Well, I will leave you now, and you calm yourself
and think things over, and to-morrow come and see me, bright and
happy. That will be enchanting! Well, good-bye, my angel. Let me
kiss you."

Marya Konstantinovna kissed Nadyezhda Fyodorovna on the forehead, made the sign of the cross over her, and softly withdrew. It was
getting dark, and Olga lighted up in the kitchen. Still crying,
Nadyezhda Fyodorovna went into the bedroom and lay down on the

bed. She began to be very feverish. She undressed without getting up, crumpled up her clothes at her feet, and curled herself up under the bedclothes. She was thirsty, and there was no one to give her something to drink.

"I'll pay it back!" she said to herself, and it seemed to her in delirium that she was sitting beside some sick woman, and recognised her as herself. "I'll pay it back. It would be stupid to imagine that it was for money. I . . . I will go away and send him the money from Petersburg. At first a hundred . . . then another hundred . . . and then the third hundred. . . ."

It was late at night when Laevsky came in.

"At first a hundred . . ." Nadyezhda Fyodorovna said to him, "then another hundred . . ."

"You ought to take some quinine," he said, and thought, "To-morrow is Wednesday; the steamer goes and I am not going in it. So I shall have to go on living here till Saturday."

Nadyezhda Fyodorovna knelt up in bed.

"I didn't say anything just now, did I?" she asked, smiling and screwing up her eyes at the light.

"No, nothing. We shall have to send for the doctor to-morrow morning. Go to sleep."

He took his pillow and went to the door. Ever since he had finally made up his mind to go away and leave Nadyezhda Fyodorovna, she had begun to raise in him pity and a sense of guilt; he felt a little ashamed in her presence, as though in the presence of a sick or old horse whom one has decided to kill. He stopped in the doorway and looked round at her.

"I was out of humour at the picnic and said something rude to you. Forgive me, for God's sake!"

Saying this, he went off to his study, lay down, and for a long while could not get to sleep.

Next morning when Samoylenko, attired, as it was a holiday, in full-dress uniform with epaulettes on his shoulders and decorations on his breast, came out of the bedroom after feeling Nadyezhda Fyodorovna's pulse and looking at her tongue, Laevsky, who was standing in the doorway, asked him anxiously: "Well? Well?"

There was an expression of terror, of extreme uneasiness, and of hope on his face.

"Don't worry yourself; there's nothing dangerous," said Samoylenko; "it's the usual fever."

"I don't mean that." Laevsky frowned impatiently. "Have you got the money?"

"My dear soul, forgive me," he whispered, looking round at the door and overcome with confusion.

"For God's sake, forgive me! No one has anything to spare, and I've only been able to collect by five- and by ten-rouble notes. . . . Only a hundred and ten in all. To-day I'll speak to some one else. Have patience."

"But Saturday is the latest date," whispered Laevsky, trembling with impatience. "By all that's sacred, get it by Saturday! If I don't get away by Saturday, nothing's any use, nothing! I can't understand how a doctor can be without money!"

"Lord have mercy on us!" Samoylenko whispered rapidly and intensely, and there was positively a breaking note in his throat. "I've been stripped of everything; I am owed seven thousand, and I'm in debt all round. Is it my fault?"

"Then you'll get it by Saturday? Yes?"

"I'll try."

"I implore you, my dear fellow! So that the money may be in my hands by Friday morning!"

Samoylenko sat down and prescribed solution of quinine and kalii bromati and tincture of rhubarb, tincturæ gentianæ, aquæ fœniculi all in one mixture, added some pink syrup to sweeten it, and went away.

XI

"You look as though you were coming to arrest me," said Von Koren, seeing Samoylenko coming in, in his full-dress uniform.

"I was passing by and thought: 'Suppose I go in and pay my respects to zoology,' " said Samoylenko, sitting down at the big table, knocked together by the zoologist himself out of plain boards. "Good-morning, holy father," he said to the deacon, who was sitting in the window, copying something. "I'll stay a minute and then run home to see about dinner. It's time. . . . I'm not hindering you?"

"Not in the least," answered the zoologist, laying out over the table slips of paper covered with small writing. "We are busy copying."

"Ah! . . . Oh, my goodness, my goodness! . . ." sighed Samoylenko. He cautiously took up from the table a dusty book on which there was lying a dead dried spider, and said: "Only fancy, though; some little green beetle is going about its business, when suddenly a monster like this swoops down upon it. I can fancy its terror."

"Yes, I suppose so."

"Is poison given it to protect it from its enemies ?"

"Yes, to protect it and enable it to attack."

"To be sure, to be sure. . . . And everything in nature, my dear fellows, is consistent and can be explained," sighed Samoylenko; "only I tell you what I don't understand. You're a man of very great intellect, so explain it to me, please. There are, you know, little beasts no bigger than rats, rather handsome to look at, but nasty and immoral in the extreme, let me tell you. Suppose such a little beast is running in the woods. He sees a bird; he catches it and devours it. He goes on and sees in the grass a nest of eggs; he does not want to eat them—he is not hungry, but yet he tastes one egg and scatters the others out of the nest with his paw. Then he meets a frog and begins to play with it; when he has tormented the frog he goes on licking himself and meets a beetle; he crushes the beetle with his paw . . . and so he spoils and destroys everything on his way. . . . He creeps into other beasts' holes, tears up the anthills, cracks the snail's shell. If he meets a rat, he fights with it; if he meets a snake or a mouse, he must strangle it; and so the whole day long. Come, tell me: what is the use of a beast like that? Why was he created?"

"I don't know what animal you are talking of," said Von Koren; "most likely one of the insectivora. Well, he got hold of the bird because it was incautious; he broke the nest of eggs because the bird was not skilful, had made the nest badly and did not know how to conceal it. The frog probably had some defect in its colouring or he would not have seen it, and so on. Your little beast only destroys the weak, the unskilful, the careless—in fact, those who have defects which nature does not think fit to hand on to posterity. Only the cleverer, the stronger, the more careful and developed survive; and so your little beast, without suspecting it, is serving the great ends of perfecting creation."

"Yes, yes, yes. . . . By the way, brother," said Samoylenko carelessly, "lend me a hundred roubles."

"Very good. There are some very interesting types among the insectivorous mammals. For instance, the mole is said to be useful because he devours noxious insects. There is a story that some German sent William I. a fur coat made of mole-skins, and the Emperor ordered him to be reproved for having destroyed so great a number of useful animals. And yet the mole is not a bit less cruel than your little beast, and is very mischievous besides, as he spoils meadows terribly."

Von Koren opened a box and took out a hundred-rouble note.

"The mole has a powerful thorax, just like the bat," he went on, shutting the box; "the bones and muscles are tremendously developed, the mouth is extraordinarily powerfully furnished. If it had the proportions of an elephant, it would be an all-destructive, invincible animal. It is interesting when two moles meet underground; they begin at once as though by agreement digging a little platform; they need the platform in order to have a battle more conveniently. When they have made it they enter upon a ferocious struggle and fight till the weaker one falls. Take the hundred roubles," said Von Koren, dropping his voice, "but only on condition that you're not borrowing it for Laevsky."

"And if it were for Laevsky," cried Samoylenko, flaring up, "what is that to you?"

"I can't give it to you for Laevsky. I know you like lending people money. You would give it to Kerim, the brigand, if he were to ask you; but, excuse me, I can't assist you in that direction."

"Yes, it is for Laevsky I am asking it," said Samoylenko, standing up and waving his right arm. "Yes! For Laevsky! And no one, fiend or devil, has a right to dictate to me how to dispose of my own money. It doesn't suit you to lend it me? No?"

The deacon began laughing.

"Don't get excited, but be reasonable," said the zoologist. "To shower benefits on Mr. Laevsky is, to my thinking, as senseless as to water weeds or to feed locusts."

"To my thinking, it is our duty to help our neighbours!" cried Samoylenko.

"In that case, help that hungry Turk who is lying under the fence! He is a workman and more useful and indispensable than your Laevsky. Give him that hundred-rouble note! Or subscribe a hundred roubles to my expedition!"

"Will you give me the money or not? I ask you!"

"Tell me openly: what does he want money for?"

"It's not a secret; he wants to go to Petersburg on Saturday."

"So that is it!" Von Koren drawled out. "Aha! . . . We understand. And is she going with him, or how is it to be?"

"She's staying here for the time. He'll arrange his affairs in Petersburg and send her the money, and then she'll go."

"That's smart!" said the zoologist, and he gave a short tenor laugh. "Smart, well planned."

He went rapidly up to Samoylenko, and standing face to face with him, and looking him in the eyes, asked: "Tell me now honestly: is he tired of her? Yes? tell me: is he tired of her? Yes?"

"Yes," Samoylenko articulated, beginning to perspire.

"How repulsive it is!" said Von Koren, and from his face it could be seen that he felt repulsion. "One of two things, Alexandr Davidditch: either you are in the plot with him, or, excuse my saying so, you are a simpleton. Surely you must see that he is taking you in like a child in the most shameless way? Why, it's as clear as day that he wants to get rid of her and abandon her here. She'll be left a burden on you. It is as clear as day that you will have to send her to Petersburg at your expense. Surely your fine friend can't have so blinded you by his dazzling qualities that you can't see the simplest thing?"

"That's all supposition," said Samoylenko, sitting down.

"Supposition? But why is he going alone instead of taking her with him? And ask him why he doesn't send her off first. The sly beast!"

Overcome with sudden doubts and suspicions about his friend, Samoylenko weakened and took a humbler tone.

"But it's impossible," he said, recalling the night Laevsky had spent at his house. "He is so unhappy!"

"What of that? Thieves and incendiaries are unhappy too!"

"Even supposing you are right . . ." said Samoylenko, hesitating. "Let us admit it. . . . Still, he's a young man in a strange place . . . a student. We have been students, too, and there is no one but us to come to his assistance."

"To help him to do abominable things, because he and you at different times have been at universities, and neither of you did anything there! What nonsense!"

"Stop; let us talk it over coolly. I imagine it will be possible to make some arrangement. . . ." Samoylenko reflected, twiddling his fingers. "I'll give him the money, you see, but make him promise on his honour that within a week he'll send Nadyezhda Fyodorovna the money for the journey."

"And he'll give you his word of honour—in fact, he'll shed tears and believe in it himself; but what's his word of honour worth? He won't keep it, and when in a year or two you meet him on the Nevsky Prospect with a new mistress on his arm, he'll excuse himself on the ground that he has been crippled by civilisation, and that he is made after the pattern of Rudin. Drop him, for God's sake! Keep away from the filth; don't stir it up with both hands!"

Samoylenko thought for a minute and said resolutely:

"But I shall give him the money all the same. As you please. I can't bring myself to refuse a man simply on an assumption."

"Very fine, too. You can kiss him if you like."

"Give me the hundred roubles, then," Samoylenko asked timidly.

"I won't."

A silence followed. Samoylenko was quite crushed; his face wore a guilty, abashed, and ingratiating expression, and it was strange to see this pitiful, childish, shamefaced countenance on a huge man wearing epaulettes and orders of merit.

"The bishop here goes the round of his diocese on horseback instead of in a carriage," said the deacon, laying down his pen. "It's extremely touching to see him sit on his horse. His simplicity and humility are full of Biblical grandeur."

"Is he a good man?" asked Von Koren, who was glad to change the conversation.

"Of course! If he hadn't been a good man, do you suppose he would have been consecrated a bishop?"

"Among the bishops are to be found good and gifted men," said Von Koren. "The only drawback is that some of them have the weakness to imagine themselves statesmen. One busies himself with Russification, another criticises the sciences. That's not their business. They had much better look into their consistory a little."

"A layman cannot judge of bishops."

"Why so, deacon? A bishop is a man just the same as you or I."

"The same, but not the same." The deacon was offended and took up his pen. "If you had been the same, the Divine Grace would have rested upon you, and you would have been bishop yourself; and since you are not bishop, it follows you are not the same."

"Don't talk nonsense, deacon," said Samoylenko dejectedly. "Listen to what I suggest," he said, turning to Von Koren. "Don't give me that hundred roubles. You'll be having your dinners with me for three months before the winter, so let me have the money beforehand for three months."

"I won't."

Samoylenko blinked and turned crimson; he mechanically drew towards him the book with the spider on it and looked at it, then he got up and took his hat.

Von Koren felt sorry for him.

"What it is to have to live and do with people like this," said the zoologist, and he kicked a paper into the corner with indignation. "You must understand that this is not kindness, it is not love, but cowardice, slackness, poison! What's gained by reason is lost by your flabby good-for-nothing hearts! When I was ill with typhoid as a schoolboy, my aunt in her sympathy gave me pickled mushrooms to eat, and I very nearly died. You, and my aunt too, must understand that love for man is not to be found in the heart or the stomach or the bowels, but here!"

Von Koren slapped himself on the forehead.

"Take it," he said, and thrust a hundred-rouble note into his hand.

"You've no need to be angry, Kolya," said Samoylenko mildly, folding up the note. "I quite understand you, but . . . you must put yourself in my place."

"You are an old woman, that's what you are."

The deacon burst out laughing.

"Hear my last request, Alexandr Daviditch," said Von Koren hotly. "When you give that scoundrel the money, make it a condition that he takes his lady with him, or sends her on ahead, and don't give it him without. There's no need to stand on ceremony with him. Tell him so, or, if you don't, I give you my word I'll go to his office and kick him downstairs, and I'll break off all acquaintance with you. So you'd better know it."

"Well! To go with her or send her on beforehand will be more convenient for him," said Samoylenko. "He'll be delighted indeed. Well, good-bye."

He said good-bye affectionately and went out, but before shutting the door after him, he looked round at Von Koren and, with a ferocious face, said:

"It's the Germans who have ruined you, brother! Yes! The Germans!"

XII

Next day, Thursday, Marya Konstantinovna was celebrating the birthday of her Kostya. All were invited to come at midday and eat pies, and in the evening to drink chocolate. When Laevsky and Nadyezhda Fyodorovna arrived in the evening, the zoologist, who was already sitting in the drawing-room, drinking chocolate, asked Samoylenko:

"Have you talked to him?"

"Not yet."

"Mind now, don't stand on ceremony. I can't understand the insolence of these people! Why, they know perfectly well the view taken by this family of their cohabitation, and yet they force themselves in here."

"If one is to pay attention to every prejudice," said Samoylenko, "one could go nowhere."

"Do you mean to say that the repugnance felt by the masses for illicit love and moral laxity is a prejudice?"

"Of course it is. It's prejudice and hate. When the soldiers see a girl of light behaviour, they laugh and whistle; but just ask them what they are themselves."

"It's not for nothing they whistle. The fact that girls strangle their illegitimate children and go to prison for it, and that Anna Karenin flung herself under the train, and that in the villages they smear the gates with tar, and that you and I, without knowing why, are pleased by Katya's purity, and that every one of us feels a vague craving for pure love, though he knows there is no such love—is all that prejudice? That is the one thing, brother, which has survived intact from natural selection, and, if it were not for that obscure force regulating the relations of the sexes, the Laevskys would have it all their own way, and mankind would degenerate in two years."

Laevsky came into the drawing-room, greeted every one, and

shaking hands with Von Koren, smiled ingratiatingly. He waited for a favourable moment and said to Samoylenko:

"Excuse me, Alexandr Daviditch, I must say two words to you."

Samoylenko got up, put his arm round Laevsky's waist, and both of them went into Nikodim Alexandritch's study.

"To-morrow's Friday," said Laevsky, biting his nails. "Have you got what you promised?"

"I've only got two hundred. I'll get the rest to-day or to-morrow. Don't worry yourself."

"Thank God . . ." sighed Laevsky, and his hands began trembling with joy. "You are saving me, Alexandr Daviditch, and I swear to you by God, by my happiness and anything you like, I'll send you the money as soon as I arrive. And I'll send you my old debt too."

"Look here, Vanya . . ." said Samoylenko, turning crimson and taking him by the button. "You must forgive my meddling in your private affairs, but . . . why shouldn't you take Nadyezhda Fyodorovna with you?"

"You queer fellow. How is that possible? One of us must stay, or our creditors will raise an outcry. You see, I owe seven hundred or more to the shops. Only wait, and I will send them the money. I'll stop their mouths, and then she can come away."

"I see. . . . But why shouldn't you send her on first?"

"My goodness, as though that were possible!" Laevsky was horrified. "Why, she's a woman; what would she do there alone? What does she know about it? That would only be a loss of time and a useless waste of money."

"That's reasonable . . ." thought Samoylenko, but remembering his conversation with Von Koren, he looked down and said sullenly: "I can't agree with you. Either go with her or send her first; otherwise . . . otherwise I won't give you the money. Those are my last words. . . ."

He staggered back, lurched backwards against the door, and went into the drawing-room, crimson, and overcome with confusion.

"Friday . . . Friday," thought Laevsky, going back into the drawing-room. "Friday. . . ."

He was handed a cup of chocolate; he burnt his lips and tongue with the scalding chocolate and thought: "Friday . . . Friday. . . ."

For some reason he could not get the word "Friday" out of his head; he could think of nothing but Friday, and the only thing that was clear to him, not in his brain but somewhere in his heart, was that he would not get off on Saturday. Before him stood Nikodim Alexandritch, very neat, with his hair combed over his temples, saying:

"Please take something to eat. . . ."

Marya Konstantinovna showed the visitors Katya's school report and said, drawling:

"It's very, very difficult to do well at school nowadays! So much is expected . . ."

"Mamma!" groaned Katya, not knowing where to hide her confusion at the praises of the company.

Laevsky, too, looked at the report and praised it. Scripture, Russian language, conduct, fives and fours, danced before his eyes, and all this, mixed with the haunting refrain of "Friday," with the carefully combed locks of Nikodim Alexandritch and the red cheeks of Katya, produced on him a sensation of such immense overwhelming boredom that he almost shrieked with despair and asked himself: "Is it possible, is it possible I shall not get away?"

They put two card tables side by side and sat down to play post. Laevsky sat down too.

"Friday . . . Friday . . ." he kept thinking, as he smiled and took a pencil out of his pocket. "Friday. . . ."

He wanted to think over his position, and was afraid to think. It was terrible to him to realise that the doctor had detected him in the deception which he had so long and carefully concealed from himself. Every time he thought of his future he would not let his thoughts have full rein. He would get into the train and set off, and thereby the problem of his life would be solved, and he did not let his thoughts go farther. Like a far-away dim light in the fields, the thought sometimes flickered in his mind that in one of the side-streets of Petersburg, in the remote future, he would have to have recourse to a tiny lie in order to get rid of Nadyezhda Fyodorovna and pay his debts; he would tell a lie only once, and then a completely new life would begin. And that was right: at the price of a small lie he would win so much truth.

Now when by his blunt refusal the doctor had crudely hinted at his deception, he began to understand that he would need deception not only in the remote future, but to-day, and to-morrow, and in a month's time, and perhaps up to the very end of his life. In fact, in order to get away he would have to lie to Nadyezhda Fyodorovna, to his creditors, and to his superiors in the Service; then, in order to get money in Petersburg, he would have to lie to his mother, to tell her that he had already broken with Nadyezhda Fyodorovna; and his mother would not give him more than five hundred roubles, so he had already deceived the doctor, as he would not be in a position to pay him back the money within a short time. Afterwards, when Nadyezhda Fyodorovna came to Petersburg, he would have to resort to a regular series of deceptions, little and big, in order to get free of her; and again there would be tears, boredom, a disgusting existence, remorse, and so there would be no new life. Deception and nothing more. A whole mountain of lies rose before Laevsky's imagination. To leap over it at one bound and not to do his lying piecemeal, he would have to bring himself to stern, uncompromising action; for instance, to getting up without saying a word, putting on his hat, and at once setting off without money and without explanation. But Laevsky felt that was impossible for him.

"Friday, Friday . . ." he thought. "Friday. . . ."

They wrote little notes, folded them in two, and put them in Nikodim Alexandritch's old top-hat. When there were a sufficient heap of notes, Kostya, who acted the part of postman, walked round the table and delivered them. The deacon, Katya, and Kostya, who received amusing notes and tried to write as funnily as they could, were highly delighted.

"We must have a little talk," Nadyezhda Fyodorovna read in a little note; she glanced at Marya Konstantinovna, who gave her an almond-oily smile and nodded.

"Talk of what?" thought Nadyezhda Fyodorovna. "If one can't tell the whole, it's no use talking."

Before going out for the evening she had tied Laevsky's cravat for him, and that simple action filled her soul with tenderness and sorrow. The anxiety in his face, his absent-minded looks, his pallor, and the incomprehensible change that had taken place in him of late, and the fact that she had a terrible revolting secret from him, and the fact that her hands trembled when she tied his cravat—all this seemed to tell her that they had not long left to be together. She looked at him as though he were an ikon, with terror and penitence, and thought: "Forgive, forgive."

Opposite her was sitting Atchmianov, and he never took his black, love-sick eyes off her. She was stirred by passion; she was ashamed of herself, and afraid that even her misery and sorrow would not prevent her from yielding to impure desire to-morrow, if not to-day—and that, like a drunkard, she would not have the strength to stop herself.

She made up her mind to go away that she might not continue this life, shameful for herself, and humiliating for Laevsky. She would beseech him with tears to let her go; and if he opposed her, she would go away secretly. She would not tell him what had happened; let him keep a pure memory of her.

"I love you, I love you, I love you," she read. It was from Atchmianov.

She would live in some far remote place, would work and send Laevsky, "anonymously," money, embroidered shirts, and tobacco, and would return to him only in old age or if he were dangerously ill and needed a nurse. When in his old age he learned what were her reasons for leaving him and refusing to be his wife, he would appreciate her sacrifice and forgive.

"You've got a long nose." That must be from the deacon or Kostya.

Nadyezhda Fyodorovna imagined how, parting from Laevsky, she would embrace him warmly, would kiss his hand, and would swear to love him all her life, all her life, and then, living in obscurity among strangers, she would every day think that somewhere she had a friend, some one she loved—a pure, noble, lofty man who kept a pure memory of her.

"If you don't give me an interview to-day, I shall take measures, I assure you on my word of honour. You can't treat decent people like this; you must understand that." That was from Kirilin.

XIII

Laevsky received two notes; he opened one and read: "Don't go away, my darling."

"Who could have written that?" he thought. "Not Samoylenko, of course. And not the deacon, for he doesn't know I want to go away. Von Koren, perhaps?"

The zoologist bent over the table and drew a pyramid. Laevsky fancied that his eyes were smiling.

"Most likely Samoylenko . . . has been gossiping," thought Laevsky.

In the other note, in the same disguised angular handwriting with long tails to the letters, was written: "Somebody won't go away on Saturday."

"A stupid gibe," thought Laevsky. "Friday, Friday. . . ."

Something rose in his throat. He touched his collar and coughed, but instead of a cough a laugh broke from his throat.

"Ha-ha-ha!" he laughed. "Ha-ha-ha! What am I laughing at? Ha-ha-ha!"

He tried to restrain himself, covered his mouth with his hand, but the laugh choked his chest and throat, and his hand could not cover his mouth.

"How stupid it is!" he thought, rolling with laughter. "Have I gone out of my mind?"

The laugh grew shriller and shriller, and became something like the bark of a lap-dog. Laevsky tried to get up from the table, but his legs would not obey him and his right hand was strangely, without his volition, dancing on the table, convulsively clutching and crumpling up the bits of paper. He saw looks of wonder, Samoylenko's grave, frightened face, and the eyes of the zoologist full of cold irony and disgust, and realised that he was in hysterics.

"How hideous, how shameful!" he thought, feeling the warmth of tears on his face. ". . . Oh, oh, what a disgrace! It has never happened to me. . . ."

They took him under his arms, and supporting his head from behind, led him away; a glass gleamed before his eyes and knocked against his teeth, and the water was spilt on his breast; he was in a little room, with two beds in the middle, side by side, covered by two snow-white quilts. He dropped on one of the beds and sobbed.

"It's nothing, it's nothing," Samoylenko kept saying; "it does happen . . . it does happen. . . ."

Chill with horror, trembling all over and dreading something awful, Nadyezhda Fyodorovna stood by the bedside and kept asking:

"What is it? What is it? For God's sake, tell me."

"Can Kirilin have written him something?" she thought.

"It's nothing," said Laevsky, laughing and crying; "go away, darling."

His face expressed neither hatred nor repulsion: so he knew noth-

66 *Anton Chekhov*

ing; Nadyezhda Fyodorovna was somewhat reassured, and she went into the drawing-room.

"Don't agitate yourself, my dear!" said Marya Konstantinovna, sitting down beside her and taking her hand. "It will pass. Men are just as weak as we poor sinners. You are both going through a crisis. . . . One can so well understand it! Well, my dear, I am waiting for an answer. Let us have a little talk."

"No, we are not going to talk," said Nadyezhda Fyodorovna, listening to Laevsky's sobs. "I feel depressed. . . . You must allow me to go home."

"What do you mean, what do you mean, my dear?" cried Marya Konstantinovna in alarm. "Do you think I could let you go without supper? We will have something to eat, and then you may go with my blessing."

"I feel miserable . . ." whispered Nadyezhda Fyodorovna, and she caught at the arm of the chair with both hands to avoid falling.

"He's got a touch of hysterics," said Von Koren gaily, coming into the drawing-room, but seeing Nadyezhda Fyodorovna, he was taken aback and retreated.

When the attack was over, Laevsky sat on the strange bed and thought.

"Disgraceful! I've been howling like some wretched girl! I must have been absurd and disgusting. I will go away by the back stairs. . . . But that would seem as though I took my hysterics too seriously. I ought to take it as a joke. . . ."

He looked in the looking-glass, sat there for some time, and went back into the drawing-room.

"Here I am," he said, smiling; he felt agonisingly ashamed, and he felt others were ashamed in his presence. "Fancy such a thing happening," he said, sitting down. "I was sitting here, and all of a sudden, do you know, I felt a terrible piercing pain in my side . . . unendurable, my nerves could not stand it, and . . . and it led to this silly performance. This is the age of nerves; there is no help for it."

At supper he drank some wine, and, from time to time, with an abrupt sigh rubbed his side as though to suggest that he still felt the pain. And no one, except Nadyezhda Fyodorovna, believed him, and he saw that.

After nine o'clock they went for a walk on the boulevard.

Nadyezhda Fyodorovna, afraid that Kirilin would speak to her, did her best to keep all the time beside Marya Konstantinovna and the children. She felt weak with fear and misery, and felt she was going to be feverish; she was exhausted and her legs would hardly move, but she did not go home, because she felt sure that she would be followed by Kirilin or Atchmianov or both at once. Kirilin walked behind her with Nikodim Alexandritch, and kept humming in an undertone:

"I don't al-low people to play with me! I don't al-low it."

From the boulevard they went back to the pavilion and walked along the beach, and looked for a long time at the phosphorescence on the water. Von Koren began telling them why it looked phosphorescent.

XIV

"It's time I went to my *vint*. . . . They will be waiting for me," said Laevsky. "Good-bye, my friends."

"I'll come with you; wait a minute," said Nadyezhda Fyodorovna, and she took his arm.

They said good-bye to the company and went away. Kirilin took leave too, and saying that he was going the same way, went along beside them.

"What will be, will be," thought Nadyezhda Fyodorovna. "So be it. . . ."

And it seemed to her that all the evil memories in her head had taken shape and were walking beside her in the darkness, breathing heavily, while she, like a fly that had fallen into the inkpot, was crawling painfully along the pavement and smirching Laevsky's side and arm with blackness.

If Kirilin should do anything horrid, she thought, not he but she would be to blame for it. There was a time when no man would have talked to her as Kirilin had done, and she had torn up her security like a thread and destroyed it irrevocably— who was to blame for it? Intoxicated by her passions she had smiled at a complete stranger, probably just because he was tall and a fine figure. After two meetings she was weary of him, had thrown him over, and did not that, she thought now, give him the right to treat her as he chose?

"Here I'll say good-bye to you, darling," said Laevsky. "Ilya Mihalitch will see you home."

He nodded to Kirilin, and, quickly crossing the boulevard, walked along the street to Sheshkovsky's, where there were lights in the windows, and then they heard the gate bang as he went in.

"Allow me to have an explanation with you," said Kirilin. "I'm not a boy, not some Atchkasov or Latchkasov, Zatchkasov. . . . I demand serious attention."

Nadyezhda Fyodorovna's heart began beating violently. She made no reply.

"The abrupt change in your behaviour to me I put down at first to coquetry," Kirilin went on; "now I see that you don't know how to behave with gentlemanly people. You simply wanted to play with me, as you are playing with that wretched Armenian boy; but I'm a gentleman and I insist on being treated like a gentleman. And so I am at your service. . . ."

"I'm miserable," said Nadyezhda Fyodorovna beginning to cry, and to hide her tears she turned away.

"I'm miserable too," said Kirilin, "but what of that?"

Kirilin was silent for a space, then he said distinctly and emphatically:

"I repeat, madam, that if you do not give me an interview this evening, I'll make a scandal this very evening."

"Let me off this evening," said Nadyezhda Fyodorovna, and she did not recognise her own voice, it was so weak and pitiful.

"I must give you a lesson. . . . Excuse me for the roughness of my tone, but it's necessary to give you a lesson. Yes, I regret to say I must give you a lesson. I insist on two interviews—to-day and to-morrow. After to-morrow you are perfectly free and can go wherever you like with any one you choose. To-day and to-morrow."

Nadyezhda Fyodorovna went up to her gate and stopped.

"Let me go," she murmured, trembling all over and seeing nothing before her in the darkness but his white tunic. "You're right: I'm a horrible woman. . . . I'm to blame, but let me go . . . I beg you." She touched his cold hand and shuddered. "I beseech you. . . ."

"Alas!" sighed Kirilin, " alas! it's not part of my plan to let you go; I only mean to give you a lesson and make you realise. And what's more, madam, I've too little faith in women."

"I'm miserable. . . ."

Nadyezhda Fyodorovna listened to the even splash of the sea, looked at the sky studded with stars, and longed to make haste and end it all, and get away from the cursed sensation of life, with its sea, stars, men, fever.

"Only not in my home," she said coldly. "Take me somewhere else."

"Come to Muridov's. That's better."

"Where's that?"

"Near the old wall."

She walked quickly along the street and then turned into the side-street that led towards the mountains. It was dark. There were pale streaks of light here and there on the pavement, from the lighted windows, and it seemed to her that, like a fly, she kept falling into the ink and crawling out into the light again. At one point he stumbled, almost fell down and burst out laughing.

"He's drunk," thought Nadyezhda Fyodorovna. "Never mind. . . . Never mind. . . . So be it."

Atchmianov, too, soon took leave of the party and followed Nadyezhda Fyodorovna to ask her to go for a row. He went to her house and looked over the fence: the windows were wide open, there were no lights.

"Nadyezhda Fyodorovna!" he called.

A moment passed, he called again.

"Who's there?" he heard Olga's voice.

"Is Nadyezhda Fyodorovna at home?"

"No, she has not come in yet."

"Strange . . . very strange," thought Atchmianov, feeling very uneasy. "She went home. . . ."

He walked along the boulevard, then along the street, and glanced in at the windows of Sheshkovsky's. Laevsky was sitting at the table without his coat on, looking attentively at his cards.

"Strange, strange," muttered Atchmianov, and remembering Laevsky's hysterics, he felt ashamed. "If she is not at home, where is she?"

He went to Nadyezhda Fyodorovna's lodgings again, and looked at the dark windows.

"It's a cheat, a cheat . . ." he thought, remembering that, meeting him at midday at Marya Konstantinovna's, she had promised to go in a boat with him that evening.

The windows of the house where Kirilin lived were dark, and there was a policeman sitting asleep on a little bench at the gate. Everything was clear to Atchmianov when he looked at the windows and the policeman. He made up his mind to go home, and set off in that direction, but somehow found himself near Nadyezhda Fyodorovna's lodgings again. He sat down on the bench near the gate and took off his hat, feeling that his head was burning with jealousy and resentment.

The clock in the town church only struck twice in the twenty-four hours—at midday and midnight. Soon after it struck midnight he heard hurried footsteps.

"To-morrow evening, then, again at Muridov's," Atchmianov heard, and he recognised Kirilin's voice. "At eight o'clock; good-bye!"

Nadyezhda Fyodorovna made her appearance near the garden. Without noticing that Atchmianov was sitting on the bench, she passed beside him like a shadow, opened the gate, and leaving it open, went into the house. In her own room she lighted the candle and quickly undressed, but instead of getting into bed, she sank on her knees before a chair, flung her arms round it, and rested her head on it.

It was past two when Laevsky came home.

XV

Having made up his mind to lie, not all at once but piecemeal, Laevsky went soon after one o'clock next day to Samoylenko to ask for the money that he might be sure to get off on Saturday. After his hysterical attack, which had added an acute feeling of shame to his depressed state of mind, it was unthinkable to remain in the town. If Samoylenko should insist on his conditions, he thought it would be possible to agree to them and take the money, and next day, just as he was starting, to say that Nadyezhda Fyodorovna refused to go. He would be able to persuade her that evening that the whole arrangement would be for her benefit. If Samoylenko, who was obviously under the influence of Von Koren, should refuse the money altogether or make fresh conditions, then he, Laevsky, would go off that very evening on a cargo vessel, or even in a sailing-boat, to Novy Athon or Novorossiisk, would send from there an humiliating telegram, and would stay there till his mother sent him the money for the journey.

When he went into Samoylenko's, he found Von Koren in the

drawing-room. The zoologist had just arrived for dinner, and, as usual, was turning over the album and scrutinising the gentlemen in top-hats and the ladies in caps.

"How very unlucky!" thought Laevsky, seeing him. "He may be in the way. Good-morning."

"Good-morning," answered Von Koren, without looking at him.

"Is Alexandr Daviditch at home?"

"Yes, in the kitchen."

Laevsky went into the kitchen, but seeing from the door that Samoylenko was busy over the salad, he went back into the drawing-room and sat down. He always had a feeling of awkwardness in the zoologist's presence, and now he was afraid there would be talk about his attack of hysterics. There was more than a minute of silence. Von Koren suddenly raised his eyes to Laevsky and asked:

"How do you feel after yesterday?"

"Very well indeed," said Laevsky, flushing. "It really was nothing much. . . ."

"Until yesterday I thought it was only ladies who had hysterics, and so at first I thought you had St. Vitus's dance."

Laevsky smiled ingratiatingly, and thought:

"How indelicate on his part! He knows quite well how unpleasant it is for me. . . ."

"Yes, it was a ridiculous performance," he said, still smiling. "I've been laughing over it the whole morning. What's so curious in an attack of hysterics is that you know it is absurd, and are laughing at it in your heart, and at the same time you sob. In our neurotic age we are the slaves of our nerves; they are our masters and do as they like with us. Civilisation has done us a bad turn in that way. . . ."

As Laevsky talked, he felt it disagreeable that Von Koren listened to him gravely, and looked at him steadily and attentively as though studying him; and he was vexed with himself that in spite of his dislike of Von Koren, he could not banish the ingratiating smile from his face.

"I must admit, though," he added, " that there were immediate causes for the attack, and quite sufficient ones too. My health has been terribly shaky of late. To which one must add boredom, constantly being hard up . . . the absence of people and general interests. . . . My position is worse than a governor's."

"Yes, your position is a hopeless one," answered Von Koren.

These calm, cold words, implying something between a jeer and an uninvited prediction, offended Laevsky. He recalled the zoologist's eyes the evening before, full of mockery and disgust. He was silent for a space and then asked, no longer smiling:

"How do you know anything of my position?"

"You were only just speaking of it yourself. Besides, your friends take such a warm interest in you, that I am hearing about you all day long."

"What friends? Samoylenko, I suppose?"

"Yes, he too."

"I would ask Alexandr Daviditch and my friends in general not to trouble so much about me."

"Here is Samoylenko; you had better ask him not to trouble so much about you."

"I don't understand your tone," Laevsky muttered, suddenly feeling as though he had only just realised that the zoologist hated and despised him, and was jeering at him, and was his bitterest and most inveterate enemy.

"Keep that tone for some one else," he said softly, unable to speak aloud for the hatred with which his chest and throat were choking, as they had been the night before with laughter.

Samoylenko came in in his shirt-sleeves, crimson and perspiring from the stifling kitchen.

"Ah, you here?" he said. "Good-morning, my dear boy. Have you had dinner? Don't stand on ceremony. Have you had dinner?"

"Alexandr Daviditch," said Laevsky, standing up, "though I did appeal to you to help me in a private matter, it did not follow that I released you from the obligation of discretion and respect for other people's private affairs."

"What's this?" asked Samoylenko, in astonishment.

"If you have no money," Laevsky went on, raising his voice and shifting from one foot to the other in his excitement, "don't give it; refuse it. But why spread abroad in every back street that my position is hopeless, and all the rest of it? I can't endure such benevolence and friend's assistance where there's a shilling-worth of talk for a ha'p'orth of help! You can boast of your benevolence as much as you please, but no one has given you the right to gossip about my private affairs!"

"What private affairs?" asked Samoylenko, puzzled and beginning to be angry. "If you've come here to be abusive, you had better clear out. You can come again afterwards!"

He remembered the rule that when one is angry with one's neighbour, one must begin to count a hundred, and one will grow calm again; and he began rapidly counting.

"I beg you not to trouble yourself about me," Laevsky went on. "Don't pay any attention to me, and whose business is it what I do and how I live? Yes, I want to go away. Yes, I get into debt, I drink, I am living with another man's wife, I'm hysterical, I'm ordinary. I am not so profound as some people, but whose business is that? Respect other people's privacy."

"Excuse me, brother," said Samoylenko, who had counted up to thirty-five, "but . . ."

"Respect other people's individuality!" interrupted Laevsky. "This continual gossip about other people's affairs, this sighing and groaning and everlasting prying, this eavesdropping, this friendly sympathy . . . damn it all! They lend me money and make conditions as though I were a schoolboy! I am treated as the devil knows what! I don't want anything," shouted Laevsky, staggering with excitement and afraid that it might end in another attack of hysterics. "I shan't get away on Saturday, then," flashed through his mind. "I want nothing. All I ask of you is to spare me your protecting care. I'm not a boy, and I'm not mad, and I beg you to leave off looking after me."

The deacon came in, and seeing Laevsky pale and gesticulating, addressing his strange speech to the portrait of Prince Vorontsov, stood still by the door as though petrified.

"This continual prying into my soul," Laevsky went on, "is insulting to my human dignity, and I beg these volunteer detectives to give up their spying! Enough!"

"What's that . . . what did you say?" said Samoylenko, who had counted up to a hundred. He turned crimson and went up to Laevsky.

"It's enough," said Laevsky, breathing hard and snatching up his cap.

"I'm a Russian doctor, a nobleman by birth, and a civil councillor," said Samoylenko emphatically. "I've never been a spy, and I allow no one to insult me!" he shouted in a breaking voice, emphasising the last word. "Hold your tongue!"

The deacon, who had never seen the doctor so majestic, so

swelling with dignity, so crimson and so ferocious, shut his mouth, ran out into the entry and there exploded with laughter.

As though through a fog, Laevsky saw Von Koren get up and, putting his hands in his trouser-pockets, stand still in an attitude of expectancy, as though waiting to see what would happen. This calm attitude struck Laevsky as insolent and insulting to the last degree.

"Kindly take back your words," shouted Samoylenko.

Laevsky, who did not by now remember what his words were, answered:

"Leave me alone! I ask for nothing. All I ask is that you and German upstarts of Jewish origin should let me alone! Or I shall take steps to make you! I will fight you!"

"Now we understand," said Von Koren, coming from behind the table. "Mr. Laevsky wants to amuse himself with a duel before he goes away. I can give him that pleasure. Mr. Laevsky, I accept your challenge."

"A challenge," said Laevsky, in a low voice, going up to the zoologist and looking with hatred at his swarthy brow and curly hair. "A challenge? By all means! I hate you! I hate you!"

"Delighted. To-morrow morning early near Kerbalay's. I leave all details to your taste. And now, clear out!"

"I hate you," Laevsky said softly, breathing hard. "I have hated you a long while! A duel! Yes!"

"Get rid of him, Alexandr Daviditch, or else I'm going," said Von Koren. "He'll bite me."

Von Koren's cool tone calmed the doctor; he seemed suddenly to come to himself, to recover his reason; he put both arms round Laevsky's waist, and, leading him away from the zoologist, muttered in a friendly voice that shook with emotion:

"My friends . . . dear, good . . . you've lost your tempers and that's enough . . . and that's enough, my friends."

Hearing his soft, friendly voice, Laevsky felt that something unheard of, monstrous, had just happened to him, as though he had been nearly run over by a train; he almost burst into tears, waved his hand, and ran out of the room.

"To feel that one is hated, to expose oneself before the man who hates one, in the most pitiful, contemptible, helpless state. My God, how hard it is!" he thought a little while afterwards as he sat in the pavilion, feeling as though his body were scarred by the hatred of which he had just been the object.

"How coarse it is, my God!"

Cold water with brandy in it revived him. He vividly pictured Von Koren's calm, haughty face; his eyes the day before, his shirt like a rug, his voice, his white hand; and heavy, passionate, hungry hatred rankled in his breast and clamoured for satisfaction. In his thoughts he felled Von Koren to the ground, and trampled him underfoot. He remembered to the minutest detail all that had happened, and wondered how he could have smiled ingratiatingly to that insignificant man, and how he could care for the opinion of wretched petty people whom nobody knew, living in a miserable little town which was not, it seemed, even on the map, and of which not one decent person in Petersburg had heard. If this wretched little town suddenly fell into ruins or caught fire, the telegram with the news would be read in Russia with no more interest than an advertisement of the sale of second-hand furniture. Whether he killed Von Koren next day or left him alive, it would be just the same, equally useless and uninteresting. Better to shoot him in the leg or hand, wound him, then laugh at him, and let him, like an insect with a broken leg lost in the grass—let him be lost with his obscure sufferings in the crowd of insignificant people like himself.

Laevsky went to Sheshkovsky, told him all about it, and asked him to be his second; then they both went to the superintendent of the postal telegraph department, and asked him, too, to be a second, and stayed to dinner with him. At dinner there was a great deal of joking and laughing. Laevsky made jests at his own expense, saying he hardly knew how to fire off a pistol, calling himself a royal archer and William Tell.

"We must give this gentleman a lesson . . ." he said.

After dinner they sat down to cards. Laevsky played, drank wine, and thought that duelling was stupid and senseless, as it did not decide the question but only complicated it, but that it was sometimes impossible to get on without it. In the given case, for instance, one could not, of course, bring an action against Von Koren. And this duel was so far good in that it made it impossible for Laevsky to remain in the town afterwards. He got a little drunk and interested in the game, and felt at ease.

But when the sun had set and it grew dark, he was possessed by a feeling of uneasiness. It was not fear at the thought of death, because while he was dining and playing cards, he had for some reason a confident belief that the duel would end in nothing; it was dread at the thought of something unknown which was to happen next morning for the first time in his life, and dread of the coming night. . . . He knew that the night would be long and sleepless, and that he would have to think not only of Von Koren and his hatred, but also of the mountain of lies which he had to get through, and which he had not strength or ability to dispense with. It was as though he had been taken suddenly ill; all at once he lost all interest in the cards and in people, grew restless, and began asking them to let him go home. He was eager to get into bed, to lie without moving, and to prepare his thoughts for the night. Sheshkovsky and the postal superintendent saw him home and went on to Von Koren's to arrange about the duel.

Near his lodgings Laevsky met Atchmianov. The young man was breathless and excited.

"I am looking for you, Ivan Andreitch," he said. "I beg you to come quickly. . . ."

"Where?"

"Some one wants to see you, some one you don't know, about very important business; he earnestly begs you to come for a minute. He wants to speak to you of something. . . . For him it's a question of life and death. . . ." In his excitement Atchmianov spoke in a strong Armenian accent.

"Who is it?" asked Laevsky.

"He asked me not to tell you his name."

"Tell him I'm busy; to-morrow, if he likes. . . ."

"How can you!" Atchmianov was aghast. "He wants to tell you something very important for you . . . very important! If you don't come, something dreadful will happen."

"Strange . . ." muttered Laevsky, unable to understand why Atchmianov was so excited and what mysteries there could be in this dull, useless little town.

"Strange," he repeated in hesitation. "Come along though; I don't care."

Atchmianov walked rapidly on ahead and Laevsky followed him. They walked down a street, then turned into an alley.

"What a bore this is!" said Laevsky.

"One minute, one minute . . . it's near."

Near the old rampart they went down a narrow alley between two empty enclosures, then they came into a sort of large yard and went towards a small house.

"That's Muridov's, isn't it?" asked Laevsky.

"Yes."

"But why we've come by the back yards I don't understand. We might have come by the street; it's nearer. . . ."

"Never mind, never mind. . . ."

It struck Laevsky as strange, too, that Atchmianov led him to a back entrance, and motioned to him as though bidding him go quietly and hold his tongue.

"This way, this way . . ." said Atchmianov, cautiously opening the door and going into the passage on tiptoe. "Quietly, quietly, I beg you . . . they may hear."

He listened, drew a deep breath and said in a whisper:

"Open that door, and go in . . . don't be afraid."

Laevsky, puzzled, opened the door and went into a room with a low ceiling and curtained windows.

There was a candle on the table.

"What do you want?" asked some one in the next room. "Is it you, Muridov?"

Laevsky turned into that room and saw Kirilin, and beside him Nadyezhda Fyodorovna.

He didn't hear what was said to him; he staggered back, and did not know how he found himself in the street. His hatred for Von Koren and his uneasiness all had vanished from his soul. As he went home he waved his right arm awkwardly and looked carefully at the ground under his feet, trying to step where it was smooth. At home in his study he walked backwards and forwards, rubbing his hands, and awkwardly shrugging his shoulders and neck, as though his jacket and shirt were too tight; then he lighted a candle and sat down to the table. . . .

XVI

"The 'humane studies' of which you speak will only satisfy human thought when, as they advance, they meet the exact sciences and progress side by side with them. Whether they will meet under a new microscope, or in the monologues of a new Hamlet, or in a new religion, I do not know, but I expect the earth will be covered with a crust of ice before it comes to pass. Of all humane learning the most durable and living is, of course, the teaching of Christ; but look how differently even that is interpreted! Some teach that we must love all our neighbours but make an exception of soldiers, criminals, and lunatics. They allow the first to be killed in war, the second to be isolated or executed, and the third they forbid to marry. Other interpreters teach that we must love all our neighbours without exception, with no distinction of *plus* or *minus*. According to their teaching, if a consumptive or a murderer or an epileptic asks your daughter in marriage, you must let him have her. If *crêtins* go to war against the physically and mentally healthy, don't defend yourselves. This advocacy of love for love's sake, like art for art's sake, if it could have power, would bring mankind in the long run to complete extinction, and so would become the vastest crime that has ever been committed upon earth. There are very many interpretations, and since there are many of them, serious thought is not satisfied by any one of them, and hastens to add its own individual interpretation to the mass. For that reason you should never put a question on a philosophical or so-called Christian basis; by so doing you only remove the question further from solution."

The deacon listened to the zoologist attentively, thought a little, and asked:

"Have the philosophers invented the moral law which is innate in every man, or did God create it together with the body?"

"I don't know. But that law is so universal among all peoples and all ages that I fancy we ought to recognise it as organically connected with man. It is not invented, but exists and will exist. I don't tell you that one day it will be seen under the microscope, but its organic connection is shown, indeed, by evidence: serious affections of the brain and all so-called mental diseases, to the best of my belief, show themselves first of all in the perversion of the moral law."

"Good. So then, just as our stomach bids us eat, our moral sense bids us love our neighbours. Is that it? But our natural man through self-love opposes the voice of conscience and reason, and this gives rise to many brain-racking questions. To whom ought we to turn for the solution of those questions if you forbid us to put them on the philosophic basis?"

"Turn to what little exact science we have. Trust to evidence and the logic of facts. It is true it is but little, but, on the other hand, it is less fluid and shifting than philosophy. The moral law, let us suppose, demands that you love your neighbour. Well? Love ought to show itself in the removal of everything which in one way or another is injurious to men and threatens them with danger in the present or in the future. Our knowledge and the evidence tells us that the morally and physically abnormal are a menace to humanity. If so you must struggle against the abnormal; if you are not able to raise them to the normal standard you must have strength and ability to render them harmless—that is, to destroy them."

"So love consists in the strong overcoming the weak."

"Undoubtedly."

"But you know the strong crucified our Lord Jesus Christ," said the deacon hotly.

"The fact is that those who crucified Him were not the strong but the weak. Human culture weakens and strives to nullify the struggle for existence and natural selection; hence the rapid advancement of the weak and their predominance over the strong. Imagine that you succeeded in instilling into bees humanitarian ideas in their crude and elementary form. What would come of it? The drones who ought to be killed would remain alive, would devour the honey, would corrupt and stifle the bees, resulting in the predominance of the weak over the strong and the degeneration of the latter. The same process is taking place now with humanity; the weak are oppressing the strong. Among savages untouched by civilisation the strongest, cleverest, and most moral takes the lead; he is the chief and the master. But we civilised men have crucified Christ, and we go on crucifying Him, so there is something lacking in us. . . . And that something one ought to raise up in ourselves, or there will be no end to these errors."

"But what criterion have you to distinguish the strong from the weak?"

"Knowledge and evidence. The tuberculous and the scrofulous are recognised by their diseases, and the insane and the immoral by their actions."

"But mistakes may be made!"

"Yes, but it's no use to be afraid of getting your feet wet when you are threatened with the deluge!"

"That's philosophy," laughed the deacon.

"Not a bit of it. You are so corrupted by your seminary philosophy that you want to see nothing but fog in everything. The abstract studies with which your youthful head is stuffed are called abstract just because they abstract your minds from what is obvious. Look the devil straight in the eye, and if he's the devil, tell him he's the devil, and don't go calling to Kant or Hegel for explanations."

The zoologist paused and went on:

"Twice two's four, and a stone's a stone. Here to-morrow we have a duel. You and I will say it's stupid and absurd, that the duel is out of date, that there is no real difference between the aristocratic duel and the drunken brawl in the pot-house, and yet we shall not stop, we shall go there and fight. So there is some force stronger than our reasoning. We shout that war is plunder, robbery, atrocity, fratricide; we cannot look upon blood without fainting; but the French or the Germans have only to insult us for us to feel at once an exaltation of spirit; in the most genuine way we shout 'Hurrah!' and rush to attack the foe. You will invoke the blessing of God on our weapons, and our valour will arouse universal and general enthusiasm. Again it follows that there is a force, if not higher, at any rate stronger, than us and our philosophy. We can no more stop it than that cloud which is moving upwards over the sea. Don't be hypocritical, don't make a long nose at it on the sly; and don't say, 'Ah, old-fashioned, stupid! Ah, it's inconsistent with Scripture!' but look it straight in the face, recognise its rational lawfulness, and when, for instance, it wants to destroy a rotten, scrofulous, corrupt race, don't hinder it with your pilules and misunderstood quotations from the Gospel. Leskov has a story of a conscientious Danila who found a leper outside the town, and fed and warmed him in the name of love and of Christ. If that Danila had really loved humanity, he would have dragged the leper as far as possible from the town, and would have flung him in a pit, and would have gone to save the healthy. Christ, I hope, taught us a rational, intelligent, practical love."

"What a fellow you are!" laughed the deacon. "You don't believe in Christ. Why do you mention His name so often?"

"Yes, I do believe in Him. Only, of course, in my own way, not in yours. Oh, deacon, deacon!" laughed the zoologist; he put his arm round the deacon's waist, and said gaily: "Well? Are you coming with us to the duel to-morrow?"

"My orders don't allow it, or else I should come."

"What do you mean by 'orders'?"

"I have been consecrated. I am in a state of grace."

"Oh, deacon, deacon," repeated Von Koren, laughing, "I love talking to you."

"You say you have faith," said the deacon. "What sort of faith is it? Why, I have an uncle, a priest, and he believes so that when in time of drought he goes out into the fields to pray for rain, he takes his umbrella and leather overcoat for fear of getting wet through on his way home. That's faith! When he speaks of Christ, his face is full of radiance, and all the peasants, men and women, weep floods of tears. He would stop that cloud and put all those forces you talk about to flight. Yes . . . faith moves mountains."

The deacon laughed and slapped the zoologist on the shoulder.

"Yes . . ." he went on; "here you are teaching all the time, fathoming the depths of the ocean, dividing the weak and the strong, writing books and challenging to duels—and everything remains as it is; but, behold! some feeble old man will mutter just one word with a holy spirit, or a new Mahomet, with a sword, will gallop from Arabia, and everything will be topsy-turvy, and in Europe not one stone will be left standing upon another."

"Well, deacon, that's on the knees of the gods."

"Faith without works is dead, but works without faith are worse still—mere waste of time and nothing more."

The doctor came into sight on the sea-front. He saw the deacon and the zoologist, and went up to them.

"I believe everything is ready," he said, breathing hard. "Govorovsky and Boyko will be the seconds. They will start at five o'clock in the morning. How it has clouded over," he said, looking at the sky. "One can see nothing; there will be rain directly."

"I hope you are coming with us?" said the zoologist.

"No, God preserve me; I'm worried enough as it is. Ustimovitch is going instead of me. I've spoken to him already."

Far over the sea was a flash of lightning, followed by a hollow roll of thunder.

"How stifling it is before a storm!" said Von Koren. "I bet you've been to Laevsky already and have been weeping on his bosom."

"Why should I go to him?" answered the doctor in confusion. "What next?"

Before sunset he had walked several times along the boulevard and the street in the hope of meeting Laevsky. He was ashamed of his hastiness and the sudden outburst of friendliness which had followed it. He wanted to apologise to Laevsky in a joking tone, to give him a good talking to, to soothe him and tell him that the duel was a survival of mediæval barbarism, but that Providence itself had brought them to the duel as a means of reconciliation; that the next day, both being splendid and highly intelligent people, they would, after exchanging shots, appreciate each other's noble qualities and would become friends. But he could not come across Laevsky.

"What should I go and see him for?" repeated Samoylenko. "I did not insult him; he insulted me. Tell me, please, why he attacked me. What harm had I done him? I go into the drawing-room, and, all of a sudden, without the least provocation: 'Spy!' There's a nice thing! Tell me, how did it begin? What did you say to him?"

"I told him his position was hopeless. And I was right. It is only honest men or scoundrels who can find an escape from any position, but one who wants to be at the same time an honest man and a scoundrel—it is a hopeless position. But it's eleven o'clock, gentlemen, and we have to be up early to-morrow."

There was a sudden gust of wind; it blew up the dust on the sea-front, whirled it round in eddies, with a howl that drowned the roar of the sea.

"A squall," said the deacon. "We must go in, our eyes are getting full of dust."

As they went, Samoylenko sighed and, holding his hat, said:

"I suppose I shan't sleep to-night."

"Don't you agitate yourself," laughed the zoologist. "You can set your mind at rest; the duel will end in nothing. Laevsky will magnanimously fire into the air—he can do nothing else; and I daresay I shall not fire at all. To be arrested and lose my time on Laevsky's account—the game's not worth the candle. By the way, what is the punishment for duelling?"

"Arrest, and in the case of the death of your opponent a maximum of three years' imprisonment in the fortress."

"The fortress of St. Peter and St. Paul?"

"No, in a military fortress, I believe."

"Though this fine gentleman ought to have a lesson!"

Behind them on the sea, there was a flash of lightning, which for an instant lighted up the roofs of the houses and the mountains. The friends parted near the boulevard. When the doctor disappeared in the darkness and his steps had died away, Von Koren shouted to him:

"I only hope the weather won't interfere with us to-morrow!"

"Very likely it will! Please God it may!"

"Good-night!"

"What about the night? What do you say?"

In the roar of the wind and the sea and the crashes of thunder, it was difficult to hear.

"It's nothing," shouted the zoologist, and hurried home.

XVII

> "Upon my mind, weighed down with woe,
>   Crowd thoughts, a heavy multitude:
>   In silence memory unfolds
>   Her long, long scroll before my eyes.
>   Loathing and shuddering I curse
>   And bitterly lament in vain,
>   And bitter though the tears I weep
>   I do not wash those lines away."

PUSHKIN.

Whether they killed him next morning, or mocked at him—that is, left him his life—he was ruined, anyway. Whether this disgraced woman killed herself in her shame and despair, or dragged on her pitiful existence, she was ruined anyway.

So thought Laevsky as he sat at the table late in the evening, still rubbing his hands. The windows suddenly blew open with a bang; a violent gust of wind burst into the room, and the papers fluttered from the table. Laevsky closed the windows and bent down to pick up the papers. He was aware of something new in his body, a sort of awkwardness he had not felt before, and his movements were strange to him. He moved timidly, jerking with his elbows and shrugging his shoulders; and when he sat down to the table again, he again began rubbing his hands. His body had lost its suppleness.

On the eve of death one ought to write to one's nearest relation. Laevsky thought of this. He took a pen and wrote with a tremulous hand:

"Mother!

He wanted to write to beg his mother, for the sake of the merciful God in whom she believed, that she would give shelter and bring a little warmth and kindness into the life of the unhappy woman who, by his doing, had been disgraced and was in solitude, poverty, and weakness, that she would forgive and forget everything, everything, everything, and by her sacrifice atone to some extent for her son's terrible sin. But he remembered how his mother, a stout, heavily-built old woman in a lace cap, used to go out into the garden in the morning, followed by her companion with the lap-dog; how she used to shout in a peremptory way to the gardener and the servants, and how proud and haughty her face was—he remembered all this and scratched out the word he had written.

There was a vivid flash of lightning at all three windows, and it was followed by a prolonged, deafening roll of thunder, beginning with a hollow rumble and ending with a crash so violent that all the window-panes rattled. Laevsky got up, went to the window, and pressed his forehead against the pane. There was a fierce, magnificent storm. On the horizon lightning-flashes were flung in white streams from the storm-clouds into the sea, lighting up the high, dark waves over the far-away expanse. And to right and to left, and, no doubt, over the house too, the lightning flashed.

"The storm!" whispered Laevsky; he had a longing to pray to some one or to something, if only to the lightning or the storm-clouds. "Dear storm!"

He remembered how as a boy he used to run out into the garden without a hat on when there was a storm, and how two fair-haired girls with blue eyes used to run after him, and how they got wet through with the rain; they laughed with delight, but when there was a loud peal of thunder, the girls used to nestle up to the boy confidingly, while he crossed himself and made haste to repeat: "Holy, holy, holy. . . ." Oh, where had they vanished to! In what sea were they drowned, those dawning days of pure, fair life? He had no fear of the storm, no love of nature now; he had no God. All the confiding girls he had ever known had by now been ruined by him and those like him. All his life he had not planted one tree in his own garden, nor grown one blade of grass; and living among the living, he had not saved one fly; he had done nothing but destroy and ruin, and lie, lie. . . .

"What in my past was not vice?" he asked himself, trying to clutch at some bright memory as a man falling down a precipice clutches at the bushes.

School? The university? But that was a sham. He had neglected his work and forgotten what he had learnt. The service of his country? That, too, was a sham, for he did nothing in the Service, took a salary for doing nothing, and it was an abominable swindling of the State for which one was not punished.

He had no craving for truth, and had not sought it; spellbound by vice and lying, his conscience had slept or been silent. Like a stranger, like an alien from another planet, he had taken no part in the common life of men, had been indifferent to their sufferings, their ideas, their religion, their sciences, their strivings, and their struggles. He had not said one good word, not written one line that was not useless and vulgar; he had not done his fellows one ha'p'orth of service, but had eaten their bread, drunk their wine, seduced their wives, lived on their thoughts, and to justify his contemptible, parasitic life in their eyes and in his own, he had always tried to assume an air of being higher and better than they. Lies, lies, lies. . . .

He vividly remembered what he had seen that evening at Muridov's, and he was in an insufferable anguish of loathing and misery. Kirilin and Atchmianov were loathsome, but they were only continuing what he had begun; they were his accomplices and his disciples. This young weak woman had trusted him more than a brother, and he had deprived her of her husband, of her friends and of her country, and had brought her here—to the heat, to fever, and to boredom; and from day to day she was bound to reflect, like a mirror, his idleness, his viciousness and falsity—and that was all she had had to fill her weak, listless, pitiable life. Then he had grown sick of her, had begun to hate her, but had not had the pluck to abandon her, and he had tried to entangle her more and more closely in a web of lies. . . . These men had done the rest.

Laevsky sat at the table, then got up and went to the window; at one minute he put out the candle and then he lighted it again. He cursed himself aloud, wept and wailed, and asked forgiveness; several times he ran to the table in despair, and wrote:

"Mother!"

Except his mother, he had no relations or near friends; but how could his mother help him? And where was she? He had an impulse to run to Nadyezhda Fyodorovna, to fall at her feet, to kiss her hands and feet, to beg her forgiveness; but she was his victim, and he was afraid of her as though she were dead.

"My life is ruined," he repeated, rubbing his hands. "Why am I still alive, my God! . . ."

He had cast out of heaven his dim star; it had fallen, and its track was lost in the darkness of night. It would never return to the sky again, because life was given only once and never came a second time. If he could have turned back the days and years of the past, he would have replaced the falsity with truth, the idleness with work, the boredom with happiness; he would have given back purity to those whom he had robbed of it. He would have found God and goodness, but that was as impossible as to put back the fallen star into the sky, and because it was impossible he was in despair.

When the storm was over he sat by the open window and thought calmly of what was before him. Von Koren would most likely kill him. The man's clear, cold theory of life justified the destruction of the rotten and the useless; if it changed at the crucial moment, it would be the hatred and the repugnance that Laevsky inspired in him that would save him. If he missed his aim or, in mockery of his hated opponent, only wounded him, or fired in the air, what could he do then? Where could he go?

"Go to Petersburg?" Laevsky asked himself. But that would mean beginning over again the old life which he cursed. And the man who seeks salvation in change of place like a migrating bird would find nothing anywhere, for all the world is alike to him. Seek salvation in men? In whom and how? Samoylenko's kindness and generosity could no more save him than the deacon's laughter or Von Koren's hatred.

He must look for salvation in himself alone, and if there were no finding it, why waste time? He must kill himself, that was all. . . .

He heard the sound of a carriage. It was getting light. The carriage passed by, turned, and crunching on the wet sand, stopped near the house. There were two men in the carriage.

"Wait a minute; I'm coming directly," Laevsky said to them out of the window. "I'm not asleep. Surely it's not time yet?"

"Yes, it's four o'clock. By the time we get there . . ."

Laevsky put on his overcoat and cap, put some cigarettes in his pocket, and stood still hesitating. He felt as though there was something else he must do. In the street the seconds talked in low voices and the horses snorted, and this sound in the damp, early morning, when everybody was asleep and light was hardly dawning in the sky, filled Laevsky's soul with a disconsolate feeling which was like a presentiment of evil. He stood for a little, hesitating, and went into the bedroom.

Nadyezhda Fyodorovna was lying stretched out on the bed, wrapped from head to foot in a rug. She did not stir, and her whole appearance, especially her head, suggested an Egyptian mummy. Looking at her in silence, Laevsky mentally asked her forgiveness, and thought that if the heavens were not empty and there really were a God, then He would save her; if there were no God, then she had better perish—there was nothing for her to live for.

All at once she jumped up, and sat up in bed. Lifting her pale face and looking with horror at Laevsky, she asked:

"Is it you? Is the storm over?"

"Yes."

She remembered; put both hands to her head and shuddered all over.

"How miserable I am!" she said. "If only you knew how miserable I am! I expected," she went on, half closing her eyes, " that you would kill me or turn me out of the house into the rain and storm, but you delay . . . delay . . ."

Warmly and impulsively he put his arms round her and covered her knees and hands with kisses. Then when she muttered something and shuddered with the thought of the past, he stroked her hair, and looking into her face, realised that this unhappy, sinful woman was the one creature near and dear to him, whom no one could replace.

When he went out of the house and got into the carriage he wanted to return home alive.

XVIII

The deacon got up, dressed, took his thick, gnarled stick and slipped quietly out of the house. It was dark, and for the first minute when he went into the street, he could not even see his white stick. There was not a single star in the sky, and it looked as though there would be rain again. There was a smell of wet sand and sea.

"It's to be hoped that the mountaineers won't attack us," thought the deacon, hearing the tap of the stick on the pavement, and noticing how loud and lonely the taps sounded in the stillness of the night.

When he got out of town, he began to see both the road and his stick. Here and there in the black sky there were dark cloudy patches, and soon a star peeped out and timidly blinked its one eye. The deacon walked along the high rocky coast and did not see the sea; it was slumbering below, and its unseen waves broke languidly and heavily on the shore, as though sighing "Ouf!" and how slowly! One wave broke—the deacon had time to count eight steps; then another broke, and six steps; later a third. As before, nothing could be seen, and in the darkness one could hear the languid, drowsy drone of the sea. One could hear the infinitely far-away, inconceivable time when God moved above chaos.

The deacon felt uncanny. He hoped God would not punish him for keeping company with infidels, and even going to look at their duels. The duel would be nonsensical, bloodless, absurd, but however that might be, it was a heathen spectacle, and it was altogether unseemly for an ecclesiastical person to be present at it. He stopped and wondered—should he go back? But an intense, restless curiosity triumphed over his doubts, and he went on.

"Though they are infidels they are good people, and will be saved," he assured himself. "They are sure to be saved," he said aloud, lighting a cigarette.

By what standard must one measure men's qualities, to judge rightly of them? The deacon remembered his enemy, the inspector of the clerical school, who believed in God, lived in chastity, and did not fight duels; but he used to feed the deacon on bread with sand in it, and on one occasion almost pulled off the deacon's ear. If human life was so artlessly constructed that every one respected this cruel and dishonest inspector who stole the Government flour, and his health and salvation were prayed for in the schools, was it just to shun such men as Von Koren and Laevsky, simply because they were unbelievers? The deacon was weighing this question, but he recalled how absurd Samoylenko had looked yesterday, and that broke the thread of his ideas. What fun they would have next day! The deacon imagined how he would sit under a bush and look on, and when Von Koren began boasting next day at dinner, he, the deacon, would begin laughing and telling him all the details of the duel.

"How do you know all about it?" the zoologist would ask.

"Well, there you are! I stayed at home, but I know all about it."

It would be nice to write a comic description of the duel. His father-in-law would read it and laugh. A good story, told or written, was more than meat and drink to his father-in-law.

The valley of the Yellow River opened before him. The stream was broader and fiercer for the rain, and instead of murmuring as before, it was raging. It began to get light. The grey, dingy morning, and the clouds racing towards the west to overtake the storm-clouds, the mountains girt with mist, and the wet trees, all struck the deacon as ugly and sinister. He washed at the brook, repeated his morning prayer, and felt a longing for tea and hot rolls, with sour cream, which were served every morning at his father-in-law's. He remembered his wife and the "Days past Recall," which she played on the piano. What sort of woman was she? His wife had been introduced, betrothed, and married to him all in one week: he had lived with her less than a month when he was ordered here, so that he had not had time to find out what she was like. All the same, he rather missed her.

"I must write her a nice letter . . ." he thought. The flag on the *duhan* hung limp, soaked by the rain, and the *duhan* itself with its wet roof seemed darker and lower than it had been before. Near the door was standing a cart; Kerbalay, with two mountaineers and a young Tatar woman in trousers—no doubt Kerbalay's wife or daughter—were bringing sacks of something out of the *duhan*, and putting them on maize straw in the cart.

Near the cart stood a pair of asses hanging their heads. When they had put in all the sacks, the mountaineers and the Tatar woman began covering them over with straw, while Kerbalay began hurriedly harnessing the asses.

"Smuggling, perhaps," thought the deacon.

Here was the fallen tree with the dried pine-needles, here was the blackened patch from the fire. He remembered the picnic and all its incidents, the fire, the singing of the mountaineers, his sweet dreams of becoming a bishop, and of the Church procession. . . . The Black River had grown blacker and broader with the rain. The deacon walked cautiously over the narrow bridge, which by now was reached by the topmost crests of the dirty water, and went up through the little copse to the drying-shed.

"A splendid head," he thought, stretching himself on the straw, and thinking of Von Koren. "A fine head—God grant him health; only there is cruelty in him. . . ."

Why did he hate Laevsky and Laevsky hate him? Why were they going to fight a duel? If from their childhood they had known poverty as the deacon had; if they had been brought up among ignorant, hard-hearted, grasping, coarse and ill-mannered people who grudged you a crust of bread, who spat on the floor and hiccoughed at dinner and at prayers; if they had not been spoilt from childhood by the pleasant surroundings and the select circle of friends they lived in—how they would have rushed at each other, how readily they would have overlooked each other's shortcomings and would have prized each other's strong points! Why, how few even outwardly decent people there were in the world! It was true that Laevsky was flighty, dissipated, queer, but he did not steal, did not spit loudly on the floor; he did not abuse his wife and say, "You'll eat till you burst, but you don't want to work;" he would not beat a child with reins, or give his servants stinking meat to eat—surely this was reason enough to be indulgent to him? Besides, he was the chief sufferer from his failings, like a sick man from his sores. Instead of being led by boredom and some sort of misunderstanding to look for degeneracy, extinction, heredity, and other such incomprehensible things in each other, would they not do better to stoop a little lower and turn their hatred and anger where whole streets resounded with moanings from coarse ignorance, greed, scolding, impurity, swearing, the shrieks of women. . . .

The sound of a carriage interrupted the deacon's thoughts. He glanced out of the door and saw a carriage and in it three persons: Laevsky, Sheshkovsky, and the superintendent of the post-office.

"Stop!" said Sheshkovsky.

All three got out of the carriage and looked at one another.

"They are not here yet," said Sheshkovsky, shaking the mud off. "Well? Till the show begins, let us go and find a suitable spot; there's not room to turn round here."

They went further up the river and soon vanished from sight. The Tatar driver sat in the carriage with his head resting on his shoulder and fell asleep. After waiting ten minutes the deacon came out of the drying-shed, and taking off his black hat that he might not be noticed, he began threading his way among the bushes and strips of maize along the bank, crouching and looking about him. The grass and maize were wet, and big drops fell on his head from the trees and bushes. "Disgraceful!" he muttered, picking up his wet and muddy skirt. "Had I realised it, I would not have come."

Soon he heard voices and caught sight of them. Laevsky was walking rapidly to and fro in the small glade with bowed back and hands thrust in his sleeves; his seconds were standing at the water's edge, rolling cigarettes.

"Strange," thought the deacon, not recognising Laevsky's walk; "he looks like an old man. . . ."

"How rude it is of them!" said the superintendent of the post-office, looking at his watch. "It may be learned manners to be late, but to my thinking it's hoggish."

Sheshkovsky, a stout man with a black beard, listened and said:

"They're coming!"

XIX

"It's the first time in my life I've seen it! How glorious!" said Von Koren, pointing to the glade and stretching out his hands to the east. "Look: green rays!"

In the east behind the mountains rose two green streaks of light, and it really was beautiful. The sun was rising.

"Good-morning!" the zoologist went on, nodding to Laevsky's seconds. "I'm not late, am I?"

He was followed by his seconds, Boyko and Govorovsky, two very young officers of the same height, wearing white tunics, and Ustimovitch, the thin, unsociable doctor; in one hand he had a bag of some sort, and in the other hand, as usual, a cane which he held behind him. Laying the bag on the ground and greeting no one, he put the other hand, too, behind his back and began pacing up and down the glade.

Laevsky felt the exhaustion and awkwardness of a man who is soon perhaps to die, and is for that reason an object of general attention. He wanted to be killed as soon as possible or taken home. He saw the sunrise now for the first time in his life; the early morning, the green rays of light, the dampness, and the men in wet boots, seemed to him to have nothing to do with his life, to be superfluous and embarrassing. All this had no connection with the night he had been through, with his thoughts and his feeling of guilt, and so he would have gladly gone away without waiting for the duel.

Von Koren was noticeably excited and tried to conceal it, pretending that he was more interested in the green light than anything. The seconds were confused, and looked at one another as though wondering why they were here and what they were to do.

"I imagine, gentlemen, there is no need for us to go further," said Sheshkovsky. "This place will do."

"Yes, of course," Von Koren agreed.

A silence followed. Ustimovitch, pacing to and fro, suddenly turned sharply to Laevsky and said in a low voice, breathing into his face:

"They have very likely not told you my terms yet. Each side is to pay me fifteen roubles, and in the case of the death of one party, the survivor is to pay thirty."

Laevsky was already acquainted with the man, but now for the first time he had a distinct view of his lustreless eyes, his stiff moustaches, and wasted, consumptive neck; he was a money-grubber, not a doctor; his breath had an unpleasant smell of beef.

"What people there are in the world!" thought Laevsky, and answered: "Very good."

The doctor nodded and began pacing to and fro again, and it was evident he did not need the money at all, but simply asked for it from hatred. Every one felt it was time to begin, or to end what had been begun, but instead of beginning or ending, they stood about, moved to and fro and smoked. The young officers, who were present at a duel for the first time in their lives, and even now hardly believed in this civilian and, to their thinking, unnecessary duel, looked critically at their tunics and stroked their sleeves. Sheshkovsky went up to them and said softly: "Gentlemen, we must use every effort to prevent this duel; they ought to be reconciled."

He flushed crimson and added:

"Kirilin was at my rooms last night complaining that Laevsky had found him with Nadyezhda Fyodorovna, and all that sort of thing."

"Yes, we know that too," said Boyko.

"Well, you see, then . . . Laevsky's hands are trembling and all that sort of thing . . . he can scarcely hold a pistol now. To fight with him is as inhuman as to fight a man who is drunk or who has typhoid. If a reconciliation cannot be arranged, we ought to put off the duel, gentlemen, or something. . . . It's such a sickening business, I can't bear to see it."

"Talk to Von Koren."

"I don't know the rules of duelling, damnation take them, and I don't want to either; perhaps he'll imagine Laevsky funks it and has sent me to him, but he can think what he likes—I'll speak to him."

Sheshkovsky hesitatingly walked up to Von Koren with a slight limp, as though his leg had gone to sleep; and as he went towards him, clearing his throat, his whole figure was a picture of indolence.

"There's something I must say to you, sir," he began, carefully scrutinising the flowers on the zoologist's shirt. "It's confidential. I don't know the rules of duelling, damnation take them, and I don't want to, and I look on the matter not as a second and that sort of thing, but as a man, and that's all about it."

"Yes. Well?"

"When seconds suggest reconciliation they are usually not listened to; it is looked upon as a formality. *Amour propre* and all that. But I humbly beg you to look carefully at Ivan Andreitch. He's not in a normal state, so to speak, to-day—not in his right mind, and a pitiable object. He has had a misfortune. I can't endure gossip. . . ."

Sheshkovsky flushed crimson and looked round.

"But in view of the duel, I think it necessary to inform you, Laevsky found his madam last night at Muridov's with . . . another gentleman."

"How disgusting!" muttered the zoologist; he turned pale, frowned, and spat loudly. "Tfoo!"

His lower lip quivered, he walked away from Sheshkovsky, unwilling to hear more, and as though he had accidentally tasted something bitter, spat loudly again, and for the first time that morning looked with hatred at Laevsky. His excitement and awkwardness passed off; he tossed his head and said aloud:

"Gentlemen, what are we waiting for, I should like to know? Why don't we begin?"

Sheshkovsky glanced at the officers and shrugged his shoulders.

"Gentlemen," he said aloud, addressing no one in particular. "Gentlemen, we propose that you should be reconciled."

"Let us make haste and get the formalities over," said Von Koren. "Reconciliation has been discussed already. What is the next formality? Make haste, gentlemen, time won't wait for us."

"But we insist on reconciliation all the same," said Sheshkovsky in a guilty voice, as a man compelled to interfere in another man's business; he flushed, laid his hand on his heart, and went on: " Gentlemen, we see no grounds for associating the offence with the duel. There's nothing in common between duelling and offences against one another of which we are sometimes guilty through human weakness. You are university men and men of culture, and no doubt you see in the duel nothing but a foolish and out-of-date formality, and all that sort of thing. That's how we look at it ourselves, or we shouldn't have come, for we cannot allow that in our presence men should fire at one another, and all that." Sheshkovsky wiped the perspiration off his face and went on: "Make an end to your misunderstanding, gentlemen; shake hands, and let us go home and drink to peace. Upon my honour, gentlemen!"

Von Koren did not speak. Laevsky, seeing that they were looking at him, said:

"I have nothing against Nikolay Vassilitch; if he considers I'm to blame, I'm ready to apologise to him."

Von Koren was offended.

"It is evident, gentlemen," he said, "you want Mr. Laevsky to return home a magnanimous and chivalrous figure, but I cannot give you and him that satisfaction. And there was no need to get up early and drive eight miles out of town simply to drink to peace, to have breakfast, and to explain to me that the duel is an out-of-date formality. A duel is a duel, and there is no need to make it more false and stupid than it is in reality. I want to fight!"

A silence followed. Boyko took a pair of pistols out of a box; one was given to Von Koren and one to Laevsky, and then there followed a difficulty which afforded a brief amusement to the zoologist and the seconds. It appeared that of all the people present not one had ever in his life been at a duel, and no one knew precisely how they ought to stand, and what the seconds ought to say and do. But then Boyko remembered and began, with a smile, to explain.

"Gentlemen, who remembers the description in Lermontov?" asked Von Koren, laughing. "In Turgenev, too, Bazarov had a duel with someone. . . . ."

"There's no need to remember," said Ustimovitch impatiently. "Measure the distance, that's all."

And he took three steps as though to show how to measure it. Boyko counted out the steps while his companion drew his sabre and scratched the earth at the extreme points to mark the barrier. In complete silence the opponents took their places.

"Moles," the deacon thought, sitting in the bushes.

Sheshkovsky said something, Boyko explained something again, but Laevsky did not hear—or rather heard, but did not understand. He cocked his pistol when the time came to do so, and raised the cold, heavy weapon with the barrel upwards. He forgot to unbutton his overcoat, and it felt very tight over his shoulder and under his arm, and his arm rose as awkwardly as though the sleeve had been cut out of tin. He remembered the hatred he had felt the night before for the swarthy brow and curly hair, and felt that even yesterday at the moment of intense hatred and anger he could not have shot a man. Fearing that the bullet might somehow hit Von Koren by accident, he raised the pistol higher and higher, and felt that this too obvious magnanimity was indelicate and anything but magnanimous, but he did not know how else to do and could do nothing else. Looking at the pale, ironically smiling face of Von Koren, who evidently had been convinced from the beginning that his opponent would fire in the air, Laevsky thought that, thank God, everything would be over directly, and all that he had to do was to press the trigger rather hard. . . .

He felt a violent shock on the shoulder; there was the sound of a shot and an answering echo in the mountains: ping-ting!

Von Koren cocked his pistol and looked at Ustimovitch, who was pacing as before with his hands behind his back, taking no notice of any one.

"Doctor," said the zoologist, "be so good as not to move to and fro like a pendulum. You make me dizzy."

The doctor stood still. Von Koren began to take aim at Laevsky.

"It's all over!" thought Laevsky.

The barrel of the pistol aimed straight at his face, the expression of hatred and contempt in Von Koren's attitude and whole figure, and the murder just about to be committed by a decent man in broad daylight, in the presence of decent men, and the stillness and the unknown force that compelled Laevsky to stand still and not to run—how mysterious it all was, how incomprehensible and terrible!

The moment while Von Koren was taking aim seemed to Laevsky longer than a night: he glanced imploringly at the seconds; they were pale and did not stir.

"Make haste and fire," thought Laevsky, and felt that his pale, quivering, and pitiful face must arouse even greater hatred in Von Koren.

"I'll kill him directly," thought Von Koren, aiming at his forehead, with his finger already on the catch. "Yes, of course I'll kill him. . . ."

"He'll kill him!" A despairing shout was suddenly heard somewhere very close at hand.

A shot rang out at once. Seeing that Laevsky remained standing where he was and did not fall, they all looked in the direction from which the shout had come, and saw the deacon. With pale face and wet hair sticking to his forehead and his cheeks, wet through and muddy, he was standing in the maize on the further bank, smiling rather queerly and waving his wet hat. Sheshkovsky laughed with joy, burst into tears, and moved away. . . .

XX

A little while afterwards, Von Koren and the deacon met near the little bridge. The deacon was excited; he breathed hard, and avoided looking in people's faces. He felt ashamed both of his terror and his muddy, wet garments.

"I thought you meant to kill him . . ." he muttered. "How contrary to human nature it is! How utterly unnatural it is!"

"But how did you come here?" asked the zoologist.

"Don't ask," said the deacon, waving his hand. "The evil one tempted me, saying: 'Go, go. . . .' So I went and almost died of fright in the maize. But now, thank God, thank God. . . . I am awfully pleased with you," muttered the deacon. "Old Grandad Tarantula will be glad. . . . It's funny, it's too funny! Only I beg of you most earnestly don't tell anybody I was there, or I may get into hot water with the authorities. They will say: 'The deacon was a second.' "

"Gentlemen," said Von Koren, "the deacon asks you not to tell any one you've seen him here. He might get into trouble."

"How contrary to human nature it is!" sighed the deacon. "Excuse my saying so, but your face was so dreadful that I thought you were going to kill him."

"I was very much tempted to put an end to that scoundrel," said Von Koren, "but you shouted close by, and I missed my aim. The whole procedure is revolting to any one who is not used to it, and it has exhausted me, deacon. I feel awfully tired. Come along. . . ."

"No, you must let me walk back. I must get dry, for I am wet and cold."

"Well, as you like," said the zoologist, in a weary tone, feeling dispirited, and, getting into the carriage, he closed his eyes. "As you like. . . ."

While they were moving about the carriages and taking their seats, Kerbalay stood in the road, and, laying his hands on his stomach, he bowed low, showing his teeth; he imagined that the gentry had come to enjoy the beauties of nature and drink tea, and could not understand why they were getting into the carriages. The party set off in complete silence and only the deacon was left by the *duhan*.

"Come to the *duhan*, drink tea," he said to Kerbalay. "Me wants to eat."

Kerbalay spoke good Russian, but the deacon imagined that the Tatar would understand him better if he talked to him in broken Russian. "Cook omelette, give cheese. . . ."

"Come, come, father," said Kerbalay, bowing. "I'll give you everything. . . . I've cheese and wine. . . . Eat what you like."

"What is 'God' in Tatar?" asked the deacon, going into the *duhan*.

"Your God and my God are the same," said Kerbalay, not understanding him. "God is the same for all men, only men are different.

Some are Russian, some are Turks, some are English—there are many sorts of men, but God is one."

"Very good. If all men worship the same God, why do you Mohammedans look upon Christians as your everlasting enemies?"

"Why are you angry?" said Kerbalay, laying both hands on his stomach. "You are a priest; I am a Mussulman: you say, 'I want to eat'— I give it you. . . . Only the rich man distinguishes your God from my God; for the poor man it is all the same. If you please, it is ready."

While this theological conversation was taking place at the *duhan*, Laevsky was driving home thinking how dreadful it had been driving there at daybreak, when the roads, the rocks, and the mountains were wet and dark, and the uncertain future seemed like a terrible abyss, of which one could not see the bottom; while now the raindrops hanging on the grass and on the stones were sparkling in the sun like diamonds, nature was smiling joyfully, and the terrible future was left behind. He looked at Sheshkovsky's sullen, tear-stained face, and at the two carriages ahead of them in which Von Koren, his seconds, and the doctor were sitting, and it seemed to him as though they were all coming back from a graveyard in which a wearisome, insufferable man who was a burden to others had just been buried.

"Everything is over," he thought of his past, cautiously touching his neck with his fingers.

On the right side of his neck was a small swelling, of the length and breadth of his little finger, and he felt a pain, as though some one had passed a hot iron over his neck. The bullet had bruised it.

Afterwards, when he got home, a strange, long, sweet day began for him, misty as forgetfulness. Like a man released from prison or from hospital, he stared at the long-familiar objects and wondered that the tables, the windows, the chairs, the light, and the sea stirred in him a keen, childish delight such as he had not known for long, long years. Nadyezhda Fyodorovna, pale and haggard, could not understand his gentle voice and strange movements; she made haste to tell him everything that had happened to her. . . . It seemed to her that very likely he scarcely heard and did not understand her, and that if he did know everything he would curse her and kill her, but he listened to her, stroked her face and hair, looked into her eyes and said:

"I have nobody but you. . . ."

Then they sat a long while in the garden, huddled close together, saying nothing, or dreaming aloud of their happy life in the future, in brief, broken sentences, while it seemed to him that he had never spoken at such length or so eloquently.

XXI

More than three months had passed.

The day came that Von Koren had fixed on for his departure. A cold, heavy rain had been falling from early morning, a north-east wind was blowing, and the waves were high on the sea. It was said that the steamer would hardly be able to come into the harbour in such weather. By the time-table it should have arrived at ten o'clock in the morning, but Von Koren, who had gone on to the sea-front at midday and again after dinner, could see nothing through the field-glass but grey waves and rain covering the horizon.

Towards the end of the day the rain ceased and the wind began to drop perceptibly. Von Koren had already made up his mind that he would not be able to get off that day, and had settled down to play chess with Samoylenko; but after dark the orderly announced that there were lights on the sea and that a rocket had been seen.

Von Koren made haste. He put his satchel over his shoulder, and kissed Samoylenko and the deacon. Though there was not the slightest necessity, he went through the rooms again, said good-bye to the orderly and the cook, and went out into the street, feeling that he had left something behind, either at the doctor's or his lodging. In the street he walked beside Samoylenko, behind them came the deacon with a box, and last of all the orderly with two portmanteaus. Only Samoylenko and the orderly could distinguish the dim lights on the sea. The others gazed into the darkness and saw nothing. The steamer had stopped a long way from the coast.

"Make haste, make haste," Von Koren hurried them. "I am afraid it will set off."

As they passed the little house with three windows, into which Laevsky had moved soon after the duel, Von Koren could not resist peeping in at the window. Laevsky was sitting, writing, bent over the table, with his back to the window.

"I wonder at him!" said the zoologist softly. "What a screw he has put on himself!"

"Yes, one may well wonder," said Samoylenko. "He sits from morning till night, he's always at work. He works to pay off his debts. And he lives, brother, worse than a beggar!"

Half a minute of silence followed. The zoologist, the doctor, and the deacon stood at the window and went on looking at Laevsky.

"So he didn't get away from here, poor fellow," said Samoylenko. "Do you remember how hard he tried?"

"Yes, he has put a screw on himself," Von Koren repeated. "His marriage, the way he works all day long for his daily bread, a new expression in his face, and even in his walk—it's all so extraordinary that I don't know what to call it."

The zoologist took Samoylenko's sleeve and went on with emotion in his voice:

"You tell him and his wife that when I went away I was full of admiration for them and wished them all happiness . . . and I beg him, if he can, not to remember evil against me. He knows me. He knows that if I could have foreseen this change, then I might have become his best friend."

"Go in and say good-bye to him."

"No, that wouldn't do."

"Why? God knows, perhaps you'll never see him again."

The zoologist reflected, and said:

"That's true."

Samoylenko tapped softly at the window. Laevsky started and looked round.

"Vanya, Nikolay Vassilitch wants to say good-bye to you," said Samoylenko. "He is just going away."

Laevsky got up from the table, and went into the passage to open the door. Samoylenko, the zoologist, and the deacon went into the house.

"I can only come for one minute," began the zoologist, taking off his goloshes in the passage, and already wishing he had not given way to his feelings and come in, uninvited. "It is as though I were forcing myself on him," he thought, "and that's stupid."

"Forgive me for disturbing you," he said as he went into the room with Laevsky, "but I'm just going away, and I had an impulse to see you. God knows whether we shall ever meet again."

"I am very glad to see you. . . . Please come in," said Laevsky, and he awkwardly set chairs for his visitors as though he wanted to bar their way, and stood in the middle of the room, rubbing his hands.

"I should have done better to have left my audience in the street," thought Von Koren, and he said firmly: "Don't remember evil against me, Ivan Andreitch. To forget the past is, of course, impossible—it is too painful, and I've not come here to apologise or to declare that I was not to blame. I acted sincerely, and I have not changed my convictions since then. . . . It is true that I see, to my great delight, that I was mistaken in regard to you, but it's easy to make a false step even on a smooth road, and, in fact, it's the natural human lot: if one is not mistaken in the main, one is mistaken in the details. Nobody knows the real truth."

"No, no one knows the truth," said Laevsky.

"Well, good-bye. . . . God give you all happiness."

Von Koren gave Laevsky his hand; the latter took it and bowed.

"Don't remember evil against me," said Von Koren. "Give my greetings to your wife, and say I am very sorry not to say good-bye to her."

"She is at home."

Laevsky went to the door of the next room, and said:

"Nadya, Nikolay Vassilitch wants to say good-bye to you."

Nadyezhda Fyodorovna came in; she stopped near the doorway and looked shyly at the visitors. There was a look of guilt and dismay on her face, and she held her hands like a schoolgirl receiving a scolding.

"I'm just going away, Nadyezhda Fyodorovna," said Von Koren, "and have come to say good-bye."

She held out her hand uncertainly, while Laevsky bowed.

"What pitiful figures they are, though!" thought Von Koren. "The life they are living does not come easy to them. I shall be in Moscow and Petersburg; can I send you anything?" he asked.

"Oh!" said Nadyezhda Fyodorovna, and she looked anxiously at her husband. "I don't think there's anything. . . ."

"No, nothing . . ." said Laevsky, rubbing his hands. "Our greetings."

Von Koren did not know what he could or ought to say, though as he went in he thought he would say a very great deal that would be warm and good and important. He shook hands with Laevsky and his wife in silence, and left them with a depressed feeling.

"What people!" said the deacon in a low voice, as he walked behind them. "My God, what people! Of a truth, the right hand of God has planted this vine! Lord! Lord! One man vanquishes thousands and another tens of thousands. Nikolay Vassilitch," he said ecstatically, "let me tell you that to-day you have conquered the greatest of man's enemies—pride."

"Hush, deacon! Fine conquerors we are! Conquerors ought to look like eagles, while he's a pitiful figure, timid, crushed; he bows like a Chinese idol and I, I am sad. . . ."

They heard steps behind them. It was Laevsky, hurrying after them to see him off. The orderly was standing on the quay with the two portmanteaus, and at a little distance stood four boatmen.

"There is a wind, though. . . . Brrr!" said Samoylenko. "There must be a pretty stiff storm on the sea now! You are not going off at a nice time, Koyla."

"I'm not afraid of sea-sickness."

"That's not the point. . . . I only hope these rascals won't upset you. You ought to have crossed in the agent's sloop. Where's the agent's sloop?" he shouted to the boatmen.

"It has gone, Your Excellency."

"And the Customs-house boat?"

"That's gone, too."

"Why didn't you let us know," said Samoylenko angrily. "You dolts!"

"It's all the same, don't worry yourself . . ." said Von Koren. "Well, good-bye. God keep you"

Samoylenko embraced Von Koren and made the sign of the cross over him three times.

"Don't forget us, Kolya. . . . Write. . . . We shall look out for you next spring."

"Good-bye, deacon," said Von Koren, shaking hands with the deacon. "Thank you for your company and for your pleasant conversation. Think about the expedition."

"Oh Lord, yes! to the ends of the earth," laughed the deacon. "I've nothing against it."

Von Koren recognised Laevsky in the darkness, and held out his hand without speaking. The boatmen were by now below, holding the boat, which was beating against the piles, though the breakwater screened it from the breakers. Von Koren went down the ladder, jumped into the boat, and sat at the helm.

"Write!" Samoylenko shouted to him. "Take care of yourself."

"No one knows the real truth," thought Laevsky, turning up the collar of his coat and thrusting his hands into his sleeves.

The boat turned briskly out of the harbour into the open sea. It vanished in the waves, but at once from a deep hollow glided up onto a high breaker, so that they could distinguish the men and even the oars. The boat moved three yards forward and was sucked two yards back.

"Write!" shouted Samoylenko; "it's devilish weather for you to go in."

"Yes, no one knows the real truth . . ." thought Laevsky, looking wearily at the dark, restless sea.

"It flings the boat back," he thought; "she makes two steps forward and one step back; but the boatmen are stubborn, they work the oars unceasingly, and are not afraid of the high waves. The boat goes on and on. Now she is out of sight, but in half an hour the boatmen will see the steamer lights distinctly, and within an hour they will be by the steamer ladder. So it is in life. . . . In the search for truth man makes two steps forward and one step back. Suffering, mistakes, and weariness of life thrust them back, but the thirst for truth and stubborn will drive them on and on. And who knows? Perhaps they will reach the real truth at last."

"Go—o—od-by—e," shouted Samoylenko.

"There's no sight or sound of them," said the deacon. "Good luck on the journey!"

It began to spot with rain.

1891

The Wife

I

I received the following letter:

DEAR SIR, PAVEL ANDREITCH!

"Not far from you—that is to say, in the village of Pestrovo—very distressing incidents are taking place, concerning which I feel it my duty to write to you. All the peasants of that village sold their cottages and all their belongings, and set off for the province of Tomsk, but did not succeed in getting there, and have come back. Here, of course, they have nothing now; everything belongs to other people. They have settled three or four families in a hut, so that there are no less than fifteen persons of both sexes in each hut, not counting the young children; and the long and the short of it is, there is nothing to eat. There is famine and there is a terrible pestilence of hunger, or spotted, typhus; literally every one is stricken. The doctor's assistant says one goes into a cottage and what does one see? Every one is sick, every one delirious, some laughing, others frantic; the huts are filthy; there is no one to fetch them water, no one to give them a drink, and nothing to eat but frozen potatoes. What can Sobol (our Zemstvo doctor) and his lady assistant do when more than medicine the peasants need bread which they have not? The District Zemstvo refuses to assist them, on the ground that their names have been taken off the register of this district, and that they are now reckoned as inhabitants of Tomsk; and, besides, the Zemstvo has no money.

"Laying these facts before you, and knowing your humanity, I beg you not to refuse immediate help.

"Your well-wisher."

Obviously the letter was written by the doctor with the animal name[1] or his lady assistant. Zemstvo doctors and their assistants go on for years growing more and more convinced every day that they can do *nothing*, and yet continue to receive their salaries from people who are living upon frozen potatoes, and consider they have a right to judge whether I am humane or not.

Worried by the anonymous letter and by the fact that peasants came every morning to the servants' kitchen and went down on their knees there, and that twenty sacks of rye had been stolen at night out of the barn, the wall having first been broken in, and by the general depression which was fostered by conversations, newspapers, and horrible weather—worried by all this, I worked listlessly and ineffectively. I was writing "A History of Railways"; I had to read a great number of Russian and foreign books, pamphlets, and articles in the magazines, to make calculations, to refer to logarithms, to think and to write; then again to read, calculate, and think; but as soon as I took up a book or began to think, my thoughts were in a muddle, my eyes began blinking, I would get up from the table with a sigh and begin walking about the big rooms of my deserted country-house. When I was tired of walking about I would stand still at my study window, and, looking across the wide courtyard, over the pond and the bare young birch-trees and the great fields covered with recently fallen, thawing snow, I saw on a low hill on the horizon a group of mud-coloured huts from which a black muddy road ran down in an irregular streak through the white field. That was Pestrovo, concerning which my anonymous correspondent had written to me. If it had not been for the crows who, foreseeing rain or snowy weather, floated cawing over the pond and the fields, and the tapping in the carpenter's shed, this bit of the world about which such a fuss was being made would have seemed like the Dead Sea; it was all so still, motionless, lifeless, and dreary!

My uneasiness hindered me from working and concentrating myself; I did not know what it was, and chose to believe it was disappointment. I had actually given up my post in the Department of Ways and Communications, and had come here into the country expressly to live in peace and to devote myself to writing on social questions. It had long been my cherished dream. And now I had to say good-bye both to

[1] *Sobol* in Russian means "sable-marten."—TRANSLATOR'S NOTE.

peace and to literature, to give up everything and think only of the peasants. And that was inevitable, because I was convinced that there was absolutely nobody in the district except me to help the starving. The people surrounding me were uneducated, unintellectual, callous, for the most part dishonest, or if they were honest, they were unreasonable and unpractical like my wife, for instance. It was impossible to rely on such people, it was impossible to leave the peasants to their fate, so that the only thing left to do was to submit to necessity and see to setting the peasants to rights myself.

I began by making up my mind to give five thousand roubles to the assistance of the starving peasants. And that did not decrease, but only aggravated my uneasiness. As I stood by the window or walked about the rooms I was tormented by the question which had not occurred to me before: how this money was to be spent. To have bread bought and to go from hut to hut distributing it was more than one man could do, to say nothing of the risk that in your haste you might give twice as much to one who was well-fed or to one who was making money out of his fellows as to the hungry. I had no faith in the local officials. All these district captains and tax inspectors were young men, and I distrusted them as I do all young people of today, who are materialistic and without ideals. The District Zemstvo, the Peasant Courts, and all the local institutions, inspired in me not the slightest desire to appeal to them for assistance. I knew that all these institutions who were busily engaged in picking out plums from the Zemstvo and the Government pie had their mouths always wide open for a bite at any other pie that might turn up.

The idea occurred to me to invite the neighbouring landowners and suggest to them to organize in my house something like a committee or a centre to which all subscriptions could be forwarded, and from which assistance and instructions could be distributed throughout the district; such an organization, which would render possible frequent consultations and free control on a big scale, would completely meet my views. But I imagined the lunches, the dinners, the suppers and the noise, the waste of time, the verbosity and the bad taste which that mixed provincial company would inevitably bring into my house, and I made haste to reject my idea.

As for the members of my own household, the last thing I could look for was help or support from them. Of my father's household, of the household of my childhood, once a big and noisy family, no one remained but the governess Mademoiselle Marie, or, as she was now called, Marya Gerasimovna, an absolutely insignificant person. She was a precise little old lady of seventy, who wore a light grey dress and a cap with white ribbons, and looked like a china doll. She always sat in the drawing-room reading.

Whenever I passed by her, she would say, knowing the reason for my brooding:

"What can you expect, Pasha? I told you how it would be before. You can judge from our servants."

My wife, Natalya Gavrilovna, lived on the lower storey, all the rooms of which she occupied. She slept, had her meals, and received her visitors downstairs in her own rooms, and took not the slightest interest in how I dined, or slept, or whom I saw. Our relations with one another were simple and not strained, but cold, empty, and dreary as relations are between people who have been so long estranged, that even living under the same roof gives no semblance of nearness. There was no trace now of the passionate and tormenting love—at one time sweet, at another bitter as wormwood—which I had once felt for Natalya Gavrilovna. There was nothing left, either, of the outbursts of the past—the loud altercations, upbraidings, complaints, and gusts of hatred which had usually ended in my wife s going abroad or to her own people, and in my sending money in small but frequent instalments that I might sting her pride oftener. (My proud and sensitive wife and her family live at my expense, and much as she would have liked to do so, my wife could not refuse my money: that afforded me satisfaction and was one comfort in my sorrow.) Now when we chanced to meet in the corridor downstairs or in the yard, I bowed, she smiled graciously. We spoke of the weather, said that it seemed time to put in the double windows, and that some one with bells on their harness had driven over the dam. And at such times I read in her face: "I am faithful to you and am not disgracing your good name which you think so much about; you are sensible and do not worry me; we are quits."

I assured myself that my love had died long ago, that I was too much absorbed in my work to think seriously of my relations with my wife. But, alas! that was only what I imagined. When my wife talked aloud downstairs I listened intently to her voice, though I could not distinguish one word. When she played the piano downstairs I stood up and listened. When her carriage or her saddle-horse was brought to the door, I went to the window and waited to see her out of the house; then I watched her get into her carriage or mount her horse and ride out of the yard. I felt that there was something wrong with me, and was afraid the expression of my eyes or my face might betray me. I looked after my wife and then watched for her to come back that I might see again from the window her face, her shoulders, her fur coat, her hat. I felt dreary, sad, infinitely regretful, and felt inclined in her absence to walk through her rooms, and longed that the problem that my wife and I had not been able to solve because our characters were incompatible, should solve itself in the natural way as soon as possible—that is, that this beautiful woman of twenty-seven might make haste and grow old, and that my head might be grey and bald.

One day at lunch my bailiff informed me that the Pestrovo peasants had begun to pull the thatch off the roofs to feed their cattle. Marya Gerasimovna looked at me in alarm and perplexity.

"What can I do?" I said to her. "One cannot fight single-handed, and I have never experienced such loneliness as I do now. I would give a great deal to find one man in the whole province on whom I could rely."

"Invite Ivan Ivanitch," said Marya Gerasimovna.

"To be sure!" I thought, delighted. "That is an idea! *C'est raison,*" I hummed, going to my study to write to Ivan Ivanitch. "*C'est raison, c'est raison.*"

II

Of all the mass of acquaintances who, in this house twenty-five to thirty-five years ago, had eaten, drunk, masqueraded, fallen in love, married, bored us with accounts of their splendid packs of hounds and horses, the only one still living was Ivan Ivanitch Bragin. At one time he had been very active, talkative, noisy, and given to falling in love, and had been famous for his extreme views and for the peculiar charm of his face, which fascinated men as well as women; now he was an old man, had grown corpulent, and was living out his days with neither views nor charm. He came the day after getting my letter, in the evening just as the samovar was brought into the dining-room and little Marya Gerasimovna had begun slicing the lemon.

"I am very glad to see you, my dear fellow," I said gaily, meeting him. "Why, you are stouter than ever."

"It isn't getting stout; it's swelling," he answered. "The bees must have stung me."

With the familiarity of a man laughing at his own fatness, he put his arms round my waist and laid on my breast his big soft head, with the hair combed down on the forehead like a Little Russian's, and went off into a thin, aged laugh.

"And you go on getting younger," he said through his laugh. "I wonder what dye you use for your hair and beard; you might let me have some of it." Sniffing and gasping, he embraced me and kissed me on the cheek. "You might give me some of it," he repeated. "Why, you are not forty, are you?"

"Alas, I am forty-six!" I said, laughing.

Ivan Ivanitch smelt of tallow candles and cooking, and that suited him. His big, puffy, slow-moving body was swathed in a long frock-coat like a coachman's full coat, with a high waist, and with hooks and eyes instead of buttons, and it would have been strange if he had smelt of eau-de-Cologne, for instance. In his long, unshaven, bluish double chin, which looked like a thistle, his goggle eyes, his shortness of breath, and in the whole of his clumsy, slovenly figure, in his voice, his laugh, and his words, it was difficult to recognize the graceful, interesting talker who used in old days to make the husbands of the district jealous on account of their wives.

"I am in great need of your assistance, my friend," I said, when we were sitting in the dining-room, drinking tea. "I want to organize relief for the starving peasants, and I don't know how to set about it. So perhaps you will be so kind as to advise me."

"Yes, yes, yes," said Ivan Ivanitch, sighing. "To be sure, to be sure, to be sure. . ."

"I would not have worried you, my dear fellow, but really there is no one here but you I can appeal to. You know what people are like about here."

"To be sure, to be sure, to be sure. . . . Yes."

I thought that as we were going to have a serious, business consultation in which any one might take part, regardless of their position or personal relations, why should I not invite Natalya Gavrilovna.

"*Tres faciunt collegium*," I said gaily. "What if we were to ask

Natalya Gavrilovna? What do you think? Fenya," I said, turning to the maid, "ask Natalya Gavrilovna to come upstairs to us, if possible at once. Tell her it's a very important matter."

A little later Natalya Gavrilovna came in. I got up to meet her and said:

"Excuse us for troubling you, Natalie. We are discussing a very important matter, and we had the happy thought that we might take advantage of your good advice, which you will not refuse to give us. Please sit down."

Ivan Ivanitch kissed her hand while she kissed his forehead; then, when we all sat down to the table, he, looking at her tearfully and blissfully, craned forward to her and kissed her hand again. She was dressed in black, her hair was carefully arranged, and she smelt of fresh scent. She had evidently dressed to go out or was expecting somebody. Coming into the dining-room, she held out her hand to me with simple friendliness, and smiled to me as graciously as she did to Ivan Ivanitch—that pleased me; but as she talked she moved her fingers, often and abruptly leaned back in her chair and talked rapidly, and this jerkiness in her words and movements irritated me and reminded me of her native town—Odessa, where the society, men and women alike, had wearied me by its bad taste.

"I want to do something for the famine-stricken peasants," I began, and after a brief pause I went on: "Money, of course, is a great thing, but to confine oneself to subscribing money, and with that to be satisfied, would be evading the worst of the trouble. Help must take the form of money, but the most important thing is a proper and sound organization. Let us think it over, my friends, and do something."

Natalya Gavrilovna looked at me inquiringly and shrugged her shoulders as though to say, "What do I know about it?"

"Yes, yes, famine . . ." muttered Ivan Ivanitch. "Certainly . . . yes."

"It's a serious position," I said, "and assistance is needed as soon as possible. I imagine the first point among the principles which we must work out ought to be promptitude. We must act on the military principles of judgment, promptitude, and energy."

"Yes, promptitude . . ." repeated Ivan Ivanitch in a drowsy and listless voice, as though he were dropping asleep. "Only one can't do anything. The crops have failed, and so what's the use of all your judgment and energy? . . . It's the elements. . . . You can't go against God and fate. . . ."

"Yes, but that's what man has a head for, to contend against the elements."

"Eh? Yes . . . that's so, to be sure. . . . Yes."

Ivan Ivanitch sneezed into his handkerchief, brightened up, and as though he had just woken up, looked round at my wife and me.

"My crops have failed, too." He laughed a thin little laugh and gave a sly wink as though this were really funny. "No money, no corn, and a yard full of labourers like Count Sheremetyev's. I want to kick them out, but I haven't the heart to"

Natalya Gavrilovna laughed, and began questioning him about his private affairs. Her presence gave me a pleasure such as I had not felt for a long time, and I was afraid to look at her for fear my eyes would betray my secret feeling. Our relations were such that that feeling might seem surprising and ridiculous.

She laughed and talked with Ivan Ivanitch without being in the least disturbed that she was in my room and that I was not laughing.

"And so, my friends, what are we to do?" I asked after waiting for a pause. "I suppose before we do anything else we had better immediately open a subscription-list. We will write to our friends in the capitals and in Odessa, Natalie, and ask them to subscribe. When we have got together a little sum we will begin buying corn and fodder for the cattle; and you, Ivan Ivanitch, will you be so kind as to undertake distributing the relief? Entirely relying on your characteristic tact and efficiency, we will only venture to express a desire that before you give any relief you make acquaintance with the details of the case on the spot, and also, which is very important, you should be careful that corn should be distributed only to those who are in genuine need, and not to the drunken, the idle, or the dishonest."

"Yes, yes, yes . . ." muttered Ivan Ivanitch. "To be sure, to be sure."

"Well, one won't get much done with that slobbering wreck," I thought, and I felt irritated.

"I am sick of these famine-stricken peasants, bother them! It's nothing but grievances with them!" Ivan Ivanitch went on, sucking the rind of the lemon. "The hungry have a grievance against those who have enough, and those who have enough have a grievance against the hungry. Yes . . . hunger stupefies and maddens a man and makes him savage; hunger is not a potato. When a man is starving he uses bad language, and steals, and may do worse. . . . One must realize that."

Ivan Ivanitch choked over his tea, coughed, and shook all over with a squeaky, smothered laughter.

" 'There was a battle at Pol . . . Poltava,' " he brought out, gesticulating with both hands in protest against the laughter and coughing which prevented him from speaking. " 'There was a battle at Poltava!' When three years after the Emancipation we had famine in two districts here, Fyodor Fyodoritch came and invited me to go to him. 'Come along, come along,' he persisted, and nothing else would satisfy him. 'Very well, let us go,' I said. And, so we set off. It was in the evening; there was snow falling. Towards night we were getting near his place, and suddenly from the wood came 'bang!' and another time 'bang!' 'Oh, damn it all!' . . . I jumped out of the sledge and I saw in the darkness a man running up to me, knee-deep in the snow. I put my arm round his shoulder, like this, and knocked the gun out of his hand. Then another one turned up; I fetched him a knock on the back of his head so that he grunted and flopped with his nose in the snow. I was a sturdy chap then, my fist was heavy; I disposed of two of them, and when I turned round Fyodor was sitting astride of a third. We did not let our three fine fellows go: we tied their hands behind their backs so that they might not do us or themselves any harm, and took the fools into the kitchen. We were angry with them and at the same time ashamed to look at them; they were peasants we knew, and were good fellows; we were sorry for them. They were quite stupid with terror. One was crying and begging our pardon, the second looked like a wild beast and kept swearing, the third knelt down and began to pray. I said to Fedya: 'Don't bear them a grudge; let them go, the rascals!' He fed them, gave them a bushel of flour each, and let them go: 'Get along with you,' he said. So that's what he did. . . . The Kingdom of Heaven be his and everlasting peace! He understood and did not bear them a grudge; but there were some who did, and how many people they ruined! Yes. . . . Why, over the affair at the Klotchkovs' tavern eleven men were sent to the disciplinary battalion. Yes. . . . And now, look, it's the same thing. Anisyin, the investigating magistrate, stayed the night with me last Thursday, and he told me about some landowner. . . . Yes. . . . They took the wall of his barn to pieces at night and carried off twenty sacks of rye. When the gentleman heard that such a crime had been committed, he sent a telegram to the Governor and another to the police captain, another to the investigating magistrate! . . . Of course, every one is afraid of a man who is fond of litigation. The authorities were in a flutter and there was a general hubbub. Two villages were searched."

"Excuse me, Ivan Ivanitch," I said. "Twenty sacks of rye were stolen from me, and it was I who telegraphed to the Governor. I telegraphed to Petersburg, too. But it was by no means out of love for litigation, as you are pleased to express it, and not because I bore them a grudge. I look at every subject from the point of view of principle. From the point of view of the law, theft is the same whether a man is hungry or not."

"Yes, yes . . ." muttered Ivan Ivanitch in confusion. "Of course. . . To be sure, yes."

Natalya Gavrilovna blushed.

"There are people . . ." she said and stopped; she made an effort to seem indifferent, but she could not keep it up, and looked into my eyes with the hatred that I know so well. "There are people," she said, "for whom famine and human suffering exist simply that they may vent their hateful and despicable temperaments upon them."

I was confused and shrugged my shoulders.

"I meant to say generally," she went on, "that there are people who are quite indifferent and completely devoid of all feeling of sympathy, yet who do not pass human suffering by, but insist on meddling for fear people should be able to do without them. Nothing is sacred for their vanity."

"There are people," I said softly, "who have an angelic character, but who express their glorious ideas in such a form that it is difficult to distinguish the angel from an Odessa market-woman."

I must confess it was not happily expressed.

My wife looked at me as though it cost her a great effort to hold her tongue. Her sudden outburst, and then her inappropriate eloquence on the subject of my desire to help the famine-stricken peasants, were, to say the least, out of place; when I had invited her to come upstairs I had expected quite a different attitude to me and my intentions. I cannot say definitely what I had expected, but I had been agreeably agitated by the expectation. Now I saw that to go on speaking about the famine would be difficult and perhaps stupid.

"Yes . . ." Ivan Ivanitch muttered inappropriately. "Burov, the merchant, must have four hundred thousand at least. I said to him: 'Hand over one or two thousand to the famine. You can't take it with you when you die, anyway.' He was offended. But we all have to die, you know. Death is not a potato."

A silence followed again.

"So there's nothing left for me but to reconcile myself to loneliness," I sighed. "One cannot fight single-handed. Well, I will try single-handed. Let us hope that my campaign against the famine will be more successful than my campaign against indifference."

"I am expected downstairs," said Natalya Gavrilovna.

She got up from the table and turned to Ivan Ivanitch.

"So you will look in upon me downstairs for a minute? I won't say good-bye to you."

And she went away.

Ivan Ivanitch was now drinking his seventh glass of tea, choking, smacking his lips, and sucking sometimes his moustache, sometimes the lemon. He was muttering something drowsily and listlessly, and I did not listen but waited for him to go. At last, with an expression that suggested that he had only come to me to take a cup of tea, he got up and began to take leave. As I saw him out I said:

"And so you have given me no advice."

"Eh? I am a feeble, stupid old man," he answered. "What use would my advice be? You shouldn't worry yourself. . . . I really don't know why you worry yourself. Don't disturb yourself, my dear fellow! Upon my word, there's no need," he whispered genuinely and affectionately, soothing me as though I were a child. "Upon my word, there is no need."

"No need? Why, the peasants are pulling the thatch off their huts, and they say there is typhus somewhere already."

"Well, what of it? If there are good crops next year, they'll thatch them again, and if we die of typhus others will live after us. Anyway, we have to die—if not now, later. Don't worry yourself, my dear."

"I can't help worrying myself," I said irritably.

We were standing in the dimly lighted vestibule. Ivan Ivanitch suddenly took me by the elbow, and, preparing to say something evidently very important, looked at me in silence for a couple of minutes.

"Pavel Andreitch!" he said softly, and suddenly in his puffy, set face and dark eyes there was a gleam of the expression for which he had once been famous and which was truly charming. "Pavel Andreitch, I speak to you as a friend: try to be different! One is ill at ease with you, my dear fellow, one really is !"

He looked intently into my face; the charming expression faded away, his eyes grew dim again, and he sniffed and muttered feebly:

"Yes, yes. . . . Excuse an old man. . . . It's all nonsense . . . yes."

As he slowly descended the staircase, spreading out his hands to balance himself and showing me his huge, bulky back and red neck, he gave me the unpleasant impression of a sort of crab.

"You ought to go away, your Excellency," he muttered. "To Petersburg or abroad. . . . Why should you live here and waste your golden days? You are young, wealthy, and healthy. . . . Yes. . . . Ah, if I were younger I would whisk away like a hare, and snap my fingers at everything."

III

My wife's outburst reminded me of our married life together. In old days after every such outburst we felt irresistibly drawn to each other; we would meet and let off all the dynamite that had accumulated in our souls. And now after Ivan Ivanitch had gone away I had a strong impulse to go to my wife. I wanted to go downstairs and tell her that her behaviour at tea had been an insult to me, that she was cruel, petty, and that her plebeian mind had never risen to a comprehension of what *I* was saying and of what *I* was doing. I walked about the rooms a long time thinking of what I would say to her and trying to guess what she would say to me.

That evening, after Ivan Ivanitch went away, I felt in a peculiarly irritating form the uneasiness which had worried me of late. I could not sit down or sit still, but kept walking about in the rooms that were lighted up and keeping near to the one in which Marya Gerasimovna was sitting. I had a feeling very much like that which I had on the North Sea during a storm when every one thought that our ship, which had no freight nor ballast, would overturn. And that evening I understood that my uneasiness was not disappointment, as I had supposed, but a different feeling, though what exactly I could not say, and that irritated me more than ever.

"I will go to her," I decided. "I can think of a pretext. I shall say that I want to see Ivan Ivanitch; that will be all."

I went downstairs and walked without haste over the carpeted floor through the vestibule and the hall. Ivan Ivanitch was sitting on the sofa in the drawing-room; he was drinking tea again and muttering something. My wife was standing opposite to him and holding on to the back of a chair. There was a gentle, sweet, and docile expression on her face, such as one sees on the faces of people listening to crazy saints or holy men when a peculiar hidden significance is imagined in their vague words and mutterings. There was something morbid, something of a nun's exaltation, in my wife's expression and attitude; and her low-pitched, half-dark rooms with their old-fashioned furniture, with her birds asleep in their cages, and with a smell of geranium, reminded me of the rooms of some abbess or pious old lady.

I went into the drawing-room. My wife showed neither surprise nor confusion, and looked at me calmly and serenely, as though she had known I should come.

"I beg your pardon," I said softly. "I am so glad you have not gone yet, Ivan Ivanitch. I forgot to ask you, do you know the Christian name of the president of our Zemstvo?"

"Andrey Stanislavovitch., Yes. . . ."

"*Merci*," I said, took out my notebook, and wrote it down.

There followed a silence during which my wife and Ivan Ivanitch were probably waiting for me to go; my wife did not believe that I wanted to know the president's name—I saw that from her eyes.

"Well, I must be going, my beauty," muttered Ivan Ivanitch, after I had walked once or twice across the drawing-room and sat down by the fire-place.

"No," said Natalya Gavrilovna quickly, touching his hand. "Stay another quarter of an hour. . . . Please do!"

Evidently she did not wish to be left alone with me without a witness.

"Oh, well, I'll wait a quarter of an hour, too," I thought.

"Why, it's snowing!" I said, getting up and looking out of window. "A good fall of snow! Ivan Ivanitch"—I went on walking about the room—"I do regret not being a sportsman. I can imagine what a pleasure it must be coursing hares or hunting wolves in snow like this!"

My wife, standing still, watched my movements, looking out of the corner of her eyes without turning her head. She looked as though she thought I had a sharp knife or a revolver in my pocket.

"Ivan Ivanitch, do take me out hunting some day," I went on softly. "I shall be very, very grateful to you."

At that moment a visitor came into the room He was a tall, thick-set gentleman whom I did not know, with a bald head, a big fair beard, and little eyes. From his baggy, crumpled clothes and his manners I took him to be a parish clerk or a teacher, but my wife introduced him to me as Dr. Sobol.

"Very, very glad to make your acquaintance," said the doctor in a loud tenor voice, shaking hands with me warmly, with a naïve smile. "Very glad!"

He sat down at the table, took a glass of tea, and said in a loud voice:

"Do you happen to have a drop of rum or brandy? Have pity on me, Olya, and look in the cupboard; I am frozen," he said, addressing the maid.

I sat down by the fire again, looked on, listened, and from time to time put in a word in the general conversation. My wife smiled graciously to the visitors and kept a sharp lookout on me, as though I were a wild beast. She was oppressed by my presence, and this aroused in me jealousy, annoyance, and an obstinate desire to wound her. "Wife, these snug rooms, the place by the fire," I thought, "are mine, have been mine for years, but some crazy Ivan Ivanitch or Sobol has for some reason more right to them than I. Now I see my wife, not out of window, but close at hand, in ordinary home surroundings that I feel the want of now I am growing older, and, in spite of her hatred for me, I miss her as years ago in my childhood I used to miss my mother and my nurse. And I feel that now, on the verge of old age, my love for her is purer and loftier than it was in the past; and that is why I want to go up to her, to stamp hard on her toe with my heel, to hurt her and smile as I do it."

"Monsieur Marten," I said, addressing the doctor, "how many hospitals have we in the district?"

"Sobol," my wife corrected.

"Two," answered Sobol .

"And how many deaths are there every year in each hospital?"

"Pavel Andreitch, I want to speak to you," said my wife.

She apologized to the visitors and went to the next room. I got up and followed her.

"You will go upstairs to your own rooms this minute," she said.

"You are ill-bred," I said to her.

"You will go upstairs to your own rooms this very minute," she repeated sharply, and she looked into my face with hatred.

She was standing so near that if I had stooped a little my beard would have touched her face.

"What is the matter?" I asked. "What harm have I done all at once?"

Her chin quivered, she hastily wiped her eyes, and, with a cursory glance at the looking-glass, whispered:

"The old story is beginning all over again. Of course you won't go away. Well, do as you like. I'll go away myself, and you stay."

We returned to the drawing-room, she with a resolute face, while I shrugged my shoulders and tried to smile. There were some more visitors—an elderly lady and a young man in spectacles. Without greeting the new arrivals or taking leave of the others, I went off to my own rooms.

After what had happened at tea and then again downstairs, it became clear to me that our "family happiness," which we had begun to forget about in the course of the last two years, was through some absurd and trivial reason beginning all over again, and that neither I nor my wife could now stop ourselves; and that next day or the day after, the outburst of hatred would, as I knew by experience of past years, be followed by something revolting which would upset the whole order of our lives. "So it seems that during these two years we have grown no wiser, colder, or calmer," I thought as I began walking about the rooms. "So there will again be tears, outcries, curses, packing up, going abroad, then the continual sickly fear that she will disgrace me with some coxcomb out there, Italian or Russian, refusing a passport, letters, utter loneliness, missing her, and in five years old age, grey hairs." I walked about, imagining what was really impossible—her, grown handsomer, stouter, embracing a man I did not know. By now convinced that that would certainly happen, "Why," I asked myself, "Why, in one of our long past quarrels, had not I given her a divorce, or why had she not at that time left me altogether? I should not have had this yearning for her now, this hatred, this anxiety; and I should have lived out my life quietly, working and not worrying about anything."

A carriage with two lamps drove into the yard, then a big sledge with three horses. My wife was evidently having a party.

Till midnight everything was quiet downstairs and I heard nothing, but at midnight there was a sound of moving chairs and a clatter of crockery. So there was supper. Then the chairs moved again, and through the floor I heard a noise; they seemed to be shouting hurrah. Marya Gerasimovna was already asleep and I was quite alone in the whole upper storey; the portraits of my forefathers, cruel, insignificant people, looked at me from the walls of the drawing-room, and the reflection of my lamp in the window winked unpleasantly. And with a feeling of jealousy and envy for what was going on downstairs, I listened and thought: "I am master here; if I like, I can in a moment turn out all that fine crew." But I knew that all that was nonsense, that I could not turn out any one, and the word "master" had no meaning. One may think oneself master, married, rich, a *kammer-junker*, as much as one likes, and at the same time not know what it means.

After supper some one downstairs began singing in a tenor voice.

"Why, nothing special has happened," I tried to persuade myself. "Why am I so upset? I won't go downstairs tomorrow, that's all; and that will be the end of our quarrel."

At a quarter past one I went to bed.

"Have the visitors downstairs gone?" I asked Alexey as he was undressing me.

"Yes, sir, they've gone."

"And why were they shouting hurrah?"

"Alexey Dmitritch Mahonov subscribed for the famine fund a thousand bushels of flour and a thousand roubles. And the old lady—I don't know her name—promised to set up a soup kitchen on her estate to feed a hundred and fifty people. Thank God . . . Natalya Gavrilovna has been pleased to arrange that all the gentry should assemble every Friday."

"To assemble here, downstairs?"

"Yes, sir. Before supper they read a list: since August up to today Natalya Gavrilovna has collected eight thousand roubles, besides corn. Thank God. . . . What I think is that if our mistress does take trouble for the salvation of her soul, she will soon collect a lot. There are plenty of rich people here."

Dismissing Alexey, I put out the light and drew the bedclothes over my head.

"After all, why am I so troubled?" I thought. "What force draws me to the starving peasants like a butterfly to a flame? I don't know them, I don't understand them; I have never seen them and I don't like them. Why this uneasiness?"

I suddenly crossed myself under the quilt.

"But what a woman she is!" I said to myself, thinking of my wife. "There's a regular committee held in the house without my knowing. Why this secrecy? Why this conspiracy? What have I done to them? Ivan Ivanitch is right—I must go away."

Next morning I woke up firmly resolved to go away. The events of the previous day—the conversation at tea, my wife, Sobol, the supper, my apprehensions—worried me, and I felt glad to think of getting away from the surroundings which reminded me of all that. While I was drinking my coffee the bailiff gave me a long report on various matters. The most agreeable item he saved for the last.

"The thieves who stole our rye have been found," he announced with a smile. "The magistrate arrested three peasants at Pestrovo yesterday."

"Go away!" I shouted at him; and à propos of nothing, I picked up the cake-basket and flung it on the floor.

IV

After lunch I rubbed my hands, and thought I must go to my wife and tell her that I was going away. Why? Who cared? Nobody cares, I answered, but why shouldn't I tell her, especially as it would give her nothing but pleasure? Besides, to go away after our yesterday's quarrel without saying a word would not be quite tactful: she might think that I was frightened of her, and perhaps the thought that she has driven me out of my house may weigh upon her. It would be just as well, too, to tell her that I subscribe five thousand, and to give her some advice about the organization, and to warn her that her inexperience in such a complicated and responsible matter might lead to most lamentable results. In short, I wanted to see my wife, and while I thought of various pretexts for going to her, I had a firm conviction in my heart that I should do so.

It was still light when I went in to her, and the lamps had not yet been lighted. She was sitting in her study, which led from the drawing-room to her bedroom, and, bending low over the table, was writing something quickly. Seeing me, she started, got up from the table, and remained standing in an attitude such as to screen her papers from me.

"I beg your pardon, I have only come for a minute," I said, and, I don't know why, I was overcome with embarrassment. "I have learnt by chance that you are organizing relief for the famine, Natalie."

"Yes, I am. But that's my business," she answered.

"Yes, it is your business," I said softly. "I am glad of it, for it just fits in with my intentions. I beg your permission to take part in it."

"Forgive me, I cannot let you do it," she said in response, and looked away.

"Why not, Natalie?" I said quietly. "Why not? I, too, am well fed and I, too, want to help the hungry."

"I don't know what it has to do with you," she said with a contemptuous smile, shrugging her shoulders. "Nobody asks you."

"Nobody asks you, either, and yet you have got up a regular committee in *my* house," I said

"I am asked, but you can have my word for it no one will ever ask you. Go and help where you are not known."

"For God's sake, don't talk to me in that tone." I tried to be mild, and besought myself most earnestly not to lose my temper. For the first few minutes I felt glad to be with my wife. I felt an atmosphere of youth, of home, of feminine softness, of the most refined elegance—exactly what was lacking on my floor and in my life altogether. My wife was wearing a pink flannel dressing-gown; it made her look much younger, and gave a softness to her rapid and sometimes abrupt movements. Her beautiful dark hair, the mere sight of which at one time stirred me to passion, had from sitting so long with her head bent come loose from the comb and was untidy, but, to my eyes, that only made it look more rich and luxuriant. All this, though, is banal to the point of vulgarity. Before me stood an ordinary woman, perhaps neither beautiful nor elegant, but this was my wife with whom I had once lived, and with whom I should have been living to this day if it had not been for her unfortunate character; she was the one human being on the terrestrial globe whom I loved. At this moment, just before going away, when I knew that I should no longer see her even through the window, she seemed to me fascinating even as she was, cold and forbidding, answering me with a proud and contemptuous mockery. I was proud of her, and confessed to myself that to go away from her was terrible and impossible.

"Pavel Andreitch," she said after a brief silence, "for two years we have not interfered with each other but have lived quietly. Why do you suddenly feel it necessary to go back to the past? Yesterday you came to insult and humiliate me," she went on, raising her voice, and her face flushed and her eyes flamed with hatred; "but restrain yourself; do not do it, Pavel Andreitch! Tomorrow I will send in a petition and they will give me a passport, and I will go away; I will go, I will go! I'll go into a convent, into a widows' home, into an almshouse. . . ."

"Into a lunatic asylum!" I cried, not able to restrain myself.

"Well, even into a lunatic asylum! That would be better, that would be better," she cried, with flashing eyes. "When I was in Pestrovo today I envied the sick and starving peasant women because they are not living with a man like you. They are free and honest, while, thanks to you, I am a parasite, I am perishing in idleness, I eat your bread, I spend your money, and I repay you with my liberty and a fidelity which is of no use to any one. Because you won't give me a passport, I must respect your good name, though it doesn't exist."

I had to keep silent. Clenching my teeth, I walked quickly into the drawing-room, but turned back at once and said:

"I beg you earnestly that there should be no more assemblies, plots, and meetings of conspirators in my house! I only admit to my house those with whom I am acquainted, and let all your crew find another place to do it if they want to take up philanthropy. I can't allow people at midnight in my house to be shouting hurrah at successfully exploiting an hysterical woman like you!"

My wife, pale and wringing her hands, took a rapid stride across the room, uttering a prolonged moan as though she had toothache. With a wave of my hand, I went into the drawing-room. I was choking with rage, and at the same time I was trembling with terror that I might not restrain myself, and that I might say or do something which I might regret all my life. And I clenched my hands tight, hoping to hold myself in.

After drinking some water and recovering my calm a little, I went

[

back to my wife. She was standing in the same attitude as before, as though barring my approach to the table with the papers. Tears were slowly trickling down her pale, cold face. I paused then and said to her bitterly but without anger:

"How you misunderstand me! How unjust you are to me! I swear upon my honour I came to you with the best of motives, with nothing but the desire to do good!"

"Pavel Andreitch!" she said, clasping her hands on her bosom, and her face took on the agonized, imploring expression with which frightened, weeping children beg not to be punished, "I know perfectly well that you will refuse me, but still I beg you. Force yourself to do one kind action in your life. I entreat you, go away from here! That's the only thing you can do for the starving peasants. Go away, and I will forgive you everything, everything!"

"There is no need for you to insult me, Natalie," I sighed, feeling a sudden rush of humility. "I had already made up my mind to go away, but I won't go until I have done something for the peasants. It's my duty!"

"Ach!" she said softly with an impatient frown. "You can make an excellent bridge or railway, but you can do nothing for the starving peasants. Do understand!"

"Indeed? Yesterday you reproached me with indifference and with being devoid of the feeling of compassion. How well you know me!" I laughed. "You believe in God—well, God is my witness that I am worried day and night. . . ."

"I see that you are worried, but the famine and compassion have nothing to do with it. You are worried because the starving peasants can get on without you, and because the Zemstvo, and in fact every one who is helping them, does not need your guidance."

I was silent, trying to suppress my irritation. Then I said:

"I came to speak to you on business. Sit down. Please sit down."

She did not sit down.

"I beg you to sit down," I repeated, and I motioned her to a chair. She sat down. I sat down, too, thought a little, and said:

"I beg you to consider earnestly what I am saying. Listen. . . . Moved by love for your fellow-creatures, you have undertaken the organization of famine relief. I have nothing against that, of course; I am completely in sympathy with you, and am prepared to co-operate with you in every way, whatever our relations may be. But, with all my respect for your mind and your heart . . . and your heart," I repeated, "I cannot allow such a difficult, complex, and responsible matter as the organization of relief to be left in your hands entirely. You are a woman, you are inexperienced, you know nothing of life, you are too confiding and expansive. You have surrounded yourself with assistants whom you know nothing about. I am not exaggerating if I say that under these conditions your work will inevitably lead to two deplorable consequences. To begin with, our district will be left unrelieved; and, secondly, you will have to pay for your mistakes and those of your assistants, not only with your purse, but with your reputation. The money deficit and other losses I could, no doubt, make good, but who could restore you your good name? When through lack of proper supervision and oversight there is a rumour that you, and consequently I, have made two hundred thousand over the famine fund, will your assistants come to your aid?"

She said nothing.

"Not from vanity, as you say," I went on, "but simply that the starving peasants may not be left unrelieved and your reputation may not be injured, I feel it my moral duty to take part in your work."

"Speak more briefly," said my wife.

"You will be so kind," I went on, "as to show me what has been subscribed so far and what you have spent. Then inform me daily of every fresh subscription in money or kind, and of every fresh outlay. You will also give me, Natalie, the list of your helpers. Perhaps they are quite decent people; I don't doubt it; but, still, it is absolutely necessary to make inquiries."

She was silent. I got up, and walked up and down the room.

"Let us set to work, then," I said, and I sat down to her table.

"Are you in earnest?" she asked, looking at me in alarm and bewilderment.

"Natalie, do be reasonable !" I said appealingly, seeing from her face that she meant to protest. "I beg you, trust my experience and my sense of honour."

"I don't understand what you want."

"Show me how much you have collected and how much you have spent."

"I have no secrets. Any one may see. Look."

On the table lay five or six school exercise books, several sheets of notepaper covered with writing, a map of the district, and a number of pieces of paper of different sizes. It was getting dusk. I lighted a candle.

"Excuse me, I don't see anything yet," I said, turning over the leaves of the exercise books. "Where is the account of the receipt of money subscriptions?"

"That can be seen from the subscription lists."

"Yes, but you must have an account," I said, smiling at her naïveté. "Where are the letters accompanying the subscriptions in money or in kind? *Pardon*, a little practical advice, Natalie: it's absolutely necessary to keep those letters. You ought to number each letter and make a special note of it in a special record. You ought to do the same with your own letters. But I will do all that myself."

"Do so, do so . . ." she said.

I was very much pleased with myself. Attracted by this living interesting work, by the little table, the naïve exercise books and the charm of doing this work in my wife's society, I was afraid that my wife would suddenly hinder me and upset everything by some sudden whim, and so I was in haste and made an effort to attach no consequence to the fact that her lips were quivering, and that she was looking about her with a helpless and frightened air like a wild creature in a trap.

"I tell you what, Natalie," I said without looking at her; "let me take all these papers and exercise books upstairs to my study. There I will look through them and tell you what I think about it tomorrow. Have you any more papers?" I asked, arranging the exercise books and sheets of papers in piles.

"Take them, take them all!" said my wife, helping me to arrange them, and big tears ran down her cheeks. "Take it all! That's all that was left me in life. . . . Take the last."

"Ach! Natalie, Natalie!" I sighed reproachfully.

She opened the drawer in the table and began flinging the papers out of it on the table at random, poking me in the chest with her elbow and brushing my face with her hair; as she did so, copper coins kept dropping upon my knees and on the floor.

"Take everything!" she said in a husky voice.

When she had thrown out the papers she walked away from me, and putting both hands to her head, she flung herself on the couch. I picked up the money, put it back in the drawer, and locked it up that

the servants might not be led into dishonesty; then I gathered up all the
papers and went off with them. As I passed my wife I stopped, and,
looking at her back and shaking shoulders, I said:

"What a baby you are, Natalie! Fie, fie! Listen, Natalie: when you
realize how serious and responsible a business it is you will be the first
to thank me. I assure you you will."

In my own room I set to work without haste. The exercise books
were not bound, the pages were not numbered. The entries were put in
all sorts of handwritings; evidently any one who liked had a hand in
managing the books. In the record of the subscriptions in kind there
was no note of their money value. But, excuse me, I thought, the rye
which is now worth one rouble fifteen kopecks may be worth two roubles fifteen kopecks in two months' time! Was that the way to do
things? Then, "Given to A. M. Sobol 32 roubles." When was it given?
For what purpose was it given? Where was the receipt? There was
nothing to show, and no making anything of it. In case of legal proceedings, these papers would only obscure the case.

"How naïve she is!" I thought with surprise. "What a child!"

I felt both vexed and amused.

V

My wife had already collected eight thousand; with my five it would
be thirteen thousand. For a start that was very good. The business
which had so worried and interested me was at last in my hands; I was
doing what the others would not and could not do; I was doing my
duty, organizing the relief fund in a practical and businesslike way.

Everything seemed to be going in accordance with my desires and
intentions; but why did my feeling of uneasiness persist? I spent four
hours over my wife's papers, making out their meaning and correcting
her mistakes, but instead of feeling soothed, I felt as though some one
were standing behind me and rubbing my back with a rough hand.
What was it I wanted? The organization of the relief fund had come
into trustworthy hands, the hungry would be fed—what more was
wanted?

The four hours of this light work for some reason exhausted me, so
that I could not sit bending over the table nor write. From below I
heard from time to time a smothered moan; it was my wife sobbing.

Alexey, invariably meek, sleepy, and sanctimonious, kept coming up to the table to see to the candles, and looked at me somewhat strangely.

"Yes, I must go away," I decided at last, feeling utterly exhausted. "As far as possible from these agreeable impressions! I will set off tomorrow."

I gathered together the papers and exercise books, and went down to my wife. As, feeling quite worn out and shattered, I held the papers and the exercise books to my breast with both hands, and passing through my bedroom saw my trunks, the sound of weeping reached me through the floor.

"Are you a *kammer-junker*?" a voice whispered in my ear. "That's a very pleasant thing. But yet you are a reptile."

"It's all nonsense, nonsense, nonsense," I muttered as I went downstairs. "Nonsense . . . and it's nonsense, too, that I am actuated by vanity or a love of display. . . . What rubbish! Am I going to get a decoration for working for the peasants or be made the director of a department? Nonsense, nonsense! And who is there to show off to here in the country?"

I was tired, frightfully tired, and something kept whispering in my ear: "Very pleasant. But, still, you are a reptile." For some reason I remembered a line out of an old poem I knew as a child: "How pleasant it is to be good!"

My wife was lying on the couch in the same attitude, on her face and with her hands clutching her head. She was crying. A maid was standing beside her with a perplexed and frightened face. I sent the maid away, laid the papers on the table, thought a moment and said:

"Here are all your papers, Natalie. It's all in order, it's all capital, and I am very much pleased. I am going away tomorrow."

She went on crying. I went into the drawing-room and sat there in the dark. My wife's sobs, her sighs, accused me of something, and to justify myself I remembered the whole of our quarrel, starting from my unhappy idea of inviting my wife to our consultation and ending with the exercise books and these tears. It was an ordinary attack of our conjugal hatred, senseless and unseemly, such as had been frequent during our married life, but what had the starving peasants to do with it? How could it have happened that they had become a bone of contention between us? It was just as though pursuing one another we had accidentally run up to the altar and had carried on a quarrel there.

"Natalie," I said softly from the drawing-room, "hush, hush!"

To cut short her weeping and make an end of this agonizing state of affairs, I ought to have gone up to my wife and comforted her, caressed her, or apologized; but how could I do it so that she would believe me? How could I persuade the wild duck, living in captivity and hating me, that it was dear to me, and that I felt for its sufferings? I had never known my wife, so I had never known how to talk to her or what to talk about. Her appearance I knew very well and appreciated it as it deserved, but her spiritual, moral world, her mind, her outlook on life, her frequent changes of mood, her eyes full of hatred, her disdain, the scope and variety of her reading which sometimes struck me, or, for instance, the nun-like expression I had seen on her face the day before—all that was unknown and incomprehensible to me. When in my collisions with her I tried to define what sort of a person she was, my psychology went no farther than deciding that she was giddy, impractical, ill-tempered, guided by feminine logic; and it seemed to me that that was quite sufficient. But now that she was crying I had a passionate desire to know more.

The weeping ceased. I went up to my wife. She sat up on the couch, and, with her head propped in both hands, looked fixedly and dreamily at the fire.

"I am going away tomorrow morning," I said.

She said nothing. I walked across the room, sighed, and said:

"Natalie, when you begged me to go away, you said: 'I will forgive you everything, everything. . . . So you think I have wronged you. I beg you calmly and in brief terms to formulate the wrong I've done you."

"I am worn out. Afterwards, some time . . ." said my wife.

"How am I to blame?" I went on. "What have I done? Tell me: you are young and beautiful, you want to live, and I am nearly twice your age and hated by you, but is that my fault? I didn't marry you by force. But if you want to live in freedom, go; I'll give you your liberty. You can go and love whom you please. . . . I will give you a divorce."

"That's not what I want," she said. "You know I used to love you and always thought of myself as older than you. That's all non-sense. . . . You are not to blame for being older or for my being younger, or that I might be able to love some one else if I were free; but because you are a difficult person, an egoist, and hate every one."

"Perhaps so. I don't know," I said.

"Please go away. You want to go on at me till the morning, but I warn you I am quite worn out and cannot answer you. You promised me to go to town. I am very grateful; I ask nothing more."

My wife wanted me to go away, but it was not easy for me to do that. I was dispirited and I dreaded the big, cheerless, chill rooms that I was so weary of. Sometimes when I had an ache or a pain as a child, I used to huddle up to my mother or my nurse, and when I hid my face in the warm folds of their dress, it seemed to me as though I were hiding from the pain. And in the same way it seemed to me now that I could only hide from my uneasiness in this little room beside my wife. I sat down and screened away the light from my eyes with my hand. . . . There was a stillness.

"How are you to blame?" my wife said after a long silence, looking at me with red eyes that gleamed with tears. "You are very well educated and very well bred, very honest, just, and high-principled, but in you the effect of all that is that wherever you go you bring suffocation, oppression, something insulting and humiliating to the utmost degree. You have a straightforward way of looking at things, and so you hate the whole world. You hate those who have faith, because faith is an expression of ignorance and lack of culture, and at the same time you hate those who have no faith for having no faith and no ideals; you hate old people for being conservative and behind the times, and young people for free-thinking. The interests of the peasantry and of Russia are dear to you, and so you hate the peasants because you suspect every one of them of being a thief and a robber. You hate every one. You are just, and always take your stand on your legal rights, and so you are always at law with the peasants and your neighbours. You have had twenty bushels of rye stolen, and your love of order has made you complain of the peasants to the Governor and all the local authorities, and to send a complaint of the local authorities to Petersburg. Legal justice!" said my wife, and she laughed. "On the ground of your legal rights and in the interests of morality, you refuse to give me a passport. Law and morality is such that a self-respecting healthy young woman has to spend her life in idleness, in depression, and in continual apprehension, and to receive in return board and lodging from a man she does not love. You have a thorough knowledge of the law, you are very honest and just, you respect marriage and family life, and the effect of all that is that all your life you have not done one kind action, that every one hates you, that you are on bad terms with every one, and the seven years that you have been married you've only lived seven months with your wife. You've had no wife and I've had no husband. To live with a man like you is impossible; there is no way of doing it. In the early years I was frightened with you, and now I am ashamed. . . . That's how my best years have been wasted. When I fought with you I ruined my temper, grew shrewish, coarse, timid, mistrustful. . . . Oh, but what's the use of talking! As though you wanted to understand! Go upstairs, and God be with you!"

My wife lay down on the couch and sank into thought.

"And how splendid, how enviable life might have been!" she said softly, looking reflectively into the fire. "What a life it might have been! There's no bringing it back now."

Any one who has lived in the country in winter and knows those long, dreary, still evenings when even the dogs are too bored to bark and even the clocks seem weary of ticking, and any one who on such evenings has been troubled by awakening conscience and has moved restlessly about, trying now to smother his conscience, now to interpret it, will understand the distraction and the pleasure my wife's voice gave me as it sounded in the snug little room, telling me I was a bad man. I did not understand what was wanted of me by my conscience, and my wife, translating it in her feminine way, made clear to me in the meaning of my agitation. As often before in the moments of intense uneasiness, I guessed that the whole secret lay, not in the starving peasants, but in my not being the sort of a man I ought to be.

My wife got up with an effort and came up to me.

"Pavel Andreitch," she said, smiling mournfully, "forgive me, I don't believe you: you are not going away, but I will ask you one more favour. Call this"—she pointed to her papers—"self-deception, feminine logic, a mistake, as you like; but do not hinder me. It's all that is left me in life." She turned away and paused. "Before this I had nothing. I have wasted my youth in fighting with you. Now I have caught at this and am living; I am happy. . . . It seems to me that I have found in this a means of justifying my existence."

"Natalie, you are a good woman, a woman of ideas," I said, looking at my wife enthusiastically, "and everything you say and do is intelligent and fine."

I walked about the room to conceal my emotion.

"Natalie," I went on a minute later, "before I go away, I beg of you as a special favour, help me to do something for the starving peasants!"

"What can I do?" said my wife, shrugging her shoulders. "Here's the subscription list."

She rummaged among the papers and found the subscription list.

"Subscribe some money," she said, and from her tone I could see that she did not attach great importance to her subscription list; "that is the only way in which you can take part in the work."

I took the list and wrote: " Anonymous, 5,000."

In this "anonymous" there was something wrong, false, conceited, but I only realized that when I noticed that my wife flushed very red and hurriedly thrust the list into the heap of papers. We both felt ashamed; I felt that I must at all costs efface this clumsiness at once, or else I should feel ashamed afterwards, in the train and at Petersburg. But how efface it? What was I to say?

"I fully approve of what you are doing, Natalie," I said genuinely, "and I wish you every success. But allow me at parting to give you one piece of advice, Natalie; be on your guard with Sobol, and with your assistants generally, and don't trust them blindly. I don't say they are not honest, but they are not gentlefolks; they are people with no ideas, no ideals, no faith, with no aim in life, no definite principles, and the whole object of their life is comprised in the rouble. Rouble, rouble, rouble!" I sighed. "They are fond of getting money easily, for nothing, and in that respect the better educated they are the more they are to be dreaded."

My wife went to the couch and lay down.

"Ideas," she brought out, listlessly and reluctantly, "ideas, ideals, objects of life, principles . . . you always used to use those words when you wanted to insult or humiliate some one, or say something unpleasant. Yes, that's your way: if with your views and such an attitude to people you are allowed to take part in anything, you would destroy it from the first day. It's time you understand that."

She sighed and paused.

"It's coarseness of character, Pavel Andreitch," she said. "You are well-bred and educated, but what a . . . Scythian you are in reality! That's because you lead a cramped life full of hatred, see no one, and read nothing but your engineering books. And, you know, there are good people, good books! Yes . . . but I am exhausted and it wearies me to talk. I ought to be in bed."

"So I am going away, Natalie," I said.

"Yes . . . yes. . . . _Merci_. . . ."

I stood still for a little while, then went upstairs. An hour later—it was half-past one—I went downstairs again with a candle in my hand to speak to my wife. I didn't know what I was going to say to her, but I felt that I must say something very important and necessary. She was not in her study, the door leading to her bedroom was closed.

"Natalie, are you asleep?" I asked softly.

There was no answer.

I stood near the door, sighed, and went into the drawing-room. There I sat down on the sofa, put out the candle, and remained sitting in the dark till the dawn.

VI

I went to the station at ten o'clock in the morning. There was no frost, but snow was falling in big wet flakes and an unpleasant damp wind was blowing.

We passed a pond and then a birch copse, and then began going uphill along the road which I could see from my window. I turned round to take a last look at my house, but I could see nothing for the snow. Soon afterwards dark huts came into sight ahead of us as in a fog. It was Pestrovo.

"If I ever go out of my mind, Pestrovo will be the cause of it," I thought. "It persecutes me."

We came out into the village street. All the roofs were intact, not one of them had been pulled to pieces; so my bailiff had told a lie. A boy was pulling along a little girl and a baby in a sledge. Another boy of three, with his head wrapped up like a peasant woman's and with huge mufflers on his hands, was trying to catch the flying snowflakes on his tongue, and laughing. Then a wagon loaded with fagots came toward us and a peasant walking beside it, and there was no telling whether his beard was white or whether it was covered with snow. He recognized my coachman, smiled at him and said something, and mechanically took off his hat to me. The dogs ran out of the yards and looked inquisitively at my horses. Everything was quiet, ordinary, as usual. The emigrants had returned, there was no bread; in the huts "some were laughing, some were delirious"; but it all looked so ordinary that one could not believe it really was so. There were no distracted faces, no voices whining for help, no weeping, nor abuse, but all around was stillness, order, life, children, sledges, dogs with dishevelled tails. Neither the children nor the peasant we met were troubled: why was I so troubled?

Looking at the smiling peasant, at the boy with the huge mufflers, at the huts, remembering my wife, I realized there was no calamity that could daunt this people; I felt as though there were already a breath of victory in the air. I felt proud and felt ready to cry out that I was with them too; but the horses were carrying us away from the village into the open country, the snow was whirling, the wind was howling, and I was left alone with my thoughts. Of the million people working for the peasantry, life itself had cast me out as a useless, incompetent, bad man. I was a hindrance, a part of the people's calamity; I was vanquished, cast out, and I was hurrying to the station to go away and hide myself in Petersburg in a hotel in Bolshaya Morskaya.

An hour later we reached the station. The coachman and a porter with a disc on his breast carried my trunks into the ladies' room. My coachman Nikanor, wearing high felt boots and the skirt of his coat tucked up through his belt, all wet with the snow and glad I was going away, gave me a friendly smile and said:

"A fortunate journey, your Excellency. God give you luck."

Every one, by the way, calls me "your Excellency," though I am only a collegiate councillor and a *kammer-junker*. The porter told me the train had not yet left the next station; I had to wait. I went outside, and with my head heavy from my sleepless night, and so exhausted I could hardly move my legs, I walked aimlessly towards the pump. There was not a soul anywhere near.

"Why am I going?" I kept asking myself. "What is there awaiting me there? The acquaintances from whom I have come away, loneliness, restaurant dinners, noise, the electric light, which makes my eyes ache. Where am I going, and what am I going for? What am I going for?"

And it seemed somehow strange to go away without speaking to my wife. I felt that I was leaving her in uncertainty. Going away, I ought to have told her that she was right, that I really was a bad man.

When I turned away from the pump, I saw in the doorway the station-master, of whom I had twice made complaints to his superiors, turning up the collar of his coat, shrinking from the wind and the snow. He came up to me, and putting two fingers to the peak of his cap, told me with an expression of helpless confusion, strained respectfulness, and hatred on his face, that the train was twenty minutes late, and asked me would I not like to wait in the warm?

"Thank you," I answered, "but I am probably not going. Send word to my coachman to wait; I have not made up my mind."

I walked to and fro on the platform and thought, should I go away or not? When the train came in I decided not to go. At home I had to expect my wife's amazement and perhaps her mockery, the dismal upper storey and my uneasiness; but, still, at my age that was easier and as it were more homelike than travelling for two days and nights with strangers to Petersburg, where I should be conscious every minute that my life was of no use to any one or to anything, and that it was approaching its end. No, better at home whatever awaited me there. . . . I went out of the station. It was awkward by daylight to return home, where every one was so glad at my going. I might spend the rest of the day till evening at some neighbour's, but with whom? With some of them I was on strained relations, others I did not know at all. I considered and thought of Ivan Ivanitch.

"We are going to Bragino!" I said to the coachman, getting into the sledge.

"It's a long way," sighed Nikanor; "it will be twenty miles, or maybe twenty-five."

"Oh, please, my dear fellow," I said in a tone as though Nikanor had the right to refuse. "Please let us go!"

Nikanor shook his head doubtfully and said slowly that we really ought to have put in the shafts, not Circassian, but Peasant or Siskin; and uncertainly, as though expecting I should change my mind, took the reins in his gloves, stood up, thought a moment, and then raised his whip.

"A whole series of inconsistent actions . . ." I thought, screening my face from the snow. "I must have gone out of my mind. Well, I don't care. . . ."

In one place, on a very high and steep slope, Nikanor carefully held the horses in to the middle of the descent, but in the middle the horses suddenly bolted and dashed downhill at a fearful rate; he raised his elbows and shouted in a wild, frantic voice such as I had never heard from him before:

"Hey! Let's give the general a drive! If you come to grief he'll buy new ones, my darlings! Hey ! look out! We'll run you down!"

Only now, when the extraordinary pace we were going at took my breath away, I noticed that he was very drunk. He must have been drinking at the station. At the bottom of the descent there was the crash of ice; a piece of dirty frozen snow thrown up from the road hit me a painful blow in the face.

The runaway horses ran up the hill as rapidly as they had downhill, and before I had time to shout to Nikanor my sledge was flying along on the level in an old pine forest, and the tall pines were stretching out their shaggy white paws to me from all directions.

"I have gone out of my mind, and the coachman's drunk," I thought. "Good!"

I found Ivan Ivanitch at home. He laughed till he coughed, laid his head on my breast, and said what he always did say on meeting me:

"You grow younger and younger. I don't know what dye you use for your hair and your beard; you might give me some of it."

"I've come to return your call, Ivan Ivanitch," I said untruthfully. "Don't be hard on me; I'm a townsman, conventional; I do keep count of calls."

"I am delighted, my dear fellow. I am an old man; I like respect. . . . Yes."

From his voice and his blissfully smiling face, I could see that he was greatly flattered by my visit. Two peasant women helped me off with my coat in the entry, and a peasant in a red shirt hung it on a book, and when Ivan Ivanitch and I went into his little study, two barefooted little girls were sitting on the floor looking at a picture-book: when they saw us they jumped up and ran away, and a tall, thin old woman in spectacles came in at once, bowed gravely to me, and picking up a pillow from the sofa and a picture-book from the floor, went away. From the adjoining rooms we heard incessant whispering and the patter of bare feet.

"I am expecting the doctor to dinner," said Ivan Ivanitch. "He promised to come from the relief centre. Yes. He dines with me every Wednesday, God bless him." He craned towards me and kissed me on the neck. "You have come, my dear fellow, so you are not vexed," he whispered, sniffing. "Don't be vexed, my dear creature. Yes. Perhaps it is annoying, but don't be cross. My only prayer to God before I die is to live in peace and harmony with all in the true way. Yes."

"Forgive me, Ivan Ivanitch, I will put my feet on a chair," I said, feeling that I was so exhausted I could not be myself; I sat further back on the sofa and put up my feet on an arm-chair. My face was burning from the snow and the wind, and I felt as though my whole body were basking in the warmth and growing weaker from it.

"It's very nice here," I went on—"warm, soft, snug . . . and goose-feather pens," I laughed, looking at the writing-table; "sand instead of blotting-paper."

"Eh? Yes . . . yes. . . . The writing-table and the mahogany cupboard here were made for my father by a self-taught cabinet-maker—Glyeb Butyga, a serf of General Zhukov's. Yes . . . a great artist in his own way."

Listlessly and in the tone of a man dropping asleep, he began telling me about cabinet-maker Butyga. I listened. Then Ivan Ivanitch went into the next room to show me a polisander wood chest of drawers remarkable for its beauty and cheapness. He tapped the chest with his fingers, then called my attention to a stove of patterned tiles, such as one never sees now. He tapped the stove, too, with his fingers. There was an atmosphere of good-natured simplicity and well-fed abundance about the chest of drawers, the tiled stove, the low chairs, the pictures embroidered in wool and silk on canvas in solid, ugly frames. When one remembers that all those objects were standing in the same places and precisely in the same order when I was a little child, and used to come here to name-day parties with my mother, it is simply unbelievable that they could ever cease to exist.

I thought what a fearful difference between Butyga and me! Butyga who made things, above all, solidly and substantially, and seeing in that his chief object, gave to length of life peculiar significance, had no thought of death, and probably hardly believed in its possibility; I, when I built my bridges of iron and stone which would last a thousand years, could not keep from me the thought, "It's not for long . . . it's no use." If in time Butyga's cupboard and my bridge should come under the notice of some sensible historian of art, he would say: "These were two men remarkable in their own way: Butyga loved his fellow-creatures and would not admit the thought that they might die and be annihilated, and so when he made his furniture he had the immortal man in his mind. The engineer Asorin did not love life or his fellow-creatures; even in the happy moments of creation, thoughts of death, of finiteness and dissolution, were not alien to him, and we see how insignificant and finite, how timid and poor, are these lines of his. . . ."

"I only heat these rooms," muttered Ivan Ivanitch, showing me his rooms. "Ever since my wife died and my son was killed in the war, I have kept the best rooms shut up. Yes . . . see . . ."

He opened a door, and I saw a big room with four columns, an old piano, and a heap of peas on the floor; it smelt cold and damp.

"The garden seats are in the next room . . . ." muttered Ivan Ivanitch. "There's no one to dance the mazurka now. . . . I've shut them up."

We heard a noise. It was Dr. Sobol arriving. While he was rubbing his cold hands and stroking his wet beard, I had time to notice in the first place that he had a very dull life, and so was pleased to see Ivan Ivanitch and me; and, secondly, that he was a naïve and simple-hearted man. He looked at me as though I were very glad to see him and very much interested in him.

"I have not slept for two nights," he said, looking at me naïvely and stroking his beard. "One night with a confinement, and the next I stayed at a peasant's with the bugs biting me all night. I am as sleepy as Satan, do you know."

With an expression on his face as though it could not afford me anything but pleasure, he took me by the arm and led me to the dining-room. His naïve eyes, his crumpled coat, his cheap tie and the smell of iodoform made an unpleasant impression upon me; I felt as though I were in vulgar company. When we sat down to table he filled my glass with vodka, and, smiling helplessly, I drank it; he put a piece of ham on my plate and I ate it submissively.

"*Repetitia est mater studiorium*," said Sobol, hastening to drink off another wineglassful. "Would you believe it, the joy of seeing good people has driven away my sleepiness? I have turned into a peasant, a savage in the wilds; I've grown coarse, but I am still an educated man, and I tell you in good earnest, it's tedious without company."

They served first for a cold course white sucking-pig with horse-radish cream, then a rich and very hot cabbage soup with pork on it, with boiled buckwheat, from which rose a column of steam. The doctor went on talking, and I was soon convinced that he was a weak, unfortunate man, disorderly in external life. Three glasses of vodka made him drunk; he grew unnaturally lively, ate a great deal, kept clearing his throat and smacking his lips, and already addressed me in Italian, "Eccellenza." Looking naïvely at me as though he were convinced that I was very glad to see and hear him, he informed me that he had long been separated from his wife and gave her three-quarters of his salary; that she lived in the town with his children, a boy and a girl, whom he adored; that he loved another woman, a widow, well educated, with an estate in the country, but was rarely able to see her, as he was busy with his work from morning till night and had not a free moment.

"The whole day long, first at the hospital, then on my rounds," he told us; "and I assure you, Eccellenza, I have not time to read a book, let alone going to see the woman I love. I've read nothing for ten years! For ten years, Eccellenza. As for the financial side of the question, ask Ivan Ivanitch: I have often no money to buy tobacco."

"On the other hand, you have the moral satisfaction of your work," I said.

"What?" he asked, and he winked. "No," he said, "better let us drink."

I listened to the doctor, and, after my invariable habit, tried to take his measure by my usual classification—materialist, idealist, filthy lucre, gregarious instincts, and so on; but no classification fitted him even approximately; and strange to say, while I simply listened and looked at him, he seemed perfectly clear to me as a person, but as soon as I began trying to classify him he became an exceptionally complex, intricate, and incomprehensible character in spite of all his candour and simplicity. "Is that man," I asked myself, "capable of wasting other people's money, abusing their confidence, being disposed to sponge on them?" And now this question, which had once seemed to me grave and important, struck me as crude, petty, and coarse.

Pie was served; then, I remember, with long intervals between, during which we drank home-made liquors, they gave us a stew of pigeons, some dish of giblets, roast sucking-pig, partridges, cauliflower, curd dumplings, curd cheese and milk, jelly, and finally pancakes and jam. At first I ate with great relish, especially the cabbage soup and the buckwheat, but afterwards I munched and swallowed mechanically, smiling helplessly and unconscious of the taste of anything. My face was burning from the hot cabbage soup and the heat of the room. Ivan Ivanitch and Sobol, too, were crimson.

"To the health of your wife," said Sobol. "She likes me. Tell her her doctor sends her his respects."

"She's fortunate, upon my word," sighed Ivan Ivanitch. "Though she takes no trouble, does not fuss or worry herself, she has become the most important person in the whole district. Almost the whole business is in her hands, and they all gather round her, the doctor, the District Captains, and the ladies. With people of the right sort that happens of itself. Yes. . . . The apple-tree need take no thought for the apple to grow on it; it will grow of itself."

"It's only people who don't care who take no thought," said I.

"Eh? Yes . . ." muttered Ivan Ivanitch, not catching what I said, "that's true. . . . One must not worry oneself. Just so, just so. . . . Only do your duty towards God and your neighbour, and then never mind what happens."

"Eccellenza," said Sobol solemnly, "just look at nature about us: if you poke your nose or your ear out of your fur collar it will be frost-bitten; stay in the fields for one hour, you'll be buried in the snow; while the village is just the same as in the days of Rurik, the same Petchenyegs and Polovtsi. It's nothing but being burnt down, starving, and struggling against nature in every way. What was I saying? Yes! If one thinks about it, you know, looks into it and analyses all this hotchpotch, if you will allow me to call it so, it's not life but more like a fire in a theatre! Any one who falls down or screams with terror, or rushes about, is the worst enemy of good order; one must stand up and look sharp, and not stir a hair! There's no time for whimpering and busying oneself with trifles. When you have to deal with elemental forces you must put out force against them, be firm and as unyielding as a stone. Isn't that right, grandfather?" He turned to Ivan Ivanitch and laughed. "I am no better than a woman myself; I am a limp rag, a flabby creature, so I hate flabbiness. I can't endure petty feelings! One mopes, another is frightened, a third will come straight in here and say: 'Fie on you! Here you've guzzled a dozen courses and you talk about the starving!' That's petty and stupid! A fourth will reproach you, Eccellenza, for being rich. Excuse me, Eccellenza," he went on in a loud voice, laying his hand on his heart, "but your having set our magistrate the task of hunting day and night for your thieves—excuse me, that's also petty on your part. I am a little drunk, so that's why I say this now, but you know, it is petty!"

"Who's asking him to worry himself? I don't understand!" I said, getting up.

I suddenly felt unbearably ashamed and mortified, and I walked round the table.

"Who asks him to worry himself? I didn't ask him to. . . . Damn him!"

"They have arrested three men and let them go again. They turned out not to be the right ones, and now they are looking for a fresh lot," said Sobol, laughing. "It's too bad!"

"I did not ask him to worry himself," said I, almost crying with excitement. "What's it all for? What's it all for? Well, supposing I was wrong, supposing I have done wrong, why do they try to put me more in the wrong?"

"Come, come, come, come!" said Sobol, trying to soothe me. "Come! I have had a drop, that is why I said it. My tongue is my enemy. Come," he sighed, "we have eaten and drunk wine, and now for a nap."

He got up from the table, kissed Ivan Ivanitch on the head, and staggering from repletion, went out of the dining-room. Ivan Ivanitch and I smoked in silence.

"I don't sleep after dinner, my dear," said Ivan Ivanitch, "but you have a rest in the lounge-room."

I agreed. In the half-dark and warmly heated room they called the lounge-room, there stood against the walls long, wide sofas, solid and heavy, the work of Butyga the cabinet-maker; on them lay high, soft, white beds, probably made by the old woman in spectacles. On one of them Sobol, without his coat and boots, already lay asleep with his face to the back of the sofa; another bed was awaiting me. I took off my coat and boots, and, overcome by fatigue, by the spirit of Butyga which hovered over the quiet lounge-room, and by the light, caressing snore of Sobol, I lay down submissively.

And at once I began dreaming of my wife, of her room, of the station-master with his face full of hatred, the heaps of snow, a fire in the theatre. . . . I dreamed of the peasants who had stolen twenty sacks of rye out of my barn. . . .

"Anyway, it's a good thing the magistrate let them go," I said.

I woke up at the sound of my own voice, looked for a moment in perplexity at Sobol's broad back, at the buckles of his waistcoat, at his thick heels, then lay down again and fell asleep.

When I woke up the second time it was quite dark. Sobol was asleep. There was peace in my heart, and I longed to make haste home. I dressed and went out of the lounge-room. Ivan Ivanitch was sitting in a big arm-chair in his study, absolutely motionless, staring at a fixed point, and it was evident that he had been in the same state of petrifaction all the while I had been asleep.

"Good!" I said, yawning. "I feel as though I had woken up after breaking the fast at Easter. I shall often come and see you now. Tell me, did my wife ever dine here?"

"So-ome-ti-mes . . . sometimes," muttered Ivan Ivanitch, making an effort to stir. "She dined here last Saturday. Yes. . . . She likes me."

After a silence I said:

"Do you remember, Ivan Ivanitch, you told me I had a disagreeable character and that it was difficult to get on with me? But what am I to do to make my character different?"

"I don't know, my dear boy. . . . I'm a feeble old man, I can't advise you. . . . Yes. . . . But I said that to you at the time because I am fond of you and fond of your wife, and I was fond of your father. . . . Yes. I shall soon die, and what need have I to conceal things from you or to tell you lies? So I tell you: I am very fond of you, but I don't respect you. No, I don't respect you."

He turned towards me and said in a breathless whisper:

"It's impossible to respect you, my dear fellow. You look like a real man. You have the figure and deportment of the French President Carnot—I saw a portrait of him the other day in an illustrated paper . . . yes. . . . You use lofty language, and you are clever, and you are high up in the service beyond all reach, but haven't real soul, my dear boy . . . there's no strength in it."

"A Scythian, in fact," I laughed. "But what about my wife? Tell me something about my wife; you know her better."

I wanted to talk about my wife, but Sobol came in and prevented me.

"I've had a sleep and a wash," he said, looking at me naïvely. "I'll have a cup of tea with some rum in it and go home."

It was by now past seven. Besides Ivan Ivanitch, women servants, the old dame in spectacles, the little girls and the peasant, all accompanied us from the hall out on to the steps, wishing us good-bye and all sorts of blessings, while near the horses in the darkness there were standing and moving about men with lanterns, telling our coachmen how and which way to drive, and wishing us a lucky journey. The horses, the men, and the sledges were white.

"Where do all these people come from?" I asked as my three horses and the doctor's two moved at a walking pace out of the yard.

"They are all his serfs," said Sobol. "The new order has not reached him yet. Some of the old servants are living out their lives with him, and then there are orphans of all sorts who have nowhere to go; there are some, too, who insist on living there, there's no turning them out. A queer old man!"

Again the flying horses, the strange voice of drunken Nikanor, the wind and the persistent snow, which got into one's eyes, one's mouth, and every fold of one's fur coat. . . .

"Well, I am running a rig," I thought, while my bells chimed in with the doctor's, the wind whistled, the coachmen shouted; and while this frantic uproar was going on, I recalled all the details of that strange wild day, unique in my life, and it seemed to me that I really had gone out of my mind or become a different man. It was as though the man I had been till that day were already a stranger to me.

The doctor drove behind and kept talking loudly with his coachman. From time to time he overtook me, drove side by side, and always, with the same naïve confidence that it was very pleasant to me, offered me a cigarette or asked for the matches. Or, overtaking me, he would lean right out of his sledge, and waving about the sleeves of his fur coat, which were at least twice as long as his arms, shout:

"Go it, Vaska! Beat the thousand roublers! Hey, my kittens!"

And to the accompaniment of loud, malicious laughter from Sobol and his Vaska the doctor's kittens raced ahead. My Nikanor took it as an affront, and held in his three horses, but when the doctor's bells had passed out of hearing, he raised his elbows, shouted, and our horses flew like mad in pursuit. We drove into a village, there were glimpses of lights, the silhouettes of huts. Some one shouted: "Ah, the devils!"

We seemed to have galloped a mile and a half, and still it was the village street and there seemed no end to it. When we caught up the doctor and drove more quietly, he asked for matches and said:

"Now try and feed that street! And, you know, there are five streets like that, sir. Stay, stay," he shouted. "Turn in at the tavern! We must get warm and let the horses rest."

They stopped at the tavern.

"I have more than one village like that in my district," said the doctor, opening a heavy door with a squeaky block, and ushering me in front of him. "If you look in broad daylight you can't see to the end of the street, and there are side-streets, too, and one can do nothing but scratch one's head. It's hard to do anything."

We went into the best room where there was a strong smell of table-cloths, and at our entrance a sleepy peasant in a waistcoat and a shirt worn outside his trousers jumped up from a bench. Sobol asked for some beer and I asked for tea.

"It's hard to do anything," said Sobol. "Your wife has faith; I respect her and have the greatest reverence for her, but I have no great faith myself. As long as our relations to the people continue to have the character of ordinary philanthropy, as shown in orphan asylums and almshouses, so long we shall only be shuffling, shamming, and deceiving ourselves, and nothing more. Our relations ought to be businesslike, founded on calculation, knowledge, and justice. My Vaska has been working for me all his life; his crops have failed, he is sick and starving. If I give him fifteen kopecks a day, by so doing I try to restore him to his former condition as a workman; that its, I am first and foremost looking after my own interests, and yet for some reason I call that fifteen kopecks relief, charity, good works. Now let us put it like this. On the most modest computation, reckoning seven kopecks a soul and five souls a family, one needs three hundred and fifty roubles a day to feed a thousand families. That sum is fixed by our practical duty to a thousand families. Meanwhile we give not three hundred and fifty a day, but only ten, and say that that is relief, charity, that that makes your wife and all of us exceptionally good people and hurrah for our humaneness. That is it, my dear soul! Ah! if we would talk less of being humane and calculated more, reasoned, and took a conscientious attitude to our duties! How many such humane, sensitive people there are among us who tear about in all good faith with subscription lists, but don't pay their tailors or their cooks. There is no logic in our life: that's what it is! No logic!"

We were silent for a while. I was making a mental calculation and said:

"I will feed a thousand families for two hundred days. Come and see me tomorrow to talk it over."

I was pleased that this was said quite simply, and was glad that Sobol answered me still more simply:

"Right."

We paid for what we had and went out of the tavern.

"I like going on like this," said Sobol, getting into the sledge. "Eccellenza, oblige me with a match. I've forgotten mine in the tavern."

A quarter of an hour later his horses fell behind, and the sound of his bells was lost in the roar of the snow-storm. Reaching home, I walked about my rooms, trying to think things over and to define my position clearly to myself; I had not one word, one phrase ready for my wife. My brain was not working.

But without thinking of anything, I went downstairs to my wife. She was in her room, in the same pink dressing-gown, and standing in the same attitude as though screening her papers from me. On her face was an expression of perplexity and irony, and it was evident that having heard of my arrival, she had prepared herself not to cry, not to entreat me, not to defend herself, as she had done the day before, but to laugh at me, to answer me contemptuously, and to act with decision. Her face was saying: "If that's how it is, good-bye."

"Natalie, I've not gone away," I said, "but it's not deception. I have gone out of my mind; I've grown old, I'm ill, I've become a different man—think as you like. . . . I've shaken off my old self with horror, with horror; I despise him and am ashamed of him, and the new man who has been in me since yesterday will not let me go away. Do not drive me away, Natalie!"

She looked intently into my face and believed me, and there was a gleam of uneasiness in her eyes. Enchanted by her presence, warmed by the warmth of her room, I muttered as in delirium, holding out my hands to her:

"I tell you, I have no one near to me but you. I have never for one minute ceased to miss you, and only obstinate vanity prevented me from owning it. The past, when we lived as husband and wife, cannot be brought back, and there's no need; but make me your servant, take all my property, and give it away to any one you like. I am at peace, Natalie, I am content. . . . I am at peace."

My wife, looking intently and with curiosity into my face, suddenly uttered a faint cry, burst into tears, and ran into the next room. I went upstairs to my own storey.

An hour later I was sitting at my table, writing my "History of Railways," and the starving peasants did not now hinder me from doing so. Now I feel no uneasiness. Neither the scenes of disorder which I saw when I went the round of the huts at Pestrovo with my wife and Sobol the other day, nor malignant rumours, nor the mistakes of the people around me, nor old age close upon me—nothing disturbs me. Just as the flying bullets do not hinder soldiers from talking of their own affairs, eating and cleaning their boots, so the starving peasants do not hinder me from sleeping quietly and looking after my personal affairs. In my house and far around it there is in full swing the work which Dr. Sobol calls "an orgy of philanthropy." My wife often comes up to me and looks about my rooms uneasily, as though looking for what more she can give to the starving peasants "to justify her existence," and I see that, thanks to her, there will soon be nothing of our property left and we shall be poor; but that does not trouble me, and I smile at her gaily. What will happen in the future I don't know.

1892

Ward No. 6

I

In the hospital yard there stands a small lodge surrounded by a perfect forest of burdocks, nettles, and wild hemp. Its roof is rusty, the chimney is tumbling down, the steps at the front-door are rotting away and overgrown with grass, and there are only traces left of the stucco. The front of the lodge faces the hospital; at the back it looks out into the open country, from which it is separated by the grey hospital fence with nails on it. These nails, with their points upwards, and the fence, and the lodge itself, have that peculiar, desolate, God-forsaken look which is only found in our hospital and prison buildings.

If you are not afraid of being stung by the nettles, come by the narrow footpath that leads to the lodge, and let us see what is going on inside. Opening the first door, we walk into the entry. Here along the walls and by the stove every sort of hospital rubbish lies littered about. Mattresses, old tattered dressing-gowns, trousers, blue striped shirts, boots and shoes no good for anything—all these remnants are piled up in heaps, mixed up and crumpled, mouldering and giving out a sickly smell.

The porter, Nikita, an old soldier wearing rusty good-conduct stripes, is always lying on the litter with a pipe between his teeth. He has a grim, surly, battered-looking face, overhanging eyebrows which give him the expression of a sheep-dog of the steppes, and a red nose; he is short and looks thin and scraggy, but he is of imposing deportment and his fists are vigorous. He belongs to the class of simple-hearted, practical, and dull-witted people, prompt in carrying out orders, who like discipline better than anything in the world, and so are convinced that it is their duty to beat people. He showers blows on the face, on the chest, on the back, on whatever comes first, and is convinced that there would be no order in the place if he did not.

Next you come into a big, spacious room which fills up the whole lodge except for the entry. Here the walls are painted a dirty blue, the ceiling is as sooty as in a hut without a chimney—it is evident that in the winter the stove smokes and the room is full of fumes. The windows are disfigured by iron gratings on the inside. The wooden floor is grey and full of splinters. There is a stench of sour cabbage, of smouldering wicks, of bugs, and of ammonia, and for the first minute this stench gives you the impression of having walked into a menagerie. . . . .

There are bedsteads screwed to the floor. Men in blue hospital dressing-gowns, and wearing nightcaps in the old style, are sitting and lying on them. These are the lunatics.

There are five of them in all here. Only one is of the upper class, the rest are all artisans. The one nearest the door—-a tall, lean workman with shining red whiskers and tear-stained eyes—sits with his head propped on his hand, staring at the same point. Day and night he grieves, shaking his head, sighing and smiling bitterly. He takes a part in conversation and usually makes no answer to questions; he eats and drinks mechanically when food is offered him. From his agonizing, throbbing cough, his thinness, and the flush on his cheeks, one may judge that he is in the first stage of consumption. Next to him is a little, alert, very lively old man, with a pointed beard and curly black hair like a negro's. By day he walks up and down the ward from window to window, or sits on his bed, cross-legged like a Turk, and, ceaselessly as a bullfinch whistles, softly sings and titters. He shows his childish gaiety and lively character at night also when he gets up to say his prayers— that is, to beat himself on the chest with his fists, and to scratch with his fingers at the door. This is the Jew Moiseika, an imbecile, who went crazy twenty years ago when his hat factory was burnt down.

And of all the inhabitants of Ward No. 6, he is the only one who is allowed to go out of the lodge, and even out of the yard into the street. He has enjoyed this privilege for years, probably because he is an old inhabitant of the hospital—a quiet, harmless imbecile, the buffoon of the town, where people are used to seeing him surrounded by boys and dogs. In his wretched gown, in his absurd night-cap, and in slippers, sometimes with bare legs and even without trousers, he walks about the streets, stopping at the gates and little shops, and begging for a copper. In one place they will give him some kvass, in another some bread, in another a copper, so that he generally goes back to the ward feeling rich and well fed. Everything that he brings back Nikita takes from him for his own benefit. The soldier does this roughly, angrily turning the Jew's pockets inside out, and calling God to witness that he will not let him go into the street again, and that breach of the regulations is worse to him than anything in the world.

Moiseika likes to make himself useful. He gives his companions water, and covers them up when they are asleep; he promises each of them to bring him back a kopeck, and to make him a new cap; he feeds with a spoon his neighbour on the left, who is paralyzed. He acts in this way, not from compassion nor from any considerations of a humane kind, but through imitation, unconsciously dominated by Gromov, his neighbour on the right hand.

Ivan Dmitritch Gromov, a man of thirty-three, who is a gentleman by birth, and has been a court usher and provincial secretary, suffers from the mania of persecution. He either lies curled up in bed, or walks from corner to corner as though for exercise; he very rarely sits down. He is always excited, agitated, and overwrought by a sort of vague, undefined expectation. The faintest rustle in the entry or shout in the yard is enough to make him raise his head and begin listening: whether they are coming for him, whether they are looking for him. And at such times his face expresses the utmost uneasiness and repulsion.

I like his broad face with its high cheek-bones, always pale and unhappy, and reflecting, as though in a mirror, a soul tormented by conflict and long-continued terror. His grimaces are strange and abnormal, but the delicate lines traced on his face by profound, genuine suffering show intelligence and sense, and there is a warm and healthy light in his eyes. I like the man himself, courteous, anxious to be of use, and extraordinarily gentle to everyone except Nikita. When anyone drops a button or a spoon, he jumps up from his bed quickly and picks it up; every day he says good-morning to his companions, and when he goes to bed he wishes them good-night.

Besides his continually overwrought condition and his grimaces, his madness shows itself in the following way also. Sometimes in the evenings he wraps himself in his dressing-gown, and, trembling all over, with his teeth chattering, begins walking rapidly from corner to corner and between the bedsteads. It seems as though he is in a violent fever. From the way he suddenly stops and glances at his companions, it can be seen that he is longing to say something very important, but, apparently reflecting that they would not listen, or would not understand him, he shakes his head impatiently and goes on pacing up and down. But soon the desire to speak gets the upper hand of every consideration, and he will let himself go and speak fervently and passionately. His talk is disordered and feverish like delirium, disconnected, and not always intelligible, but, on the other hand, something extremely fine may be felt in it, both in the words and the voice. When he talks you recognize in him the lunatic and the man. It is difficult to reproduce on paper his insane talk. He speaks of the baseness of mankind, of violence trampling on justice, of the glorious life which will one day be upon earth, of the window-gratings, which remind him every minute of the stupidity and cruelty of oppressors. It makes a disorderly, incoherent potpourri of themes old but not yet out of date.

II

Some twelve or fifteen years ago an official called Gromov, a highly respectable and prosperous person, was living in his own house in the principal street of the town. He had two sons, Sergey and Ivan. When Sergey was a student in his fourth year he was taken ill with galloping consumption and died, and his death was, as it were, the first of a whole series of calamities which suddenly showered on the Gromov family. Within a week of Sergey's funeral the old father was put on trial for fraud and misappropriation, and he died of typhoid in the prison hospital soon afterwards. The house, with all their belongings, was sold by auction, and Ivan Dmitritch and his mother were left entirely without means.

Hitherto in his father's lifetime, Ivan Dmitritch, who was studying in the University of Petersburg, had received an allowance of sixty or seventy roubles a month, and had had no conception of poverty; now he had to make an abrupt change in his life. He had to spend his time from morning to night giving lessons for next to nothing, to work at copying, and with all that to go hungry, as all his earnings were sent to keep his mother. Ivan Dmitritch could not stand such a life; he lost heart and strength, and, giving up the university, went home.

Here, through interest, he obtained the post of teacher in the district school, but could not get on with his colleagues, was not liked by the boys, and soon gave up the post. His mother died. He was for six months without work, living on nothing but bread and water; then he became a court usher. He kept this post until he was dismissed owing to his illness.

He had never even in his young student days given the impression of being perfectly healthy. He had always been pale, thin, and given to catching cold; he ate little and slept badly. A single glass of wine went to his head and made him hysterical. He always had a craving for society, but, owing to his irritable temperament and suspiciousness, he never became very intimate with anyone, and had no friends. He always spoke with contempt of his fellow-townsmen, saying that their coarse ignorance and sleepy animal existence seemed to him loathsome and horrible. He spoke in a loud tenor, with heat, and invariably either with scorn and indignation, or with wonder and enthusiasm, and always with perfect sincerity. Whatever one talked to him about he always brought it round to the same subject: that life was dull and stifling in the town; that the townspeople had no lofty interests, but lived a dingy, meaningless life, diversified by violence, coarse profligacy, and hypocrisy; that scoundrels were well fed and clothed, while honest men lived from hand to mouth; that they needed schools, a progressive local paper, a theatre, public lectures, the co-ordination of the intellectual elements; that society must see its failings and be horrified. In his criticisms of people he laid on the colours thick, using only black and white, and no fine shades; mankind was divided for him into honest men and scoundrels: there was nothing in between. He always spoke with passion and enthusiasm of women and of love, but he had never been in love.

In spite of the severity of his judgments and his nervousness, he was liked, and behind his back was spoken of affectionately as Vanya. His innate refinement and readiness to be of service, his good breeding, his moral purity, and his shabby coat, his frail appearance and family misfortunes, aroused a kind, warm, sorrowful feeling. Moreover, he was well educated and well read; according to the townspeople's notions, he knew everything, and was in their eyes something like a walking encyclopædia.

He had read a great deal. He would sit at the club, nervously pulling at his beard and looking through the magazines and books; and from his face one could see that he was not reading, but devouring the pages without giving himself time to digest what he read. It must be supposed that reading was one of his morbid habits, as he fell upon anything that came into his hands with equal avidity, even last year's newspapers and calendars. At home he always read lying down.

III

One autumn morning Ivan Dmitritch, turning up the collar of his greatcoat and splashing through the mud, made his way by side-streets and back lanes to see some artisan, and to collect some payment that was owing. He was in a gloomy mood, as he always was in the morning. In one of the side-streets he was met by two convicts in fetters and four soldiers with rifles in charge of them. Ivan Dmitritch had very often met convicts before, and they had always excited feelings of compassion and discomfort in him; but now this meeting made a peculiar, strange impression on him. It suddenly seemed to him for some reason that he, too, might be put into fetters and led through the mud to prison like that. After visiting the artisan, on the way home he met near the post office a police superintendent of his acquaintance, who greeted him and walked a few paces along the street with him, and for some reason this seemed to him suspicious. At home he could not get the convicts or the soldiers with their rifles out of his head all day, and an unaccountable inward agitation prevented him from reading or concentrating his mind. In the evening he did not light his lamp, and at night he could not sleep, but kept thinking that he might be arrested, put into fetters, and thrown into prison. He did not know of any harm he had done, and could be certain that he would never be guilty of murder, arson, or theft in the future either; but was it not easy to commit a crime by accident, unconsciously, and was not false witness always possible, and, indeed, miscarriage of justice? It was not without good reason that the agelong experience of the simple people teaches that beggary and prison are ills none can be safe from. A judicial mistake is very possible as legal proceedings are conducted nowadays, and there is nothing to be wondered at in it. People who have an official, professional relation to other men's sufferings—for instance, judges, police officers, doctors—in course of time, through habit, grow so callous that they cannot, even if they wish it, take any but a formal attitude to their clients; in this respect they are not different from the peasant who slaughters sheep and calves in the back-yard, and does not notice the blood. With this formal, soulless attitude to human personality the judge needs but one thing—time—in order to deprive an innocent man of all rights of property, and to condemn him to penal servitude. Only the time spent on performing certain formalities for which the judge is paid his salary, and then—it is all over. Then you may look in vain for justice and protection in this dirty, wretched little town a hundred and fifty miles from a railway station! And, indeed, is it not absurd even to think of justice when every kind of violence is accepted by society as a rational and consistent necessity, and every act of mercy—for instance, a verdict of acquittal—calls forth a perfect outburst of dissatisfied and revengeful feeling?

In the morning Ivan Dmitritch got up from his bed in a state of horror, with cold perspiration on his forehead, completely convinced that he might be arrested any minute. Since his gloomy thoughts of yesterday had haunted him so long, he thought, it must be that there was some truth in them. They could not, indeed, have come into his mind without any grounds whatever.

A policeman walking slowly passed by the windows: that was not for nothing. Here were two men standing still and silent near the house. Why were they silent? And agonizing days and nights followed for Ivan Dmitritch. Everyone who passed by the windows or came into the yard seemed to him a spy or a detective. At midday the chief of the police usually drove down the street with a pair of horses; he was going from his estate near the town to the police department; but Ivan Dmitritch fancied every time that he was driving especially quickly, and that he had a peculiar expression: it was evident that he was in haste to announce that there was a very important criminal in the town. Ivan Dmitritch started at every ring at the bell and knock at the gate, and was agitated whenever he came upon anyone new at his landlady's; when he met police officers and gendarmes he smiled and began whistling so as to seem unconcerned. He could not sleep for whole nights in succession expecting to be arrested, but he snored loudly and sighed as though in deep sleep, that his landlady might think he was asleep; for if he could not sleep it meant that he was tormented by the stings of conscience—what a piece of evidence! Facts and common sense persuaded him that all these terrors were nonsense and morbidity, that if one looked at the matter more broadly there was nothing really terrible in arrest and imprisonment—so long as the conscience is at ease; but the more sensibly and logically he reasoned, the more acute and agonizing his mental distress became. It might be compared with the story of a hermit who tried to cut a dwelling-place for himself in a virgin forest; the more zealously he worked with his axe, the thicker the forest grew. In the end Ivan Dmitritch, seeing it was useless, gave up reasoning altogether, and abandoned himself entirely to despair and terror.

He began to avoid people and to seek solitude. His official work had been distasteful to him before: now it became unbearable to him. He was afraid they would somehow get him into trouble, would put a bribe in his pocket unnoticed and then denounce him, or that he would accidentally make a mistake in official papers that would appear to be fraudulent, or would lose other people's money. It is strange that his imagination had never at other times been so agile and inventive as now, when every day he thought of thousands of different reasons for being seriously anxious over his freedom and honour; but, on the other hand, his interest in the outer world, in books in particular, grew sensibly fainter, and his memory began to fail him.

In the spring when the snow melted there were found in the ravine near the cemetery two half-decomposed corpses—the bodies of an old woman and a boy bearing the traces of death by violence. Nothing was talked of but these bodies and their unknown murderers. That people might not think he had been guilty of the crime, Ivan Dmitritch walked about the streets, smiling, and when he met acquaintances he turned pale, flushed, and began declaring that there was no greater crime than the murder of the weak and defenceless. But this duplicity soon exhausted him, and after some reflection he decided that in his position the best thing to do was to hide in his landlady's cellar. He sat in the cellar all day and then all night, then another day, was fearfully cold, and waiting till dusk, stole secretly like a thief back to his room. He stood in the middle of the room till day-break, listening without stirring. Very early in the morning, before sunrise, some workmen came into the house. Ivan Dmitritch knew perfectly well that they had come to mend the stove in the kitchen, but terror told him that they were police officers disguised as workmen. He slipped stealthily out of the flat, and, overcome by terror, ran along the street without his cap and coat. Dogs raced after him barking, a peasant shouted somewhere behind him, the wind whistled in his ears, and it seemed to Ivan Dmitritch that the force and violence of the whole world was massed together behind his back and was chasing after him.

He was stopped and brought home, and his landlady sent for a doctor. Doctor Andrey Yefimitch, of whom we shall have more to say hereafter, prescribed cold compresses on his head and laurel drops, shook his head, and went away, telling the landlady he should not come again, as one should not interfere with people who are going out of their minds. As he had not the means to live at home and be nursed, Ivan Dmitritch was soon sent to the hospital, and was there put into the ward for venereal patients. He could not sleep at night, was full of whims and fancies, and disturbed the patients, and was soon afterwards, by Andrey Yefimitch's orders, transferred to Ward No. 6.

Within a year Ivan Dmitritch was completely forgotten in the town, and his books, heaped up by his landlady in a sledge in the shed, were pulled to pieces by boys.

IV

Ivan Dmitritch's neighbour on the left hand is, as I have said already, the Jew Moiseika; his neighbour on the right hand is a peasant so rolling in fat that he is almost spherical, with a blankly stupid face, utterly devoid of thought. This is a motionless, gluttonous, unclean animal who has long ago lost all powers of thought or feeling. An acrid, stifling stench always comes from him.

Nikita, who has to clean up after him, beats him terribly with all his might, not sparing his fists; and what is dreadful is not his being beaten—that one can get used to—but the fact that this stupefied creature does not respond to the blows with a sound or a movement, nor by a look in the eyes, but only sways a little like a heavy barrel.

The fifth and last inhabitant of Ward No. 6 is a man of the artisan class who had once been a sorter in the post office, a thinnish, fair little man with a good-natured but rather sly face. To judge from the clear, cheerful look in his calm and intelligent eyes, he has some pleasant idea in his mind, and has some very important and agreeable secret.

He has under his pillow and under his mattress something that he never shows anyone, not from fear of its being taken from him and stolen, but from modesty. Sometimes he goes to the window, and turning his back to his companions, puts something on his breast, and bending his head, looks at it; if you go up to him at such a moment, he is overcome with confusion and snatches something off his breast. But it is not difficult to guess his secret.

"Congratulate me," he often says to Ivan Dmitritch; "I have been presented with the Stanislav order of the second degree with the star. The second degree with the star is only given to foreigners, but for some reason they want to make an exception for me," he says with a smile, shrugging his shoulders in perplexity. "That I must confess I did not expect."

"I don't understand anything about that," Ivan Dmitritch replies morosely.

"But do you know what I shall attain to sooner or later?" the former sorter persists, screwing up his eyes slyly. "I shall certainly get the Swedish 'Polar Star.' That's an order it is worth working for, a white cross with a black ribbon. It's very beautiful."

Probably in no other place is life so monotonous as in this ward. In the morning the patients, except the paralytic and the fat peasant, wash in the entry at a big tub and wipe themselves with the skirts of their dressing-gowns; after that they drink tea out of tin mugs which Nikita brings them out of the main building. Everyone is allowed one mugful. At midday they have soup made out of sour cabbage and boiled grain, in the evening their supper consists of grain left from dinner. In the intervals they lie down, sleep, look out of window, and walk from one corner to the other. And so every day. Even the former sorter always talks of the same orders.

Fresh faces are rarely seen in Ward No. 6. The doctor has not taken in any new mental cases for a long time, and the people who are fond of visiting lunatic asylums are few in this world. Once every two months Semyon Lazaritch, the barber, appears in the ward. How he cuts the patients' hair, and how Nikita helps him to do it, and what a trepidation the lunatics are always thrown into by the arrival of the drunken, smiling barber, we will not describe.

No one even looks into the ward except the barber. The patients are condemned to see day after day no one but Nikita.

A rather strange rumour has, however, been circulating in the hospital of late.

It is rumoured that the doctor has begun to visit Ward No. 6.

V

A strange rumour!

Dr. Andrey Yefimitch Ragin is a strange man in his way. They say that when he was young he was very religious, and prepared himself for a clerical career, and that when he had finished his studies at the high school in 1863 he intended to enter a theological academy, but that his father, a surgeon and doctor of medicine, jeered at him and declared point-blank that he would disown him if he became a priest. How far this is true I don't know, but Andrey Yefimitch himself has more than once confessed that he has never had a natural bent for medicine or science in general.

However that may have been, when he finished his studies in the medical faculty he did not enter the priesthood. He showed no special devoutness, and was no more like a priest at the beginning of his medical career than he is now.

His exterior is heavy, coarse like a peasant's, his face, his beard, his flat hair, and his coarse, clumsy figure, suggest an overfed, intemperate, and harsh innkeeper on the highroad. His face is surly-looking and covered with blue veins, his eyes are little and his nose is red. With his height and broad shoulders he has huge hands and feet; one would think that a blow from his fist would knock the life out of anyone, but his step is soft, and his walk is cautious and insinuating; when he meets anyone in a narrow passage he is always the first to stop and make way, and to say, not in a bass, as one would expect, but in a high, soft tenor: "I beg your pardon!" He has a little swelling on his neck which prevents him from wearing stiff starched collars, and so he always goes about in soft linen or cotton shirts. Altogether he does not dress like a doctor. He wears the same suit for ten years, and the new clothes, which he usually buys at a Jewish shop, look as shabby and crumpled on him as his old ones; he sees patients and dines and pays visits all in the same coat; but this is not due to niggardliness, but to complete carelessness about his appearance.

When Andrey Yefimitch came to the town to take up his duties the "institution founded to the glory of God" was in a terrible condition. One could hardly breathe for the stench in the wards, in the passages, and in the courtyards of the hospital. The hospital servants, the nurses, and their children slept in the wards together with the patients. They complained that there was no living for beetles, bugs, and mice. The surgical wards were never free from erysipelas. There were only two scalpels and not one thermometer in the whole hospital; potatoes were kept in the baths. The superintendent, the housekeeper, and the medical assistant robbed the patients, and of the old doctor, Andrey Yefimitch's predecessor, people declared that he secretly sold the hospital alcohol, and that he kept a regular harem consisting of nurses and female patients. These disorderly proceedings were perfectly well known in the town, and were even exaggerated, but people took them calmly; some justified them on the ground that there were only peasants and working men in the hospital, who could not be dissatisfied, since they were much worse off at home than in the hospital—they couldn't be fed on woodcocks! Others said in excuse that the town alone, without help from the Zemstvo, was not equal to maintaining a good hospital; thank God for having one at all, even a poor one. And the newly formed Zemstvo did not open infirmaries either in the town or the neighbourhood, relying on the fact that the town already had its hospital.

After looking over the hospital Andrey Yefimitch came to the conclusion that it was an immoral institution and extremely prejudicial to the health of the townspeople. In his opinion the most sensible thing that could be done was to let out the patients and close the hospital. But he reflected that his will alone was not enough to do this, and that it would be useless; if physical and moral impurity were driven out of one place, they would only move to another; one must wait for it to wither away of itself. Besides, if people open a hospital and put up with having it, it must be because they need it; superstition and all the nastiness and abominations of daily life were necessary, since in process of time they worked out to something sensible, just as manure turns into black earth. There was nothing on earth so good that it had not something nasty about its first origin.

When Andrey Yefimitch undertook his duties he was apparently not greatly concerned about the irregularities at the hospital. He only asked the attendants and nurses not to sleep in the wards, and had two cupboards of instruments put up; the superintendent, the housekeeper, the medical assistant, and the erysipelas remained unchanged.

Andrey Yefimitch loved intelligence and honesty intensely, but he had no strength of will nor belief in his right to organize an intelligent and honest life about him. He was absolutely unable to give orders, to forbid things, and to insist. It seemed as though he had taken a vow never to raise his voice and never to make use of the imperative. It was difficult for him to say. "Fetch" or "Bring"; when he wanted his meals he would cough hesitatingly and say to the cook, "How about tea? . . ." or "How about dinner? . . ." To dismiss the superintendent or to tell him to leave off stealing, or to abolish the unnecessary parasitic post altogether, was absolutely beyond his powers. When Andrey Yefimitch was deceived or flattered, or accounts he knew to be cooked were brought him to sign, he would turn as red as a crab and feel guilty, but yet he would sign the accounts. When the patients complained to him of being hungry or of the roughness of the nurses, he would be confused and mutter guiltily: "Very well, very well, I will go into it later. . . . Most likely there is some misunderstanding. . . ."

At first Andrey Yefimitch worked very zealously. He saw patients every day from morning till dinner-time, performed operations, and even attended confinements. The ladies said of him that he was attentive and clever at diagnosing diseases, especially those of women and children. But in process of time the work unmistakably wearied him by its monotony and obvious uselessness. To-day one sees thirty patients, and to-morrow they have increased to thirty-five, the next day forty, and so on from day to day, from year to year, while the mortality in the town did not decrease and the patients did not leave off coming. To be any real help to forty patients between morning and dinner was not physically possible, so it could but lead to deception. If twelve thousand patients were seen in a year it meant, if one looked at it simply, that twelve thousand men were deceived. To put those who were seriously ill into wards, and to treat them according to the principles of science, was impossible, too, because though there were principles there was no science; if he were to put aside philosophy and pedantically follow the rules as other doctors did, the things above all necessary were cleanliness and ventilation instead of dirt, wholesome nourishment instead of broth made of stinking, sour cabbage, and good assistants instead of thieves; and, indeed, why hinder people dying if death is the normal and legitimate end of everyone? What is gained if some shop-keeper or clerk lives an extra five or ten years? If the aim of medicine is by drugs to alleviate suffering, the question forces itself on one: why alleviate it? In the first place, they say that suffering leads man to perfection; and in the second, if mankind really learns to alleviate its sufferings with pills and drops, it will completely abandon religion and philosophy, in which it has hitherto found not merely protection from all sorts of trouble, but even happiness. Pushkin suffered terrible agonies before his death, poor Heine lay paralyzed for several years; why, then, should not some Andrey Yefimitch or Matryona Savishna be ill, since their lives had nothing of importance in them, and would have been entirely empty and like the life of an amoeba except for suffering?

Oppressed by such reflections, Andrey Yefimitch relaxed his efforts and gave up visiting the hospital every day.

VI

His life was passed like this. As a rule he got up at eight o'clock in the morning, dressed, and drank his tea. Then he sat down in his study to read, or went to the hospital. At the hospital the out-patients were sitting in the dark, narrow little corridor waiting to be seen by the doctor. The nurses and the attendants, tramping with their boots over the brick floors, ran by them; gaunt-looking patients in dressing-gowns passed; dead bodies and vessels full of filth were carried by; the children were crying, and there was a cold draught. Andrey Yefimitch knew that such surroundings were torture to feverish, consumptive, and impressionable patients; but what could be done? In the consulting-room he was met by his assistant, Sergey Sergeyitch—a fat little man with a plump, well-washed shaven face, with soft, smooth manners, wearing a new loosely cut suit, and looking more like a senator than a medical assistant. He had an immense practice in the town, wore a white tie, and considered himself more proficient than the doctor, who had no practice. In the corner of the consulting-room there stood a large ikon in a shrine with a heavy lamp in front of it, and near it a candle-stand with a white cover on it. On the walls hung portraits of bishops, a view of the Svyatogorsky Monastery, and wreaths of dried cornflowers. Sergey Sergeyitch was religious, and liked solemnity and decorum. The ikon had been put up at his expense; at his instructions some one of the patients read the hymns of praise in the consulting-room on Sundays, and after the reading Sergey Sergeyitch himself went through the wards with a censer and burned incense.

There were a great many patients, but the time was short, and so the work was confined to the asking of a few brief questions and the administration of some drugs, such as castor-oil or volatile ointment. Andrey Yefimitch would sit with his cheek resting in his hand, lost in thought and asking questions mechanically. Sergey Sergeyitch sat down too, rubbing his hands, and from time to time putting in his word.

"We suffer pain and poverty," he would say, "because we do not pray to the merciful God as we should. Yes!"

Andrey Yefimitch never performed any operation when he was seeing patients; he had long ago given up doing so, and the sight of blood upset him. When he had to open a child's mouth in order to look at its throat, and the child cried and tried to defend itself with its little hands, the noise in his ears made his head go round and brought tears to his eyes. He would make haste to prescribe a drug, and motion to the woman to take the child away.

He was soon wearied by the timidity of the patients and their incoherence, by the proximity of the pious Sergey Sergeyitch, by the portraits on the walls, and by his own questions which he had asked over and over again for twenty years. And he would go away after seeing five or six patients. The rest would be seen by his assistant in his absence.

With the agreeable thought that, thank God, he had no private practice now, and that no one would interrupt him, Andrey Yefimitch sat down to the table immediately on reaching home and took up a book. He read a great deal and always with enjoyment. Half his salary went on buying books, and of the six rooms that made up his abode three were heaped up with books and old magazines. He liked best of all works on history and philosophy; the only medical publication to which he subscribed was *The Doctor*, of which he always read the last pages first. He would always go on reading for several hours without a break and without being weary. He did not read as rapidly and impulsively as Ivan Dmitritch had done in the past, but slowly and with concentration, often pausing over a passage which he liked or did not find intelligible. Near the books there always stood a decanter of vodka, and a salted cucumber or a pickled apple lay beside it, not on a plate, but on the baize table-cloth. Every half-hour he would pour himself out a glass of vodka and drink it without taking his eyes off the book. Then without looking at it he would feel for the cucumber and bite off a bit.

At three o'clock he would go cautiously to the kitchen door, cough, and say, "Daryushka, what about dinner? . . ."

After his dinner—a rather poor and untidily served one—Andrey Yefimitch would walk up and down his rooms with his arms folded, thinking. The clock would strike four, then five, and still he would be walking up and down thinking. Occasionally the kitchen door would creak, and the red and sleepy face of Daryushka would appear.

"Andrey Yefimitch, isn't it time for you to have your beer?" she would ask anxiously.

"No, it's not time yet . . ." he would answer. "I'll wait a little. . . . I'll wait a little. . . ."

Towards the evening the postmaster, Mihail Averyanitch, the only man in town whose society did not bore Andrey Yefimitch, would come in. Mihail Averyanitch had once been a very rich landowner, and had served in the calvary, but had come to ruin, and was forced by poverty to take a job in the post office late in life. He had a hale and hearty appearance, luxuriant grey whiskers, the manners of a well-bred man, and a loud, pleasant voice. He was good-natured and emotional, but hot-tempered. When anyone in the post office made a protest, expressed disagreement, or even began to argue, Mihail Averyanitch would turn crimson, shake all over, and shout in a voice of thunder, "Hold your tongue!" so that the post office had long enjoyed the reputation of an institution which it was terrible to visit. Mihail Averyanitch liked and respected Andrey Yefimitch for his culture and the loftiness of his soul; he treated the other inhabitants of the town superciliously, as though they were his subordinates.

"Here I am," he would say, going in to Andrey Yefimitch. "Good evening, my dear fellow! I'll be bound, you are getting sick of me, aren't you?"

"On the contrary, I am delighted," said the doctor. "I am always glad to see you."

The friends would sit on the sofa in the study and for some time would smoke in silence.

"Daryushka, what about the beer?" Andrey Yefimitch would say.

They would drink their first bottle still in silence, the doctor brooding and Mihail Averyanitch with a gay and animated face, like a man who has something very interesting to tell. The doctor was always the one to begin the conversation.

"What a pity," he would say quietly and slowly, not looking his friend in the face (he never looked anyone in the face)—"what a great pity it is that there are no people in our town who are capable of carrying on intelligent and interesting conversation, or care to do so. It is an immense privation for us. Even the educated class do not rise above vulgarity; the level of their development, I assure you, is not a bit higher than that of the lower orders."

"Perfectly true. I agree."

"You know, of course," the doctor went on quietly and deliberately, "that everything in this world is insignificant and uninteresting except the higher spiritual manifestations of the human mind. Intellect draws a sharp line between the animals and man, suggests the divinity of the latter, and to some extent even takes the place of the immortality which does not exist. Consequently the intellect is the only possible source of enjoyment. We see and hear of no trace of intellect about us, so we are deprived of enjoyment. We have books, it is true, but that is not at all the same as living talk and converse. If you will allow me to make a not quite apt comparison: books are the printed score, while talk is the singing."

"Perfectly true."

A silence would follow. Daryushka would come out of the kitchen and with an expression of blank dejection would stand in the doorway to listen, with her face propped on her fist.

"Eh!" Mihail Averyanitch would sigh. "To expect intelligence of this generation!"

And he would describe how wholesome, entertaining, and interesting life had been in the past. How intelligent the educated class in Russia used to be, and what lofty ideas it had of honour and friendship; how they used to lend money without an IOU, and it was thought a disgrace not to give a helping hand to a comrade in need; and what campaigns, what adventures, what skirmishes, what comrades, what women! And the Caucasus, what a marvellous country! The wife of a battalion commander, a queer woman, used to put on an officer's uniform and drive off into the mountains in the evening, alone, without a guide. It was said that she had a love affair with some princeling in the native village.

"Queen of Heaven, Holy Mother . . ." Daryushka would sigh.

"And how we drank! And how we ate! And what desperate liberals we were!"

Andrey Yefimitch would listen without hearing; he was musing as he sipped his beer.

"I often dream of intellectual people and conversation with them," he said suddenly, interrupting Mihail Averyanitch. "My father gave me an excellent education, but under the influence of the ideas of the sixties made me become a doctor. I believe if I had not obeyed him then, by now I should have been in the very centre of the intellectual movement. Most likely I should have become a member of some university. Of course, intellect, too, is transient and not eternal, but you know why I cherish a partiality for it. Life is a vexatious trap; when a thinking man reaches maturity and attains to full consciousness he cannot help feeling that he is in a trap from which there is no escape. Indeed, he is summoned without his choice by fortuitous circumstances from non-existence into life . . . what for? He tries to find out the meaning and object of his existence; he is told nothing, or he is told absurdities; he knocks and it is not opened to him; death comes to him—also without his choice. And so, just as in prison men held together by common misfortune feel more at ease when they are together, so one does not notice the trap in life when people with a bent for analysis and generalization meet together and pass their time in the interchange of proud and free ideas. In that sense the intellect is the source of an enjoyment nothing can replace."

"Perfectly true."

Not looking his friend in the face, Andrey Yefimitch would go on, quietly and with pauses, talking about intellectual people and conversation with them, and Mihail Averyanitch would listen attentively and agree: "Perfectly true."

"And you do not believe in the immortality of the soul?" he would ask suddenly.

"No, honoured Mihail Averyanitch; I do not believe it, and have no grounds for believing it."

"I must own I doubt it too. And yet I have a feeling as though I should never die. Oh, I think to myself: 'Old fogey, it is time you were dead!' But there is a little voice in my soul says: 'Don't believe it; you won't die.' "

Soon after nine o'clock Mihail Averyanitch would go away. As he put on his fur coat in the entry he would say with a sigh:

"What a wilderness fate has carried us to, though, really! What's most vexatious of all is to have to die here. Ech! . . ."

VII

After seeing his friend out Andrey Yefimitch would sit down at the table and begin reading again. The stillness of the evening, and afterwards of the night, was not broken by a single sound, and it seemed as though time were standing still and brooding with the doctor over the book, and as though there were nothing in existence but the books and the lamp with the green shade. The doctor's coarse peasant-like face was gradually lighted up by a smile of delight and enthusiasm over the progress of the human intellect. Oh, why is not man immortal? he thought. What is the good of the brain centres and convolutions, what is the good of sight, speech, self-consciousness, genius, if it is all destined to depart into the soil, and in the end to grow cold together with the earth's crust, and then for millions of years to fly with the earth round the sun with no meaning and no object? To do that there was no need at all to draw man with his lofty, almost godlike intellect out of non-existence, and then, as though in mockery, to turn him into clay. The transmutation of substances! But what cowardice to comfort oneself with that cheap substitute for immortality! The unconscious processes that take place in nature are lower even than the stupidity of man, since in stupidity there is, anyway, consciousness and will, while in those processes there is absolutely nothing. Only the coward who has more fear of death than dignity can comfort himself with the fact that his body will in time live again in the grass, in the stones, in the toad. To find one's immortality in the transmutation of substances is as strange as to prophesy a brilliant future for the case after a precious violin has been broken and become useless.

When the clock struck, Andrey Yefimitch would sink back into his chair and close his eyes to think a little. And under the influence of the fine ideas of which he had been reading he would, unawares, recall his past and his present. The past was hateful—better not to think of it.

And it was the same in the present as in the past. He knew that at the very time when his thoughts were floating together with the cooling earth round the sun, in the main building beside his abode people were suffering in sickness and physical impurity: someone perhaps could not sleep and was making war upon the insects, someone was being infected by erysipelas, or moaning over too tight a bandage; perhaps the patients were playing cards with the nurses and drinking vodka. According to the yearly return, twelve thousand people had been deceived; the whole hospital rested as it had done twenty years ago on thieving, filth, scandals, gossip, on gross quackery, and, as before, it was an immoral institution extremely injurious to the health of the inhabitants. He knew that Nikita knocked the patients about behind the barred windows of Ward No. 6, and that Moiseika went about the town every day begging alms.

On the other hand, he knew very well that a magical change had taken place in medicine during the last twenty-five years. When he was studying at the university he had fancied that medicine would soon be overtaken by the fate of alchemy and metaphysics; but now when he was reading at night the science of medicine touched him and excited his wonder, and even enthusiasm. What unexpected brilliance, what a revolution! Thanks to the antiseptic system operations were performed such as the great Pirogov had considered impossible even *in spe*. Ordinary Zemstvo doctors were venturing to perform the resection of the kneecap; of abdominal operations only one per cent. was fatal; while stone was considered such a trifle that they did not even write about it. A radical cure for syphilis had been discovered. And the theory of heredity, hypnotism, the discoveries of Pasteur and of Koch, hygiene based on statistics, and the work of Zemstvo doctors!

Psychiatry with its modern classification of mental diseases, methods of diagnosis, and treatment, was a perfect Elborus in comparison with what had been in the past. They no longer poured cold water on the heads of lunatics nor put strait-waistcoats upon them; they treated them with humanity, and even, so it was stated in the papers, got up balls and entertainments for them. Andrey Yefimitch knew that with modern tastes and views such an abomination as Ward No. 6 was possible only a hundred and fifty miles from a railway in a little town where the mayor and all the town council were half-illiterate tradesmen who looked upon the doctor as an oracle who must be believed without any criticism even if he had poured molten lead into their mouths; in any other place the public and the newspapers would long ago have torn this little Bastille to pieces.

"But, after all, what of it?" Andrey Yefimitch would ask himself, opening his eyes. "There is the antiseptic system, there is Koch, there is Pasteur, but the essential reality is not altered a bit; ill-health and mortality are still the same. They get up balls and entertainments for the mad, but still they don't let them go free; so it's all nonsense and vanity, and there is no difference in reality between the best Vienna clinic and my hospital." But depression and a feeling akin to envy prevented him from feeling indifferent; it must have been owing to exhaustion. His heavy head sank on to the book, he put his hands under his face to make it softer, and thought: "I serve in a pernicious institution and receive a salary from people whom I am deceiving. I am not honest, but then, I of myself am nothing, I am only part of an inevitable social evil: all local officials are pernicious and receive their salary for doing nothing. . . . And so for my dishonesty it is not I who am to blame, but the times. . . . If I had been born two hundred years later I should have been different. . . ."

When it struck three he would put out his lamp and go into his bedroom; he was not sleepy.

VIII

Two years before, the Zemstvo in a liberal mood had decided to allow three hundred roubles a year to pay for additional medical service in the town till the Zemstvo hospital should be opened, and the district doctor, Yevgeny Fyodoritch Hobotov, was invited to the town to assist Andrey Yefimitch. He was a very young man—not yet thirty—tall and dark, with broad cheek-bones and little eyes; his forefathers had probably come from one of the many alien races of Russia. He arrived in the town without a farthing, with a small portmanteau, and a plain young woman whom he called his cook. This woman had a baby at the breast. Yevgeny Fyodoritch used to go about in a cap with a peak, and in high boots, and in the winter wore a sheepskin. He made great friends with Sergey Sergeyitch, the medical assistant, and with the treasurer, but held aloof from the other officials, and for some reason called them aristocrats. He had only one book in his lodgings, "The Latest Pre-scriptions of the Vienna Clinic for 1881." When he went to a patient he always took this book with him. He played billiards in the evening at the club: he did not like cards. He was very fond of using in conver-sation such expressions as "endless bobbery," "canting soft soap," "shut up with your finicking...."

He visited the hospital twice a week, made the round of the wards, and saw out-patients. The complete absence of antiseptic treatment and the cupping roused his indignation, but he did not introduce any new system, being afraid of offending Andrey Yefimitch. He regarded his colleague as a sly old rascal, suspected him of being a man of large means, and secretly envied him. He would have been very glad to have his post.

IX

On a spring evening towards the end of March, when there was no snow left on the ground and the starlings were singing in the hospital garden, the doctor went out to see his friend the postmaster as far as the gate. At that very moment the Jew Moiseika, returning with his booty, came into the yard. He had no cap on, and his bare feet were thrust into goloshes; in his hand he had a little bag of coppers.

"Give me a kopeck!" he said to the doctor, smiling, and shivering with cold. Andrey Yefimitch, who could never refuse anyone anything, gave him a ten-kopeck piece.

"How bad that is!" he thought, looking at the Jew's bare feet with their thin red ankles. "Why, it's wet."

And stirred by a feeling akin both to pity and disgust, he went into the lodge behind the Jew, looking now at his bald head, now at his ankles. As the doctor went in, Nikita jumped up from his heap of lit-ter and stood at attention.

"Good-day, Nikita," Andrey Yefimitch said mildly. "That Jew should be provided with boots or something, he will catch cold."

"Certainly, your honour. I'll inform the superintendent."

"Please do; ask him in my name. Tell him that I asked."

The door into the ward was open. Ivan Dmitritch, lying propped on his elbow on the bed, listened in alarm to the unfamiliar voice, and suddenly recognized the doctor. He trembled all over with anger, jumped up, and with a red and wrathful face, with his eyes starting out of his head, ran out into the middle of the road.

"The doctor has come!" he shouted, and broke into a laugh. "At last! Gentlemen, I congratulate you. The doctor is honouring us with a visit! Cursed reptile!" he shrieked, and stamped in a frenzy such as had never been seen in the ward before. "Kill the reptile! No, killing's too good. Drown him in the midden-pit!"

Andrey Yefimitch, hearing this, looked into the ward from the entry and asked gently: "What for?"

"What for?" shouted Ivan Dmitritch, going up to him with a menacing air and convulsively wrapping himself in his dressing-gown. "What for? Thief!" he said with a look of repulsion, moving his lips as though he would spit at him. "Quack! hangman!"

"Calm yourself," said Andrey Yefimitch, smiling guiltily. "I assure you I have never stolen anything; and as to the rest, most likely you greatly exaggerate. I see you are angry with me. Calm yourself, I beg, if you can, and tell me coolly what are you angry for?"

"What are you keeping me here for?"

"Because you are ill."

"Yes, I am ill. But you know dozens, hundreds of madmen are walking about in freedom because your ignorance is incapable of distinguishing them from the sane. Why am I and these poor wretches to be shut up here like scapegoats for all the rest? You, your assistant, the superintendent, and all your hospital rabble, are immeasurably inferior to every one of us morally; why then are we shut up and you not? Where's the logic of it?"

"Morality and logic don't come in, it all depends on chance. If anyone is shut up he has to stay, and if anyone is not shut up he can walk about, that's all. There is neither morality nor logic in my being a doctor and your being a mental patient, there is nothing but idle chance."

"That twaddle I don't understand . . ." Ivan Dmitritch brought out in a hollow voice, and he sat down on his bed.

Moiseika, whom Nikita did not venture to search in the presence of the doctor, laid out on his bed pieces of bread, bits of paper, and little bones, and, still shivering with cold, began rapidly in a singsong voice saying something in Yiddish. He most likely imagined that he had opened a shop.

"Let me out," said Ivan Dmitritch, and his voice quivered.

"I cannot."

"But why, why?"

"Because it is not in my power. Think, what use will it be to you if I do let you out? Go. The townspeople or the police will detain you or bring you back."

"Yes, yes, that's true," said Ivan Dmitritch, and he rubbed his forehead. "It's awful! But what am I to do, what?"

Andrey Yefimitch liked Ivan Dmitritch's voice and his intelligent young face with its grimaces. He longed to be kind to the young man and soothe him; he sat down on the bed beside him, thought, and said:

"You ask me what to do. The very best thing in your position would be to run away. But, unhappily, that is useless. You would be taken up. When society protects itself from the criminal, mentally deranged, or otherwise inconvenient people, it is invincible. There is only one thing left for you: to resign yourself to the thought that your presence here is inevitable."

"It is no use to anyone."

"So long as prisons and madhouses exist someone must be shut up in them. If not you, I. If not I, some third person. Wait till in the distant future prisons and madhouses no longer exist, and there will be neither bars on the windows nor hospital gowns. Of course, that time will come sooner or later."

Ivan Dmitritch smiled ironically.

"You are jesting," he said, screwing up his eyes. "Such gentlemen as you and your assistant Nikita have nothing to do with the future, but you may be sure, sir, better days will come! I may express myself cheaply, you may laugh, but the dawn of a new life is at hand; truth and justice will triumph, and—our turn will come! I shall not live to see it, I shall perish, but some people's great-grandsons will see it. I greet them with all my heart and rejoice, rejoice with them! Onward! God be your help, friends!"

With shining eyes Ivan Dmitritch got up, and stretching his hands towards the window, went on with emotion in his voice:

"From behind these bars I bless you! Hurrah for truth and justice! I rejoice!"

"I see no particular reason to rejoice," said Andrey Yefimitch, who thought Ivan Dmitritch's movement theatrical, though he was delighted by it. "Prisons and madhouses there will not be, and truth, as you have just expressed it, will triumph; but the reality of things, you know, will not change, the laws of nature will still remain the same. People will suffer pain, grow old, and die just as they do now. However magnificent a dawn lighted up your life, you would yet in the end be nailed up in a coffin and thrown into a hole."

"And immortality?"

"Oh, come, now!"

"You don't believe in it, but I do. Somebody in Dostoevsky or Voltaire said that if there had not been a God men would have invented him. And I firmly believe that if there is no immortality the great intellect of man will sooner or later invent it."

"Well said," observed Andrey Yefimitch, smiling with pleasure; "it's a good thing you have faith. With such a belief one may live happily even shut up within walls. You have studied somewhere, I presume?"

"Yes, I have been at the university, but did not complete my studies."

"You are a reflecting and a thoughtful man. In any surroundings you can find tranquillity in yourself. Free and deep thinking which strives for the comprehension of life, and complete contempt for the foolish bustle of the world—those are two blessings beyond any that man has ever known. And you can possess them even though you lived behind threefold bars. Diogenes lived in a tub, yet he was happier than all the kings of the earth."

"Your Diogenes was a blockhead," said Ivan Dmitritch morosely. "Why do you talk to me about Diogenes and some foolish comprehension of life?" he cried, growing suddenly angry and leaping up. "I love life; I love it passionately. I have the mania of persecution, a continual agonizing terror; but I have moments when I am overwhelmed by the thirst for life, and then I am afraid of going mad. I want dreadfully to live, dreadfully!"

He walked up and down the ward in agitation, and said, dropping his voice:

"When I dream I am haunted by phantoms. People come to me, I hear voices and music, and I fancy I am walking through woods or by the seashore, and I long so passionately for movement, for interests. . . . Come, tell me, what news is there?" asked Ivan Dmitritch; "what's happening?"

"Do you wish to know about the town or in general?"

"Well, tell me first about the town, and then in general."

"Well, in the town it is appallingly dull. . . . There's no one to say a word to, no one to listen to. There are no new people. A young doctor called Hobotov has come here recently."

"He had come in my time. Well, he is a low cad, isn't he?"

"Yes, he is a man of no culture. It's strange, you know. . . . Judging by every sign, there is no intellectual stagnation in our capital cities; there is a movement—so there must be real people there too; but for some reason they always send us such men as I would rather not see. It's an unlucky town!"

"Yes, it is an unlucky town," sighed Ivan Dmitritch, and he laughed. "And how are things in general? What are they writing in the papers and reviews?"

It was by now dark in the ward. The doctor got up, and, standing, began to describe what was being written abroad and in Russia, and the tendency of thought that could be noticed now. Ivan Dmitritch listened attentively and put questions, but suddenly, as though recalling something terrible, clutched at his head and lay down on the bed with his back to the doctor.

"What's the matter?" asked Andrey Yefimitch.

"You will not hear another word from me," said Ivan Dmitritch rudely. "Leave me alone."

"Why so?"

"I tell you, leave me alone. Why the devil do you persist?"

Andrey Yefimitch shrugged his shoulders, heaved a sigh, and went out. As he crossed the entry he said: "You might clear up here, Nikita . . . there's an awfully stuffy smell."

"Certainly, your honour."

"What an agreeable young man!" thought Andrey Yefimitch, going back to his flat. "In all the years I have been living here I do believe he is the first I have met with whom one can talk. He is capable of reasoning and is interested in just the right things."

While he was reading, and afterwards, while he was going to bed, he kept thinking about Ivan Dmitritch, and when he woke next morning he remembered that he had the day before made the acquaintance of an intelligent and interesting man, and determined to visit him again as soon as possible.

X

Ivan Dmitritch was lying in the same position as on the previous day, with his head clutched in both hands and his legs drawn up. His face was not visible.

"Good-day, my friend," said Andrey Yefimitch. "You are not asleep, are you?"

"In the first place, I am not your friend," Ivan Dmitritch articulated into the pillow; "and in the second, your efforts are useless; you will not get one word out of me."

"Strange," muttered Andrey Yefimitch in confusion. "Yesterday we talked peacefully, but suddenly for some reason you took offence and broke off all at once. . . . Probably I expressed myself awkwardly, or perhaps gave utterance to some idea which did not fit in with your convictions. . . ."

"Yes, a likely idea!" said Ivan Dmitritch, sitting up and looking at the doctor with irony and uneasiness. His eyes were red. "You can go and spy and probe somewhere else, it's no use your doing it here. I knew yesterday what you had come for."

"A strange fancy," laughed the doctor. "So you suppose me to be a spy?"

"Yes, I do. . . . A spy or a doctor who has been charged to test me—it's all the same—"

"Oh excuse me, what a queer fellow you are really!"

The doctor sat down on the stool near the bed and shook his head reproachfully.

"But let us suppose you are right," he said, "let us suppose that I am treacherously trying to trap you into saying something so as to betray you to the police. You would be arrested and then tried. But would you be any worse off being tried and in prison than you are here? If you are banished to a settlement, or even sent to penal servitude, would it be worse than being shut up in this ward? I imagine it would be no worse. . . . What, then, are you afraid of?"

These words evidently had an effect on Ivan Dmitritch. He sat down quietly.

It was between four and five in the afternoon—the time when Andrey Yefimitch usually walked up and down his rooms, and

Daryushka asked whether it was not time for his beer. It was a still, bright day.

"I came out for a walk after dinner, and here I have come, as you see," said the doctor. "It is quite spring."

"What month is it? March?" asked Ivan Dmitritch.

"Yes, the end of March."

"Is it very muddy?"

"No, not very. There are already paths in the garden."

"It would be nice now to drive in an open carriage somewhere into the country," said Ivan Dmitritch, rubbing his red eyes as though he were just awake, "then to come home to a warm, snug study, and . . . and to have a decent doctor to cure one's headache. . . . It's so long since I have lived like a human being. It's disgusting here! Insufferably disgusting!"

After his excitement of the previous day he was exhausted and listless, and spoke unwillingly. His fingers twitched, and from his face it could be seen that he had a splitting headache.

"There is no real difference between a warm, snug study and this ward," said Andrey Yefimitch. "A man's peace and contentment do not lie outside a man, but in himself."

"What do you mean?"

"The ordinary man looks for good and evil in external things— that is, in carriages, in studies—but a thinking man looks for it in himself."

"You should go and preach that philosophy in Greece, where it's warm and fragrant with the scent of pomegranates, but here it is not suited to the climate. With whom was it I was talking of Diogenes? Was it with you?"

"Yes, with me yesterday."

"Diogenes did not need a study or a warm habitation; it's hot there without. You can lie in your tub and eat oranges and olives. But bring him to Russia to live: he'd be begging to be let indoors in May, let alone December. He'd be doubled up with the cold."

"No. One can be insensible to cold as to every other pain. Marcus Aurelius says: 'A pain is a vivid idea of pain; make an effort of will to change that idea, dismiss it, cease to complain, and the pain will disappear.' That is true. The wise man, or simply the reflecting, thoughtful man, is distinguished precisely by his contempt for suffering; he is always contented and surprised at nothing."

"Then I am an idiot, since I suffer and am discontented and surprised at the baseness of mankind."

"You are wrong in that; if you will reflect more on the subject you will understand how insignificant is all that external world that agitates us. One must strive for the comprehension of life, and in that is true happiness."

"Comprehension . . ." repeated Ivan Dmitritch frowning. "External, internal. . . . Excuse me, but I don t understand it. I only know," he said, getting up and looking angrily at the doctor—"I only know that God has created me of warm blood and nerves, yes, indeed! If organic tissue is capable of life it must react to every stimulus. And I do! To pain I respond with tears and outcries, to baseness with indignation, to filth with loathing. To my mind, that is just what is called life. The lower the organism, the less sensitive it is, and the more feebly it reacts to stimulus; and the higher it is, the more responsively and vigorously it reacts to reality. How is it you don't know that? A doctor, and not know such trifles! To despise suffering, to be always contented, and to be surprised at nothing, one must reach this condition"—and Ivan Dmitritch pointed to the peasant who was a mass of fat—"or to harden oneself by suffering to such a point that one loses all sensibility to it—that is, in other words, to cease to live. You must excuse me, I am not a sage or a philosopher," Ivan Dmitritch continued with irritation, "and I don't understand anything about it. I am not capable of reasoning."

"On the contrary, your reasoning is excellent."

"The Stoics, whom you are parodying, were remarkable people, but their doctrine crystallized two thousand years ago and has not advanced, and will not advance, an inch forward, since it is not practical or living. It had a success only with the minority which spends its life in savouring all sorts of theories and ruminating over them; the majority did not understand it. A doctrine which advocates indifference to wealth and to the comforts of life, and a contempt for suffering and death, is quite unintelligible to the vast majority of men, since that majority has never known wealth or the comforts of life; and to despise suffering would mean to it despising life itself, since the whole existence of man is made up of the sensations of hunger, cold, injury, loss, and a Hamlet-like dread of death. The whole of life lies in these sensations; one may be oppressed by it, one may hate it, but one cannot despise it. Yes, so, I repeat, the doctrine of the Stoics can never have a future; from the beginning of time up to to-day you see continually increasing the struggle, the sensibility to pain, the capacity of responding to stimulus."

Ivan Dmitritch suddenly lost the thread of his thoughts, stopped, and rubbed his forehead with vexation.

"I meant to say something important, but I have lost it," he said. "What was I saying? Oh, yes! This is what I mean: one of the Stoics sold himself into slavery to redeem his neighbour, so, you see, even a Stoic did react to stimulus, since, for such a generous act as the destruction of oneself for the sake of one's neighbour, he must have had a soul capable of pity and indignation. Here in prison I have forgotten everything I have learned, or else I could have recalled something else. Take Christ, for instance: Christ responded to reality by weeping, smiling, being sorrowful and moved to wrath, even overcome by misery. He did not go to meet His sufferings with a smile, He did not despise death, but prayed in the Garden of Gethsemane that this cup might pass Him by."

Ivan Dmitritch laughed and sat down.

"Granted that a man's peace and contentment lie not outside but in himself," he said, "granted that one must despise suffering and not be surprised at anything, yet on what ground do you preach the theory? Are you a sage? A philosopher?"

"No, I am not a philosopher, but everyone ought to preach it because it is reasonable."

"No, I want to know how it is that you consider yourself competent to judge of 'comprehension,' contempt for suffering, and so on. Have you ever suffered? Have you any idea of suffering? Allow me to ask you, were you ever thrashed in your childhood?"

"No, my parents had an aversion for corporal punishment."

"My father used to flog me cruelly; my father was a harsh, sickly Government clerk with a long nose and a yellow neck. But let us talk of you. No one has laid a finger on you all your life, no one has scared you nor beaten you; you are as strong as a bull. You grew up under your father's wing and studied at his expense, and then you dropped at once into a sinecure. For more than twenty years you have lived rent free with heating, lighting, and service all provided, and had the right to work how you pleased and as much as you pleased, even to do nothing. You were naturally a flabby, lazy man, and so you have tried to arrange your life so that nothing should disturb you or make you move. You have handed over your work to the assistant and the rest of the rabble while you sit in peace and warmth, save money, read, amuse yourself with reflections, with all sorts of lofty nonsense, and" (Ivan Dmitritch looked at the doctor's red nose) "with boozing; in fact, you have seen nothing of life, you know absolutely nothing of it, and are only theoretically acquainted with reality; you despise suffering and are surprised at nothing for a very simple reason: vanity of vanities, the external and the internal, contempt for life, for suffering and for death, comprehension, true happiness—that's the philosophy that suits the Russian sluggard best. You see a peasant beating his wife, for instance. Why interfere? Let him beat her, they will both die sooner or later, anyway; and, besides, he who beats injures by his blows, not the person he is beating, but himself. To get drunk is stupid and unseemly, but if you drink you die, and if you don't drink you die. A peasant woman comes with toothache . . . well, what of it? Pain is the idea of pain, and besides 'there is no living in this world without illness; we shall all die, and so, go away, woman, don't hinder me from thinking and drinking vodka.' A young man asks advice, what he is to do, how he is to live; anyone else would think before answering, but you have got the answer ready: strive for 'comprehension' or for true happiness. And what is that fantastic 'true happiness'? There's no answer, of course. We are kept here behind barred windows, tortured, left to rot; but that is very good and reasonable, because there is no difference at all between this ward and a warm, snug study. A convenient philosophy. You can do nothing, and your conscience is clear, and you feel you are wise. . . . No, sir, it is not philosophy, it's not thinking, it's not breadth of vision, but laziness, fakirism, drowsy stupefaction. Yes," cried Ivan Dmitritch, getting angry again, "you despise suffering, but I'll be bound if you pinch your finger in the door you will howl at the top of your voice."

"And perhaps I shouldn't howl," said Andrey Yefimitch, with a gentle smile.

"Oh, I dare say! Well, if you had a stroke of paralysis, or supposing some fool or bully took advantage of his position and rank to insult you in public, and if you knew he could do it with impunity, then you would understand what it means to put people off with comprehension and true happiness.

"That's original," said Andrey Yefimitch, laughing with pleasure and rubbing his hands. "I am agreeably struck by your inclination for drawing generalizations, and the sketch of my character you have just drawn is simply brilliant. I must confess that talking to you gives me great pleasure. Well, I've listened to you, and now you must graciously listen to me."

XI

The conversation went on for about an hour longer, and apparently made a deep impression on Andrey Yefimitch. He began going to the ward every day. He went there in the mornings and after dinner, and often the dusk of evening found him in conversation with Ivan Dmitritch. At first Ivan Dmitritch held aloof from him, suspected him of evil designs, and openly expressed his hostility. But afterwards he got used to him, and his abrupt manner changed to one of condescending irony.

Soon it was all over the hospital that the doctor, Andrey Yefimitch, had taken to visiting Ward No. 6. No one—neither Sergey Sergeyitch, nor Nikita, nor the nurses—could conceive why he went there, why he stayed there for hours together, what he was talking about, and why he did not write prescriptions. His actions seemed strange. Often Mihail Averyanitch did not find him at home, which had never happened in the past, and Daryushka was greatly perturbed, for the doctor drank his beer now at no definite time, and sometimes was even late for dinner.

One day—it was at the end of June—Dr. Hobotov went to see Andrey Yefimitch about something. Not finding him at home, he proceeded to look for him in the yard; there he was told that the old doctor had gone to see the mental patients. Going into the lodge and stopping in the entry, Hobotov heard the following conversation:

"We shall never agree, and you will not succeed in converting me to your faith," Ivan Dmitritch was saying irritably; "you are utterly ignorant of reality, and you have never known suffering, but have only like a leech fed beside the sufferings of others, while I have been in continual suffering from the day of my birth till to-day. For that reason, I tell you frankly, I consider myself superior to you and more competent in every respect. It's not for you to teach me."

"I have absolutely no ambition to convert you to my faith," said Andrey Yefimitch gently, and with regret that the other refused to understand him. "And that is not what matters, my friend; what matters is not that you have suffered and I have not. Joy and suffering are passing; let us leave them, never mind them. What matters is that you and I think; we see in each other people who are capable of thinking and reasoning, and that is a common bond between us however different our views. If you knew, my friend, how sick I am of the universal senselessness, ineptitude, stupidity, and with what delight I always talk with you! You are an intelligent man, and I enjoyed your company."

Hobotov opened the door an inch and glanced into the ward; Ivan Dmitritch in his night-cap and the doctor Andrey Yefimitch were sitting side by side on the bed. The madman was grimacing, twitching, and convulsively wrapping himself in his gown, while the doctor sat motionless with bowed head, and his face was red and look helpless and sorrowful. Hobotov shrugged his shoulders, grinned, and glanced at Nikita. Nikita shrugged his shoulders too.

Next day Hobotov went to the lodge, accompanied by the assistant. Both stood in the entry and listened.

"I fancy our old man has gone clean off his chump!" said Hobotov as he came out of the lodge.

"Lord have mercy upon us sinners!" sighed the decorous Sergey Sergeyitch, scrupulously avoiding the puddles that he might not muddy his polished boots. "I must own, honoured Yevgeny Fyodoritch, I have been expecting it for a long time."

XII

After this Andrey Yefimitch began to notice a mysterious air in all around him. The attendants, the nurses, and the patients looked at him inquisitively when they met him, and then whispered together. The superintendent's little daughter Masha, whom he liked to meet in the hospital garden, for some reason ran away from him now when he went up with a smile to stroke her on the head. The postmaster no longer said, "Perfectly true," as he listened to him, but in unaccountable confusion muttered, "Yes, yes, yes . . ." and looked at him with a grieved and thoughtful expression; for some reason he took to advising his friend to give up vodka and beer, but as a man of delicate feeling he did not say this directly, but hinted it, telling him first about the commanding officer of his battalion, an excellent man, and then about the priest of the regiment, a capital fellow, both of whom drank and fell ill, but on giving up drinking completely regained their health. On two or three occasions Andrey Yefimitch was visited by his colleague Hobotov, who also advised him to give up spirituous liquors, and for no apparent reason recommended him to take bromide.

In August Andrey Yefimitch got a letter from the mayor of the town asking him to come on very important business. On arriving at the town hall at the time fixed, Andrey Yefimitch found there the military commander, the superintendent of the district school, a member of the town council, Hobotov, and a plump, fair gentleman who was introduced to him as a doctor. This doctor, with a Polish surname difficult to pronounce, lived at a pedigree stud-farm twenty miles away, and was now on a visit to the town.

"There's something that concerns you," said the member of the town council, addressing Andrey Yefimitch after they had all greeted one another and sat down to the table. "Here Yevgeny Fyodoritch says that there is not room for the dispensary in the main building, and that it ought to be transferred to one of the lodges. That's of no consequence—of course it can be transferred, but the point is that the lodge wants doing up"

"Yes, it would have to be done up," said Andrey Yefimitch after a moment's thought. "If the corner lodge, for instance, were fitted up as a dispensary, I imagine it would cost at least five hundred roubles. An unproductive expenditure!"

Everyone was silent for a space.

"I had the honour of submitting to you ten years ago," Andrey Yefimitch went on in a low voice, "that the hospital in its present form is a luxury for the town beyond its means. It was built in the forties, but things were different then. The town spends too much on unnecessary buildings and superfluous staff. I believe with a different system two model hospitals might be maintained for the same money."

"Well, let us have a different system, then!" the member of the town council said briskly.

"I have already had the honour of submitting to you that the medical department should be transferred to the supervision of the Zemstvo."

"Yes, transfer the money to the Zemstvo and they will steal it," laughed the fair-haired doctor.

"That's what it always comes to," the member of the council assented, and he also laughed.

Andrey Yefimitch looked with apathetic, lustreless eyes at the fair-haired doctor and said: "One should be just."

Again there was silence. Tea was brought in. The military commander, for some reason much embarrassed, touched Andrey Yefimitch's hand across the table and said: "You have quite forgotten us, doctor. But of course you are a hermit: you don't play cards and don't like women. You would be dull with fellows like us."

They all began saying how boring it was for a decent person to live in such a town. No theatre, no music, and at the last dance at the club there had been about twenty ladies and only two gentlemen. The young men did not dance, but spent all the time crowding round the refreshment bar or playing cards.

Not looking at anyone and speaking slowly in a low voice, Andrey Yefimitch began saying what a pity, what a terrible pity it was that the townspeople should waste their vital energy, their hearts, and their minds on cards and gossip, and should have neither the power nor the inclination to spend their time in interesting conversation and reading, and should refuse to take advantage of the enjoyments of the mind. The mind alone was interesting and worthy of attention, all the rest was low and petty. Hobotov listened to his colleague attentively and suddenly asked:

"Andrey Yefimitch, what day of the month is it?"

Having received an answer, the fair-haired doctor and he, in the tone of examiners conscious of their lack of skill, began asking Andrey Yefimitch what was the day of the week, how many days there were in the year, and whether it was true that there was a remarkable prophet living in Ward No. 6.

In response to the last question Andrey Yefimitch turned rather red and said: "Yes, he is mentally deranged, but he is an interesting young man."

They asked him no other questions.

When he was putting on his overcoat in the entry, the military commander laid a hand on his shoulder and said with a sigh:

"It's time for us old fellows to rest!"

As he came out of the hall, Andrey Yefimitch understood that it had been a committee appointed to enquire into his mental condition. He recalled the questions that had been asked him, flushed crimson, and for some reason, for the first time in his life, felt bitterly grieved for medical science.

"My God . . ." he thought, remembering how these doctors had just examined him; "why, they have only lately been hearing lectures on mental pathology; they had passed an examination—what's the explanation of this crass ignorance? They have not a conception of mental pathology!"

And for the first time in his life he felt insulted and moved to anger.

In the evening of the same day Mihail Averyanitch came to see him. The postmaster went up to him without waiting to greet him, took him by both hands, and said in an agitated voice:

"My dear fellow, my dear friend, show me that you believe in my genuine affection and look on me as your friend!" And preventing Andrey Yefimitch from speaking, he went on, growing excited: "I love you for your culture and nobility of soul. Listen to me, my dear fellow. The rules of their profession compel the doctors to conceal the truth from you, but I blurt out the plain truth like a soldier. You are not well! Excuse me, my dear fellow, but it is the truth; everyone about you has been noticing it for a long time. Dr. Yevgeny Fyodoritch has just told me that it is essential for you to rest and distract your mind for the sake of your health. Perfectly true! Excellent! In a day or two I am taking a holiday and am going away for a sniff of a different atmosphere. Show that you are a friend to me, let us go together! Let us go for a jaunt as in the good old days."

"I feel perfectly well," said Andrey Yefimitch after a moment's thought. "I can't go away. Allow me to show you my friendship in some other way."

To go off with no object, without his books, without his Daryushka, without his beer, to break abruptly through the routine of life, established for twenty years—the idea for the first minute struck him as wild and fantastic, but he remembered the conversation at the Zemstvo committee and the depressing feelings with which he had returned home, and the thought of a brief absence from the town in which stupid people looked on him as a madman was pleasant to him.

"And where precisely do you intend to go?" he asked.

"To Moscow, to Petersburg, to Warsaw. . . . I spent the five happiest years of my life in Warsaw. What a marvellous town! Let us go, my dear fellow!"

XIII

A week later it was suggested to Andrey Yefimitch that he should have a rest—that is, send in his resignation—a suggestion he received with indifference, and a week later still, Mihail Averyanitch and he were sitting in a posting carriage driving to the nearest railway station. The days were cool and bright, with a blue sky and a transparent distance. They were two days driving the hundred and fifty miles to the railway station, and stayed two nights on the way. When at the posting station the glasses given them for their tea had not been properly washed, or the drivers were slow in harnessing the horses, Mihail Averyanitch would turn crimson, and quivering all over would shout:

"Hold your tongue! Don't argue!"

And in the carriage he talked without ceasing for a moment, describing his campaigns in the Caucasus and in Poland. What adventures he had had, what meetings! He talked loudly and opened his eyes so wide with wonder that he might well be thought to be lying. Moreover, as he talked he breathed in Andrey Yefimitch's face and laughed into his ear. This bothered the doctor and prevented him from thinking or concentrating his mind.

In the train they travelled, from motives of economy, third-class in a non-smoking compartment. Half the passengers were decent people. Mihail Averyanitch soon made friends with everyone, and moving from one seat to another, kept saying loudly that they ought not to travel by these appalling lines. It was a regular swindle! A very different thing riding on a good horse: one could do over seventy miles a day and feel fresh and well after it. And our bad harvests were due to the draining of the Pinsk marshes; altogether, the way things were done was dreadful. He got excited, talked loudly, and would not let others speak. This endless chatter to the accompaniment of loud laughter and expressive gestures wearied Andrey Yefimitch.

"Which of us is the madman?" he thought with vexation. "I, who try not to disturb my fellow-passengers in any way, or this egoist who thinks that he is cleverer and more interesting than anyone here, and so will leave no one in peace?"

In Moscow Mihail Averyanitch put on a military coat without epaulettes and trousers with red braid on them. He wore a military cap and overcoat in the street, and soldiers saluted him. It seemed to Andrey Yefimitch, now, that his companion was a man who had flung away all that was good and kept only what was bad of all the characteristics of a country gentleman that he had once possessed. He liked to be waited on even when it was quite unnecessary. The matches would be lying before him on the table, and he would see them and shout to the waiter to give him the matches; he did not hesitate to appear before a maidservant in nothing but his underclothes; he used the familiar mode of address to all footmen indiscriminately, even old men, and when he was angry called them fools and blockheads. This, Andrey Yefimitch thought, was like a gentleman, but disgusting.

First of all Mihail Averyanitch led his friend to the Iversky Madonna. He prayed fervently, shedding tears and bowing down to the earth, and when he had finished, heaved a deep sigh and said:

"Even though one does not believe it makes one somehow easier when one prays a little. Kiss the ikon, my dear fellow."

Andrey Yefimitch was embarrassed and he kissed the image, while Mihail Averyanitch pursed up his lips and prayed in a whisper, and again tears came into his eyes. Then they went to the Kremlin and looked there at the Tsar-cannon and the Tsar-bell, and even touched them with their fingers, admired the view over the river, visited St. Saviour's and the Rumyantsev museum.

They dined at Tyestov's. Mihail Averyanitch looked a long time at the menu, stroking his whiskers, and said in the tone of a gourmand accustomed to dine in restaurants:

"We shall see what you give us to eat to-day, angel!"

XIV

The doctor walked about, looked at things, ate and drank, but he had all the while one feeling: annoyance with Mihail Averyanitch. He longed to have a rest from his friend, to get away from him, to hide himself, while the friend thought it was his duty not to let the doctor move a step away from him, and to provide him with as many distractions as possible. When there was nothing to look at he entertained him with conversation. For two days Andrey Yefimitch endured it, but on the third he announced to his friend that he was ill and wanted to stay at home for the whole day; his friend replied that in that case he would stay too—that really he needed rest, for he was run off his legs already. Andrey Yefimitch lay on the sofa, with his face to the back, and clenching his teeth, listened to his friend, who assured him with heat that sooner or later France would certainly thrash Germany, that there were a great many scoundrels in Moscow, and that it was impossible to judge of a horse's quality by its outward appearance. The doctor began to have a buzzing in his ears and palpitations of the heart, but out of delicacy could not bring himself to beg his friend to go away or hold his tongue. Fortunately Mihail Averyanitch grew weary of sitting in the hotel room, and after dinner he went out for a walk.

As soon as he was alone Andrey Yefimitch abandoned himself to a feeling of relief. How pleasant to lie motionless on the sofa and to know that one is alone in the room! Real happiness is impossible without solitude. The fallen angel betrayed God probably because he longed for solitude, of which the angels know nothing. Andrey Yefimitch wanted to think about what he had seen and heard during the last few days, but he could not get Mihail Averyanitch out of his head.

"Why, he has taken a holiday and come with me out of friendship, out of generosity," thought the doctor with vexation; "nothing could be worse than this friendly supervision. I suppose he is good-natured and generous and a lively fellow, but he is a bore. An insufferable bore. In the same way there are people who never say anything but what is clever and good, yet one feels that they are dull-witted people."

For the following days Andrey Yefimitch declared himself ill and would not leave the hotel room; he lay with his face to the back of the sofa, and suffered agonies of weariness when his friend entertained him with conversation, or rested when his friend was absent. He was vexed with himself for having come, and with his friend, who grew every day more talkative and more free-and-easy; he could not succeed in attuning his thoughts to a serious and lofty level.

"This is what I get from the real life Ivan Dmitritch talked about," he thought, angry at his own pettiness. "It's of no consequence, though. . . . I shall go home, and everything will go on as before. . . ."

It was the same thing in Petersburg too; for whole days together he did not leave the hotel room, but lay on the sofa and only got up to drink beer.

Mihail Averyanitch was all haste to get to Warsaw.

"My dear man, what should I go there for?" said Andrey Yefimitch in an imploring voice. "You go alone and let me get home! I entreat you!"

"On no account," protested Mihail Averyanitch. "It's a marvellous town."

Andrey Yefimitch had not the strength of will to insist on his own way, and much against his inclination went to Warsaw. There he did not leave the hotel room, but lay on the sofa, furious with himself, with his friend, and with the waiters, who obstinately refused to understand Russian; while Mihail Averyanitch, healthy, hearty, and full of spirits as usual, went about the town from morning to night, looking for his old acquaintances. Several times he did not return home at night. After one night spent in some unknown haunt he returned home early in the morning, in a violently excited condition, with a red face and tousled hair. For a long time he walked up and down the rooms muttering something to himself, then stopped and said:

"Honour before everything."

After walking up and down a little longer he clutched his head in both hands and pronounced in a tragic voice: "Yes, honour before everything! Accursed be the moment when the idea first entered my head to visit this Babylon! My dear friend," he added, addressing the doctor, "you may despise me, I have played and lost; lend me five hundred roubles!"

Andrey Yefimitch counted out five hundred roubles and gave them to his friend without a word. The latter, still crimson with shame and anger, incoherently articulated some useless vow, put on his cap, and went out. Returning two hours later he flopped into an easy-chair, heaved a loud sigh, and said:

"My honour is saved. Let us go, my friend; I do not care to remain another hour in this accursed town. Scoundrels! Austrian spies!"

By the time the friends were back in their own town it was November, and deep snow was lying in the streets. Dr. Hobotov had Andrey

Yefimitch's post; he was still living in his old lodgings, waiting for
Andrey Yefimitch to arrive and clear out of the hospital apartments.
The plain woman whom he called his cook was already established in
one of the lodges.

Fresh scandals about the hospital were going the round of the
town. It was said that the plain woman had quarrelled with the superintendent, and that the latter had crawled on his knees before her begging forgiveness. On the very first day he arrived Andrey Yefimitch had
to look out for lodgings.

"My friend," the postmaster said to him timidly, "excuse an indis-
creet question: what means have you at your disposal?"

Andrey Yefimitch, without a word, counted out his money and
said: "Eighty-six roubles."

"I don't mean that," Mihail Averyanitch brought out in confusion,
misunderstanding him; "I mean, what have you to live on?"

"I tell you, eighty-six roubles . . . I have nothing else."

Mihail Averyanitch looked upon the doctor as an honourable man,
yet he suspected that he had accumulated a fortune of at least twenty
thousand. Now learning that Andrey Yefimitch was a beggar, that he
had nothing to live on he was for some reason suddenly moved to tears
and embraced his friend.

XV

Andrey Yefimitch now lodged in a little house with three windows.
There were only three rooms besides the kitchen in the little house.
The doctor lived in two of them which looked into the street, while
Daryushka and the landlady with her three children lived in the third
room and the kitchen. Sometimes the landlady's lover, a drunken
peasant who was rowdy and reduced the children and Daryushka to
terror, would come for the night. When he arrived and established
himself in the kitchen and demanded vodka, they all felt very uncomfortable, and the doctor would be moved by pity to take the crying
children into his room and let them lie on his floor, and this gave him
great satisfaction.

He got up as before at eight o'clock, and after his morning tea sat
down to read his old books and magazines: he had no money for new
ones. Either because the books were old, or perhaps because of the

change in his surroundings, reading exhausted him, and did not grip his attention as before. That he might not spend his time in idleness he made a detailed catalogue of his books and gummed little labels on their backs, and this mechanical, tedious work seemed to him more interesting than reading. The monotonous, tedious work lulled his thoughts to sleep in some unaccountable way, and the time passed quickly while he thought of nothing. Even sitting in the kitchen, peeling potatoes with Daryushka or picking over the buckwheat grain, seemed to him interesting. On Saturdays and Sundays he went to church. Standing near the wall and half closing his eyes, he listened to the singing and thought of his father, of his mother, of the university, of the religions of the world; he felt calm and melancholy, and as he went out of the church afterwards he regretted that the service was so soon over. He went twice to the hospital to talk to Ivan Dmitritch. But on both occasions Ivan Dmitritch was unusually excited and ill-humoured; he bade the doctor leave him in peace, as he had long been sick of empty chatter, and declared, to make up for all his sufferings, he asked from the damned scoundrels only one favour—solitary confinement. Surely they would not refuse him even that? On both occasions when Andrey Yefimitch was taking leave of him and wishing him good-night, he answered rudely and said:

"Go to hell!"

And Andrey Yefimitch did not know now whether to go to him for the third time or not. He longed to go.

In old days Andrey Yefimitch used to walk about his rooms and think in the interval after dinner, but now from dinner-time till evening tea he lay on the sofa with his face to the back and gave himself up to trivial thoughts which he could not struggle against. He was mortified that after more than twenty years of service he had been given neither a pension nor any assistance. It is true that he had not done his work honestly, but, then, all who are in the Service get a pension without distinction whether they are honest or not. Contemporary justice lies precisely in the bestowal of grades, orders, and pensions, not for moral qualities or capacities, but for service whatever it may have been like. Why was he alone to be an exception? He had no money at all. He was ashamed to pass by the shop and look at the woman who owned it. He owed thirty-two roubles for beer already. There was money owing to the landlady also. Daryushka sold old clothes and books on the sly, and told lies to the landlady, saying that the doctor was just going to receive a large sum of money.

He was angry with himself for having wasted on travelling the thousand roubles he had saved up. How useful that thousand roubles would have been now! He was vexed that people would not leave him in peace. Hobotov thought it his duty to look in on his sick colleague from time to time. Everything about him was revolting to Andrey Yefimitch—his well-fed face and vulgar, condescending tone, and his use of the word "colleague," and his high top-boots; the most revolting thing was that he thought it was his duty to treat Andrey Yefimitch, and thought that he really was treating him. On every visit he brought a bottle of bromide and rhubarb pills.

Mihail Averyanitch, too, thought it his duty to visit his friend and entertain him. Every time he went in to Andrey Yefimitch with an affectation of ease, laughed constrainedly, and began assuring him that he was looking very well to-day, and that, thank God, he was on the highroad to recovery, and from this it might be concluded that he looked on his friend's condition as hopeless. He had not yet repaid his Warsaw debt, and was overwhelmed by shame; he was constrained, and so tried to laugh louder and talk more amusingly. His anecdotes and descriptions seemed endless now, and were an agony both to Andrey Yefimitch and himself.

In his presence Andrey Yefimitch usually lay on the sofa with his face to the wall, and listened with his teeth clenched; his soul was oppressed with rankling disgust, and after every visit from his friend he felt as though this disgust had risen higher, and was mounting into his throat.

To stifle petty thoughts he made haste to reflect that he himself, and Hobotov, and Mihail Averyanitch, would all sooner or later perish without leaving any trace on the world. If one imagined some spirit flying by the earthly globe in space in a million years he would see nothing but clay and bare rocks. Everything—culture and the moral law—would pass away and not even a burdock would grow out of them. Of what consequence was shame in the presence of a shopkeeper, of what consequence was the insignificant Hobotov or the wearisome friendship of Mihail Averyanitch? It was all trivial and nonsensical.

But such reflections did not help him now. Scarcely had he imagined the earthly globe in a million years, when Hobotov in his high top-boots or Mihail Averyanitch with his forced laugh would appear from behind a bare rock, and he even heard the shamefaced whisper: "The Warsaw debt. . . . I will repay it in a day or two, my dear fellow, without fail. . . ."

XVI

One day Mihail Averyanitch came after dinner when Andrey Yefimitch was lying on the sofa. It so happened that Hobotov arrived at the same time with his bromide. Andrey Yefimitch got up heavily and sat down, leaning both arms on the sofa.

"You have a much better colour to-day than you had yesterday, my dear man," began Mihail Averyanitch. "Yes, you look jolly. Upon my soul, you do!"

"It's high time you were well, dear colleague," said Hobotov, yawning. "I'll be bound, you are sick of this bobbery."

"And we shall recover," said Mihail Averyanitch cheerfully. "We shall live another hundred years! To be sure!"

"Not a hundred years, but another twenty," Hobotov said reassuringly. "It's all right, all right, colleague; don't lose heart. . . . Don't go piling it on!"

"We'll show what we can do," laughed Mihail Averyanitch, and he slapped his friend on the knee. "We'll show them yet! Next summer, please God, we shall be off to the Caucasus, and we will ride all over it on horseback—trot, trot, trot! And when we are back from the Caucasus I shouldn't wonder if we will all dance at the wedding." Mihail Averyanitch gave a sly wink. "We'll marry you, my dear boy, we'll marry you. . . ."

Andrey Yefimitch felt suddenly that the rising disgust had mounted to his throat, his heart began beating violently.

"That's vulgar," he said, getting up quickly and walking away to the window. "Don't you understand that you are talking vulgar nonsense?"

He meant to go on softly and politely, but against his will he suddenly clenched his fists and raised them above his head.

"Leave me alone," he shouted in a voice unlike his own, blushing crimson and shaking all over. "Go away, both of you!"

Mihail Averyanitch and Hobotov got up and stared at him first with amazement and then with alarm.

"Go away, both!" Andrey Yefimitch went on shouting. "Stupid people! Foolish people! I don't want either your friendship or your medicines, stupid man! Vulgar! Nasty!"

Hobotov and Mihail Averyanitch, looking at each other in bewilderment, staggered to the door and went out. Andrey Yefimitch snatched up the bottle of bromide and flung it after them; the bottle broke with a crash on the door-frame.

"Go to the devil!" he shouted in a tearful voice, running out into the passage. "To the devil!"

When his guests were gone Andrey Yefimitch lay down on the sofa, trembling as though in a fever, and went on for a long while repeating: "Stupid people! Foolish people!"

When he was calmer, what occurred to him first of all was the thought that poor Mihail Averyanitch must be feeling fearfully ashamed and depressed now, and that it was all dreadful. Nothing like this had ever happened to him before. Where was his intelligence and his tact? Where was his comprehension of things and his philosophical indifference?

The doctor could not sleep all night for shame and vexation with himself, and at ten o'clock next morning he went to the post office and apologized to the postmaster.

"We won't think again of what has happened," Mihail Averyanitch, greatly touched, said with a sigh, warmly pressing his hand. "Let bygones be bygones. Lyubavkin," he suddenly shouted so loud that all the postmen and other persons present started, "hand a chair; and you wait," he shouted to a peasant woman who was stretching out a registered letter to him through the grating. "Don't you see that I am busy? We will not remember the past," he went on, affectionately addressing Andrey Yefimitch; "sit down, I beg you, my dear fellow."

For a minute he stroked his knees in silence, and then said:

"I have never had a thought of taking offence. Illness is no joke, I understand. Your attack frightened the doctor and me yesterday, and we had a long talk about you afterwards. My dear friend, why won't you treat your illness seriously? You can't go on like this. . . . Excuse me speaking openly as a friend," whispered Mihail Averyanitch. "You live in the most unfavourable surroundings, in a crowd, in uncleanliness, no one to look after you, no money for proper treatment. . . . My dear friend, the doctor and I implore you with all our hearts, listen to our advice: go into the hospital! There you will have wholesome food and attendance and treatment. Though, between ourselves, Yevgeny Fyodoritch is *mauvais ton*, yet he does understand his work, you can fully rely upon him. He has promised me he will look after you."

Andrey Yefimitch was touched by the postmaster's genuine sympathy and the tears which suddenly glittered on his cheeks.

"My honoured friend, don't believe it!" he whispered, laying his hand on his heart; "don't believe them. It's all a sham. My illness is only that in twenty years I have only found one intelligent man in the whole town, and he is mad. I am not ill at all, it's simply that I have got into an enchanted circle which there is no getting out of. I don't care; I am ready for anything."

"Go into the hospital, my dear fellow."

"I don't care if it were into the pit."

"Give me your word, my dear man, that you will obey Yevgeny Fyodoritch in everything."

"Certainly I will give you my word. But I repeat, my honoured friend, I have got into an enchanted circle. Now everything, even the genuine sympathy of my friends, leads to the same thing—to my ruin. I am going to my ruin, and I have the manliness to recognize it."

"My dear fellow, you will recover."

"What's the use of saying that?" said Andrey Yefimitch, with irritation. "There are few men who at the end of their lives do not experience what I am experiencing now. When you are told that you have something such as diseased kidneys or enlarged heart, and you begin being treated for it, or are told you are mad or a criminal—that is, in fact, when people suddenly turn their attention to you—you may be sure you have got into an enchanted circle from which you will not escape. You will try to escape and make things worse. You had better give in, for no human efforts can save you. So it seems to me."

Meanwhile the public was crowding at the grating. That he might not be in their way, Andrey Yefimitch got up and began to take leave. Mihail Averyanitch made him promise on his honour once more, and escorted him to the outer door.

Towards evening on the same day Hobotov, in his sheepskin and his high top-boots, suddenly made his appearance, and said to Andrey Yefimitch in a tone as though nothing had happened the day before:

"I have come on business, colleague. I have come to ask you whether you would not join me in a consultation. Eh?"

Thinking that Hobotov wanted to distract his mind with an outing, or perhaps really to enable him to earn something, Andrey Yefimitch put on his coat and hat, and went out with him into the street. He was glad of the opportunity to smooth over his fault of the previous day and to be reconciled, and in his heart thanked Hobotov, who did not even allude to yesterday's scene and was evidently sparing him. One would never have expected such delicacy from this uncultured man.

"Where is your invalid?" asked Andrey Yefimitch.

"In the hospital. . . . I have long wanted to show him to you. A very interesting case."

They went into the hospital yard, and going round the main building, turned towards the lodge where the mental cases were kept, and all this, for some reason, in silence. When they went into the lodge Nikita as usual jumped up and stood at attention.

"One of the patients here has a lung complication." Hobotov said in an undertone, going into the yard with Andrey Yefimitch. "You wait here, I'll be back directly. I am going for a stethoscope."

And he went away.

XVII

It was getting dusk. Ivan Dmitritch was lying on his bed with his face thrust unto his pillow; the paralytic was sitting motionless, crying quietly and moving his lips. The fat peasant and the former sorter were asleep. It was quiet.

Andrey Yefimitch sat down on Ivan Dmitritch's bed and waited. But half an hour passed, and instead of Hobotov, Nikita came into the ward with a dressing-gown, some underlinen, and a pair of slippers in a heap on his arm.

"Please change your things, your honour," he said softly. "Here is your bed; come this way," he added, pointing to an empty bedstead which had obviously recently been brought into the ward. "It's all right; please God, you will recover."

Andrey Yefimitch understood it all. Without saying a word he crossed to the bed to which Nikita pointed and sat down; seeing that

Nikita was standing waiting, he undressed entirely and he felt ashamed. Then he put on the hospital clothes; the drawers were very short, the shirt was long, and the dressing-gown smelt of smoked fish.

"Please God, you will recover," repeated Nikita, and he gathered up Andrey Yefimitch's clothes into his arms, went out, and shut the door after him.

"No matter . . ." thought Andrey Yefimitch, wrapping himself in his dressing-gown in a shamefaced way and feeling that he looked like a convict in his new costume. "It's no matter. . . . It does not matter whether it's a dress-coat or a uniform or this dressing-gown. . . ."

But how about his watch? And the notebook that was in the side-pocket? And his cigarettes? Where had Nikita taken his clothes? Now perhaps to the day of his death he would not put on trousers, a waist-coat, and high boots. It was all somehow strange and even incomprehensible at first. Andrey Yefimitch was even now convinced that there was no difference between his landlady's house and Ward No. 6, that everything in this world was nonsense and vanity of vanities. And yet his hands were trembling, his feet were cold, and he was filled with dread at the thought that soon Ivan Dmitritch would get up and see that he was in a dressing-gown. He got up and walked across the room and sat down again.

Here he had been sitting already half an hour, an hour, and he was miserably sick of it: was it really possible to live here a day, a week, and even years like these people? Why, he had been sitting here, had walked about and sat down again; he could get up and look out of win-dow and walk from corner to corner again, and then what? Sit so all the time, like a post, and think? No, that was scarcely possible.

Andrey Yefimitch lay down, but at once got up, wiped the cold sweat from his brow with his sleeve and felt that his whole face smelt of smoked fish. He walked about again.

"It's some misunderstanding . . ." he said, turning out the palms of his hands in perplexity. "It must be cleared up. There is a misun-derstanding. . . ."

Meanwhile Ivan Dmitritch woke up; he sat up and propped his cheeks on his fists. He spat. Then he glanced lazily at the doctor, and apparently for the first minute did not understand; but soon his sleepy face grew malicious and mocking.

"Aha! so they have put you in here, too, old fellow?" he said in a voice husky from sleepiness, screwing up one eye. "Very glad to see you. You sucked the blood of others, and now they will suck yours. Excellent!"

"It's a misunderstanding . . ." Andrey Yefimitch brought out, frightened by Ivan Dmitritch's words; he shrugged his shoulders and repeated: "It's some misunderstanding. . . ."

Ivan Dmitritch spat again and lay down.

"Cursed life," he grumbled, "and what's bitter and insulting, this life will not end in compensation for our sufferings, it will not end with apotheosis as it would in an opera, but with death; peasants will come and drag one's dead body by the arms and the legs to the cellar. Ugh! Well, it does not matter. . . . We shall have our good time in the other world. . . . I shall come here as a ghost from the other world and frighten these reptiles. I'll turn their hair grey."

Moiseika returned, and, seeing the doctor, held out his hand.

"Give me one little kopeck," he said.

XVIII

Andrey Yefimitch walked away to the window and looked out into the open country. It was getting dark, and on the horizon to the right a cold crimson moon was mounting upwards. Not far from the hospital fence, not much more than two hundred yards away, stood a tall white house shut in by a stone wall. This was the prison.

"So this is real life," thought Andrey Yefimitch, and he felt frightened.

The moon and the prison, and the nails on the fence, and the faraway flames at the bone-charring factory were all terrible. Behind him there was the sound of a sigh. Andrey Yefimitch looked round and saw a man with glittering stars and orders on his breast, who was smiling and slyly winking. And this, too, seemed terrible.

Andrey Yefimitch assured himself that there was nothing special about the moon or the prison, that even sane persons wear orders, and that everything in time will decay and turn to earth, but he was suddenly overcome with desire; he clutched at the grating with both hands and shook it with all his might. The strong grating did not yield.

Then that it might not be so dreadful he went to Ivan Dmitritch's bed and sat down.

"I have lost heart, my dear fellow," he muttered, trembling and wiping away the cold sweat, "I have lost heart."

"You should be philosophical," said Ivan Dmitritch ironically.

"My God, my God. . . . Yes, yes. . . . You were pleased to say once that there was no philosophy in Russia, but that all people, even the paltriest, talk philosophy. But you know the philosophizing of the paltriest does not harm anyone," said Andrey Yefimitch in a tone as if he wanted to cry and complain. "Why, then, that malignant laugh, my friend, and how can these paltry creatures help philosophizing if they are not satisfied? For an intelligent, educated man, made in God's image, proud and loving freedom, to have no alternative but to be a doctor in a filthy, stupid, wretched little town, and to spend his whole life among bottles, leeches, mustard plasters! Quackery, narrowness, vulgarity! Oh, my God!"

"You are talking nonsense. If you don't like being a doctor you should have gone in for being a statesman."

"I could not, I could not do anything. We are weak, my dear friend. . . . I used to be indifferent. I reasoned boldly and soundly, but at the first coarse touch of life upon me I have lost heart. . . . Prostration. . . . We are weak, we are poor creatures . . . and you, too, my dear friend, you are intelligent, generous, you drew in good impulses with your mother's milk, but you had hardly entered upon life when you were exhausted and fell ill. . . . Weak, weak!"

Andrey Yefimitch was all the while at the approach of evening tormented by another persistent sensation besides terror and the feeling of resentment. At last he realized that he was longing for a smoke and for beer.

"I am going out, my friend," he said. "I will tell them to bring a light; I can't put up with this. . . . I am not equal to it. . . ."

Andrey Yefimitch went to the door and opened it, but at once Nikita jumped up and barred his way.

"Where are you going? You can't, you can't!" he said. "It's bed-time."

"But I'm only going out for a minute to walk about the yard," said Andrey Yefimitch.

"You can't, you can't; it's forbidden. You know that yourself."

"But what difference will it make to anyone if I do go out?" asked Andrey Yefimitch, shrugging his shoulders. "I don't understand. Nikita, I must go out!" he said in a trembling voice. "I must."

"Don't be disorderly, it's not right," Nikita said peremptorily.

"This is beyond everything," Ivan Dmitritch cried suddenly, and he jumped up. "What right has he not to let you out? How dare they keep us here? I believe it is clearly laid down in the law that no one can be deprived of freedom without trial! It's an outrage! It's tyranny!"

"Of course it's tyranny," said Andrey Yefimitch, encouraged by Ivan Dmitritch's outburst. "I must go out, I want to. He has no right! Open, I tell you.

"Do you hear, you dull-witted brute?" cried Ivan Dmitritch, and he banged on the door with his fist. "Open the door, or I will break it open! Torturer!"

"Open the door," cried Andrey Yefimitch, trembling all over; "I insist!"

"Talk away!" Nikita answered through the door, "talk away. . . ."

"Anyhow, go and call Yevgeny Fyodoritch! Say that I beg him to come for a minute!"

"His honour will come of himself to-morrow."

"They will never let us out," Ivan Dmitritch was going on meanwhile. "They will leave us to rot here! Oh, Lord, can there really be no hell in the next world, and will these wretches be forgiven? Where is justice? Open the door, you wretch! I am choking!" he cried in a hoarse voice, and flung himself upon the door. "I'll dash out my brains, murderers!"

Nikita opened the door quickly, and roughly with both his hands and his knee shoved Andrey Yefimitch back, then swung his arm and punched him in the face with his fist. It seemed to Andrey Yefimitch as though a huge salt wave enveloped him from his head downwards and dragged him to the bed; there really was a salt taste in his mouth: most likely the blood was running from his teeth. He waved his arms as though he were trying to swim out and clutched at a bedstead, and at the same moment felt Nikita hit him twice on the back.

Ivan Dmitritch gave a loud scream. He must have been beaten too.

Then all was still, the faint moonlight came through the grating, and a shadow like a net lay on the floor. It was terrible. Andrey Yefimitch lay and held his breath: he was expecting with horror to be struck again. He felt as though someone had taken a sickle, thrust it into him, and turned it round several times in his breast and bowels. He bit the pillow from pain and clenched his teeth, and all at once through the chaos in his brain there flashed the terrible unbearable thought that these people, who seemed now like black shadows in the moonlight, had to endure such pain day by day for years. How could it have happened that for more than twenty years he had not known it and had refused to know it? He knew nothing of pain, had no conception of it, so he was not to blame, but his conscience, as inexorable and as rough as Nikita, made him turn cold from the crown of his head to his heels. He leaped up, tried to cry out with all his might, and to run in haste to kill Nikita, and then Hobotov, the superintendent and the assistant, and then himself; but no sound came from his chest, and his legs would not obey him. Gasping for breath, he tore at the dressing-gown and the shirt on his breast, rent them, and fell senseless on the bed.

XIX

Next morning his head ached, there was a droning in his ears and a feeling of utter weakness all over. He was not ashamed at recalling his weakness the day before. He had been cowardly, had even been afraid of the moon, had openly expressed thoughts and feelings such as he had not expected in himself before; for instance, the thought that the paltry people who philosophized were really dissatisfied. But now nothing mattered to him.

He ate nothing; he drank nothing. He lay motionless and silent.

"It is all the same to me, he thought when they asked him questions. "I am not going to answer. . . . It's all the same to me."

After dinner Mihail Averyanitch brought him a quarter pound of tea and a pound of fruit pastilles. Daryushka came too and stood for a whole hour by the bed with an expression of dull grief on her face. Dr. Hobotov visited him. He brought a bottle of bromide and told Nikita to fumigate the ward with something.

Towards evening Andrey Yefimitch died of an apoplectic stroke. At first he had a violent shivering fit and a feeling of sickness; something revolting as it seemed, penetrating through his whole body, even to his finger-tips, strained from his stomach to his head and flooded his eyes and ears. There was a greenness before his eyes. Andrey Yefimitch understood that his end had come, and remembered that Ivan Dmitritch, Mihail Averyanitch, and millions of people believed in immortality. And what if it really existed? But he did not want immortality, and he thought of it only for one instant. A herd of deer, extraordinarily beautiful and graceful, of which he had been reading the day before, ran by him; then a peasant woman stretched out her hand to him with a registered letter. . . . Mihail Averyanitch said something, then it all vanished, and Andrey Yefimitch sank into oblivion for ever.

The hospital porters came, took him by his arms and legs, and carried him away to the chapel.

There he lay on the table, with open eyes, and the moon shed its light upon him at night. In the morning Sergey Sergeyitch came, prayed piously before the crucifix, and closed his former chief's eyes.

Next day Andrey Yefimitch was buried. Mihail Averyanitch and Daryushka were the only people at the funeral.

1892

An Anonymous Story

I

Through causes which it is not the time to go into in detail, I had to enter the service of a Petersburg official called Orlov, in the capacity of a footman. He was about five and thirty, and was called Georgy[1] Ivanitch.

I entered this Orlov's service on account of his father, a prominent political man, whom I looked upon as a serious enemy of my cause. I reckoned that, living with the son, I should—from the conversations I should hear, and from the letters and papers I should find on the table—learn every detail of the father's plans and intentions.

As a rule at eleven o'clock in the morning the electric bell rang in my footman's quarters to let me know that my master was awake. When I went into the bedroom with his polished shoes and brushed clothes, Georgy Ivanitch would be sitting in his bed with a face that looked, not drowsy, but rather exhausted by sleep, and he would gaze off in one direction without any sign of satisfaction at having waked. I helped him to dress, and he let me do it with an air of reluctance without speaking or noticing my presence; then with his head wet with washing, smelling of fresh scent, he used to go into the dining-room to drink his coffee. He used to sit at the table, sipping his coffee and glancing through the newspapers, while the maid Polya and I stood respectfully at the door gazing at him. Two grown-up persons had to stand watching with the gravest attention a third drinking coffee and munching rusks. It was probably ludicrous and grotesque, but I saw nothing humiliating in having to stand near the door, though I was quite as well born and well educated as Orlov himself.

[1] Both *g*'s hard, as in "Gorgon"; *e* like *ai* in *rain*.

I was in the first stage of consumption, and was suffering from something else, possibly even more serious than consumption. I don't know whether it was the effect of my illness or of an incipient change in my philosophy of life of which I was not conscious at the time, but I was, day by day, more possessed by a passionate, irritating longing for ordinary everyday life. I yearned for mental tranquillity, health, fresh air, good food. I was becoming a dreamer, and, like a dreamer, I did not know exactly what I wanted. Sometimes I felt inclined to go into a monastery, to sit there for days together by the window and gaze at the trees and the fields; sometimes I fancied I would buy fifteen acres of land and settle down as a country gentleman; sometimes I inwardly vowed to take up science and become a professor at some provincial university. I was a retired navy lieutenant; I dreamed of the sea, of our squadron, and of the corvette in which I had made the cruise round the world. I longed to experience again the indescribable feeling when, walking in the tropical forest or looking at the sunset in the Bay of Bengal, one is thrilled with ecstasy and at the same time homesick. I dreamed of mountains, women, music, and, with the curiosity of a child, I looked into people's faces, listened to their voices. And when I stood at the door and watched Orlov sipping his coffee, I felt not a footman, but a man interested in everything in the world, even in Orlov.

In appearance Orlov was a typical Petersburger, with narrow shoulders, a long waist, sunken temples, eyes of an indefinite colour, and scanty, dingy-coloured hair, beard and moustaches. His face had a stale, unpleasant look, though it was studiously cared for. It was particularly unpleasant when he was asleep or lost in thought. It is not worth while describing a quite ordinary appearance; besides, Petersburg is not Spain, and a man's appearance is not of much consequence even in love affairs, and is only of value to a handsome footman or coachman. I have spoken of Orlov's face and hair only because there was something in his appearance worth mentioning. When Orlov took a newspaper or book, whatever it might be, or met people, whoever they might be, an ironical smile began to come into his eyes, and his whole countenance assumed an expression of light mockery in which there was no malice. Before reading or hearing anything he always had his irony in readiness, as a savage has his shield. It was an habitual irony, like some old liquor brewed years ago, and now it came into his face probably without any participation of his will, as it were by reflex action. But of that later.

Soon after midday he took his portfolio, full of papers, and drove to his office. He dined away from home and returned after eight o'clock. I used to light the lamp and candles in his study, and he would sit down in a low chair with his legs stretched out on another chair, and, reclining in that position, would begin reading. Almost every day he brought in new books with him or received parcels of them from the shops, and there were heaps of books in three languages, to say nothing of Russian, which he had read and thrown away, in the corners of my room and under my bed. He read with extraordinary rapidity. They say: "Tell me what you read, and I'll tell you who you are." That may be true, but it was absolutely impossible to judge of Orlov by what he read. It was a regular hotchpotch. Philosophy, French novels, political economy, finance, new poets, and publications of the firm *Posrednik*[2] — and he read it all with the same rapidity and with the same ironical expression in his eyes.

After ten o'clock he carefully dressed, often in evening dress, very rarely in his *kammer-junker*'s uniform, and went out, returning in the morning.

Our relations were quiet and peaceful, and we never had any misunderstanding. As a rule he did not notice my presence, and when he talked to me there was no expression of irony on his face—he evidently did not look upon me as a human being.

I only once saw him angry. One day—it was a week after I had entered his service—he came back from some dinner at nine o'clock; his face looked ill-humoured and exhausted. When I followed him into his study to light the candles, he said to me:

"There's a nasty smell in the flat."

"No, the air is fresh," I answered.

"I tell you, there's a bad smell," he answered irritably.

"I open the movable panes every day."

"Don't argue, blockhead!" he shouted.

I was offended, and was on the point of answering, and goodness

---

[2] *I.e.*, Tchertkov and others, publishers of Tolstoy, who issued good literature for peasants' reading.

knows how it would have ended if Polya, who knew her master better than I did, had not intervened.

"There really is a disagreeable smell," she said, raising her eyebrows. "What can it be from? Stepan, open the pane in the drawing-room, and light the fire."

With much bustle and many exclamations, she went through all the rooms, rustling her skirts and squeezing the sprayer with a hissing sound. And Orlov was still out of humour; he was obviously restraining himself not to vent his ill-temper aloud. He was sitting at the table and rapidly writing a letter. After writing a few lines he snorted angrily and tore it up, then he began writing again.

"Damn them all!" he muttered. "They expect me to have an abnormal memory!"

At last the letter was written; he got up from the table and said, turning to me:

"Go to Znamensky Street and deliver this letter to Zinaida Fyodorovna Krasnovsky in person. But first ask the porter whether her husband—that is, Mr. Krasnovsky—has returned yet. If he has returned, don't deliver the letter, but come back. Wait a minute! . . . If she asks whether I have any one here, tell her that there have been two gentlemen here since eight o'clock, writing something."

I drove to Znamensky Street. The porter told me that Mr. Krasnovsky had not yet come in, and I made my way up to the third storey. The door was opened by a tall, stout, drab-coloured flunkey with black whiskers, who in a sleepy, churlish, and apathetic voice, such as only flunkeys use in addressing other flunkeys, asked me what I wanted. Before I had time to answer, a lady dressed in black came hurriedly into the hall. She screwed up her eyes and looked at me.

"Is Zinaida Fyodorovna at home?" I asked.

"That is me," said the lady.

"A letter from Georgy Ivanitch."

She tore the letter open impatiently, and holding it in both hands, so that I saw her sparkling diamond rings, she began reading. I made out a pale face with soft lines, a prominent chin, and long dark lashes. From her appearance I should not have judged the lady to be more than five and twenty.

"Give him my thanks and my greetings," she said when she had finished the letter. "Is there any one with Georgy Ivanitch?" she asked softly, joyfully, and as though ashamed of her mistrust.

"Two gentlemen," I answered. "They're writing something."

"Give him my greetings and thanks," she repeated, bending her head sideways, and, reading the letter as she walked, she went noiselessly out.

I saw few women at that time, and this lady of whom I had a passing glimpse made an impression on me. As I walked home I recalled her face and the delicate fragrance about her, and fell to dreaming. By the time I got home Orlov had gone out.

II

And so my relations with my employer were quiet and peaceful, but still the unclean and degrading element which I so dreaded on becoming a footman was conspicuous and made itself felt every day. I did not get on with Polya. She was a well-fed and pampered hussy who adored Orlov because he was a gentleman and despised me because I was a footman. Probably, from the point of view of a real flunkey or cook, she was fascinating, with her red cheeks, her turned-up nose, her coquettish glances, and the plumpness, one might almost say fatness, of her person. She powdered her face, coloured her lips and eyebrows, laced herself in, and wore a bustle, and a bangle made of coins. She walked with little tripping steps; as she walked she swayed, or, as they say, wriggled her shoulders and back. The rustle of her skirts, the creaking of her stays, the jingle of her bangle and the vulgar smell of lip salve, toilet vinegar, and scent stolen from her master, aroused in me whilst I was doing the rooms with her in the morning a sensation as though I were taking part with her in some abomination.

Either because I did not steal as she did, or because I displayed no desire to become her lover, which she probably looked upon as an insult, or perhaps because she felt that I was a man of a different order, she hated me from the first day. My inexperience, my appearance—so unlike a flunkey—and my illness, seemed to her pitiful and excited her disgust. I had a bad cough at that time, and sometimes at night I prevented her from sleeping, as our rooms were only divided by a wooden partition, and every morning she said to me:

"Again you didn't let me sleep. You ought to be in hospital instead of in service."

She so genuinely believed that I was hardly a human being, but something infinitely below her, that, like the Roman matrons who were not ashamed to bathe before their slaves, she sometimes went about in my presence in nothing but her chemise.

Once when I was in a happy, dreamy mood, I asked her at dinner (we had soup and roast meat sent in from a restaurant every day):

"Polya, do you believe in God?"

"Why, of course!"

"Then," I went on, "you believe there will be a day of judgment, and that we shall have to answer to God for every evil action?"

She gave me no reply, but simply made a contemptuous grimace, and, looking that time at her cold eyes and over-fed expression, I realised that for her complete and finished personality no God, no conscience, no laws existed, and that if I had had to set fire to the house, to murder or to rob, I could not have hired a better accomplice.

In my novel surroundings I felt very uncomfortable for the first week at Orlov's before I got used to being addressed as "thou," and being constantly obliged to tell lies (saying "My master is not at home" when he was). In my flunkey's shallow-tail I felt as though I were in armour. But I grew accustomed to it in time. Like a genuine footman, I waited at table, tidied the rooms, ran and drove about on errands of all sorts. When Orlov did not want to keep an appointment with Zinaida Fyodorovna, or when he forgot that he had promised to go and see her, I drove to Znametlsky Street, put a letter into her hands and told a lie. And the result of it all was quite different from what I had expected when I became a footman. Every day of this new life of mine was wasted for me and my cause, as Orlov never spoke of his father, nor did his visitors, and all I could learn of the stateman's doings was, as before, what I could glean from the newspapers or from correspondence with my comrades. The hundreds of notes and papers I used to find in the study and read had not the remotest connection with what I was looking for. Orlov was absolutely uninterested in his father's political work, and looked as though he had never heard of it, or as though his father had long been dead.

III

Every Thursday we had visitors.

I ordered a piece of roast beef from the restaurant and telephoned to Eliseyev's to send us caviare, cheese, oysters, and so on. I bought playing-cards. Polya was busy all day getting ready the tea-things and the dinner service. To tell the truth, this spurt of activity came as a pleasant change in our idle life, and Thursdays were for us the most interesting days.

Only three visitors used to come. The most important and perhaps the most interesting was the one called Pekarsky—a tall, lean man of five and forty, with a long hooked nose, with a big black beard, and a bald patch on his head. His eyes were large and prominent, and his expression was grave and thoughtful like that of a Greek philosopher. He was on the board of management of some railway, and also had some post in a bank; he was a consulting lawyer in some important Government institution, and had business relations with a large number of private persons as a trustee, chairman of committees, and so on. He was of quite a low grade in the service, and modestly spoke of himself as a lawyer, but he had vast influence. A note or card from him was enough to make a celebrated doctor, a director of a railway, or a great dignitary see any one without waiting; and it was said that through his protection one might obtain even a post of the Fourth Class, and get any sort of unpleasant business hushed up. He was looked upon as a very intelligent man, but his was a strange, peculiar intelligence. he was able to multiply 213 by 373 in his head instantaneously, or turn English pounds into German marks without help of pencil or paper; he understood finance and railway business thoroughly, and the machinery of Russian administration had no secrets for him; he was a most skilful pleader in civil suits, and it was not easy to get the better of him at law. But that exceptional intelligence could not grasp many things which are understood even by some stupid people. For instance, he was absolutely unable to understand why people are depressed, why they weep, shoot themselves, and even kill others; why they fret about things that do not affect them personally, and why they laugh when they read Gogol or Shtchedrin. . . . Everything abstract, everything belonging to the domain of thought and feeling, was to him boring and incomprehensible, like music to one who has no ear. He looked at people simply from the business point of view, and divided them into competent and incompetent. No other classification existed for him. Honesty and rectitude were only signs of competence. Drinking, gambling, and debauchery were permissible, but must not be allowed to interfere with business. Believing in God was rather stupid, but religion ought to be safeguarded, as the common people must have some principle to restrain them, otherwise they would not work. Punishment is only necessary as a deterrent. There was no need to go away for holidays, as it was just as nice in town. And so on. He was a widower and had no children, but lived on a large scale, as though he had a family, and paid three thousand roubles a year for his flat.

The second visitor, Kukushkin, an actual civil councillor though a young man, was short, and was conspicuous for his extremely unpleasant appearance, which was due to the disproportion between his fat, puffy body and his lean little face. His lips were puckered up suavely, and his little trimmed moustaches looked as though they had been fixed on with glue. He was a man with the manners of a lizard. He did not walk, but, as it were, crept along with tiny steps, squirming and sniggering, and when he laughed he showed his teeth. He was a clerk on special commissions, and did nothing, though he received a good salary, especially in the summer, when special and lucrative jobs were found for him. He was a man of personal ambition, not only to the marrow of his bones, but more fundamentally—to the last drop of his blood; but even in his ambitions he was petty and did not rely on himself, but was building his career on the chance favour flung him by his superiors. For the sake of obtaining some foreign decoration, or for the sake of having his name mentioned in the newspapers as having been present at some special service in the company of other great personages, he was ready to submit to any kind of humiliation, to beg, to flatter, to promise. He flattered Orlov and Pekarsky from cowardice, because he thought they were powerful; he flattered Polya and me because we were in the service of a powerful man. Whenever I took off his fur coat he tittered and asked me: "Stepan, are you married?" and then unseemly vulgarities followed—by way of showing me special attention. Kukushkin flattered Orlov's weaknesses, humoured his corrupted and blasé ways; to please him he affected malicious raillery and atheism, in his company criticised persons before whom in other places he would slavishly grovel. When at supper they talked of love and women, he pretended to be a subtle and perverse voluptuary. As a rule, one may say, Petersburg rakes are fond of talking of their abnormal tastes. Some young actual civil councillor is perfectly satisfied with the embraces of his cook or of some unhappy street-walker on the Nevsky Prospect, but to listen to him you would think he was contaminated by all the vices of East and West combined, that he was an honourary member of a dozen iniquitous secret societies and was already marked by the police. Kukushkin lied about himself in an unconscionable way, and they did not exactly disbelieve him, but paid little heed to his incredible stories.

The third guest was Gruzin, the son of a worthy and learned general; a man of Orlov's age, with long hair, short-sighted eyes, and gold spectacles. I remember his long white fingers, that looked like a pianist's; and, indeed, there was something of a musician, of a virtuoso, about his whole figure. The first violins in orchestras look just like that. He used to cough, suffered from migraine, and seemed altogether invalidish and delicate. Probably at home he was dressed and undressed like a baby. He had finished at the College of Jurisprudence, and had at first served in the Department of Justice, then he was transferred to the Senate; he left that, and through patronage had received a post in the Department of Crown Estates, and had soon afterwards given that up. In my time he was serving in Orlov's department; he was his head-clerk, but he said that he should soon exchange into the Department of Justice again. He took his duties and his shifting about from one post to another with exceptional levity, and when people talked before him seriously of grades in the service, decorations, salaries, he smiled good-naturedly and repeated Prutkov's aphorism: "It's only in the Government service you learn the truth." He had a little wife with a wrinkled face, who was very jealous of him, and five weedy-looking children. He was unfaithful to his wife, he was only fond of his children when he saw them, and on the whole was rather indifferent to his family, and made fun of them. He and his family existed on credit, borrowing wherever they could at every opportunity, even from his superiors in the office and porters in people's houses. His was a flabby nature; he was so lazy that he did not care what became of himself, and drifted along heedless where or why he was going. He went where he was taken. If he was taken to some low haunt, he went; if wine was set before him, he drank— if it were not put before him, he abstained; if wives were abused in his presence, he abused his wife, declaring she had ruined his life— when wives were praised, he praised his and said quite sincerely: "I am very fond of her, poor thing!" He had no fur coat and always wore a rug which smelt of the nursery. When at supper he rolled balls of bread and drank a great deal of red wine, absorbed in thought, strange to say, I used to feel almost certain that there was something in him of which perhaps he had a vague sense, though in the bustle and vulgarity of his daily life he had not time to understand and appreciate it. He played a little on the piano. Sometimes he would sit down at the piano, play a chord or two, and begin singing softly:

"What does the coming day bring to me?"

But at once, as though afraid, he would get up and walk from the piano.

The visitors usually arrived about ten o'clock. They played cards in Orlov's study, and Polya and I handed them tea. It was only on these occasions that I could gauge the full sweetness of a flunkey's life. Standing for four or five hours at the door, watching that no one's glass should be empty, changing the ash-trays, running to the table to pick up the chalk or a card when it was dropped, and, above all, standing, waiting, being attentive without venturing to speak, to cough, to smile—is harder, I assure you, is harder than the hardest of field labor. I have stood on watch at sea for four hours at a stretch on stormy winter nights, and to my thinking it is an infinitely easier duty.

They used to play cards till two, sometimes till three o'clock at night, and then, stretching, they would go into the dining-room to supper, or, as Orlov said, for a snack of something. At supper there was conversation. It usually began by Orlov's speaking with laughing eyes of some acquaintance, of some book he had lately been reading, of a new appointment or Government scheme. Kukushkin, always ingratiating, would fall into his tone, and what followed was to me, in my mood at that time, a revolting exhibition. The irony of Orlov and his friends knew no bounds, and spared no one and nothing. If they spoke of religion, it was with irony; they spoke of philosophy, of the significance and object of life—irony again, if any one began about the peasantry, it was with irony.

There is in Petersburg a species of men whose speciality it is to jeer at every aspect of life; they cannot even pass by a starving man or a suicide without saying something vulgar. But Orlov and his friends did not jeer or make jokes, they talked ironically. They used to say that there was no God, and personality was completely lost at death; the immortals only existed in the French Academy. Real good did not and could not possibly exist, as its existence was conditional upon human perfection, which was a logical absurdity. Russia was a country as poor and dull as Persia. The intellectual class was hopeless; in Pekarsky's opinion the overwhelming majority in it were incompetent persons, good for nothing. The people were drunken, lazy, thievish, and degenerate. We had no science, our literature was uncouth, our commerce rested on swindling—"No selling without cheating." And everything was in that style, and everything was a subject for laughter.

Towards the end of supper the wine made them more good-humoured, and they passed to more lively conversation. They laughed over Gruzin's family life, over Kukushkin's conquests, or at Pekarsky, who had, they said, in his account book one page headed *Charity* and another *Physiological Necessities.* They said that no wife was faithful; that there was no wife from whom one could not, with practice, obtain caresses without leaving her drawing-room while her husband was sitting in his study close by; that girls in their teens were perverted and knew everything. Orlov had preserved a letter of a schoolgirl of fourteen: on her way home from school she had "hooked an officer on the Nevsky," who had, it appears, taken her home with him, and had only let her go late in the evening; and she hastened to write about this to her school friend to share her joy with her. They maintained that there was not and never had been such a thing as moral purity, and that evidently it was unnecessary; mankind had so far done very well without it. The harm done by so-called vice was undoubtedly exaggerated. Vices which are punished by our legal code had not prevented Diogenes from being a philosopher and a teacher. Cæsar and Cicero were profligates and at the same time great men. Cato in his old age married a young girl, and yet he was regarded as a great ascetic and a pillar of morality.

At three or four o'clock the party broke up or they went off together out of town, or to Officers' Street, to the house of a certain Varvara Ossipovna, while I retired to my quarters, and was kept awake a long while by coughing and headache.

IV

Three weeks after I entered Orlov's service—it was Sunday morning, I remember—somebody rang the bell. It was not yet eleven, and Orlov was still asleep. I went to open the door. You can imagine my astonishment when I found a lady in a veil standing at the door on the landing.

"Is Georgy Ivanitch up?" she asked.

From her voice I recognised Zinaida Fyodorovna, to whom I had taken letters in Znamensky Street. I don't remember whether I had time or self-possession to answer her—I was taken aback at seeing her. And, indeed, she did not need my answer. In a flash she had darted by me, and, filling the hall with the fragrance of her perfume, which I remember to this day, she went on, and her footsteps died away. For at least half an hour afterwards I heard nothing. But again some one rang. This time it was a smartly dressed girl, who looked like a maid in a wealthy family, accompanied by our house porter. Both were out of breath, carrying two trunks and a dress-basket.

"These are for Zinaida Fyodorovna," said the girl.

And she went down without saying another word. All this was mysterious, and made Polya, who had a deep admiration for the pranks of her betters, smile slyly to herself; she looked as though she would like to say, "So that's what we're up to," and she walked about the whole time on tiptoe. At last we heard footsteps; Zinaida Fyodorovna came quickly into the hall, and seeing me at the door of my room, said:

"Stepan, take Georgy Ivanitch his things."

When I went in to Orlov with his clothes and his boots, he was sitting on the bed with his feet on the bearskin rug. There was an air of embarrassment about his whole figure. He did not notice me, and my menial opinion did not interest him; he was evidently perturbed and embarrassed before himself, before his inner eye. He dressed, washed, and used his combs and brushes silently and deliberately, as though allowing himself time to think over his position and to reflect, and even from his back one could see he was troubled and dissatisfied with himself.

They drank coffee together. Zinaida Fyodorovna poured out coffee for herself and for Orlov, then she put her elbows on the table and laughed.

"I still can't believe it," she said. "When one has been a long while on one's travels and reaches a hotel at last, it's difficult to believe that one hasn't to go on. It is pleasant to breathe freely."

With the expression of a child who very much wants to be mischievous, she sighed with relief and laughed again.

"You will excuse me," said Orlov, nodding towards the coffee. "Reading at breakfast is a habit I can't get over. But I can do two things at once—read and listen."

"Read away. . . . You shall keep your habits and your freedom. But why do you look so solemn ? Are you always like that in the morning, or is it only to-day ? Aren't you glad?"

"Yes, I am. But I must own I am a little overwhelmed."

"Why? You had plenty of time to prepare yourself for my descent upon you. I've been threatening to come every day."

"Yes, but I didn't expect you to carry out your threat to-day."

"I didn't expect it myself, but that's all the better. It's all the better, my dear. It's best to have an aching tooth out and have done with it."

"Yes, of course."

"Oh, my dear," she said, closing her eyes, "all is well that ends well; but before this happy ending, what suffering there has been! My laughing means nothing; I am glad, I am happy, but I feel more like crying than laughing. Yesterday I had to fight a regular battle," she went on in French. "God alone knows how wretched I was. But I laugh because I can't believe in it. I keep fancying that my sitting here drinking coffee with you is not real, but a dream."

Then, still speaking French, she described how she had broken with her husband the day before, and her eyes were alternately full of tears and of laughter while she gazed with rapture at Orlov. She told him her husband had long suspected her, but had avoided explanations; they had frequent quarrels, and usually at the most heated moment he would suddenly subside into silence and depart to his study for fear that in his exasperation he might give utterance to his suspicions or she might herself begin to speak openly. And she had felt guilty, worthless, incapable of taking a bold and serious step, and that had made her hate herself and her husband more every day, and she had suffered the torments of hell. But the day before, when during a quarrel he had cried out in a tearful voice, "My God, when will it end?" and had walked off to his study, she had run after him like a cat after a mouse, and, preventing him from shutting the door, she had cried that she hated him with her whole soul. Then he let her come into the study and she had told him everything, had confessed that she loved some one else, that that some one else was her real, most lawful husband, and that she thought it her true duty to go away to him that very day, whatever might happen, if she were to be shot for it.

"There's a very romantic streak in you," Orlov interrupted, keeping his eyes fixed on the newspaper.

She laughed and went on talking without touching her coffee. Her cheeks glowed and she was a little embarrassed by it, and she looked in confusion at Polya and me. From what she went on to say I learnt that her husband had answered her with threats, reproaches, and finally tears, and that it would have been more accurate to say that she, and not he, had been the attacking party.

"Yes, my dear, so long as I was worked up, everything went all right," she told Orlov; "but as night came on, my spirits sank. You don't believe in God, *George*, but I do believe a little, and I fear retribution. God requires of us patience, magnanimity, self-sacrifice, and here I am refusing to be patient and want to remodel my life to suit myself. Is that right? What if from the point of view of God it's wrong? At two o'clock in the night my husband came to me and said: 'You dare not go away. I'll fetch you back through the police and make a scandal.' And soon afterwards I saw him like a shadow at my door. 'Have mercy on me! Your elopement may injure me in the service.' Those words had a coarse effect upon me and made me feel stiff all over. I felt as though the retribution were beginning already; I began crying and trembling with terror. I felt as though the ceiling would fall upon me, that I should be dragged off to the police-station at once, that you would grow cold to me—all sorts of things, in fact ! I thought I would go into a nunnery or become a nurse, and give up all thought of happiness, but then I remembered that you loved me, and that I had no right to dispose of myself without your knowledge; and everything in my mind was in a tangle—I was in despair and did not know what to do or think. But the sun rose and I grew happier. As soon as it was morning I dashed off to you. Ah, what I've been through, dear one ! I haven't slept for two nights!"

She was tired out and excited. She was sleepy, and at the same time she wanted to talk endlessly, to laugh and to cry, and to go to a restaurant to lunch that she might feel her freedom.

"You have a cosy flat, but I am afraid it may be small for the two of us," she said, walking rapidly through all the rooms when they had finished breakfast. "What room will you give me? I like this one because it is next to your study."

At one o'clock she changed her dress in the room next to the study, which from that time she called hers, and she went off with Orlov to lunch. They dined, too, at a restaurant, and spent the long interval between lunch and dinner in shopping. Till late at night I was opening the door to messengers and errand-boys from the shops. They bought, among other things, a splendid pier-glass, a dressing-table, a bedstead, and a gorgeous tea service which we did not need. They bought a regular collection of copper saucepans, which we set in a row on the shelf in our cold, empty kitchen. As we were unpacking the tea service Polya's eyes gleamed, and she looked at me two or three times with hatred and fear that I, not she, would be the first to steal one of these charming cups. A lady's writing-table, very expensive and inconvenient, came too. It was evident that Zinaida Fyodorovna contemplated settling with us for good, and meant to make the flat her home.

She came back with Orlov between nine and ten. Full of proud consciousness that she had done something bold and out of the common, passionately in love, and, as she imagined, passionately loved, exhausted, looking forward to a sweet sound sleep, Zinaida Fyodorovna was revelling in her new life. She squeezed her hands together in the excess of her joy, declared that everything was delightful, and swore that she would love Orlov for ever; and these vows, and the naïve, almost childish confidence that she too was deeply loved and would be loved for ever, made her at least five years younger. She talked charming nonsense and laughed at herself.

"There is no other blessing greater than freedom!" she said, forcing herself to say something serious and edifying. "How absurd it is when you think of it! We attach no value to our own opinion even when it is wise, but tremble before the opinion of all sorts of stupid people. Up to the last minute I was afraid of what other people would say, but as soon as I followed my own instinct and made up my mind to go my own way, my eyes were opened, I overcame my silly fears, and now I am happy and wish every one could be as happy!"

But her thoughts immediately took another turn, and she began talking of another flat, of wallpapers, horses, a trip to Switzerland and Italy. Orlov was tired by the restaurants and the shops, and was still suffering from the same uneasiness that I had noticed in the morning. He smiled, but more from politeness than pleasure, and when she spoke of anything seriously, he agreed ironically: "Oh, yes."

"Stepan, make haste and find us a good cook," she said to me.

"There's no need to be in a hurry over the kitchen arrangements," said Orlov, looking at me coldly. "We must first move into another flat."

We had never had cooking done at home nor kept horses, because, as he said, "he did not like disorder about him," and only put up with having Polya and me in his flat from necessity. The so-called domestic hearth with its everyday joys and its petty cares offended his taste as vulgarity; to be with child, or to have children and talk about them, was bad form, like a petty bourgeois. And I began to feel very curious to see how these two creatures would get on together in one flat—she, domestic and home-loving with her copper saucepans and her dreams of a good cook and horses; and he, fond of saying to his friends that a decent and orderly man's flat ought, like a warship, to have nothing in it superfluous—no women, no children, no rags, no kitchen utensils.

V

Then I will tell you what happened the following Thursday. That day Zinaida Fyodorovna dined at Content's or Donon's. Orlov returned home alone, and Zinaida Fyodorovna, as I learnt afterwards, went to the Petersburg Side to spend with her old governess the time visitors were with us. Orlov did not care to show her to his friends. I realised that at breakfast, when he began assuring her that for the sake of her peace of mind it was essential to give up his Thursday evenings.

As usual the visitors arrived at almost the same time.

"Is your mistress at home, too?" Kukushkin asked me in a whisper.

"No, sir," I answered.

He went in with a sly, oily look in his eyes, smiling mysteriously, rubbing his hands, which were cold from the frost.

"I have the honour to congratulate you," he said to Orlov, shaking all over with ingratiating, obsequious laughter. "May you increase and multiply like the cedars of Lebanon."

The visitors went into the bedroom, and were extremely jocose on the subject of a pair of feminine slippers, the rug that had been put down between the two beds, and a grey dressing-jacket that hung at the foot of the bedstead. They were amused that the obstinate man who despised all the common place details of love had been caught in feminine snares in such a simple and ordinary way.

"He who pointed the finger of scorn is bowing the knee in homage," Kukushkin repeated several times. He had, I may say in parenthesis, an unpleasant habit of adorning his conversation with texts in Church Slavonic. "Sh-sh!" he said as they went from the bedroom into the room next to the study. "Sh-sh! Here Gretchen is dreaming of her Faust."

He went off into a peal of laughter as though he had said something very amusing. I watched Gruzin, expecting that his musical soul would not endure this laughter, but I was mistaken. His thin, good-natured face beamed with pleasure. When they sat down to play cards, he, lisping and choking with laughter, said that all that "dear George" wanted to complete his domestic felicity was a cherry-wood pipe and a guitar. Pekarsky laughed sedately, but from his serious expression one could see that Orlov's new love affair was distasteful to him. He did not understand what had happened exactly.

"But how about the husband?" he asked in perplexity, after they had played three rubbers.

"I don't know," answered Orlov.

Pekarsky combed his big beard with his fingers and sank into thought, and he did not speak again till supper-time. When they were seated at supper, he began deliberately, drawling every word:

"Altogether, excuse my saying so, I don't understand either of you. You might love each other and break the seventh commandment to your heart's content—that I understand. Yes, that's comprehensible. But why make the husband a party to your secrets? Was there any need for that?"

"But does it make any difference?"

"Hm! . . ." Pekarsky mused. "Well, then, let me tell you this, my friend," he went on, evidently thinking hard: "if I ever marry again and you take it into your head to seduce my wife, please do it so that I don't notice it. It's much more honest to deceive a man than to break up his family life and injure his reputation. I understand. You both imagine that in living together openly you are doing something exceptionally honourable and advanced, but I can't agree with that . . . what shall I call it ? . . . romantic attitude?"

Orlov made no reply. He was out of humour and disinclined to talk. Pekarsky, still perplexed, drummed on the table with his fingers, thought a little, and said:

"I don't understand you, all the same. You are not a student and she is not a dressmaker. You are both of you people with means. I should have thought you might have arranged a separate flat for her."

"No, I couldn't. Read Turgenev."

"Why should I read him? I have read him already."

"Turgenev teaches us in his novels that every exalted, noble-minded girl should follow the man she loves to the ends of the earth, and should serve his idea," said Orlov, screwing up his eyes ironically. "The ends of the earth are poetic license; the earth and all its ends can be reduced to the flat of the man she loves. . . . And so not to live in the same flat with the woman who loves you is to deny her her exalted vocation and to refuse to share her ideals. Yes, my dear fellow, Turgenev wrote, and I have to suffer for it."

"What Turgenev has got to do with it I don't understand," said Gruzin softly, and he shrugged his shoulders. "Do you remember, *George*, how in 'Three Meetings' he is walking late in the evening somewhere in Italy, and suddenly hears, ' *Vieni pensando a me segretamente*,' " Gruzin hummed. "It's fine."

"But she hasn't come to settle with you by force," said Pekarsky. "It was your own wish."

"What next! Far from wishing it, I never imagined that this would ever happen. When she said she was coming to live with me, I thought it was a charming joke on her part."

Everybody laughed.

"I couldn't have wished for such a thing," said Orlov in the tone of a man compelled to justify himself. "I am not a Turgenev hero, and if I ever wanted to free Bulgaria I shouldn't need a lady's company. I look upon love primarily as a necessity of my physical nature, degrading and antagonistic to my spirit; it must either be satisfied with discretion or renounced altogether, otherwise it will bring into one's life elements as unclean as itself. For it to be an enjoyment and not a torment, I will try to make it beautiful and to surround it with a mass of illusions. I should never go and see a woman unless I were sure beforehand that she would be beautiful and fascinating; and I should never go unless I were in the mood. And it is only in that way that we succeed in deceiving one another, and fancying that we are in love and happy. But can I wish for copper saucepans and untidy hair, or like to be seen myself when I am unwashed or out of humour? Zinaida Fyodorovna in the simplicity of her heart wants me to love what I have been shunning all my life. She wants my flat to smell of cooking and washing up; she wants all the fuss of moving into another flat, of driving about with her own horses; she wants to count over my linen and to look after my health; she wants to meddle in my personal life at every instant, and to watch over every step; and at the same time she assures me genuinely that my habits and my freedom will be untouched. She is persuaded that, like a young couple, we shall very soon go for a honeymoon—that is, she wants to be with me all the time in trains and hotels, while I like to read on the journey and cannot endure talking in trains."

"You should give her a talking to," said Pekarsky.

"What! Do you suppose she would understand me? Why, we think so differently. In her opinion, to leave one's papa and mamma or one's husband for the sake of the man one loves is the height of civic virtue, while I look upon it as childish. To fall in love and run away with a man to her means beginning a new life, while to my mind it means nothing at all. Love and man constitute the chief interest of her life, and possibly it is the philosophy of the unconscious at work in her. Try and make her believe that love is only a simple physical need, like the need of food or clothes; that it doesn't mean the end of the world if wives and husbands are unsatisfactory; that a man may be a profligate and a libertine, and yet a man of honour and a genius; and that, on the other hand, one may abstain from the pleasures of love and at the same time be a stupid, vicious animal! The civilised man of to-day, even among the lower classes—for instance, the French workman—spends ten *sous* on dinner, five *sous* on his wine, and five or ten *sous* on a woman, and devotes his brains and nerves entirely to his work. But Zinaida Fyodarovna assigns to love not so many *sous*, but her whole soul. I might give her a talking to, but she would raise a wail in answer, and declare in all sincerity that I had ruined her, that she had nothing left to live for.

"Don't say anything to her," said Pekarsky, "but simply take a separate flat for her, that's all."

"That's easy to say. . . ."

There was a brief silence.

"But she is charming," said Kukushkin. "She is exquisite. Such women imagine that they will be in love for ever, and abandon themselves with tragic intensity."

"But one must keep a head on one's shoulders," said Orlov; "one must be reasonable. All experience gained from everyday life and handed down in innumerable novels and plays, uniformly confirms the fact that adultery and cohabitation of any sort between decent people never lasts longer than two or at most three years, however great the love may have been at the beginning. That she ought to know. And so all this business of moving, of saucepans, hopes of eternal love and harmony, are nothing but a desire to delude herself and me. She is charming and exquisite—who denies it? But she has turned my life upside down; what I have regarded as trivial and nonsensical till now she has forced me to raise to the level of a serious problem; I serve an idol whom I have never looked upon as God. She is charming—exquisite, but for some reason now when I am going home, I feel uneasy, as though I expected to meet with something inconvenient at home, such as workmen pulling the stove to pieces and blocking up the place with heaps of bricks. In fact, I am no longer giving up to love a *sous*, but part of my peace of mind and my nerves. And that's bad."

"And she doesn't hear this villain!" sighed Kukushkin. "My dear sir," he said theatrically, "I will relieve you from the burdensome obligation to love that adorable creature! I will wrest Zinaida Fyodorovna from you!"

"You may . . ." said Orlov carelessly.

For half a minute Kukushkin laughed a shrill little laugh, shaking all over, then he said:

"Look out; I am in earnest! Don't you play the Othello afterwards!"

They all began talking of Kukushkin's indefatigable energy in love affairs, how irresistible he was to women, and what a danger he was to husbands; and how the devil would roast him in the other world for his immorality in this. He screwed up his eyes and remained silent, and when the names of ladies of their acquaintance were mentioned, he held up his little finger as though to say they mustn't give away other people's secrets.

Orlov suddenly looked at his watch.

His friends understood, and began to take their leave. I remember that Gruzin, who was a little drunk, was wearisomely long in getting off. He put on his coat, which was cut like children's coats in poor families, pulled up the collar, and began telling some long-winded story; then, seeing he was not listened to, he flung the rug that smelt of the nursery over one shoulder, and with a guilty and imploring face begged me to find his hat.

"*George*, my angel," he said tenderly. "Do as I ask you, dear boy; come out of town with us!"

"You can go, but I can't. I am in the position of a married man now."

"She is a dear, she won't be angry. My dear chief, come along! It's glorious weather; there's snow and frost. . . . Upon my word, you want shaking up a bit; you are out of humour. I don't know what the devil is the matter with you. . . ."

Orlov stretched, yawned, and looked at Pekarsky.

"Are you going?" he said, hesitating.

"I don't know. Perhaps."

"Shall I get drunk? All right, I'll come," said Orlov after some hesitation. "Wait a minute; I'll get some money."

He went into the study, and Gruzin slouched in, too, dragging his rug after him. A minute later both came back into the hall. Gruzin, a little drunk and very pleased, was crumpling a ten-rouble note in his hands.

"We'll settle up to-morrow," he said. "And she is kind, she won't be cross. . . . She is my Lisotchka's godmother; I am fond of her, poor thing! Ah, my dear fellow!" he laughed joyfully, and pressing his forehead on Pekarsky's back. "Ah, Pekarsky, my dear fellow! Advocatissimus—as dry as a biscuit, but you bet he is fond of women. . . ."

"Fat ones," said Orlov, putting on his fur coat. "But let us get off, or we shall be meeting her on the doorstep."

" '*Vieni pensando a me segretamente*,' " hummed Gruzin.

At last they drove off: Orlov did not sleep at home, and returned next day at dinner-time.

VI

Zinaida Fyodorovna had lost her gold watch, a present from her father. This loss surprised and alarmed her. She spent half a day going through the rooms, looking helplessly on all the tables and on all the windows. But the watch had disappeared completely.

Only three days afterwards Zinaida Fyodorovna, on coming in, left her purse in the hall. Luckily for me, on that occasion it was not I but Polya who helped her off with her coat. When the purse was missed, it could not be found in the hall.

"Strange," said Zinaida Fyodorovna in bewilderment. "I distinctly remember taking it out of my pocket to pay the cabman . . . and then I put it here near the looking-glass. It's very odd!"

I had not stolen it, but I felt as though I had stolen it and had been caught in the theft. Tears actually came into my eyes. When they were seated at dinner, Zinaida Fyodorovna said to Orlov in French:

"There seem to be spirits in the flat. I lost my purse in the hall today, and now, lo and behold, it is on my table. But it's not quite a disinterested trick of the spirits. They took out a gold coin and twenty roubles in notes."

"You are always losing something; first it's your watch and then it's your money . . ." said Orlov. "Why is it nothing of the sort ever happens to me?"

A minute later Zinaida Fyodorovna had forgotten the trick played by the spirits, and was telling with a laugh how the week before she had ordered some notepaper and had forgotten to give her new address, and the shop had sent the paper to her old home at her husband's, who had to pay twelve roubles for it. And suddenly she turned her eyes on Polya and looked at her intently. She blushed as she did so, and was so confused that she began talking of something else.

When I took in the coffee to the study, Orlov was standing with his back to the fire and she was sitting in an arm-chair facing him.

"I am not in a bad temper at all," she was saying in French. "But I have been putting things together, and now I see it clearly. I can give you the day and the hour when she stole my watch. And the purse ? There can be no doubt about it. Oh!" she laughed as she took the coffee from me. "Now I understand why I am always losing my handkerchiefs and gloves. Whatever you say, I shall dismiss the magpie to-morrow and send Stepan for my Sofya. She is not a thief and has not got such a . . . repulsive appearance."

"You are out of humour. To-morrow you will feel differently, and will realise that you can't discharge people simply because you suspect them."

"It's not suspicion; it's certainty," said Zinaida Fyodorovna. "So long as I suspected that unhappy-faced, poor-looking valet of yours, I said nothing. It's too bad of you not to believe me, *George*."

"If we think differently about anything, it doesn't follow that I don't believe you. You may be right," said Orlov, turning round and flinging his cigarette-end into the fire, "but there is no need to be excited about it, anyway. In fact, I must say, I never expected my humble establishment would cause you so much serious worry and agitation. You've lost a gold coin: never mind—you may have a hundred of mine; but to change my habits, to pick up a new housemaid, to wait till she is used to the place—all that's a tedious, tiring business and does not suit me. Our present maid certainly is fat, and has, perhaps, a weakness for gloves and handkerchiefs, but she is perfectly well behaved, well trained, and does not shriek when Kukushkin pinches her."

"You mean that you can't part with her? . . . Why don't you say so?"

"Are you jealous?"

"Yes, I am," said Zinaida Fyodorovna, decidedly.

"Thank you."

"Yes, I am jealous," she repeated, and tears glistened in her eyes. "No, it's something worse . . . which I find it difficult to find a name for." She pressed her hands on her temples, and went on impulsively. "You men are so disgusting! It's horrible!"

"I see nothing horrible about it."

"I've not seen it; I don't know; but they say that you men begin with housemaids as boys, and get so used to it that you feel no repugnance. I don't know, I don't know, but I have actually read . . . *George*, of course you are right," she said, going up to Orlov and changing to a caressing and imploring tone. "I really am out of humour to-day. But, you must understand, I can't help it. She disgusts me and I am afraid of her. It makes me miserable to see her."

"Surely you can rise above such paltriness?" said Orlov, shrugging his shoulders in perplexity, and walking away from the fire. "Nothing could be simpler: take no notice of her, and then she won't disgust you, and you won't need to make a regular tragedy out of a trifle."

I went out of the study, and I don't know what answer Orlov received. Whatever it was, Polya remained. After that Zinaida Fyodorovna never applied to her for anything, and evidently tried to dispense with her services. When Polya handed her anything or even passed by her, jingling her bangle and rustling her skirts, she shuddered.

I believe that if Gruzin or Pekarsky had asked Orlov to dismiss Polya he would have done so without the slightest hesitation, without troubling about any explanations. He was easily persuaded, like all indifferent people. But in his relations with Zinaida Fyodorovna he displayed for some reason, even in trifles, an obstinacy which sometimes was almost irrational. I knew beforehand that if Zinaida Fyodorovna liked anything, it would be certain not to please Orlov. When on coming in from shopping she made haste to show him with pride some new purchase, he would glance at it and say coldly that the more unnecessary objects they had in the flat, the less airy it would be. It sometimes happened that after putting on his dress clothes to go out somewhere, and after saying good-bye to Zinaida Fyodorovna, he would suddenly change his mind and remain at home from sheer perversity. I used to think that he remained at home then simply in order to feel injured.

"Why are you staying?" said Zinaida Fyodorovna, with a show of vexation, though at the same time she was radiant with delight. "Why do you? You are not accustomed to spending your evenings at home, and I don't want you to alter your habits on my account. Do go out as usual, if you don't want me to feel guilty."

"No one is blaming you," said Orlov.

With the air of a victim he stretched himself in his easy-chair in the study, and shading his eyes with his hand, took up a book. But soon the book dropped from his hand, he turned heavily in his chair, and again screened his eyes as though from the sun. Now he felt annoyed that he had not gone out.

"May I come in?" Zinaida Fyodorovna would say, coming irresolutely into the study. "Are you reading? I felt dull by myself, and have come just for a minute . . . to have a peep at you."

I remember one evening she went in like that, irresolutely and inappropriately, and sank on the rug at Orlov's feet, and from her soft, timid movements one could see that she did not understand his mood and was afraid.

"You are always reading . . ." she said cajolingly, evidently wishing to flatter him. ' Do you know, *George*, what is one of the secrets of your success? You are very clever and well-read. What book have you there?"

Orlov answered. A silence followed for some minutes which seemed to me very long. I was standing in the drawing-room, from which I could watch them, and was afraid of coughing.

"There is something I wanted to tell you," said Zinaida Fyodorovna, and she laughed; "shall I? Very likely you'll laugh and say that I flatter myself. You know I want, I want horribly to believe that you are staying at home to-night for my sake . . . that we might spend the evening together. Yes? May I think so?"

"Do," he said, screening his eyes. "The really happy man is he who thinks not only of what is, but of what is not."

"That was a long sentence which I did not quite understand. You mean happy people live in their imagination. Yes, that's true. I love to sit in your study in the evening and let my thoughts carry me far, far away. . . . It's pleasant sometimes to dream. Let us dream aloud, *George*."

"I've never been at a girls' boarding-school; I never learnt the art."

"You are out of humour?" said Zinaida Fyodorovna, taking Orlov's hand. "Tell me why. When you are like that, I'm afraid. I don't know whether your head aches or whether you are angry with me. . . ."

Again there was a silence lasting several long minutes.

"Why have you changed?" she said softly. "Why are you never so tender or so gay as you used to be at Znamensky Street ? I've been with you almost a month, but it seems to me as though we had not yet begun to live, and have not yet talked of anything as we ought to. You always answer me with jokes or else with a long cold lecture like a teacher. And there is something cold in your jokes. . . . Why have you given up talking to me seriously?"

"I always talk seriously."

"Well, then, let us talk. For God's sake, *George*. . . . Shall we?"

"Certainly, but about what?"

"Let us talk of our life, of our future," said Zinaida Fyodorovna dreamily. "I keep making plans for our life, plans and plans—and I enjoy doing it so! *George*, I'll begin with the question, when are you going to give up your post?"

"What for?" asked Orlov, taking his hand from his forehead.

"With your views you cannot remain in the service. You are out of place there."

"My views?" Orlov repeated. "My views? In conviction and temperament I am an ordinary official, one of Shtchedrin's heroes. You take me for something different, I venture to assure you."

"Joking again, *George!*"

"Not in the least. The service does not satisfy me, perhaps; but, anyway, it is better for me than anything else. I am used to it, and in it I meet men of my own sort; I am in my place there and find it tolerable."

"You hate the service and it revolts you."

"Indeed? If I resign my post, take to dreaming aloud and letting myself be carried away into another world, do you suppose that that world would be less hateful to me than the service?"

"You are ready to libel yourself in order to contradict me." Zinaida Fyodorovna was offended and got up. "I am sorry I began this talk."

"Why are you angry? I am not angry with you for not being an official. Every one lives as he likes best."

"Why, do you live as you like best? Are you free ? To spend your life writing documents that are opposed to your own ideas," Zinaida Fyodorovna went on, clasping her hands in despair: "to submit to authority, congratulate your superiors at the New Year, and then cards and nothing but cards: worst of all, to be working for a system which must be distasteful to you—no, *George*, no! You should not make such horrid jokes. It's dreadful. You are a man of ideas, and you ought to be working for your ideas and nothing else."

"You really take me for quite a different person from what I am," sighed Orlov.

"Say simply that you don't want to talk to me. You dislike me, that's all," said Zinaida Fyodorovna through her tears.

"Look here, my dear," said Orlov admonishingly, sitting up in his chair. "You were pleased to observe yourself that I am a clever, well-read man, and to teach one who knows does nothing but harm. I know very well all the ideas, great and small, which you mean when you call me a man of ideas. So if I prefer the service and cards to those ideas, you may be sure I have good grounds for it. That's one thing. Secondly, you have, so far as I know, never been in the service, and can only have drawn your ideas of Government service from anecdotes and indifferent novels. So it would not be amiss for us to make a compact, once for all, not to talk of things we know already or of things about which we are not competent to speak."

"Why do you speak to me like that?" said Zinaida Fyodorovna, stepping back as though in horror. "What for? *George*, for God's sake, think what you are saying!"

Her voice quivered and broke; she was evidently trying to restrain her tears, but she suddenly broke into sobs.

"*George*, my darling, I am perishing!" she said in French, dropping down before Orlov, and laying her head on his knees. "I am miserable, I am exhausted. I can't bear it, I can't bear it. . . . In my childhood my hateful, depraved stepmother, then my husband, now you . . . you! . . . You meet my mad love with coldness and irony. . . . And that horrible, insolent servant," she went on, sobbing. "Yes, yes, I see: I am not your wife nor your friend, but a woman you don't respect because she has become your mistress. . . . I shall kill myself!"

I had not expected that her words and her tears would make such an impression on Orlov. He flushed, moved uneasily in his chair, and instead of irony, his face wore a look of stupid, schoolboyish dismay.

"My darling, you misunderstood me," he muttered helplessly, touching her hair and her shoulders. "Forgive me, I entreat you. I was unjust . . . and I hate myself."

"I insult you with my whining and complaints. . . . You are a true, generous . . . rare man—I am conscious of it every minute; but I've been horribly depressed for the last few days. . .

Zinaida Fyodorovna impulsively embraced Orlov and kissed him on the cheek.

"Only please don't cry," he said.

"No, no. . . . I've had my cry, and now I am better."

"As for the servant, she shall be gone to-morrow," he said, still moving uneasily in his chair.

"No, she must stay, *George!* Do you hear? I am not afraid of her now. . . . One must rise above trifles and not imagine silly things. You are right! You are a wonderful, rare person!"

She soon left off crying. With tears glistening on her eyelashes, sitting on Orlov's knee, she told him in a low voice something touching, something like a reminiscence of childhood and youth. She stroked his face, kissed him, and carefully examined his hands with the rings on them and the charms on his watch-chain. She was carried away by what she was saying, and by being near the man she loved, and probably because her tears had cleared and refreshed her soul, there was a note of wonderful candour and sincerity in her voice. And Orlov played with her chestnut hair and kissed her hands, noiselessly pressing them to his lips.

Then they had tea in the study, and Zinaida Fyodorovna read aloud some letters. Soon after midnight they went to bed.

I had a fearful pain in my side that night, and could not get warm or go to sleep till morning. I could hear Orlov go from the bedroom into his study. After sitting there about an hour, he rang the bell. In my pain and exhaustion I forgot all the rules and conventions, and went to his study in my night attire, barefooted. Orlov, in his dressing-gown and cap, was standing in the doorway, waiting for me.

"When you are sent for you should come dressed," he said sternly. "Bring some fresh candles."

I was about to apologise, but suddenly broke into a violent cough, and clutched at the side of the door to save myself from falling.

"Are you ill?" said Orlov.

I believe it was the first time of our acquaintance that he addressed me not in the singular—goodness knows why. Most likely, in my night clothes and with my face distorted by coughing, I played my part poorly, and was very little like a flunkey.

"If you are ill, why do you take a place?" he said.

"That I may not die of starvation," I answered.

"How disgusting it all is, really!" he said softly, going up to his table.

While hurriedly getting into my coat, I put up and lighted fresh candles. He was sitting at the table, with feet stretched out on a low chair, cutting a book.

I left him deeply engrossed, and the book did not drop out of his hands as it had done in the evening.

VII

Now that I am writing these lines I am restrained by that dread of appearing sentimental and ridiculous, in which I have been trained from childhood; when I want to be affectionate or to say anything tender, I don't know how to be natural. And it is that dread, together with lack of practice, that prevents me from being able to express with perfect clearness what was passing in my soul at that time.

I was not in love with Zinaida Fyodorovna, but in the ordinary human feeling I had for her, there was far more youth, freshness, and joyousness than in Orlov's love.

As I worked in the morning, cleaning boots or sweeping the rooms, I waited with a thrill at my heart for the moment when I should hear her voice and her footsteps. To stand watching her as she drank her coffee in the morning or ate her lunch, to hold her fur coat for her in the hall, and to put the goloshes on her little feet while she rested her hand on my shoulder; then to wait till the hall porter rang up for me, to meet her at the door, cold, and rosy, powdered with the snow, to listen to her brief exclamations about the frost or the cabman—if only you knew how much all that meant to me! I longed to be in love, to have a wife and child of my own. I wanted my future wife to have just such a face, such a voice. I dreamed of it at dinner, and in the street when I was sent on some errand, and when I lay awake at night. Orlov rejected with disgust children, cooking, copper saucepans, and feminine knickknacks, and I gathered them all up, tenderly cherished them in my dreams, loved them, and begged them of destiny. I had visions of a wife, a nursery, a little house with garden paths. . . .

I knew that if I did love her I could never dare to hope for the miracle of her returning my love, but that reflection did not worry me. In my quiet, modest feeling akin to ordinary affection, there was no jealousy of Orlov or even envy of him, since I realised that for a wreck like me happiness was only to be found in dreams.

When Zinaida Fyodorovna sat up night after night for her *George*, looking immovably at a book of which she never turned a page, or when she shuddered and turned pale at Polya's crossing the room, I suffered with her, and the idea occurred to me to lance this festering wound as quickly as possible by letting her know what was said here at supper on Thursdays; but—how was it to be done? More and more often I saw her tears. For the first weeks she laughed and sang to herself, even when Orlov was not at home, but by the second month there was a mournful stillness in our flat broken only on Thursday evenings.

She flattered Orlov, and to wring from him a counterfeit smile or kiss, was ready to go on her knees to him, to fawn on him like a dog. Even when her heart was heaviest, she could not resist glancing into a looking-glass if she passed one and straightening her hair. It seemed strange to me that she could still take an interest in clothes and go into ecstasies over her purchases. It did not seem in keeping with her genuine grief. She paid attention to the fashions and ordered expensive dresses. What for ? On whose account ? I particularly remember one dress which cost four hundred roubles. To give four hundred roubles for an unnecessary, useless dress while women for their hard day's work get only twenty kopecks a day without food, and the makers of Venice and Brussels lace are only paid half a franc a day on the supposition that they can earn the rest by immorality! And it seemed strange to me that Zinaida Fyodorovna was not conscious of it; it vexed me. But she had only to go out of the house for me to find excuses and explanations for everything, and to be waiting eagerly for the hall porter to ring for me.

She treated me as a flunkey, a being of a lower order. One may pat a dog, and yet not notice it; I was given orders and asked questions, but my presence was not observed. My master and mistress thought it unseemly to say more to me than is usually said to servants; if when waiting at dinner I had laughed or put in my word in the conversation, they would certainly have thought I was mad and have dismissed me. Zinaida Fyodorovna was favourably disposed to me, all the same. When she was sending me on some errand or explaining to me the working of a new lamp or anything of that sort, her face was extraordinarily kind, frank, and cordial, and her eyes looked me straight in the face. At such moments I always fancied she remembered with gratitude how I used to bring her letters to Znamensky Street. When she rang the bell, Polya, who considered me her favourite and hated me for it, used to say with a jeering smile:

"Go along, *your* mistress wants you."

Zinaida Fyodorovna considered me as a being of a lower order, and did not suspect that if any one in the house were in a humiliating position it was she. She did not know that I, a footman, was unhappy on her account, and used to ask myself twenty times a day what was in store for her and how it would all end. Things were growing visibly worse day by day. After the evening on which they had talked of his official work, Orlov, who could not endure tears, unmistakably began to avoid conversation with her; whenever Zinaida Fyodorovna began to argue, or to beseech him, or seemed on the point of crying, he seized some plausible excuse for retreating to his study or going out. He more and more rarely slept at home, and still more rarely dined there: on Thursdays he was the one to suggest some expedition to his friends. Zinaida Fyodorovna was still dreaming of having the cooking done at home, of moving to a new flat, of travelling abroad, but her dreams remained dreams. Dinner was sent in from the restaurant. Orlov asked her not to broach the question of moving until after they had come back from abroad, and apropos of their foreign tour, declared that they could not go till his hair had grown long, as one could not go trailing from hotel to hotel and serving the idea without long hair.

To crown it all, in Orlov's absence, Kukushkin began calling at the flat in the evening. There was nothing exceptional in his behaviour, but I could never forget the conversation in which he had offered to cut Orlov out. He was regaled with tea and red wine, and he used to titter and, anxious to say something pleasant, would declare that a free union was superior in every respect to legal marriage, and that all decent people ought really to come to Zinaida Fyodorovna and fall at her feet.

VIII

Christmas was spent drearily in vague anticipations of calamity. On New Year's Eve Orlov unexpectedly announced at breakfast that he was being sent to assist a senator who was on a revising commission in a certain province.

"I don't want to go, but I can't find an excuse to get off," he said with vexation. "I must go; there's nothing for it."

Such news instantly made Zinaida Fyodorovna's eyes look red. "Is it for long?" she asked.

"Five days or so."

"I am glad, really, you are going," she said after a moment's thought. "It will be a change for you. You will fall in love with someone on the way, and tell me about it afterwards."

At every opportunity she tried to make Orlov feel that she did restrict his liberty in any way, and that he could do exactly as he and this artless, transparent strategy deceived no one, and only essarily reminded Orlov that he was not free.

"I am going this evening," he said, and began reading

Zinaida Fyodorovna wanted to see him off at the station, but he dissuaded her, saying that he was not going to America, and not going to be away five years, but only five days—possibly less.

The parting took place between seven and eight. He put one arm round her, and kissed her on the lips and on the forehead.

"Be a good girl, and don't be depressed while I am away," he said in a warm, affectionate tone which touched even me. "God keep you!"

She looked greedily into his face, to stamp his dear features on her memory, then she put her arms gracefully round his neck and laid her head on his breast.

"Forgive me our misunderstandings," she said in French. "Husband and wife cannot help quarrelling if they love each other, and I love you madly. Don't forget me. . . . Wire to me often and fully."

Orlov kissed her once more, and, without saying a word, went out in confusion. When he heard the click of the lock as the door closed, he stood still in the middle of the staircase in hesitation and glanced upwards. It seemed to me that if a sound had reached him at that moment from above, he would have turned back. But all was quiet. He straightened his coat and went downstairs irresolutely.

The sledges had been waiting a long while at the door. Orlov got into one, I got into the other with two portmanteaus. It was a hard frost and there were fires smoking at the cross-roads. The cold wind nipped my face and hands, and took my breath away as we drove rapidly along; and, closing my eyes, I thought what a splendid woman she was. How she loved him! Even useless rubbish is collected in the courtyards nowadays and used for some purpose, even broken glass is considered a useful commodity, but something so precious, so rare, as the love of a refined, young, intelligent, and good woman is utterly thrown away and ....d. One of the early sociologists regarded every evil passion as a ....ich might by judicious management be turned to good, while ....en a fine, noble passion springs up and dies away in impo- ....no account, misunderstood or vulgarised. Why is it? ....pped unexpectedly. I opened my eyes and I saw that ....still in Sergievsky Street, near a big house where ....ut of the sledge and vanished into the entry. ....'s footman came out, bareheaded, and, ...to me: ....cabmen and go upstairs. You are wanted!"

At a complete loss, I went to the first storey. I had been to Pekarskey's flat before—that is, I had stood in the hall and looked into the drawing-room, and, after the damp, gloomy street, it always struck me by the brilliance of its picture-frames, its bronzes and expensive furniture. To-day in the midst of this splendor I saw Gruzin, Kukushkin, and, after a minute, Orlov.

"Look here, Stepan," he said, coming up to me. "I shall be staying here till Friday or Saturday. If any letters or telegrams come, you must bring them here every day. At home, of course, you will say that I have gone, and send my greetings. Now you can go."

When I reached home Zinaida Fyodorovna was lying on the sofa in the drawing-room, eating a pear. There was only one candle burning in the candelabra.

"Did you catch the train?" asked Zinaida Fyodorovna.

"Yes, madam. His honour sends his greetings."

I went into my room and I, too, lay down. I had nothing to do, and I did not want to read. I was not surprised and I was not indignant. I only racked my brains to think why this deception was necessary. It is only boys in their teens who deceive their mistresses like that. How was it that a man who had thought and read so much could not imagine anything more sensible? I must confess I had by no means a poor opinion of his intelligence. I believe if he had had to deceive his minister or any other influential person he would have put a great deal of skill and energy into doing so; but to deceive a woman, the first idea that occurred to him was evidently good enough. If it succeeded—well and good; if it did not, there would be no harm done—he could tell some other lie just as quickly and simply, with no mental effort.

At midnight when the people on the floor overhead were moving their chairs and shouting hurrah to welcome the New Year, Zinaida Fyodorovna rang for me from the room next to the study. Languid from lying down so long, she was sitting at the table, writing something on a scrap of paper.

"I must send a telegram," she said, with a smile. "Go to the station as quick as you can and ask them to send it after him."

Going out into the street, I read on the scrap of paper:

"May the New Year bring new happiness. Make haste and telegraph; I miss you dreadfully. It seems an eternity. I am only

sorry I can't send a thousand kisses and my very heart by telegraph. Enjoy yourself, my darling.—ZINA."

I sent the telegram, and next morning I gave her the
receipt.

IX

The worst of it was that Orlov had thoughtlessly let Polya, too, into the
secret of his deception, telling her to bring his shirts to Sergievsky
Street. After that, she looked at Zinaida Fyodorovna with a malignant
joy and hatred I could not understand, and was never tired of snorting
with delight to herself in her own room and in the hall.

"She's outstayed her welcome; it's time she took herself off!" she
would say with zest. "She ought to realise that herself. . . ."

She already divined by instinct that Zinaida Fyodorovna would
not be with us much longer, and, not to let the chance slip, carried
off everything she set her eyes on—smelling-bottles, tortoise-shell
hairpins, handkerchiefs, shoes! On the day after New Year's Day,
Zinaida Fyodorovna summoned me to her room and told me in a low
voice that she missed her black dress. And then she walked through all
the rooms, with a pale, frightened, and indignant face, talking to herself:

"It's too much! It's beyond everything. Why, it's unheard-of insolence!"

At dinner she tried to help herself to soup, but could not—her
hands were trembling. Her lips were trembling, too. She looked helplessly at the soup and at the little pies, waiting for the trembling to pass
off and suddenly she could not resist looking at Polya.

"You can go, Polya," she said. "Stepan is enough by himself."

"I'll stay; I don't mind," answered Polya

"There's no need for you to stay. You go away altogether," Zinaida
Fyodorovna went on, getting up in great agitation. "You may look out
for another place. You can go at once."

"I can't go away without the master's orders. He engaged me. It
must be as he orders."

"You can take orders from me, too! I am mistress here! said
Zinaida Fyodorovna, and she flushed crimson.

"You may be the mistress, but only the master can dismiss me. It was he engaged me."

"You dare not stay here another minute!" cried Zinaida Fyodorovna, and she struck the plate with her knife. "You are a thief! Do you hear?"

Zinaida Fyodorovna flung her dinner-napkin on the table, and with a pitiful, suffering face, went quickly out of the room. Loudly sobbing and wailing something indistinct, Polya, too, went away. The soup and the grouse got cold. And for some reason all the restaurant dainties on the table struck me as poor, thievish, like Polya. Two pies on a plate had a particularly miserable and guilty air. "We shall be taken back to the restaurant to-day," they seemed to be saying, "and to-morrow we shall be put on the table again for some official or celebrated singer."

"She is a fine lady, indeed," I heard uttered in Polya s room. "I could have been a lady like that long ago, but I have some self-respect! We'll see which of us will be the first to go?"

Zinaida Fyodorovna rang the bell. She was sitting in her room, in the corner, looking as though she had been put in the corner as a punishment.

"No telegram has come?" she asked.

"No, madam."

"Ask the porter; perhaps there is a telegram. And don't leave the house," she called after me. "I am afraid to be left alone."

After that I had to run down almost every hour to ask the porter whether a telegram had come. I must own it was a dreadful time! To avoid seeing Polya, Zinaida Fyodorovna dined and had tea in her own room; it was here that she slept, too, on a short sofa like a half-moon, and she made her own bed. For the first days I took the telegrams; but, getting no answer, she lost her faith in me and began telegraphing herself. Looking at her, I, too, began impatiently hoping for a telegram. I hoped he would contrive some deception, would make arrangements, for instance, that a telegram should be sent to her from some station. If he were too much engrossed with cards or had been attracted by some other woman, I thought that both Gruzin and Kukushkin would remind him of us. But our expectations were vain. Five times a day I would go in to Zinaida Fyodorovna, intending to tell her the truth, but her eyes looked piteous as a fawn's, her shoulders seemed to droop, her lips were moving, and I went away again without saying a word. Pity and sympathy seemed to rob me of all manliness. Polya, as cheerful and well satisfied with herself as though nothing had happened, was tidying the master's study and the bedroom, rummaging in the cupboards, and making the crockery jingle, and when she passed Zinaida Fyodorovna's door, she hummed something and coughed. She was pleased that her mistress was hiding from her. In the evening she would go out somewhere, and rang at two or three o'clock in the morning, and I had to open the door to her and listen to remarks about my cough. Immediately afterwards I would hear another ring; I would run to the room next to the study, and Zinaida Fyodorovna, putting her head out of the door, would ask, "Who was it rung?" while she looked at my hands to see whether I had a telegram.

When at last on Saturday the bell rang below and she heard the familiar voice on the stairs, she was so delighted that she broke into sobs. She rushed to meet him, embraced him, kissed him on the breast and sleeves, said something one could not understand. The hall porter brought up the portmanteaus; Polya's cheerful voice was heard. It was as though some one had come home for the holidays.

"Why didn't you wire?" asked Zinaida Fyodorovna, breathless with joy. "Why was it? I have been in misery; I don't know how I've lived through it. . . . Oh, my God!"

"It was very simple! I returned with the senator to Moscow the very first day, and didn't get your telegrams," said Orlov. "After dinner, my love I'll give you a full account of my doings, but now I must sleep and sleep. . . . I am worn out with the journey."

It was evident that he had not slept all night; he had probably been playing cards and drinking freely. Zinaida Fyodorovna put him to bed, and we all walked about on tiptoe all that day. The dinner went off quite satisfactorily, but when they went into the study and had coffee the explanation began. Zinaida Fyodorovna began talking of something rapidly in a low voice; she spoke in French, and her words flowed like a stream. Then I heard a loud sigh from Orlov, and his voice.

"My God!" he said in French. "Have you really nothing fresher to tell me than this everlasting tale of your servant's misdeeds?"

"But, my dear, she robbed me and said insulting things to me."

"But why is it she doesn't rob me or say insulting things to me? Why is it I never notice the maids nor the porters nor the footmen?

My dear, you are simply capricious and refuse to know your own mind. . . . I really begin to suspect that you must be in a certain condition. When I offered to let her go, you insisted on her remaining, and now you want me to turn her away. I can be obstinate, too, in such cases. You want her to go, but I want her to remain. That's the only way to cure you of your nerves."

"Oh, very well, very well," said Zinaida Fyodorovna in alarm. "Let us say no more about that. . . . Let us put it off till to-morrow. . . . Now tell me about Moscow. . . . What is going on in Moscow?"

X

After lunch next day—it was the seventh of January, St. John the Baptist's Day—Orlov put on his black dress coat and his decoration to go to visit his father and congratulate him on his name day. He had to go at two o'clock, and it was only half-past one when he had finished dressing. What was he to do for that half-hour ? He walked about the drawing-room, declaiming some congratulatory verses which he had recited as a child to his father and mother.

Zinaida Fyodorovna, who was just going out to a dressmaker's or to the shops, was sitting, listening to him with a smile. I don't know how their conversation began, but when I took Orlov his gloves, he was standing before her with a capricious, beseeching face, saying:

"For God's sake, in the name of everything that's holy, don't talk of things that everybody knows! What an unfortunate gift our intellectual thoughtful ladies have for talking with enthusiasm and an air of profundity of things that every schoolboy is sick to death of! Ah, if only you would exclude from our conjugal programme all these serious questions! How grateful I should be to you!"

"We women may not dare, it seems, to have views of our own."

"I give you full liberty to be as liberal as you like, and quote from any authors you choose, but make me one concession: don't hold forth in my presence on either of two subjects: the corruption of the upper classes and the evils of the marriage system. Do understand me, at last. The upper class is always abused in contrast with the world of tradesmen, priests, workmen and peasants, Sidors and Nikitas of all sorts. I detest both classes, but if I had honesty to choose between the two, I should without hesitation, prefer the upper class, and there would be no falsity or affectation about it, since all my tastes are in that direction. Our world is trivial and empty, but at any rate we speak French decently, read something, and don't punch each other in the ribs even in our most violent quarrels, while the Sidors and the Nikitas and their worships in trade talk about 'being quite agreeable,' 'in a jiffy,' 'blast your eyes,' and display the utmost license of pothouse manners and the most degrading superstition."

"The peasant and the tradesman feed you."

"Yes, but what of it? That's not only to my discredit, but to theirs too. They feed me and take off their caps to me, so it seems they have not the intelligence and honesty to do otherwise. I don't blame or praise any one: I only mean that the upper class and the lower are as bad as one another. My feelings and my intelligence are opposed to both, but my tastes lie more in the direction of the former. Well, now for the evils of marriage," Orlov went on, glancing at his watch. "It's high time for you to understand that there are no evils in the system itself; what is the matter is that you don't know yourselves what you want from marriage. What is it you want? In legal and illegal cohabitation, in every sort of union and cohabitation, good or bad, the underlying reality is the same. You ladies live for that underlying reality alone: for you it's everything; your existence would have no meaning for you without it. You want nothing but that, and you get it; but since you've taken to reading novels you are ashamed of it: you rush from pillar to post, you recklessly change your men, and to justify this turmoil you have begun talking of the evils of marriage. So long as you can't and won't renounce what underlies it all, your chief foe, your devil—so long as you serve that slavishly, what use is there in discussing the matter seriously? Everything you may say to me will be falsity and affectation. I shall not believe you."

I went to find out from the hall porter whether the sledge was at the door, and when I came back I found it had become a quarrel. As sailors say, a squall had blown up.

"I see you want to shock me by your cynicism today," said Zinaida Fyodorovna, walking about the drawing-room in great emotion. "It revolts me to listen to you. I am pure before God and man, and have nothing to repent of. I left my husband and came to you, and am proud of it. I swear, on my honour, I am proud of it!"

"Well, that's all right, then!"

"If you are a decent, honest man, you, too, ought to be proud of what I did. It raises you and me above thousands of people who would like to do as we have done, but do not venture through cowardice or petty prudence. But you are not a decent man. You are afraid of freedom, and you mock the promptings of genuine feeling, from fear that some ignoramus may suspect you of being sincere. You are afraid to show me to your friends; there's no greater infliction for you than to go about with me in the street. . . . Isn't that true? Why haven't you introduced me to your father or your cousin all this time ? Why is it ? No, I am sick of it at last," cried Zinaida Fyodorovna, stamping. "I demand what is mine by right. You must present me to your father."

"If you want to know him, go and present yourself. He receives visitors every morning from ten till half-past."

"How base you are!" said Zinaida Fyodorovna, wringing her hands in despair. "Even if you are not sincere, and are not saying what you think, I might hate you for your cruelty. Oh, how base you are!"

"We keep going round and round and never reach the real point. The real point is that you made a mistake, and you won't acknowledge it aloud. You imagined that I was a hero, and that I had some extraordinary ideas and ideals, and it has turned out that I am a most ordinary official, a card-player, and have no partiality for ideas of any sort. I am a worthy representative of the rotten world from which you have run away because you were revolted with its triviality and emptiness. Recognise it and be just: don't be indignant with me, but with yourself, as it is your mistake, and not mine."

"Yes, I admit I was mistaken."

"Well, that's all right, then. We've reached that point at last, thank God. Now hear something more, if you please: I can't rise to your level—I am too depraved; you can't descend to my level, either, for you are too exalted. So there is only one thing left to do. . . ."

"What?" Zinaida Fyodorovna asked quickly, holding her breath and turning suddenly as white as a sheet of paper.

"To call logic to our aid. . . ."

"Georgy, why are you torturing me?" Zinaida Fyodorovna said suddenly in Russian in a breaking voice. "What is it for? Think of my misery. . . ."

Orlov, afraid of tears, went quickly into his study, and I don't know why—whether it was that he wished to cause her extra pain, or whether he remembered it was usually done in such cases—he locked the door after him. She cried out and ran after him with a rustle of her skirt.

"What does this mean?" she cried, knocking at his door. "What . . . what does this mean?" she repeated in a shrill voice breaking with indignation. "Ah, so this is what you do! Then let me tell you I hate you, I despise you! Everything is over between us now."

I heard hysterical weeping mingled with laughter. Something small in the drawing-room fell off the table and was broken. Orlov went out into the hall by another door, and, looking round him nervously, he hurriedly put on his great-coat and went out.

Half an hour passed, an hour, and she was still weeping. I remembered that she had no father or mother, no relations, and here she was living between a man who hated her and Polya, who robbed her—and how desolate her life seemed to me! I do not know why, but I went into the drawing-room to her. Weak and helpless, looking with her lovely hair like an embodiment of tenderness and grace, she was in anguish, as though she were ill; she was lying on a couch, hiding her face, and quivering all over.

"Madam, shouldn't I fetch a doctor?" I asked gently.

"No, there's no need . . . it's nothing," she said, and she looked at me with her tear-stained eyes. "I have a little headache. . . . Thank you."

I went out, and in the evening she was writing letter after letter, and sent me out first to Pekarsky, then to Gruzin, then to Kukushkin, and finally anywhere I chose, if only I could find Orlov and give him the letter. Every time I came back with the letter she scolded me, entreated me, thrust money into my hand—as though she were in a fever. And all the night she did not sleep, but sat in the drawing-room, talking to herself.

Orlov returned to dinner next day, and they were reconciled.

The first Thursday afterwards Orlov complained to his friends of the intolerable life he led; he smoked a great deal, and said with irritation:

"It is no life at all; it's the rack. Tears, wailing, intellectual conversations, begging for forgiveness, again tears and wailing; and the long and the short of it is that I have no flat of my own now. I am wretched, and I make her wretched. Surely I haven't to live another month or two like this ? How can I ? But yet I may have to?"

"Why don't you speak, then?" said Pekarsky.

"I've tried, but I can't. One can boldly tell the truth, whatever it may be, to an independent, rational man; but in this case one has to do with a creature who has no will, no strength of character, and no logic. I cannot endure tears; they disarm me. When she cries, I am ready to swear eternal love and cry myself."

Pekarsky did not understand; he scratched his broad forehead in perplexity and said:

"You really had better take another flat for her. It's so simple!"

"She wants me, not the flat. But what's the good of talking?" sighed Orlov?" I only hear endless conversations, but no way out of my position. It certainly is a case of 'being guilty without guilt.' I don't claim to be a mushroom, but it seems I've got to go into the basket. The last thing I've ever set out to be is a hero. I never could endure Turgenev's novels; and now, all of a sudden, as though to spite me, I've heroism forced upon me. I assure her on my honour that I'm not a hero at all, I adduce irrefutable proofs of the same, but she doesn't believe me. Why doesn't she believe me? I suppose I really must have something of the appearance of a hero."

"You go off on a tour of inspection in the provinces," said Kukushkin, laughing.

"Yes, that's the only thing left for me."

A week after this conversation Orlov announced that he was again ordered to attend the senator, and the same evening he went off with his portmanteaus to Pekarsky.

XI

An old man of sixty, in a long fur coat reaching to the ground, and a beaver cap, was standing at the door.

"Is Georgy Ivanitch at home?" he asked.

At first I thought it was one of the moneylenders, Gruzin's creditors, who sometimes used to come to Orlov for small payments on account; but when he came into the hall and flung open his coat, I saw the thick brows and the characteristically compressed lips which I knew so well from the photographs, and two rows of stars on the uniform. I recognised him: it was Orlov's father, the distinguished statesman.

I answered that Georgy Ivanitch was not at home. The old man pursed up his lips tightly and looked into space, reflecting, showing me his dried-up, toothless profile.

"I'll leave a note," he said; "show me in."

He left his goloshes in the hall, and, without taking off his long, heavy fur coat, went into the study. There he sat down before the table, and, before taking up the pen, for three minutes he pondered, shading his eyes with his hand as though from the sun—exactly as his son did when he was out of humour. His face was sad, thoughtful, with that look of resignation which I have only seen on the faces of the old and religious. I stood behind him, gazed at his bald head and at the hollow at the nape of his neck, and it was clear as daylight to me that this weak old man was now in my power. There was not a soul in the flat except my enemy and me. I had only to use a little physical violence, then snatch his watch to disguise the object of the crime, and to get off by the back way, and I should have gained infinitely more than I could have imagined possible when I took up the part of a footman. I thought that I could hardly get a better opportunity. But instead of acting, I looked quite unconcernedly, first at his bald patch and then at his fur, and calmly meditated on this man's relation to his only son, and on the fact that people spoiled by power and wealth probably don't want to die. . . .

"Have you been long in my son's service?" he asked, writing a large hand on the paper.

"Three months, your High Excellency."

He finished the letter and stood up. I still had time. I urged myself on and clenched my fists, trying to wring out of my soul some trace of my former hatred; I recalled what a passionate, implacable, obstinate hate I had felt for him only a little while before. . . . But it is difficult to strike a match against a crumbling stone. The sad old face and the cold glitter of his stars roused in me nothing but petty, cheap, unnecessary thoughts of the transitoriness of everything earthly, of the nearness of death. . . .

"Good-day, brother," said the old man. He put on his cap and went out.

There could be no doubt about it: I had undergone a change; I had become different. To convince myself, I began to recall the past, but at once I felt uneasy, as though I had accidentally peeped into a dark, damp corner. I remembered my comrades and friends, and my first thought was how I should blush in confusion if ever I met any of them. What was I now? What had I to think of and to do? Where was I to go? What was I living for?

I could make nothing of it. I only knew one thing—that I must make haste to pack my things and be off. Before the old man's visit my position as a flunkey had a meaning; now it was absurd. Tears dropped into my open portmanteau; I felt insufferably sad; but how I longed to live! I was ready to embrace and include in my short life every possibility open to man. I wanted to speak, to read, and to hammer in some big factory, and to stand on watch, and to plough. I yearned for the Nevsky Prospect, for the sea and the fields—for every place to which my imagination travelled. When Zinaida Fyodorovna came in, I rushed to open the door for her, and with peculiar tenderness took off her fur coat. The last time!

We had two other visitors that day besides the old man. In the evening when it was quite dark, Gruzin came to fetch some papers for Orlov. He opened the table-drawer, took the necessary papers, and, rolling them up, told me to put them in the hall beside his cap while he went in to see Zinaida Fyodorovna. She was lying on the sofa in the drawing-room, with her arms behind her head. Five or six days had already passed since Orlov went on his tour of inspection, and no one knew when he would be back, but this time she did not send telegrams and did not expect them. She did not seem to notice the presence of Polya, who was still living with us. "So be it, then," was what I read on her passionless and very pale face. Like Orlov, she wanted to be unhappy out of obstinacy. To spite herself and everything in the world, she lay for days together on the sofa, desiring and expecting nothing but evil for herself. Probably she was picturing to herself Orlov's return and the inevitable quarrels with him; then his growing indifference to her, his infidelities; then how they would separate; and perhaps these agonising thoughts gave her satisfaction. But what would she have said if she found out the actual truth?

"I love you, Godmother," said Gruzin, greeting her and kissing her hand. "You are so kind! And so dear *George* has gone away," he lied. "He has gone away, the rascal!"

He sat down with a sigh and tenderly stroked her hand.

"Let me spend an hour with you, my dear," he said. I don't want to go home, and it's too early to go to the Birshovs'. The Birshovs are keeping their Katya's birthday to-day. She is a nice child!"

I brought him a glass of tea and a decanter of brandy. He slowly and with obvious reluctance drank the tea, and returning the glass to me, asked timidly:

"Can you give me . . . something to eat, my friend? I have had no dinner."

We had nothing in the flat. I went to the restaurant and brought him the ordinary rouble dinner.

"To your health, my dear," he said to Zinaida Fyodorovna, and he tossed off a glass of vodka. "My little girl, your godchild, sends you her love. Poor child! she's rickety. Ah, children, children!" he sighed. "Whatever you may say, Godmother, it is nice to be a father. Dear *George* can't understand that feeling."

He drank some more. Pale and lean, with his dinner-napkin over his chest like a little pinafore, he ate greedily, and raising his eyebrows, kept looking guiltily, like a little boy, first at Zinaida Fyodorovna and then at me. It seemed as though he would have begun crying if I had not given him the grouse or the jelly. When he had satisfied his hunger he grew more lively, and began laughingly telling some story about the Birshov household, but perceiving that it was tiresome and that Zinaida Fyodorovna was not laughing, he ceased. And there was a sudden feeling of dreariness. After he had finished his dinner they sat in the drawing-room by the light of a single lamp, and did not speak; it was painful to him to lie to her, and she wanted to ask him something, but could not make up her mind to. So passed half an hour. Gruzin glanced at his watch.

"I suppose it's time for me to go."

"No, stay a little. . . . We must have a talk."

Again they were silent. He sat down to the piano, struck one chord, then began playing, and sang softly, "What does the coming day bring me?" but as usual he got up suddenly and tossed his head.

"Play something," Zinaida Fyodorovna asked him.

"What shall I play?" he asked, shrugging his shoulders. "I have forgotten everything. I've given it up long ago."

Looking at the ceiling as though trying to remember, he played two pieces of Tchaikovsky with exquisite expression, with such warmth, such insight! His face was just as usual—neither stupid nor intelligent—and it seemed to me a perfect marvel that a man whom I was accustomed to see in the midst of the most degrading, impure surroundings, was capable of such purity, of rising to a feeling so lofty, so far beyond my reach. Zinaida Fyodorovna's face glowed, and she walked about the drawing-room in emotion.

"Wait a bit, Godmother; if I can remember it, I will play you something," he said; "I heard it played on the violoncello."

Beginning timidly and picking out the notes, and then gathering confidence, he played Saint-Saëns's "Swan Song." He played it through, and then played it a second time.

"It's nice, isn't it?" he said.

Moved by the music, Zinaida Fyodorovna stood beside him and asked:

"Tell me honestly, as a friend, what do you think about me?"

"What am I to say?" he said, raising his eyebrows. "I love you and think nothing but good of you. But if you wish that I should speak generally about the question that interests you," he went on, rubbing his sleeve near the elbow and frowning, "then, my dear, you know. . . . To follow freely the promptings of the heart does not always give good people happiness. To feel free and at the same time to be happy, it seems to me, one must not conceal from oneself that life is coarse, cruel, and merciless in its conservatism, and one must retaliate with what it deserves—that is, be as coarse and as merciless in one's striving for freedom. That's what I think."

"That's beyond me," said Zinaida Fyodorovna, with a mournful smile. "I am exhausted already. I am so exhausted that I wouldn't stir a finger for my own salvation."

"Go into a nunnery."

He said this in jest, but after he had said it, tears glistened in Zinaida Fyodorovna's eyes and then in his.

"Well," he said, "we've been sitting and sitting, and now we must go. Good-bye, dear Godmother. God give you health."

He kissed both her hands, and stroking them tenderly, said that he should certainly come to see her again in a day or two. In the hall, as he was putting on his overcoat, that was so like a child's pelisse, he fumbled long in his pockets to find a tip for me, but found nothing there.

"Good-bye, my dear fellow," he said sadly, and went away.

I shall never forget the feeling that this man left behind him.

Zinaida Fyodorovna still walked about the room in her excitement. That she was walking about and not still lying down was so much to the good. I wanted to take advantage of this mood to speak to her openly and then to go away, but I had hardly seen Gruzin out when I heard a ring. It was Kukushkin.

"Is Georgy Ivanitch at home?" he said. "Has he come back? You say no? What a pity! In that case, I'll go in and kiss your mistress's hand, and go away. Zinaida Fyodorovna, may I come in?" he cried. "I want to kiss your hand. Excuse my being so late."

He was not long in the drawing-room, not more than ten minutes, but I felt as though he were staying a long while and would never go away. I bit my lips from indignation and annoyance, and already hated Zinaida Fyodorovna. "Why does she not turn him out?" I thought indignantly, though it was evident that she was bored by his company.

When I held his fur coat for him he asked me, as a mark of special good-will, how I managed to get on without a wife.

"But I don't suppose you waste your time," he said, laughingly. "I've no doubt Polya and you are as thick as thieves. . . . You rascal!"

In spite of my experience of life, I knew very little of mankind at that time, and it is very likely that I often exaggerated what was of little consequence and failed to observe what was important. It seemed to me it was not without motive that Kukushkin tittered and flattered me. Could it be that he was hoping that I, like a flunkey, would gossip in other kitchens and servants' quarters of his coming to see us in the evenings when Orlov was away, and staying with Zinaida Fyodorovna till late at night ? And when my tittle-tattle came to the ears of his acquaintance, he would drop his eyes in confusion and shake his little finger. And would not he, I thought, looking at his little honeyed face, this very evening at cards pretend and perhaps declare that he had already won Zinaida Fyodorovna from Orlov?

That hatred which failed me at midday when the old father had come, took possession of me now. Kukushkin went away at last, and as I listened to the shuffle of his leather goloshes, I felt greatly tempted to fling after him, as a parting shot, some coarse word of abuse, but I restrained myself. And when the steps had died away on the stairs, I went back to the hall, and, hardly conscious of what I was doing, took up the roll of papers that Gruzin had left behind, and ran headlong downstairs. Without cap or overcoat, I ran down into the street. It was not cold, but big flakes of snow were falling and it was windy.

"Your Excellency!" I cried, catching up Kukushkin. "Your Excellency!"

He stopped under a lamp-post and looked round with surprise.

"Your Excellency!" I said breathless, "your Excellency!"

And not able to think of anything to say, I hit him two or three times on the face with the roll of paper. Completely at a loss, and hardly wondering—I had so completely taken him by surprise—he leaned his back against the lamp-post and put up his hands to protect his face. At that moment an army doctor passed, and saw how I was beating the man, but he merely looked at us in astonishment and went on. I felt ashamed and I ran back to the house.

XII

With my head wet from the snow, and gasping for breath, I ran to my room, and immediately flung off my swallow-tails, put on a reefer jacket and an overcoat, and carried my portmanteau out into the passage; I must get away! But before going I hurriedly sat down and began writing to Orlov:

"I leave you my false passport," I began. "I beg you to keep it as a memento, you false man, you Petersburg official!

"To steal into another man's house under a false name, to watch under the mask of a flunkey this person's intimate life, to hear everything, to see everything in order later on, unasked, to accuse a man of lying—all this, you will say, is on a level with theft. Yes, but I care nothing for fine feelings now. I have endured dozens of your dinners and suppers when you said and did what you liked, and I had to hear, to look on, and be silent. I don't want to make you a present of my silence. Besides, if there is not a living soul at hand who dares to tell you the truth without flattery, let your flunkey Stepan wash your magnificent countenance for you."

I did not like this beginning, but I did not care to alter it. Besides, what did it matter?

The big windows with their dark curtains, the bed, the crumpled dress coat on the floor, and my wet footprints, looked gloomy and forbidding. And there was a peculiar stillness.

Possibly because I had run out into the street without my cap and goloshes I was in a high fever. My face burned, my legs ached. . . . My heavy head drooped over the table, and there was that kind of division in my thought when every idea in the brain seemed dogged by its shadow.

"I am ill, weak, morally cast down," I went on; "I cannot write to you as I should like to. From the first moment I desired to insult and humiliate you, but now I do not feel that I have the right to do so. You and I have both fallen, and neither of us will ever rise up again; and even if my letter were eloquent, terrible, and passionate, it would still seem like beating on the lid of a coffin: however one knocks upon it, one will not wake up the dead! No efforts could warm your accursed cold blood, and you know that better than I do. Why write? But my mind and heart are burning, and I go on writing; for some reason I am moved as though this letter still might save you and me. I am so feverish that my thoughts are disconnected, and my pen scratches the paper without meaning; but the question I want to put to you stands before me as clear as though in letters of flame.

"Why I am prematurely weak and fallen is not hard to explain. Like Samson of old, I have taken the gates of Gaza on my shoulders to carry them to the top of the mountain, and only when I was exhausted, when youth and health were quenched in me forever, I noticed that that burden was not for my shoulders, and that I had deceived myself. I have been, moreover, in cruel and continual pain. I have endured cold, hunger, illness, and loss of liberty. Of personal happiness I know and have known nothing. I have no home; my memories are bitter, and my conscience is often in dread of them. But why have you fallen—you? What fatal, diabolical causes hindered your life from blossoming into full flower? Why, almost before beginning life, were you in such haste to cast off the image and likeness of God, and to become a cowardly beast who backs and scares others because he is afraid himself? You are afraid of life—as afraid of it as an Oriental who sits all day on a cushion smoking his hookah. Yes, you read a great deal, and a European coat fits you well, but yet with what tender, purely Oriental, pasha-like care you protect yourself from hunger, cold, physical effort, from pain and uneasiness! How early your soul has taken to its dressing-gown! What a cowardly part you have played towards real life and nature, with which every healthy and normal man struggles! How soft, how snug, how warm, how comfortable—and how bored you are! Yes, it is deathly boredom, unrelieved by one ray of light, as in solitary confinement; but you try to hide from that enemy, too, you play cards eight hours out of twenty-four.

"And your irony? Oh, but how well I understand it! Free, bold, living thought is searching and dominating; for an indolent, sluggish mind it is intolerable. That it may not disturb your peace, like thousands of your contemporaries, you made haste in youth to put it under bar and bolt. Your ironical attitude to life, or whatever you like to call it, is your armour; and your thought, fettered and frightened, dare not leap over the fence you have put round it; and when you jeer at ideas which you pretend to know all about, you are like the deserter fleeing from the field of battle, and, to stifle his shame, sneering at war and at valour. Cynicism stifles pain. In some novel of Dostoevsky's an old man tramples underfoot the portrait of his dearly loved daughter because he had been unjust to her, and you vent your foul and vulgar jeers upon the ideas of goodness and truth because you have not the strength to follow them. You are frightened of every honest and truthful hint at your degradation, and you purposely surround yourself with people who do nothing but flatter your weaknesses. And you may well, you may well dread the sight of tears!

"By the way, your attitude to women. Shamelessness has been handed down to us in our flesh and blood, and we are trained to shamelessness; but that is what we are men for—to subdue the beast in us. When you reached manhood and *all* ideas became known to you, you could not have failed to see the truth; you knew it, but you did not follow it; you were afraid of it, and to deceive your conscience you began loudly assuring yourself that it was not you but woman that was to blame, that she was as degraded as your attitude to her. Your cold, scabrous anecdotes, your coarse laughter, all your innumerable theories concerning the underlying reality of marriage and the definite demands made upon it, concerning the ten *sous* the French workman pays his woman; your everlasting attacks on female logic, lying, weakness and so on—doesn't it all look like a desire at all costs to force woman down into the mud that she may be on the same level as your attitude toward her? You are a weak, unpleasant person!"

Zinaida Fyodorovna began playing the piano in the drawing-room, trying to recall the song of Saint-Saëns that Gruzin had played.

I went and lay on my bed, but remembering that it was time for me to go, I got up with an effort and with a heavy, burning head went to the table again.

"But this is the question," I went on. "Why are we worn out? Why are we, at first so passionate, so bold, so noble, and so full of faith, complete bankrupts at thirty or thirty-five? Why does one waste in consumption, another put a bullet through his brains, a third seek forgetfulness in vodka and cards, while the fourth tries to stifle his fear and misery by cynically trampling underfoot the pure image of his fair youth? Why is it that, having once fallen, we do not try to rise up again, and, losing one thing, do not seek something else? Why is it?

"The thief hanging on the Cross could bring back the joy of life and the courage of confident hope, though perhaps he had not more than an hour to live. You have long years before you, and I shall probably not die so soon as one might suppose. What if by a miracle the present turned out to be a dream, a horrible nightmare, and we should wake up renewed, pure, strong, proud of our righteousness? Sweet visions fire me, and I am almost breathless with emotion. I have a terrible longing to live. I long for our life to be holy, lofty, and majestic as the heavens above. Let us live! The sun doesn't rise twice a day, and life is not given to us again—clutch at what is left of your life and save it. . . ."

I did not write another word. I had a multitude of thoughts in my mind, but I could not connect them and get them on to paper. Without finishing the letter, I signed it with my name and rank, and went into the study. It was dark. I felt for the table and put the letter on it. I must have stumbled against the furniture in the dark and made a noise.

"Who is there?" I heard an alarmed voice in the drawing-room.

And the clock on the table softly struck one at the moment.

XIII

For at least half a minute I fumbled at the door in the dark, feeling for the handle; then I slowly opened it and walked into the drawing-room. Zinaida Fyodorovna was lying on the couch, and raising herself on her elbow, she looked towards me. Unable to bring myself to speak, I walked slowly by, and she followed me with her eyes. I stood for a little time in the dining-room and then walked by her again, and she looked at me intently and with perplexity, even with alarm. At last I stood still and said with an effort:

"He is not coming back."

She quickly got on to her feet, and looked at me without understanding.

"He is not coming back," I repeated, and my heart beat violently. "He will not come back, for he has not left Petersburg. He is staying at Pekarsky's."

She understood and believed me—I saw that from her sudden pallor, and from the way she laid her arms upon her bosom in terror and entreaty. In one instant all that had happened of late flashed through her mind; she reflected, and with pitiless clarity she saw the whole truth. But at the same time she remembered that I was a flunkey, a being of a lower order. . . . A casual stranger, with hair ruffled, with face flushed with fever, perhaps drunk, in a common overcoat, was coarsely intruding into her intimate life, and that offended her. She said to me sternly:

"It's not your business: go away."

"Oh, believe me!" I cried impetuously, holding out my hands to her. "I am not a footman; I am as free as you."

I mentioned my name, and, speaking very rapidly that she might not interrupt me or go away, explained to her who I was and why I was living there. This new discovery struck her more than the first. Till then she had hoped that her footman had lied or made a mistake or been silly, but now after my confession she had no doubts left. From the expression of her unhappy eyes and face, which suddenly lost its softness and beauty and looked old, I saw that she was insufferably miserable, and that the conversation would lead to no good; but I went on impetuously:

"The senator and the tour of inspection were invented to deceive you. In January, just as now, he did not go away, but stayed at Pekarsky's, and I saw him every day and took part in the deception. He was weary of you, he hated your presence here, he mocked at you. . . . If you could have heard how he and his friends here jeered at you and your love, you would not have remained here one minute! Go away from here! Go away."

"Well," she said in a shaking voice, and moved her hand over her hair. "Well, so be it."

Her eyes were full of tears, her lips were quivering, and her whole face was strikingly pale and distorted with anger. Orlov's coarse, petty lying revolted her and seemed to her contemptible, ridiculous: she smiled and I did not like that smile.

"Well," she repeated, passing her hand over her hair again, "so be it. He imagines that I shall die of humiliation, and instead of that I am . . . amused by it. There's no need for him to hide." She walked away from the piano and said, shrugging her shoulders: "There's no need. . . . It would have been simpler to have it out with me instead of keeping in hiding in other people's flats. I have eyes; I saw it myself long ago. . . . I was only waiting for him to come back to have things out once for all."

Then she sat down on a low chair by the table, and, leaning her head on the arm of the sofa, wept bitterly. In the drawing-room there was only one candle burning in the candelabra, and the chair where she was sitting was in darkness; but I saw how her head and shoulders were quivering, and how her hair, escaping from her combs, covered her neck, her face, her arms. . . . Her quiet, steady weeping, which was not hysterical but a woman's ordinary weeping, expressed a sense of insult, of wounded pride, of injury, and of something helpless, hopeless, which one could not set right and to which one could not get used. Her tears stirred an echo in my troubled and suffering heart; I forgot my illness and everything else in the world; I walked about the drawing-room and muttered distractedly:

"Is this life ? . . . Oh, one can't go on living like this, one can't. . . . Oh, it's madness, wickedness, not life."

"What humiliation!" she said through her tears. "To live together, to smile at me at the very time when I was burdensome to him, ridiculous in his eyes! Oh, how humiliating!"

She lifted up her head, and looking at me with tear-stained eyes through her hair, wet with her tears, and pushing it back as it prevented her seeing me, she asked:

"They laughed at me?"

"To these men you were laughable—you and your love and Turgenev; they said your head was full of him. And if we both die at once in despair, that will amuse them, too; they will make a funny anecdote of it and tell it at your requiem service. But why talk of them?" I said impatiently. "We must get away from here—I cannot stay here one minute longer."

She began crying again, while I walked to the piano and sat down. "What are we waiting for?" I asked dejectedly. "It's two o'clock."

"I am not waiting for anything," she said. "I am utterly lost."

"Why do you talk like that? We had better consider together what we are to do. Neither you nor I can stay here. Where do you intend to go?"

Suddenly there was a ring at the bell. My heart stood still. Could it be Orlov, to whom perhaps Kukushkin had complained of me? How should we meet? I went to open the door. It was Polya. She came in shaking the snow off her pelisse, and went into her room without saying a word to me. When I went back to the drawing-room, Zinaida Fyodorovna, pale as death, was standing in the middle of the room, looking towards me with big eyes.

"Who was it?" she asked softly.

"Polya," I answered.

She passed her hand over her hair and closed her eyes wearily.

"I will go away at once," she said. "Will you be kind and take me to the Petersburg Side? What time is it now?"

"A quarter to three."

XIV

When, a little afterwards, we went out of the house, it was dark and deserted in the street. Wet snow was falling and a damp wind lashed in one's face. I remember it was the beginning of March; a thaw had set in, and for some days past the cabmen had been driving on wheels. Under the impression of the back stairs, of the cold, of the midnight darkness, and the porter in his sheepskin who had questioned us before letting us out of the gate, Zinaida Fyodorovna was utterly cast down and dispirited. When we got into the cab and the hood was put up, trembling all over, she began hurriedly saying how grateful she was to me.

"I do not doubt your good-will, but I am ashamed that you should be troubled," she muttered. "Oh, I understand, I understand. . . . When Gruzin was here to-day, I felt that he was lying and concealing something. Well, so be it. But I am ashamed, anyway, that you should be troubled."

She still had her doubts. To dispel them finally, I asked the cabman to drive through Sergievsky Street; stopping him at Pekarsky's door, I got out of the cab and rang. When the porter came to the door, I asked aloud, that Zinaida Fyodorovna might hear, whether Georgy Ivanitch was at home.

"Yes," was the answer, "he came in half an hour ago. He must be in bed by now. What do you want?"

Zinaida Fyodorovna could not refrain from putting her head out.

"Has Georgy Ivanitch been staying here long?" she asked.

"Going on for three weeks."

"And he's not been away?"

"No," answered the porter, looking at me with surprise.

"Tell him, early to-morrow," I said, "that his sister has arrived from Warsaw. Good-bye."

Then we drove on. The cab had no apron, the snow fell on us in big flakes, and the wind, especially on the Neva, pierced us through and through. I began to feel as though we had been driving for a long time, that for ages we had been suffering, and that for ages I had been listening to Zinaida Fyodorovna's shuddering breath. In semi-delirium, as though half asleep, I looked back upon my strange, incoherent life, and for some reason recalled a melodrama, "The Parisian Beggars," which I had seen once or twice in my childhood. And when to shake off that semi-delirium I peeped out from the hood and saw the dawn, all the images of the past, all my misty thoughts, for some reason, blended in me into one distinct, overpowering thought: everything was irrevocably over for Zinaida Fyodorovna and for me. This was as certain a conviction as though the cold blue sky contained a prophecy, but a minute later I was already thinking of something else and believed differently.

"What am I now?" said Zinaida Fyodorovna, in a voice husky with the cold and the damp. "Where am I to go? What am I to do? Gruzin told me to go into a nunnery. Oh, I would! I would change my dress, my face, my name, my thoughts . . . everything—everything, and would hide myself for ever. But they will not take me into a nunnery. I am with child."

"We will go abroad together to-morrow," I said.

"That's impossible. My husband won't give me a passport."

"I will take you without a passport."

The cabman stopped at a wooden house of two storeys, painted a dark colour. I rang. Taking from me her small light basket—the only luggage we had brought with us—Zinaida Fyodorovna gave a wry smile and said:

"These are my *bijoux*."

But she was so weak that she could not carry these *bijoux*.

It was a long while before the door was opened. After the third or fourth ring a light gleamed in the windows, and there was a sound of steps, coughing and whispering; at last the key grated in the lock, and a stout peasant woman with a frightened red face appeared at the door. Some distance behind her stood a thin little old woman with short grey hair, carrying a candle in her hand. Zinaida Fyodorovna ran into the passage and flung her arms round the old woman's neck.

"Nina, I've been deceived," she sobbed loudly." I've been coarsely, foully deceived! Nina, Nina!"

I handed the basket to the peasant woman. The door was closed, but still I heard her sobs and the cry "Nina!"

I got into the cab and told the man to drive slowly to the Nevsky Prospect. I had to think of a night's lodging for myself.

Next day towards evening I went to see Zinaida Fyodorovna. She was terribly changed. There were no traces of tears on her pale, terribly sunken face, and her expression was different. I don't know whether it was that I saw her now in different surroundings, far from luxurious, and that our relations were by now different, or perhaps that intense grief had already set its mark upon her; she did not strike me as so elegant and well dressed as before. Her figure seemed smaller; there was an abruptness and excessive nervousness about her as though she were in a hurry, and there was not the same softness even in her smile. I was dressed in an expensive suit which I had bought during the day. She looked first of all at that suit and at the hat in my hand, then turned an impatient, searching glance upon my face as though studying it.

"Your transformation still seems to me a sort of miracle," she said. "Forgive me for looking at you with such curiosity. You are an extraordinary man, you know."

I told her again who I was, and why I was living at Orlov's, and I told her at greater length and in more detail than the day before. She listened with great attention, and said without letting me finish:

"Everything there is over for me. You know, I could not refrain from writing a letter. Here is the answer."

On the sheet which she gave there was written in Orlov's hand:

"I am not going to justify myself. But you must own that it was your mistake, not mine. I wish you happiness, and beg you to make haste and forget.

Yours sincerely,

"G.O.

"P.S.—I am sending on your things."

The trunks and baskets despatched by Orlov were standing in the passage, and my poor little portmanteau was there beside them.

"So . . ." Zinaida Fyodorovna began, but she did not finish.

We were silent. She took the note and held it for a couple of minutes before her eyes, and during that time her face wore the same haughty, contemptuous, proud, and harsh expression as the day before at the beginning of our explanation; tears came into her eyes—not timid, bitter tears, but proud, angry tears.

"Listen," she said, getting up abruptly and moving away to the window that I might not see her face. "I have made up my mind to go abroad with you to-morrow."

"I am very glad. I am ready to go to-day."

"Accept me as a recruit. Have you read Balzac?" she asked suddenly, turning round. "Have you? At the end of his novel 'Père Goriot' the hero looks down upon Paris from the top of a hill and threatens the town: ' Now we shall settle our account,' and after this he begins a new life. So when I look out of the train window at Petersburg for the last time, I shall say, 'Now we shall settle our account! ' "

Saying this, she smiled at her jest, and for some reason shuddered all over.

XV

At Venice I had an attack of pleurisy. Probably I had caught cold in the evening when we were rowing from the station to the Hotel Bauer. I had to take to my bed and stay there for a fortnight. Every morning while I was ill Zinaida Fyodorovna came from her room to drink coffee with me, and afterwards read aloud to me French and Russian books, of which we had bought a number at Vienna. These books were either long, long familiar to me or else had no interest for me, but I had the sound of a sweet, kind voice beside me, so that the meaning of all of them was summed up for me in the one thing—I was not alone. She would go out for a walk, come back in her light grey dress, her light straw hat, gay, warmed by the spring sun; and sitting by my bed, bending low down over me, would tell me something about Venice or read me those books—and I was happy.

At night I was cold, ill, and dreary, but by day I revelled in life—I can find no better expression for it. The brilliant warm sunshine beating in at the open windows and at the door upon the balcony, the shouts below, the splash of oars, the tinkle of bells, the prolonged boom of the cannon at midday, and the feeling of perfect, perfect freedom, did wonders with me; I felt as though I were growing strong, broad wings which were bearing me God knows whither. And what charm, what joy at times at the thought that another life was so close to mine! that I was the servant, the guardian, the friend, the indispensable fellow-traveller of a creature, young, beautiful, wealthy, but weak, lonely, and insulted! It is pleasant even to be ill when you know that there are people who are looking forward to your convalescence as to a holiday. One day I heard her whispering behind the door with my doctor, and then she came in to me with tear-stained eyes. It was a bad sign, but I was touched, and there was a wonderful lightness in my heart.

But at last they allowed me to go out on the balcony. The sunshine and the breeze from the sea caressed and fondled my sick body. I looked down at the familiar gondolas, which glide with feminine grace smoothly and majestically as though they were alive, and felt all the luxury of this original, fascinating civilisation. There was a smell of the sea. Some one was playing a stringed instrument and two voices were singing. How delightful it was! How unlike it was to that Petersburg night when the wet snow was falling and beating so rudely on our faces. If one looks straight across the canal, one sees the sea, and on the wide expanse towards the horizon the sun glittered on the water so dazzlingly that it hurt one's eyes to look at it. My soul yearned towards that lovely sea, which was so akin to me and to which I had given up my youth. I longed to live—to live— and nothing more.

A fortnight later I began walking freely. I loved to sit in the sun, and to listen to the gondoliers without understanding them, and for hours together to gaze at the little house where, they said, Desdemona lived—a naïve, mournful little house with a demure expression, as light as lace, so light that it looked as though one could lift it from its place with one hand. I stood for a long time by the tomb of Canova, and could not take my eyes off the melancholy lion. And in the Palace of the Doges I was always drawn to the corner where the portrait of the unhappy Marino Faliero was painted over with black. "It is fine to be an artist, a poet, a dramatist," I thought, "but since that is not vouchsafed to me, if only I could go in for mysticism! If only I had a grain of some faith to add to the unruffled peace and serenity that fills the soul!"

In the evening we ate oysters, drank wine, and went out in a gondola. I remember our black gondola swayed softly in the same place while the water faintly gurgled under it. Here and there the reflection of the stars and the lights on the bank quivered and trembled. Not far from us in a gondola, hung with coloured lanterns which were reflected in the water, there were people singing. The sounds of guitars, of violins, of mandolins, of men's and women's voices, were audible in the dark. Zinaida Fyodorovna, pale, with a grave, almost stern face, was sitting beside me, compressing her lips and clenching her hands. She was thinking about something; she did not stir an eyelash, nor hear me. Her face, her attitude, and her fixed, expressionless gaze, and her incredibly miserable, dreadful, and icy-cold memories, and around her the gondolas, the lights, the music, the song with its vigorous passionate cry of *"Jam-mo! Jam-mo!"*—what contrasts in life! When she sat like that, with tightly clasped hands, stony, mournful, I used to feel as though we were both characters in some novel in the old-fashioned style called "The Ill-fated," "The Abandoned," or something of the sort. Both of us: she—the ill-fated, the abandoned; and I—the faithful, devoted friend, the dreamer, and, if you like it, a superfluous man, a failure capable of nothing but coughing and dreaming, and perhaps sacrificing myself. . . But who and what needed my sacrifices now? And what had I to sacrifice, indeed ?

When we came in in the evening we always drank tea in her room and talked. We did not shrink from touching on old, unhealed wounds—on the contrary, for some reason I felt a positive pleasure in telling her about my life at Orlov's, or referring openly to relations which I knew and which could not have been concealed from me.

"At moments I hated you," I said to her. "When he was capricious, condescending, told you lies, I marvelled how it was you did not see, did not understand, when it was all so clear! You kissed his hands, you knelt to him, you flattered him. . . ."

"When I . . . kissed his hands and knelt to him, I loved him . . ." she said, blushing crimson.

"Can it have been so difficult to see through him? A fine sphinx! A sphinx indeed—a *kammer-junker!* I reproach you for nothing, God forbid," I went on, feeling I was coarse, that I had not the tact, the delicacy which are so essential when you have to do with a fellow-creature's soul; in early days before I knew her I had not noticed this defect in myself. "But how could you fail to see what he was?" I went on, speaking more softly and more diffidently, however.

"You mean to say you despise my past, and you are right," she said, deeply stirred. "You belong to a special class of men who cannot be judged by ordinary standards; your moral requirements are exceptionally rigorous, and I understand you can't forgive things. I understand you, and if sometimes I say the opposite, it doesn't mean that I look at things differently from you; I speak the same old nonsense simply because I haven't had time yet to wear out my old clothes and prejudices. I, too, hate and despise my past, and Orlov and my love. . . . What was that love? It's positively absurd now," she said, going to the window and looking down at the canal. "All this love only clouds the conscience and confuses the mind. The meaning of life is to be found only in one thing—fighting. To get one's heel on the vile head of the serpent and to crush it! That's the meaning of life. In that alone or in nothing."

I told her long stories of my past, and described my really astounding adventures. But of the change that had taken place in me I did not say one word. She always listened to me with great attention, and at interesting places she rubbed her hands as though vexed that it had not yet been her lot to experience such adventures, such joys and terrors. Then she would suddenly fall to musing and retreat into herself, and I could see from her face that she was not attending to me.

I closed the windows that looked out on the canal and asked whether we should not have the fire lighted.

"No, never mind. I am not cold," she said, smiling listlessly. "I only feel weak. Do you know, I fancy I have grown much wiser lately. I have extraordinary, original ideas now. When I think of my past, of my life then . . . people in general, in fact, it is all summed up for me in the image of my stepmother. Coarse, insolent, soulless, false, depraved, and a morphia maniac too. My father, who was feeble and weak-willed, married my mother for her money and drove her into consumption; but his second wife, my stepmother, he loved passionately, insanely. . . . What I had to put up with! But what is the use of talking! And so, as I say, it is all summed up in her image. . . . And it vexes me that my stepmother is dead. I should like to meet her now!"

"Why?"

"I don't know," she answered with a laugh and a graceful movement of her head. "Good-night. You must get well. As soon as you are well, we'll take up our work. . . . It's time to begin."

After I had said good-night and had my hand on the door-handle, she said:

"What do you think? Is Polya still living there?"

"Probably."

And I went off to my room. So we spent a whole month. One grey morning when we both stood at my window, looking at the clouds which were moving up from the sea, and at the darkening canal, expecting every minute that it would pour with rain, and when a thick, narrow streak of rain covered the sea as though with a muslin veil, we both felt suddenly dreary. The same day we both set off for Florence.

XVI

It was autumn, at Nice. One morning when I went into her room she was sitting on a low chair, bent together and huddled up, with her legs crossed and her face hidden in her hands. She was weeping bitterly, with sobs, and her long, unbrushed hair fell on her knees. The impression of the exquisite marvellous sea which I had only just seen and of which I wanted to tell her, left me all at once, and my heart ached.

"What is it?" I asked; she took one hand from her face and motioned me to go away. "What is it?" I repeated, and for the first time during our acquaintance I kissed her hand.

"No, it's nothing, nothing," she said quickly. "Oh, it's nothing, nothing. . . . Go away. . . . You see, I'm not dressed."

I went out overwhelmed. The calm and serene mood in which I

had been for so long was poisoned by compassion. I had a passionate longing to fall at her feet, to entreat her not to weep in solitude, but to share her grief with me, and the monotonous murmur of the sea already sounded a gloomy prophecy in my ears, and I foresaw fresh tears, fresh troubles, and fresh losses in the future. "What is she crying about? What is it?" I wondered, recalling her face and her agonised look. I remembered she was with child. She tried to conceal her condition from other people, and also from herself. At home she went about in a loose wrapper or in a blouse with extremely full folds over the bosom, and when she went out anywhere she laced herself in so tightly that on two occasions she fainted when we were out. She never spoke to me of her condition, and when I hinted that it might be as well to see a doctor, she flushed crimson and said not a word.

When I went to see her next time she was already dressed and had her hair done.

"There, there," I said, seeing that she was ready to cry again. "We had better go to the sea and have a talk."

"I can't talk. Forgive me, I am in the mood now when one wants to be alone. And, if you please, Vladimir Ivanitch, another time you want to come into my room, be so good as to give a knock at the door."

That "be so good" had a peculiar, unfeminine sound. I went away. My accursed Petersburg mood came back, and all my dreams were crushed and crumpled up like leaves by the heat. I felt I was alone again and there was no nearness between us. I was no more to her than that cobweb to that palm-tree, which hangs on it by chance and which will be torn off and carried away by the wind. I walked about the square where the band was playing, went into the Casino; there I looked at overdressed and heavily perfumed women, and every one of them glanced at me as though she would say: "You are alone; that's all right." Then I went out on the terrace and looked for a long time at the sea. There was not one sail on the horizon. On the left bank, in the lilac-coloured mist, there were mountains, gardens, towers, and houses, the sun was sparkling over it all, but it was all alien, indifferent, an incomprehensible tangle.

XVII

She used as before to come into my room in the morning to coffee, but we no longer dined together, as she said she was not hungry; and she lived only on coffee, tea, and various trifles such as oranges and caramels.

And we no longer had conversations in the evening. I don't know why it was like this. Ever since the day when I had found her in tears she had treated me somehow lightly, at times casually, even ironically, and for some reason called me "My good sir." What had before seemed to her terrible, heroic, marvellous, and had stirred her envy and enthusiasm, did not touch her now at all, and usually after listening to me, she stretched and said:

"Yes, 'great things were done in days of yore,' my good sir."

It sometimes happened even that I did not see her for days together. I would knock timidly and guiltily at her door and get no answer; I would knock again—still silence. . . . I would stand near the door and listen; then the chambermaid would pass and say coldly, *"Madame est partie."* Then I would walk about the passages of the hotel, walk and walk. . . . English people, full-bosomed ladies, waiters in swallow-tails. . . . And as I keep gazing at the long striped rug that stretches the whole length of the corridor, the idea occurs to me that I am playing in the life of this woman a strange, probably false part, and that it is beyond my power to alter that part. I run to my room and fall on my bed, and think and think, and can come to no conclusion; and all that is clear to me is that I want to live, and that the plainer and the colder and the harder her face grows, the nearer she is to me, and the more intensely and painfully I feel our kinship. Never mind "My good sir," never mind her light careless tone, never mind anything you like, only don't leave me, my treasure. I am afraid to be alone.

Then I go out into the corridor again, listen in a tremor. . . . I have no dinner; I don't notice the approach of evening. At last about eleven I hear the familiar footstep, and at the turn near the stairs Zinaida Fyodorovna comes into sight.

"Are you taking a walk?" she would ask as she passes me. "You had better go out into the air. . . . Good-night!"

"But shall we not meet again to-day?"

"I think it's late. But as you like."

"Tell me, where have you been?" I would ask, following her into the room.

"Where? To Monte Carlo." She took ten gold coins out of her pocket and said: "Look, my good sir; I have won. That's at roulette."

"Nonsense! As though you would gamble."

"Why not? I am going again to-morrow."

I imagined her with a sick and morbid face, in her condition, tightly laced, standing near the gaming-table in a crowd of cocottes, of old women in their dotage who swarm round the gold like flies round the honey. I remembered she had gone off to Monte Carlo for some reason in secret from me.

"I don't believe you," I said one day. "You wouldn't go there."

"Don't agitate yourself. I can't lose much."

"It's not the question of what you lose," I said with annoyance. "Has it never occurred to you while you were playing there that the glitter of gold, all these women, young and old, the croupiers, all the surroundings—that it is all a vile, loathsome mockery at the toiler's labour, at his bloody sweat?"

"If one doesn't play, what is one to do here?" she asked. "The toiler's labour and his bloody sweat—all that eloquence you can put off till another time; but now, since you have begun, let me go on. Let me ask you bluntly, what is there for me to do here, and what am I to do?"

"What are you to do?" I said, shrugging my shoulders. "That's a question that can't be answered straight off."

"I beg you to answer me honestly, Vladimir Ivanitch," she said, and her face looked angry. "Once I have brought myself to ask you this question, I am not going to listen to stock phrases. I am asking you," she went on, beating her hand on the table, as though marking time, "what ought I to do here? And not only here at Nice, but in general?"

I did not speak, but looked out of window to the sea. My heart was beating terribly.

"Vladimir Ivanitch." she said softly and breathlessly; it was hard for her to speak—"Vladimir Ivanitch, if you do not believe in the cause yourself, if you no longer think of going back to it, why . . . why did you drag me out of Petersburg? Why did you make me promises, why did you rouse mad hopes? Your convictions have changed; you have become a different man, and nobody blames you for it—our convictions are not always in our power. But . . . but, Vladimir Ivanitch, for God's sake, why are you not sincere?" she went on softly, coming up to me. "All these months when I have been dreaming aloud, raving, going into raptures over my plans, remodelling my life on a new pattern, why didn't you tell me the truth? Why were you silent or encouraged me by your stories; and behaved as though you were in complete sympathy with me? Why was it? Why was it necessary?"

"It's difficult to acknowledge one's bankruptcy," I said, turning round, but not looking at her. "Yes, I have no faith; I am worn out. I have lost heart. . . . It is difficult to be truthful—very difficult, and I held my tongue. God forbid that any one should have to go through what I have been through."

I felt that I was on the point of tears, and ceased speaking.

"Vladimir Ivanitch," she said, and took me by both hands, "you have been through so much and seen so much of life, you know more than I do; think seriously, and tell me, what am I to do? Teach me! If you haven't the strength to go forward yourself and take others with you, at least show me where to go. After all, I am a living, feeling, thinking being. To sink into a false position . . . to play an absurd part . . . is painful to me. I don't reproach you, I don't blame you; I only ask you."

Tea was brought in.

"Well?" said Zinaida Fyodorovna, giving me a glass. "What do you say to me?"

"There is more light in the world than you see through your window," I answered. "And there are other people besides me, Zinaida Fyodorovna."

"Then tell me who they are," she said eagerly. "That's all I ask of you."

"And I want to say, too," I went on, "one can serve an idea in more than one calling. If one has made a mistake and lost faith in one, one may find another. The world of ideas is large and cannot be exhausted."

"The world of ideas!" she said, and she looked into my face sarcastically. "Then we had better leave off talking. What's the use? . . ."

She flushed.

"The world of ideas!" she repeated. She threw her dinner-napkin aside, and an expression of indignation and contempt came into her face. "All your fine ideas, I see, lead up to one inevitable, essential step: I ought to become your mistress. That's what's wanted. To be taken up with ideas without being the mistress of an honourable, progressive man, is as good as not understanding the ideas. One has to begin with that . . . that is, with being your mistress, and the rest will come of itself."

"You are irritated, Zinaida Fyodorovna," I said.

"No, I am sincere!" she cried, breathing hard. "I am sincere!"

"You are sincere, perhaps, but you are in error, and it hurts me to hear you."

"I am in error?" she laughed. "Any one else might say that, but not you, my dear sir! I may seem to you indelicate, cruel, but I don't care: you love me? You love me, don't you?"

I shrugged my shoulders.

"Yes, shrug your shoulders!" she went on sarcastically. "When you were ill I heard you in your delirium, and ever since these adoring eyes, these sighs, and edifying conversations about friendship, about spiritual kinship. . . . But the point is, why haven't you been sincere? Why have you concealed what is and talked about what isn't? Had you said from the beginning what ideas exactly led you to drag me from Petersburg, I should have known. I should have poisoned myself then as I meant to, and there would have been none of this tedious farce. . . . But what's the use of talking!"

With a wave of the hand she sat down

"You speak to me as though you suspected me of dishonourable intentions," I said, offended.

"Oh, very well. What's the use of talking! I don't suspect you of intentions, but of having no intentions. If you had any, I should have known them by now. You had nothing but ideas and love. For the present—ideas and love, and in prospect—me as your mistress. That's in the order of things both in life and in novels. . . . Here you abused him," she said, and she slapped the table with her hand, "but one can't help agreeing with him. He has good reasons for despising these ideas."

"He does not despise ideas; he is afraid of them," I cried. "He is a coward and a liar."

"Oh, very well. He is a coward and a liar, and deceived me. And you? Excuse my frankness; what are you? He deceived me and left me to take my chance in Petersburg, and you have deceived me and abandoned me here. But he did not mix up ideas with his deceit, and you . . ."

"For goodness' sake, why are you saying this?" I cried in horror, wringing my hands and going up to her quickly. "No, Zinaida Fyodorovna, this is cynicism. You must not be so despairing; listen to me," I went on, catching at a thought which flashed dimly upon me, and which seemed to me might still save us both. "Listen. I have passed through so many experiences in my time that my head goes round at the thought of them, and I have realised with my mind, with my racked soul, that man finds his true destiny in nothing if not in self-sacrificing love for his neighbour. It is towards that we must strive, and that is our destination! That is my faith!"

I wanted to go on to speak of mercy, of forgiveness, but there was an insincere note in my voice, and I was embarrassed.

"I want to live!" I said genuinely. "To live, to live! I want peace, tranquillity; I want warmth—this sea here—to have you near. Oh, how I wish I could rouse in you the same thirst for life! You spoke just now of love, but it would be enough for me to have you near, to hear your voice, to watch the look in your face . . . !"

She blushed crimson, and to hinder my speaking, said quickly:

"You love life, and I hate it. So our ways lie apart."

She poured herself out some tea, but did not touch it, went into the bedroom, and lay down.

"I imagine it is better to cut short this conversation," she said to me from within. "Everything is over for me, and I want nothing. . . . What more is there to say?"

"No, it's not all over!"

"Oh, very well! . . . I know! I am sick of it. . . . That's enough."

I got up, took a turn from one end of the room to the other, and went out into the corridor. When late at night I went to her door and listened, I distinctly heard her crying.

Next morning the waiter, handing me my clothes, informed me, with a smile, that the lady in number thirteen was confined. I dressed somehow, and almost fainting with terror ran to Zinaida Fyodorovna. In her room I found a doctor, a midwife, and an elderly Russian lady from Harkov, called Darya Milhailovna. There was a smell of ether. I had scarcely crossed the threshold when from the room where she was lying I heard a low, plaintive moan, and, as though it had been wafted me by the wind from Russia, I thought of Orlov, his irony, Polya, the Neva, the drifting snow, then the cab without an apron, the prediction I had read in the cold morning sky, and the despairing cry "Nina! Nina!"

"Go in to her," said the lady.

I went in to see Zinaida Fyodorovna, feeling as though I were the father of the child. She was lying with her eyes closed, looking thin and pale, wearing a white cap edged with lace. I remember there were two expressions on her face: one—cold, indifferent, apathetic; the other—a look of childish helplessness given her by the white cap. She did not hear me come in, or heard, perhaps, but did not pay attention. I stood, looked at her, and waited.

But her face was contorted with pain; she opened her eyes and gazed at the ceiling, as though wondering what was happening to her. . . . There was a look of loathing on her face.

"It's horrible . . ." she whispered.

"Zinaida Fyodorovna." I spoke her name softly. She looked at me indifferently, listlessly, and closed her eyes. I stood there a little while, then went away.

At night, Darya Mihailovna informed me that the child, a girl, was born, but that the mother was in a dangerous condition. Then I heard noise and bustle in the passage. Darya Mihailovna came to me again and with a face full of despair, wringing her hands, said:

"Oh, this is awful! The doctor suspects that she has taken poison! Oh, how badly Russians do behave here!"

And at twelve o'clock the next day Zinaida Fyodorovna died.

XVIII

Two years had passed. Circumstances had changed; I had come to Petersburg again and could live here openly. I was no longer afraid of being and seeming sentimental, and gave myself up entirely to the fatherly, or rather idolatrous feeling roused in me by Sonya, Zinaida Fyodorovna's child. I fed her with my own hands, gave her her bath, put her to bed, never took my eyes off her for nights together, and screamed when it seemed to me that the nurse was just going to drop her. My thirst for normal ordinary life had become stronger and more acute as time went on, but wider visions stopped short at Sonya, as though I had found in her at last just what I needed. I loved the child madly. In her I saw the continuation of my life, and it was not exactly that I fancied, but I felt, I almost believed, that when I had cast off at last my long, bony, bearded frame, I should go on living in those little blue eyes, that silky flaxen hair, those dimpled pink hands which stroked my face so lovingly and were clasped round my neck.

Sonya's future made me anxious. Orlov was her father; in her birth certificate she was called Krasnovsky, and the only person who knew of her existence, and took interest in her—that is, I—was at death's door. I had to think about her seriously.

The day after I arrived in Petersburg I went to see Orlov. The door was opened to me by a stout old fellow with red whiskers and no moustache, who looked like a German. Polya, who was tidying the drawing-room, did not recognize me, but Orlov knew me at once.

"Ah, Mr. Revolutionist!" he said, looking at me with curiosity, and laughing. "What fate has brought you?"

He was not changed in the least: the same well-groomed, unpleasant face, the same irony. And a new book was lying on the table just as of old, with an ivory paper-knife thrust in it. He had evidently been reading before I came in. He made me sit down, offered me a cigar, and with a delicacy found only in well-bred people, concealing the unpleasant feeling aroused by my face and my wasted figure, observed casually that I was not in the least changed, and that he would have known me anywhere in spite of my having grown a beard. We talked of the weather, of Paris. To dispose as quickly as possible of the oppressive, inevitable question, which weighed upon him and me, he asked:

"Zinaida Fyodorovna is dead?"

"Yes," I answered.

"In childbirth?"

"Yes, in childbirth. The doctor suspected another cause of death, but . . . it is more comforting for you and for me to think that she died in childbirth."

He sighed decorously and was silent. The angel of silence passed over us, as they say.

"Yes. And here everything is as it used to be—no changes," he said briskly, seeing that I was looking about the room. "My father, as you know, has left the service and is living in retirement; I am still in the same department. Do you remember Pekarsky? He is just the same as ever. Gruzin died of diphtheria a year ago. . . . Kukushkin is alive, and often speaks of you. By the way," said Orlov, dropping his eyes with an air of reserve, "when Kukushkin heard who you were, he began telling every one you had attacked him and tried to murder him . . . and that he only just escaped with his life."

I did not speak.

"Old servants do not forget their masters. . . . It's very nice of you," said Orlov jocosely. "Will you have some wine and some coffee, though? I will tell them to make some."

"No, thank you. I have come to see you about a very important matter, Georgy Ivanitch."

"I am not very fond of important matters, but I shall be glad to be of service to you. What do you want?"

"You see," I began, growing agitated, "I have here with me Zinaida Fyodorovna's daughter. . . . Hitherto I have brought her up, but, as you see, before many days I shall be an empty sound. I should like to die with the thought that she is provided for."

Orlov coloured a little, frowned a little, and took a cursory and sullen glance at me. He was unpleasantly affected, not so much by the "important matter" as by my words about death, about becoming an empty sound.

"Yes, it must be thought about," he said, screening his eyes as though from the sun. "Thank you. You say it's a girl?"

"Yes, a girl. A wonderful child!"

"Yes. Of course, it's not a lap-dog, but a human being. I understand we must consider it seriously. I am prepared to do my part, and am very grateful to you."

He got up, walked about, biting his nails, and stopped before a picture.

"We must think about it," he said in a hollow voice, standing with his back to me. "I shall go to Pekarsky's to-day and will ask him to go to Krasnovsky's. I don't think he will make much ado about consenting to take the child."

"But, excuse me, I don't see what Krasnovsky has got to do with it," I said, also getting up and walking to a picture at the other end of the room.

"But she bears his name, of course!" said Orlov.

"Yes, he may be legally obliged to accept the child—I don't know; but I came to you, Georgy Ivanitch, not to discuss the legal aspect."

"Yes, yes, you are right," he agreed briskly. "I believe I am talking nonsense. But don't excite yourself. We will decide the matter to our mutual satisfaction. If one thing won't do, we'll try another; and if that won't do, we'll try a third—one way or another this delicate question shall be settled. Pekarsky will arrange it all. Be so good as to leave me your address and I will let you know at once what we decide. Where are you living?"

Orlov wrote down my address, sighed, and said with a smile:

"Oh, Lord, what a job it is to be the father of a little daughter! But Pekarsky will arrange it all. He is a sensible man. Did you stay long in Paris?"

"Two months."

We were silent. Orlov was evidently afraid I should begin talking of the child again, and to turn my attention in another direction, said:

"You have probably forgotten your letter by now. But I have kept it. I understand your mood at the time, and, I must own, I respect that letter. 'Damnable cold blood,' 'Asiatic,' 'coarse laugh'—that was charming and characteristic," he went on with an ironical smile. "And the fundamental thought is perhaps near the truth, though one might dispute the question endlessly. That is," he hesitated, "not dispute the thought itself, but your attitude to the question—your temperament, so to say. Yes, my life is abnormal, corrupted, of no use to any one, and what prevents me from beginning a new life is cowardice—there you are quite right. But that you take it so much to heart, are troubled, and reduced to despair by it—that's irrational; there you are quite wrong."

"A living man cannot help being troubled and reduced to despair when he sees that he himself is going to ruin and others are going to ruin round him."

"Who doubts it! I am not advocating indifference; all I ask for is an objective attitude to life. The more objective, the less danger of falling into error. One must look into the root of things, and try to see in every phenomenon a cause of all the other causes. We have grown feeble, slack—degraded, in fact. Our generation is entirely composed of neurasthenics and whimperers; we do nothing but talk of fatigue and exhaustion. But the fault is neither yours nor mine; we are of too little consequence to affect the destiny of a whole generation. We must suppose for that larger, more general causes with a solid *raison d'être* from the biological point of view. We are neurasthenics, flabby, renegades, but perhaps it's necessary and of service for generations that will come after us. Not one hair falls from the head without the will of the Heavenly Father—in other words, nothing happens by chance in Nature and in human environment. Everything has its cause and is inevitable. And if so, why should we worry and write despairing letters?"

"That's all very well," I said, thinking a little. "I believe it will be easier and clearer for the generations to come; our experience will be at their service. But one wants to live apart from future generations and not only for their sake. Life is only given us once, and one wants to live it boldly, with full consciousness and beauty. One wants to play a striking, independent, noble part; one wants to make history so that those generations may not have the right to say of each of us that we were nonentities or worse. . . . I believe what is going on about us is inevitable and not without a purpose, but what have I to do with that inevitability? Why should my *ego* be lost?"

"Well, there's no help for it," sighed Orlov, getting up and, as it were, giving me to understand that our conversation was over.

I took my hat.

"We've only been sitting here half an hour, and how many questions we have settled, when you come to think of it!" said Orlov, seeing me into the hall. "So I will see to that matter. . . . I will see Pekarsky to-day. . . . Don't be uneasy."

He stood waiting while I put on my coat, and was obviously relieved at the feeling that I was going away.

"Georgy Ivanitch, give me back my letter," I said.

"Certainly."

He went to his study, and a minute later returned with the letter. I thanked him and went away.

The next day I got a letter from him. He congratulated me on the satisfactory settlement of the question. Pekarsky knew a lady, he wrote, who kept a school, something like a kindergarten, where she took quite little children. The lady could be entirely depended upon, but before concluding anything with her it would be as well to discuss the matter with Krasnovsky—it was a matter of form. He advised me to see Pekarsky at once and to take the birth certificate with me, if I had it. "Rest assured of the sincere respect and devotion of your humble servant. . . ."

I read this letter, and Sonya sat on the table and gazed at me attentively without blinking, as though she knew her fate was being decided.

1893

The Black Monk

I

Andrey Vassilitch Kovrin, who held a master's degree at the University, had exhausted himself, and had upset his nerves. He did not send for a doctor, but casually, over a bottle of wine, he spoke to a friend who was a doctor, and the latter advised him to spend the spring and summer in the country. Very opportunely a long letter came from Tanya Pesotsky, who asked him to come and stay with them at Borissovka. And he made up his mind that he really must go.

To begin with—that was in April—he went to his own home, Kovrinka, and there spent three weeks in solitude; then, as soon as the roads were in good condition, he set off, driving in a carriage, to visit Pesotsky, his former guardian, who had brought him up, and was a horticulturist well known all over Russia. The distance from Kovrinka to Borissovka was reckoned only a little over fifty miles. To drive along a soft road in May in a comfortable carriage with springs was a real pleasure.

Pesotsky had an immense house with columns and lions, off which the stucco was peeling, and with a footman in swallow-tails at the entrance. The old park, laid out in the English style, gloomy and severe, stretched for almost three-quarters of a mile to the river, and there ended in a steep, precipitous clay bank, where pines grew with bare roots that looked like shaggy paws; the water shone below with an unfriendly gleam, and the peewits flew up with a plaintive cry, and there one always felt that one must sit down and write a ballad. But near the house itself, in the courtyard and orchard, which together with the nurseries covered ninety acres, it was all life and gaiety even in bad weather. Such marvellous roses, lilies, camellias; such tulips of all possible shades, from glistening white to sooty black—such a wealth of flowers, in fact, Kovrin had never seen anywhere as at Pesotsky's. It was only the beginning of spring, and the real glory of the flower-beds was still hidden away in the hot-houses. But even the flowers along the avenues, and here and there in the flower-beds, were enough to make one feel, as one walked about the garden, as though one were in a realm of tender colours, especially in the early morning when the dew was glistening on every petal.

What was the decorative part of the garden, and what Pesotsky contemptuously spoke of as rubbish, had at one time in his childhood given Kovrin an impression of fairyland.

Every sort of caprice, of elaborate monstrosity and mockery at Nature was here. There were espaliers of fruit-trees, a pear-tree in the shape of a pyramidal poplar, spherical oaks and lime-trees, an apple-tree in the shape of an umbrella, plum-trees trained into arches, crests, candelabra, and even into the number 1862—the year when Pesotsky first took up horticulture. One came across, too, lovely, graceful trees with strong, straight stems like palms, and it was only by looking intently that one could recognise these trees as gooseberries or currants. But what made the garden most cheerful and gave it a lively air, was the continual coming and going in it, from early morning till evening; people with wheelbarrows, shovels, and watering-cans swarmed round the trees and bushes, in the avenues and the flower-beds, like ants. . . .

Kovrin arrived at Pesotsky's at ten o'clock in the evening. He found Tanya and her father, Yegor Semyonitch, in great anxiety. The clear starlight sky and the thermometer foretold a frost towards morning, and meanwhile Ivan Karlitch, the gardener, had gone to the town, and they had no one to rely upon. At supper they talked of nothing but the morning frost, and it was settled that Tanya should not go to bed, and between twelve and one should walk through the garden, and see that everything was done properly, and Yegor Semyonitch should get up at three o'clock or even earlier.

Kovrin sat with Tanya all the evening, and after midnight went out with her into the garden. It was cold. There was a strong smell of burning already in the garden. In the big orchard, which was called the commercial garden, and which brought Yegor Semyonitch several thousand clear profit, a thick, black, acrid smoke was creeping over the ground and, curling round the trees, was saving those thousands from the frost. Here the trees were arranged as on a chessboard, in straight and regular rows like ranks of soldiers, and this severe pedantic regularity, and the fact that the trees were of the same size, and had tops and trunks all exactly alike, made them look monotonous and even dreary. Kovrin and Tanya walked along the rows where fires of dung, straw, and all sorts of refuse were smouldering, and from time to time they were met by labourers who wandered in the smoke like shadows. The only trees in flower were the cherries, plums, and certain sorts of apples, but the whole garden was plunged in smoke, and it was only near the nurseries that Kovrin could breathe freely.

"Even as a child I used to sneeze from the smoke here," he said, shrugging his shoulders, "but to this day I don't understand how smoke can keep off frost."

"Smoke takes the place of clouds when there are none . . ." answered Tanya.

"And what do you want clouds for?"

"In overcast and cloudy weather there is no frost."

"You don't say so."

He laughed and took her arm. Her broad, very earnest face, chilled with the frost, with her delicate black eyebrows, the turned-up collar of her coat, which prevented her moving her head freely, and the whole of her thin, graceful figure, with her skirts tucked up on account of the dew, touched him.

"Good heavens! she is grown up," he said. "When I went away from here last, five years ago, you were still a child. You were such a thin, long-legged creature, with your hair hanging on your shoulders; you used to wear short frocks, and I used to tease you, calling you a heron. . . . What time does!"

"Yes, five years!" sighed Tanya. "Much water has flowed since then. Tell me, Andryusha, honestly," she began eagerly, looking him in the face: "do you feel strange with us now? But why do I ask you? You are a man, you live your own interesting life, you are somebody. . . . To grow apart is so natural! But however that may be, Andryusha, I want you to think of us as your people. We have a right to that."

"I do, Tanya."

"On your word of honour?"

"Yes, on my word of honour."

"You were surprised this evening that we have so many of your photographs. You know my father adores you. Sometimes it seems to me that he loves you more than he does me. He is proud of you. You are a clever, extraordinary man, you have made a brilliant career for yourself, and he is persuaded that you have turned out like this because he brought you up. I don't try to prevent him from thinking so. Let him."

Dawn was already beginning, and that was especially perceptible from the distinctness with which the coils of smoke and the tops of the trees began to stand out in the air.

"It's time we were asleep, though," said Tanya, "and it's cold, too." She took his arm. "Thank you for coming, Andryusha. We have only uninteresting acquaintances, and not many of them. We have only the garden, the garden, the garden, and nothing else. Standards, half-standards," she laughed. "Aports, Reinettes, Borovinkas, budded stocks, grafted stocks. . . . All, all our life has gone into the garden. I never even dream of anything but apples and pears. Of course, it is very nice and useful, but sometimes one longs for something else for variety. I remember that when you used to come to us for the summer holidays, or simply a visit, it always seemed to be fresher and brighter in the house, as though the covers had been taken off the lustres and the furniture. I was only a little girl then, but yet I understood it."

She talked a long while and with great feeling. For some reason the idea came into his head that in the course of the summer he might grow fond of this little, weak, talkative creature, might be carried away and fall in love; in their position it was so possible and natural! This thought touched and amused him; he bent down to her sweet, preoccupied face and hummed softly:

" 'Onyegin, I won't conceal it;
I madly love Tatiana. . . .' "

By the time they reached the house, Yegor Semyonitch had got up. Kovrin did not feel sleepy; he talked to the old man and went to the garden with him. Yegor Semyonitch was a tall, broad-shouldered, corpulent man, and he suffered from asthma, yet he walked so fast that it was hard work to hurry after him. He had an extremely preoccupied air; he was always hurrying somewhere, with an expression that suggested that if he were one minute late all would be ruined!

"Here is a business, brother . . ." he began, standing still to take breath. "On the surface of the ground, as you see, is frost; but if you raise the thermometer on a stick fourteen feet above the ground, there it is warm. . . . Why is that?"

"I really don't know," said Kovrin, and he laughed.

"H'm! . . . One can't know everything, of course. . . . However large the intellect may be, you can't find room for everything in it. I suppose you still go in chiefly for philosophy?"

"Yes, I lecture in psychology; I am working at philosophy in general."

"And it does not bore you?"

"On the contrary, it's all I live for."

"Well, God bless you! . . ." said Yegor Semyonitch, meditatively stroking his grey whiskers. "God bless you! . . . I am delighted about you . . . delighted, my boy. . . ."

But suddenly he listened, and, with a terrible face, ran off and quickly disappeared behind the trees in a cloud of smoke.

"Who tied this horse to an apple-tree?" Kovrin heard his despairing, heart-rending cry. "Who is the low scoundrel who has dared to tie this horse to an apple-tree ? My God, my God! They have ruined everything; they have spoilt everything; they have done everything filthy, horrible, and abominable. The orchard's done for, the orchard's ruined. My God!"

When he came back to Kovrin, his face looked exhausted and mortified.

"What is one to do with these accursed people?" he said in a tearful voice, flinging up his hands. "Styopka was carting dung at night, and tied the horse to an apple-tree! He twisted the reins round it, the rascal, as tightly as he could, so that the bark is rubbed off in three places. What do you think of that! I spoke to him and he stands like a post and only blinks his eyes. Hanging is too good for him."

Growing calmer, he embraced Kovrin and kissed him on the cheek.

"Well, God bless you! . . . God bless you! . . ." he muttered. "I am very glad you have come. Unutterably glad. . . . Thank you."

Then, with the same rapid step and preoccupied face, he made the round of the whole garden, and showed his former ward all his greenhouses and hot-houses, his covered-in garden, and two apiaries which he called the marvel of our century.

While they were walking the sun rose, flooding the garden with brilliant light. It grew warm. Foreseeing a long, bright, cheerful day, Kovrin recollected that it was only the beginning of May, and that he had before him a whole summer as bright, cheerful, and long; and suddenly there stirred in his bosom a joyous, youthful feeling, such as he used to experience in his childhood, running about in that garden. And he hugged the old man and kissed him affectionately. Both of them, feeling touched, went indoors and drank tea out of old-fashioned china cups, with cream and satisfying krendels made with milk and eggs; and these trifles reminded Kovrin again of his childhood and boyhood. The delightful present was blended with the impressions of the past that stirred within him; there was a tightness at his heart; yet he was happy.

He waited till Tanya was awake and had coffee with her, went for a walk, then went to his room and sat down to work. He read attentively, making notes, and from time to time raised his eyes to look out at the open windows or at the fresh, still dewy flowers in the vases on the table; and again he dropped his eyes to his book, and it seemed to him as though every vein in his body was quivering and fluttering with pleasure.

II

In the country he led just as nervous and restless a life as in town. He read and wrote a great deal, he studied Italian, and when he was out for a walk, thought with pleasure that he would soon sit down to work again. He slept so little that every one wondered at him; if he accidentally dozed for half an hour in the daytime, he would lie awake all night, and, after a sleepless night, would feel cheerful and vigorous as though nothing had happened.

He talked a great deal, drank wine, and smoked expensive cigars. Very often, almost every day, young ladies of neighbouring families would come to the Pesotskys', and would sing and play the piano with Tanya; sometimes a young neighbour who was a good violinist would come, too. Kovrin listened with eagerness to the music and singing, and was exhausted by it, and this showed itself by his eyes closing and his head falling to one side.

One day he was sitting on the balcony after evening tea, reading.

At the same time, in the drawing-room, Tanya taking soprano, one of the young ladies a contralto, and the young man with his violin, were practising a well-known serenade of Braga's. Kovrin listened to the words—they were Russian—and could not understand their meaning. At last, leaving his book and listening attentively, he understood: a maiden, full of sick fancies, heard one night in her garden mysterious sounds, so strange and lovely that she was obliged to recognise them as a holy harmony which is unintelligible to us mortals, and so flies back to heaven. Kovrin's eyes began to close. He got up, and in exhaustion walked up and down the drawing-room, and then the dining-room. When the singing was over he took Tanya's arm, and with her went out on the balcony.

"I have been all day thinking of a legend," he said. "I don't remember whether I have read it somewhere or heard it, but it is a strange and almost grotesque legend. To begin with, it is somewhat obscure. A thousand years ago a monk, dressed in black, wandered about the desert, somewhere in Syria or Arabia. . . . Some miles from where he was, some fisherman saw another black monk, who was moving slowly over the surface of a lake. This second monk was a mirage. Now forget all the laws of optics, which the legend does not recognise, and listen to the rest. From that mirage there was cast another mirage, then from that other a third, so that the image of the black monk began to be repeated endlessly from one layer of the atmosphere to another. So that he was seen at one time in Africa, at another in Spain, then in Italy, then in the Far North. . . . Then he passed out of the atmosphere of the earth, and now he is wandering all over the universe, still never coming into conditions in which he might disappear. Possibly he may be seen now in Mars or in some star of the Southern Cross. But, my dear, the real point on which the whole legend hangs lies in the fact that, exactly a thousand years from the day when the monk walked in the desert, the mirage will return to the atmosphere of the earth again and will appear to men. And it seems that the thousand years is almost up. . . . According to the legend, we may look out for the black monk to-day or to-morrow."

"A queer mirage," said Tanya, who did not like the legend.

"But the most wonderful part of it all, laughed Kovrin, "is that I simply cannot recall where I got this legend from. Have I read it somewhere? Have I heard it? Or perhaps I dreamed of the black monk. I swear I don't remember. But the legend interests me. I have been thinking about it all day."

Letting Tanya go back to her visitors, he went out of the house, and, lost in meditation, walked by the flower-beds. The sun was already setting. The flowers, having just been watered, gave forth a damp, irritating fragrance. Indoors they began singing again, and in the distance the violin had the effect of a human voice. Kovrin, racking his brains to remember where he had read or heard the legend, turned slowly towards the park, and unconsciously went as far as the river. By a little path that ran along the steep bank, between the bare roots, he went down to the water, disturbed the peewits there and frightened two ducks. The last rays of the setting sun still threw light here and there on the gloomy pines, but it was quite dark on the surface of the river. Kovrin crossed to the other side by the narrow bridge. Before him lay a wide field covered with young rye not yet in blossom. There was no living habitation, no living soul in the distance, and it seemed as though the little path, if one went along it, would take one to the unknown, mysterious place where the sun had just gone down, and where the evening glow was flaming in immensity and splendour.

"How open, how free, how still it is here!" thought Kovrin, walking along the path. "And it feels as though all the world were watching me, hiding and waiting for me to understand it. . . ."

But then waves began running across the rye, and a light evening breeze softly touched his uncovered head. A minute later there was another gust of wind, but stronger—the rye began rustling, and he heard behind him the hollow murmur of the pines. Kovrin stood still in amazement. From the horizon there rose up to the sky, like a whirlwind or a water-spout, a tall black column. Its outline was indistinct, but from the first instant it could be seen that it was not standing still, but moving with fearful rapidity, moving straight towards Kovrin, and the nearer it came the smaller and the more distinct it was. Kovrin moved aside into the rye to make way for it, and only just had time to do so.

A monk, dressed in black, with a grey head and black eyebrows, his arms crossed over his breast, floated by him. . . . His bare feet did not touch the earth. After he had floated twenty feet beyond him, he looked round at Kovrin, and nodded to him with a friendly but sly smile. But what a pale, fearfully pale, thin face! Beginning to grow larger again, he flew across the river, collided noiselessly with the clay bank and pines, and passing through them, vanished like smoke.

"Why, you see," muttered Kovrin, "there must be truth in the legend."

Without trying to explain to himself the strange apparition, glad that he had succeeded in seeing so near and so distinctly, not only the monk's black garments, but even his face and eyes, agreeably excited, he went back to the house.

In the park and in the garden people were moving about quietly, in the house they were playing—so he alone had seen the monk. He had an intense desire to tell Tanya and Yegor Semyonitch, but he reflected that they would certainly think his words the ravings of delirium, and that would frighten them; he had better say nothing.

He laughed aloud, sang, and danced the mazurka; he was in high spirits, and all of them, the visitors and Tanya, thought he had a peculiar look, radiant and inspired, and that he was very interesting.

III

After supper, when the visitors had gone, he went to his room and lay down on the sofa: he wanted to think about the monk. But a minute later Tanya came in.

"Here, Andryusha; read father's articles," she said, giving him a bundle of pamphlets and proofs. "They are splendid articles. He writes capitally."

"Capitally, indeed!" said Yegor Semyonitch, following her and smiling constrainedly; he was ashamed. "Don't listen to her, please; don't read them! Though, if you want to go to sleep, read them by all means; they are a fine soporific."

"I think they are splendid articles," said Tanya, with deep conviction. "You read them, Andryusha, and persuade father to write oftener. He could write a complete manual of horticulture."

Yegor Semyonitch gave a forced laugh, blushed, and began uttering the phrases usually made use of by an embarrassed author. At last he began to give way.

"In that case, begin with Gaucher's article and these Russian articles," he muttered, turning over the pamphlets with a trembling hand, "or else you won't understand. Before you read my objections, you must know what I am objecting to. But it's all nonsense . . . tiresome stuff. Besides, I believe it's bedtime."

Tanya went away. Yegor Semyonitch sat down on the sofa by Kovrin and heaved a deep sigh.

"Yes, my boy . . ." he began after a pause. "That's how it is, my dear lecturer. Here I write articles, and take part in exhibitions, and receive medals. . . . Pesotsky, they say, has apples the size of a head, and Pesotsky, they say, has made his fortune with his garden. In short, 'Kotcheby is rich and glorious.' But one asks oneself: what is it all for? The garden is certainly fine, a model. It's not really a garden, but a regular institution, which is of the greatest public importance because it marks, so to say, a new era in Russian agriculture and Russian industry. But, what's it for? What's the object of it?"

"The fact speaks for itself."

"I do not mean in that sense. I meant to ask: what will happen to the garden when I die? In the condition in which you see it now, it would not be maintained for one month without me. The whole secret of success lies not in its being a big garden or a great number of labourers being employed in it, but in the fact that I love the work. Do you understand? I love it perhaps more than myself. Look at me; I do everything myself. I work from morning to night: I do all the grafting myself, the pruning myself, the planting myself. I do it all myself: when any one helps me I am jealous and irritable till I am rude. The whole secret lies in loving it—that is, in the sharp eye of the master; yes, and in the master's hands, and in the feeling that makes one, when one goes anywhere for an hour's visit, sit, ill at ease, with one's heart far away, afraid that something may have happened in the garden. But when I die, who will look after it? Who will work? The gardener? The labourers? Yes ? But I tell you, my dear fellow, the worst enemy in the garden is not a hare, not a cockchafer, and not the frost, but any outside person."

"And Tanya?" asked Kovrin, laughing. "She can't be more harmful than a hare? She loves the work and understands it."

"Yes, she loves it and understands it. If after my death the garden goes to her and she is the mistress, of course nothing better could be wished. But if, which God forbid, she should marry," Yegor Semyonitch whispered, and looked with a frightened look at Kovrin, "that's just it. If she marries and children come, she will have no time to think about the garden. What I fear most is: she will marry some fine gentleman, and he will be greedy, and he will let the garden to people who will run it for profit, and everything will go to the devil the very first year! In our work females are the scourge of God!"

Yegor Semyonitch sighed and paused for a while.

"Perhaps it is egoism, but I tell you frankly: I don't want Tanya to get married. I am afraid of it! There is one young dandy comes to see us, bringing his violin and scraping on it; I know Tanya will not marry him, I know it quite well; but I can't bear to see him! Altogether, my boy, I am very queer. I know that."

Yegor Semyonitch got up and walked about the room in excitement, and it was evident that he wanted to say something very important, but could not bring himself to it.

"I am very fond of you, and so I am going to speak to you openly," he decided at last, thrusting his hands into his pockets. "I deal plainly with certain delicate questions, and say exactly what I think, and I cannot endure so-called hidden thoughts. I will speak plainly: you are the only man to whom I should not be afraid to marry my daughter. You are a clever man with a good heart, and would not let my beloved work go to ruin; and the chief reason is that I love you as a son, and I am proud of you. If Tanya and you could get up a romance somehow, then—well! I should be very glad and even happy. I tell you this plainly, without mincing matters, like an honest man."

Kovrin laughed. Yegor Semyonitch opened the door to go out, and stood in the doorway.

"If Tanya and you had a son, I would make a horticulturist of him," he said, after a moment's thought. "However, this is idle dreaming. Good-night."

Left alone, Kovrin settled himself more comfortably on the sofa and took up the articles. The title of one was "On Intercropping"; of another, "A Few Words on the Remarks of Monsieur Z. concerning the Trenching of the Soil for a New Garden"; a third, "Additional Matter concerning Grafting with a Dormant Bud"; and they were all of the same sort. But what a restless, jerky tone! What nervous, almost hysterical passion! Here was an article, one would have thought, with most peaceable and impersonal contents: the subject of it was the Russian Antonovsky Apple. But Yegor Semyonitch began it with "Audiatur altera pars," and finished it with "Sapienti sat"; and between these two quotations a perfect torrent of venomous phrases directed "at the learned ignorance of our recognised horticultural authorities, who observe Nature from the height of their university chairs," or at Monsieur Gaucher, "whose success has been the work of the vulgar and the dilettanti." And then followed an inappropriate, affected, and insincere regret that peasants who stole fruit and broke the branches could not nowadays be flogged.

"It is beautiful, charming, healthy work, but even in this there is strife and passion," thought Kovrin. "I suppose that everywhere and in all careers men of ideas are nervous, and marked by exaggerated sensitiveness. Most likely it must be so."

He thought of Tanya, who was so pleased with Yegor Semyonitch's articles. Small, pale, and so thin that her shoulder-blades stuck out, her eyes, wide and open, dark and intelligent, had an intent gaze, as though looking for something. She walked like her father with a little hurried step. She talked a great deal and was fond of arguing, accompanying every phrase, however insignificant, with expressive mimicry and gesticulation. No doubt she was nervous in the extreme.

Kovrin went on reading the articles, but he understood nothing of them, and flung them aside. The same pleasant excitement with which he had earlier in the evening danced the mazurka and listened to the music was now mastering him again and rousing a multitude of thoughts. He got up and began walking about the room, thinking about the black monk. It occurred to him that if this strange, supernatural monk had appeared to him only, that meant that he was ill and had reached the point of having hallucinations. This reflection frightened him, but not for long.

"But I am all right, and I am doing no harm to any one; so there is no harm in my hallucinations," he thought; and he felt happy again.

He sat down on the sofa and clasped his hands round his head. Restraining the unaccountable joy which filled his whole being, he then paced up and down again, and sat down to his work. But the thought that he read in the book did not satisfy him. He wanted something gigantic, unfathomable, stupendous. Towards morning he undressed and reluctantly went to bed: he ought to sleep.

When he heard the footsteps of Yegor Semyonitch going out into the garden, Kovrin rang the bell and asked the footman to bring him some wine. He drank several glasses of Lafitte, then wrapped himself up, head and all; his consciousness grew clouded and he fell asleep.

IV

Yegor Semyonitch and Tanya often quarrelled and said nasty things to each other.

They quarrelled about something that morning. Tanya burst out crying and went to her room. She would not come down to dinner nor to tea. At first Yegor Semyonitch went about looking sulky and dignified, as though to give every one to understand that for him the claims of justice and good order were more important than anything else in the world; but he could not keep it up for long, and soon sank into depression. He walked about the park dejectedly, continually sighing: "Oh, my God! My God!" and at dinner did not eat a morsel. At last, guilty and conscience-stricken, he knocked at the locked door and called timidly:

"Tanya! Tanya!"

And from behind the door came a faint voice, weak with crying but still determined:

"Leave me alone, if you please."

The depression of the master and mistress was reflected in the whole household, even in the labourers working in the garden. Kovrin was absorbed in his interesting work, but at last he, too, felt dreary and uncomfortable. To dissipate the general ill-humour in some way, he made up his mind to intervene, and towards evening he knocked at Tanya's door. He was admitted.

"Fie, fie, for shame!" he began playfully, looking with surprise at Tanya's tear-stained, woebegone face, flushed in patches with crying. "Is it really so serious ? Fie, fie!"

"But if you knew how he tortures me!" she said, and floods of scalding tears streamed from her big eyes. "He torments me to death," she went on, wringing her hands. "I said nothing to him . . . nothing . . . I only said that there was no need to keep . . . too many labourers . . . if we could hire them by the day when we wanted them. You know . . . you know the labourers have been doing nothing for a whole week. . . . I . . . I . . . only said that, and he shouted and . . . said . . . a lot of horrible insulting things to me. What for?"

"There, there," said Kovrin, smoothing her hair. "You've quarrelled with each other, you've cried, and that's enough. You must not be angry for long—that's wrong . . . all the more as he loves you beyond everything."

282

"He has . . . has spoiled my whole life," Tanya went on, sobbing. "I hear nothing but abuse and . . . insults. He thinks I am of no use in the house. Well! He is right. I shall go away to-morrow; I shall become a telegraph clerk. . . . I don't care. . . ."

"Come, come, come. . . . You mustn't cry, Tanya. You mustn't, dear. . . . You are both hot-tempered and irritable, and you are both to blame. Come along; I will reconcile you."

Kovrin talked affectionately and persuasively, while she went on crying, twitching her shoulders and wringing her hands, as though some terrible misfortune had really befallen her. He felt all the sorrier for her because her grief was not a serious one, yet she suffered extremely. What trivialities were enough to make this little creature miserable for a whole day, perhaps for her whole life! Comforting Tanya, Kovrin thought that, apart from this girl and her father, he might hunt the world over and would not find people who would love him as one of themselves, as one of their kindred. If it had not been for those two he might very likely, having lost his father and mother in early childhood, never to the day of his death have known what was meant by genuine affection and that naïve, uncritical love which is only lavished on very close blood relations; and he felt that the nerves of this weeping, shaking girl responded to his half-sick, overstrained nerves like iron to a magnet. He never could have loved a healthy, strong, rosy-cheeked woman, but pale, weak, unhappy Tanya attracted him.

And he liked stroking her hair and her shoulders, pressing her hand and wiping away her tears. . . . At last she left off crying. She went on for a long time complaining of her father and her hard, insufferable life in that house, entreating Kovrin to put himself in her place; then she began, little by little, smiling, and sighing that God had given her such a bad temper. At last, laughing aloud, she called herself a fool, and ran out of the room.

When a little later Kovrin went into the garden, Yegor Semyonitch and Tanya were walking side by side along an avenue as though nothing had happened, and both were eating rye bread with salt on it, as both were hungry.

V

Glad that he had been so successful in the part of peacemaker, Kovrin went into the park. Sitting on a garden seat, thinking, he heard the rattle of a carriage and a feminine laugh—visitors were arriving. When the shades of evening began falling on the garden, the sounds of the violin and singing voices reached him indistinctly, and that reminded him of the black monk. Where, in what land or in what planet, was that optical absurdity moving now?

Hardly had he recalled the legend and pictured in his imagination the dark apparition he had seen in the rye-field, when, from behind a pine-tree exactly opposite, there came out noiselessly, without the slightest rustle, a man of medium height with uncovered grey head, all in black, and barefooted like a beggar, and his black eyebrows stood out conspicuously on his pale, death-like face. Nodding his head graciously, this beggar or pilgrim came noiselessly to the seat and sat down, and Kovrin recognised him as the black monk.

For a minute they looked at one another, Kovrin with amazement, and the monk with friendliness and, just as before, a little slyness, as though he were thinking something to himself.

"But you are a mirage," said Kovrin. "Why are you here and sitting still? That does not fit in with the legend."

"That does not matter," the monk answered in a low voice, not immediately turning his face towards him. "The legend, the mirage, and I are all the products of your excited imagination. I am a phantom."

"Then you don't exist?" said Kovrin

"You can think as you like," said the monk, with a faint smile. "I exist in your imagination, and your imagination is part of nature, so I exist in nature.

"You have a very old, wise, and extremely expressive face, as though you really had lived more than a thousand years," said Kovrin. "I did not know that my imagination was capable of creating such phenomena. But why do you look at me with such enthusiasm? Do you like me?"

"Yes, you are one of those few who are justly called the chosen of God. You do the service of eternal truth. Your thoughts, your designs, the marvellous studies you are engaged in, and all your life, bear the

Divine, the heavenly stamp, seeing that they are consecrated to the rational and the beautiful—that is, to what is eternal."

"You said 'eternal truth.' . . . But is eternal truth of use to man and within his reach, if there is no eternal life?"

"There is eternal life," said the monk.

"Do you believe in the immortality of man?"

"Yes, of course. A grand, brilliant future is in store for you men. And the more there are like you on earth, the sooner will this future be realised. Without you who serve the higher principle and live in full understanding and freedom, mankind would be of little account; developing in a natural way, it would have to wait a long time for the end of its earthly history. You will lead it some thousands of years earlier into the kingdom of eternal truth—and therein lies your supreme service. You are the incarnation of the blessing of God, which rests upon men."

"And what is the object of eternal life?" asked Kovrin.

"As of all life—enjoyment. True enjoyment lies in knowledge, and eternal life provides innumerable and inexhaustible sources of knowledge, and in that sense it has been said: 'In My Father's house there are many mansions.' "

"If only you knew how pleasant it is to hear you!" said Kovrin, rubbing his hands with satisfaction.

"I am very glad."

"But I know that when you go away I shall be worried by the question of your reality. You are a phantom, an hallucination. So I am mentally deranged, not normal?"

"What if you are ? Why trouble yourself ? You are ill because you have overworked and exhausted yourself, and that means that you have sacrificed your health to the idea, and the time is near at hand when you will give up life itself to it. What could be better? That is the goal towards which all divinely endowed, noble natures strive."

"If I know I am mentally affected, can I trust myself?"

"And are you sure that the men of genius, whom all men trust, did not see phantoms, too? The learned say now that genius is allied to madness. My friend, healthy and normal people are only the common herd. Reflections upon the neurasthenia of the age, nervous exhaustion and degeneracy, et cetera, can only seriously agitate those who place the object of life in the present—that is, the common herd."

"The Romans used to say: *Mens sana in corpore sano.*"

"Not everything the Greeks and the Romans said is true. Exaltation, enthusiasm, ecstasy—all that distinguishes prophets, poets, martyrs for the idea, from the common folk—is repellent to the animal side of man—that is, his physical health. I repeat, if you want to be healthy and normal, go to the common herd."

"Strange that you repeat what often comes into my mind," said Kovrin. "It is as though you had seen and overheard my secret thoughts. But don't let us talk about me. What do you mean by 'eternal truth'?"

The monk did not answer. Kovrin looked at him and could not distinguish his face. His features grew blurred and misty. Then the monk's head and arms disappeared; his body seemed merged into the seat and the evening twilight, and he vanished altogether.

"The hallucination is over," said Kovrin; and he laughed. "It's a pity."

He went back to the house, light-hearted and happy. The little the monk had said to him had flattered, not his vanity, but his whole soul, his whole being. To be one of the chosen, to serve eternal truth, to stand in the ranks of those who could make mankind worthy of the kingdom of God some thousands of years sooner—that is, to free men from some thousands of years of unnecessary struggle, sin, and suffering; to sacrifice to the idea everything—youth, strength, health; to be ready to die for the common weal—what an exalted, what a happy lot! He recalled his past—pure, chaste, laborious; he remembered what he had learned himself and what he had taught to others, and decided that there was no exaggeration in the monk's words.

Tanya came to meet him in the park: she was by now wearing a different dress.

"Are you here?" she said. "And we have been looking and looking for you. . . . But what is the matter with you?" she asked in wonder, glancing at his radiant, ecstatic face and eyes full of tears. "How strange you are, Andryusha!"

"I am pleased, Tanya," said Kovrin, laying his hand on her shoulders. "I am more than pleased: I am happy. Tanya, darling Tanya, you are an extraordinary, nice creature. Dear Tanya, I am so glad, I am so glad!"

He kissed both her hands ardently, and went on:

"I have just passed through an exalted, wonderful, unearthly moment. But I can't tell you all about it or you would call me mad and not believe me. Let us talk of you. Dear, delightful Tanya! I love you, and am used to loving you. To have you near me, to meet you a dozen times a day, has become a necessity of my existence; I don't know how I shall get on without you when I go back home."

"Oh," laughed Tanya, "you will forget about us in two days. We are humble people and you are a great man."

"No; let us talk in earnest!" he said. "I shall take you with me, Tanya. Yes? Will you come with me? Will you be mine?"

"Come," said Tanya, and tried to laugh again, but the laugh would not come, and patches of colour came into her face.

She began breathing quickly and walked very quickly, but not to the house, but further into the park.

"I was not thinking of it . . . I was not thinking of it," she said, wringing her hands in despair.

And Kovrin followed her and went on talking, with the same radiant, enthusiastic face:

"I want a love that will dominate me altogether; and that love only you, Tanya, can give me. I am happy! I am happy!"

She was overwhelmed, and huddling and shrinking together, seemed ten years older all at once, while he thought her beautiful and expressed his rapture aloud:

"How lovely she is!"

VI

Learning from Kovrin that not only a romance had been got up, but that there would even be a wedding, Yegor Semyonitch spent a long time in pacing from one corner of the room to the other, trying to conceal his agitation. His hands began trembling, his neck swelled and turned purple, he ordered his racing droshky and drove off somewhere. Tanya, seeing how he lashed the horse, and seeing how he pulled his cap over his ears, understood what he was feeling, shut herself up in her room, and cried the whole day.

In the hot-houses the peaches and plums were already ripe; the packing and sending off of these tender and fragile goods to Moscow took a great deal of care, work, and trouble. Owing to the fact that the summer was very hot and dry, it was necessary to water every tree, and a great deal of time and labour was spent on doing it. Numbers of caterpillars made their appearance, which, to Kovrin's disgust, the labourers and even Yegor Semyonitch and Tanya squashed with their fingers. In spite of all that, they had already to book autumn orders for fruit and trees, and to carry on a great deal of correspondence. And at the very busiest time, when no one seemed to have a free moment, the work of the fields carried off more than half their labourers from the garden. Yegor Semyonitch, sunburnt, exhausted, ill-humoured, galloped from the fields to the garden and back again; cried that he was being torn to pieces, and that he should put a bullet through his brains.

Then came the fuss and worry of the trousseau, to which the Pesotskys attached a good deal of importance. Every one's head was in a whirl from the snipping of the scissors, the rattle of the sewing-machine, the smell of hot irons, and the caprices of the dressmaker, a huffy and nervous lady. And, as ill-luck would have it, visitors came every day, who had to be entertained, fed, and even put up for the night. But all this hard labour passed unnoticed as though in a fog. Tanya felt that love and happiness had taken her unawares, though she had, since she was fourteen, for some reason been convinced that Kovrin would marry her and no one else. She was bewildered, could not grasp it, could not believe herself. . . . At one minute such joy would swoop down upon her that she longed to fly away to the clouds and there pray to God, at another moment she would remember that in August she would have to part from her home and leave her father; or, goodness knows why, the idea would occur to her that she was worthless—insignificant and unworthy of a great man like Kovrin—and she would go to her room, lock herself in, and cry bitterly for several hours. When there were visitors, she would suddenly fancy that Kovrin looked extraordinarily handsome, and that all the women were in love with him and envying her, and her soul was filled with pride and rapture, as though she had vanquished the whole world; but he had only to smile politely at any young lady for her to be trembling with jealousy, to retreat to her room—and tears again These new sensations mastered her completely; she helped her father mechanically, without noticing peaches, caterpillars or labourers, or how rapidly the time was passing.

It was almost the same with Yegor Semyonitch. He worked from morning till night, was always in a hurry, was irritable, and flew into rages, but all of this was in a sort of spellbound dream. It seemed as though there were two men in him: one was the real Yegor Semyonitch, who was moved to indignation, and clutched his head in despair when he heard of some irregularity from Ivan Karlovitch the gardener; and another—not the real one—who seemed as though he were half drunk, would interrupt a business conversation at half a word, touch the gardener on the shoulder, and begin muttering:

"Say what you like, there is a great deal in blood. His mother was a wonderful woman, most high-minded and intelligent. It was a pleasure to look at her good, candid, pure face; it was like the face of an angel. She drew splendidly, wrote verses, spoke five foreign languages, sang. . . . Poor thing! she died of consumption. The Kingdom of Heaven be hers."

The unreal Yegor Semyonitch sighed, and after a pause went on:

"When he was a boy and growing up in my house, he had the same angelic face, good and candid. The way he looks and talks and moves is as soft and elegant as his mother's. And his intellect! We were always struck with his intelligence. To be sure, it's not for nothing he's a Master of Arts! It's not for nothing! And wait a bit, Ivan Karlovitch, what will he be in ten years' time? He will be far above us!"

But at this point the real Yegor Semyonitch, suddenly coming to himself, would make a terrible face, would clutch his head and cry:

"The devils! They have spoilt everything! They have ruined everything! They have spoilt everything! The garden's done for, the garden's ruined!"

Kovrin, meanwhile, worked with the same ardour as before, and did not notice the general commotion. Love only added fuel to the flames. After every talk with Tanya he went to his room, happy and triumphant, took up his book or his manuscript with the same passion with which he had just kissed Tanya and told her of his love. What the black monk had told him of the chosen of God, of eternal truth, of the brilliant future of mankind and so on, gave peculiar and extraordinary significance to his work, and filled his soul with pride and the consciousness of his own exalted consequence. Once or twice a week, in the park or in the house, he met the black monk and had long conversations with him, but this did not alarm him, but, on the contrary, delighted him, as he was now firmly persuaded that such apparitions only visited the elect few who rise up above their fellows and devote themselves to the service of the idea.

One day the monk appeared at dinner-time and sat in the dining-room window. Kovrin was delighted, and very adroitly began a conversation with Yegor Semyonitch and Tanya of what might be of interest to the monk; the black-robed visitor listened and nodded his head graciously, and Yegor Semyonitch and Tanya listened, too, and smiled gaily without suspecting that Kovrin was not talking to them but to his hallucination.

Imperceptibly the fast of the Assumption was approaching, and soon after came the wedding, which, at Yegor Semyonitch's urgent desire, was celebrated with "a flourish"—that is, with senseless festivities that lasted for two whole days and nights. Three thousand roubles' worth of food and drink was consumed, but the music of the wretched hired band, the noisy toasts, the scurrying to and fro of the footmen, the uproar and crowding, prevented them from appreciating the taste of the expensive wines and wonderful delicacies ordered from Moscow.

VII

One long winter night Kovrin was lying in bed, reading a French novel. Poor Tanya, who had headaches in the evenings from living in town, to which she was not accustomed, had been asleep a long while, and, from time to time, articulated some incoherent phrase in her restless dreams.

It struck three o'clock. Kovrin put out the light and lay down to sleep, lay for a long time with his eyes closed, but could not get to sleep because, as he fancied, the room was very hot and Tanya talked in her sleep. At half-past four he lighted the candle again, and this time he saw the black monk sitting in an arm-chair near the bed.

"Good-morning," said the monk, and after a brief pause he asked: "What are you thinking of now?"

"Of fame," answered Kovrin. "In the French novel I have just been reading, there is a description of a young *savant*, who does silly things and pines away through worrying about fame. I can't understand such anxiety."

"Because you are wise. Your attitude towards fame is one of indifference, as towards a toy which no longer interests you."

"Yes, that is true."

"Renown does not allure you now. What is there flattering, amusing, or edifying in their carving your name on a tombstone, then time rubbing off the inscription together with the gilding? Moreover, happily there are too many of you for the weak memory of mankind to be able to retain your names."

"Of course," assented Kovrin. "Besides, why should they be remembered? But let us talk of something else. Of happiness, for instance. What is happiness?"

When the clock struck five, he was sitting on the bed, dangling his feet to the carpet, talking to the monk:

"In ancient times a happy man grew at last frightened of his happiness—it was so great!—and to propitiate the gods he brought as a sacrifice his favourite ring. Do you know, I, too, like Polykrates, begin to be uneasy of my happiness. It seems strange to me that from morning to night I feel nothing but joy; it fills my whole being and smothers all other feelings. I don't know what sadness, grief, or boredom is. Here I am not asleep; I suffer from sleeplessness, but I am not dull. I say it in earnest; I begin to feel perplexed."

"But why?" the monk asked in wonder. "Is joy a supernatural feeling? Ought it not to be the normal state of man? The more highly a man is developed on the intellectual and moral side, the more independent he is, the more pleasure life gives him. Socrates, Diogenes, and Marcus Aurelius, were joyful, not sorrowful. And the Apostle tells us: ' Rejoice continually'; 'Rejoice and be glad.' "

"But will the gods be suddenly wrathful?" Kovrin jested; and he laughed. "If they take from me comfort and make me go cold and hungry, it won't be very much to my taste."

Meanwhile Tanya woke up, and looked with amazement and horror at her husband. He was talking, addressing the arm-chair, laughing and gesticulating; his eyes were gleaming, and there was something strange in his laugh.

"Andryusha, whom are you talking to?" she asked, clutching the hand he stretched out to the monk. "Andryusha! Whom?"

"Oh! Whom?" said Kovrin in confusion. "Why, to him. . . . He is sitting here," he said, pointing to the black monk.

"There is no one here . . . no one! Andryusha, you are ill!"

Tanya put her arm round her husband and held him tight, as

though protecting him from the apparition, and put her hand over his eyes.

"You are ill!" she sobbed, trembling all over. "Forgive me, my precious, my dear one, but I have noticed for a long time that your mind is clouded in some way. . . . You are mentally ill, Andryusha."

Her trembling infected him, too. He glanced once more at the arm-chair, which was now empty, felt a sudden weakness in his arms and legs, was frightened, and began dressing.

"It s nothing, Tanya; it's nothing," he muttered, shivering. "I really am not quite well . . . it's time to admit that."

"I have noticed it for a long time . . . and father has noticed it," she said, trying to suppress her sobs. "You talk to yourself, smile somehow strangely . . . and can't sleep. Oh, my God, my God, save us!" she said in terror. "But don't be frightened, Andryusha; for God's sake don't be frightened. . . ."

She began dressing, too. Only now, looking at her, Kovrin realised the danger of his position—realised the meaning of the black monk and his conversations with him. It was clear to him now that he was mad.

Neither of them knew why they dressed and went into the dining-room: she in front and he following her. There they found Yegor Semyonitch standing in his dressing-gown and with a candle in his hand. He was staying with them, and had been awakened by Tanya's sobs.

"Don't be frightened, Andryusha," Tanya was saying, shivering as though in a fever; "don't be frightened. . . . Father, it will all pass over . . . it will all pass over. . . ."

Kovrin was too much agitated to speak. He wanted to say to his father-in-law in a playful tone: "Congratulate me; it appears I have gone out of my mind"; but he could only move his lips and smile bitterly.

At nine o'clock in the morning they put on his jacket and fur coat, wrapped him up in a shawl, and took him in a carriage to a doctor.

VIII

Summer had come again, and the doctor advised their going into the country. Kovrin had recovered; he had left off seeing the black monk, and he had only to get up his strength. Staying at his father-in-law's, he drank a great deal of milk, worked for only two hours out of the twenty-four, and neither smoked nor drank wine.

On the evening before Elijah's Day they had an evening service in the house. When the deacon was handing the priest the censer the immense old room smelt like a graveyard, and Kovrin felt bored. He went out into the garden. Without noticing the gorgeous flowers, he walked about the garden, sat down on a seat, then strolled about the park; reaching the river, he went down and then stood lost in thought, looking at the water. The sullen pines with their shaggy roots, which had seen him a year before so young, so joyful and confident, were not whispering now, but standing mute and motionless, as though they did not recognise him. And, indeed, his head was closely cropped, his beautiful long hair was gone, his step was lagging, his face was fuller and paler than last summer.

He crossed by the footbridge to the other side. Where the year before there had been rye the oats stood, reaped, and lay in rows. The sun had set and there was a broad stretch of glowing red on the horizon, a sign of windy weather next day. It was still. Looking in the direction from which the year before the black monk had first appeared, Kovrin stood for twenty minutes, till the evening glow had begun to fade. . . .

When, listless and dissatisfied, he returned home the service was over. Yegor Semyonitch and Tanya were sitting on the steps of the verandah, drinking tea. They were talking of something, but, seeing Kovrin, ceased at once, and he concluded from their faces that their talk had been about him.

"I believe it is time for you to have your milk," Tanya said to her husband.

"No, it is not time yet . . ." he said, sitting down on the bottom step. "Drink it yourself; I don't want it."

Tanya exchanged a troubled glance with her father, and said in a guilty voice:

"You notice yourself that milk does you good."

"Yes, a great deal of good!" Kovrin laughed. "I congratulate you: I have gained a pound in weight since Friday." He pressed his head tightly in his hands and said miserably: "Why, why have you cured me? Preparations of bromide, idleness, hot baths, supervision, cowardly consternation at every mouthful, at every step—all this will reduce me at last to idiocy. I went out of my mind, I had megalomania; but then

I was cheerful, confident, and even happy; I was interesting and original. Now I have become more sensible and stolid, but I am just like every one else: I am—mediocrity; I am weary of life. . . . Oh, how cruelly you have treated me! . . . I saw hallucinations, but what harm did that do to any one? I ask, what harm did that do any one?"

"Goodness knows what you are saying!" sighed Yegor Semyonitch. "It's positively wearisome to listen to it."

"Then don't listen."

The presence of other people, especially Yegor Semyonitch, irritated Kovrin now; he answered him drily, coldly, and even rudely, never looked at him but with irony and hatred, while Yegor Semyonitch was overcome with confusion and cleared his throat guiltily, though he was not conscious of any fault in himself. At a loss to understand why their charming and affectionate relations had changed so abruptly, Tanya huddled up to her father and looked anxiously in his face; she wanted to understand and could not understand, and all that was clear to her was that their relations were growing worse and worse every day, that of late her father had begun to look much older, and her husband had grown irritable, capricious, quarrelsome and uninteresting. She could not laugh or sing; at dinner she ate nothing; did not sleep for nights together, expecting something awful, and was so worn out that on one occasion she lay in a dead faint from dinner-time till evening. During the service she thought her father was crying, and now while the three of them were sitting together on the terrace she made an effort not to think of it.

"How fortunate Buddha, Mahomed, and Shakespeare were that their kind relations and doctors did not cure them of their ecstasy and their inspiration," said Kovrin. "If Mahomed had taken bromide for his nerves, had worked only two hours out of the twenty-four, and had drunk milk, that remarkable man would have left no more trace after him than his dog. Doctors and kind relations will succeed in stupefying mankind, in making mediocrity pass for genius and in bringing civilisation to ruin. If only you knew," Kovrin said with annoyance, "how grateful I am to you."

He felt intense irritation, and to avoid saying too much, he got up quickly and went into the house. It was still, and the fragrance of the tobacco plant and the marvel of Peru floated in at the open window. The moonlight lay in green patches on the floor and on the piano in the big dark dining-room. Kovrin remembered the raptures of the previous summer when there had been the same scent of the marvel of Peru and the moon had shone in at the window. To bring back the mood of last year he went quickly to his study, lighted a strong cigar, and told the footman to bring him some wine. But the cigar left a bitter and disgusting taste in his mouth, and the wine had not the same flavour as it had the year before. And so great is the effect of giving up a habit, the cigar and the two gulps of wine made him giddy, and brought on palpitations of the heart, so that he was obliged to take bromide.

Before going to bed, Tanya said to him:

"Father adores you. You are cross with him about something, and it is killing him. Look at him; he is aging, not from day to day, but from hour to hour. I entreat you, Andryusha, for God's sake, for the sake of your dead father, for the sake of my peace of mind, be affectionate to him."

"I can't, I don't want to."

"But why?" asked Tanya, beginning to tremble all over. "Explain why."

"Because he is antipathetic to me, that's all," said Kovrin carelessly; and he shrugged his shoulders. "But we won't talk about him: he is your father."

"I can't understand, I can't," said Tanya, pressing her hands to her temples and staring at a fixed point. "Something incomprehensible, awful, is going on in the house. You have changed, grown unlike yourself. . . . You, clever, extraordinary man as you are, are irritated over trifles, meddle in paltry nonsense. . . . Such trivial things excite you, that sometimes one is simply amazed and can't believe that it is you. Come, come, don't be angry, don't be angry," she went on, kissing his hands, frightened of her own words. "You are clever, kind, noble. You will be just to father. He is so good."

"He is not good; he is just good-natured. Burlesque old uncles like your father, with well-fed, good-natured faces, extraordinarily hospitable and queer, at one time used to touch me and amuse me in novels and in farces and in life; now I dislike them. They are egoists to the marrow of their bones. What disgusts me most of all is their being so well-fed, and that purely bovine, purely hoggish optimism of a full stomach."

Tanya sat down on the bed and laid her head on the pillow.

"This is torture," she said, and from her voice it was evident that she was utterly exhausted, and that it was hard for her to speak. "Not one moment of peace since the winter. . . . Why, it's awful! My God! I am wretched."

"Oh, of course, I am Herod, and you and your father are the innocents. Of course."

His face seemed to Tanya ugly and unpleasant. Hatred and an ironical expression did not suit him. And, indeed, she had noticed before that there was something lacking in his face, as though ever since his hair had been cut his face had changed, too. She wanted to say something wounding to him, but immediately she caught herself in this antagonistic feeling, she was frightened and went out of the bedroom.

IX

Kovrin received a professorship at the University. The inaugural address was fixed for the second of December, and a notice to that effect was hung up in the corridor at the University. But on the day appointed he informed the students' inspector, by telegram, that he was prevented by illness from giving the lecture.

He had hæmorrhages from the throat. He was often spitting blood, but it happened two or three times a month that there was a considerable loss of blood, and then he grew extremely weak and sank into a drowsy condition. This illness did not particularly frighten him, as he knew that his mother had lived for ten years or longer suffering from the same disease, and the doctors assured him that there was no danger, and had only advised him to avoid excitement, to lead a regular life, and to speak as little as possible.

In January again his lecture did not take place owing to the same reason, and in February it was too late to begin the course. It had to be postponed to the following year.

By now he was living not with Tanya, but with another woman, who was two years older than he was, and who looked after him as though he were a baby. He was in a calm and tranquil state of mind; he readily gave in to her, and when Varvara Nikolaevna—that was the name of his friend—decided to take him to the Crimea, he agreed, though he had a presentiment that no good would come of the trip.

They reached Sevastopol in the evening and stopped at an hotel to rest and go on the next day to Yalta. They were both exhausted by the journey. Varvara Nikolaevna had some tea, went to bed and was soon asleep. But Kovrin did not go to bed. An hour before starting for the station, he had received a letter from Tanya, and had not brought himself to open it, and now it was lying in his coat pocket, and the thought of it excited him disagreeably. At the bottom of his heart he genuinely considered now that his marriage to Tanya had been a mistake. He was glad that their separation was final, and the thought of that woman who in the end had turned into a living relic, still walking about though everything seemed dead in her except her big, staring, intelligent eyes—the thought of her roused in him nothing but pity and disgust with himself. The handwriting on the envelope reminded him how cruel and unjust he had been two years before, how he had worked off his anger at his spiritual emptiness, his boredom, his loneliness, and his dissatisfaction with life by revenging himself on people in no way to blame. He remembered, also, how he had torn up his dissertation and all the articles he had written during his illness, and how he had thrown them out of window, and the bits of paper had fluttered in the wind and caught on the trees and flowers. In every line of them he saw strange, utterly groundless pretension, shallow defiance, arrogance, megalomania; and they made him feel as though he were reading a description of his vices. But when the last manuscript had been torn up and sent flying out of window, he felt, for some reason, suddenly bitter and angry; he went to his wife and said a great many unpleasant things to her. My God, how he had tormented her! One day, wanting to cause her pain, he told her that her father had played a very unattractive part in their romance, that he had asked him to marry her. Yegor Semyonitch accidentally overheard this, ran into the room, and, in his despair, could not utter a word, could only stamp and make a strange, bellowing sound as though he had lost the power of speech, and Tanya, looking at her father, had uttered a heart-rending shriek and had fallen into a swoon. It was hideous.

All this came back into his memory as he looked at the familiar writing. Kovrin went out on to the balcony; it was still warm weather and there was a smell of the sea. The wonderful bay reflected the moonshine and the lights, and was of a colour for which it was difficult to find a name. It was a soft and tender blending of dark blue and green; in places the water was like blue vitriol, and in places it seemed as though the moonlight were liquefied and filling the bay instead of water. And what harmony of colours, what an atmosphere of peace, calm, and sublimity!

In the lower storey under the balcony the windows were probably open, for women's voices and laughter could be heard distinctly. Apparently there was an evening party.

Kovrin made an effort, tore open the envelope, and, going back into his room, read:

"My father is just dead. I owe that to you, for you have killed him. Our garden is being ruined; strangers are managing it already—that is, the very thing is happening that poor father dreaded. That, too, I owe to you. I hate you with my whole soul, and I hope you may soon perish. Oh, how wretched I am! Insufferable anguish is burning my soul. . . . My curses on you. I took you for an extraordinary man, a genius; I loved you, and you have turned out a madman. . . ."

Kovrin could read no more, he tore up the letter and threw it away. He was overcome by an uneasiness that was akin to terror. Varvara Nikolaevna was asleep behind the screen, and he could hear her breathing. From the lower storey came the sounds of laughter and women's voices, but he felt as though in the whole hotel there were no living soul but him. Because Tanya, unhappy, broken by sorrow, had cursed him in her letter and hoped for his perdition, he felt eerie and kept glancing hurriedly at the door, as though he were afraid that the uncomprehended force which two years before had wrought such havoc in his life and in the life of those near him might come into the room and master him once more.

He knew by experience that when his nerves were out of hand the best thing for him to do was to work. He must sit down to the table and force himself, at all costs, to concentrate his mind on some one thought. He took from his red portfolio a manuscript containing a sketch of a small work of the nature of a compilation, which he had planned in case he should find it dull in the Crimea without work. He sat down to the table and began working at this plan, and it seemed to him that his calm, peaceful, indifferent mood was coming back. The manuscript with the sketch even led him to meditation on the vanity of the world. He thought how much life exacts for the worthless or very commonplace blessings it can give a man. For instance, to gain, before forty, a university chair, to be an ordinary professor, to expound ordinary and secondhand thoughts in dull, heavy, insipid language—in fact, to gain the position of a mediocre learned man, he, Kovrin, had had to study for fifteen years, to work day and night, to endure a terrible mental illness, to experience an unhappy marriage, and to do a great number of stupid and unjust things which it would have been pleasant not to remember. Kovrin recognised clearly, now, that he was a mediocrity, and readily resigned himself to it, as he considered that every man ought to be satisfied with what he is.

The plan of the volume would have soothed him completely, but the torn letter showed white on the floor and prevented him from concentrating his attention. He got up from the table, picked up the pieces of the letter and threw them out of window, but there was a light wind blowing from the sea, and the bits of paper were scattered on the window-sill. Again he was overcome by uneasiness akin to terror, and he felt as though in the whole hotel there were no living soul but himself. . . . He went out on the balcony. The bay, like a living thing, looked at him with its multitude of light blue, dark blue, turquoise and fiery eyes, and seemed beckoning to him. And it really was hot and oppressive, and it would not have been amiss to have a bathe.

Suddenly in the lower storey under the balcony a violin began playing, and two soft feminine voices began singing. It was something familiar. The song was about a maiden, full of sick fancies, who heard one night in her garden mysterious sounds, so strange and lovely that she was obliged to recognise them as a holy harmony which is unintelligible to us mortals, and so flies back to heaven. . . . Kovrin caught his breath and there was a pang of sadness at his heart, and a thrill of the sweet, exquisite delight he had so long forgotten began to stir in his breast.

A tall black column, like a whirlwind or a waterspout, appeared on the further side of the bay. It moved with fearful rapidity across the bay, towards the hotel, growing smaller and darker as it came, and Kovrin only just had time to get out of the way to let it pass. . . . The monk with bare grey head, black eyebrows, barefoot, his arms crossed over his breast, floated by him, and stood still in the middle of the room.

"Why did you not believe me?" he asked reproachfully, looking affectionately at Kovrin. "If you had believed me then, that you were a genius, you would not have spent these two years so gloomily and so wretchedly."

Kovrin already believed that he was one of God's chosen and a genius; he vividly recalled his conversations with the monk in the past and tried to speak, but the blood flowed from his throat on to his breast, and not knowing what he was doing, he passed his hands over his breast, and his cuffs were soaked with blood. He tried to call Varvara Nikolaevna, who was asleep behind the screen; he made an effort and said:

"Tanya!"

He fell on the floor, and propping himself on his arms, called again:

"Tanya!"

He called Tanya, called to the great garden with the gorgeous flowers sprinkled with dew, called to the park, the pines with their shaggy roots, the rye-field, his marvellous learning, his youth, courage, joy—called to life, which was so lovely. He saw on the floor near his face a great pool of blood, and was too weak to utter a word, but an unspeakable, infinite happiness flooded his whole being. Below, under the balcony, they were playing the serenade, and the black monk whispered to him that he was a genius, and that he was dying only because his frail human body had lost its balance and could no longer serve as the mortal garb of genius.

When Varvara Nikolaevna woke up and came out from behind the screen, Kovrin was dead, and a blissful smile was set upon his face.

1894

A Woman's Kingdom

I

Christmas Eve

Here was a thick roll of notes. It came from the bailiff at the forest villa; he wrote that he was sending fifteen hundred roubles, which he had been awarded as damages, having won an appeal. Anna Akimovna disliked and feared such words as "awarded damages" and "won the suit." She knew that it was impossible to do without the law, but for some reason, whenever Nazaritch, the manager of the factory, or the bailiff of her villa in the country, both of whom frequently went to law, used to win lawsuits of some sort for her benefit, she always felt uneasy and, as it were, ashamed. On this occasion, too, she felt uneasy and awkward, and wanted to put that fifteen hundred roubles further away that it might be out of her sight.

She thought with vexation that other girls of her age—she was in her twenty-sixth year—were now busy looking after their households, were weary and would sleep sound, and would wake up tomorrow morning in holiday mood; many of them had long been married and had children. Only she, for some reason, was compelled to sit like an old woman over these letters, to make notes upon them, to write answers, then to do nothing the whole evening till midnight, but wait till she was sleepy; and tomorrow they would all day long be coming with Christmas greetings and asking for favours; and the day after tomorrow there would certainly be some scandal at the factory—some one would be beaten or would die of drinking too much vodka, and she would be fretted by pangs of conscience; and after the holidays Nazaritch would turn off some twenty of the workpeople for absence from work, and all of the twenty would hang about at the front door, without their caps on, and she would be ashamed to go out to them, and they would be driven away like dogs. And all her acquaintances would say behind her back, and write to her in anonymous letters, that she was a millionaire and exploiter—that she was devouring other men's lives and sucking the blood of the workers.

Here there lay a heap of letters read through and laid aside already. They were all begging letters. They were from people who were hungry, drunken, dragged down by large families, sick, degraded, despised. . . . Anna Akimovna had already noted on each letter, three roubles to be paid to one, five to another; these letters would go the same day to the office, and next the distribution of assistance would take place, or, as the clerks used to say, the beasts would be fed.

They would distribute also in small sums four hundred and seventy roubles—the interest on a sum bequeathed by the late Akim Ivanovitch for the relief of the poor and needy. There would be a hideous crush. From the gates to the doors of the office there would stretch a long file of strange people with brutal faces, in rags, numb with cold, hungry and already drunk, in husky voices calling down blessings upon Anna Akimovna, their benefactress, and her parents: those at the back would press upon those in front, and those in front would abuse them with bad language. The clerk would get tired of the noise, the swearing, and the sing-song whining and blessing; would fly out and give some one a box on the ear to the delight of all. And her own people, the factory hands, who received nothing at Christmas but their wages, and had already spent every farthing of it, would stand in the middle of the yard, looking on and laughing—some enviously, others ironically.

"Merchants, and still more their wives, are fonder of beggars than they are of their own workpeople," thought Anna Akimovna. "It's always so."

Her eye fell upon the roll of money. It would be nice to distribute that hateful, useless money among the workpeople tomorrow, but it did not do to give the workpeople anything for nothing, or they would demand it again next time. And what would be the good of fifteen hundred roubles when there were eighteen hundred workmen in the factory besides their wives and children? Or she might, perhaps, pick out one of the writers of those begging letters—some luckless man who had long ago lost all hope of anything better— and give him the fifteen hundred. The money would come upon the poor creature like a thun-

der-clap, and perhaps for the first time in his life he would feel happy.
This idea struck Anna Akimovna as original and amusing, and it fascinated her. She took one letter at random out of the pile and read it.
Some petty official called Tchalikov had long been out of a situation,
was ill, and living in Gushtchin's Buildings; his wife was in consumption, and he had five little girls. Anna Akimovna knew well the four-
storeyed house, Gushtchin's Buildings, in which Tchalikov lived. Oh, it
was a horrid, foul, unhealthy house!

"Well, I will give it to that Tchalikov," she decided. "I won't send
it; I had better take it myself to prevent unnecessary talk. Yes," she
reflected, as she put the fifteen hundred roubles in her pocket, "and I'll
have a look at them, and perhaps I can do something for the little
girls."

She felt light-hearted; she rang the bell and ordered the horses to
be brought round.

When she got into the sledge it was past six o'clock in the evening.
The windows in all the blocks of buildings were brightly lighted up,
and that made the huge courtyard seem very dark: at the gates, and at
the far end of the yard near the warehouses and the workpeople's barracks, electric lamps were gleaming.

Anna Akimovna disliked and feared those huge dark buildings,
warehouses, and barracks where the workmen lived. She had only once
been in the main building since her father's death. The high ceilings
with iron girders; the multitude of huge, rapidly turning wheels, con-
necting straps and levers; the shrill hissing; the clank of steel; the rattle of the trolleys; the harsh puffing of steam; the faces—pale, crimson,
or black with coal-dust; the shirts soaked with sweat; the gleam of steel,
of copper, and of fire; the smell of oil and coal; and the draught, at
times very hot and at times very cold—gave her an impression of hell.
It seemed to her as though the wheels, the levers, and the hot hissing
cylinders were trying to tear themselves away from their fastenings to
crush the men, while the men, not hearing one another, ran about with
anxious faces, and busied themselves about the machines, trying to stop
their terrible movement. They showed Anna Akimovna something and
respectfully explained it to her. She remembered how in the forge a
piece of red-hot iron was pulled out of the furnace; and how an old
man with a strap round his head, and another, a young man in a blue
shirt with a chain on his breast, and an angry face, probably one of the

foremen, struck the piece of iron with hammers; and how the golden sparks had been scattered in all directions; and how, a little afterwards, they had dragged out a huge piece of sheet-iron with a clang. The old man had stood erect and smiled, while the young man had wiped his face with his sleeve and explained something to her. And she remembered, too, how in another department an old man with one eye had been filing a piece of iron, and how the iron filings were scattered about; and how a red-haired man in black spectacles, with holes in his shirt, had been working at a lathe, making something out of a piece of steel: the lathe roared and hissed and squeaked, and Anna Akimovna felt sick at the sound, and it seemed as though they were boring into her ears. She looked, listened, did not understand, smiled graciously, and felt ashamed. To get hundreds of thousands of roubles from a business which one does not understand and cannot like—how strange it is!

And she had not once been in the workpeople's barracks. There, she was told, it was damp; there were bugs, debauchery, anarchy. It was an astonishing thing: a thousand roubles were spent annually on keeping the barracks in good order, yet, if she were to believe the anonymous letters, the condition of the workpeople was growing worse and worse every year.

"There was more order in my father's day," thought Anna Akimovna, as she drove out of the yard, "because he had been a workman himself. I know nothing about it and only do silly things."

She felt depressed again, and was no longer glad that she had come, and the thought of the lucky man upon whom fifteen hundred roubles would drop from heaven no longer struck her as original and amusing. To go to some Tchalikov or other, when at home a business worth a million was gradually going to pieces and being ruined, and the workpeople in the barracks were living worse than convicts, meant doing something silly and cheating her conscience. Along the highroad and across the fields near it, workpeople from the neighbouring cotton and paper factories were walking towards the lights of the town. There was the sound of talk and laughter in the frosty air. Anna Akimovna looked at the women and young people, and she suddenly felt a longing for a plain rough life among a crowd. She recalled vividly that faraway time when she used to be called Anyutka, when she was a little girl and used to lie under the same quilt with her mother, while a washerwoman who lodged with them used to wash clothes in the next room;

while through the thin walls there came from the neighbouring flats sounds of laughter, swearing, children's crying, the accordion, and the whirr of carpenters' lathes and sewing-machines; while her father, Akim Ivanovitch, who was clever at almost every craft, would be soldering something near the stove, or drawing or planing, taking no notice whatever of the noise and stuffiness. And she longed to wash, to iron, to run to the shop and the tavern as she used to do every day when she lived with her mother. She ought to have been a work-girl and not the factory owner! Her big house with its chandeliers and pictures; her footman Mishenka, with his glossy moustache and swallow-tail coat; the devout and dignified Varvarushka, and smooth-tongued Agafyushka; and the young people of both sexes who came almost every day to ask her for money, and with whom she always for some reason felt guilty; and the clerks, the doctors, and the ladies who were charitable at her expense, who flattered her and secretly despised her for her humble origin—how wearisome and alien it all was to her!

Here was the railway crossing and the city gate; then came houses alternating with kitchen gardens; and at last the broad street where stood the renowned Gushtchin's Buildings. The street, usually quiet, was now on Christmas Eve full of life and movement. The eating-houses and beer-shops were noisy. If some one who did not belong to that quarter but lived in the centre of the town had driven through the street now, he would have noticed nothing but dirty, drunken, and abusive people; but Anna Akimovna, who had lived in those parts all her life, was constantly recognizing in the crowd her own father or mother or uncle. Her father was a soft fluid character, a little fantastical, frivolous, and irresponsible. He did not care for money, respectability, or power; he used to say that a working man had no time to keep the holy-days and go to church; and if it had not been for his wife, he would probably never have gone to confession, taken the sacrament or kept the fasts. While her uncle, Ivan Ivanovitch, on the contrary, was like flint; in everything relating to religion, politics, and morality, he was harsh and relentless, and kept a strict watch, not only over himself, but also over all his servants and acquaintances. God forbid that one should go into his room without crossing oneself before the ikon! The luxurious mansion in which Anna Akimovna now lived he had always kept locked up, and only opened it on great holidays for important visitors, while he lived himself in the office, in a little room covered with ikons. He had leanings towards the Old Believers, and was continually entertaining priests and bishops of the old ritual, though he had been christened, and married, and had buried his wife in accordance with the Orthodox rites. He disliked Akim, his only brother and his heir, for his frivolity, which he called simpleness and folly, and for his indifference to religion. He treated him as inferior, kept him in the position of a workman, paid him sixteen roubles a month. Akim addressed his brother with formal respect, and on the days of asking forgiveness, he and his wife and daughter bowed down to the ground before him. But three years before his death Ivan Ivanovitch had drawn closer to his brother, forgave his shortcomings, and ordered him to get a governess for Anyutka.

There was a dark, deep, evil-smelling archway under Gushtchin's Buildings; there was a sound of men coughing near the walls. Leaving the sledge in the street, Anna Akimovna went in at the gate and there inquired how to get to No. 46 to see a clerk called Tchalikov. She was directed to the furthest door on the right in the third storey. And in the courtyard and near the outer door, and even on the stairs, there was still the same loathesome smell as under the archway. In Anna Aki-movna's childhood, when her father was a simple workman, she used to live in a building like that, and afterwards, when their circumstances were different, she had often visited them in the character of a Lady Bountiful. The narrow stone staircase with its steep dirty steps, with landings at every story; the greasy swinging lanterns; the stench; the troughs, pots, and rags on the landings near the doors,—all this had been familiar to her long ago. . . . One door was open, and within could be seen Jewish tailors in caps, sewing. Anna Akimovna met people on the stairs, but it never entered her head that people might be rude to her. She was no more afraid of peasants or workpeople, drunk or sober, than of her acquaintances of the educated class.

There was no entry at No. 46; the door opened straight into the kitchen. As a rule the dwellings of workmen and mechanics smell of varnish, tar, hides, smoke, according to the occupation of the tenant; the dwellings of persons of noble or official class who have come to poverty may be known by a peculiar rancid, sour smell. This disgusting smell enveloped Anna Akimovna on all sides, and as yet she was only on the threshold. A man in a black coat, no doubt Tchalikov himself, was sitting in a corner at the table with his back to the door, and with him were five little girls. The eldest, a broad-faced thin girl with a comb in her hair, looked about fifteen, while the youngest, a chubby child with hair that stood up like a hedge-hog, was not more than three. All the six were eating. Near the stove stood a very thin little woman with a yellow face, far gone in pregnancy. She was wearing a skirt and a white blouse, and had an oven fork in her hand.

"I did not expect you to be so disobedient, Liza," the man was saying reproachfully. "Fie, fie, for shame! Do you want papa to whip you—eh?"

Seeing an unknown lady in the doorway, the thin woman started, and put down the fork.

"Vassily Nikititch!" she cried, after a pause, in a hollow voice, as though she could not believe her eyes.

The man looked round and jumped up. He was a flat-chested, bony man with narrow shoulders and sunken temples. His eyes were small and hollow with dark rings round them, he had a wide mouth, and a long nose like a bird's beak—a little bit bent to the right. His beard was parted in the middle, his moustache was shaven, and this made him look more like a hired footman than a government clerk.

"Does Mr. Tchalikov live here?" asked Anna Akimovna.

"Yes, madam," Tchalikov answered severely, but immediately recognizing Anna Akimovna, he cried: "Anna Akimovna!" and all at once he gasped and clasped his hands as though in terrible alarm. "Benefactress!"

With a moan he ran to her, grunting inarticulately as though he were paralyzed—there was cabbage on his beard and he smelt of vodka—pressed his forehead to her muff, and seemed as though he were in a swoon.

"Your hand, your holy hand!" he brought out breathlessly. "It's a dream, a glorious dream! Children, awaken me!"

He turned towards the table and said in a sobbing voice, shaking his fists:

"Providence has heard us! Our saviour, our angel, has come! We are saved! Children, down on your knees! on your knees !"

Madame Tchalikov and the little girls, except the youngest one, began for some reason rapidly clearing the table.

"You wrote that your wife was very ill," said Anna Akimovna, and she felt ashamed and annoyed. "I am not going to give them the fifteen hundred," she thought.

"Here she is, my wife," said Tchalikov in a thin feminine voice, as though his tears had gone to his head. "Here she is, unhappy creature! With one foot in the grave! But we do not complain, madam. Better death than such a life. Better die, unhappy woman!"

"Why is he playing these antics?" thought Anna Akimovna with annoyance. "One can see at once he is used to dealing with merchants."

"Speak to me like a human being," she said. "I don't care for farces."

"Yes, madam; five bereaved children round their mother's coffin with funeral candles—that's a farce? Eh?" said Tchalikov bitterly, and turned away.

"Hold your tongue," whispered his wife, and she pulled at his sleeve. "The place has not been tidied up, madam," she said, addressing Anna Akimovna; "please excuse it . . . you know what it is where there are children. A crowded hearth, but harmony."

"I am not going to give them the fifteen hundred," Anna Akimovna thought again.

And to escape as soon as possible from these people and from the sour smell, she brought out her purse and made up her mind to leave them twenty-five roubles, not more; but she suddenly felt ashamed that she had come so far and disturbed people for so little.

"If you give me paper and ink, I will write at once to a doctor who is a friend mine to come and see you," she said, flushing red. "He is a very good doctor. And I will leave you some money for medicine."

Madame Tchalikov was hastening to wipe the table.

"It's messy here! What are you doing?" hissed Tchalikov, looking at her wrathfully. "Take her to the lodger's room! I make bold to ask you, madam, to step into the lodger's room," he said, addressing Anna Akimovna. "It's clean there."

"Osip Ilyitch told us not to go into his room!" said one of the little girls, sternly.

But they had already led Anna Akimovna out of the kitchen, through a narrow passage room between two bedsteads: it was evident from the arrangement of the beds that in one two slept lengthwise, and in the other three slept across the bed. In the lodger's room, that came next, it really was clean. A neat-looking bed with a red woollen quilt, a pillow in a white pillow-case, even a slipper for the watch, a table covered with a hempen cloth and on it, an inkstand of milky-looking glass, pens, paper, photographs in frames—everything as it ought to be; and another table for rough work, on which lay tidily arranged a watchmaker's tools and watches taken to pieces. On the walls hung hammers, pliers, awls, chisels, nippers, and so on, and there were three hanging clocks which were ticking; one was a big clock with thick weights, such as one sees in eating-houses.

As she sat down to write the letter, Anna Akimovna saw facing her on the table the photographs of her father and of herself. That surprised her.

"Who lives here with you?" she asked.

"Our lodger, madam, Pimenov. He works in your factory."

"Oh, I thought he must be a watchmaker."

"He repairs watches privately, in his leisure hours. He is an amateur."

After a brief silence during which nothing could be heard but the ticking of the clocks and the scratching of the pen on the paper, Tchalikov heaved a sigh and said ironically, with indignation:

"It's a true saying: gentle birth and a grade in the service won't put a coat on your back. A cockade in your cap and a noble title, but nothing to eat. To my thinking, if any one of humble class helps the poor he is much more of a gentleman than any Tchalikov who has sunk into poverty and vice."

To flatter Anna Akimovna, he uttered a few more disparaging phrases about his gentle birth, and it was evident that he was humbling himself because he considered himself superior to her. Meanwhile she had finished her letter and had sealed it up. The letter would be thrown away and the money would not be spent on medicine—that she knew, but she put twenty-five roubles on the table all the same, and after a moment's thought, added two more red notes. She saw the wasted, yellow hand of Madame Tchalikov, like the claw of a hen, dart out and clutch the money tight.

"You have graciously given this for medicine," said Tchalikov in a quivering voice, "but hold out a helping hand to me also . . . and the children!" he added with a sob. "My unhappy children! I am not afraid for myself; it is for my daughters I fear! It's the hydra of vice that I fear!"

Trying to open her purse, the catch of which had gone wrong, Anna Akimovna was confused and turned red. She felt ashamed that people should be standing before her, looking at her hands and waiting, and most likely at the bottom of their hearts laughing at her. At that instant some one came into the kitchen and stamped his feet, knocking the snow off.

"The lodger has come in," said Madame Tchalikov.

Anna Akimovna grew even more confused. She did not want any one from the factory to find her in this ridiculous position. As ill-luck would have it, the lodger came in at the very moment when, having broken the catch at last, she was giving Tchalikov some notes, and Tchalikov, grunting as though he were paralyzed, was feeling about with his lips where he could kiss her. In the lodger she recognized the workman who had once clanked the sheet-iron before her in the forge, and had explained things to her. Evidently he had come in straight from the factory; his face looked dark and grimy, and on one cheek near his nose was a smudge of soot. His hands were perfectly black, and his unbelted shirt shone with oil and grease. He was a man of thirty, of medium height, with black hair and broad shoulders, and a look of great physical strength. At the first glance Anna Akimovna perceived that he must be a foreman, who must be receiving at least thirty-five roubles a month, and a stern, loud-voiced man who struck the workmen in the face; all this was evident from his manner of standing, from the attitude he involuntarily assumed at once on seeing a lady in his room, and most of all from the fact that he did not wear top-boots, that he had breast pockets, and a pointed, picturesquely clipped beard. Her father, Akim Ivanovitch, had been the brother of the factory owner, and yet he had been afraid of foremen like this lodger and had tried to win their favour.

"Excuse me for having come in here in your absence," said Anna Akimovna.

The workman looked at her in surprise, smiled in confusion and did not speak.

"You must speak a little louder, madam . . ." said Tchalikov softly. "When Mr. Pimenov comes home from the factory in the evenings he is a little hard of hearing."

But Anna Akimovna was by now relieved that there was nothing more for her to do here; she nodded to them and went rapidly out of the room. Pimenov went to see her out.

"Have you been long in our employment?" she asked in a loud voice, without turning to him.

"From nine years old. I entered the factory in your uncle's time."

"That's a long while! My uncle and my father knew all the workpeople, and I know hardly any of them. I had seen you before, but I did not know your name was Pimenov."

Anna Akimovna felt a desire to justify herself before him, to pretend that she had just given the money not seriously, but as a joke.

"Oh, this poverty," she sighed. "We give charity on holidays and working days, and still there is no sense in it. I believe it is useless to help such people as this Tchalikov."

"Of course it is useless," he agreed. "However much you give him, he will drink it all away. And now the husband and wife will be snatching it from one another and fighting all night," he added with a laugh.

"Yes, one must admit that our philanthropy is useless, boring, and absurd. But still, you must agree, one can't sit with one's hand in one's lap; one must do something. What's to be done with the Tchalikovs, for instance?"

She turned to Pimenov and stopped, expecting an answer from him; he, too, stopped and slowly, without speaking, shrugged his shoulders. Obviously he knew what to do with the Tchalikovs, but the treatment would have been so coarse and inhuman that he did not venture to put it into words. And the Tchalikovs were to him so utterly uninteresting and worthless, that a moment later he had forgotten them; looking into Anna Akimovna's eyes, he smiled with pleasure, and his face wore an expression as though he were dreaming about something very pleasant. Only, now standing close to him, Anna Akimovna saw from his face, and especially from his eyes, how exhausted and sleepy he was.

"Here, I ought to give him the fifteen hundred roubles!" she thought, but for some reason this idea seemed to her incongruous and insulting to Pimenov.

"I am sure you are aching all over after your work, and you come to the door with me," she said as they went down the stairs. "Go home."

But he did not catch her words. When they came out into the street, he ran on ahead, unfastened the cover of the sledge, and helping Anna Akimovna in, said:

"I wish you a happy Christmas!"

II

Christmas Morning

"They have left off ringing ever so long! It's dreadful; you won't be there before the service is over! Get up!"

"Two horses are racing, racing . . ." said Anna Akimovna, and she woke up; before her, candle in hand, stood her maid, red-haired Masha. "Well, what is it?"

"Service is over already," said Masha with despair. "I have called you three times! Sleep till evening for me, but you told me yourself to call you!"

Anna Akimovna raised herself on her elbow and glanced towards the window. It was still quite dark outside, and only the lower edge of the window-frame was white with snow. She could hear a low, mellow chime of bells; it was not the parish church, but somewhere further away. The watch on the little table showed three minutes past six.

"Very well, Masha. . . . In three minutes . . ." said Anna Akimovna in an imploring voice, and she snuggled under the bed-clothes.

She imagined the snow at the front door, the sledge, the dark sky, the crowd in the church, and the smell of juniper, and she felt dread at the thought; but all the same, she made up her mind that she would get up at once and go to early service. And while she was warm in bed and struggling with sleep—which seems, as though to spite one, particularly sweet when one ought to get up—and while she had visions of an immense garden on a mountain and then Gushtchin's Buildings, she was worried all the time by the thought that she ought to get up that very minute and go to church.

But when she got up it was quite light, and it turned out to be half-past nine. There had been a heavy fall of snow in the night; the trees were clothed in white, and the air was particularly light, transparent, and tender, so that when Anna Akimovna looked out of the window her first impulse was to draw a deep, deep breath. And when she had washed, a relic of far-away childish feelings—joy that today was Christmas—suddenly stirred within her; after that she felt light-hearted, free and pure in soul, as though her soul, too, had been washed or plunged in the white snow. Masha came in, dressed up and tightly laced, and wished her a happy Christmas; then she spent a long time combing her

312

mistress's hair and helping her to dress. The fragrance and feeling of the new, gorgeous, splendid dress, its faint rustle, and the smell of fresh scent, excited Anna Akimovna.

"Well, it's Christmas," she said gaily to Masha. "Now we will try our fortunes."

"Last year, I was to marry an old man. It turned up three times the same."

"Well, God is merciful."

"Well, Anna Akimovna, what I think is, rather than neither one thing nor the other, I'd marry an old man," said Masha mournfully, and she heaved a sigh. "I am turned twenty; it's no joke."

Every one in the house knew that red-haired Masha was in love with Mishenka, the footman, and this genuine, passionate, hopeless love had already lasted three years.

"Come, don't talk nonsense," Anna Akimovna consoled her. "I am going on for thirty, but I am still meaning to marry a young man."

While his mistress was dressing, Mishenka, in a new swallow-tail and polished boots, walked about the hall and drawing-room and waited for her to come out, to wish her a happy Christmas. He had a peculiar walk, stepping softly and delicately; looking at his feet, his hands, and the bend of his head, it might be imagined that he was not simply walking, but learning to dance the first figure of a quadrille. In spite of his fine velvety moustache and handsome, rather flashy appearance, he was steady, prudent, and devout as an old man. He said his prayers, bowing down to the ground, and liked burning incense in his room. He respected people of wealth and rank and had a reverence for them; he despised poor people, and all who came to ask favours of any kind, with all the strength of his cleanly flunkey soul. Under his starched shirt he wore a flannel, winter and summer alike, being very careful of his health; his ears were plugged with cotton-wool.

When Anna Akimovna crossed the hall with Masha, he bent his head downwards a little and said in his disagreeable, honeyed voice:

"I have to congratulate you, Anna Akimovna, on the most solemn feast of the birth of our Lord."

Anna Akimovna gave him five roubles, while poor Masha was numb with ecstasy. His holiday get-up, his attitude, his voice, and what he said, impressed her by their beauty and elegance; as she followed her mistress she could think of nothing, could see nothing, she could only smile, first blissfully, and then bitterly. The upper story of the house was called the best or visitors' half, while the name of the business part—old people's or simply women's part—was given to the rooms on the lower story where Aunt Tatyana Ivanovna kept house. In the upper part the gentry and educated visitors were entertained; in the lower story, simpler folk and the aunt's personal friends. Handsome, plump, and healthy, still young and fresh, and feeling she had on a magnificent dress which seemed to her to diffuse a sort of radiance all about her, Anna Akimovna went down to the lower story. Here she was met with reproaches for forgetting God now that she was so highly educated, for sleeping too late for the service, and for not coming downstairs to break the fast, and they all clasped their hands and exclaimed with perfect sincerity that she was lovely, wonderful; and she believed it, laughed, kissed them, gave one a rouble, another three or five according to their position. She liked being downstairs. Wherever one looked there were shrines, ikons, little lamps, portraits of ecclesiastical personages—the place smelt of monks; there was a rattle of knives in the kitchen, and already a smell of something savoury, exceedingly appetizing, was pervading all the rooms. The yellow-painted floors shone, and from the doors narrow rugs with bright blue stripes ran like little paths to the ikon corner, and the sunshine was simply pouring in at the windows.

In the dining-room some old women, strangers, were sitting; in Varvarushka's room, too, there were old women, and with them a deaf and dumb girl, who seemed abashed about something and kept saying, "Bli, bli! . . ." Two skinny-looking little girls who had been brought to the orphanage for Christmas came up to kiss Anna Akimovna's hand, and stood before her transfixed with admiration of her splendid dress; she noticed that one of the girls squinted, and in the midst of her light-hearted holiday mood she felt a sick pang at her heart at the thought that young men would despise the girl, and that she would never marry. In the cook Agafya's room, five huge peasants in new shirts were sitting round the samovar; these were not workmen from the factory, but relations of the cook. Seeing Anna Akimovna, all the peasants jumped up from their seats, and from regard for decorum, ceased munching, though their mouths were full. The cook Stepan, in a white cap, with a knife in his hand, came into the room and gave her his greetings; porters in high felt boots came in, and they, too, offered their greetings. The water-carrier peeped in with icicles on his beard, but did not venture to come in.

Anna Akimovna walked through the rooms followed by her retinue—the aunt, Varvarushka, Nikandrovna, the sewing-maid Marfa Petrovna, and the downstairs Masha. Varvarushka—a tall, thin, slender woman, taller than any one in the house, dressed all in black, smelling of cypress and coffee—crossed herself in each room before the ikon, bowing down from the waist. And whenever one looked at her one was reminded that she had already prepared her shroud and that lottery tickets were hidden away by her in the same box.

"Anyutinka, be merciful at Christmas," she said, opening the door into the kitchen. "Forgive him, bless the man! Have done with it!"

The coachman Panteley, who had been dismissed for drunkenness in November, was on his knees in the middle of the kitchen. He was a good-natured man, but he used to be unruly when he was drunk, and could not go to sleep, but persisted in wandering about the buildings and shouting in a threatening voice, "I know all about it!" Now from his beefy and bloated face and from his bloodshot eyes it could be seen that he had been drinking continually from November till Christmas.

"Forgive me, Anna Akimovna," he brought out in a hoarse voice, striking his forehead on the floor and showing his bull-like neck.

"It was Auntie dismissed you; ask her."

"What about auntie?" said her aunt, walking into the kitchen, breathing heavily; she was very stout, and on her bosom one might have stood a tray of teacups and a samovar. "What about auntie now? You are mistress here, give your own orders; though these rascals might be all dead for all I care. Come, get up, you hog!" she shouted at Panteley, losing patience. "Get out of my sight! It's the last time I forgive you, but if you transgress again—don't ask for mercy!"

Then they went into the dining-room to coffee. But they had hardly sat down, when the downstairs Masha rushed headlong in, saying with horror, "The singers!" and ran back again. They heard some one blowing his nose, a low bass cough, and footsteps that sounded like horses' iron-shod hoofs tramping about the entry near the hall. For half a minute all was hushed. . . . The singers burst out so suddenly and loudly that every one started. While they were singing, the priest from the almshouses with the deacon and the sexton arrived. Putting on the stole, the priest slowly said that when they were ringing for matins it was snowing and not cold, but that the frost was sharper towards morning, God bless it! and now there must be twenty degrees of frost.

"Many people maintain, though, that winter is healthier than summer," said the deacon; then immediately assumed an austere expression and chanted after the priest. "Thy Birth, O Christ our Lord. . . ."

Soon the priest from the workmen's hospital came with the deacon, then the Sisters from the hospital, children from the orphanage, and then singing could be heard almost uninterruptedly. They sang, had lunch, and went away.

About twenty men from the factory came to offer their Christmas greetings. They were only the foremen, mechanicians, and their assistants, the pattern-makers, the accountant, and so on—all of good appearance, in new black coats. They were all first-rate men, as it were picked men; each one knew his value—that is, knew that if he lost his berth today, people would be glad to take him on at another factory. Evidently they liked Auntie, as they behaved freely in her presence and even smoked, and when they had all trooped in to have something to eat, the accountant put his arm round her immense waist. They were free-and-easy, perhaps, partly also because Varvarushka, who under the old masters had wielded great power and had kept watch over the morals of the clerks, had now no authority whatever in the house; and perhaps because many of them still remembered the time when Auntie Tatyana Ivanovna, whose brothers kept a strict hand over her, had been dressed like a simple peasant woman like Agafya, and when Anna Akimovna used to run about the yard near the factory buildings and every one used to call her Anyutya.

The foremen ate, talked, and kept looking with amazement at Anna Akimovna, how she had grown up and how handsome she had become! But this elegant girl, educated by governesses and teachers, was a stranger to them; they could not understand her, and they instinctively kept closer to "Auntie," who called them by their names, continually pressed them to eat and drink, and, clinking glasses with them, had already drunk two wineglasses of rowan-berry wine with them. Anna Akimovna was always afraid of their thinking her proud, an upstart, or a crow in peacock's feathers; and now while the foremen were crowding round the food, she did not leave the dining-room, but took part in the conversation. She asked Pimenov, her acquaintance of the previous day:

"Why have you so many clocks in your room?"

"I mend clocks," he answered. "I take the work up between times, on holidays, or when I can't sleep."

"So if my watch goes wrong I can bring it to you to be repaired?" Anna Akimovna asked, laughing.

"To be sure, I will do it with pleasure," said Pimenov, and there was an expression of tender devotion in his face, when, not herself knowing why, she unfastened her magnificent watch from its chain and handed it to him; he looked at it in silence and gave it back. "To be sure, I will do it with pleasure," he repeated. "I don't mend watches now. My eyes are weak, and the doctors have forbidden me to do fine work. But for you I can make an exception."

"Doctors talk nonsense," said the accountant. They all laughed. "Don't you believe them," he went on, flattered by the laughing; "last year a tooth flew out of a cylinder and hit old Kalmykov such a crack on the head that you could see his brains, and the doctor said he would die; but he is alive and working to this day, only he has taken to stammering since that mishap."

"Doctors do talk nonsense, they do, but not so much," sighed Auntie. "Pyotr Andreyitch, poor dear, lost his sight. Just like you, he used to work day in day out at the factory near the hot furnace, and he went blind. The eyes don't like heat. But what are we talking about?" she said, rousing herself. "Come and have a drink. My best wishes for Christmas, my dears. I never drink with any one else, but I drink with you, sinful woman as I am. Please God!"

Anna Akimovna fancied that after yesterday Pimenov despised her as a philanthropist, but was fascinated by her as a woman. She looked at him and thought that he behaved very charmingly and was nicely dressed. It is true that the sleeves of his coat were not quite long enough, and the coat itself seemed short-waisted, and his trousers were not wide and fashionable, but his tie was tied carelessly and with taste and was not as gaudy as the others'. And he seemed to be a good-natured man, for he ate submissively whatever Auntie put on his plate. She remembered how black he had been the day before, and how sleepy, and the thought of it for some reason touched her.

When the men were preparing to go, Anna Akimovna put out her hand to Pimenov. She wanted to ask him to come in sometimes to see her, without ceremony, but she did not know how to—her tongue would not obey her; and that they might not think she was attracted by Pimenov, she shook hands with his companions, too.

Then the boys from the school of which she was a patroness came. They all had their heads closely cropped and all wore grey blouses of the same pattern. The teacher—a tall, beardless young man with patches of red on his face—was visibly agitated as he formed the boys into rows; the boys sang in tune, but with harsh, disagreeable voices. The manager of the factory, Nazaritch, a bald, sharp-eyed Old Believer, could never get on with the teachers, but the one who was now anxiously waving his hands he despised and hated, though he could not have said why. He behaved rudely and condescendingly to the young man, kept back his salary, meddled with the teaching, and had finally tried to dislodge him by appointing, a fortnight before Christmas, as porter to the school a drunken peasant, a distant relation of his wife's, who disobeyed the teacher and said rude things to him before the boys.

Anna Akimovna was aware of all this, but she could be of no help, for she was afraid of Nazaritch herself. Now she wanted at least to be very nice to the schoolmaster, to tell him she was very much pleased with him; but when after the sitting he began apologizing for something in great confusion, and Auntie began to address him familiarly as she drew him without ceremony to the table, she felt, for some reason, bored and awkward, and giving orders that the children should be given sweets, went upstairs.

"In reality there is something cruel in these Christmas customs," she said a little while afterwards, as it were to herself, looking out of window at the boys, who were flocking from the house to the gates and shivering with cold, putting their coats on as they ran. "At Christmas one wants to rest, to sit at home with one's own people, and the poor boys, the teacher, and the clerks and foremen, are obliged for some reason to go through the frost, then to offer their greetings, show their respect, be put to confusion . . ."

Mishenka, who was standing at the door of the drawing-room and overheard this, said:

"It has not come from us, and it will not end with us. Of course, I am not an educated man, Anna Akimovna, but I do understand that the poor must always respect the rich. It is well said, 'God marks the rogue.' In prisons, night refuges, and pot-houses you never see any but the poor, while decent people, you may notice, are always rich. It has been said of the rich, 'Deep calls to deep.' "

"You always express yourself so tediously and incomprehensibly," said Anna Akimovna, and she walked to the other end of the big drawing-room.

It was only just past eleven. The stillness of the big room, only broken by the singing that floated up from below, made her yawn. The bronzes, the albums, and the pictures on the walls, representing a ship at sea, cows in a meadow, and views of the Rhine, were so absolutely stale that her eyes simply glided over them without observing them. The holiday mood was already growing tedious. As before, Anna Akimovna felt that she was beautiful, good-natured, and wonderful, but now it seemed to her that that was of no use to any one; it seemed to her that she did not know for whom and for what she had put on this expensive dress, too, and, as always happened on all holidays, she began to be fretted by loneliness and the persistent thought that her beauty, her health, and her wealth, were a mere cheat, since she was not wanted, was of no use to any one, and nobody loved her. She walked through all the rooms, humming and looking out of window; stopping in the drawing-room, she could not resist beginning to talk to Mishenka.

"I don't know what you think of yourself, Misha," she said, and heaved a sigh. "Really, God might punish you for it."

"What do you mean?"

"You know what I mean. Excuse my meddling in your affairs. But it seems you are spoiling your own life out of obstinacy. You'll admit that it is high time you got married, and she is an excellent and deserving girl. You will never find any one better. She's a beauty, clever, gentle, and devoted. . . . And her appearance! . . . If she belonged to our circle or a higher one, people would be falling in love with her for her red hair alone. See how beautifully her hair goes with her complexion. Oh, goodness! You don't understand anything, and don't know what you want," Anna Akimovna said bitterly, and tears came into her eyes. "Poor girl, I am so sorry for her! I know you want a wife with money, but I have told you already I will give Masha a dowry."

Mishenka could not picture his future spouse in his imagination except as a tall, plump, substantial, pious woman, stepping like a peacock, and, for some reason, with a long shawl over her shoulders; while Masha was thin, slender, tightly laced, and walked with little steps, and, worst of all, she was too fascinating and at times extremely attractive to Mishenka, and that, in his opinion, was incongruous with matrimony and only in keeping with loose behaviour. When Anna Akimovna had promised to give Masha a dowry, he had hesitated for a time; but once a poor student in a brown overcoat over his uniform, coming with a letter for Anna Akimovna, was fascinated by Masha, and could not resist embracing her near the hat-stand, and she had uttered a faint shriek; Mishenka, standing on the stairs above, had seen this, and from that time had begun to cherish a feeling of disgust for Masha. A poor student! Who knows, if she had been embraced by a rich student or an officer the consequences might have been different.

"Why don't you wish it?" Anna Akimovna asked. "What more do you want?"

Mishenka was silent and looked at the arm-chair fixedly, and raised his eyebrows.

"Do you love some one else?"

Silence. The red-haired Masha came in with letters and visiting cards on a tray. Guessing that they were talking about her, she blushed to tears.

"The postmen have come," she muttered. "And there is a clerk called Tchalikov waiting below. He says you told him to come to-day for something."

"What insolence!" said Anna Akimovna, moved to anger. "I gave him no orders. Tell him to take himself off; say I am not at home!"

A ring was heard. It was the priests from her parish. They were always shown into the aristocratic part of the house—that is, upstairs. After the priests, Nazaritch, the manager of the factory, came to pay his visit, and then the factory doctor; then Mishenka announced the inspector of the elementary schools. Visitors kept arriving.

When there was a moment free, Anna Akimovna sat down in a deep arm-chair in the drawing-room, and shutting her eyes, thought that her loneliness was quite natural because she had not married and never would marry. . . . But that was not her fault. Fate itself had flung her out of the simple working-class surroundings in which, if she could trust her memory, she had felt so snug and at home, into these immense rooms, where she could never think what to do with herself, and could not understand why so many people kept passing before her eyes. What was happening now seemed to her trivial, useless, since it did not and could not give her happiness for one minute.

"If I could fall in love," she thought, stretching; the very thought of this sent a rush of warmth to her heart. "And if I could escape from the factory . . ." she mused, imagining how the weight of those factory buildings, barracks, and schools would roll off her conscience, roll off her mind. . . . Then she remembered her father, and thought if he had lived longer he would certainly have married her to a working man— to Pimenov, for instance. He would have told her to marry, and that would have been all about it. And it would have been a good thing; then the factory would have passed into capable hands.

She pictured his curly head, his bold profile, his delicate, ironical lips and the strength, the tremendous strength, in his shoulders, in his arms, in his chest, and the tenderness with which he had looked at her watch that day.

"Well," she said, "it would have been all right. . . . I would have married him."

"Anna Akimovna," said Mishenka, coming noiselessly into the drawing-room.

"How you frightened me!" she said, trembling all over. "What do you want?"

"Anna Akimovna," he said, laying his hand on his heart and raising his eyebrows, "you are my mistress and my benefactress, and no one but you can tell me what I ought to do about marriage, for you are as good as a mother to me. . . . But kindly forbid them to laugh and jeer at me downstairs. They won't let me pass without it."

"How do they jeer at you?"

"They call me Mashenka's Mishenka."

"Pooh, what nonsense!" cried Anna Akimovna indignantly. "How stupid you all are! What a stupid you are, Misha! How sick I am of you! I can't bear the sight of you."

III

Dinner

Just as the year before, the last to pay her visits were Krylin, an actual civil councillor, and Lysevitch, a well-known barrister. It was already dark when they arrived. Krylin, a man of sixty, with a wide mouth and with grey whiskers close to his ears, with a face like a lynx, was wearing a uniform with an Anna ribbon, and white trousers. He held Anna Akimovna's hand in both of his for a long while, looked intently in her face, moved his lips, and at last said, drawling upon one note:

"I used to respect your uncle . . . and your father, and enjoyed the privilege of their friendship. Now I feel it an agreeable duty, as you see, to present my Christmas wishes to their honoured heiress . . . in spite of my infirmities and the distance I have to come. . . . And I am very glad to see you in good health."

The lawyer Lysevitch, a tall, handsome fair man, with a slight sprinkling of grey on his temples and beard, was distinguished by exceptionally elegant manners; he walked with a swaying step, bowed as it were reluctantly, and shrugged his shoulders as he talked, and all this with an indolent grace, like a spoiled horse fresh from the stable. He was well fed, extremely healthy, and very well off; on one occasion he had won forty thousand roubles, but concealed the fact from his friends. He was fond of good fare, especially cheese, truffles, and grated radish with hemp oil; while in Paris he had eaten, so he said, baked but unwashed guts. He spoke smoothly, fluently, without hesitation, and only occasionally, for the sake of effect, permitted himself to hesitate and snap his fingers as if picking up a word. He had long ceased to believe in anything he had to say in the law courts, or perhaps he did believe in it, but attached no kind of significance to it; it had all so long been familiar, stale, ordinary. . . . He believed in nothing but what was original and unusual. A copy-book moral in an original form would move him to tears. Both his notebooks were filled with extraordinary expressions which he had read in various authors; and when he needed to look up any expression, he would search nervously in both books, and usually failed to find it. Anna Akimovna's father had in a good-humoured moment ostentatiously appointed him legal adviser in matters concerning the factory, and had assigned him a salary of twelve thousand roubles. The legal business of the factory had been confined to two or three trivial actions for recovering debts, which Lysevitch handed to his assistants.

Anna Akimovna knew that he had nothing to do at the factory, but she could not dismiss him—she had not the moral courage; and besides, she was used to him. He used to call himself her legal adviser, and his salary, which he invariably sent for on the first of the month punctually, he used to call "stern prose." Anna Akimovna knew that when, after her father's death, the timber of her forest was sold for railway sleepers, Lysevitch had made more than fifteen thousand out of the transaction, and had shared it with Nazaritch. When first she found out they had cheated her she had wept bitterly, but afterwards she had grown used to it.

Wishing her a happy Christmas, and kissing both her hands, he looked her up and down, and frowned.

"You mustn't," he said with genuine disappointment. "I have told you, my dear, you mustn't!"

"What do you mean, Viktor Nikolaitch?"

"I have told you you mustn't get fat. All your family have an unfortunate tendency to grow fat. You mustn't," he repeated in an imploring voice, and kissed her hand. "You are so handsome! You are so splendid! Here, your Excellency, let me introduce the one woman in the world whom I have ever seriously loved."

"There is nothing surprising in that. To know Anna Akimovna at your age and not to be in love with her, that would be impossible."

"I adore her," the lawyer continued with perfect sincerity, but with his usual indolent grace. "I love her, but not because I am a man and she is a woman. When I am with her I always feel as though she belongs to some third sex, and I to a fourth, and we float away together into the domain of the subtlest shades, and there we blend into the spectrum. Leconte de Lisle defines such relations better than any one. He has a superb passage, a marvellous passage. . . ."

Lysevitch rummaged in one notebook, then in the other, and, not finding the quotation, subsided. They began talking of the weather, of the opera, of the arrival, expected shortly, of Duse. Anna Akimovna remembered that the year before Lysevitch and, she fancied, Krylin had dined with her, and now when they were getting ready to go away, she began with perfect sincerity pointing out to them in an imploring voice that as they had no more visits to pay, they ought to remain to dinner with her. After some hesitation the visitors agreed.

In addition to the family dinner, consisting of cabbage soup, sucking pig, goose with apples, and so on, a so-called "French" or "chef's" dinner used to be prepared in the kitchen on great holidays, in case any visitor in the upper story wanted a meal. When they heard the clatter of crockery in the dining-room, Lysevitch began to betray a noticeable excitement; he rubbed his hands, shrugged his shoulders, screwed up his eyes, and described with feeling what dinners her father and uncle used to give at one time, and a marvellous *matelote* of turbots the cook here could make: it was not a *matelote*, but a veritable revelation! He was already gloating over the dinner, already eating it in imagination and enjoying it. When Anna Akimovna took his arm and led him to the dining-room, he tossed off a glass of vodka and put a piece of salmon in his mouth; he positively purred with pleasure. He munched loudly, disgustingly, emitting sounds from his nose, while his eyes grew oily and rapacious.

The *hors d'oeuvres* were superb; among other things, there were fresh white mushrooms stewed in cream, and *sauce provençale* made of fried oysters and crayfish, strongly flavoured with some bitter pickles. The dinner, consisting of elaborate holiday dishes, was excellent, and so were the wines. Mishenka waited at table with enthusiasm. When he laid some new dish on the table and lifted the shining cover, or poured out the wine, he did it with the solemnity of a professor of black magic, and, looking at his face and his movements suggesting the first figure of a quadrille, the lawyer thought several times, "What a fool!"

After the third course Lysevitch said, turning to Anna Akimovna:

"The *fin de siècle* woman—I mean when she is young, and of course wealthy—must be independent, clever, elegant, intellectual, bold, and a little depraved. Depraved within limits, a little; for excess, you know, is wearisome. You ought not to vegetate, my dear; you ought not to live like every one else, but to get the full savour of life, and a slight flavour of depravity is the sauce of life. Revel among flowers of intoxicating fragrance, breathe the perfume of musk, eat hashish, and best of all, love, love, love. . . . To begin with, in your place I would set up seven lovers—one for each day of the week; and one I would call Monday, one Tuesday, the third Wednesday, and so on, so that each might know his day."

This conversation troubled Anna Akimovna; she ate nothing and only drank a glass of wine.

"Let me speak at last," she said. "For myself personally, I can't conceive of love without family life. I am lonely, lonely as the moon in the sky, and a waning moon, too; and whatever you may say, I am convinced, I feel that this waning can only be restored by love in its ordinary sense. It seems to me that such love would define my duties, my work, make clear my conception of life. I want from love peace of soul, tranquillity; I want the very opposite of musk, and spiritualism, and *fin de siècle* . . . in short"—she grew embarrassed—"a husband and children."

"You want to be married? Well, you can do that, too," Lysevitch assented. "You ought to have all experiences: marriage, and jealousy, and the sweetness of the first infidelity, and even children. . . . But make haste and live—make haste, my dear: time is passing; it won't wait."

"Yes, I'll go and get married!" she said, looking angrily at his well-fed, satisfied face. "I will marry in the simplest, most ordinary way and be radiant with happiness. And, would you believe it, I will marry some plain working man, some mechanic or draughtsman."

"There is no harm in that, either. The Duchess Josiana loved Gwinplin, and that was permissible for her because she was a grand duchess. Everything is permissible for you, too, because you are an exceptional woman: if, my dear, you want to love a negro or an Arab, don't scruple; send for a negro. Don't deny yourself anything. You ought to be as bold as your desires; don't fall short of them."

"Can it be so hard to understand me?" Anna Akimovna asked with amazement, and her eyes were bright with tears. "Understand, I have an immense business on my hands—two thousand workmen, for whom I must answer before God. The men who work for me grow blind and deaf. I am afraid to go on like this; I am afraid! I am wretched, and you have the cruelty to talk to me of negroes and . . . and you smile!" Anna Akimovna brought her fist down on the table. "To go on living the life I am living now, or to marry some one as idle and incompetent as myself, would be a crime. I can't go on living like this," she said hotly, "I cannot!"

"How handsome she is!" said Lysevitch, fascinated by her. "My God, how handsome she is! But why are you angry, my dear? Perhaps I am wrong; but surely you don't imagine that if, for the sake of ideas

Anton Chekhov

for which I have the deepest respect, you renounce the joys of life and lead a dreary existence, your workmen will be any the better for it? Not a scrap! No, frivolity, frivolity!" he said decisively. "It's essential for you; it's your duty to be frivolous and depraved! Ponder that, my dear, ponder it."

Anna Akimovna was glad she had spoken out, and her spirits rose. She was pleased she had spoken so well, and that her ideas were so fine and just, and she was already convinced that if Pimenov, for instance, loved her, she would marry him with pleasure.

Mishenka began to pour out champagne.

"You make me angry, Viktor Nikolaitch," she said, clinking glasses with the lawyer. "It seems to me you give advice and know nothing of life yourself. According to you, if a man be a mechanic or a draughtsman, he is bound to be a peasant and an ignoramus! But they are the cleverest people! Extraordinary people!"

"Your uncle and father . . . I knew them and respected them . . ." Krylin said, pausing for emphasis (he had been sitting upright as a post, and had been eating steadily the whole time), "were people of considerable intelligence and . . . of lofty spiritual qualities."

"Oh, to be sure, we know all about their qualities," the lawyer muttered, and asked permission to smoke.

When dinner was over Krylin was led away for a nap. Lysevitch finished his cigar, and, staggering from repletion, followed Anna Akimovna into her study. Cosy corners with photographs and fans on the walls, and the inevitable pink or pale blue lanterns in the middle of the ceiling, he did not like, as the expression of an insipid and unoriginal character; besides, the memory of certain of his love affairs of which he was now ashamed was associated with such lanterns. Anna Akimovna's study with its bare walls and tasteless furniture pleased him exceedingly. It was snug and comfortable for him to sit on a Turkish divan and look at Anna Akimovna, who usually sat on the rug before the fire, clasping her knees and looking into the fire and thinking of something; and at such moments it seemed to him that her peasant Old Believer blood was stirring within her.

Every time after dinner when coffee and liqueurs were handed, he grew livelier and began telling her various bits of literary gossip. He spoke with eloquence and inspiration, and was carried away by his own stories; and she listened to him and thought every time that for such enjoyment it was worth paying not only twelve thousand, but three times that sum, and forgave him everything she disliked in him. He sometimes told her the story of some tale or novel he had been reading, and then two or three hours passed unnoticed like a minute. Now he began rather dolefully in a failing voice with his eyes shut.

"It's ages, my dear, since I have read anything," he said when she asked him to tell her something. "Though I do sometimes read Jules Verne."

"I was expecting you to tell me something new."

"H'm! . . . new," Lysevitch muttered sleepily, and he settled himself further back in the corner of the sofa. "None of the new literature, my dear, is any use for you or me. Of course, it is bound to be such as it is, and to refuse to recognize it is to refuse to recognize—would mean refusing to recognize the natural order of things, and I do recognize it, but . . ." Lysevitch seemed to have fallen asleep. But a minute later his voice was heard again:

"All the new literature moans and howls like the autumn wind in the chimney. 'Ah, unhappy wretch! Ah, your life may be likened to a prison! Ah, how damp and dark it is in your prison! Ah, you will certainly come to ruin, and there is no chance of escape for you!' That's very fine, but I should prefer a literature that would tell us how to escape from prison. Of all contemporary writers, however, I prefer Maupassant." Lysevitch opened his eyes. "A fine writer, a perfect writer!" Lysevitch shifted in his seat. "A wonderful artist! A terrible, prodigious, supernatural artist!" Lysevitch got up from the sofa and raised his right arm. "Maupassant!" he said rapturously. "My dear, read Maupassant! one page of his gives you more than all the riches of the earth! Every line is a new horizon. The softest, tenderest impulses of the soul alternate with violent tempestuous sensations; your soul, as though under the weight of forty thousand atmospheres, is transformed into the most insignificant little bit of some great thing of an undefined rosy hue which I fancy, if one could put it on one's tongue, would yield a pungent, voluptuous taste. What a fury of transitions, of motives, of melodies! You rest peacefully on the lilies and the roses, and suddenly a thought—a terrible, splendid, irresistible thought—swoops down upon you like a locomotive, and bathes you in hot steam and deafens you with its whistle. Read Maupassant, dear girl; I insist on it."

Lysevitch waved his arms and paced from corner to corner in violent excitement.

"Yes, it is inconceivable," he pronounced, as though in despair; "his last thing overwhelmed me, intoxicated me! But I am afraid you will not care for it. To be carried away by it you must savour it, slowly suck the juice from each line, drink it in. . . . You must drink it in! . . ."

After a long introduction, containing many words such as dæmonic sensuality, a network of the most delicate nerves, simoom, crystal, and so on, he began at last telling the story of the novel. He did not tell the story so whimsically, but told it in minute detail, quoting from memory whole descriptions and conversations; the characters of the novel fascinated him, and to describe them he threw himself into attitudes, changed the expression of his face and voice like a real actor. He laughed with delight at one moment in a deep bass, and at another, on a high shrill note, clasped his hands and clutched at his head with an expression which suggested that it was just going to burst. Anna Akimovna listened enthralled, though she had already read the novel, and it seemed to her ever so much finer and more subtle in the lawyer's version than in the book itself. He drew her attention to various subtleties, and emphasized the felicitous expressions and the profound thoughts, but she saw in it, only life, life, life and herself, as though she had been a character in the novel. Her spirits rose, and she, too, laughing and clasping her hands, thought that she could not go on living such a life, that there was no need to have a wretched life when one might have a splendid one. She remembered her words and thoughts at dinner, and was proud of them; and when Pimenov suddenly rose up in her imagination, she felt happy and longed for him to love her.

When he had finished the story, Lysevitch sat down on the sofa, exhausted.

"How splendid you are! How handsome!" he began, a little while afterwards in a faint voice as if he were ill. "I am happy near you, dear girl, but why am I forty-two instead of thirty? Your tastes and mine do not coincide: you ought to be depraved, and I have long passed that phase, and want a love as delicate and immaterial as a ray of sunshine— that is, from the point of view of a woman of your age, I am of no earthly use."

In his own words, he loved Turgenev, the singer of virginal love and purity, of youth, and of the melancholy Russian landscape; but he loved virginal love, not from knowledge but from hearsay, as something abstract, existing outside real life. Now he assured himself that he loved Anna Akimovna platonically, ideally, though he did not know what those words meant. But he felt comfortable, snug, warm. Anna Akimovna seemed to him enchanting, original, and he imagined that the pleasant sensation that was aroused in him by these surroundings was the very thing that was called platonic love.

He laid his cheek on her hand and said in the tone commonly used in coaxing little children:

"My precious, why have you punished me?"

"How? When?"

"I have had no Christmas present from you."

Anna Akimovna had never heard before of their sending a Christmas box to the lawyer, and now she was at a loss how much to give him. But she must give him something, for he was expecting it, though he looked at her with eyes full of love.

"I suppose Nazaritch forgot it," she said, "but it is not too late to set it right."

She suddenly remembered the fifteen hundred she had received the day before, which was now lying in the toilet drawer in her bedroom. And when she brought that ungrateful money and gave it to the lawyer, and he put it in his coat pocket with indolent grace, the whole incident passed off charmingly and naturally. The sudden reminder of a Christmas box and this fifteen hundred was not unbecoming in Lysevitch.

"Merci," he said, and kissed her finger.

Krylin came in with blissful, sleepy face, but without his decorations.

Lysevitch and he stayed a little longer and drank a glass of tea each, and began to get ready to go. Anna Akimovna was a little embarrassed. . . . She had utterly forgotten in what department Krylin served, and whether she had to give him money or not; and if she had to, whether to give it now or send it afterwards in an envelope.

"Where does he serve?" she whispered to Lysevitch.

"Goodness knows," muttered Lysevitch, yawning.

She reflected that if Krylin used to visit her father and her uncle and respected them, it was probably not for nothing: apparently he had been charitable at their expense, serving in some charitable institution. As she said good-bye she slipped three hundred roubles into his hand; he seemed taken aback, and looked at her for a minute in silence with his pewtery eyes, but then seemed to understand and said:

"The receipt, honoured Anna Akimovna, you can only receive on the New Year."

Lysevitch had become utterly limp and heavy, and he staggered when Mishenka put on his overcoat.

As he went downstairs he looked like a man in the last stage of exhaustion, and it was evident that he would drop asleep as soon as he got into his sledge.

"Your Excellency," he said languidly to Krylin, stopping in the middle of the staircase, "has it ever happened to you to experience a feeling as though some unseen force were drawing you out longer and longer? You are drawn out and turn into the finest wire. Subjectively this finds expression in a curious voluptuous feeling which is impossible to compare with anything."

Anna Akimovna, standing at the top of the stairs, saw each of them give Mishenka a note.

"Good-bye! Come again!" she called to them, and ran into her bedroom.

She quickly threw off her dress, that she was weary of already, put on a dressing-gown, and ran downstairs; and as she ran downstairs she laughed and thumped with her feet like a school-boy; she had a great desire for mischief.

IV

Evening

Auntie, in a loose print blouse, Varvarushka and two old women, were sitting in the dining-room having supper. A big piece of salt meat, a ham, and various savouries, were lying on the table before them, and clouds of steam were rising from the meat, which looked particularly fat and appetizing. Wine was not served on the lower story, but they made up for it with a great number of spirits and home-made liqueurs. Agafyushka, the fat, white-skinned, well-fed cook, was standing with her arms crossed in the doorway and talking to the old women, and the dishes were being handed by the downstairs Masha, a dark girl with a crimson ribbon in her hair. The old women had had enough to eat before the morning was over, and an hour before supper had had tea and buns, and so they were now eating with effort—as it were, from a sense of duty.

"Oh, my girl!" sighed Auntie, as Anna Akimovna ran into the dining-room and sat down beside her. "You've frightened me to death!"

Every one in the house was pleased when Anna Akimovna was in good spirits and played pranks; this always reminded them that the old men were dead and that the old women had no authority in the house, and any one could do as he liked without any fear of being sharply called to account for it. Only the two old women glanced askance at Anna Akimovna with amazement: she was humming, and it was a sin to sing at table.

"Our mistress, our beauty, our picture," Agafyushka began chanting with sugary sweetness. "Our precious jewel! The people, the people that have come to-day to look at our queen. Lord have mercy upon us! Generals, and officers and gentlemen. . . . I kept looking out of window and counting and counting till I gave it up."

"I'd as soon they did not come at all," said Auntie; she looked sadly at her niece and added: "They only waste the time for my poor orphan girl."

Anna Akimovna felt hungry, as she had eaten nothing since the morning. They poured her out some very bitter liqueur; she drank it off, and tasted the salt meat with mustard, and thought it extraordinarily nice. Then the downstairs Masha brought in the turkey, the pickled apples and the gooseberries. And that pleased her, too. There was only one thing that was disagreeable: there was a draught of hot air from the tiled stove; it was stiflingly close and every one's cheeks were burning. After supper the cloth was taken off and plates of peppermint biscuits, walnuts, and raisins were brought in.

"You sit down, too . . . no need to stand there!" said Auntie to the cook.

Agafyushka sighed and sat down to the table; Masha set a wineglass of liqueur before her, too, and Anna Akimovna began to feel as though Agafyushka's white neck were giving out heat like the stove. They were all talking of how difficult it was nowadays to get married, and saying that in old days, if men did not court beauty, they paid attention to money, but now there was no making out what they wanted; and while hunchbacks and cripples used to be left old maids, nowadays men would not have even the beautiful and wealthy. Auntie began to set this down to immorality, and said that people had no fear of God, but she suddenly remembered that Ivan Ivanitch, her brother, and Varvarushka— both people of holy life—had feared God, but all the same had had children on the sly, and had sent them to the Foundling Asylum. She pulled herself up and changed the conversation, telling them about a suitor she had once had, a factory hand, and how she had loved him, but her brothers had forced her to marry a widower, an ikon-painter, who, thank God, had died two years after. The downstairs Masha sat down to the table, too, and told them with a mysterious air that for the last week some unknown man with a black moustache, in a great-coat with an astrachan collar, had made his appearance every morning in the yard, had stared at the windows of the big house, and had gone on further— to the buildings; the man was all right, nice-looking. . . .

All this conversation made Anna Akimovna suddenly long to be married—long intensely, painfully; she felt as though she would give half her life and all her fortune only to know that upstairs there was a man who was closer to her than any one in the world, that he loved her warmly and was missing her; and the thought of such closeness, ecstatic and inexpressible in words, troubled her soul. And the instinct of youth and health flattered her with lying assurances that the real poetry of life was not over but still to come, and she believed it, and leaning back in her chair (her hair fell down as she did so), she began laughing, and, looking at her, the others laughed, too. And it was a long time before this careless laughter died down in the dining-room.

She was informed that the Stinging Beetle had come. This was a pilgrim woman called Pasha or Spiridonovna—a thin little woman of fifty, in a black dress with a white kerchief, with keen eyes, sharp nose, and a sharp chin; she had sly, viperish eyes and she looked as though she could see right through every one. Her lips were shaped like a heart. Her viperishness and hostility to every one had earned her the nickname of the Stinging Beetle.

Going into the dining-room without looking at any one, she made for the ikons and chanted in a high voice "Thy Holy Birth," then she sang "The Virgin today gives birth to the Son," then "Christ is born," then she turned round and bent a piercing gaze upon all of them.

"A happy Christmas," she said, and she kissed Anna Akimovna on the shoulder. "It's all I could do, all I could do to get to you, my kind friends." She kissed Auntie on the shoulder. "I should have come to you this morning, but I went in to some good people to rest on the way. 'Stay, Spiridonovna, stay,' they said, and I did not notice that evening was coming on."

As she did not eat meat, they gave her salmon and caviare. She ate looking from under her eyelids at the company, and drank three glasses of vodka. When she had finished she said a prayer and bowed down to Anna Akimovna's feet.

They began to play a game of "kings," as they had done the year before, and the year before that, and all the servants in both stories crowded in at the doors to watch the game. Anna Akimovna fancied she caught a glimpse once or twice of Mishenka, with a patronizing smile on his face, among the crowd of peasant men and women. The first to be king was Stinging Beetle, and Anna Akimovna as the soldier paid her tribute; and then Auntie was king and Anna Akimovna was peasant, which excited general delight, and Agafyushka was prince, and was quite abashed with pleasure. Another game was got up at the other end of the table—played by the two Mashas, Varvarushka, and the sewing-maid Marfa Ptrovna, who was waked on purpose to play "kings," and whose face looked cross and sleepy.

While they were playing they talked of men, and of how difficult it was to get a good husband nowadays, and which state was to be preferred—that of an old maid or a widow.

"You are a handsome, healthy, sturdy lass," said Stinging Beetle to Anna Akimovna. "But I can't make out for whose sake you are holding back."

"What's to be done if nobody will have me?"

"Or maybe you have taken a vow to remain a maid?" Stinging Beetle went on, as though she did not hear. "Well, that's a good deed. . . . Remain one," she repeated, looking intently and maliciously at her cards. "All right, my dear, remain one. . . . Yes . . . only maids, these saintly maids, are not all alike." She heaved a sigh and played the king. "Oh, no, my girl, they are not all alike! Some really watch over themselves like nuns, and butter would not melt in their mouths; and if such a one does sin in an hour of weakness, she is worried to death, poor thing! so it would be a sin to condemn her. While others will go dressed in black and sew their shroud, and yet love rich old men on the sly. Yes, y-es, my canary birds, some hussies will bewitch an old man and rule over him, my doves, rule over him and turn his head; and when they've saved up money and lottery tickets enough, they will bewitch him to his death."

Varvarushka's only response to these hints was to heave a sigh and look towards the ikons. There was an expression of Christian meekness on her countenance.

"I know a maid like that, my bitterest enemy," Stinging Beetle went on, looking round at every one in triumph; "she is always sighing, too, and looking at the ikons, the she-devil. When she used to rule in a certain old man's house, if one went to her she would give one a crust, and bid one bow down to the ikons while she would sing: 'In conception Thou dost abide a Virgin . . . !' On holidays she will give one a bite, and on working days she will reproach one for it. But nowadays I will make merry over her! I will make as merry as I please, my jewel."

Varvarushka glanced at the ikons again and crossed herself.

"But no one will have me, Spiridonovna," said Anna Akimovna to change the conversation. "What's to be done?"

"It's your own fault. You keep waiting for highly educated gentlemen, but you ought to marry one of your own sort, a merchant."

"We don't want a merchant," said Auntie, all in a flutter. "Queen of Heaven, preserve us! A gentleman will spend your money, but then he will be kind to you, you poor little fool. But a merchant will be so strict that you won't feel at home in your own house. You'll be wanting to fondle him and he will be counting his money, and when you sit down to meals with him, he'll grudge you every mouthful, though it's your own, the lout! . . . Marry a gentleman."

They all talked at once, loudly interrupting one another, and Auntie tapped on the table with the nutcrackers and said, flushed and angry:

"We won't have a merchant; we won't have one! If you choose a merchant I shall go to an almshouse."

"Sh . . . Sh! . . . Hush!" cried Stinging Beetle; when all were silent she screwed up one eye and said: "Do you know what, Annushka, my birdie . . . ? There is no need for you to get married really like every one else. You're rich and free, you are your own mistress; but yet, my child, it doesn't seem the right thing for you to be an old maid. I'll find you, you know, some trumpery and simple-witted man. You'll marry him for appearances and then have your fling, bonny lass! You can hand him five thousand or ten maybe, and pack him off where he came from, and you will be mistress in your own house—you can love whom you like and no one can say anything to you. And then you can love your highly educated gentleman. You'll have a jolly time!" Stinging Beetle snapped her fingers and gave a whistle.

"It's sinful," said Auntie.

"Oh, sinful," laughed Stinging Beetle. "She is educated, she understands. To cut some one's throat or bewitch an old man—that's a sin, that's true; but to love some charming young friend is not a sin at all. And what is there in it, really? There's no sin in it at all! The old pilgrim women have invented all that to make fools of simple folk. I, too, say everywhere it's a sin; I don't know myself why it's a sin." Stinging Beetle emptied her glass and cleared her throat. "Have your fling, bonny lass," this time evidently addressing herself. "For thirty years, wenches, I have thought of nothing but sins and been afraid, but now I see I have wasted my time, I've let it slip by like a ninny! Ah, I have been a fool, a fool!" She sighed. "A woman's time is short and every day is precious. You are handsome, Annushka, and very rich; but as soon as thirty-five or forty strikes for you your time is up. Don't listen to any one, my girl; live, have your fling till you are forty, and then you will have time to pray forgiveness—there will be plenty of time to bow down and to sew your shroud. A candle to God and a poker to the devil! You can do both at once! Well, how is it to be? Will you make some little man happy?"

"I will," laughed Anna Akimovna. "I don't care now; I would marry a working man."

"Well, that would do all right! Oh, what a fine fellow you would choose then!" Stinging Beetle screwed up her eyes and shook her head. "O—o—oh!"

"I tell her myself," said Auntie, "it's no good waiting for a gentleman, so she had better marry, not a gentleman, but some one humbler; anyway we should have a man in the house to look after things. And there are lots of good men. She might have some one out of the factory. They are all sober, steady men. . . ."

"I should think so," Stinging Beetle agreed. "They are capital fellows. If you like, Aunt, I will make a match for her with Vassily Lebedinsky?"

"Oh, Vasya's legs are so long," said Auntie seriously. "He is so lanky. He has no looks."

There was laughter in the crowd by the door.

"Well, Pimenov? Would you like to marry Pimenov?" Stinging Beetle asked Anna Akimovna.

"Very good. Make a match for me with Pimenov."

"Really?"

"Yes, do!" Anna Akimovna said resolutely, and she struck her fist on the table. "On my honour, I will marry him."

"Really?"

Anna Akimovna suddenly felt ashamed that her cheeks were burning and that every one was looking at her; she flung the cards together on the table and ran out of the room. As she ran up the stairs and, reaching the upper story, sat down to the piano in the drawing-room, a murmur of sound reached her from below like the roar of the sea; most likely they were talking of her and of Pimenov, and perhaps Stinging Beetle was taking advantage of her absence to insult Varvarushka and was putting no check on her language.

The lamp in the big room was the only light burning in the upper story, and it sent a glimmer through the door into the dark drawing-room. It was between nine and ten, not later. Anna Akimovna played a waltz, then another, then a third; she went on playing without stopping. She looked into the dark corner beyond the piano, smiled, and inwardly called to it, and the idea occurred to her that she might drive off to the town to see some one, Lysevitch for instance, and tell him what was passing in her heart. She wanted to talk without ceasing, to laugh, to play the fool, but the dark corner was sullenly silent, and all round in all the rooms of the upper story it was still and desolate.

She was fond of sentimental songs, but she had a harsh, untrained voice, and so she only played the accompaniment and sang hardly audibly, just above her breath. She sang in a whisper one song after another, for the most part about love, separation, and frustrated hopes, and she imagined how she would hold out her hands to him and say with entreaty, with tears, "Pimenov, take this burden from me!" And then, just as though her sins had been forgiven, there would be joy and comfort in her soul, and perhaps a free, happy life would begin. In an anguish of anticipation she leant over the keys, with a passionate longing for the change in her life to come at once without delay, and was terrified at the thought that her old life would go on for some time longer. Then she played again and sang hardly above her breath, and all was stillness about her. There was no noise coming from downstairs now, they must have gone to bed. It had struck ten some time before. A long, solitary, wearisome night was approaching.

Anna Akimovna walked through all the rooms, lay down for a while on the sofa, and read in her study the letters that had come that evening; there were twelve letters of Christmas greetings and three anonymous letters. In one of them some workman complained in a horrible, almost illegible handwriting that Lenten oil sold in the factory shop was rancid and smelt of paraffin; in another, some one respectfully informed her that over a purchase of iron Nazaritch had lately taken a bribe of a thousand roubles from some one; in a third she was abused for her inhumanity.

The excitement of Christmas was passing off, and to keep it up Anna Akimovna sat down at the piano again and softly played one of the new waltzes, then she remembered how cleverly and creditably she had spoken at dinner today. She looked round at the dark windows, at the walls with the pictures, at the faint light that came from the big room, and all at once she began suddenly crying, and she felt vexed that she was so lonely, and that she had no one to talk to and consult. To cheer herself she tried to picture Pimenov in her imagination, but it was unsuccessful.

It struck twelve. Mishenka, no longer wearing his swallow-tail but in his reefer jacket, came in, and without speaking lighted two candles; then he went out and returned a minute later with a cup of tea on a tray.

"What are you laughing at?" she asked, noticing a smile on his face.

"I was downstairs and heard the jokes you were making about Pimenov . . ." he said, and put his hand before his laughing mouth. "If he were sat down to dinner today with Viktor Nikolaevitch and the general, he'd have died of fright." Mishenka's shoulders were shaking with laughter. "He doesn't know even how to hold his fork, I bet."

The footman's laughter and words, his reefer jacket and moustache, gave Anna Akimovna a feeling of uncleanness. She shut her eyes to avoid seeing him, and, against her own will, imagined Pimenov dining with Lysevitch and Krylin, and his timid, unintellectual figure seemed to her pitiful and helpless, and she felt repelled by it. And only now, for the first time in the whole day, she realized clearly that all she had said and thought about Pimenov and marrying a workman was nonsense, folly, and wilfulness. To convince herself of the opposite, to overcome her repulsion, she tried to recall what she had said at dinner, but now she could not see anything in it: shame at her own thoughts and actions, and the fear that she had said something improper during the day, and disgust at her own lack of spirit, overwhelmed her completely. She took up a candle and, as rapidly as if some one were pursuing her, ran downstairs, woke Spiridonovna, and began assuring her she had been joking. Then she went to her bedroom. Red-haired Masha, who was dozing in an arm-chair near the bed, jumped up and began shaking up the pillows. Her face was exhausted and sleepy, and her magnificent hair had fallen on one side.

"Tchalikov came again this evening," she said, yawning, "but I did not dare to announce him; he was very drunk. He says he will come again tomorrow."

"What does he want with me?" said Anna Akimovna, and she flung her comb on the floor. "I won't see him, I won't."

She made up her mind she had no one left in life but this Tchalikov, that he would never leave off persecuting her, and would remind her every day how uninteresting and absurd her life was. So all she was fit for was to help the poor. Oh, how stupid it was!

She lay down without undressing, and sobbed with shame and depression: what seemed to her most vexatious and stupid of all was that her dreams that day about Pimenov had been right, lofty, honourable, but at the same time she felt that Lysevitch and even Krylin were nearer to her than Pimenov and all the workpeople taken together. She thought that if the long day she had just spent could have been represented in a picture, all that had been bad and vulgar—as, for instance, the dinner, the lawyer's talk, the game of "kings"—would have been true, while her dreams and talk about Pimenov would have stood out from the whole as something false, as out of drawing; and she thought, too, that it was too late to dream of happiness, that everything was over for her, and it was impossible to go back to the life when she had slept under the same quilt with her mother, or to devise some new special sort of life.

Red-haired Masha was kneeling before the bed, gazing at her in mournful perplexity; then she, too, began crying, and laid her face against her mistress's arm, and without words it was clear why she was so wretched.

"We are fools!" said Anna Akimovna, laughing and crying. "We are fools! Oh, what fools we are!"

1894

Three Years

I

It was dark, and already lights had begun to gleam here and there in the houses, and a pale moon was rising behind the barracks at the end of the street. Laptev was sitting on a bench by the gate waiting for the end of the evening service at the Church of St. Peter and St. Paul. He was reckoning that Yulia Sergeyevna would pass by on her way from the service, and then he would speak to her, and perhaps spend the whole evening with her.

He had been sitting there for an hour and a half already, and all that time his imagination had been busy picturing his Moscow rooms, his Moscow friends, his man Pyotr, and his writing-table. He gazed half wonderingly at the dark, motionless trees, and it seemed strange to him that he was living now, not in his summer villa at Sokolniki, but in a provincial town in a house by which a great herd of cattle was driven every morning and evening, accompanied by terrible clouds of dust and the blowing of a horn. He thought of long conversations in which he had taken part quite lately in Moscow—conversations in which it had been maintained that one could live without love, that passionate love was an obsession, that finally there is no such love, but only a physical attraction between the sexes—and so on, in the same style; he remembered them and thought mournfully that if he were asked now what love was, he could not have found an answer.

The service was over, the people began to appear. Laptev strained his eyes gazing at the dark figures. The bishop had been driven by in his carriage, the bells had stopped ringing, and the red and green lights in the belfry were one after another extinguished—there had been an illumination, as it was dedication day—but the people were still coming out, lingering, talking, and standing under the windows. But at last

Laptev heard a familiar voice, his heart began beating violently, and he was overcome with despair on seeing that Yulia Sergeyevna was not alone, but walking with two ladies.

"It's awful, awful!" he whispered, feeling jealous. "It's awful!"

At the corner of the lane, she stopped to say good-bye to the ladies, and while doing so glanced at Laptev.

"I was coming to see you," he said. "I'm coming for a chat with your father. Is he at home?"

"Most likely," she answered. "It's early for him to have gone to the club."

There were gardens all along the lane, and a row of lime-trees growing by the fence cast a broad patch of shadow in the moonlight, so that the gate and the fences were completely plunged in darkness on one side, from which came the sounds of women whispering, smothered laughter, and someone playing softly on a balalaika. There was a fragrance of lime-flowers and of hay. This fragrance and the murmur of the unseen whispers worked upon Laptev. He was all at once overwhelmed with a passionate longing to throw his arms round his companion, to shower kisses on her face, her hands, her shoulders, to burst into sobs, to fall at her feet and to tell her how long he had been waiting for her. A faint, scarcely perceptible scent of incense hung about her; and that scent reminded him of the time when he, too, believed in God and used to go to evening service, and when he used to dream so much of pure romantic love. And it seemed to him that, because this girl did not love him, all possibility of the happiness he had dreamed of then was lost to him forever.

She began speaking sympathetically of the illness of his sister, Nina Fyodorovna. Two months before his sister had undergone an operation for cancer, and now every one was expecting a return of the disease.

"I went to see her this morning," said Yulia Sergeyevna, "and it seemed to me that during the last week she has, not exactly grown thin, but has, as it were, faded."

"Yes, yes," Laptev agreed. "There's no return of the symptoms, but every day I notice she grows weaker and weaker, and is wasting before my eyes. I don't understand what's the matter with her."

"Oh dear! And how strong she used to be, plump and rosy!" said Yulia Sergeyevna after a moment's silence. "Every one here used to call her the Moscow lady. How she used to laugh! On holidays she used to dress up like a peasant girl, and it suited her so well."

Doctor Sergey Borisovitch was at home; he was a stout, red-faced man, wearing a long coat that reached below his knees, and looking as though he had short legs. He was pacing up and down his study, with his hands in his pockets, and humming to himself in an undertone, "Ru-ru-ru-ru." His grey whiskers looked unkempt, and his hair was unbrushed, as though he had just got out of bed. And his study with pillows on the sofa, with stacks of papers in the corners, and with a dirty invalid poodle lying under the table, produced the same impression of unkemptness and untidiness as himself.

"M. Laptev wants to see you," his daughter said to him, going into his study.

"Ru-ru-ru-ru," he hummed louder than ever, and turning into the drawing-room, gave his hand to Laptev, and asked: "What good news have you to tell me?"

It was dark in the drawing-room. Laptev, still standing with his hat in his hand, began apologising for disturbing him; he asked what was to be done to make his sister sleep at night, and why she was growing so thin; and he was embarrassed by the thought that he had asked those very questions at his visit that morning.

"Tell me," he said, "wouldn't it be as well to send for some specialist on internal diseases from Moscow? What do you think of it?"

The doctor sighed, shrugged his shoulders, and made a vague gesture with his hands.

It was evident that he was offended. He was a very huffy man, prone to take offence, and always ready to suspect that people did not believe in him, that he was not recognised or properly respected, that his patients exploited him, and that his colleagues showed him ill-will. He was always jeering at himself, saying that fools like him were only made for the public to ride rough-shod over them.

Yulia Sergeyevna lighted the lamp. She was tired out with the service, and that was evident from her pale, exhausted face, and her weary step. She wanted to rest. She sat down on the sofa, put her hands on her lap, and sank into thought. Laptev knew that he was ugly, and now he felt as though he were conscious of his ugliness all over his body. He was short, thin, with ruddy cheeks, and his hair had grown so thin that his head felt cold. In his expression there was none of that refined simplicity which makes even rough, ugly faces attractive; in the society of women, he was awkward, over-talkative, affected. And now he almost despised himself for it. He must talk that Yulia Sergeyevna might not be bored in his company. But what about? About his sister's illness again?

And he began to talk about medicine, saying what is usually said. He approved of hygiene, and said that he had long ago wanted to found a night-refuge in Moscow—in fact, he had already calculated the cost of it. According to his plan the workmen who came in the evening to the night-refuge were to receive a supper of hot cabbage soup with bread, a warm, dry bed with a rug, and a place for drying their clothes and their boots.

Yulia Sergeyevna was usually silent in his presence, and in a strange way, perhaps by the instinct of a lover, he divined her thoughts and intentions. And now, from the fact that after the evening service she had not gone to her room to change her dress and drink tea, he deduced that she was going to pay some visit elsewhere.

"But I'm in no hurry with the night-refuge," he went on, speaking with vexation and irritability, and addressing the doctor, who looked at him, as it were, blankly and in perplexity, evidently unable to understand what induced him to raise the question of medicine and hygiene. "And most likely it will be a long time, too, before I make use of our estimate. I fear our night-shelter will fall into the hands of our pious humbugs and philanthropic ladies, who always ruin any undertaking."

Yulia Sergeyevna got up and held out her hand to Laptev.

"Excuse me," she said, "it's time for me to go. Please give my love to your sister."

"Ru-ru-ru-ru," hummed the doctor. "Ru-ru-ru-ru."

Yulia Sergeyevna went out, and after staying a little longer, Laptev said good-bye to the doctor and went home. When a man is dissatisfied and feels unhappy, how trivial seem to him the shapes of the lime-trees, the shadows, the clouds, all the beauties of nature, so complacent, so indifferent! By now the moon was high up in the sky, and the clouds were scudding quickly below. "But how naïve and provincial the moon is, how threadbare and paltry the clouds!" thought Laptev. He felt ashamed of the way he had talked just now about medicine, and the night-refuge. He felt with horror that next day he would not have will enough to resist trying to see her and talk to her again, and would again be convinced that he was nothing to her. And the day after—it would be the same. With what object? And how and when would it all end?

At home he went in to see his sister. Nina Fyodorovna still looked strong and gave the impression of being a well-built, vigorous woman, but her striking pallor made her look like a corpse, especially when, as now, she was lying on her back with her eyes closed; her eldest daughter Sasha, a girl of ten years old, was sitting beside her reading aloud from her reading-book.

"Alyosha has come," the invalid said softly to herself.

There had long been established between Sasha and her uncle a tacit compact, to take turns in sitting with the patient. On this occasion Sasha closed her reading-book, and without uttering a word, went softly out of the room. Laptev took an historical novel from the chest of drawers, and looking for the right page, sat down and began reading it aloud.

Nina Fyodorovna was born in Moscow of a merchant family. She and her two brothers had spent their childhood and early youth, living at home in Pyatnitsky Street. Their childhood was long and wearisome; her father treated her sternly, and had even on two or three occasions flogged her, and her mother had had a long illness and died. The servants were coarse, dirty, and hypocritical; the house was frequented by priests and monks, also hypocritical; they ate and drank and coarsely flattered her father, whom they did not like. The boys had the good-fortune to go to school, while Nina was left practically uneducated. All her life she wrote an illegible scrawl, and had read nothing but historical novels. Seventeen years ago, when she was twenty-two, on a summer holiday at Himki, she made the acquaintance of her present husband, a landowner called Panaurov, had fallen in love with him, and married him secretly against her father's will. Panaurov, a handsome, rather impudent fellow, who whistled and lighted his cigarette from the holy lamp, struck the father as an absolutely worthless person. And when the son-in-law began in his letters demanding a dowry, the old man wrote to his daughter that he would send her furs, silver, and various articles that had been left at her mother's death, as well as thirty thousand roubles, but without his paternal blessing. Later he sent another twenty thousand. This money, as well as the dowry, was spent; the estate had been sold and Panaurov moved with his family to the

town and got a job in a provincial government office. In the town he
formed another tie, and had a second family, and this was the subject of
much talk, as his illicit family was not a secret.

Nina Fyodorovna adored her husband. And now, listening to the
historical novel, she was thinking how much she had gone through in
her life, how much she had suffered, and that if any one were to
describe her life it would make a very pathetic story. As the tumour was
in her breast, she was persuaded that love and her domestic grief were
the cause of her illness, and that jealousy and tears had brought her to
her hopeless state.

At last Alexey Fyodorovitch closed the book and said:

"That's the end, and thank God for it. To-morrow we'll begin a
new one."

Nina Fyodorovna laughed. She had always been given to laughter, but of late Laptev had begun to notice that at moments her mind
seemed weakened by illness, and she would laugh at the smallest trifle, and even without any cause at all.

"Yulia came before dinner while you were out," she said. "So far as
I can see, she hasn't much faith in her papa. 'Let papa go on treating
you,' she said, 'but write in secret to the holy elder to pray for you, too.'
There is a holy man somewhere here. Yulia forgot her parasol here; you
must take it to her to-morrow," she went on after a brief pause. "No,
when the end comes, neither doctors nor holy men are any help."

"Nina, why can't you sleep at night?" Laptev asked, to change the
subject.

"Oh, well, I don't go to sleep—that's all. I lie and think."

"What do you think about, dear?"

"About the children, about you . . . about my life. I've gone through
a great deal, Alyosha, you know. When one begins to remember and
remember. . . . My God!" She laughed. "It's no joke to have borne five
children as I have, to have buried three. . . . Sometimes I was expecting
to be confined while my Grigory Nikolaitch would be sitting at that
very time with another woman. There would be no one to send for the
doctor or the midwife. I would go into the passage or the kitchen for the
servant, and there Jews, tradesmen, moneylenders, would be waiting for
him to come home. My head used to go round. . . . He did not love me,
though he never said so openly. Now I've grown calmer—it doesn't
weigh on my heart; but in old days, when I was younger, it hurt me—

ach! how it hurt me, darling! Once—while we were still in the country—I found him in the garden with a lady, and I walked away. . . . I walked on aimlessly, and I don't know how, but I found myself in the church porch. I fell on my knees: 'Queen of Heaven!' I said. And it was night, the moon was shining. . . ."

She was exhausted, she began gasping for breath. Then, after resting a little, she took her brother's hand and went on in a weak, toneless voice:

"How kind you are, Alyosha! . . . And how clever! . . . What a good man you've grown up into!"

At midnight Laptev said good-night to her, and as he went away he took with him the parasol that Yulia Sergeyevna had forgotten. In spite of the late hour, the servants, male and female, were drinking tea in the dining-room. How disorderly! The children were not in bed, but were there in the dining-room, too. They were all talking softly in undertones, and had not noticed that the lamp was smoking and would soon go out. All these people, big and little, were disturbed by a whole succession of bad omens and were in an oppressed mood. The glass in the hall had been broken, the samovar had been buzzing every day, and, as though on purpose, was even buzzing now. They were describing how a mouse had jumped out of Nina Fyodorovna's boot when she was dressing. And the children were quite aware of the terrible significance of these omens. The elder girl, Sasha, a thin little brunette, was sitting motionless at the table, and her face looked scared and woebegone, while the younger, Lida, a chubby fair child of seven, stood beside her sister looking from under her brows at the light.

Laptev went downstairs to his own rooms in the lower storey, where under the low ceilings it was always close and smelt of geraniums. In his sitting-room, Panaurov, Nina Fyodorovna's husband, was sitting reading the newspaper. Laptev nodded to him and sat down opposite. Both sat still and said nothing. They used to spend whole evenings like this without speaking, and neither of them was in the least put out by this silence.

The little girls came down from upstairs to say good-night. Deliberately and in silence, Panaurov made the sign of the cross over them several times, and gave them his hand to kiss. They dropped curtsies, and then went up to Laptev, who had to make the sign of the cross and give them his hand to kiss also. This ceremony with the hand-kissing and curtsying was repeated every evening.

When the children had gone out Panaurov laid aside the newspaper and said:

"It's not very lively in our God-fearing town! I must confess, my dear fellow," he added with a sigh, "I'm very glad that at last you've found some distraction."

"What do you mean?" asked Laptev.

"I saw you coming out of Dr. Byelavin's just now. I expect you don't go there for the sake of the papa."

"Of course not," said Laptev, and he blushed.

"Well, of course not. And by the way, you wouldn't find such another old brute as that papa if you hunted by daylight with a candle. You can't imagine what a foul, stupid, clumsy beast he is! You cultured people in the capitals are still interested in the provinces only on the lyrical side, only from the *paysage* and *Poor Anton* point of view, but I can assure you, my boy, there's nothing logical about it; there's nothing but barbarism, meanness, and nastiness—that's all. Take the local devotees of science—the local intellectuals, so to speak. Can you imagine there are here in this town twenty-eight doctors? They've all made their fortunes, and they are living in houses of their own, and meanwhile the population is in just as helpless a condition as ever. Here, Nina had to have an operation, quite an ordinary one really, yet we were obliged to get a surgeon from Moscow; not one doctor here would undertake it. It's beyond all conception. They know nothing, they understand nothing. They take no interest in anything. Ask them, for instance, what cancer is—what it is, what it comes from."

And Panaurov began to explain what cancer was. He was a specialist on all scientific subjects, and explained from a scientific point of view everything that was discussed. But he explained it all in his own way. He had a theory of his own about the circulation of the blood, about chemistry, about astronomy. He talked slowly, softly, convincingly.

"It's beyond all conception," he pronounced in an imploring voice, screwing up his eyes, sighing languidly, and smiling as graciously as a king, and it was evident that he was very well satisfied with himself, and never gave a thought to the fact that he was fifty.

"I am rather hungry," said Laptev. "I should like something savoury."

"Well, that can easily be managed."

Not long afterwards Laptev and his brother-in-law were sitting upstairs in the dining-room having supper. Laptev had a glass of vodka, and then began drinking wine. Panaurov drank nothing. He never drank, and never gambled, yet in spite of that he had squandered all his own and his wife's property, and had accumulated debts. To squander so much in such a short time, one must have, not passions, but a special talent. Panaurov liked dainty fare, liked a handsome dinner service, liked music after dinner, speeches, bowing footmen, to whom he would carelessly fling tips of ten, even twenty-five roubles. He always took part in all lotteries and subscriptions, sent bouquets to ladies of his acquaintance on their birthdays, bought cups, stands for glasses, studs, ties, walking-sticks, scents, cigarette-holders, pipes, lap-dogs, parrots, Japanese bric-à-brac, antiques; he had silk nightshirts, and a bedstead made of ebony inlaid with mother-of-pearl. His dressing-gown was a genuine Bokhara, and everything was to correspond; and on all this there went every day, as he himself expressed, "a deluge" of money.

At supper he kept sighing and shaking his head.

"Yes, everything on this earth has an end," he said softly, screwing up his dark eyes. "You will fall in love and suffer. You will fall out of love; you'll be deceived, for there is no woman who will not deceive; you will suffer, will be brought to despair, and will be faithless too. But the time will come when all this will be a memory, and when you will reason about it coldly and look upon it as utterly trivial. . . ."

Laptev, tired, a little drunk, looked at his handsome head, his clipped black beard, and seemed to understand why women so loved this pampered, conceited, and physically handsome creature.

After supper Panaurov did not stay in the house, but went off to his other lodgings. Laptev went out to see him on his way. Panaurov was the only man in the town who wore a top-hat, and his elegant, dandified figure, his top-hat and tan gloves, beside the grey fences, the pitiful little houses, with their three windows and the thickets of nettles, always made a strange and mournful impression.

After saying good-bye to him Laptev returned home without hurrying. The moon was shining brightly; one could distinguish every straw on the ground, and Laptev felt as though the moonlight were caressing his bare head, as though some one were passing a feather over his hair.

"I love!" he pronounced aloud, and he had a sudden longing to run to overtake Panaurov, to embrace him, to forgive him, to make him a present of a lot of money, and then to run off into the open country, into a wood, to run on and on without looking back.

At home he saw lying on the chair the parasol Yulia Sergeyevna had forgotten; he snatched it up and kissed it greedily. The parasol was a silk one, no longer new, tied round with old elastic. The handle was a cheap one, of white bone. Laptev opened it over him, and he felt as though there were the fragrance of happiness about him.

He settled himself more comfortably in his chair, and still keeping hold of the parasol, began writing to Moscow to one of his friends:

"DEAR PRECIOUS KOSTYA,

"Here is news for you: I'm in love again! I say *again*, because six years ago I fell in love with a Moscow actress, though I didn't even succeed in making her acquaintance, and for the last year and a half I have been living with a certain person you know—a woman neither young nor good-looking. Ah, my dear boy, how unlucky I am in love. I've never had any success with women, and if I say *again* it's simply because it's rather sad and mortifying to acknowledge even to myself that my youth has passed entirely without love, and that I'm in love in a real sense now for the first time in my life, at thirty-four. Let it stand that I love *again*.

"If only you knew what a girl she was! She couldn't be called a beauty—she has a broad face, she is very thin, but what a wonderful expression of goodness she has when she smiles! When she speaks, her voice is as clear as a bell. She never carries on a conversation with me—I don't know her; but when I'm beside her I feel she's a striking, exceptional creature, full of intelligence and lofty aspirations. She is religious, and you cannot imagine how deeply this touches me and exalts her in my eyes. On that point I am ready to argue with you endlessly. You may be right, to your thinking; but, still, I love to see her praying in church. She is a provincial, but she was educated in Moscow. She loves our Moscow; she dresses in the Moscow style, and I love her for that—love her, love her. . . . I see you frowning and getting up to read me a long lecture on what love is, and what sort of woman one can love, and what sort one cannot, and so on, and so on. But, dear Kostya, before I was in love I, too, knew quite well what love was.

"My sister thanks you for your message. She often recalls how she used to take Kostya Kotchevoy to the preparatory class, and never speaks of you except as *poor Kostya*, as she still thinks of you as the little orphan boy she remembers. And so, poor orphan, I'm in love. While it's a secret, don't say anything to a 'certain person.' I think it will all come right of itself, or, as the footman says in Tolstoy, will 'come round.' "

When he had finished his letter Laptev went to bed. He was so tired that he couldn't keep his eyes open, but for some reason he could not get to sleep; the noise in the street seemed to prevent him. The cattle were driven by to the blowing of a horn, and soon afterwards the bells began ringing for early mass. At one minute a cart drove by creaking; at the next, he heard the voice of some woman going to market. And the sparrows twittered the whole time.

II

The next morning was a cheerful one; it was a holiday. At ten o'clock Nina Fyodorovna, wearing a brown dress and with her hair neatly arranged, was led into the drawing-room, supported on each side. There she walked about a little and stood by the open window, and her smile was broad and naïve, and, looking at her, one recalled a local artist, a great drunkard, who wanted her to sit to him for a picture of the Russian carnival. And all of them—the children, the servants, her brother, Alexey Fyodorovitch, and she herself—were suddenly convinced, that she was certainly going to get well. With shrieks of laughter the children ran after their uncle, chasing him and catching him, and filling the house with noise.

People called to ask how she was, brought her holy bread, told her that in almost all the churches they were offering up prayers for her that day. She had been conspicuous for her benevolence in the town, and was liked. She was very ready with her charity, like her brother Alexey, who gave away his money freely, without considering whether it was necessary to give it or not. Nina Fyodorovna used to pay the school fees for poor children; used to give away tea, sugar, and jam to old women; used to provide trousseaux for poor brides; and if she picked up a newspaper, she always looked first of all to see if there were any appeals for charity or a paragraph about somebody's being in a destitute condition.

She was holding now in her hand a bundle of notes, by means of which various poor people, her protégés, had procured goods from a grocer's shop. They had been sent her the evening before by the shopkeeper with a request for the payment of the total—eighty-two roubles.

"My goodness, what a lot they've had! They've no conscience!" she said, deciphering with difficulty her ugly handwriting. "It's no joke! Eighty-two roubles! I declare I won't pay it."

"I'll pay it to-day," said Laptev.

"Why should you? Why should you?" cried Nina Fyodorovna in agitation. "It's quite enough for me to take two hundred and fifty every month from you and our brother. God bless you!" she added, speaking softly, so as not to be overheard by the servants.

"Well, but I spend two thousand five hundred a month," he said. "I tell you again, dear: you have just as much right to spend it as I or Fyodor. Do understand that, once for all. There are three of us, and of every three kopecks of our father's money, one belongs to you."

But Nina Fyodorovna did not understand, and her expression looked as though she were mentally solving some very difficult problem. And this lack of comprehension in pecuniary matters, always made Laptev feel uneasy and troubled. He suspected that she had private debts in addition which worried her and of which she scrupled to tell him.

Then came the sound of footsteps and heavy breathing; it was the doctor coming up the stairs, dishevelled and unkempt as usual.

"Ru-ru-ru," he was humming. "Ru-ru."

To avoid meeting him, Laptev went into the dining-room, and then went downstairs to his own room. It was clear to him that to get on with the doctor and to drop in at his house without formalities was impossible; and to meet the "old brute," as Panaurov called him, was distasteful. That was why he so rarely saw Yulia. He reflected now that the father was not at home, that if he were to take Yulia Sergeyevna her parasol, he would be sure to find her at home alone, and his heart ached with joy. Haste, haste!

He took the parasol and, violently agitated, flew on the wings of love. It was hot in the street. In the big courtyard of the doctor's house, overgrown with coarse grass and nettles, some twenty urchins were playing ball. These were all the children of working-class families who tenanted the three disreputable-looking lodges, which the doctor was always meaning to have done up, though he put it off from year to year. The yard resounded with ringing, healthy voices. At some distance on one side, Yulia Sergeyevna was standing at her porch, her hands folded, watching the game.

"Good-morning!" Laptev called to her.

She looked round. Usually he saw her indifferent, cold, or tired as she had been the evening before. Now her face looked full of life and frolic, like the faces of the boys who were playing ball.

"Look, they never play so merrily in Moscow," she said, going to meet him. "There are no such big yards there, though; they've no place to run there. Papa has only just gone to you," she added, looking round at the children.

"I know; but I've not come to see him, but to see you," said Laptev, admiring her youthfulness, which he had not noticed till then, and seemed only that day to have discovered in her; it seemed to him as though he were seeing her slender white neck with the gold chain for the first time. "I've come to see you . . ." he repeated. "My sister has sent you your parasol; you forgot it yesterday."

She put out her hand to take the parasol, but he pressed it to his bosom and spoke passionately, without restraint, yielding again to the sweet ecstasy he had felt the night before, sitting under the parasol.

"I entreat you, give it me. I shall keep it in memory of you . . . of our acquaintance. It's so wonderful!"

"Take it," she said, and blushed; "but there's nothing wonderful about it."

He looked at her in ecstasy, in silence, not knowing what to say.

"Why am I keeping you here in the heat?" she said after a brief pause, laughing. "Let us go indoors."

"I am not disturbing you?"

They went into the hall. Yulia Sergeyevna ran upstairs, her white dress with blue flowers on it rustling as she went.

"I can't be disturbed," she answered, stopping on the landing. "I never do anything. Every day is a holiday for me, from morning till night."

"What you say is inconceivable to me," he said, going up to her. "I grew up in a world in which every one without exception, men and women alike, worked hard every day."

"But if one has nothing to do? "she asked.

"One has to arrange one's life under such conditions, that work is inevitable. There can be no clean and happy life without work."

Again he pressed the parasol to his bosom, and to his own surprise spoke softly, in a voice unlike his own:

"If you would consent to be my wife I would give everything—I would give everything. There's no price I would not pay, no sacrifice I would not make."

She started and looked at him with wonder and alarm.

"What are you saying!" she brought out, turning pale. "It's impossible, I assure you. Forgive me."

Then with the same rustle of her skirts she went up higher, and vanished through the doorway.

Laptev grasped what this meant, and his mood was transformed, completely, abruptly, as though a light in his soul had suddenly been extinguished.

Filled with the shame of a man humiliated, of a man who is disdained, who is not liked, who is distasteful, perhaps disgusting, who is shunned, he walked out of the house.

"I would give everything," he thought, mimicking himself as he went home through the heat and recalled the details of his declaration. "I would give everything—like a regular tradesman. As though she wanted your *everything!*"

All he had just said seemed to him repulsively stupid. Why had he lied, saying that he had grown up in a world where every one worked, without exception? Why had he talked to her in a lecturing tone about a clean and happy life? It was not clever, not interesting; it was false—false in the Moscow style. But by degrees there followed that mood of indifference into which criminals sink after a severe sentence. He began thinking that, thank God! everything was at an end and that the terrible uncertainty was over; that now there was no need to spend whole days in anticipation, in pining, in thinking always of the same thing. Now everything was clear; he must give up all hope of personal happiness, live without desires, without hopes, without dreams, or expectations, and to escape that dreary sadness which he was so sick of trying to soothe, he could busy himself with other people's affairs, other people's happiness, and old age would come on imperceptibly, and life would reach its end—and nothing more was wanted. He did not care, he wished for nothing, and could reason about it coolly, but there was a sort of heaviness in his face especially under his eyes, his forehead felt drawn tight like elastic—and tears were almost starting into his eyes. Feeling weak all over, he lay down on his bed, and in five minutes was sound asleep.

III

The proposal Laptev had made so suddenly threw Yulia Sergeyevna into despair.

She knew Laptev very little, had made his acquaintance by chance; he was a rich man, a partner in the well-known Moscow firm of "Fyodor Laptev and Sons"; always serious, apparently clever, and anxious about his sister's illness. It had seemed to her that he took no notice of her whatever, and she did not care about him in the least— and then all of a sudden that declaration on the stairs, that pitiful, ecstatic face. . . .

The offer had overwhelmed her by its suddenness and by the fact that the word *wife* had been uttered, and by the necessity of rejecting it. She could not remember what she had said to Laptev, but she still felt traces of the sudden, unpleasant feeling with which she had rejected him. He did not attract her, he looked like a shopman; he was not interesting; she could not have answered him except with a refusal, and yet she felt uncomfortable, as though she had done wrong.

"My God! without waiting to get into the room, on the stairs," she said to herself in despair, addressing the ikon which hung over her pillow; "and no courting beforehand, but so strangely, so oddly. . . ."

In her solitude her agitation grew more intense every hour, and it was beyond her strength to master this oppressive feeling alone. She needed some one to listen to her story and to tell her that she had done right. But she had no one to talk to. She had lost her mother long before; she thought her father a queer man, and could not talk to him seriously. He worried her with his whims, his extreme readiness to take offence, and his meaningless gestures; and as soon as one began to talk to him, he promptly turned the conversation on himself. And in her prayer she was not perfectly open, because she did not know for certain what she ought to pray for.

The samovar was brought in. Yulia Sergeyevna, very pale and tired, looking dejected, came into the dining-room to make tea—it was one of her duties—and poured out a glass for her father. Sergey Borisovitch, in his long coat that reached below his knees, with his red face and unkempt hair, walked up and down the room with his hands in his pockets, pacing, not from corner to corner, but backwards and forwards at random, like a wild beast in its cage. He would stand still by the table, sip his glass of tea with relish, and pace about again, lost in thought.

"Laptev made me an offer to-day," said Yulia Sergeyevna, and she blushed crimson.

The doctor looked at her and did not seem to understand.

"Laptev?" he queried. "Panaurov's brother-in-law?"

He was fond of his daughter; it was most likely that she would sooner or later be married, and leave him, but he tried not to think about that. He was afraid of being alone, and for some reason fancied, that if he were left alone in that great house, he would have an apoplectic stroke, but he did not like to speak of this directly.

"Well, I'm delighted to hear it," he said, shrugging his shoulders. "I congratulate you with all my heart. It offers you a splendid opportunity for leaving me, to your great satisfaction. And I quite understand your feelings. To live with an old father, an invalid, half crazy, must be very irksome at your age. I quite understand you. And the sooner I'm laid out and in the devil's clutches, the better every one will be pleased. I congratulate you with all my heart."

"I refused him."

The doctor felt relieved, but he was unable to stop himself and went on:

"I wonder, I've long wondered, why I've not yet been put into a madhouse—why I'm still wearing this coat instead of a strait-waist-coat? I still have faith in justice, in goodness. I am a fool, an idealist, and nowadays that's insanity, isn't it? And how do they repay me for my honesty? They almost throw stones at me and ride rough-shod over me. And even my nearest kith and kin do nothing but try to get the better of me. It's high time the devil fetched an old fool like me. . . ."

"There's no talking to you like a rational being!" said Yulia.

She got up from the table impulsively, and went to her room in great wrath, remembering how often her father had been unjust to her. But a little while afterwards she felt sorry for her father, too, and when he was going to the club she went downstairs with him, and shut the door after him. It was a rough and stormy night; the door shook with the violence of the wind, and there were draughts in all directions in the passage, so that the candle was almost blown out. In her own domain upstairs Yulia Sergeyevna went the round of all the rooms, making the sign of the cross over every door and window; the wind howled, and it sounded as though some one were walking on the roof. Never had it been so dreary, never had she felt so lonely.

She asked herself whether she had done right in rejecting a man, simply because his appearance did not attract her. It was true he was a man she did not love, and to marry him would mean renouncing forever her dreams, her conceptions of happiness in married life, but would she ever meet the man of whom she dreamed, and would he love her? She was twenty-one already. There were no eligible young men in the town. She pictured all the men she knew—government clerks, schoolmasters, officers, and some of them were married already, and their domestic life was conspicuous for its dreariness and triviality; others were uninteresting, colourless, unintelligent, immoral. Laptev was, anyway, a Moscow man, had taken his degree at the university, spoke French. He lived in the capital, where there were lots of clever, noble, remarkable people; where there was noise and bustle, splendid theatres, musical evenings, first-rate dressmakers, confectioners. . . . In the Bible it was written that a wife must love her husband, and great importance was given to love in novels, but wasn't there exaggeration in it? Was it out of the question to enter upon married life without love? It was said, of course, that love soon passed away, and that nothing was left but habit, and that the object of married life was not to be found in love, nor in happiness, but in duties, such as the bringing up of one's children, the care of one's household, and so on. And perhaps what was meant in the Bible was love for one's husband as one's neighbour, respect for him, charity.

At night Yulia Sergeyevna read the evening prayers attentively, then knelt down, and pressing her hands to her bosom, gazing at the flame of the lamp before the ikon, said with feeling:

"Give me understanding, Holy Mother, our Defender! Give me understanding, O Lord!"

She had in the course of her life come across elderly maiden ladies, poor and of no consequence in the world, who bitterly repented and openly confessed their regret that they had refused suitors in the past. Would not the same thing happen to her? Had not she better go into a convent or become a Sister of Mercy?

She undressed and got into bed, crossing herself and crossing the air around her. Suddenly the bell rang sharply and plaintively in the corridor.

"Oh, my God!" she said, feeling a nervous irritation all over her at the sound. She lay still and kept thinking how poor this provincial life was in events, monotonous and yet not peaceful. One was constantly having to tremble, to feel apprehensive, angry or guilty, and in the end one's nerves were so strained, that one was afraid to peep out of the bedclothes.

A little while afterwards the bell rang just as sharply again. The servant must have been asleep and had not heard. Yulia Sergeyevna lighted a candle, and feeling vexed with the servant, began with a shiver to dress, and when she went out into the corridor, the maid was already closing the door downstairs.

"I thought it was the master, but it's some one from a patient," she said.

Yulia Sergeyevna went back to her room. She took a pack of cards out of the chest of drawers, and decided that if after shuffling the cards well and cutting, the bottom card turned out to be a red one, it would mean *yes*—that is, she would accept Laptev's offer; and that if it was a black, it would mean *no*. The card turned out to be the ten of spades.

That relieved her mind—she fell asleep; but in the morning, she was wavering again between *yes* and *no*, and she was dwelling on the thought that she could, if she chose, change her life. The thought harassed her, she felt exhausted and unwell; but yet, soon after eleven, she dressed and went to see Nina Fyodorovna. She wanted to see Laptev: perhaps now he would seem more attractive to her; perhaps she had been wrong about him hitherto. . . .

She found it hard to walk against the wind. She struggled along, holding her hat on with both hands, and could see nothing for the dust.

IV

Going into his sister's room, and seeing to his surprise Yulia Sergeyevna, Laptev had again the humiliating sensation of a man who feels himself an object of repulsion. He concluded that if after what had happened yesterday she could bring herself so easily to visit his sister and meet him, it must be because she was not concerned about him, and regarded him as a complete nonentity. But when he greeted her, and with a pale face and dust under her eyes she looked at him mournfully and remorsefully, he saw that she, too, was miserable.

She did not feel well. She only stayed ten minutes, and began saying good-bye. And as she went out she said to Laptev:

"Will you see me home, Alexey Fyodorovitch? "

They walked along the street in silence, holding their hats, and he, walking a little behind, tried to screen her from the wind. In the lane it was more sheltered, and they walked side by side.

"Forgive me if I was not nice yesterday"; and her voice quavered as though she were going to cry. "I was so wretched! I did not sleep all night."

"I slept well all night," said Laptev, without looking at her; "but that doesn't mean that I was happy. My life is broken. I'm deeply unhappy, and after your refusal yesterday I go about like a man poisoned. The most difficult thing was said yesterday. To-day I feel no embarrassment and can talk to you frankly. I love you more than my sister, more than my dead mother. . . . I can live without my sister, and without my mother, and I have lived without them, but life without you—is meaningless to me; I can't face it. . . ."

And now too, as usual, he guessed her intention. He realised that she wanted to go back to what had happened the day before, and with that object had asked him to accompany her, and now was taking him home with her. But what could she add to her refusal? What new idea had she in her head? From everything, from her glances, from her smile, and even from her tone, from the way she held her head and shoulders as she walked beside him, he saw that, as before, she did not love him, that he was a stranger to her. What more did she want to say?

Doctor Sergey Borisovitch was at home.

"You are very welcome. I'm always glad to see you, Fyodor Alexeyitch," he said, mixing up his Christian name and his father's. "Delighted, delighted!"

He had never been so polite before, and Laptev saw that he knew of his offer; he did not like that either. He was sitting now in the drawing-room, and the room impressed him strangely, with its poor, common decorations, its wretched pictures, and though there were arm-chairs in it, and a huge lamp with a shade over it, it still looked like an uninhabited place, a huge barn, and it was obvious that no one could feel at home in such a room, except a man like the doctor. The next room, almost twice as large, was called the reception-room, and in it there were only rows of chairs, as though for a dancing class. And while Laptev was sitting in the drawing-room talking to the doctor about his sister, he began to be tortured by a suspicion. Had not Yulia Sergeyevna been to his sister Nina's, and then brought him here to tell him that she would accept him? Oh, how awful it was! But the most awful thing of all was that his soul was capable of such a suspicion. And he imagined how the father and the daughter had spent the evening, and perhaps the night before, in prolonged consultation, perhaps dispute, and at last had come to the conclusion that Yulia had acted thoughtlessly in refusing a rich man. The words that parents use in such cases kept ringing in his ears:

"It is true you don't love him, but think what good you could do!"

The doctor was going out to see patients. Laptev would have gone with him, but Yulia Sergeyevna said:

"I beg you to stay."

She was distressed and dispirited, and told herself now that to refuse an honourable, good man who loved her, simply because he was not attractive, especially when marrying him would make it possible for her to change her mode of life, her cheerless, monotonous, idle life in which youth was passing with no prospect of anything better in the future—to refuse him under such circumstances was madness, caprice and folly, and that God might even punish her for it.

The father went out. When the sound of his steps had died away, she suddenly stood up before Laptev and said resolutely, turning horribly white as she did so:

"I thought for a long time yesterday, Alexey Fyodorovitch. . . . I accept your offer."

He bent down and kissed her hand. She kissed him awkwardly on the head with cold lips.

He felt that in this love scene the chief thing—her love—was lacking, and that there was a great deal that was not wanted; and he longed to cry out, to run away, to go back to Moscow at once. But she was close to him, and she seemed to him so lovely, and he was suddenly overcome by passion. He reflected that it was too late for deliberation now; he embraced her passionately, and muttered some words, calling her *thou*; he kissed her on the neck, and then on the cheek, on the head. . . .

She walked away to the window, dismayed by these demonstrations, and both of them were already regretting what they had said and both were asking themselves in confusion:

"Why has this happened?"

"If only you knew how miserable I am!" she said, wringing her hands.

"What is it?" he said, going up to her, wringing his hands too. "My dear, for God's sake, tell me—what is it? Only tell the truth, I entreat you—nothing but the truth!"

"Don't pay any attention to it," she said, and forced herself to smile. "I promise you I'll be a faithful, devoted wife. . . . Come this evening."

Sitting afterwards with his sister and reading aloud an historical novel, he recalled it all and felt wounded that his splendid, pure, rich feeling was met with such a shallow response. He was not loved, but his offer had been accepted—in all probability because he was rich: that is, what was thought most of in him was what he valued least of all in himself. It was quite possible that Yulia, who was so pure and believed in God, had not once thought of his money; but she did not love him—did not love him, and evidently she had interested motives, vague, perhaps, and not fully thought out—still, it was so. The doctor's house with its common furniture was repulsive to him, and he looked upon the doctor himself as a wretched, greasy miser, a sort of operatic Gaspard from "Les Cloches de Corneville." The very name "Yulia" had a vulgar sound. He imagined how he and his Yulia would stand at their wedding, in reality complete strangers to one another, without a trace of feeling on her side, just as though their marriage had been made by a professional matchmaker; and the only consolation left him now, as commonplace as the marriage itself, was the reflection that he was not the first, and would not be the last; that thousands of people were married like that; and that with time, when Yulia came to know him better, she would perhaps grow fond of him.

"Romeo and Juliet!" he said, as he shut the novel, and he laughed. "I am Romeo, Nina. You may congratulate me. I made an offer to Yulia Byelavin to-day."

Nina Fyodorovna thought he was joking, but when she believed it, she began to cry; she was not pleased at the news.

"Well, I congratulate you," she said. "But why is it so sudden?"

"No, it's not sudden. It's been going on since March, only you don't notice anything. . . . I fell in love with her last March when I made her acquaintance here, in your rooms."

"I thought you would marry some one in our Moscow set," said Nina Fyodorovna after a pause. "Girls in our set are simpler. But what matters, Alyosha, is that you should be happy—that matters most. My Grigory Nikolaitch did not love me, and there's no concealing it; you can see what our life is. Of course any woman may love you for your goodness and your brains, but, you see, Yulitchka is a girl of good family from a high-class boarding-school; goodness and brains are not enough for her. She is young, and, you, Alyosha, are not so young, and are not good-looking."

To soften the last words, she stroked his head and said:

"You're not good-looking, but you're a dear."

She was so agitated that a faint blush came into her cheeks, and she began discussing eagerly whether it would be the proper thing for her to bless Alyosha with the ikon at the wedding. She was, she reasoned, his elder sister, and took the place of his mother; and she kept trying to convince her dejected brother that the wedding must be celebrated in proper style, with pomp and gaiety, so that no one could find fault with it.

Then he began going to the Byelavins' as an accepted suitor, three or four times a day; and now he never had time to take Sasha's place and read aloud the historical novel. Yulia used to receive him in her two rooms, which were at a distance from the drawing-room and her father's study, and he liked them very much. The walls in them were dark; in the corner stood a case of ikons; and there was a smell of good scent and of the oil in the holy lamp. Her rooms were at the furthest end of the house; her bedstead and dressing-table were shut off by a screen. The doors of the bookcase were covered on the inside with a green curtain, and there were rugs on the floor, so that her footsteps were noiseless—and from this he concluded that she was of a reserved character, and that she liked a quiet, peaceful, secluded life. In her own home she was treated as though she were not quite grown up. She had no money of her own, and sometimes when they were out for walks together, she was overcome with confusion at not having a farthing. Her father allowed her very little for dress and books, hardly ten pounds a year. And, indeed, the doctor himself had not much money in spite of his good practice. He played cards every night at the club, and always lost. Moreover, he bought mortgaged houses through a building society, and let them. The tenants were irregular in paying the rent, but he was convinced that such speculations were profitable. He had mortgaged his own house in which he and his daughter were living, and with the money so raised had bought a piece of waste ground, and had already begun to build on it a large two-storey house, meaning to mortgage it, too, as soon as it was finished.

Laptev now lived in a sort of cloud, feeling as though he were not himself, but his double, and did many things which he would never have brought himself to do before. He went three or four times to the club with the doctor, had supper with him, and offered him money for house-building. He even visited Panaurov at his other establishment. It somehow happened that Panaurov invited him to dinner, and without thinking, Laptev accepted. He was received by a lady of five-and-thirty. She was tall and thin, with hair touched with grey, and black eyebrows, apparently not Russian. There were white patches of powder on her face. She gave him a honeyed smile and pressed his hand jerkily, so that the bracelets on her white hands tinkled. It seemed to Laptev that she smiled like that because she wanted to conceal from herself and from others that she was unhappy. He also saw two little girls, aged five and three, who had a marked likeness to Sasha. For dinner they had milk-soup, cold veal, and chocolate. It was insipid and not good; but the table was splendid, with gold forks, bottles of Soyer, and cayenne pepper, an extraordinary bizarre cruet-stand, and a gold pepper-pot.

It was only as he was finishing the milk-soup that Laptev realised how very inappropriate it was for him to be dining there. The lady was embarrassed, and kept smiling, showing her teeth. Panaurov expounded didactically what being in love was, and what it was due to.

"We have in it an example of the action of electricity," he said in French, addressing the lady. "Every man has in his skin microscopic glands which contain currents of electricity. If you meet with a person whose currents are parallel with your own, then you get love."

When Laptev went home and his sister asked him where he had been he felt awkward, and made no answer.

He felt himself in a false position right up to the time of the wedding. His love grew more intense every day, and Yulia seemed to him a poetic and exalted creature; but, all the same, there was no mutual love, and the truth was that he was buying her and she was selling herself. Sometimes, thinking things over, he fell into despair and asked himself: should he run away? He did not sleep for nights together, and kept thinking how he should meet in Moscow the lady whom he had called in his letters "a certain person," and what attitude his father and his brother, difficult people, would take towards his marriage and towards Yulia. He was afraid that his father would say something rude to Yulia at their first meeting. And something strange had happened of late to his brother Fyodor. In his long letters he had taken to writing of the importance of health, of the effect of illness on the mental condition, of the meaning of religion, but not a word about Moscow or business. These letters irritated Laptev, and he thought his brother's character was changing for the worse.

The wedding was in September. The ceremony took place at the Church of St. Peter and St. Paul, after mass, and the same day the young couple set off for Moscow. When Laptev and his wife, in a black dress with a long train, already looking not a girl but a married woman, said good-bye to Nina Fyodorovna, the invalid's face worked, but there was no tear in her dry eyes. She said:

"If—which God forbid—I should die, take care of my little girls."

"Oh, I promise!" answered Yulia Sergeyevna, and her lips and eyelids began quivering too.

"I shall come to see you in October," said Laptev, much moved. "You must get better, my darling."

They travelled in a special compartment. Both felt depressed and uncomfortable. She sat in the corner without taking off her hat, and made a show of dozing, and he lay on the seat opposite, and he was dis-

turbed by various thoughts—of his father, of "a certain person,"
whether Yulia would like her Moscow flat. And looking at his wife, who
did not love him, he wondered dejectedly "why this had happened."

V

The Laptevs had a wholesale business in Moscow, dealing in fancy
goods: fringe, tape, trimmings, crochet cotton, buttons, and so on. The
gross receipts reached two millions a year; what the net profit was, no
one knew but the old father. The sons and the clerks estimated the
profits at approximately three hundred thousand, and said that it would
have been a hundred thousand more if the old man had not "been too
free-handed"—that is, had not allowed credit indiscriminately. In the
last ten years alone the bad debts had mounted up to the sum of a million; and when the subject was referred to, the senior clerk would wink
slyly and deliver himself of sentences the meaning of which was not
clear to every one:

"The psychological sequences of the age."

Their chief commercial operations were conducted in the town
market in a building which was called the warehouse. The entrance to
the warehouse was in the yard, where it was always dark, and smelt of
matting and where the dray-horses were always stamping their hoofs
on the asphalt. A very humble-looking door, studded with iron, led
from the yard into a room with walls discoloured by damp and
scrawled over with charcoal, lighted up by a narrow window covered
by an iron grating. Then on the left was another room larger and
cleaner with an iron stove and a couple of chairs, though it, too, had a
prison window: this was the office, and from it a narrow stone staircase led up to the second storey, where the principal room was. This
was rather a large room, but owing to the perpetual darkness, the low-
pitched ceiling, the piles of boxes and bales, and the numbers of men
that kept flitting to and fro in it, it made as unpleasant an impression
on a newcomer as the others. In the offices on the top storey the goods
lay in bales, in bundles and in cardboard boxes on the shelves; there
was no order nor neatness in the arrangement of it, and if crimson
threads, tassels, ends of fringe, had not peeped out here and there from
holes in the paper parcels, no one could have guessed what was being
bought and sold here. And looking at these crumpled paper parcels and

boxes, no one would have believed that a million was being made out of such trash, and that fifty men were employed every day in this warehouse, not counting the buyers.

When at midday, on the day after his arrival at Moscow, Laptev went into the warehouse, the workmen packing the goods were hammering so loudly that in the outer room and the office no one heard him come in. A postman he knew was coming down the stairs with a bundle of letters in his hand; he was wincing at the noise, and he did not notice Laptev either. The first person to meet him upstairs was his brother Fyodor Fyodorovitch, who was so like him that they passed for twins. This resemblance always reminded Laptev of his own personal appearance, and now, seeing before him a short, red-faced man with rather thin hair, with narrow plebeian hips, looking so uninteresting and so unintellectual, he asked himself:

"Can I really look like that?"

"How glad I am to see you!" said Fyodor, kissing his brother and pressing his hand warmly. "I have been impatiently looking forward to seeing you every day, my dear fellow. When you wrote that you were getting married, I was tormented with curiosity, and I've missed you, too, brother. Only fancy, it's six months since we saw each other. Well? How goes it? Nina's very bad? Awfully bad?"

"Awfully bad."

"It's in God's hands," sighed Fyodor. "Well, what of your wife? She's a beauty, no doubt? I love her already. Of course, she is my little sister now. We'll make much of her between us."

Laptev saw the broad, bent back—so familiar to him—of his father, Fyodor Stepanovitch. The old man was sitting on a stool near the counter, talking to a customer.

"Father, God has sent us joy!" cried Fyodor. "Brother has come!"

Fyodor Stepanovitch was a tall man of exceptionally powerful build, so that, in spite of his wrinkles and eighty years, he still looked a hale and vigorous man. He spoke in a deep, rich, sonorous voice, that resounded from his broad chest as from a barrel. He wore no beard, but a short-clipped military moustache, and smoked cigars. As he was always too hot, he used all the year round to wear a canvas coat at home and at the warehouse. He had lately had an operation for cataract. His sight was bad, and he did nothing in the business but talk to the customers and have tea and jam with them.

Laptev bent down and kissed his head and then his lips.

"It's a good long time since we saw you, honoured sir," said the old man—"a good long time. Well, am I to congratulate you on entering the state of holy matrimony? Very well, then; I congratulate you."

And he put his lips out to be kissed. Laptev bent down and kissed him.

"Well, have you brought your young lady?" the old man asked, and without waiting for an answer, he said, addressing the customer: " 'Herewith I beg to inform you, father, that I'm going to marry such and such a young lady.' Yes. But as for asking for his father's counsel or blessing, that's not in the rules nowadays. Now they go their own way. When I married I was over forty, but I went on my knees to my father and asked his advice. Nowadays we've none of that."

The old man was delighted to see his son, but thought it unseemly to show his affection or make any display of his joy. His voice and his manner of saying "your young lady" brought back to Laptev the depression he had always felt in the warehouse. Here every trifling detail reminded him of the past, when he used to be flogged and put on Lenten fare; he knew that even now boys were thrashed and punched in the face till their noses bled, and that when those boys grew up they would beat others. And before he had been five minutes in the warehouse, he always felt as though he were being scolded or punched in the face.

Fyodor slapped the customer on the shoulder and said to his brother:

"Here, Alyosha, I must introduce our Tambov benefactor, Grigory Timofeitch. He might serve as an example for the young men of the day; he's passed his fiftieth birthday, and he has tiny children."

The clerks laughed, and the customer, a lean old man with a pale face, laughed too.

"Nature above the normal capacity," observed the head-clerk, who was standing at the counter close by. "It always comes out when it's there."

The head-clerk—a tall man of fifty, in spectacles, with a dark beard, and a pencil behind his ear—usually expressed his ideas vaguely in roundabout hints, while his sly smile betrayed that he attached particular significance to his words. He liked to obscure his utterances with bookish words, which he understood in his own way, and many

such words he used in a wrong sense. For instance, the word "except."
When he had expressed some opinion positively and did not want to be
contradicted, he would stretch out his hand and pronounce:

"Except!"

And what was most astonishing, the customers and the other clerks
understood him perfectly. His name was Ivan Vassilitch Potchatkin,
and he came from Kashira. Now, congratulating Laptev, he expressed
himself as follows:

"It's the reward of valour, for the female heart is a strong opponent."

Another important person in the warehouse was a clerk called
Makeitchev—a stout, solid, fair man with whiskers and a perfectly bald
head. He went up to Laptev and congratulated him respectfully in a
low voice:

"I have the honour, sir. . . . The Lord has heard your parent's
prayer. Thank God."

Then the other clerks began coming up to congratulate him on his
marriage. They were all fashionably dressed, and looked like perfectly
well-bred, educated men. Since between every two words they put in
a "sir," their congratulations—something like "Best wishes, sir, for
happiness, sir," uttered very rapidly in a low voice—sounded rather like
the hiss of a whip in the air—"Shshsh-s s s s!" Laptev was soon bored
and longing to go home, but it was awkward to go away. He was
obliged to stay at least two hours at the warehouse to keep up appearances. He walked away from the counter and began asking Makeitchev
whether things had gone well while he was away, and whether anything
new had turned up, and the clerk answered him respectfully, avoiding
his eyes. A boy with a cropped head, wearing a grey blouse, handed
Laptev a glass of tea without a saucer; not long afterwards another boy,
passing by, stumbled over a box, and almost fell down, and
Makeitchev's face looked suddenly spiteful and ferocious like a wild
beast's, and he shouted at him:

"Keep on your feet!"

The clerks were pleased that their young master was married and
had come back at last; they looked at him with curiosity and friendly
feeling, and each one thought it his duty to say something agreeable
when he passed him. But Laptev was convinced that it was not genuine,
and that they were only flattering him because they were afraid of him.

He never could forget how fifteen years before, a clerk, who was mentally deranged, had run out into the street with nothing on but his shirt and shaking his fists at the windows, shouted that he had been ill-treated; and how, when the poor fellow had recovered, the clerks had jeered at him for long afterwards, reminding him how he had called his employers "planters" instead of "exploiters." Altogether the employés at Laptevs' had a very poor time of it, and this fact was a subject of conversation for the whole market. The worst of it was that the old man, Fyodor Stepanovitch, maintained something of an Asiatic despotism in his attitude to them. Thus, no one knew what wages were paid to the old man's favourites, Potchatkin and Makeitchev. They received no more than three thousand a year, together with bonuses, but he made out that he paid them seven. The bonuses were given to all the clerks every year, but privately, so that the man who got little was bound from vanity to say he had got more. Not one boy knew when he would be promoted to be a clerk; not one of the men knew whether his employer was satisfied with him or not. Nothing was directly forbidden, and so the clerks never knew what was allowed, and what was not. They were not forbidden to marry, but they did not marry for fear of displeasing their employer and losing their place. They were allowed to have friends and pay visits, but the gates were shut at nine o'clock, and every morning the old man scanned them all suspiciously, and tried to detect any smell of vodka about them: "Now then, breathe," he would say.

Every clerk was obliged to go to early service, and to stand in church in such a position that the old man could see them all. The fasts were strictly observed. On great occasions, such as the birthday of their employer or of any member of his family, the clerks had to subscribe and present a cake from Fley's, or an album. The clerks lived three or four in a room in the lower storey, and in the lodges of the house in Pyatnitsky Street, and at dinner ate from a common bowl, though there was a plate set before each of them. If one of the family came into the room while they were at dinner, they all stood up.

Laptev was conscious that only, perhaps, those among them who had been corrupted by the old man's training could seriously regard him as their benefactor; the others must have looked on him as an enemy and a "planter." Now, after six months' absence, he saw no change for the better; there was indeed something new which boded nothing good. His brother Fyodor, who had always been quiet, thoughtful, and extremely refined, was now running about the ware-house with a pencil behind his ear making a show of being very busy and businesslike, slapping customers on the shoulder and shouting "Friends!" to the clerks. Apparently he had taken up a new role, and Alexey did not recognise him in the part.

The old man's voice boomed unceasingly. Having nothing to do, he was laying down the law to a customer, telling him how he should order his life and his business, always holding himself up as an example. That boastfulness, that aggressive tone of authority, Laptev had heard ten, fifteen, twenty years ago. The old man adored himself; from what he said it always appeared that he had made his wife and all her rela-tions happy, that he had been munificent to his children, and a bene-factor to his clerks and employés, and that every one in the street and all his acquaintances remembered him in their prayers. Whatever he did was always right, and if things went wrong with people it was because they did not take his advice; without his advice nothing could succeed. In church he stood in the foremost place, and even made observations to the priests, if in his opinion they were not conducting the service properly, and believed that this was pleasing God because God loved him.

At two o'clock every one in the warehouse was hard at work, except the old man, who still went on booming in his deep voice. To avoid standing idle, Laptev took some trimmings from a workgirl and let her go; then listened to a customer, a merchant from Vologda, and told a clerk to attend to him.

"T.V.A.!" resounded on all sides (prices were denoted by letters in the warehouse and goods by numbers). "R.I.T.!" As he went away, Laptev said good-bye to no one but Fyodor.

"I shall come to Pyatnitsky Street with my wife to-morrow," he said; "but I warn you, if father says a single rude thing to her, I shall not stay there another minute."

"You're the same as ever," sighed Fyodor. "Marriage has not changed you. You must be patient with the old man. So till eleven o'clock, then. We shall expect you impatiently. Come directly after mass, then."

"I don't go to mass."

"That does not matter. The great thing is not to be later than eleven, so you may be in time to pray to God and to lunch with us.

Give my greetings to my little sister and kiss her hand for me. I have a presentiment that I shall like her," Fyodor added with perfect sincerity. "I envy you, brother!" he shouted after him as Alexey went downstairs.

"And why does he shrink into himself in that shy way as though he fancied he was naked?" thought Laptev, as he walked along Nikolsky Street, trying to understand the change that had come over his brother. "And his language is new, too: 'Brother, dear brother, God has sent us joy; to pray to God'—just like Iudushka in Shtchedrin."

VI

At eleven o'clock the next day, which was Sunday, he was driving with his wife along Pyatnitsky Street in a light, one-horse carriage. He was afraid of his father's doing something outrageous, and was already ill at ease. After two nights in her husband's house Yulia Sergeyevna considered her marriage a mistake and a calamity, and if she had had to live with her husband in any other town but Moscow, it seemed to her that she could not have endured the horror of it. Moscow entertained her— she was delighted with the streets, the churches; and if it had been possible to drive about Moscow in those splendid sledges with expensive horses, to drive the whole day from morning till night, and with the swift motion to feel the cold autumn air blowing upon her, she would perhaps not have felt herself so unhappy.

Near a white, lately stuccoed two-storey house the coachman pulled up his horse, and began to turn to the right. They were expected, and near the gate stood two policemen and the porter in a new full-skirted coat, high boots, and goloshes. The whole space, from the middle of the street to the gates and all over the yard from the porch, was strewn with fresh sand. The porter took off his hat, the policemen saluted. Near the entrance Fyodor met them with a very serious face.

"Very glad to make your acquaintance, little sister," he said, kissing Yulia's hand. "You're very welcome."

He led her upstairs on his arm, and then along a corridor through a crowd of men and women. The anteroom was crowded too, and smelt of incense.

"I will introduce you to our father directly," whispered Fyodor in the midst of a solemn, deathly silence. "A venerable old man, *pater-familias*."

In the big drawing-room, by a table prepared for service, Fyodor Stepanovitch stood, evidently waiting for them, and with him the priest in a calotte, and a deacon. The old man shook hands with Yulia without saying a word. Every one was silent. Yulia was overcome with confusion.

The priest and the deacon began putting on their vestments. A censer was brought in, giving off sparks and fumes of incense and charcoal. The candles were lighted. The clerks walked into the drawing-room on tiptoe and stood in two rows along the wall. There was perfect stillness, no one even coughed.

"The blessing of God," began the deacon.

The service was read with great solemnity; nothing was left out and two canticles were sung—to sweetest Jesus and the most Holy Mother of God. The singers sang very slowly, holding up the music before them. Laptev noticed how confused his wife was. While they were singing the canticles, and the singers in different keys brought out "Lord have mercy on us," he kept expecting in nervous suspense that the old man would make some remark such as, "You don't know how to cross yourself," and he felt vexed. Why this crowd, and why this ceremony with priests and choristers? It was too bourgeois. But when she, like the old man, put her head under the gospel and afterwards several times dropped upon her knees, he realised that she liked it all, and was reassured.

At the end of the service, during "Many, many years," the priest gave the old man and Alexey the cross to kiss, but when Yulia went up, he put his hand over the cross, and showed he wanted to speak. Signs were made to the singers to stop.

"The prophet Samuel," began the priest, "went to Bethlehem at the bidding of the Lord, and there the elders of the town with fear and trembling asked him: 'Comest thou peaceably?' And the prophet answered: 'Peaceably: I am come to sacrifice unto the Lord: sanctify yourselves and come with me to the sacrifice.' Even so, Yulia, servant of God, shall we ask of thee, Dost thou come bringing peace into this house?"

Yulia flushed with emotion. As he finished, the priest gave her the cross to kiss, and said in quite a different tone of voice:

"Now Fyodor Fyodorovitch must be married; it's high time."

The choir began singing once more, people began moving, and

the room was noisy again. The old man, much touched, with his eyes full of tears, kissed Yulia three times, made the sign of the cross over her face, and said:

"This is your home. I'm an old man and need nothing."

The clerks congratulated her and said something, but the choir was singing so loud that nothing else could be heard. Then they had lunch and drank champagne. She sat beside the old father, and he talked to her, saying that families ought not to be parted but live together in one house; that separation and disunion led to permanent rupture.

"I've made money and the children only do the spending of it," he said. "Now, you live with me and save money. It's time for an old man like me to rest."

Yulia had all the time a vision of Fyodor flitting about so like her husband, but shyer and more restless; he fussed about her and often kissed her hand.

"We are plain people, little sister," he said, and patches of red came into his face as he spoke. "We live simply in Russian style, like Christians, little sister."

As they went home, Laptev felt greatly relieved that everything had gone off so well, and that nothing outrageous had happened as he had expected. He said to his wife:

"You're surprised that such a stalwart, broad-shouldered father should have such stunted, narrow-chested sons as Fyodor and me. Yes; but it's easy to explain! My father married my mother when he was forty-five, and she was only seventeen. She turned pale and trembled in his presence. Nina was born first—born of a comparatively healthy mother, and so she was finer and sturdier than we were. Fyodor and I were begotten and born after mother had been worn out by terror. I can remember my father correcting me—or, to speak plainly, beating me—before I was five years old. He used to thrash me with a birch, pull my ears, hit me on the head, and every morning when I woke up my first thought was whether he would beat me that day. Play and childish mischief was forbidden us. We had to go to morning service and to early mass. When we met priests or monks we had to kiss their hands; at home we had to sing hymns. Here you are religious and love all that, but I'm afraid of religion, and when I pass a church I remember my childhood, and am overcome with horror. I was taken to the warehouse as soon as I was eight years old. I worked like a working boy, and it was bad for my health, for I used to be beaten there every day. Afterwards when I went to the high school, used to go to school till dinner-time, and after dinner I had to sit in that warehouse till evening; and things went on like that till I was twenty-two, till I got to know Yartsev, and he persuaded me to leave my father's house. That Yartsev did a great deal for me. I tell you what," said Laptev, and he laughed with pleasure: "let us go and pay Yartsev a visit at once. He's a very fine fellow! How touched he will be!"

VII

On a Saturday in November Anton Rubinstein was conducting in a symphony concert. It was very hot and crowded. Laptev stood behind the columns, while his wife and Kostya Kotchevoy were sitting in the third or fourth row some distance in front. At the very beginning of an interval a "certain person," Polina Nikolaevna Razsudin, quite unexpectedly passed by him. He had often since his marriage thought with trepidation of a possible meeting with her. When now she looked at him openly and directly, he realised that he had all this time shirked having things out with her, or writing her two or three friendly lines, as though he had been hiding from her; he felt ashamed and blushed crimson. She pressed his hand tightly and impulsively and asked:

"Have you seen Yartsev?"

And without waiting for an answer she went striding on impetuously as though some one were pushing her on from behind.

She was very thin and plain, with a long nose; her face always looked tired, and exhausted, and it seemed as though it were an effort to her to keep her eyes open, and not to fall down. She had fine, dark eyes, and an intelligent, kind, sincere expression, but her movements were awkward and abrupt. It was hard to talk to her, because she could not talk or listen quietly. Loving her was not easy. Sometimes when she was alone with Laptev she would go on laughing for a long time, hiding her face in her hands, and would declare that love was not the chief thing in life for her, and would be as whimsical as a girl of seventeen; and before kissing her he would have to put out all the candles. She was thirty. She was married to a schoolmaster, but had not lived with her husband for years. She earned her living by giving music lessons and playing in quartettes.

During the ninth symphony she passed again as though by accident, but the crowd of men standing like a thick wall behind the columns prevented her going further, and she remained beside him. Laptev saw that she was wearing the same little velvet blouse she had worn at concerts last year and the year before. Her gloves were new, and her fan, too, was new, but it was a common one. She was fond of fine clothes, but she did not know how to dress, and grudged spending money on it. She dressed so badly and untidily that when she was going to her lessons striding hurriedly down the street, she might easily have been taken for a young monk.

The public applauded and shouted encore.

"You'll spend the evening with me," said Polina Nikolaevna, going up to Laptev and looking at him severely. "When this is over we'll go and have tea. Do you hear? I insist on it. You owe me a great deal, and haven't the moral right to refuse me such a trifle."

"Very well; let us go," Laptev assented.

Endless calls followed the conclusion of the concert. The audience got up from their seats and went out very slowly, and Laptev could not go away without telling his wife. He had to stand at the door and wait.

"I'm dying for some tea," Polina Nikolaevna said plaintively. "My very soul is parched."

"You can get something to drink here," said Laptev. "Let's go to the buffet."

"Oh, I've no money to fling away on waiters. I'm not a shopkeeper."

He offered her his arm; she refused, in a long, wearisome sentence which he had heard many times, to the effect that she did not class herself with the feebler fair sex, and did not depend on the services of gentlemen.

As she talked to him she kept looking about at the audience and greeting acquaintances; they were her fellow-students at the higher courses and at the conservatorium, and her pupils. She gripped their hands abruptly, as though she were tugging at them. But then she began twitching her shoulders, and trembling as though she were in a fever, and at last said softly, looking at Laptev with horror:

"Who is it you've married? Where were your eyes, you mad fellow? What did you see in that stupid, insignificant girl? Why, I loved you for your mind, for your soul, but that china doll wants nothing but your money!"

"Let us drop that, Polina," he said in a voice of supplication. "All that you can say to me about my marriage I've said to myself many times already. . . . Don't cause me unnecessary pain."

Yulia Sergeyevna made her appearance, wearing a black dress with a big diamond brooch, which her father-in-law had sent her after the service. She was followed by her suite—Kotchevoy, two doctors of their acquaintance, an officer, and a stout young man in student's uniform, called Kish.

"You go on with Kostya," Laptev said to his wife. "I'm coming later."

Yulia nodded and went on. Polina Nikolaevna gazed after her, quivering all over and twitching nervously, and in her eyes there was a look of repulsion, hatred, and pain.

Laptev was afraid to go home with her, foreseeing an unpleasant discussion, cutting words, and tears, and he suggested that they should go and have tea at a restaurant. But she said:

"No, no. I want to go home. Don't dare to talk to me of restaurants."

She did not like being in a restaurant, because the atmosphere of restaurants seemed to her poisoned by tobacco smoke and the breath of men. Against all men she did not know she cherished a strange prejudice, regarding them all as immoral rakes, capable of attacking her at any moment. Besides, the music played at restaurants jarred on her nerves and gave her a headache.

Coming out of the Hall of Nobility, they took a sledge in Ostozhenka and drove to Savelovsky Lane, where she lodged. All the way Laptev thought about her. It was true that he owed her a great deal. He had made her acquaintance at the flat of his friend Yartsev, to whom she was giving lessons in harmony. Her love for him was deep and perfectly disinterested, and her relations with him did not alter her habits; she went on giving her lessons and wearing herself out with work as before. Through her he came to understand and love music, which he had scarcely cared for till then.

"Half my kingdom for a cup of tea!" she pronounced in a hollow voice, covering her mouth with her muff that she might not catch cold. "I've given five lessons, confound them! My pupils are as stupid as posts;

I nearly died of exasperation. I don't know how long this slavery can go on. I'm worn out. As soon as I can scrape together three hundred roubles, I shall throw it all up and go to the Crimea, to lie on the beach and drink in ozone. How I love the sea—oh, how I love the sea!"

"You'll never go," said Laptev. " To begin with, you'll never save the money; and, besides, you'd grudge spending it. Forgive me, I repeat again: surely it's quite as humiliating to collect the money by far-things from idle people who have music lessons to while away their time, as to borrow it from your friends."

"I haven't any friends," she said irritably. " And please don't talk nonsense. The working class to which I belong has one privilege: the consciousness of being incorruptible—the right to refuse to be indebted to wretched little shopkeepers, and to treat them with scorn. No, indeed, you don't buy me! I'm not a Yulitchka!"

Laptev did not attempt to pay the driver, knowing that it would call forth a perfect torrent of words, such as he had often heard before. She paid herself.

She had a little furnished room in the flat of a solitary lady who provided her meals. Her big Becker piano was for the time at Yartsev's in Great Nikitsky Street, and she went there every day to play on it. In her room there were arm-chairs in loose covers, a bed with a white summer quilt, and flowers belonging to the landlady; there were oleo-graphs on the walls, and there was nothing that would have suggested that there was a woman, and a woman of university education, living in it. There was no toilet table; there were no books; there was not even a writing-table. It was evident that she went to bed as soon as she got home, and went out as soon as she got up in the morning.

The cook brought in the samovar. Polina Nikolaevna made tea, and, still shivering—the room was cold—began abusing the singers who had sung in the ninth symphony. She was so tired she could hardly keep her eyes open. She drank one glass of tea, then a second, and then a third.

"And so you are married," she said. "But don't be uneasy; I'm not going to pine away. I shall be able to tear you out of my heart. Only it's annoying and bitter to me that you are just as contemptible as every one else; that what you want in a woman is not brains or intellect, but simply a body, good looks, and youth. . . . Youth!" she pronounced through her nose, as though mimicking some one, and she laughed.

"Youth! You must have purity, *reinheit! reinheit!*" she laughed, throwing herself back in her chair. "*Reinheit!*"

When she left off laughing her eyes were wet with tears.

"You're happy, at any rate?" she asked.

"No."

"Does she love you?"

"No."

Laptev, agitated, and feeling miserable, stood up and began walking about the room.

"No," he repeated. " If you want to know, Polina, I'm very unhappy. There's no help for it; I've done the stupid thing, and there's no correcting it now. I must look at it philosophically. She married me without love, stupidly, perhaps with mercenary motives, but without understanding, and now she evidently sees her mistake and is miserable. I see it. At night we sleep together, but by day she is afraid to be left alone with me for five minutes, and tries to find distraction, society. With me she feels ashamed and frightened."

"And yet she takes money from you?"

"That's stupid, Polina!" cried Laptev. "She takes money from me because it makes absolutely no difference to her whether she has it or not. She is an honest, pure girl. She married me simply because she wanted to get away from her father, that's all."

"And are you sure she would have married you if you had not been rich?" asked Polina.

"I'm not sure of anything," said Laptev dejectedly. "Not of anything. I don't understand anything. For God's sake, Polina, don't let us talk about it."

"Do you love her?"

"Desperately."

A silence followed. She drank a fourth glass, while he paced up and down, thinking that by now his wife was probably having supper at the doctors' club.

"But is it possible to love without knowing why?" asked Polina, shrugging her shoulders. "No; it's the promptings of animal passion! You are poisoned, intoxicated by that beautiful body, that *reinheit!* Go away from me; you are unclean! Go to her!"

She brandished her hand at him, then took up his hat and hurled it at him. He put on his fur coat without speaking and went out, but she ran after him into the passage, clutched his arm above the elbow, and broke into sobs.

"Hush, Polina! Don't!" he said, and could not unclasp her fingers. "Calm yourself, I entreat you."

She shut her eyes and turned pale, and her long nose became an unpleasant waxy colour like a corpse's, and Laptev still could not unclasp her fingers. She had fainted. He lifted her up carefully, laid her on her bed, and sat by her for ten minutes till she came to herself. Her hands were cold, her pulse was weak and uneven.

"Go home," she said, opening her eyes. "Go away, or I shall begin howling again. I must take myself in hand."

When he came out, instead of going to the doctors' club where his friends were expecting him, he went home. All the way home he was asking himself reproachfully why he had not settled down to married life with that woman who loved him so much, and was in reality his wife and friend. She was the one human being who was devoted to him; and, besides, would it not have been a grateful and worthy task to give happiness, peace, and a home to that proud, clever, overworked creature? Was it for him, he asked himself, to lay claim to youth and beauty, to that happiness which could not be, and which, as though in punishment or mockery, had kept him for the last three months in a state of gloom and oppression. The honeymoon was long over, and he still, absurd to say, did not know what sort of person his wife was. To her school friends and her father she wrote long letters of five sheets, and was never at a loss for something to say to them, but to him she never spoke except about the weather or to tell him that dinner was ready, or that it was supper-time. When at night she said her lengthy prayers and then kissed her crosses and ikons, he thought, watching her with hatred, "Here she's praying. What's she praying about? What about?" In his thoughts he showered insults on himself and her, telling himself that when he got into bed and took her into his arms, he was taking what he had paid for; but it was horrible. If only it had been a healthy, reckless, sinful woman; but here he had youth, piety, meekness, the pure eyes of innocence. . . . While they were engaged her piety had touched him; now the conventional definiteness of her views and convictions seemed to him a barrier, behind which the real truth could not be seen. Already everything in his married life was agonising. When his wife, sitting beside him in the theatre, sighed or laughed

besought some one to go for her father, then she put on a coat and a
kerchief, and ran into the street. From the servants she knew already
that her father had another wife and two children with whom he lived
in Bazarny Street. She ran out of the gate and turned to the left, crying,
and frightened of unknown people. She soon began to sink into the
snow and grew numb with cold.

She met an empty sledge, but she did not take it: perhaps, she
thought, the man would drive her out of town, rob her, and throw her
into the cemetery (the servants had talked of such a case at tea) She
went on and on, sobbing and panting with exhaustion. When she got
into Bazarny Street, she inquired where M. Panaurov lived. An
unknown woman spent a long time directing her, and seeing that she
did not understand, took her by the hand and led her to a house of one
storey that stood back from the street. The door stood open. Sasha
ran through the entry, along the corridor, and found herself at last in
a warm, lighted room where her father was sitting by the samovar with
a lady and two children. But by now she was unable to utter a word,
and could only sob. Panaurov understood.

"Mother's worse?" he asked. "Tell me, child: is mother worse?"

He was alarmed and sent for a sledge.

When they got home, Nina Fyodorovna was sitting propped up
with pillows, with a candle in her hand. Her face looked dark and her
eyes were closed. Crowding in the doorway stood the nurse, the cook,
the housemaid, a peasant called Prokofy and a few persons of the humbler class, who were complete strangers. The nurse was giving them
orders in a whisper, and they did not understand. Inside the room at
the window stood Lida, with a pale and sleepy face, gazing severely at
her mother.

Panaurov took the candle out of Nina Fyodorovna's hand, and,
frowning contemptuously, flung it on the chest of drawers.

"This is awful!" he said, and his shoulders quivered. "Nina, you
must lie down," he said affectionately. "Lie down, dear."

She looked at him, but did not know him. . . . They laid her down
on her back.

When the priest and the doctor, Sergey Borisovitch, arrived, the
servants crossed themselves devoutly and prayed for her.

"What a sad business!" said the doctor thoughtfully, coming out
into the drawing-room. "Why, she was still young—not yet forty."

They heard the loud sobbing of the little girls. Panaurov, with a pale face and moist eyes, went up to the doctor and said in a faint, weak voice:

"Do me a favour, my dear fellow. Send a telegram to Moscow. I'm not equal to it."

The doctor fetched the ink and wrote the following telegram to his daughter:

"Madame Panaurov died at eight o'clock this evening. Tell your husband: a mortgaged house for sale in Dvoryansky Street, nine thousand cash. Auction on twelfth. Advise him not miss opportunity."

IX

Laptev lived in one of the turnings out of Little Dmitrovka. Besides the big house facing the street, he rented also a two-storey lodge in the yard at the back of his friend Kotchevoy, a lawyer's assistant whom all the Laptevs called Kostya, because he had grown up under their eyes. Facing this lodge stood another, also of two storeys, inhabited by a French family consisting of a husband and wife and five daughters.

There was a frost of twenty degrees. The windows were frozen over. Waking up in the morning, Kostya, with an anxious face, took twenty drops of a medicine; then, taking two dumb-bells out of the bookcase, he did gymnastic exercises. He was tall and thin, with big reddish moustaches; but what was most noticeable in his appearance was the length of his legs.

Pyotr, a middle-aged peasant in a reefer jacket and cotton breeches tucked into his high boots, brought in the samovar and made the tea.

"It's very nice weather now, Konstantin Ivanovitch," he said.

"It is, but I tell you what, brother, it's a pity we can't get on, you and I, without such exclamations."

Pyotr sighed from politeness.

"What are the little girls doing?" asked Kotchevoy.

"The priest has not come. Alexey Fyodorovitch is giving them their lesson himself."

Kostya found a spot in the window that was not covered with frost, and began looking through a field-glass at the windows of the house where the French family lived.

"There's no seeing," he said.

Meanwhile Alexey Fyodorovitch was giving Sasha and Lida a scripture lesson below. For the last six weeks they had been living in Moscow, and were installed with their governess in the lower storey of the lodge. And three times a week a teacher from a school in the town, and a priest, came to give them lessons. Sasha was going through the New Testament and Lida was going through the Old. The time before Lida had been set the story up to Abraham to learn by heart.

"And so Adam and Eve had two sons," said Laptev. "Very good. But what were they called? Try to remember them!"

Lida, still with the same severe face, gazed dumbly at the table. She moved her lips, but without speaking; and the elder girl, Sasha, looked into her face, frowning.

"You know it very well, only you mustn't be nervous," said Laptev. "Come, what were Adam's sons called?"

"Abel and Canel," Lida whispered.

"Cain and Abel," Laptev corrected her.

A big tear rolled down Lida's cheek and dropped on the book. Sasha looked down and turned red, and she, too, was on the point of tears. Laptev felt a lump in his throat, and was so sorry for them he could not speak. He got up from the table and lighted a cigarette. At that moment Kotchevoy came down the stairs with a paper in his hand. The little girls stood up, and without looking at him, made curtsies.

"For God's sake, Kostya, give them their lessons," said Laptev, turning to him. "I'm afraid I shall cry, too, and I have to go to the warehouse before dinner."

"All right."

Alexey Fyodorovitch went away. Kostya, with a very serious face, sat down to the table and drew the Scripture history towards him.

"Well," he said; "where have you got to?"

"She knows about the Flood," said Sasha.

"The Flood? All right. Let's peg in at the Flood. Fire away about the Flood." Kostya skimmed through a brief description of the Flood in the book, and said: "I must remark that there really never was a Flood such as is described here. And there was no such person as Noah. Some thousands of years before the birth of Christ, there was an extraordinary inundation of the earth, and that's not only mentioned in the Jewish Bible, but in the books of other ancient peoples: the Greeks, the

Chaldeans, the Hindoos. But whatever the inundation may have been, it couldn't have covered the whole earth. It may have flooded the plains, but the mountains must have remained. You can read this book, of course, but don't put too much faith in it."

Tears trickled down Lida's face again. She turned away and suddenly burst into such loud sobs, that Kostya started and jumped up from his seat in great confusion.

"I want to go home," she said, "to papa and to nurse."

Sasha cried too. Kostya went upstairs to his own room, and spoke on the telephone to Yulia Sergeyevna.

"My dear soul," he said, "the little girls are crying again; there's no doing anything with them."

Yulia Sergeyevna ran across from the big house in her indoor dress, with only a knitted shawl over her shoulders, and chilled through by the frost, began comforting the children.

"Do believe me, do believe me," she said in an imploring voice, hugging first one and then the other. "Your papa's coming to-day; he has sent a telegram. You're grieving for mother, and I grieve too. My heart's torn, but what can we do? We must bow to God's will!"

When they left off crying, she wrapped them up and took them out for a drive. They stopped near the Iverskoy chapel, put up candles at the shrine, and, kneeling down, prayed. On the way back they went in Filippov's, and had cakes sprinkled with poppy-seeds.

The Laptevs had dinner between two and three. Pyotr handed the dishes. This Pyotr waited on the family, and by day ran to the post, to the warehouse, to the law courts for Kostya; he spent his evenings making cigarettes, ran to open the door at night, and before five o'clock in the morning was up lighting the stoves, and no one knew where he slept. He was very fond of opening seltzer-water bottles and did it easily, without a bang and without spilling a drop.

"With God's blessing," said Kostya, drinking off a glass of vodka before the soup.

At first Yulia Sergeyevna did not like Kostya; his bass voice, his phrases such as "Landed him one on the beak," "filth," "produce the samovar," etc., his habit of clinking glasses and making sentimental speeches, seemed to her trivial. But as she got to know him better, she began to feel very much at home with him. He was open with her; he liked talking to her in a low voice in the evening, and even gave her novels of his own composition to read, though these had been kept a secret even from such friends as Laptev and Yartsev. She read these novels and praised them, so that she might not disappoint him, and he was delighted because he hoped sooner or later to become a distinguished author.

In his novels he described nothing but country-house life, though he had only seen the country on rare occasions when visiting friends at a summer villa, and had only been in a real country-house once in his life, when he had been to Volokolamsk on law business. He avoided any love interest as though he were ashamed of it; he put in frequent descriptions of nature, and in them was fond of using such expressions as, "the capricious lines of the mountains, the miraculous forms of the clouds, the harmony of mysterious rhythms. . . ." His novels had never been published, and this he attributed to the censorship.

He liked the duties of a lawyer, but yet he considered that his most important pursuit was not the law but these novels. He believed that he had a subtle, æsthetic temperament, and he always had leanings towards art. He neither sang nor played on any musical instrument, and was absolutely without an ear for music, but he attended all the symphony and philharmonic concerts, got up concerts for charitable objects, and made the acquaintance of singers. . . .

They used to talk at dinner.

"It's a strange thing," said Laptev, "my Fyodor took my breath away again! He said we must find out the date of the centenary of our firm, so as to try and get raised to noble rank; and he said it quite seriously. What can be the matter with him? I confess I begin to feel worried about him."

They talked of Fyodor, and of its being the fashion nowadays to adopt some pose or other. Fyodor, for instance, tried to appear like a plain merchant, though he had ceased to be one; and when the teacher came from the school, of which old Laptev was the patron, to ask Fyodor for his salary, the latter changed his voice and deportment, and behaved with the teacher as though he were some one in authority.

There was nothing to be done; after dinner they went into the study. They talked about the decadents, about "The Maid of Orleans," and Kostya delivered a regular monologue; he fancied that he was very successful in imitating Ermolova. Then they sat down and played whist. The little girls had not gone back to the lodge but were sitting together in one arm-chair, with pale and mournful faces, and were listening to every noise in the street, wondering whether it was their father coming. In the evening when it was dark and the candles were lighted, they felt deeply dejected. The talk over the whist, the footsteps of Pyotr, the crackling in the fireplace, jarred on their nerves, and they did not like to look at the fire. In the evenings they did not want to cry, but they felt strange, and there was a load on their hearts. They could not understand how people could talk and laugh when their mother was dead.

"What did you see through the field-glasses today?" Yulia Sergeyevna asked Kostya.

"Nothing to-day, but yesterday I saw the old Frenchman having his bath."

At seven o'clock Yulia and Kostya went to the Little Theatre. Laptev was left with the little girls.

"It's time your father was here," he said, looking at his watch. "The train must be late."

The children sat in their arm-chair dumb and huddling together like animals when they are cold, while he walked about the room looking impatiently at his watch. It was quiet in the house. But just before nine o'clock some one rang at the bell. Pyotr went to open the door.

Hearing a familiar voice, the children shrieked, burst into sobs, and ran into the hall. Panaurov was wearing a sumptuous coat of antelope skin, and his head and moustaches were white with hoar frost. "In a minute, in a minute," he muttered, while Sasha and Lida, sobbing and laughing, kissed his cold hands, his hat, his antelope coat. With the languor of a handsome man spoilt by too much love, he fondled the children without haste, then went into the study and said, rubbing his hands:

"I've not come to stay long, my friends. I'm going to Petersburg to-morrow. They've promised to transfer me to another town."

He was staying at the Dresden Hotel.

X

A friend who was often at the Laptevs' was Ivan Gavrilitch Yartsev. He was a strong, healthy man with black hair and a clever, pleasant face. He was considered to be handsome, but of late he had begun to grow stout, and that rather spoilt his face and figure; another thing that spoilt him was that he wore his hair cut so close that the skin showed through.

At the University his tall figure and physical strength had won him the nickname of "the pounder" among the students. He had taken his degree with the Laptev brothers in the faculty of philology—then he went in for science and now had the degree of *magister* in chemistry. But he had never given a lecture or even been a demonstrator. He taught physics and natural history in the modern school, and in two girls' high schools. He was enthusiastic over his pupils, especially the girls, and used to maintain that a remarkable generation was growing up. At home he spent his time studying sociology and Russian history, as well as chemistry, and he sometimes published brief notes in the newspapers and magazines, signing them "Y." When he talked of some botanical or zoological subject, he spoke like an historian; when he was discussing some historical question, he approached it as a man of science.

Kish, nicknamed "the eternal student," was also like one of the family at the Laptevs'. He had been for three years studying medicine. Then he took up mathematics, and spent two years over each year's course. His father, a provincial druggist, used to send him forty roubles a month, to which his mother, without his father's knowledge, added another ten. And this sum was not only sufficient for his board and lodging, but even for such luxuries as an overcoat lined with Polish beaver, gloves, scent, and photographs (he often had photographs taken of himself and used to distribute them among his friends). He was neat and demure, slightly bald, with golden side-whiskers, and he had the air of a man nearly always ready to oblige. He was always busy looking after other people's affairs. At one time he would be rushing about with a subscription list; at another time he would be freezing in the early morning at a ticket office to buy tickets for ladies of his acquaintance, or at somebody's request would be ordering a wreath or a bouquet. People simply said of him: "Kish will go, Kish will do it, Kish will buy it." He was usually unsuccessful in carrying out his commissions. Reproaches were showered upon him, people frequently forgot to pay him for the things he bought, but he simply sighed in hard cases and never protested. He was never particularly delighted nor disappointed; his stories were always long and boring; and his jokes invariably provoked laughter just because they were not funny. Thus, one day, for instance, intending to make a joke, he said to Pyotr: "Pyotr, you're not a sturgeon"; and this aroused a general laugh, and he, too, laughed for a long time, much pleased at having made such a successful jest. Whenever one of the professors was buried, he walked in front with the mutes.

Yartsev and Kish usually came in the evening to tea. If the Laptevs were not going to the theatre or a concert, the evening tea lingered on till supper. One evening in February the following conversation took place:

"A work of art is only significant and valuable when there are some serious social problems contained in its central idea," said Kostya, looking wrathfully at Yartsev. "If there is in the work a protest against serfdom, or the author takes up arms against the vulgarity of aristocratic society, the work is significant and valuable. The novels that are taken up with 'Ach!' and 'Och!' and 'she loved him, while he ceased to love her,' I tell you, are worthless, and damn them all, I say!"

"I agree with you, Konstantin Ivanovitch," said Yulia Sergeyevna. "One describes a love scene; another, a betrayal; and the third, meeting again after separation. Are there no other subjects? Why, there are many people sick, unhappy, harassed by poverty, to whom reading all that must be distasteful."

It was disagreeable to Laptev to hear his wife, not yet twenty-two, speaking so seriously and coldly about love. He understood why this was so.

"If poetry does not solve questions that seem so important," said Yartsev, "you should turn to works on technical subjects, criminal law, or finance, read scientific pamphlets. What need is there to discuss in 'Romeo and Juliet,' liberty of speech, or the disinfecting of prisons, instead of love, when you can find all that in special articles and textbooks?"

"That's pushing it to the extreme," Kostya interrupted. "We are not talking of giants like Shakespeare or Goethe; we are talking of the hundreds of talented mediocre writers, who would be infinitely more valuable if they would let love alone, and would employ themselves in spreading knowledge and humane ideas among the masses."

Kish, lisping and speaking a little through his nose, began telling the story of a novel he had lately been reading. He spoke circumstantially and without haste. Three minutes passed, then five, then ten, and no one could make out what he was talking about, and his face grew more and more indifferent, and his eyes more and more blank.

"Kish, do be quick over it," Yulia Sergeyevna could not resist saying; "it's really agonizing!"

"Shut up, Kish!" Kostya shouted to him.

They all laughed, and Kish with them.

Fyodor came in. Flushing red in patches, he greeted them all in a nervous flurry, and led his brother away into the study. Of late he had taken to avoiding the company of more than one person at once.

"Let the young people laugh, while we speak from the heart in here," he said, settling himself in a deep arm-chair at a distance from the lamp. "It's a long time, my dear brother, since we've seen each other. How long is it since you were at the warehouse? I think it must be a week."

"Yes, there's nothing for me to do there. And I must confess that the old man wearies me."

"Of course, they could get on at the warehouse without you and me, but one must have some occupation. 'In the sweat of thy brow thou shalt eat bread,' as it is written. God loves work."

Pyotr brought in a glass of tea on a tray. Fyodor drank it without sugar, and asked for more. He drank a great deal of tea, and could get through as many as ten glasses in the evening.

"I tell you what, brother," he said, getting up and going to his brother. "Laying aside philosophic subtleties, you must get elected on to the town council, and little by little we will get you on to the local Board, and then to be an alderman. And as time goes on—you are a clever man and well-educated—you will be noticed in Petersburg and asked to go there—active men on the provincial assemblies and town councils are all the fashion there now and before you are fifty you'll be a privy councillor, and have a ribbon across your shoulders."

Laptev made no answer; he knew that all this—being a privy councillor and having a ribbon over his shoulder—was what Fyodor desired for himself, and he did not know what to say.

The brothers sat still and said nothing. Fyodor opened his watch and for a long, long time gazed into it with strained attention, as though he wanted to detect the motion of the hand, and the expression of his face struck Laptev as strange.

They were summoned to supper. Laptev went into the dining-room, while Fyodor remained in the study. The argument was over and Yartsev was speaking in the tones of a professor giving a lecture:

"Owing to differences of climate, of energy, of tastes, of age, equality among men is physically impossible. But civilised man can make this inequality innocuous, as he has already done with bogs and bears. A learned man succeeded in making a cat, a mouse, a falcon, a sparrow, all eat out of one plate; and education, one must hope, will do the same thing with men. Life continually progresses, civilisation makes enormous advances before our eyes, and obviously a time will come when we shall think, for instance, the present condition of the factory population as absurd as we now do the state of serfdom, in which girls were exchanged for dogs."

"That won't be for a long while, a very long while," said Kostya, with a laugh, "not till Rothschild thinks his cellars full of gold absurd, and till then the workers may bend their backs and die of hunger. No; that's not it. We mustn't wait for it; we must struggle for it. Do you suppose because the cat eats out of the same saucer as the mouse—do you suppose that she is influenced by a sense of conscious intelligence? Not a bit of it! She's made to do it by force."

"Fyodor and I are rich; our father's a capitalist, a millionaire. You will have to struggle with us," said Laptev, rubbing his forehead with his hand. "Struggle with me is an idea I cannot grasp. I am rich, but what has money given me so far? What has this power given me? In what way am I happier than you? My childhood was slavery, and money did not save me from the birch. When Nina was ill and died, my money did not help her. If people don't care for me, I can't make them like me if I spend a hundred million."

"But you can do a great deal of good," said Kish.

"Good, indeed! You spoke to me yesterday of a mathematical man who is looking for a job. Believe me, I can do as little for him as you can. I can give money, but that's not what he wants. I asked a well-known musician to help a poor violinist, and this is what he answered: 'You apply to me just because you are not a musician yourself.' In the same way I say to you that you apply for help to me so confidently because you've never been in the position of a rich man."

"Why you bring in the comparison with a well-known musician I don't understand!" said Yulia Sergeyevna, and she flushed crimson. "What has the well-known musician to do with it!"

Her face was quivering with hatred, and she dropped her eyes to conceal the feeling. And not only her husband, but all the men sitting at the table, knew what the look in her face meant.

"What has the well-known musician got to do with it?" she said slowly. "Why, nothing's easier than helping some one poor."

Silence followed. Pyotr handed the woodcock, but they all refused it, and ate nothing but salad. Laptev did not remember what he had said, but it was clear to him that it was not his words that were hateful, but the fact of his meddling in the conversation at all.

After supper he went into his study; intently, with a beating heart, expecting further humiliation, he listened to what was going on in the hall. An argument had sprung up there again. Then Yartsev sat down to the piano and played a sentimental song. He was a man of varied accomplishments; he could play and sing, and even perform conjuring tricks.

"You may please yourselves, my friends, but I'm not going to stay at home," said Yulia. "We must go somewhere."

They decided to drive out of town, and sent Kish to the merchant's club to order a three-horse sledge. They did not ask Laptev to go with them because he did not usually join these expeditions, and because his brother was sitting with him; but he took it to mean that his society bored them, and that he was not wanted in their light-hearted youthful company. And his vexation, his bitter feeling, was so intense that he almost shed tears. He was positively glad that he was treated so ungraciously, that he was scorned, that he was a stupid, dull husband, a money-bag; and it seemed to him, that he would have been even more glad if his wife were to deceive him that night with his best friend, and were afterwards to acknowledge it, looking at him with hatred. . . . He was jealous on her account of their student friends, of actors, of singers, of Yartsev, even of casual acquaintances; and now he had a passionate longing for her really to be unfaithful to him. He longed to find her in another man's arms, and to be rid of this nightmare forever. Fyodor was drinking tea, gulping it noisily. But he, too, got up to go.

"Our old father must have got cataract," he said, as he put on his fur coat. "His sight has become very poor."

Laptev put on his coat, too, and went out. After seeing his brother part of the way home, he took a sledge and drove to Yar's.

"And this is family happiness!" he said, jeering at himself. "This is love!"

His teeth were chattering, and he did not know if it were jealousy or something else. He walked about near the tables; listened to a comic singer in the hall. He had not a single phrase ready should he meet his own party; and he felt sure beforehand that if he met his wife, he would only smile pitifully and not cleverly, and that every one would understand what feeling had induced him to come here. He was bewildered by the electric light, the loud music, the smell of powder, and the fact that the ladies he met looked at him. He stood at the doors trying to see and to hear what was going on in the private rooms, and it seemed to him that he was somehow playing a mean, contemptible part on a level with the comic singers and those ladies. Then he went to Strelna, but he found none of his circle there, either; and only when on the way home he was again driving up to Yar's, a three-horse sledge noisily overtook him. The driver was drunk and shouting, and he could hear Yartsev laughing: "Ha, ha, ha!"

Laptev returned home between three and four. Yulia Sergeyevna was in bed. Noticing that she was not asleep, he went up to her and said sharply:

"I understand your repulsion, your hatred, but you might spare me before other people; you might conceal your feelings."

She got up and sat on the bed with her legs dangling. Her eyes looked big and black in the lamplight.

"I beg your pardon," she said.

He could not utter a single word from excitement and the trembling of his whole body; he stood facing her and was dumb. She trembled, too, and sat with the air of a criminal waiting for explanations.

"How I suffer!" he said at last, and he clutched his head. "I'm in hell, and I'm out of my mind."

"And do you suppose it's easy for me?" she asked, with a quiver in her voice. "God alone knows what I go through."

"You've been my wife for six months, but you haven't a spark of love for me in your heart. There's no hope, not one ray of light! Why did you marry me?" Laptev went on with despair. "Why? What demon thrust you into my arms? What did you hope for? What did you want?"

She looked at him with terror, as though she were afraid he would kill her.

"Did I attract you? Did you like me?" he went on, gasping for breath. "No. Then what? What? Tell me what?" he cried. "Oh, the cursed money! The cursed money!"

"I swear to God, no!" she cried, and she crossed herself. She seemed to shrink under the insult, and for the first time he heard her crying. "I swear to God, no!" she repeated. "I didn't think about your money; I didn't want it. I simply thought I should do wrong if I refused you. I was afraid of spoiling your life and mine. And now I am suffering for my mistake. I'm suffering unbearably!"

She sobbed bitterly, and he saw that she was hurt; and not knowing what to say, dropped down on the carpet before her.

"That's enough; that's enough," he muttered. "I insulted you because I love you madly." He suddenly kissed her foot and passionately hugged it. "If only a spark of love," he muttered. "Come, lie to me; tell me a lie! Don't say it's a mistake! . . ."

But she went on crying, and he felt that she was only enduring his caresses as an inevitable consequence of her mistake. And the foot he had kissed she drew under her like a bird. He felt sorry for her.

She got into bed and covered her head over; he undressed and got into bed, too. In the morning they both felt confused and did not know what to talk about, and he even fancied she walked unsteadily on the foot he had kissed.

Before dinner Panaurov came to say good-bye. Yulia had an irresistible desire to go to her own home; it would be nice, she thought, to go away and have a rest from married life, from the embarrassment and the continual consciousness that she had done wrong. It was decided at dinner that she should set off with Panaurov, and stay with her father for two or three weeks until she was tired of it.

XI

She travelled with Panaurov in a reserved compartment; he had on his head an astrachan cap of peculiar shape.

"Yes, Petersburg did not satisfy me," he said, drawling, with a sigh. "They promise much, but nothing definite. Yes, my dear girl. I have been a Justice of the Peace, a member of the local Board, chairman of the Board of Magistrates, and finally councillor of the provincial administration. I think I have served my country and have earned the right to receive attention; but—would you believe it?—I can never succeed in wringing from the authorities a post in another town. . . ."

Panaurov closed his eyes and shook his head.

"They don't recognise me," he went on, as though dropping asleep. "Of course I'm not an administrator of genius, but, on the other hand, I'm a decent, honest man, and nowadays even that's something rare. I regret to say I have not been always quite straightforward with women, but in my relations with the Russian government I've always been a gentleman. But enough of that," he said, opening his eyes; "let us talk of you. What put it into your head to visit your papa so suddenly?"

"Well. . . . I had a little misunderstanding with my husband," said Yulia, looking at his cap.

"Yes. What a queer fellow he is! All the Laptevs are queer. Your husband's all right—he's nothing out of the way, but his brother Fyodor is a perfect fool."

Panaurov sighed and asked seriously:

"And have you a lover yet?"

Yulia looked at him in amazement and laughed.

"Goodness knows what you're talking about."

It was past ten o'clock when they got out at a big station and had supper. When the train went on again Panaurov took off his greatcoat and his cap, and sat down beside Yulia.

"You are very charming, I must tell you," he began. "Excuse me for the eating-house comparison, but you remind me of fresh salted cucumber; it still smells of the hotbed, so to speak, and yet has a smack of the salt and a scent of fennel about it. As time goes on you will make a magnificent woman, a wonderful, exquisite woman. If this trip of ours had happened five years ago," he sighed, "I should have felt it my duty to join the ranks of your adorers, but now, alas, I'm a veteran on the retired list."

He smiled mournfully, but at the same time graciously, and put his arm round her waist.

"You must be mad!" she said; she flushed crimson and was so frightened that her hands and feet turned cold.

"Leave off, Grigory Nikolaevitch!"

"What are you afraid of, dear?" he asked softly. "What is there dreadful about it? It's simply that you're not used to it."

If a woman protested he always interpreted it as a sign that he had made an impression on her and attracted her. Holding Yulia round the waist, he kissed her firmly on the cheek, then on the lips, in the full conviction that he was giving her intense gratification. Yulia recovered from her alarm and confusion, and began laughing. He kissed her once more and said, as he put on his ridiculous cap:

"That is all that the old veteran can give you. A Turkish Pasha, a kind-hearted old fellow, was presented by some one—or inherited, I fancy it was—a whole harem. When his beautiful young wives drew up in a row before him, he walked round them, kissed each one of them, and said: 'That is all that I am equal to giving you.' And that's just what I say, too."

All this struck her as stupid and extraordinary, and amused her. She felt mischievous. Standing up on the seat and humming, she got a box of sweets from the shelf, and throwing him a piece of chocolate, shouted:

"Catch !"

He caught it. With a loud laugh she threw him another sweet, then a third, and he kept catching them and putting them into his mouth, looking at her with imploring eyes; and it seemed to her that in his face, his features, his expression, there was a great deal that was feminine and childlike. And when, out of breath, she sat down on the seat and looked at him, laughing, he tapped her cheek with two fingers, and said as though he were vexed:

"Naughty girl!"

"Take it," she said, giving him the box. "I don't care for sweet things."

He ate up the sweets—every one of them, and locked the empty box in his trunk; he liked boxes with pictures on them.

"That's mischief enough, though," he said. "It's time for the veteran to go bye-bye."

He took out of his hold-all a Bokhara dressing-gown and a pillow, lay down, and covered himself with the dressing-gown.

"Good-night, darling!" he said softly, and sighed as though his whole body ached.

And soon a snore was heard. Without the slightest feeling of constraint, she, too, lay down and went to sleep.

When next morning she drove through her native town from the station homewards, the streets seemed to her empty and deserted. The snow looked grey, and the houses small, as though some one had squashed them. She was met by a funeral procession: the dead body was carried in an open coffin with banners.

"Meeting a funeral, they say, is lucky," she thought.

There were white bills pasted in the windows of the house where Nina Fyodorovna used to live.

With a sinking at her heart she drove into her own courtyard and rang at the door. It was opened by a servant she did not know—a plump, sleepy-looking girl wearing a warm wadded jacket. As she went upstairs Yulia remembered how Laptev had declared his love there, but now the staircase was unscrubbed, covered with foot-marks. Upstairs in the cold passage patients were waiting in their out-door coats. And for some reason her heart beat violently, and she was so excited she could scarcely walk.

The doctor, who had grown even stouter, was sitting with a brick-red face and dishevelled hair, drinking tea. Seeing his daughter, he was greatly delighted, and even lachrymose. She thought that she was the only joy in this old man's life, and much moved, she embraced him warmly, and told him she would stay a long time—till Easter. After taking off her things in her own room, she went back to the dining-room to have tea with him. He was pacing up and down with his hands in his pockets, humming, "Ru—ru—ru"; this meant that he was dissatisfied with something.

"You have a gay time of it in Moscow," he said. "I am very glad for your sake. . . . I'm an old man and I need nothing. I shall soon give up the ghost and set you all free. And the wonder is that my hide is so tough, that I'm alive still! It's amazing!"

He said that he was a tough old ass that every one rode on. They had thrust on him the care of Nina Fyodorovna, the worry of her children, and of her burial; and that coxcomb Panaurov would not trouble himself about it, and had even borrowed a hundred roubles from him and had never paid it back.

"Take me to Moscow and put me in a madhouse," said the doctor. "I'm mad; I'm a simple child, as I still put faith in truth and justice."

Then he found fault with her husband for his short-sightedness in not buying houses that were being sold so cheaply. And now it seemed to Yulia that she was not the one joy in this old man's life. While he was seeing his patients, and afterwards going his rounds, she walked through all the rooms, not knowing what to do or what to think about. She had already grown strange to her own town and her own home. She felt no inclination to go into the streets or see her friends; and at the thought of her old friends and her life as a girl, she felt no sadness nor regret for the past.

In the evening she dressed a little more smartly and went to the evening service. But there were only poor people in the church, and her splendid fur coat and hat made no impression. And it seemed to her that there was some change in the church as well as in herself. In old days she had loved it when they read the prayers for the day at evening service, and the choir sang anthems such as "I will open my lips." She liked moving slowly in the crowd to the priest who stood in the middle of the church, and then to feel the holy oil on her forehead; now she only waited for the service to be over. And now, going out of the church, she was only afraid that beggars would ask for alms; it was such a bore to have to stop and feel for her pockets; besides, she had no coppers in her pocket now—nothing but roubles.

She went to bed early, and was a long time in going to sleep. She kept dreaming of portraits of some sort, and of the funeral procession she had met that morning. The open coffin with the dead body was carried into the yard, and brought to a standstill at the door; then the coffin was swung backwards and forwards on a sheet, and dashed violently against the door. Yulia woke and jumped up in alarm. There really was a bang at the door, and the wire of the bell rustled against the wall, though no ring was to be heard.

The doctor coughed. Then she heard the servant go downstairs, and then come back.

"Madam!" she said, and knocked at the door. "Madam!"

"What is it?" said Yulia.

"A telegram for you!"

Yulia went out to her with a candle. Behind the servant stood the doctor, in his night-clothes and greatcoat, and he, too, had a candle in his hand.

"Our bell is broken," he said, yawning sleepily. "It ought to have been mended long ago."

Yulia broke open the telegram and read:

"We drink to your health.—YARTSEV, KOTCHEVOY."

"Ah, what idiots!" she said, and burst out laughing; and her heart felt light and gay.

Going back into her room, she quietly washed and dressed, then she spent a long time in packing her things, until it was daylight, and at midday she set off for Moscow.

XII

In Holy Week the Laptevs went to an exhibition of pictures in the school of painting. The whole family went together in the Moscow fashion, the little girls, the governess, Kostya, and all.

Laptev knew the names of all the well-known painters, and never missed an exhibition. He used sometimes to paint little landscape paintings when he was in the country in the summer, and he fancied he had a good deal of taste, and that if he had studied he might have made a good painter. When he was abroad he sometimes used to go to curio shops, examining the antiques with the air of a connoisseur and giving his opinion on them. When he bought any article he gave just what the shopkeeper liked to ask for it and his purchase remained afterwards in a box in the coach-house till it disappeared altogether. Or going into a print shop, he would slowly and attentively examine the engravings and the bronzes, making various remarks on them, and would buy a common frame or a box of wretched prints. At home he had pictures always of large dimensions but of inferior quality; the best among them were badly hung. It had happened to him more than once to pay large sums for things which had afterwards turned out to be forgeries of the grossest kind. And it was remarkable that, though as a rule timid in the affairs of life, he was exceedingly bold and self-confident at a picture exhibition. Why?

Yulia Sergeyevna looked at the pictures as her husband did, through her open fist or an opera-glass, and was surprised that the people in the pictures were like live people, and the trees like real trees. But she did not understand art, and it seemed to her that many pictures in the exhibition were alike, and she imagined that the whole object in painting was that the figures and objects should stand out as though they were real, when you looked at the picture through your open fist.

"That forest is Shiskin's," her husband explained to her. "He always paints the same thing. . . . But notice snow's never such a lilac colour as that. . . . And that boy's left arm is shorter than his right."

When they were all tired and Laptev had gone to look for Kostya, that they might go home, Yulia stopped indifferently before a small landscape. In the foreground was a stream, over it a little wooden bridge; on the further side a path that disappeared in the dark grass; a field on the right; a copse; near it a camp fire—no doubt of watchers by night; and in the distance there was a glow of the evening sunset.

Yulia imagined walking herself along the little bridge, and then along the little path further and further, while all round was stillness, the drowsy landrails calling and the fire flickering in the distance. And for some reason she suddenly began to feel that she had seen those very clouds that stretched across the red part of the sky, and that copse, and that field before, many times before. She felt lonely, and longed to walk on and on along the path; and there, in the glow of sunset was the calm reflection of something unearthly, eternal.

"How finely that's painted!" she said, surprised that the picture had suddenly become intelligible to her.

"Look, Alyosha! Do you see how peaceful it is?"

She began trying to explain why she liked the landscape so much, but neither Kostya nor her husband understood her. She kept looking at the picture with a mournful smile, and the fact that the others saw nothing special in it troubled her. Then she began walking through the rooms and looking at the pictures again. She tried to understand them and no longer thought that a great many of them were alike. When, on returning home, for the first time she looked attentively at the big picture that hung over the piano in the drawing-room, she felt a dislike for it, and said:

"What an idea to have pictures like that!"

And after that the gilt cornices, the Venetian looking-glasses with flowers on them, the pictures of the same sort as the one that hung over the piano, and also her husband's and Kostya's reflections upon art, aroused in her a feeling of dreariness and vexation, even of hatred.

Life went on its ordinary course from day to day with no promise of anything special. The theatrical season was over, the warm days had come. There was a long spell of glorious weather. One morning the Laptevs attended the district court to hear Kostya, who had been appointed by the court to defend some one. They were late in starting, and reached the court after the examination of the witnesses had begun. A soldier in the reserve was accused of theft and housebreaking. There were a great number of witnesses, washerwomen; they all testified that the accused was often in the house of their employer—a woman who kept a laundry. At the Feast of the Exaltation of the Cross he came late in the evening and began asking for money; he wanted a pick-me-up, as he had been drinking, but no one gave him anything. Then he went away, but an hour afterwards he came back, and brought with him some beer and a soft gingerbread cake for the little girl. They drank and sang songs almost till daybreak, and when in the morning they looked about, the lock of the door leading up into the attic was broken, and of the linen three men's shirts, a petticoat, and two sheets were missing. Kostya asked each witness sarcastically whether she had not drunk the beer the accused had brought. Evidently he was insinuating that the washerwomen had stolen the linen themselves. He delivered his speech without the slightest nervousness, looking angrily at the jury.

He explained what robbery with housebreaking meant, and the difference between that and simple theft. He spoke very circumstantially and convincingly, displaying an unusual talent for speaking at length and in a serious tone about what had been known to every one long before. And it was difficult to make out exactly what he was aiming at. From his long speech the foreman of the jury could only have deduced "that it was housebreaking but not robbery, as the washerwomen had sold the linen for drink themselves; or, if there had been robbery, there had not been housebreaking." But obviously, he said just what was wanted, as his speech moved the jury and the audience, and was very much liked. When they gave a verdict of acquittal, Yulia nodded to Kostya, and afterwards pressed his hand warmly.

In May the Laptevs moved to a country villa at Sokolniki. By that time Yulia was expecting a baby.

XIII

More than a year had passed. Yulia and Yartsev were lying on the grass at Sokolniki not far from the embankment of the Yaroslav railway; a little distance away Kotchevoy was lying with hands under his head, looking at the sky. All three had been for a walk, and were waiting for the six o'clock train to pass to go home to tea.

"Mothers see something extraordinary in their children, that is ordained by nature," said Yulia. "A mother will stand for hours together by the baby's cot looking at its little ears and eyes and nose, and fascinated by them. If any one else kisses her baby the poor thing imagines that it gives him immense pleasure. And a mother talks of nothing but her baby. I know that weakness in mothers, and I keep watch over myself, but my Olga really is exceptional. How she looks at me when I'm nursing her! How she laughs! She's only eight months old, but, upon my word, I've never seen such intelligent eyes in a child of three."

"Tell me, by the way," asked Yartsev: "which do you love most—your husband or your baby?"

Yulia shrugged her shoulders.

"I don't know," she said. "I never was so very fond of my husband, and Olga is in reality my first love. You know that I did not marry Alexey for love. In old days I was foolish and miserable, and thought that I had ruined my life and his, and now I see that love is not necessary—that it is all nonsense."

"But if it is not love, what feeling is it that binds you to your husband? Why do you go on living with him?"

"I don't know. . . . I suppose it must be habit. I respect him, I miss him when he's away for long, but that's—not love. He is a clever, honest man, and that's enough to make me happy. He is very kind and good-hearted. . . ."

"Alyosha's intelligent, Alyosha's good," said Kostya, raising his head lazily; "but, my dear girl, to find out that he is intelligent, good, and interesting, you have to eat a hundredweight of salt with him. . . . And what's the use of his goodness and intelligence? He can fork out money as much as you want, but when character is needed to resist insolence or aggressiveness, he is faint-hearted and overcome with nervousness. People like your amiable Alyosha are splendid people, but they are no use at all for fighting. In fact, they are no use for anything."

At last the train came in sight. Coils of perfectly pink smoke from the funnels floated over the copse, and two windows in the last compartment flashed so brilliantly in the sun, that it hurt their eyes to look at it.

"Tea-time!" said Yulia Sergeyevna, getting up.

She had grown somewhat stouter of late, and her movements were already a little matronly, a little indolent.

"It's bad to be without love though," said Yartsev, walking behind her. "We talk and read of nothing else but love, but we do very little loving ourselves, and that's really bad."

"All that's nonsense, Ivan Gavrilitch," said Yulia. "That's not what gives happiness."

They had tea in the little garden, where mignonette, stocks, and tobacco plants were in flower, and spikes of early gladiolus were just opening. Yartsev and Kotchevoy could see from Yulia's face that she was passing through a happy period of inward peace and serenity, that she wanted nothing but what she had, and they, too, had a feeling of peace and comfort in their hearts. Whatever was said sounded apt and clever; the pines were lovely—the fragrance of them was exquisite as it had never been before; and the cream was very nice; and Sasha was a good, intelligent child.

After tea Yartsev sang songs, accompanying himself on the piano, while Yulia and Kotchevoy sat listening in silence, though Yulia got up from time to time, and went softly indoors, to take a look at the baby and at Lida, who had been in bed for the last two days feverish and eating nothing.

"My friend, my tender friend," sang Yartsev. "No, my friends, I'll be hanged if I understand why you are all so against love!" he said, flinging back his head. "If I weren't busy for fifteen hours of the twenty-four, I should certainly fall in love."

Supper was served on the verandah; it was warm and still, but Yulia wrapped herself in a shawl and complained of the damp. When it got dark, she seemed not quite herself; she kept shivering and begging her visitors to stay a little longer. She regaled them with wine, and after supper ordered brandy to keep them from going. She didn't want to be left alone with the children and the servants.

"We summer visitors are getting up a performance for the children," she said. "We have got everything—a stage and actors; we are only at a loss for a play. Two dozen plays of different sorts have been sent us, but there isn't one that is suitable. Now, you are fond of the theatre, and are so good at history," she said, addressing Yartsev. "Write an historical play for us."

"Well, I might."

The men drank up all the brandy, and prepared to go.

It was past ten, and for summer-villa people that was late.

"How dark it is! One can't see a bit," said Yulia, as she went with them to the gate. "I don't know how you'll find your way. But, isn't it cold?"

She wrapped herself up more closely and walked back to the porch.

"I suppose my Alexey's playing cards somewhere," she called to them. "Good-night!"

After the lighted rooms nothing could be seen. Yartsev and Kostya groped their way like blind men to the railway embankment and crossed it.

"One can't see a thing," said Kostya in his bass voice, standing still and gazing at the sky. "And the stars, the stars, they are like new three-penny-bits. Gavrilitch!"

"Ah?" Yartsev responded somewhere in the darkness.

"I say, one can't see a thing. Where are you?"

Yartsev went up to him whistling, and took his arm.

"Hi, there, you summer visitors!" Kostya shouted at the top of his voice. "We've caught a socialist."

When he was exhilarated he was always very rowdy, shouting, wrangling with policemen and cabdrivers, singing, and laughing violently.

"Nature be damned," he shouted.

"Come, come," said Yartsev, trying to pacify him. "You mustn't. Please don't."

Soon the friends grew accustomed to the darkness, and were able to distinguish the outlines of the tall pines and telegraph posts. From time to time the sound of whistles reached them from the station and the telegraph wires hummed plaintively. From the copse itself there came no sound, and there was a feeling of pride, strength, and mystery in its silence, and on the right it seemed that the tops of the pines were almost touching the sky. The friends found their path and walked along it. There it was quite dark, and it was only from the long strip of sky dotted with stars, and from the firmly trodden earth under their feet, that they could tell they were walking along a path. They walked along side by side in silence, and it seemed to both of them that people were coming to meet them. Their tipsy exhilaration passed off. The fancy came into Yartsev's mind that perhaps that copse was haunted by the spirits of the Muscovite Tsars, boyars, and patriarchs, and he was on the point of telling Kostya about it, but he checked himself.

When they reached the town gate there was a faint light of dawn in the sky. Still in silence, Yartsev and Kotchevoy walked along the wooden pavement, by the cheap summer cottages, eating-houses, timber-stacks. Under the arch of interlacing branches, the damp air was fragrant of lime-trees, and then a broad, long street opened before them, and on it, not a soul, not a light. . . . When they reached the Red Pond, it was daylight.

"Moscow—it's a town that will have to suffer a great deal more," said Yartsev, looking at the Alexyevsky Monastery.

"What put that into your head?"

"I don't know. I love Moscow."

Both Yartsev and Kostya had been born in Moscow, and adored the town, and felt for some reason antagonistic to every other town. Both were convinced that Moscow was a remarkable town, and Russia a remarkable country. In the Crimea, in the Caucasus, and abroad, they felt dull, uncomfortable, and ill at ease, and they thought their grey Moscow weather very pleasant and healthy. And when the rain lashed at the window-panes and it got dark early, and when the walls of the churches and houses looked a drab, dismal colour, days when one doesn't know what to put on when one is going out—such days excited them agreeably.

At last near the station they took a cab.

"It really would be nice to write an historical play," said Yartsev, "but not about the Lyapunovs or the Godunovs, but of the times of Yaroslav or of Monomach. . . . I hate all historical plays except the monologue of Pimen. When you have to do with some historical authority or even read a textbook of Russian history, you feel that every one in Russia is exceptionally talented, gifted, and interesting; but when I see an historical play at the theatre, Russian life begins to seem stupid, morbid, and not original."

Near Dmitrovka the friends separated, and Yartsev went on to his lodging in Nikitsky Street. He sat half dozing, swaying from side to side, and pondering on the play. He suddenly imagined a terrible din, a clanging noise, and shouts in some unknown language, that might have been Kalmuck, and a village wrapped in flames, and forests near covered with hoarfrost and soft pink in the glow of the fire, visible for miles around, and so clearly that every little fir-tree could be distinguished, and savage men darting about the village on horseback and on foot, and as red as the glow in the sky.

"The Polovtsy," thought Yartsev.

One of them, a terrible old man with a bloodstained face all scorched from the fire, binds to his saddle a young girl with a white Russian face, and the girl looks sorrowful, understanding. . . . Yartsev flung back his head and woke up.

"My friend, my tender friend . . ." he hummed.

As he paid the cabman and went up his stairs, he could not shake off his dreaminess; he saw the flames catching the village, and the forest beginning to crackle and smoke. A huge, wild bear frantic with terror rushed through the village. . . . And the girl tied to the saddle was still looking.

When at last he went into his room it was broad daylight. Two candles were burning by some open music on the piano. On the sofa lay Polina Razsudin wearing a black dress and a sash, with a newspaper in her hand, fast asleep. She must have been playing late, waiting for Yartsev to come home, and, tired of waiting, fell asleep.

"Hullo, she's worn out," he thought.

Carefully taking the newspaper out of her hands, he covered her with a rug. He put out the candles and went into his bedroom. As he got into bed, he still thought of his historical play, and the tune of "My friend, my tender friend" was still ringing in his head. . . .

Two days later Laptev looked in upon him for a moment to tell him that Lida was ill with diphtheria, and that Yulia Sergeyevna and her baby had caught it from her, and five days later came the news that Lida and Yulia were recovering, but the baby was dead, and that the Laptevs had left their villa at Sokolniki and had hastened back to Moscow.

XIV

It had become distasteful to Laptev to be long at home. His wife was constantly away in the lodge declaring that she had to look after the little girls, but he knew that she did not go to the lodge to give them lessons but to cry in Kostya's room. The ninth day came, then the twentieth, and then the fortieth, and still he had to go to the cemetery to listen to the requiem, and then to wear himself out for a whole day and night thinking of nothing but that unhappy baby, and trying to comfort his wife with all sorts of commonplace expressions. He went rarely to the warehouse now, and spent most of his time in charitable work, seizing upon every pretext requiring his attention, and he was glad when he had for some trivial reason to be out for the whole day. He had been intending of late to go abroad, to study night-refuges, and that idea attracted him now.

It was an autumn day. Yulia had just gone to the lodge to cry, while Laptev lay on a sofa in the study thinking where he could go. Just at that moment Pyotr announced Polina Razsudin. Laptev was delighted; he leapt up and went to meet the unexpected visitor, who had been his closest friend, though he had almost begun to forget her. She had not changed in the least since that evening when he had seen her for the last time, and was just the same as ever.

"Polina," he said, holding out both hands to her. "What ages! If you only knew how glad I am to see you! Do come in!"

Polina greeted him, jerked him by the hand, and without taking off her coat and hat, went into the study and sat down.

"I've come to you for one minute," she said. "I haven't time to talk of any nonsense. Sit down and listen. Whether you are glad to see me or not is absolutely nothing to me, for I don't care a straw for the gracious attentions of you lords of creation. I've only come to you because I've been to five other places already to-day, and everywhere I was met with a refusal, and it's a matter that can't be put off. Listen," she went on, looking into his face. "Five students of my acquaintance, stupid, unintelligent people, but certainly poor, have neglected to pay their fees, and are being excluded from the university. Your wealth makes it your duty to go straight to the university and pay for them."

"With pleasure, Polina."

"Here are their names," she said, giving him a list. "Go this minute; you'll have plenty of time to enjoy your domestic happiness afterwards."

At that moment a rustle was heard through the door that led into

the drawing-room; probably the dog was scratching itself. Polina
turned crimson and jumped up.

"Your Dulcinea's eavesdropping," she said. "That's horrid!"

Laptev was offended at this insult to Yulia.

"She's not here; she's in the lodge," he said. "And don't speak of her
like that. Our child is dead, and she is in great distress."

"You can console her," Polina scoffed, sitting down again; "she'll
have another dozen. You don't need much sense to bring children into
the world."

Laptev remembered that he had heard this, or something very like
it, many times in old days, and it brought back a whiff of the romance
of the past, of solitary freedom, of his bachelor life, when he was young
and thought he could do anything he chose, when he had neither love
for his wife nor memory of his baby.

"Let us go together," he said, stretching.

When they reached the university Polina waited at the gate, while
Laptev went into the office; he came back soon afterwards and handed
Polina five receipts.

"Where are you going now?" he asked.

"To Yartsev's."

"I'll come with you."

"But you'll prevent him from writing."

"No, I assure you I won't," he said, and looked at her imploringly.

She had on a black hat trimmed with crape, as though she were in
mourning, and a short, shabby coat, the pockets of which stuck out.
Her nose looked longer than it used to be, and her face looked bloodless in spite of the cold. Laptev liked walking with her, doing what she
told him, and listening to her grumbling. He walked along thinking
about her, what inward strength there must be in this woman, since,
though she was so ugly, so angular, so restless, though she did not know
how to dress, and always had untidy hair, and was always somehow out
of harmony, she was yet so fascinating.

They went into Yartsev's flat by the back way through the kitchen,
where they were met by the cook, a clean little old woman with grey
curls; she was overcome with embarrassment, and with a honeyed
smile which made her little face look like a pie, said:

"Please walk in."

Yartsev was not at home. Polina sat down to the piano, and beginning upon a tedious, difficult exercise, told Laptev not to hinder her. And without distracting her attention by conversation, he sat on one side and began turning over the pages of a "The Messenger of Europe." After practising for two hours—it was the task she set herself every day—she ate something in the kitchen and went out to her lessons. Laptev read the continuation of a story, then sat for a long time without reading and without being bored, glad to think that he was too late for dinner at home.

"Ha, ha, ha!" came Yartsev's laugh, and he walked in with ruddy cheeks, looking strong and healthy, wearing a new coat with bright buttons. "Ha, ha, ha!"

The friends dined together. Then Laptev lay on the sofa while Yartsev sat near and lighted a cigar. It got dark.

"I must be getting old," said Laptev." Ever since my sister Nina died, I've taken to constantly thinking of death."

They began talking of death, of the immortality of the soul, of how nice it would be to rise again and fly off somewhere to Mars, to be always idle and happy, and, above all, to think in a new special way, not as on earth.

"One doesn't want to die," said Yartsev softly. "No sort of philosophy can reconcile me to death, and I look on it simply as annihilation. One wants to live."

"You love life, Gavrilitch?"

"Yes, I love it."

"Do you know, I can never understand myself about that. I'm always in a gloomy mood or else indifferent. I'm timid, without self-confidence; I have a cowardly conscience; I never can adapt myself to life, or become its master. Some people talk nonsense or cheat, and even so enjoy life, while I consciously do good, and feel nothing but uneasiness or complete indifference. I explain all that, Gavrilitch, by my being a slave, the grandson of a serf. Before we plebeians fight our way into the true path, many of our sort will perish on the way."

"That's all quite right, my dear fellow," said Yartsev, and he sighed. "That only proves once again how rich and varied Russian life is. Ah, how rich it is! Do you know, I feel more convinced every day that we are on the eve of the greatest triumph, and I should like to live to take part in it. Whether you like to believe it or not, to my thinking a remarkable generation is growing up. It gives me great enjoyment to teach the children, especially the girls. They are wonderful children!"

Yartsev went to the piano and struck a chord.

"I'm a chemist, I think in chemical terms, and I shall die a chemist," he went on. "But I am greedy, and I am afraid of dying unsatisfied; and chemistry is not enough for me, and I seize upon Russian history, history of art, the science of teaching music. . . . Your wife asked me in the summer to write an historical play, and now I'm longing to write and write. I feel as though I could sit for three days and three nights without moving, writing all the time. I am worn out with ideas—my brain's crowded with them, and I feel as though there were a pulse throbbing in my head. I don't in the least want to become anything special, to create something great. I simply want to live, to dream, to hope, to be in the midst of everything. . . . Life is short, my dear fellow, and one must make the most of everything."

After this friendly talk, which was not over till midnight, Laptev took to coming to see Yartsev almost every day. He felt drawn to him. As a rule he came towards evening, lay down on the sofa, and waited patiently for Yartsev to come in, without feeling in the least bored. When Yartsev came back from his work, he had dinner, and sat down to work; but Laptev would ask him a question, a conversation would spring up, and there was no more thought of work and at midnight the friends parted very well pleased with one another.

But this did not last long. Arriving one day at Yartsev's, Laptev found no one there but Polina, who was sitting at the piano practising her exercises. She looked at him with a cold, almost hostile expression, and asked without shaking hands:

"Tell me, please: how much longer is this going on?"

"This? What?" asked Laptev, not understanding.

"You come here every day and hinder Yartsev from working. Yartsev is not a tradesman; he is a scientific man, and every moment of his life is precious. You ought to understand and to have some little delicacy!"

"If you think that I hinder him," said Laptev, mildly, disconcerted, "I will give up my visits."

"Quite right, too. You had better go, or he may be home in a minute and find you here."

The tone in which this was said, and the indifference in Polina's eyes, completely disconcerted him. She had absolutely no sort of feeling for him now, except the desire that he should go as soon as possible—and what a contrast it was to her old love for him! He went out without shaking hands with her, and he fancied she would call out to him, bring him back, but he heard the scales again, and as he slowly went down the stairs he realised that he had become a stranger to her now.

Three days later Yartsev came to spend the evening with him.

"I have news," he said, laughing. "Polina Nikolaevna has moved into my rooms altogether." He was a little confused, and went on in a low voice: "Well, we are not in love with each other, of course, but I suppose that . . . that doesn't matter. I am glad I can give her a refuge and peace and quiet, and make it possible for her not to work if she's ill. She fancies that her coming to live with me will make things more orderly, and that under her influence I shall become a great scientist. That's what she fancies. And let her fancy it. In the South they have a saying: 'Fancy makes the fool a rich man.' Ha, ha, ha!"

Laptev said nothing. Yartsev walked up and down the study, looking at the pictures he had seen so many times before, and said with a sigh:

"Yes, my dear fellow, I am three years older than you are, and it's too late for me to think of real love, and in reality a woman like Polina Nikolaevna is a godsend to me, and, of course, I shall get on capitally with her till we're both old people; but, goodness knows why, one still regrets something, one still longs for something, and I still feel as though I am lying in the Vale of Daghestan and dreaming of a ball. In short, man's never satisfied with what he has."

He went into the drawing-room and began singing as though nothing had happened, and Laptev sat in his study with his eyes shut, and tried to understand why Polina had gone to live with Yartsev. And then he felt sad that there were no lasting, permanent attachments. And he felt vexed that Polina Nikolaevna had gone to live with Yartsev, and vexed with himself that his feeling for his wife was not what it had been.

XV

Laptev sat reading and swaying to and fro in a rocking-chair; Yulia was in the study, and she, too, was reading. It seemed there was nothing to talk about; they had both been silent all day. From time to time he looked at her from over his book and thought: "Whether one marries from passionate love, or without love at all, doesn't it come to the same thing?" And the time when he used to be jealous, troubled, distressed, seemed to him far away. He had succeeded in going abroad, and now he was resting after the journey and looking forward to another visit in the spring to England, which he had very much liked.

And Yulia Sergeyevna had grown used to her sorrow, and had left off going to the lodge to cry. That winter she had given up driving out shopping, had given up the theatres and concerts, and had stayed at home. She never cared for big rooms, and always sat in her husband's study or in her own room, where she had shrines of ikons that had come to her on her marriage, and where there hung on the wall the landscape that had pleased her so much at the exhibition. She spent hardly any money on herself, and was almost as frugal now as she had been in her father's house.

The winter passed cheerlessly. Card-playing was the rule every-where in Moscow, and if any other recreation was attempted, such as singing, reading, drawing, the result was even more tedious. And since there were few talented people in Moscow, and the same singers and reciters performed at every entertainment, even the enjoyment of art gradually palled and became for many people a tiresome and monoto-nous social duty.

Moreover, the Laptevs never had a day without something vexa-tious happening. Old Laptev's eyesight was failing; he no longer went to the warehouse, and the oculist told them that he would soon be blind. Fyodor had for some reason given up going to the warehouse and spent his time sitting at home writing something. Panaurov had got a post in another town, and had been promoted an actual civil councillor, and was now staying at the Dresden. He came to the Laptevs' almost every day to ask for money. Kish had finished his stud-ies at last, and while waiting for Laptev to find him a job, used to spend whole days at a time with them, telling them long, tedious stories. All this was irritating and exhausting, and made daily life unpleasant.

Pyotr came into the study, and announced an unknown lady. On the card he brought in was the name "Josephina Iosefovna Milan."

Yulia Sergeyevna got up languidly and went out limping slightly, as her foot had gone to sleep. In the doorway appeared a pale, thin lady with dark eyebrows, dressed altogether in black. She clasped her hands on her bosom and said supplicatingly:

"M. Laptev, save my children!"

The jingle of her bracelets sounded familiar to him, and he knew the face with patches of powder on it; he recognised her as the lady with whom he had once so inappropriately dined before his marriage. It was Panaurov's second wife.

"Save my children," she repeated, and her face suddenly quivered and looked old and pitiful. "You alone can save us, and I have spent my last penny coming to Moscow to see you! My children are starving!"

She made a motion as though she were going to fall on her knees. Laptev was alarmed, and clutched her by the arm.

"Sit down, sit down . . ." he muttered, making her sit down. "I beg you to be seated."

"We have no money to buy bread," she said. "Grigory Nikolae-vitch is going away to a new post, but he will not take the children and me with him, and the money which you so generously send us he spends only on himself. What are we to do ? What? My poor, unhappy children!"

"Calm yourself, I beg. I will give orders that that money shall be made payable to you."

She began sobbing, and then grew calmer, and he noticed that the tears had made little pathways through the powder on her cheeks, and that she was growing a moustache.

"You are infinitely generous, M. Laptev. But be our guardian angel, our good fairy, persuade Grigory Nikolaevitch not to abandon me, but to take me with him. You know I love him—I love him insanely; he's the comfort of my life."

Laptev gave her a hundred roubles, and promised to talk to Panau-rov, and saw her out to the hall in trepidation the whole time, for fear she should break into sobs or fall on her knees.

After her, Kish made his appearance. Then Kostya came in with his photographic apparatus. Of late he had been attracted by photog-raphy and took photographs of every one in the house several times a day. This new pursuit caused him many disappointments, and he had actually grown thinner.

Before evening tea Fyodor arrived. Sitting in a corner in the study, he opened a book and stared for a long time at a page, obviously not reading. Then he spent a long time drinking tea; his face turned red. In his presence Laptev felt a load on his heart; even his silence was irksome to him.

"Russia may be congratulated on the appearance of a new author," said Fyodor. "Joking apart, though, brother, I have turned out a little article—the firstfruits of my pen, so to say—and I've brought it to show you. Read it, dear boy, and tell me your opinion—but sincerely."

He took a manuscript out of his pocket and gave it to his brother. The article was called "The Russian Soul"; it was written tediously, in the colourless style in which people with no talent, but full of secret vanity, usually write. The leading idea of it was that the intellectual man has the right to disbelieve in the supernatural, but it is his duty to conceal his lack of faith, that he may not be a stumbling-block and shake the faith of others. Without faith there is no idealism, and idealism is destined to save Europe and guide humanity into the true path.

"But you don't say what Europe has to be saved from," said Laptev.

"That's intelligible of itself."

"Nothing is intelligible," said Laptev, and he walked about the room in agitation. "It's not intelligible to me why you wrote it. But that's your business."

"I want to publish it in pamphlet form."

"That's your affair."

They were silent for a minute. Fyodor sighed and said:

"It's an immense regret to me, dear brother, that we think differently. Oh, Alyosha, Alyosha, my darling brother! You and I are true Russians, true believers, men of broad nature; all of these German and Jewish crochets are not for us. You and I are not wretched upstarts, you know, but representatives of a distinguished merchant family."

"What do you mean by a distinguished family?" said Laptev, restraining his irritation. "A distinguished family! The landowners beat our grandfather and every low little government clerk punched him in the face. Our grandfather thrashed our father, and our father thrashed us. What has your distinguished family done for us? What sort of nerves, what sort of blood, have we inherited? For nearly three years you've been arguing like an ignorant deacon, and talking all sorts of nonsense, and now you've written—this slavish drivel here! While I, while I! Look at me. . . . No elasticity, no boldness, no strength of will; I tremble over every step I take as though I should be flogged for it. I am timid before nonentities, idiots, brutes, who are immeasurably my inferiors mentally and morally; I am afraid of porters, doorkeepers, policemen, gendarmes. I am afraid of every one, because I was born of a mother who was terrified, and because from a child I was beaten and frightened! . . . You and I will do well to have no children. Oh, God, grant that this distinguished merchant family may die with us!"

Yulia Sergeyevna came into the study and sat down at the table.

"Are you arguing about something here?" she asked. "Am I interrupting?"

"No, little sister," answered Fyodor. "Our discussion was of principles. Here, you are abusing the family," he added, turning to his brother. "That family has created a business worth a million, though. That stands for something, anyway!"

"A great distinction—a business worth a million! A man with no particular brains, without abilities, by chance becomes a trader, and then when he has grown rich he goes on trading from day to day, with no sort of system, with no aim, without having any particular greed for money. He trades mechanically, and money comes to him of itself, without his going to meet it. He sits all his life at his work, likes it only because he can domineer over his clerks and get the better of his customers. He's a churchwarden because he can domineer over the choristers and keep them under his thumb; he's the patron of a school because he likes to feel the teacher is his subordinate and enjoys lording it over him. The merchant does not love trading, he loves dominating, and your warehouse is not so much a commercial establishment as a torture chamber! And for a business like yours, you want clerks who have been deprived of individual character and personal life—and you make them such by forcing them in childhood to lick the dust for a crust of bread, and you've trained them from childhood to believe that you are their benefactors. No fear of your taking a university man into your warehouse!"

"University men are not suitable for our business."

"That's not true," cried Laptev. "It's a lie!"

"Excuse me, it seems to me you spit into the well from which you drink yourself," said Fyodor, and he got up. "Our business is hateful to you, yet you make use of the income from it."

"Aha! We've spoken our minds," said Laptev, and he laughed,

looking angrily at his brother. "Yes, if I didn't belong to your distinguished family—if I had an ounce of will and courage, I should long ago have flung away that income, and have gone to work for my living. But in your warehouse you've destroyed all character in me from a child! I'm your product."

Fyodor looked at the clock and began hurriedly saying good-bye. He kissed Yulia's hand and went out, but instead of going into the hall, walked into the drawing-room, then into the bedroom.

"I've forgotten how the rooms go," he said in extreme confusion. "It's a strange house. Isn't it a strange house!"

He seemed utterly overcome as he put on his coat, and there was a look of pain on his face. Laptev felt no more anger; he was frightened, and at the same time felt sorry for Fyodor, and the warm, true love for his brother, which seemed to have died down in his heart during those three years, awoke, and he felt an intense desire to express that love.

"Come to dinner with us to-morrow, Fyodor," he said, and stroked him on the shoulder. "Will you come?"

"Yes, yes; but give me some water."

Laptev ran himself to the dining-room to take the first thing he could get from the sideboard. This was a tall beer-jug. He poured water into it and brought it to his brother. Fyodor began drinking, but bit a piece out of the jug; they heard a crunch, and then sobs. The water ran over his fur coat and his jacket, and Laptev, who had never seen men cry, stood in confusion and dismay, not knowing what to do. He looked on helplessly while Yulia and the servant took off Fyodor's coat and helped him back again into the room, and went with him, feeling guilty.

Yulia made Fyodor lie down on the sofa and knelt beside him.

"It's nothing," she said, trying to comfort him. "It's your nerves. . . ."

"I'm so miserable, my dear!" he said. "I am so unhappy, unhappy . . . but all the time I've been hiding it, I've been hiding it!"

He put his arm round her neck and whispered in her ear:

"Every night I see my sister Nina. She comes and sits in the chair near my bed. . . ."

When, an hour later, he put on his fur coat in the hall, he was smiling again and ashamed to face the servant. Laptev went with him to Pyatnitsky Street.

"Come and have dinner with us to-morrow," he said on the way, holding him by the arm, "and at Easter we'll go abroad together. You absolutely must have a change, or you'll be getting quite morbid!"

When he got home Laptev found his wife in a state of great nervous agitation. The scene with Fyodor had upset her, and she could not recover her composure. She wasn't crying but kept tossing on the bed, clutching with cold fingers at the quilt, at the pillows, at her husband's hands. Her eyes looked big and frightened.

"Don't go away from me, don't go away," she said to her husband. "Tell me, Alyosha, why have I left off saying my prayers? What has become of my faith? Oh, why did you talk of religion before me? You've shaken my faith, you and your friends. I never pray now."

He put compresses on her forehead, chafed her hands, gave her tea to drink, while she huddled up to him in terror. . . .

Towards morning she was worn out and fell asleep, while Laptev sat beside her and held her hand. So that he could get no sleep. The whole day afterwards he felt shattered and dull, and wandered listlessly about the rooms without a thought in his head.

XVI

The doctor said that Fyodor's mind was affected. Laptev did not know what to do in his father's house, while the dark warehouse in which neither his father nor Fyodor ever appeared now seemed to him like a sepulchre. When his wife told him that he absolutely must go every day to the warehouse and also to his father's, he either said nothing, or began talking irritably of his childhood, saying that it was beyond his power to forgive his father for his past, that the warehouse and the house in Pyatnitsky Street were hateful to him, and so on.

One Sunday morning Yulia went herself to Pyatnitsky Street. She found old Fyodor Stepanovitch in the same big drawing-room in which the service had been held on her first arrival. Wearing slippers, and without a cravat, he was sitting motionless in his arm-chair, blinking with his sightless eyes.

"It's I—your daughter-in-law," she said, going up to him. "I've come to see how you are."

He began breathing heavily with excitement.

Touched by his affliction and his loneliness, she kissed his hand;

and he passed his hand over her face and head, and having satisfied himself that it was she, made the sign of the cross over her.

"Thank you, thank you," he said. "You know I've lost my eyes and can see nothing. . . . I can dimly see the window and the fire, but people and things I cannot see at all. Yes, I'm going blind, and Fyodor has fallen ill, and without the master's eye things are in a bad way now. If there is any irregularity there's no one to look into it; and folks soon get spoiled. And why is it Fyodor has fallen ill? Did he catch cold? Here I have never ailed in my life and never taken medicine. I never saw anything of doctors."

And, as he always did, the old man began boasting. Meanwhile the servants hurriedly laid the table and brought in lunch and bottles of wine. Ten bottles were put on the table; one of them was in the shape of the Eiffel Tower. There was a whole dish of hot pies smelling of jam, rice, and fish.

"I beg my dear guest to have lunch," said the old man.

She took him by the arm, led him to the table, and poured him out a glass of vodka.

"I will come to you again to-morrow," she said, "and I'll bring your grandchildren, Sasha and Lida. They will be sorry for you, and fondle you."

"There's no need. Don't bring them. They are illegitimate."

"Why are they illegitimate? Why, their father and mother were married."

"Without my permission. I do not bless them, and I don't want to know them. Let them be."

"You speak strangely, Fyodor Stepanovitch," said Yulia, with a sigh.

"It is written in the Gospel: children must fear and honour their parents."

"Nothing of the sort. The Gospel tells us that we must forgive even our enemies."

"One can't forgive in our business. If you were to forgive every one, you would come to ruin in three years."

"But to forgive, to say a kind, friendly word to any one, even a sinner, is something far above business, far above wealth."

Yulia longed to soften the old man, to awaken a feeling of compassion in him, to move him to repentance; but he only listened condescendingly to all she said, as a grown-up person listens to a child.

"Fyodor Stepanovitch," said Yulia resolutely, "you are an old man, and God soon will call you to Himself. He won't ask you how you managed your business, and whether you were successful in it, but whether you were gracious to people; or whether you were harsh to those who were weaker than you, such as your servants, your clerks."

"I was always the benefactor of those that served me; they ought to remember me in their prayers forever," said the old man, with conviction, but touched by Yulia's tone of sincerity, and anxious to give her pleasure, he said: "Very well; bring my grandchildren to-morrow. I will tell them to buy me some little presents for them."

The old man was slovenly in his dress, and there was cigar ash on his breast and on his knees; apparently no one cleaned his boots, or brushed his clothes. The rice in the pies was half cooked, the tablecloth smelt of soap, the servants tramped noisily about the room. And the old man and the whole house had a neglected look, and Yulia, who felt this, was ashamed of herself and of her husband.

"I will be sure to come and see you to-morrow," she said.

She walked through the rooms, and gave orders for the old man's bedroom to be set to rights, and the lamp to be lighted under the ikons in it. Fyodor, sitting in his own room, was looking at an open book without reading it. Yulia talked to him and told the servants to tidy his room, too; then she went downstairs to the clerks. In the middle of the room where the clerks used to dine, there was an unpainted wooden post to support the ceiling and to prevent its coming down. The ceilings in the basement were low, the walls covered with cheap paper, and there was a smell of charcoal fumes and cooking. As it was a holiday, all the clerks were at home, sitting on their bedsteads waiting for dinner. When Yulia went in they jumped up, and answered her questions timidly, looking up at her from under their brows like convicts.

"Good heavens! What a horrid room you have!" she said, throwing up her hands. "Aren't you crowded here?"

"Crowded, but not aggrieved," said Makeitchev. "We are greatly indebted to you, and will offer up our prayers for you to our Heavenly Father."

"The congruity of life with the conceit of the personality," said Potchatkin.

And noticing that Yulia did not understand Potchatkin, Makeitchev hastened to explain:

"We are humble people and must live according to our position."

She inspected the boys' quarters, and then the kitchen, made acquaintance with the housekeeper, and was thoroughly dissatisfied.

When she got home she said to her husband:

"We ought to move into your father's house and settle there for good as soon as possible. And you will go every day to the warehouse."

Then they both sat side by side in the study without speaking. His heart was heavy, and he did not want to move into Pyatnitsky Street or to go into the warehouse; but he guessed what his wife was thinking, and could not oppose her. He stroked her cheek and said:

"I feel as though our life is already over, and that a grey half-life is beginning for us. When I knew that my brother Fyodor was hopelessly ill, I shed tears; we spent our childhood and youth together, when I loved him with my whole soul. And now this catastrophe has come, and it seems, too, as though, losing him, I am finally cut away from my past. And when you said just now that we must move into the house in Pyatnitsky Street, to that prison, it began to seem to that to me that there was no future for me either."

He got up and walked to the window.

"However that may be, one has to give up all thoughts of happiness," he said, looking out into the street. "There is none. I never have had any, and I suppose it doesn't exist at all. I was happy once in my life, though, when I sat at night under your parasol. Do you remember how you left your parasol at Nina's?" he asked, turning to his wife. "I was in love with you then, and I remember I spent all night sitting under your parasol, and was perfectly blissful."

Near the book-case in the study stood a mahogany chest with bronze fittings where Laptev kept various useless things, including the parasol. He took it out and handed it to his wife.

"Here it is."

Yulia looked for a minute at the parasol, recognised it, and smiled mournfully.

"I remember," she said. "When you proposed to me you held it in your hand." And seeing that he was preparing to go out, she said: "Please come back early if you can. I am dull without you."

And then she went into her own room, and gazed for a long time at the parasol.

XVII

In spite of the complexity of the business and the immense turnover, there were no bookkeepers in the warehouse, and it was impossible to make anything out of the books kept by the cashier in the office. Every day the warehouse was visited by agents, German and English, with whom the clerks talked politics and religion. A man of noble birth, ruined by drink, an ailing, pitiable creature, used to come to translate the foreign correspondence in the office; the clerks used to call him a midge, and put salt in his tea. And altogether the whole concern struck Laptev as a very queer business.

He went to the warehouse every day and tried to establish a new order of things; he forbade them to thrash the boys and to jeer at the buyers, and was violently angry when the clerks gleefully despatched to the provinces worthless shop-soiled goods as though they were new and fashionable. Now he was the chief person in the warehouse, but still, as before, he did not know how large his fortune was, whether his business was doing well, how much the senior clerks were paid, and so on. Potchatkin and Makeitchev looked upon him as young and inexperienced, concealed a great deal from him, and whispered mysteriously every evening with his blind old father.

It somehow happened at the beginning of June that Laptev went into the Bubnovsky restaurant with Potchatkin to talk business with him over lunch. Potchatkin had been with the Laptevs a long while, and had entered their service at eight years old. He seemed to belong to them—they trusted him fully; and when on leaving the warehouse he gathered up all the takings from the till and thrust them into his pocket, it never aroused the slightest suspicion. He was the head man in the business and in the house, and also in the church, where he performed the duties of churchwarden in place of his old master. He was nicknamed Malyuta Skuratov on account of his cruel treatment of the boys and clerks under him.

When they went into the restaurant he nodded to a waiter and said:

"Bring us, my lad, half a bodkin and twenty-four unsavouries."

After a brief pause the waiter brought on a tray half a bottle of vodka and some plates of various kinds of savouries.

"Look here, my good fellow," said Potchatkin. "Give us a plateful of the source of all slander and evil-speaking, with mashed potatoes."

The waiter did not understand; he was puzzled, and would have said something, but Potchatkin looked at him sternly and said:

"Except."

The waiter thought intently, then went to consult with his colleagues, and in the end guessing what was meant, brought a plateful of tongue. When they had drunk a couple of glasses and had had lunch, Laptev asked:

"Tell me, Ivan Vassilitch, is it true that our business has been dropping off for the last year?"

"Not a bit of it."

"Tell me frankly and honestly what income we have been making and are making, and what our profits are. We can't go on in the dark. We had a balancing of the accounts at the warehouse lately, but, excuse me, I don't believe in it; you think fit to conceal something from me and only tell the truth to my father. You have been used to being diplomatic from your childhood, and now you can't get on without it. And what's the use of it? So I beg you to be open. What is our position?"

"It all depends upon the fluctuation of credit," Potchatkin answered after a moment's pause.

"What do you understand by the fluctuation of credit?"

Potchatkin began explaining, but Laptev could make nothing of it, and sent for Makeitchev. The latter promptly made his appearance, had some lunch after saying grace, and in his sedate, mellow baritone began saying first of all that the clerks were in duty bound to pray night and day for their benefactors.

"By all means, only allow me not to consider myself your benefactor," said Laptev.

"Every man ought to remember what he is, and to be conscious of his station. By the grace of God you are a father and benefactor to us, and we are your slaves."

"I am sick of all that!" said Laptev, getting angry. "Please be a benefactor to me now. Please explain the position of our business. Give up looking upon me as a boy, or to-morrow I shall close the business. My father is blind, my brother is in the asylum, my nieces are only children. I hate the business; I should be glad to go away, but there's no one to take my place, as you know. For goodness' sake, drop your diplomacy!"

They went to the warehouse to go into the accounts; then they went on with them at home in the evening, the old father himself assisting. Initiating his son into his commercial secrets, the old man spoke as though he were engaged, not in trade, but in sorcery. It appeared that the profits of the business were increasing approximately ten per cent. per annum, and that the Laptevs' fortune, reckoning only money and paper securities, amounted to six million roubles.

When at one o'clock at night, after balancing the accounts, Laptev went out into the open air, he was still under the spell of those figures. It was a still, sultry, moonlight night. The white walls of the houses beyond the river, the heavy barred gates, the stillness and the black shadows, combined to give the impression of a fortress, and nothing was wanting to complete the picture but a sentinel with a gun. Laptev went into the garden and sat down on a seat near the fence, which divided them from the neighbour's yard, where there was a garden, too. The bird-cherry was in bloom. Laptev remembered that the tree had been just as gnarled and just as big when he was a child, and had not changed at all since then. Every corner of the garden and of the yard recalled the far-away past. And in his childhood, too, just as now, the whole yard bathed in moonlight could be seen through the sparse trees, the shadows had been mysterious and forbidding, a black dog had lain in the middle of the yard, and the clerks' windows had stood wide open. And all these were cheerless memories.

The other side of the fence, in the neighbour's yard, there was a sound of light steps.

"My sweet, my precious . . ." said a man's voice so near the fence that Laptev could hear the man's breathing.

Now they were kissing. Laptev was convinced that the millions and the business which was so distasteful to him were ruining his life, and would make him a complete slave. He imagined how, little by little, he would grow accustomed to his position; would, little by little, enter into the part of the head of a great firm; would begin to grow dull and old, die in the end, as the average man usually does die, in a decrepit, soured old age, making every one about him miserable and depressed. But what hindered him from giving up those millions and that business, and leaving that yard and garden which had been hateful to him from his childhood?

The whispering and kisses the other side of the fence disturbed him. He moved into the middle of the yard, and, unbuttoning his shirt over his chest, looked at the moon, and it seemed to him that he would order the gate to be unlocked, and would go out and never come back again. His heart ached sweetly with the foretaste of freedom; he laughed joyously, and pictured how exquisite, poetical, and even holy, life might be. . . .

But he still stood and did not go away, and kept asking himself: "What keeps me here?" And he felt angry with himself and with the black dog, which still lay stretched on the stone yard, instead of running off to the open country, to the woods, where it would have been free and happy. It was clear that that dog and he were prevented from leaving the yard by the same thing; the habit of bondage, of servitude. . . .

At midday next morning he went to see his wife, and that he might not be dull, asked Yartsev to go with him. Yulia Sergeyevna was staying in a summer villa at Butovo, and he had not been to see her for five days. When they reached the station the friends got into a carriage, and all the way there Yartsev was singing and in raptures over the exquisite weather. The villa was in a great park not far from the station. At the beginning of an avenue, about twenty paces from the gates, Yulia Sergeyevna was sitting under a broad, spreading poplar, waiting for her guests. She had on a light, elegant dress of a pale cream colour trimmed with lace, and in her hand she had the old familiar parasol. Yartsev greeted her and went on to the villa from which came the sound of Sasha's and Lida's voices, while Laptev sat down beside her to talk of business matters.

"Why is it you haven't been for so long?" she said, keeping his hand in hers. "I have been sitting here for days watching for you to come. I miss you so when you are away!"

She stood up and passed her hand over his hair, and scanned his face, his shoulders, his hat, with interest.

"You know I love you," she said, and flushed crimson. "You are precious to me. Here you've come. I see you, and I'm so happy I can't tell you. Well, let us talk. Tell me something."

She had told him she loved him, and he could only feel as though he had been married to her for ten years, and that he was hungry for his lunch. She had put her arm round his neck, tickling his cheek with the silk of her dress; he cautiously removed her hand, stood up, and without uttering a single word, walked to the villa. The little girls ran to meet him.

"How they have grown!" he thought. "And what changes in these three years. . . . But one may have to live another thirteen years, another thirty years. . . . What is there in store for us in the future? If we live, we shall see."

He embraced Sasha and Lida, who hung upon his neck, and said:

"Grandpapa sends his love. . . . Uncle Fyodor is dying. Uncle Kostya has sent a letter from America and sends you his love in it. He's bored at the exhibition and will soon be back. And Uncle Alyosha is hungry."

Then he sat on the verandah and saw his wife walking slowly along the avenue towards the house. She was deep in thought; there was a mournful, charming expression in her face, and her eyes were bright with tears. She was not now the slender, fragile, pale-faced girl she used to be; she was a mature, beautiful, vigorous woman. And Laptev saw the enthusiasm with which Yartsev looked at her when he met her, and the way her new, lovely expression was reflected in his face, which looked mournful and ecstatic too. One would have thought that he was seeing her for the first time in his life. And while they were at lunch on the verandah, Yartsev smiled with a sort of joyous shyness, and kept gazing at Yulia and at her beautiful neck. Laptev could not help watching them while he thought that he had perhaps another thirteen, another thirty years of life before him. . . . And what would he have to live through in that time? What is in store for us in the future?

And he thought:

"Let us live, and we shall see."

1895

The Murder

I

The evening service was being celebrated at Progonnaya Station. Before the great ikon, painted in glaring colours on a background of gold, stood the crowd of railway servants with their wives and children, and also of the timbermen and sawyers who worked close to the railway line. All stood in silence, fascinated by the glare of the lights and the howling of the snow-storm which was aimlessly disporting itself outside, regardless of the fact that it was the Eve of the Annunciation. The old priest from Vedenyapino conducted the service; the sacristan and Matvey Terehov were singing.

Matvey's face was beaming with delight; he sang stretching out his neck as though he wanted to soar upwards. He sang tenor and chanted the "Praises" too in a tenor voice with honied sweetness and persuasiveness. When he sang "Archangel Voices," he waved his arms like a conductor, and trying to second the sacristan's hollow bass with his tenor, achieved something extremely complex, and from his face it could be seen that he was experiencing great pleasure.

At last the service was over, and they all quietly dispersed, and it was dark and empty again, and there followed that hush which is only known in stations that stand solitary in the open country or in the forest when the wind howls and nothing else is heard, and when all the emptiness around, all the dreariness of life slowly ebbing away is felt.

Matvey lived not far from the station at his cousin's tavern. But he did not want to go home. He sat down at the refreshment bar and began talking to the waiter in a low voice.

"We had our own choir in the tile factory. And I must tell you that though we were only workmen, our singing was first-rate, splendid.

425

We were often invited to the town, and when the Deputy Bishop, Father Ivan, took the service at Trinity Church, the bishop's singers sang in the right choir and we in the left. Only they complained in the town that we kept the singing on too long: 'the factory choir drag it out,' they used to say. It is true we began St. Andrey's prayers and the Praises between six and seven, and it was past eleven when we finished, so that it was sometimes after midnight when we got home to the factory. It was good," sighed Matvey. "Very good it was, indeed, Sergey Nikanoritch! But here in my father's house it is anything but joyful. The nearest church is four miles away; with my weak health I can't get so far; there are no singers there. And there is no peace or quiet in our family; day in day out, there is an uproar, scolding, uncleanliness; we all eat out of one bowl like peasants; and there are beetles in the cabbage soup. . . . God has not given me health, else I would have gone away long ago, Sergey Nikanoritch."

Matvey Terehov was a middle-aged man about forty-five, but he had a look of ill-health; his face was wrinkled and his lank, scanty beard was quite grey, and that made him seem many years older. He spoke in a weak voice, circumspectly, and held his chest when he coughed, while his eyes assumed the uneasy and anxious look one sees in very apprehensive people. He never said definitely what was wrong with him, but he was fond of describing at length how once at the factory he had lifted a heavy box and had ruptured himself, and how this had led to "the gripes" and had forced him to give up his work in the tile factory and come back to his native place; but he could not explain what he meant by "the gripes."

"I must own I am not fond of my cousin," he went on, pouring himself out some tea. "He is my elder; it is a sin to censure him, and I fear the Lord, but I cannot bear it in patience. He is a haughty, surly, abusive man; he is the torment of his relations and workmen, and constantly out of humour. Last Sunday I asked him in an amiable way, 'Brother, let us go to Pahomovo for the Mass!' but he said, 'I am not going; the priest there is a gambler'; and he would not come here today because, he said, the priest from Vedenyapino smokes and drinks vodka. He doesn't like the clergy! He reads Mass himself and the Hours and the Vespers, while his sister acts as sacristan; he says, 'Let us pray unto the Lord!' and she, in a thin little voice like a turkey-hen, 'Lord, have mercy upon us! . . .' It's a sin, that's what it is. Every day I say to him, 'Think what you are doing, brother! Repent, brother!' and he takes no notice."

Sergey Nikanoritch, the waiter, poured out five glasses of tea and carried them on a tray to the waiting room. He had scarcely gone in when there was a shout:

"Is that the way to serve it, pig's face? You don't know how to wait!"

It was the voice of the station-master. There was a timid mutter, then again a harsh and angry shout:

"Get along!"

The waiter came back, greatly crestfallen.

"There was a time when I gave satisfaction to counts and princes," he said in a low voice; "but now I don't know how to serve tea. . . . He called me names before the priest and the ladies!"

The waiter, Sergey Nikanoritch, had once had money of his own, and had kept a buffet at a first-class station, which was a junction in the principal town of a province. There he had worn a swallow-tail coat and a gold chain. But things had gone ill with him; he had squandered all his own money over expensive fittings and service; he had been robbed by his staff, and, getting gradually into difficulties, had moved to another station less bustling. Here his wife had left him, taking with her all the silver, and he moved to a third station of a still lower class, where no hot dishes were served. Then to a fourth. Frequently changing his situation and sinking lower and lower, he had at last come to Progonnaya, and here he used to sell nothing but tea and cheap vodka, and for lunch hard-boiled eggs and dry sausages, which smelt of tar, and which he himself sarcastically said were only fit for the orchestra. He was bald all over the top of his head, and had prominent blue eyes and thick bushy whiskers, which he often combed out, looking into the little looking-glass. Memories of the past haunted him continually; he could never get used to sausage "only fit for the orchestra," to the rudeness of the station-master, and to the peasants who used to haggle over the prices, and in his opinion it was as unseemly to haggle over prices in a refreshment room as in a chemist's shop. He was ashamed of his poverty and degradation, and that shame was now the leading interest of his life.

"Spring is late this year," said Matvey, listening. "It's a good job; I don't like spring. In spring it is very muddy, Sergey Nikanoritch. In books they write: Spring, the birds sing, the sun is setting, but what is there pleasant in that? A bird is a bird, and nothing more. I am fond of good company, of listening to folks, of talking of religion or singing something agreeable in chorus; but as for nightingales and flowers— bless them, I say!"

He began again about the tile factory, about the choir, but Sergey Nikanoritch could not get over his mortification, and kept shrugging his shoulders and muttering. Matvey said good-bye and went home.

There was no frost, and the snow was already melting on the roofs, though it was still falling in big flakes; they were whirling rapidly round and round in the air and chasing one another in white clouds along the railway lines. And the oak forest on both sides of the line, in the dim light of the moon, which was hidden somewhere high up in the clouds, resounded with a prolonged sullen murmur. When a violent storm shakes the trees, how terrible they are! Matvey walked along the causeway beside the line, covering his face and his hands, while the wind beat on his back. All at once a little nag, plastered all over with snow, came into sight; a sledge scraped along the bare stones of the causeway, and a peasant, white all over, too, with his head muffled up, cracked his whip. Matvey looked round after him, but at once, as though it had been a vision, there was neither sledge nor peasant to be seen, and he hastened his steps, suddenly scared, though he did not know why.

Here was the crossing and the dark little house where the signal-man lived. The barrier was raised, and by it perfect mountains had drifted and clouds of snow were whirling round like witches on broomsticks. At that point the line was crossed by an old highroad, which was still called " the track." On the right, not far from the crossing, by the roadside stood Terehov's tavern, which had been a posting inn. Here there was always a light twinkling at night.

When Matvey reached home there was a strong smell of incense in all the rooms and even in the entry. His cousin Yakov Ivanitch was still reading the evening service. In the prayer-room where this was going on, in the corner opposite the door, there stood a shrine of old-fashioned ancestral ikons in gilt settings, and both walls to right and to left were decorated with ikons of ancient and modern fashion, in shrines and without them. On the table, which was draped to the floor, stood an ikon of the Annunciation, and close by a cyprus-wood cross and the censer; wax candles were burning. Beside the table was a reading desk. As he passed by the prayer-room, Matvey stopped and glanced in at the door. Yakov Ivanitch was reading at the desk at that moment; his sister Aglaia, a tall lean old woman in a dark-blue dress and white kerchief, was praying with him. Yakov Ivanitch's daughter Dashutka, an ugly freckled girl of eighteen, was there, too, barefoot as usual, and wearing the dress in which she had at nightfall taken water to the cattle.

"Glory to Thee Who hast shown us the light!" Yakov Ivanitch boomed out in a chant, bowing low.

Aglaia propped her chin on her hand and chanted in a thin, shrill, drawling voice. And upstairs, above the ceiling, there was the sound of vague voices which seemed menacing or ominous of evil. No one had lived on the storey above since a fire there a long time ago. The windows were boarded up, and empty bottles lay about on the floor between the beams. Now the wind was banging and droning, and it seemed as though someone were running and stumbling over the beams.

Half of the lower storey was used as a tavern, while Terehov's family lived in the other half, so that when drunken visitors were noisy in the tavern every word they said could be heard in the rooms. Matvey lived in a room next the kitchen, with a big stove, in which, in old days, when this had been a posting inn, bread had been baked every day. Dashutka, who had no room of her own, lived in the same room behind the stove. A cricket chirped there always at night and mice ran in and out.

Matvey lighted a candle and began reading a book which he had borrowed from the station policeman. While he was sitting over it the service ended, and they all went to bed. Dashutka lay down, too. She began snoring at once, but soon woke up and said, yawning:

"You shouldn't burn a candle for nothing, Uncle Matvey."

"It's my candle," answered Matvey; "I bought it with my own money."

Dashutka turned over a little and fell asleep again. Matvey sat up a good time longer—he was not sleepy—and when he had finished the last page he took a pencil out of a box and wrote on the book:

"I, Matvey Terehov, have read this book, and think it the very best of all books I have read, for which I express my gratitude to the noncommissioned officer of the Police Department of Railways, Kuzma Nikolaev Zhukov, as the possessor of this priceless book."

He considered it an obligation of politeness to make such inscriptions in other people's books.

II

On Annunciation Day, after the mail train had been seen off, Matvey was sitting in the refreshment bar, talking and drinking tea with lemon in it.

The waiter and Zhukov the policeman were listening to him.

"I was, I must tell you," Matvey was saying, "inclined to religion from my earliest childhood. I was only twelve years old when I used to read the epistle in church, and my parents were greatly delighted, and every summer I used to go on a pilgrimage with my dear mother. Sometimes other lads would be singing songs and catching crayfish, while I would be all the time with my mother. My elders commended me, and, indeed, I was pleased myself that I was of such good behaviour. And when my mother sent me with her blessing to the factory, I used between working hours to sing tenor there in our choir, and nothing gave me greater pleasure. I needn't say, I drank no vodka, I smoked no tobacco, and lived in chastity; but we all know such a mode of life is displeasing to the enemy of mankind, and he, the unclean spirit, once tried to ruin me and began to darken my mind, just as now with my cousin. First of all, I took a vow to fast every Monday and not to eat meat any day, and as time went on all sorts of fancies came over me. For the first week of Lent down to Saturday the holy fathers have ordained a diet of dry food, but it is no sin for the weak or those who work hard even to drink tea, yet not a crumb passed into my mouth till the Sunday, and afterwards all through Lent I did not allow myself a drop of oil, and on Wednesdays and Fridays I did not touch a morsel at all. It was the same in the lesser fasts. Sometimes in St. Peter's fast our factory lads would have fish soup, while I would sit a little apart from them and suck a dry crust. Different people have different powers, of course, but I can say of myself I did not find fast days hard, and, indeed, the greater the zeal the easier it seems. You are only hungry on the first days of the fast, and then you get used to it; it goes on getting easier, and by the end of a week you don't mind it at all, and there is a numb feeling in your legs as though you were not on earth, but in the clouds. And, besides that, I laid all sorts of penances on myself; I used to get up in the night and pray, bowing down to the ground, used to drag heavy stones from place to place, used to go out barefoot in the snow, and I even wore chains, too. Only, as time went on, you know, I was confessing one day to the priest and suddenly this reflection occurred to me: why, this priest, I thought, is married, he eats meat and smokes tobacco—how can he confess me, and what power has he to absolve my sins if he is more sinful than I? I even scruple to eat Lenten oil, while he eats sturgeon, I dare say. I went to another priest, and he, as ill-luck would have it, was a fat fleshy man, in a silk cassock; he rustled like a lady, and he smelt of tobacco, too. I went to fast and confess in the monastery, and my heart was not at ease even there; I kept fancying the monks were not living according to their rules. And after that I could not find a service to my mind: in one place they read the service too fast, in another they sang the wrong prayer, in a third the sacristan stammered. Sometimes, the Lord forgive me a sinner, I would stand in church and my heart would throb with anger. How could one pray, feeling like that? And I fancied that the people in the church did not cross themselves properly, did not listen properly; wherever I looked it seemed to me that they were all drunkards, that they broke the fast, smoked, lived loose lives and played cards. I was the only one who lived according to the commandments. The wily spirit did not slumber; it got worse as it went on. I gave up singing in the choir and I did not go to church at all; since my notion was that I was a righteous man and that the church did not suit me owing to its imperfections—that is, indeed, like a fallen angel, I was puffed up in my pride beyond all belief. After this I began attempting to make a church for myself. I hired from a deaf woman a tiny little room, a long way out of town near the cemetery, and made a prayer-room like my cousin's, only I had big church candlesticks, too, and a real censer. In this prayer-room of mine I kept the rules of holy Mount Athos—that is, every day my matins began at midnight without fail, and on the eve of the chief of the twelve great holy days my midnight service lasted ten hours and sometimes even twelve. Monks are allowed by rule to sit during the singing of the Psalter and the reading of the Bible, but I wanted to be better than the monks, and so I used to stand all through. I used to read and sing slowly, with tears and sighing, lifting up my hands, and I used to go straight from prayer to work without sleeping; and, indeed, I was always praying at my work, too. Well, it got all over the town 'Matvey is a saint; Matvey heals the sick and the senseless.' I never had healed anyone, of course, but we all know wherever any heresy or false doctrine springs up there's no keeping the female sex away. They are just like flies on the honey. Old maids and females of all sorts came trailing to me, bowing down to my feet, kissing my hands and crying out I was a saint and all the rest of it, and one even saw a halo round my head. It was too crowded in the prayer-room. I took a bigger room, and then we had a regular tower of Babel. The devil got hold of me completely and screened the light from my eyes with his unclean hoofs. We all behaved as though we were frantic. I read, while the old maids and other females sang, and then after standing on their legs for twenty-four hours or longer without eating or drinking, suddenly a trembling would come over them as though they were in a fever; after that, one would begin screaming and then another—it was horrible! I, too, would shiver all over like a Jew in a frying-pan, I don't know myself why, and our legs began to prance about. It's a strange thing, indeed: you don't want to, but you prance about and waggle your arms; and after that, screaming and shrieking, we all danced and ran after one another—ran till we dropped; and in that way, in wild frenzy, I fell into fornication."

The policeman laughed, but, noticing that no one else was laughing, became serious and said:

"That's Molokanism. I have heard they are all like that in the Caucasus."

"But I was not killed by a thunderbolt," Matvey went on, crossing himself before the ikon and moving his lips. "My dead mother must have been praying for me in the other world. When everyone in the town looked upon me as a saint, and even ladies and gentlemen of good family used to come to me in secret for consolation, I happened to go in to our landlord, Osip Varlamitch, to ask forgiveness—it was the Day of Forgiveness—and he fastened the door with the hook, and we were left alone face to face. And he began to reprove me, and I must tell you Osip Varlamitch was a man of brains, though without education, and everyone respected and feared him, for he was a man of stern, God-fearing life and worked hard. He had been the mayor of the town, and a warden of the church for twenty years maybe, and had done a great deal of good; he had covered all the New Moscow Road with gravel, had painted the church, and had decorated the columns to look like malachite. Well, he fastened the door, and—'I have been wanting to get at you for a long time, you rascal, . . .' he said. 'You think you are a saint,' he said. 'No, you are not a saint, but a backslider from God, a heretic and an evildoer! . . .' And he went on and on. . . . I can't tell you how he said it, so eloquently and cleverly, as though it were all written down, and so touchingly. He talked for two hours. His words penetrated my soul; my eyes were opened. I listened, listened and— burst into sobs! 'Be an ordinary man,' he said, 'eat and drink, dress and pray like everyone else. All that is above the ordinary is of the devil. Your chains,' he said, 'are of the devil; your fasting is of the devil; your prayer-room is of the devil. It is all pride,' he said. Next day, on Monday in Holy Week, it pleased God I should fall ill. I ruptured myself and was taken to the hospital. I was terribly worried, and wept bitterly and trembled. I thought there was a straight road before me from the hospital to hell, and I almost died. I was in misery on a bed of sickness for six months, and when I was discharged the first thing I did I confessed, and took the sacrament in the regular way and became a man again. Osip Varlamitch saw me off home and exhorted me: 'Remember, Matvey, that anything above the ordinary is of the devil.' And now I eat and drink like everyone else and pray like everyone else. . . . If it happens now that the priest smells of tobacco or vodka I don't venture to blame him, because the priest, too, of course, is an ordinary man. But as soon as I am told that in the town or in the village a saint has set up who does not eat for weeks, and makes rules of his own, I know whose work it is. So that is how I carried on in the past, gentlemen. Now, like Osip Varlamitch, I am continually exhorting my cousins and reproaching them, but I am a voice crying in the wilderness. God has not vouchsafed me the gift."

Matvey's story evidently made no impression whatever. Sergey Nikanoritch said nothing, but began clearing the refreshments off the counter, while the policeman began talking of how rich Matvey's cousin was.

"He must have thirty thousand at least," he said.

Zhukov the policeman, a sturdy, well-fed, red-haired man with a full face (his cheeks quivered when he walked), usually sat lolling and crossing his legs when not in the presence of his superiors. As he talked he swayed to and fro and whistled carelessly, while his face had a self-satisfied, replete air, as though he had just had dinner. He was making money, and he always talked of it with the air of a connoisseur. He undertook jobs as an agent, and when anyone wanted to sell an estate, a horse or a carriage, they applied to him.

"Yes, it will be thirty thousand, I dare say," Sergey Nikanoritch assented. "Your grandfather had an immense fortune," he said, addressing Matvey. "Immense it was; all left to your father and your uncle. Your father died as a young man and your uncle got hold of it all, and afterwards, of course, Yakov Ivanitch. While you were going pilgrimages with your mamma and singing tenor in thc factory, they didn't let the grass grow under their feet."

"Fifteen thousand comes to your share," said the policeman, swaying from side to side. "The tavern belongs to you in common, so the capital is in common. Yes. If I were in your place I should have taken it into court long ago. I would have taken it into court for one thing, and while the case was going on I'd have knocked his face to a jelly."

Yakov Ivanitch was disliked because, when anyone believes differently from others, it upsets even people who are indifferent to religion. The policeman disliked him also because he, too, sold horses and carriages.

" You don't care about going to law with your cousin because you have plenty of money of your own," said the waiter to Matvey, looking at him with envy. "It is all very well for anyone who has means, but here I shall die in this position, I suppose. . . ."

Matvey began declaring that he hadn't any money at all, but Sergey Nikanoritch was not listening. Memories of the past and of the insults which he endured every day came showering upon him. His bald head began to perspire; he flushed and blinked.

"A cursed life!" he said with vexation, and he banged the sausage on the floor.

III

The story ran that the tavern had been built in the time of Alexander I., by a widow who had settled here with her son; her name was Avdotya Terehov. The dark roofed-in courtyard and the gates always kept locked excited, especially on moonlight nights, a feeling of depression and unaccountable uneasiness in people who drove by with posting-horses, as though sorcerers or robbers were living in it; and the driver always looked back after he had passed, and whipped up his horses. Travellers did not care to put up here, as the people of the house were always unfriendly and charged heavily. The yard was muddy even in summer; huge fat pigs used to lie there in the mud, and the horses in which the Terehovs dealt wandered about untethered, and often it happened that they ran out of the yard and dashed along the road like mad creatures, terrifying the pilgrim women. At that time there was a great deal of traffic on the road; long trains of loaded waggons trailed by, and all sorts of adventures happened, such as, for instance, that thirty years ago some waggoners got up a quarrel with a passing merchant and killed him, and a slanting cross is standing to this day half a mile from the tavern; posting-chaises with bells and the heavy *dormeuses* of country gentlemen drove by; and herds of horned cattle passed, bellowing and stirring up clouds of dust.

When the railway came there was at first at this place only a platform, which was called simply a halt; ten years afterwards the present station, Progonnaya, was built. The traffic on the old posting-road almost ceased, and only local landowners and peasants drove along it now, but the working people walked there in crowds in spring and autumn. The posting-inn was transformed into a restaurant; the upper storey was destroyed by fire, the roof had grown yellow with rust, the roof over the yard had fallen by degrees, but huge fat pigs, pink and revolting, still wallowed in the mud in the yard. As before, the horses sometimes ran away and, lashing their tails, dashed madly along the road. In the tavern they sold tea, hay, oats and flour, as well as vodka and beer, to be drunk on the premises and also to be taken away; they sold spirituous liquors warily, for they had never taken out a licence.

The Terehovs had always been distinguished by their piety, so much so that they had even been given the nickname of the "Godlies." But perhaps because they lived apart like bears, avoided people and thought out all their ideas for themselves, they were given to dreams and to doubts and to changes of faith, and almost each generation had a peculiar faith of its own. The grandmother Avdotya, who had built the inn, was an Old Believer; her son and both her grandsons (the fathers of Matvey and Yakov) went to the Orthodox church, entertained the clergy, and worshipped before the new ikons as devoutly as they had done before the old. The son in old age refused to eat meat and imposed upon himself the rule of silence, considering all conversation as sin; it was the peculiarity of the grandsons that they interpreted the Scripture not simply, but sought in it a hidden meaning, declaring that every sacred word must contain a mystery.

Avdotya's great-grandson Matvey had struggled from early childhood with all sorts of dreams and fancies, and had been almost ruined by it; the other great-grandson, Yakov Ivanitch, was orthodox, but after his wife's death he gave up going to church and prayed at home. Following his example, his sister Aglaia had turned, too; she did not go to church herself, and did not let Dashutka go. Of Aglaia it was told that in her youth she used to attend the Flagellant meetings in Vedenyapino, and that she was still a Flagellant in secret, and that was why she wore a white kerchief.

Yakov Ivanitch was ten years older than Matvey; he was a very handsome tall old man with a big grey beard almost to his waist, and bushy eyebrows which gave his face a stern, even ill-natured expression. He wore a long jerkin of good cloth or a black sheepskin coat, and altogether tried to be clean and neat in dress; he wore goloshes even in dry weather. He did not go to church, because, to his thinking, the services were not properly celebrated and because the priests drank wine at unlawful times and smoked tobacco. Every day he read and sang the service at home with Aglaia. At Vedenyapino they left out the "Praises" at early matins, and had no evening service even on great holidays, but he used to read through at home everything that was laid down for every day, without hurrying or leaving out a single line, and in his spare time read aloud the Lives of the Saints. And in everyday life he adhered strictly to the rules of the church; thus, if wine were allowed on some day in Lent, "for the sake of the vigil," then he never failed to drink wine, even if he were not inclined.

He read, sang, burned incense and fasted, not for the sake of receiving blessings of some sort from God, but for the sake of good order. Man cannot live without religion, and religion ought to be expressed from year to year and from day to day in a certain order, so that every morning and every evening a man might turn to God with exactly those words and thoughts that were befitting that special day and hour. One must live and, therefore, also pray as is pleasing to God, and so every day one must read and sing what is pleasing to God—that is, what is laid down in the rule of the church. Thus the first chapter of St. John must only be read on Easter Day, and "It is most meet" must not be sung from Easter to Ascension, and so on. The consciousness of this order and its importance afforded Yakov Ivanitch great gratification during his religious exercises. When he was forced to break this order by some necessity—to drive to town or to the bank, for instance—his conscience was uneasy and he felt miserable.

When his cousin Matvey had returned unexpectedly from the factory and settled in the tavern as though it were his home, he had from the very first day disturbed this settled order. He refused to pray with them, had meals and drank tea at wrong times, got up late, drank milk on Wednesdays and Fridays on the pretext of weak health; almost every day he went into the prayer-room while they were at prayers and cried: "Think what you are doing, brother! Repent, brother!" These words threw Yakov into a fury, while Aglaia could not refrain from beginning to scold; or at night Matvey would steal into the prayer-room and say softly: "Cousin, your prayer is not pleasing to God. For it is written, First be reconciled with thy brother and then offer thy gift. You lend money at usury, you deal in vodka—repent!"

In Matvey's words Yakov saw nothing but the usual evasions of empty-headed and careless people who talk of loving your neighbour, of being reconciled with your brother, and so on, simply to avoid praying, fasting and reading holy books, and who talk contemptuously of profit and interest simply because they don't like working. Of course, to be poor, save nothing, and put by nothing was a great deal easier than being rich.

But yet he was troubled and could not pray as before. As soon as he went into the prayer-room and opened the book he began to be afraid his cousin would come in and hinder him; and, in fact, Matvey did soon appear and cry in a trembling voice: "Think what you are doing, brother! Repent, brother!" Aglaia stormed and Yakov, too, flew into a passion and shouted: "Go out of my house!" while Matvey answered him: "The house belongs to both of us."

Yakov would begin singing and reading again, but he could not regain his calm, and unconsciously fell to dreaming over his book. Though he regarded his cousin's words as nonsense, yet for some reason it had of late haunted his memory that it is hard for a rich man to enter the kingdom of heaven, that the year before last he had made a very good bargain over buying a stolen horse, that one day when his wife was alive a drunkard had died of vodka in his tavern. . . .

He slept badly at nights now and woke easily, and he could hear that Matvey, too, was awake, and continually sighing and pining for his tile factory. And while Yakov turned over from one side to another at night he thought of the stolen horse and the drunken man, and what was said in the gospels about the camel.

It looked as though his dreaminess were coming over him again. And as ill-luck would have it, although it was the end of March, every day it kept snowing, and the forest roared as though it were winter, and there was no believing that spring would ever come. The weather disposed one to depression, and to quarrelling and to hatred, and in the night, when the wind droned over the ceiling, it seemed as though someone were living overhead in the empty storey; little by little the broodings settled like a burden on his mind, his head burned and he could not sleep.

IV

On the morning of the Monday before Good Friday, Matvey heard from his room Dashutka say to Aglaia:

"Uncle Matvey said, the other day, that there is no need to fast."

Matvey remembered the whole conversation he had had the evening before with Dashutka, and he felt hurt all at once.

"Girl, don't do wrong!" he said in a moaning voice, like a sick man. "You can't do without fasting; our Lord Himself fasted forty days. I only explained that fasting does a bad man no good."

" You should just listen to the factory hands; they can teach you goodness," Aglaia said sarcastically as she washed the floor (she usually washed the floors on working days and was always angry with everyone when she did it). "We know how they keep the fasts in the factory. You had better ask that uncle of yours—ask him about his 'Darling,' how he used to guzzle milk on fast days with her, the viper. He teaches others; he forgets about his viper. But ask him who was it he left his money with— who was it?"

Matvey had carefully concealed from everyone, as though it were a foul sore, that during that period of his life when old women and unmarried girls had danced and run about with him at their prayers he had formed a connection with a working woman and had had a child by her. When he went home he had given this woman all he had saved at the factory, and had borrowed from his landlord for his journey, and now he had only a few roubles which he spent on tea and candles. The "Darling" had informed him later on that the child was dead, and asked him in a letter what she should do with the money. This letter was brought from the station by the labourer. Aglaia intercepted it and read it, and had reproached Matvey with his "Darling" every day since.

"Just fancy, nine hundred roubles," Aglaia went on. " You gave nine hundred roubles to a viper, no relation, a factory jade, blast you!" She had flown into a passion by now and was shouting shrilly: "Can't you speak? I could tear you to pieces, wretched creature! Nine hundred roubles as though it were a farthing. You might have left it to Dashutka—she is a relation, not a stranger—or else have sent it to Byelev for Marya's poor orphans. And your viper did not choke, may she be thrice accursed, the she-devil! May she never look upon the light of day!"

Yakov Ivanitch called to her; it was time to begin the "Hours." She washed, put on a white kerchief, and by now quiet and meek, went into the prayer-room to the brother she loved. When she spoke to Matvey or served peasants in the tavern with tea she was a gaunt, keen-eyed, ill-humoured old woman; in the prayer-room her face was serene and softened, she looked younger altogether, she curtsied affectedly, and even pursed up her lips.

Yakov Ivanitch began reading the service softly and dolefully, as he always did in Lent. After he had read a little he stopped to listen to the stillness that reigned through the house, and then went on reading again, with a feeling of gratification; he folded his hands in supplication, rolled his eyes, shook his head, sighed. But all at once there was the sound of voices. The policeman and Sergey Nikanoritch had come to see Matvey. Yakov Ivanitch was embarrassed at reading aloud and singing when there were strangers in the house, and now, hearing voices, he began reading in a whisper and slowly. He could hear in the prayer-room the waiter say:

"The Tatar at Shtchepovo is selling his business for fifteen hundred. He'll take five hundred down and an I.O.U. for the rest. And so, Matvey Vassilitch, be so kind as to lend me that five hundred roubles. I will pay you two per cent. a month."

"What money have I got?" cried Matvey, amazed. "I have no money!"

"Two per cent. a month will be a godsend to you," the policeman explained. "While lying by, your money is simply eaten by the moth, and that's all that you get from it."

Afterwards the visitors went out and a silence followed. But Yakov Ivanitch had hardly begun reading and singing again when a voice was heard outside the door:

"Brother, let me have a horse to drive to Vedenyapino."

It was Matvey. And Yakov was troubled again.

"Which can you go with?" he asked after a moment's thought. "The man has gone with the sorrel to take the pig, and I am going with the little stallion to Shuteykino as soon as I have finished."

"Brother, why is it you can dispose of the horses and not I?" Matvey asked with irritation.

"Because I am not taking them for pleasure, but for work."

"Our property is in common, so the horses are in common, too, and you ought to understand that, brother."

A silence followed. Yakov did not go on praying, but waited for Matvey to go away from the door.

"Brother," said Matvey, "I am a sick man. I don't want possessions—let them go; you have them, but give me a small share to keep me in my illness. Give it me and I'll go away."

Yakov did not speak. He longed to be rid of Matvey, but he could not give him money, since all the money was in the business; besides, there had never been a case of the family dividing in the whole history of the Terehovs. Division means ruin.

Yakov said nothing, but still waited for Matvey to go away, and kept looking at his sister, afraid that she would interfere, and that there would be a storm of abuse again, as there had been in the morning. When at last Matvey did go Yakov went on reading, but now he had no pleasure in it. There was a heaviness in his head and a darkness before his eyes from continually bowing down to the ground, and he was weary of the sound of his soft dejected voice. When such a depression of spirit came over him at night, he put it down to not being able to sleep; by day it frightened him, and he began to feel as though devils were sitting on his head and shoulders.

Finishing the service after a fashion, dissatisfied and ill-humoured, he set off for Shuteykino. In the previous autumn a gang of navvies had dug a boundary ditch near Progonnaya, and had run up a bill at the tavern for eighteen roubles, and now he had to find their foreman in Shuteykino and get the money from him. The road had been spoilt by the thaw and the snowstorm; it was of a dark colour and full of holes, and in parts it had given way altogether. The snow had sunk away at the sides below the road, so that he had to drive, as it were, upon a narrow causeway, and it was very difficult to turn off it when he met anything. The sky had been overcast ever since the morning and a damp wind was blowing. . . .

A long train of sledges met him; peasant women were carting bricks. Yakov had to turn off the road. His horse sank into the snow up to its belly; the sledge lurched over to the right, and to avoid falling out he bent over to the left, and sat so all the time the sledges moved slowly by him. Through the wind he heard the creaking of the sledge poles and the breathing of the gaunt horses, and the women saying about him, "There's Godly coming," while one, gazing with compassion at his horse, said quickly:

"It looks as though the snow will be lying till Yegory's Day! They are worn out with it!"

Yakov sat uncomfortably huddled up, screwing up his eyes on account of the wind, while horses and red bricks kept passing before him. And perhaps because he was uncomfortable and his side ached, he felt all at once annoyed, and the business he was going about seemed to him unimportant, and he reflected that he might send the labourer next day to Shuteykino. Again, as in the previous sleepless night, he thought of the saying about the camel, and then memories of all sorts crept into his mind: of the peasant who had sold him the stolen horse, of the drunken man, of the peasant women who had brought their samovars to him to pawn. Of course, every merchant tries to get as much as he can, but Yakov felt depressed that he was in trade; he longed to get somewhere far away from this routine, and he felt dreary at the thought that he would have to read the evening service that day. The wind blew straight into his face and soughed in his collar, and it seemed as though it were whispering to him all these thoughts, bringing them from the broad white plain. . . . Looking at that plain, familiar to him from childhood, Yakov remembered that he had had just this same trouble and these same thoughts in his young days when dreams and imaginings had come upon him and his faith had wavered.

He felt miserable at being alone in the open country; he turned back and drove slowly after the sledges, and the women laughed and said: "Godly has turned back."

At home nothing had been cooked and the samovar was not heated, owing to the fast, and this made the day seem very long. Yakov Ivanitch had long ago taken the horse to the stable, dispatched the flour to the station, and twice taken up the Psalms to read, and yet the evening was still far off. Aglaia had already washed all the floors, and, having nothing to do, was tidying up her chest, the lid of which was pasted over on the inside with labels off bottles. Matvey, hungry and melancholy, sat reading, or went up to the Dutch stove and slowly scrutinized the tiles which reminded him of the factory. Dashutka was asleep; then, waking up, she went to take water to the cattle. When she was getting water from the well the cord broke and the pail fell in. The labourer began looking for a boathook to get the pail out, and Dashutka, barefooted, with legs as red as a goose's, followed him about in the muddy snow, repeating: "It's too far!" She meant to say that the well was too deep for the hook to reach the bottom, but the labourer did not understand her, and evidently she bothered him, so that he suddenly turned round and abused her in unseemly language. Yakov Ivanitch, coming out that moment into the yard, heard Dashutka answer the labourer in a long rapid stream of choice abuse, which she could only have learned from drunken peasants in the tavern.

"What are you saying, shameless girl!" he cried to her, and he was positively aghast. "What language!"

And she looked at her father in perplexity, dully, not understanding why she should not use those words. He would have admonished her, but she struck him as so savage and benighted; and for the first time he realized that she had no religion. And all this life in the forest, in the snow, with drunken peasants, with coarse oaths, seemed to him as savage and benighted as this girl, and instead of giving her a lecture he only waved his hand and went back into the room.

At that moment the policeman and Sergey Nikanoritch came in again to see Matvey. Yakov Ivanitch thought that these people, too, had no religion, and that that did not trouble them in the least; and human life began to seem to him as strange, senseless and unenlightened as a dog's. Bareheaded he walked about the yard, then he went out on to the road, clenching his fists. Snow was falling in big flakes at the time. His beard was blown about in the wind. He kept shaking his head, as though there were something weighing upon his head and shoulders, as though devils were sitting on them; and it seemed to him that it was not himself walking about, but some wild beast, a huge terrible beast, and that if he were to cry out his voice would be a roar that would sound all over the forest and the plain, and would frighten everyone. . . .

V

When he went back into the house the policeman was no longer there, but the waiter was sitting with Matvey, counting something on the reckoning beads. He was in the habit of coming often, almost every day, to the tavern; in old days he had come to see Yakov Ivanitch, now he came to see Matvey. He was continually reckoning on the beads, while his face perspired and looked strained, or he would ask for money or, stroking his whiskers, would describe how he had once been in a first-class station and used to prepare champagne punch for officers, and at grand dinners served the sturgeon soup with his own hands. Nothing in this world interested him but refreshment bars, and he could only talk about things to eat, about wines and the paraphernalia of the dinner-table. On one occasion, handing a cup of tea to a young woman who was nursing her baby and wishing to say something agreeable to her, he expressed himself in this way:

"The mother's breast is the baby's refreshment bar."

Reckoning with the beads in Matvey's room, he asked for money; said he could not go on living at Progonnaya, and several times repeated in a tone of voice that sounded as though he were just going to cry:

"Where am I to go? Where am I to go now? Tell me that, please."

Then Matvey went into the kitchen and began peeling some boiled potatoes which he had probably put away from the day before. It was quiet, and it seemed to Yakov Ivanitch that the waiter was gone. It was past the time for evening service; he called Aglaia, and, thinking there was no one else in the house, sang out aloud without embarrassment. He sang and read, but was inwardly pronouncing other words, "Lord, forgive me! Lord, save me!" and, one after another, without ceasing, he made low bows to the ground as though he wanted to exhaust himself, and he kept shaking his head, so that Aglaia looked at him with wonder. He was afraid Matvey would come in, and was certain that he would come in, and felt an anger against him which he could overcome neither by prayer nor by continually bowing down to the ground.

Matvey opened the door very softly and went into the prayer-room.

"It's a sin, such a sin!" he said reproachfully, and heaved a sigh. "Repent! Think what you are doing, brother!"

Yakov Ivanitch, clenching his fists and not looking at him for fear of striking him, went quickly out of the room. Feeling himself a huge terrible wild beast, just as he had done before on the road, he crossed the passage into the grey, dirty room, reeking with smoke and fog, in which the peasants usually drank tea, and there he spent a long time walking from one corner to the other, treading heavily, so that the crockery jingled on the shelves and the tables shook. It was clear to him now that he was himself dissatisfied with his religion, and could not pray as he used to do. He must repent, he must think things over, reconsider, live and pray in some other way. But how pray? And perhaps all this was a temptation of the devil, and nothing of this was necessary? . . . How was it to be? What was he to do? Who could guide him? What helplessness! He stopped and, clutching at his head, began to think, but Matvey's being near him prevented him from reflecting calmly. And he went rapidly into the room.

Matvey was sitting in the kitchen before a bowl of potato, eating. Close by, near the stove, Aglaia and Dashutka were sitting facing one another, spinning yarn. Between the stove and the table at which Matvey was sitting was stretched an ironing-board; on it stood a cold iron.

"Sister," Matvey asked, "let me have a little oil!"

"Who eats oil on a day like this?" asked Aglaia.

"I am not a monk, sister, but a layman. And in my weak health I may take not only oil but milk."

"Yes, at the factory you may have anything."

Aglaia took a bottle of Lenten oil from the shelf and banged it angrily down before Matvey, with a malignant smile, evidently pleased that he was such a sinner.

"But I tell you, you can't eat oil!" shouted Yakov.

Aglaia and Dashutka started, but Matvey poured the oil into the bowl and went on eating as though he had not heard.

"I tell you, you can't eat oil!" Yakov shouted still more loudly; he turned red all over, snatched up the bowl, lifted it higher than his head, and dashed it with all his force to the ground, so that it flew into fragments. "Don't dare to speak!" he cried in a furious voice, though Matvey had not said a word. "Don't dare!" he repeated, and struck his fist on the table.

Matvey turned pale and got up.

"Brother!" he said, still munching—"brother, think what you are about!"

"Out of my house this minute!" shouted Yakov; he loathed Matvey's wrinkled face, and his voice, and the crumbs on his moustache, and the fact that he was munching. "Out, I tell you! "

"Brother, calm yourself! The pride of hell has confounded you!"

"Hold your tongue!" (Yakov stamped.) "Go away, you devil!"

"If you care to know," Matvey went on in a loud voice, as he, too, began to get angry, "you are a backslider from God and a heretic. The accursed spirits have hidden the true light from you; your prayer is not acceptable to God. Repent before it is too late! The deathbed of the sinner is terrible! Repent, brother!"

Yakov seized him by the shoulders and dragged him away from the table, while he turned whiter than ever, and, frightened and bewildered, began muttering, "What is it? What's the matter?" and, struggling and making efforts to free himself from Yakov's hands, he accidentally caught hold of his shirt near the neck and tore the collar, and it seemed to Aglaia that he was trying to beat Yakov. She uttered a shriek, snatched up the bottle of Lenten oil and with all her force brought it down straight on the skull of the cousin she hated. Matvey reeled, and in one instant his face became calm and indifferent. Yakov, breathing heavily, excited, and feeling pleasure at the gurgle the bottle had made, like a living thing, when it had struck the head, kept him from falling and several times (he remembered this very distinctly) motioned Aglaia towards the iron with his finger; and only when the blood began trickling through his hands and he heard Dashutka's loud wail, and when the ironing-board fell with a crash, and Matvey rolled heavily on it, Yakov left off feeling anger and understood what had happened.

"Let him rot, the factory buck!" Aglaia brought out with repulsion, still keeping the iron in her hand. The white bloodstained kerchief slipped on to her shoulders and her grey hair fell in disorder. "He's got what he deserved!"

Everything was terrible. Dashutka sat on the floor near the stove with the yarn in her hands, sobbing, and continually bowing down, uttering at each bow a gasping sound. But nothing was so terrible to Yakov as the potato in the blood, on which he was afraid of stepping, and there was something else terrible which weighed upon him like a bad dream and seemed the worst danger, though he could not take it in for the first minute. This was the waiter, Sergey Nikanoritch, who was standing in the doorway with the reckoning beads in his hands, very pale, looking with horror at what was happening in the kitchen. Only when he turned and went quickly into the passage and from there outside, Yakov grasped who it was and followed him.

Wiping his hands on the snow as he went, he reflected. The idea flashed through his mind that their labourer had gone away long before and had asked leave to stay the night at home in the village; the day before they had killed a pig, and there were huge bloodstains in the snow and on the sledge, and even one side of the top of the well was spattered with blood, so that it could not have seemed suspicious even if the whole of Yakov's family had been stained with blood. To conceal the murder would be agonizing, but for the policeman, who would whistle and smile ironically, to come from the station, for the peasants to arrive and bind Yakov's and Aglaia's hands, and take them solemnly to the district courthouse and from there to the town, while everyone on the way would point at them and say mirthfully, "They are taking the Godlies!"—this seemed to Yakov more agonizing than anything, and he longed to lengthen out the time somehow, so as to endure this shame not now, but later, in the future.

"I can lend you a thousand roubles, . . ." he said, overtaking Sergey Nikanoritch. "If you tell anyone, it will do no good. . . . There's no bringing the man back, anyway"; and with difficulty keeping up with the waiter, who did not look round, but tried to walk away faster than ever, he went on: "I can give you fifteen hundred. . . ."

He stopped because he was out of breath, while Sergey Nikanoritch walked on as quickly as ever, probably afraid that he would be killed, too. Only after passing the railway crossing and going half the way from the crossing to the station, he furtively looked round and walked more slowly. Lights, red and green, were already gleaming in the station and along the line; the wind had fallen, but flakes of snow were still coming down and the road had turned white again. But just at the station Sergey Nikanoritch stopped, thought a minute, and turned resolutely back. It was growing dark.

"Oblige me with the fifteen hundred, Yakov Ivanitch," he said, trembling all over. "I agree."

VI

Yakov Ivanitch's money was in the bank of the town and was invested in second mortgages; he only kept a little at home, just what was wanted for necessary expenses. Going into the kitchen, he felt for the match-box, and while the sulphur was burning with a blue light he had time to make out the figure of Matvey, which was still lying on the floor near the table, but now it was covered with a white sheet, and nothing could be seen but his boots. A cricket was chirruping. Aglaia and Dashutka were not in the room, they were both sitting behind the counter in the tea-room, spinning yarn in silence. Yakov Ivanitch crossed to his own room with a little lamp in his hand, and pulled from under the bed a lit-tle box in which he kept his money. This time there were in it four hundred and twenty-one rouble notes and silver to the amount of thirty-five roubles; the notes had an unpleasant heavy smell. Putting the money together in his cap, Yakov Ivanitch went out into the yard and then out of the gate. He walked looking from side to side, but there was no sign of the waiter.

"Hi!" cried Yakov.

A dark figure stepped out from the barrier at the railway crossing and came irresolutely towards him.

"Why do you keep walking about?" said Yakov with vexation, as he recognized the waiter. "Here you are; there is a little less than five hun-dred. . . . I've no more in the house."

"Very well; . . . very grateful to you," muttered Sergey Nikanoritch, taking the money greedily and stuffing it into his pockets. He was trem-bling all over, and that was perceptible in spite of the darkness. " Don't worry yourself, Yakov Ivanitch. . . . What should I chatter for? I came and went away, that's all I've to do with it. As the saying is, I know nothing and I can tell nothing. . . ." And at once he added with a sigh: "Cursed life!"

For a minute they stood in silence, without looking at each other.

"So it all came from a trifle, goodness knows how, . . ." said the waiter, trembling. "I was sitting counting to myself when all at once a noise. . . . I looked through the door, and just on account of Lenten oil you . . . Where is he now?"

"Lying there in the kitchen."

"You ought to take him away somewhere. . . . Why put it off?"

Yakov accompanied him to the station without a word, then went home again and harnessed the horse to take Matvey to Limarovo. He had decided to take him to the forest of Limarovo, and to leave him there on the road, and then he would tell everyone that Matvey had gone off to Vedenyapino and had not come back, and then everybody would think that he had been killed by someone on the road. He knew there was no deceiving anyone by this, but to move, to do something, to be active was not so agonizing as to sit still and wait. He called Dashutka, and with her carried Matvey out. Aglaia stayed behind to clean up the kitchen.

When Yakov and Dashutka turned back they were detained at the railway crossing by the barrier being let down. A long goods train was passing, dragged by two engines, breathing heavily, and flinging puffs of crimson fire out of their funnels.

The foremost engine uttered a piercing whistle at the crossing in sight of the station.

"It's whistling, . . ." said Dashutka.

The train had passed at last, and the signalman lifted the barrier without haste.

"Is that you, Yakov Ivanitch? I didn't know you, so you'll be rich."

And then when they had reached home they had to go to bed.

Aglaia and Dashutka made themselves a bed in the tea-room and lay down side by side, while Yakov stretched himself on the counter. They neither said their prayers nor lighted the ikon lamp before lying down to sleep. All three lay awake till morning, but did not utter a single word, and it seemed to them that all night someone was walking about in the empty storey overhead.

Two days later a police inspector and the examining magistrate came from the town and made a search, first in Matvey's room and then in the whole tavern. They questioned Yakov first of all, and he testified that on the Monday Matvey had gone to Vedenyapino to confess, and that he must have been killed by the sawyers who were working on the line.

And when the examining magistrate had asked him how it had happened that Matvey was found on the road, while his cap had turned up at home—surely he had not gone to Vedenyapino without his cap?—and why they had not found a single drop of blood beside him in the snow on the road though his head was smashed in and his face and chest were black with blood, Yakov was confused, lost his head and answered:

" I cannot tell."

And just what Yakov had so feared happened: the policeman came, the district police officer smoked in the prayer-room, and Aglaia fell upon him with abuse and was rude to the police inspector; and afterwards when Yakov and Aglaia were led out of the yard, the peasants crowded at the gates and said, "They are taking the Godlies!" and it seemed that they were all glad.

At the inquiry the policeman stated positively that Yakov and Aglaia had killed Matvey in order not to share with him, and that Matvey had money of his own, and that if it was not found at the search evidently Yakov and Aglaia had got hold of it. And Dashutka was questioned. She said that Uncle Matvey and Aunt Aglaia quarrelled and almost fought every day over money, and that Uncle Matvey was rich, so much so that he had given someone—"his Darling"—nine hundred roubles.

Dashutka was left alone in the tavern. No one came now to drink tea or vodka, and she divided her time between cleaning up the rooms, drinking mead and eating rolls; but a few days later they questioned the signalman at the railway crossing, and he said that late on Monday evening he had seen Yakov and Dashutka driving from Limarovo. Dashutka, too, was arrested, taken to the town and put in prison. It soon became known, from what Aglaia said, that Sergey Nikanoritch had been present at the murder. A search was made in his room, and money was found in an unusual place, in his snowboots under the stove, and the money was all in small change, three hundred one-rouble notes. He swore he had made this money himself, and that he hadn't been in the tavern for a year, but witnesses testified that he was poor and had been in great want of money of late, and that he used to go every day to the tavern to borrow from Matvey; and the policeman described how on the day of the murder he had himself gone twice to the tavern with the waiter to help him to borrow. It was recalled at this juncture that on Monday evening Sergey Nikanoritch had not been there to meet the passenger train, but had gone off somewhere. And he, too, was arrested and taken to the town.

The trial took place eleven months later.

Yakov Ivanitch looked much older and much thinner, and spoke in a low voice like a sick man. He felt weak, pitiful, lower in stature than anyone else, and it seemed as though his soul, too, like his body, had grown older and wasted, from the pangs of his conscience and from the dreams and imaginings which never left him all the while he was in prison. When it came out that he did not go to church the president of the court asked him:

"Are you a dissenter?"

"I can't tell," he answered.

He had no religion at all now; he knew nothing and understood nothing; and his old belief was hateful to him now, and seemed to him darkness and folly. Aglaia was not in the least subdued, and she still went on abusing the dead man, blaming him for all their misfortunes. Sergey Nikanoritch had grown a beard instead of whiskers. At the trial he was red and perspiring, and was evidently ashamed of his grey prison coat and of sitting on the same bench with humble peasants. He defended himself awkwardly, and, trying to prove that he had not been to the tavern for a whole year, got into an altercation with every witness, and the spectators laughed at him. Dashutka had grown fat in prison. At the trial she did not understand the questions put to her, and only said that when they killed Uncle Matvey she was dreadfully frightened, but afterwards she did not mind.

All four were found guilty of murder with mercenary motives. Yakov Ivanitch was sentenced to penal servitude for twenty years; Aglaia for thirteen and a half; Sergey Nikanoritch to ten; Dashutka to six.

VII

Late one evening a foreign steamer stopped in the roads of Dué in Sahalin and asked for coal. The captain was asked to wait till morning, but he did not want to wait over an hour, saying that if the weather changed for the worse in the night there would be a risk of his having to go off without coal. In the Gulf of Tartary the weather is liable to violent changes in the course of half an hour, and then the shores of Sahalin are dangerous. And already it had turned fresh, and there was a considerable sea running.

A gang of convicts were sent to the mine from the Voevodsky Prison, the grimmest and most forbidding of all the prisons in Sahalin. The coal had to be loaded upon barges, and then they had to be towed by a steam-cutter alongside the steamer which was anchored more than a quarter of a mile from the coast, and then the unloading and reloading had to begin—an exhausting task when the barge kept rocking against the steamer and the men could scarcely keep on their legs for sea-sickness. The convicts, only just roused from their sleep, still drowsy, went along the shore, stumbling in the darkness and clanking their fetters. On the left, scarcely visible, was a tall, steep, extremely gloomy-looking cliff, while on the right there was a thick impenetrable mist, in which the sea moaned with a prolonged monotonous sound, "Ah! . . . ah! . . . ah! . . . ah! . . ." And it was only when the overseer was lighting his pipe, casting as he did so a passing ray of light on the escort with a gun and on the coarse faces of two or three of the nearest convicts, or when he went with his lantern close to the water that the white crests of the foremost waves could be discerned.

One of this gang was Yakov Ivanitch, nicknamed among the convicts the "Brush," on account of his long beard. No one had addressed him by his name or his father's name for a long time now; they called him simply Yashka.

He was here in disgrace, as, three months after coming to Siberia, feeling an intense irresistible longing for home, he had succumbed to temptation and run away; he had soon been caught, had been sentenced to penal servitude for life and given forty lashes. Then he was punished by flogging twice again for losing his prison clothes, though on each occasion they were stolen from him. The longing for home had begun from the very time he had been brought to Odessa, and the convict train had stopped in the night at Progonnaya; and Yakov, pressing to the window, had tried to see his own home, and could see nothing in the darkness. He had no one with whom to talk of home. His sister Aglaia had been sent right across Siberia, and he did not know where she was now. Dashutka was in Sahalin, but she had been sent to live with some ex-convict in a far-away settlement; there was no news of her except that once a settler who had come to the Voevodsky Prison told Yakov that Dashutka had three children. Sergey Nikanoritch was serving as a footman at a government official's at Dué, but he could not reckon on ever seeing him, as he was ashamed of being acquainted with convicts of the peasant class.

The gang reached the mine, and the men took their places on the quay. It was said there would not be any loading, as the weather kept getting worse and the steamer was meaning to set off. They could see three lights. One of them was moving: that was the steam-cutter going to the steamer, and it seemed to be coming back to tell them whether the work was to be done or not. Shivering with the autumn cold and the damp sea mist, wrapping himself in his short torn coat, Yakov Ivanitch looked intently without blinking in the direction in which lay his home. Ever since he had lived in prison together with men banished here from all ends of the earth—with Russians, Ukrainians, Tatars, Georgians, Chinese, Gypsies, Jews—and ever since he had listened to their talk and watched their sufferings, he had begun to turn again to God, and it seemed to him at last that he had learned the true faith for which all his family, from his grandmother Avdotya down, had so thirsted, which they had sought so long and which they had never found. He knew it all now and understood where God was, and how He was to be served, and the only thing he could not understand was why men's destinies were so diverse, why this simple faith which other men receive from God for nothing and together with their lives, had cost him such a price that his arms and legs trembled like a drunken man's from all the horrors and agonies which as far as he could see would go on without a break to the day of his death. He looked with strained eyes into the darkness, and it seemed to him that through the thousand miles of that mist he could see home, could see his native province, his district, Progonnaya, could see the darkness, the savagery, the heartlessness, and dull, sullen, animal indifference of the men he had left there. His eyes were dimmed with tears; but still he gazed into the distance where the pale lights of the steamer faintly gleamed, and his heart ached with yearning for home, and he longed to live, to go back home to tell them there of his new faith and to save from ruin if only one man, and to live without suffering if only for one day.

The cutter arrived, and the overseer announced in a loud voice that there would be no loading.

"Back!" he commanded. "Steady!"

They could hear the hoisting of the anchor chain on the steamer. A strong piercing wind was blowing by now; somewhere on the steep cliff overhead the trees were creaking. Most likely a storm was coming.

1895

My Life

The Story of a Provincial

I

The Superintendent said to me: "I only keep you out of regard for your worthy father; but for that you would have been sent flying long ago." I replied to him: "You flatter me too much, your Excellency, in assuming that I am capable of flying." And then I heard him say: "Take that gentleman away; he gets upon my nerves."

Two days later I was dismissed. And in this way I have, during the years I have been regarded as grown up, lost nine situations, to the great mortification of my father, the architect of our town. I have served in various departments, but all these nine jobs have been as alike as one drop of water is to another: I had to sit, write, listen to rude or stupid observations, and go on doing so till I was dismissed.

When I came in to my father he was sitting buried in a low armchair with his eyes closed. His dry, emaciated face, with a shade of dark blue where it was shaved (he looked like an old Catholic organist), expressed meekness and resignation. Without responding to my greeting or opening his eyes, he said:

"If my dear wife and your mother were living, your life would have been a source of continual distress to her. I see the Divine Providence in her premature death. I beg you, unhappy boy," he continued, opening his eyes, "tell me: what am I to do with you?"

In the past when I was younger my friends and relations had known what to do with me: some of them used to advise me to volunteer for the army, others to get a job in a pharmacy, and others in the telegraph department; now that I am over twenty-five, that grey hairs are beginning to show on my temples, and that I have been already in the army, and in a pharmacy, and in the telegraph department, it would seem that all earthly possibilities have been exhausted, and people have given up advising me, and merely sigh or shake their heads.

"What do you think about yourself?" my father went on. "By the time they are your age, young men have a secure social position, while look at you: you are a proletarian, a beggar, a burden on your father!"

And as usual he proceeded to decree that the young people of to-day were on the road to perdition through infidelity, materialism, and self-conceit, and that amateur theatricals ought to be prohibited, because they seduced young people from religion and their duties.

"To-morrow we shall go together, and you shall apologize to the superintendent, and promise him to work conscientiously," he said in conclusion. "You ought not to remain one single day with no regular position in society."

"I beg you to listen to me," I said sullenly, expecting nothing good from this conversation. "What you call a position in society is the privilege of capital and education. Those who have neither wealth nor education earn their daily bread by manual labour, and I see no grounds for my being an exception."

"When you begin talking about manual labour it is always stupid and vulgar!" said my father with irritation. "Understand, you dense fellow—understand, you addle-pate, that besides coarse physical strength you have the divine spirit, a spark of the holy fire, which distinguishes you in the most striking way from the ass or the reptile, and brings you nearer to the Deity! This fire is the fruit of the efforts of the best of mankind during thousands of years. Your great-grandfather Poloznev, the general, fought at Borodino; your grandfather was a poet, an orator, and a Marshal of Nobility; your uncle is a schoolmaster; and lastly, I, your father, am an architect! All the Poloznevs have guarded the sacred fire for you to put it out!"

"One must be just," I said. "Millions of people put up with manual labour."

"And let them put up with it! They don't know how to do anything else! Anybody, even the most abject fool or criminal, is capable of manual labour; such labour is the distinguishing mark of the slave and the barbarian, while the holy fire is vouchsafed only to a few!"

To continue this conversation was unprofitable. My father worshipped himself, and nothing was convincing to him but what he said himself. Besides, I knew perfectly well that the disdain with which he talked of physical toil was founded not so much on reverence for the sacred fire as on a secret dread that I should become a workman, and should set the whole town talking about me; what was worse, all my contemporaries had long ago taken their degrees and were getting on well, and the son of the manager of the State Bank was already a collegiate assessor, while I, his only son, was nothing! To continue the conversation was unprofitable and unpleasant, but I still sat on and feebly retorted, hoping that I might at last be understood. The whole question, of course, was clear and simple, and only concerned with the means of my earning my living; but the simplicity of it was not seen, and I was talked to in mawkishly rounded phrases of Borodino, of the sacred fire, of my uncle a forgotten poet, who had once written poor and artificial verses; I was rudely called an addle-pate and a dense fellow. And how I longed to be understood! In spite of everything, I loved my father and my sister and it had been my habit from childhood to consult them—a habit so deeply rooted that I doubt whether I could ever have got rid of it; whether I were in the right or the wrong, I was in constant dread of wounding them, constantly afraid that my father's thin neck would turn crimson and that he would have a stroke.

"To sit in a stuffy room," I began, "to copy, to compete with a typewriter, is shameful and humiliating for a man of my age. What can the sacred fire have to do with it?"

"It's intellectual work, anyway," said my father. "But that's enough; let us cut short this conversation, and in any case I warn you: if you don't go back to your work again, but follow your contemptible propensities, then my daughter and I will banish you from our hearts. I shall strike you out of my will, I swear by the living God!"

With perfect sincerity to prove the purity of the motives by which I wanted to be guided in all my doings, I said:

"The question of inheritance does not seem very important to me. I shall renounce it all beforehand."

For some reason or other, quite to my surprise, these words were deeply resented by my father. He turned crimson.

"Don't dare to talk to me like that, stupid!" he shouted in a thin, shrill voice. "Wastrel!" and with a rapid, skilful, and habitual movement he slapped me twice in the face. "You are forgetting yourself."

When my father beat me as a child I had to stand up straight, with my hands held stiffly to my trouser seams, and look him straight in the face. And now when he hit me I was utterly overwhelmed, and, as though I were still a child, drew myself up and tried to look him in the face. My father was old and very thin but his delicate muscles must have been as strong as leather, for his blows hurt a good deal.

I staggered back into the passage, and there he snatched up his umbrella, and with it hit me several times on the head and shoulders; at that moment my sister opened the drawing-room door to find out what the noise was, but at once turned away with a look of horror and pity without uttering a word in my defence.

My determination not to return to the Government office, but to begin a new life of toil, was not to be shaken. All that was left for me to do was to fix upon the special employment, and there was no particular difficulty about that, as it seemed to me that I was very strong and fitted for the very heaviest labour. I was faced with a monotonous life of toil in the midst of hunger, coarseness, and stench, continually preoccupied with earning my daily bread. And—who knows?—as I returned from my work along Great Dvoryansky Street, I might very likely envy Dolzhikov the engineer, who lived by intellectual work, but, at the moment, thinking over all my future hardships made me light-hearted. At times I had dreamed of spiritual activity, imagining myself a teacher, a doctor, or a writer, but these dreams remained dreams. The taste for intellectual pleasures—for the theatre, for instance, and for reading—was a passion with me, but whether I had any ability for intellectual work I don't know. At school I had had an unconquerable aversion for Greek, so that I was only in the fourth class when they had to take me from school. For a long while I had coaches preparing me for the fifth class. Then I served in various Government offices, spending the greater part of the day in complete idleness, and I was told that was intellectual work. My activity in the scholastic and official sphere had required neither mental application nor talent, nor special qualifications, nor creative impulse; it was mechanical. Such intellectual work I put on a lower level than physical toil; I despise it, and I don't think that for one moment it could serve as a justification for an idle, careless life, as it is indeed nothing but a sham, one of the forms of that same idleness. Real intellectual work I have in all probability never known.

Evening came on. We lived in Great Dvoryansky Street; it was the principal street in the town, and in the absence of decent public gardens our *beau monde* used to use it as a promenade in the evenings. This charming street did to some extent take the place of a public garden, as on each side of it there was a row of poplars which smelt sweet, particularly after rain, and acacias, tall bushes of lilac, wild-cherries and apple-trees hung over the fences and palings. The May twilight, the tender young greenery with its shifting shades, the scent of the lilac, the buzzing of the insects, the stillness, the warmth—how fresh and marvellous it all is, though spring is repeated every year! I stood at the garden gate and watched the passers-by. With most of them I had grown up and at one time played pranks; now they might have been disconcerted by my being near them, for I was poorly and unfashionably dressed, and they used to say of my very narrow trousers and huge, clumsy boots that they were like sticks of macaroni stuck in boats. Besides, I had a bad reputation in the town because I had no decent social position, and used often to play billiards in cheap taverns, and also, perhaps, because I had on two occasions been hauled up before an officer of the police, though I had done nothing whatever to account for this.

In the big house opposite someone was playing the piano at Dolzhikov's. It was beginning to get dark, and stars were twinkling in the sky. Here my father, in an old top-hat with wide upturned brim, walked slowly by with my sister on his arm, bowing in response to greetings.

"Look up," he said to my sister, pointing to the sky with the same umbrella with which he had beaten me that afternoon. "Look up at the sky! Even the tiniest stars are all worlds! How insignificant is man in comparison with the universe!"

And he said this in a tone that suggested that it was particularly agreeable and flattering to him that he was so insignificant. How absolutely devoid of talent and imagination he was! Sad to say, he was the only architect in the town, and in the fifteen to twenty years that I could remember not one single decent house had been built in it. When any one asked him to plan a house, he usually drew first the reception hall and drawing-room: just as in old days the boarding-school misses always started from the stove when they danced, so his artistic ideas could only begin and develop from the hall and drawing-room. To them he tacked on a dining-room, a nursery, a study, linking the rooms together with doors, and so they all inevitably turned into passages, and every one of them had two or even three unnecessary doors. His imagination must have been lacking in clearness, extremely muddled, curtailed. As though feeling that something was lacking, he invariably had recourse to all sorts of outbuildings, planting one beside another; and I can see now the narrow entries, the poky little passages, the crooked staircases leading to half-landings where one could not stand upright, and where, instead of a floor, there were three huge steps like the shelves of a bath-house; and the kitchen was invariably in the basement with a brick floor and vaulted ceilings. The front of the house had a harsh, stubborn expression; the lines of it were stiff and timid; the roof was low-pitched and, as it were, squashed down; and the fat, well-fed-looking chimneys were invariably crowned by wire caps with squeaking black cowls. And for some reason all these houses, built by my father exactly like one another, vaguely reminded me of his top-hat and the back of his head, stiff and stubborn-looking. In the course of years they have grown used in the town to the poverty of my father's imagination. It has taken root and become our local style.

This same style my father had brought into my sister's life also, beginning with christening her Kleopatra (just as he had named me Misail). When she was a little girl he scared her by references to the stars, to the sages of ancient times, to our ancestors, and discoursed at length on the nature of life and duty; and now, when she was twenty-six, he kept up the same habits, allowing her to walk arm in arm with no one but himself, and imagining for some reason that sooner or later a suitable young man would be sure to appear, and to desire to enter into matrimony with her from respect for his personal qualities. She adored my father, feared him, and believed in his exceptional intelligence.

It was quite dark, and gradually the street grew empty. The music had ceased in the house opposite; the gate was thrown wide open, and a team with three horses trotted frolicking along our street with a soft tinkle of little bells. That was the engineer going for a drive with his daughter. It was bedtime.

I had my own room in the house, but I lived in a shed in the yard, under the same roof as a brick barn which had been built some time or other, probably to keep harness in; great hooks were driven into the wall. Now it was not wanted, and for the last thirty years my father had stowed away in it his newspapers, which for some reason he had bound in half-yearly volumes and allowed nobody to touch. Living here, I was less liable to be seen by my father and his visitors, and I fancied that if I did not live in a real room, and did not go into the house every day to dinner, my father's words that I was a burden upon him did not sound so offensive.

My sister was waiting for me. Unseen by my father, she had brought me some supper: not a very large slice of cold veal and a piece of bread. In our house such sayings as: "A penny saved is a penny gained," and "Take care of the pence and the pounds will take care of themselves," and so on, were frequently repeated, and my sister, weighed down by these vulgar maxims, did her utmost to cut down the expenses, and so we fared badly. Putting the plate on the table, she sat down on my bed and began to cry.

"Misail," she said, "what a way to treat us!"

She did not cover her face; her tears dropped on her bosom and hands, and there was a look of distress on her face. She fell back on the pillow, and abandoned herself to her tears, sobbing and quivering all over.

"You have left the service again . . ." she articulated. "Oh, how awful it is!"

"But do understand, sister, do understand . . ." I said, and I was overcome with despair because she was crying.

As ill-luck would have it, the kerosene in my little lamp was exhausted; it began to smoke, and was on the point of going out, and the old hooks on the walls looked down sullenly, and their shadows flickered.

"Have mercy on us," said my sister, sitting up. "Father is in terrible distress and I am ill; I shall go out of my mind. What will become of you?" she said, sobbing and stretching out her arms to me. "I beg you, I implore you, for our dear mother's sake, I beg you to go back to the office!"

"I can't, Kleopatra!" I said, feeling that a little more and I should give way. "I cannot!"

"Why not?" my sister went on. "Why not? Well, if you can't get on with the Head, look out for another post. Why shouldn't you get a situation on the railway, for instance? I have just been talking to Anyuta Blagovo; she declares they would take you on the railway line, and even promised to try and get a post for you. For God's sake, Misail, think a little! Think a little, I implore you."

We talked a little longer and I gave way. I said that the thought of a job on the railway that was being constructed had never occurred to me, and that if she liked I was ready to try it.

She smiled joyfully through her tears and squeezed my hand, and then went on crying because she could not stop, while I went to the kitchen for some kerosene.

II

Among the devoted supporters of amateur theatricals, concerts and *tableaux vivants* for charitable objects the Azhogins, who lived in their own house in Great Dvoryansky Street, took a foremost place; they always provided the room, and took upon themselves all the troublesome arrangements and the expenses. They were a family of wealthy landowners who had an estate of some nine thousand acres in the district and a capital house, but they did not care for the country, and lived winter and summer alike in the town. The family consisted of the mother, a tall, spare, refined lady, with short hair, a short jacket, and a flat-looking skirt in the English fashion, and three daughters who, when they were spoken of, were called not by their names but simply: the eldest, the middle, and the youngest. They all had ugly sharp chins, and were short-sighted and round-shouldered. They were dressed like their mother, they lisped disagreeably, and yet, in spite of that, infallibly took part in every performance and were continually doing something with a charitable object—acting, reciting, singing. They were very serious and never smiled, and even in a musical comedy they played without the faintest trace of gaiety, with a businesslike air, as though they were engaged in bookkeeping.

I loved our theatricals, especially the numerous, noisy, and rather incoherent rehearsals, after which they always gave a supper. In the choice of the plays and the distribution of the parts I had no hand at all. The post assigned to me lay behind the scenes. I painted the scenes, copied out the parts, prompted, made up the actors' faces; and I was entrusted, too, with various stage effects such as thunder, the singing of nightingales, and so on. Since I had no proper social position and no decent clothes, at the rehearsals I held aloof from the rest in the shadows of the wings and maintained a shy silence.

I painted the scenes at the Azhogins' either in the barn or in the yard. I was assisted by Andrey Ivanov, a house painter, or, as he called himself, a contractor for all kinds of house decorations, a tall, very thin, pale man of fifty, with a hollow chest, with sunken temples, with blue rings round his eyes, rather terrible to look at in fact. He was afflicted with some internal malady, and every autumn and spring people said that he wouldn't recover, but after being laid up for a while he would get up and say afterwards with surprise: "I have escaped dying again."

In the town he was called Radish, and they declared that this was his real name. He was as fond of the theatre as I was, and as soon as rumours reached him that a performance was being got up he threw aside all his work and went to the Azhogins, to paint scenes.

The day after my talk with my sister, I was working at the Azhogins' from morning till night. The rehearsal was fixed for seven o'clock in the evening, and an hour before it began all the amateurs were gathered together in the hall, and the eldest, the middle, and the youngest Azhogins were pacing about the stage, reading from manuscript books. Radish, in a long rusty-red overcoat and a scarf muffled round his neck, already stood leaning with his head against the wall, gazing with a devout expression at the stage. Madame Azhogin went up first to one and then to another guest, saying something agreeable to each. She had a way of gazing into one's face and speaking softly as though telling a secret.

"It must be difficult to paint scenery," she said softly, coming up to me. "I was just talking to Madame Mufke about superstitions when I saw you come in. My goodness, my whole life I have been waging war against superstitions! To convince the servants what nonsense all their terrors are, I always light three candles, and begin all my important undertakings on the thirteenth of the month."

Dolzhikov's daughter came in, a plump, fair beauty, dressed, as people said, in everything from Paris. She did not act, but a chair was set for her on the stage at the rehearsals, and the performances never began till she had appeared in the front row, dazzling and astounding everyone with her fine clothes. As a product of the capital she was allowed to make remarks during the rehearsals; and she did so with a sweet indulgent smile, and one could see that she looked upon our performance as a childish amusement. It was said she had studied singing at the Petersburg Conservatoire, and even sang for a whole winter in a private opera. I thought her very charming, and I usually watched her through the rehearsals and performances without taking my eyes off her.

I had just picked up the manuscript book to begin prompting when my sister suddenly made her appearance. Without taking off her cloak or hat, she came up to me and said:

"Come along, I beg you."

I went with her. Anyuta Blagovo, also in her hat and wearing a dark veil, was standing behind the scenes at the door. She was the daughter of the Assistant President of the Court, who had held that office in our town almost ever since the establishment of the circuit court. Since she was tall and had a good figure, her assistance was considered indispensable for *tableaux vivants*, and when she represented a fairy or something like Glory her face burned with shame; but she took no part in dramatic performances, and came to the rehearsals only for a moment on some special errand, and did not go into the hall. Now, too, it was evident that she had only looked in for a minute.

"My father was speaking about you," she said drily, blushing and not looking at me. "Dolzhikov has promised you a post on the railway-line. Apply to him to-morrow; he will be at home."

I bowed and thanked her for the trouble she had taken.

"And you can give up this," she said, indicating the exercise book.

My sister and she went up to Madame Azhogin and for two minutes they were whispering with her looking towards me; they were consulting about something.

"Yes, indeed," said Madame Azhogin, softly coming up to me and looking intently into my face. "Yes, indeed, if this distracts you from serious pursuits"—she took the manuscript book from my hands—"you can hand it over to someone else; don't distress yourself, my friend, go home, and good luck to you."

I said good-bye to her, and went away overcome with confusion. As I went down the stairs I saw my sister and Anyuta Blagovo going away; they were hastening along, talking eagerly about something, probably about my going into the railway service. My sister had never been at a rehearsal before, and now she was most likely conscience-stricken, and afraid her father might find out that, without his permission, she had been to the Azhogins'!

I went to Dolzhikov's next day between twelve and one. The footman conducted me into a very beautiful room, which was the engineer's drawing-room, and, at the same time, his working study. Everything here was soft and elegant, and, for a man so unaccustomed to luxury as I was, it seemed strange. There were costly rugs, huge arm-chairs, bronzes, pictures, gold and plush frames; among the photographs scattered about the walls there were very beautiful women, clever, lovely faces, easy attitudes; from the drawing-room there was a door leading straight into the garden on to a verandah: one could see lilac-trees; one could see a table laid for lunch, a number of bottles, a bouquet of roses; there was a fragrance of spring and expensive cigars, a fragrance of happiness—and everything seemed as though it would say: "Here is a man who has lived and laboured, and has attained at last the happiness possible on earth." The engineer's daughter was sitting at the writing-table, reading a newspaper.

"You have come to see my father?" she asked. "He is having a shower bath; he will be here directly. Please sit down and wait."

I sat down.

"I believe you live opposite?" she questioned me, after a brief silence.

"Yes."

"I am so bored that I watch you every day out of the window; you must excuse me," she went on, looking at the newspaper, "and I often see your sister; she always has such a look of kindness and concentration."

Dolzhikov came in. He was rubbing his neck with a towel.

"Papa, Monsieur Poloznev," said his daughter.

"Yes, yes, Blagovo was telling me," he turned briskly to me without giving me his hand. "But listen, what can I give you? What sort of posts have I got? You are a queer set of people!" he went on aloud in a tone as though he were giving me a lecture. "A score of you keep coming to me every day; you imagine I am the head of a department! I am constructing a railway-line, my friends; I have employment for heavy labour: I need mechanics, smiths, navvies, carpenters, well-sinkers, and none of you can do anything but sit and write! You are all clerks."

And he seemed to me to have the same air of happiness as his rugs and easy chairs. He was stout and healthy, ruddy-cheeked and broad-chested, in a print cotton shirt and full trousers like a toy china sledge-driver. He had a curly, round beard—and not a single grey hair—a hooked nose, and clear, dark, guileless eyes.

"What can you do?" he went on. "There is nothing you can do! I am an engineer. I am a man of an assured position, but before they gave me a railway-line I was for years in harness; I have been a practical mechanic. For two years I worked in Belgium as an oiler. You can judge for yourself, my dear fellow, what kind of work can I offer you?"

"Of course that is so . . ." I muttered in extreme confusion, unable to face his clear, guileless eyes.

"Can you work the telegraph, any way?" he asked, after a moment's thought.

"Yes, I have been a telegraph clerk."

"Hm! Well, we will see then. Meanwhile, go to Dubetchnya. I have got a fellow there, but he is a wretched creature."

"And what will my duties consist of?" I asked.

"We shall see. Go there; meanwhile I will make arrangements. Only please don't get drunk, and don't worry me with requests of any sort, or I shall send you packing."

He turned away from me without even a nod.

I bowed to him and his daughter who was reading a newspaper, and went away. My heart felt so heavy, that when my sister began asking me how the engineer had received me, I could not utter a single word.

I got up early in the morning, at sunrise, to go to Dubetchnya. There was not a soul in our Great Dvoryansky Street; everyone was asleep, and my footsteps rang out with a solitary, hollow sound. The poplars, covered with dew, filled the air with soft fragrance. I was sad, and did not want to go away from the town. I was fond of my native town. It seemed to be so beautiful and so snug! I loved the fresh green-ery, the still, sunny morning, the chiming of our bells; but the people with whom I lived in this town were boring, alien to me, sometimes even repulsive. I did not like them nor understand them.

I did not understand what these sixty-five thousand people lived for and by. I knew that Kimry lived by boots, that Tula made samovars and guns, that Odessa was a sea-port, but what our town was, and what it did, I did not know. Great Dvoryansky Street and the two other smartest streets lived on the interest of capital, or on salaries received by officials from the public treasury; but what the other eight streets, which ran parallel for over two miles and vanished beyond the hills, lived upon, was always an insoluble riddle to me. And the way those people lived one is ashamed to describe! No garden, no theatre, no decent band; the public library and the club library were only visited by Jewish youths, so that the magazines and new books lay for months uncut; rich and well-educated people slept in close, stuffy bedrooms, on wooden bedsteads infested with bugs; their children were kept in revoltingly dirty rooms called nurseries, and the servants, even the old and respected ones, slept on the floor in the kitchen, covered with rags. On ordinary days the houses smelt of beetroot soup, and on fast days of sturgeon cooked in sunflower oil. The food was not good, and the drinking water was unwholesome. In the town council, at the governor's, at the head priest's, on all sides in private houses, people had been saying for years and years that our town had not a good and cheap water-supply, and that it was necessary to obtain a loan of two hundred thousand from the Treasury for laying on water; very rich people, of whom three dozen could have been counted up in our town, and who at times lost whole estates at cards, drank the polluted water, too, and talked all their lives with great excitement of a loan for the water-supply—and I did not understand that; it seemed to me it would have been simpler to take the two hundred thousand out of their own pockets and lay it out on that object.

I did not know one honest man in the town. My father took bribes, and imagined that they were given him out of respect for his moral qualities; at the high school, in order to be moved up rapidly from class to class, the boys went to board with their teachers, who charged them exorbitant sums; the wife of the military commander took bribes from the recruits when they were called up before the board and even deigned to accept refreshments from them, and on one occasion could not get up from her knees in church because she was drunk; the doctors took bribes, too, when the recruits came up for examination, and the town doctor and the veterinary surgeon levied a regular tax on the butchers' shops and the restaurants; at the district school they did a trade in certificates, qualifying for partial exemption from military service; the higher clergy took bribes from the humbler priests and from the church elders; at the Municipal, the Artisans', and all the other

Boards every petitioner was pursued by a shout: "Don't forget your thanks!" and the petitioner would turn back to give sixpence or a shilling. And those who did not take bribes, such as the higher officials of the Department of Justice, were haughty, offered two fingers instead of shaking hands, were distinguished by the frigidity and narrowness of their judgments, spent a great deal of time over cards, drank to excess, married heiresses, and undoubtedly had a pernicious corrupting influence on those around them. It was only the girls who had still the fresh fragrance of moral purity; most of them had higher impulses, pure and honest hearts; but they had no understanding of life, and believed that bribes were given out of respect for moral qualities, and after they were married grew old quickly, let themselves go completely, and sank hopelessly in the mire of vulgar, petty bourgeois existence.

III

A railway-line was being constructed in our neighbourhood. On the eve of feast days the streets were thronged with ragged fellows whom the townspeople called "navvies," and of whom they were afraid. And more than once I had seen one of these tatterdemalions with a blood-stained countenance being led to the police station, while a samovar or some linen, wet from the wash, was carried behind by way of material evidence. The navvies usually congregated about the taverns and the market-place; they drank, ate, and used bad language, and pursued with shrill whistles every woman of light behaviour who passed by. To entertain this hungry rabble our shopkeepers made cats and dogs drunk with vodka, or tied an old kerosene can to a dog's tail; a hue and cry was raised, and the dog dashed along the street, jingling the can, squealing with terror; it fancied some monster was close upon its heels; it would run far out of the town into the open country and there sink exhausted. There were in the town several dogs who went about trembling with their tails between their legs; and people said this diversion had been too much for them, and had driven them mad.

A station was being built four miles from the town. It was said that the engineers asked for a bribe of fifty thousand roubles for bringing the line right up to the town, but the town council would only consent to give forty thousand; they could not come to an agreement over the difference, and now the townspeople regretted it, as they had to make a road to the station and that, it was reckoned, would cost more. The sleepers and rails had been laid throughout the whole length of the line, and trains ran up and down it, bringing building materials and labourers, and further progress was only delayed on account of the bridges which Dolzhikov was building, and some of the stations were not yet finished.

Dubetchnya, as our first station was called, was a little under twelve miles from the town. I walked. The cornfields, bathed in the morning sunshine, were bright green. It was a flat, cheerful country, and in the distance there were the distinct outlines of the station, of ancient barrows, and far-away homesteads. . . . How nice it was out there in the open! I And how I longed to be filled with the sense of freedom, if only for that one morning, that I might not think of what was being done in the town, not think of my needs, not feel hungry! Nothing has so marred my existence as an acute feeling of hunger, which made images of buckwheat porridge, rissoles, and baked fish mingle strangely with my best thoughts. Here I was standing alone in the open country, gazing upward at a lark which hovered in the air at the same spot, trilling as though in hysterics, and meanwhile I was thinking: "How nice it would be to eat a piece of bread and butter!" Or I would sit down by the roadside to rest, and shut my eyes to listen to the delicious sounds of May, and what haunted me was the smell of hot potatoes. Though I was tall and strongly built, I had as a rule little to eat, and so the predominant sensation throughout the day was hunger, and perhaps that was why I knew so well how it is that such multitudes of people toil merely for their daily bread, and can talk of nothing but things to eat.

At Dubetchnya they were plastering the inside of the station, and building a wooden upper storey to the pumping shed. It was hot; there was a smell of lime, and the workmen sauntered listlessly between the heaps of shavings and mortar rubble. The pointsman lay asleep near his sentry box, and the sun was blazing full on his face. There was not a single tree. The telegraph wire hummed faintly and hawks were perching on it here and there. I, wandering, too, among the heaps of rubbish, and not knowing what to do, recalled how the engineer, in answer to my question what my duties would consist in, had said: "We shall see when you are there"; but what could one see in that wilderness?

The plasterers spoke of the foreman, and of a certain Fyodot Vasilyev. I did not understand, and gradually I was overcome by depression—the physical depression in which one is conscious of one's arms and legs and huge body, and does not know what to do with them or where to put them.

After I had been walking about for at least a couple of hours, I noticed that there were telegraph poles running off to the right from the station, and that they ended a mile or a mile and a half away at a white stone wall. The workmen told me the office was there, and at last I reflected that that was where I ought to go.

It was a very old manor house, deserted long ago. The wall round it, of porous white stone, was mouldering and had fallen away in places, and the lodge, the blank wall of which looked out on the open country, had a rusty roof with patches of tin-plate gleaming here and there on it. Within the gates could be seen a spacious courtyard overgrown with rough weeds, and an old manor house with sunblinds on the windows, and a high roof red with rust. Two lodges, exactly alike, stood one on each side of the house to right and to left: one had its windows nailed up with boards; near the other, of which the windows were open, there was washing on the line, and there were calves moving about. The last of the telegraph poles stood in the courtyard, and the wire from it ran to the window of the lodge, of which the blank wall looked out into the open country. The door stood open; I went in. By the telegraph apparatus a gentleman with a curly dark head, wearing a reefer coat made of sailcloth, was sitting at a table; he glanced at me morosely from under his brows, but immediately smiled and said:

"Hello, Better-than-nothing!"

It was Ivan Tcheprakov, an old schoolfellow of mine, who had been expelled from the second class for smoking. We used at one time, during autumn, to catch goldfinches, finches, and linnets together, and to sell them in the market early in the morning, while our parents were still in their beds. We watched for flocks of migrating starlings and shot at them with small shot, then we picked up those that were wounded, and some of then died in our hands in terrible agonies (I remember to this day how they moaned in the cage at night); those that recovered we sold, and swore with the utmost effrontery that they were all cocks. On one occasion at the market I had only one starling left, which I had offered to purchasers in vain, till at last I sold it for a farthing. "Anyway, it's better than nothing," I said to comfort myself, as I put the farthing in my pocket, and from that day the street urchins and the schoolboys called after me: "Better-than-nothing"; and to this day the street boys and the shopkeepers mock at me with the nickname, though no one remembers how it arose.

Tcheprakov was not of robust constitution: he was narrow-chested, round-shouldered, and long-legged. He wore a silk cord for a tie, had no trace of a waistcoat, and his boots were worse than mine, with the heels trodden down on one side. He stared, hardly even blinking, with a strained expression, as though he were just going to catch something, and he was always in a fuss.

"You wait a minute," he would say fussily. "You listen. . . . Whatever was I talking about?"

We got into conversation. I learned that the estate on which I now was had until recently been the property of the Tcheprakovs, and had only the autumn before passed into the possession of Dolzhikov, who considered it more profitable to put his money into land than to keep it in notes, and had already bought up three good-sized mortgaged estates in our neighbourhood. At the sale Tcheprakov's mother had reserved for herself the right to live for the next two years in one of the lodges at the side, and had obtained a post for her son in the office.

"I should think he could buy!" Tcheprakov said of the engineer. "See what he fleeces out of the contractors alone! He fleeces everyone!"

Then he took me to dinner, deciding fussily that I should live with him in the lodge, and have my meals from his mother.

"She is a bit stingy," he said, "but she won't charge you much."

It was very cramped in the little rooms in which his mother lived; they were all, even the passage and the entry, piled up with furniture which had been brought from the big house after the sale; and the furniture was all old-fashioned mahogany. Madame Tcheprakov, a very stout middle-aged lady with slanting Chinese eyes, was sitting in a big arm-chair by the window, knitting a stocking. She received me ceremoniously.

"This is Poloznev, mamma," Tcheprakov introduced me. "He is going to serve here."

"Are you a nobleman? " she asked in a strange, disagreeable voice: it seemed to me to sound as though fat were bubbling in her throat.

"Yes," I answered.

"Sit down."

The dinner was a poor one. Nothing was served but pies filled with bitter curd, and milk soup. Elena Nikiforovna, who presided, kept blinking in a queer way, first with one eye and then with the other. She talked, she ate, but yet there was something deathly about her whole figure, and one almost fancied the faint smell of a corpse. There was only a glimmer of life in her, a glimmer of consciousness that she had been a lady who had once had her own serfs, that she was the widow of a general whom the servants had to address as "your Excellency"; and when these feeble relics of life flickered up in her for an instant she would say to her son:

"Jean, you are not holding your knife properly!"

Or she would say to me, drawing a deep breath, with the mincing air of a hostess trying to entertain a visitor:

"You know we have sold our estate. Of course, it is a pity, we are used to the place, but Dolzhikov has promised to make Jean station-master of Dubetchnya, so we shall not have to go away; we shall live here at the station, and that is just the same as being on our own property! The engineer is so nice! Don't you think he is very handsome?"

Until recently the Tcheprakovs had lived in a wealthy style, but since the death of the general everything had been changed. Elena Nikiforovna had taken to quarrelling with the neighbours, to going to law, and to not paying her bailiffs or her labourers; she was in constant terror of being robbed, and in some ten years Dubetchnya had become unrecognizable.

Behind the great house was an old garden which had already run wild, and was overgrown with rough weeds and bushes. I walked up and down the verandah, which was still solid and beautiful; through the glass doors one could see a room with parquetted floor, probably the drawing-room; an old-fashioned piano and pictures in deep mahogany frames—there was nothing else. In the old flower-beds all that remained were peonies and poppies, which lifted their white and bright red heads above the grass. Young maples and elms, already nibbled by the cows, grew beside the paths, drawn up and hindering each other's growth. The garden was thickly overgrown and seemed impassable, but this was only near the house where there stood poplars, fir-trees, and old lime-trees, all of the same age, relics of the former avenues.

Further on, beyond them the garden had been cleared for the sake of hay, and here it was not moist and stuffy, and there were no spiders' webs in one's mouth and eyes. A light breeze was blowing. The further one went the more open it was, and here in the open space were cherries, plums, and spreading apple-trees, disfigured by props and by canker; and pear-trees so tall that one could not believe they were pear-trees. This part of the garden was let to some shopkeepers of the town, and it was protected from thieves and starlings by a feeble-minded peasant who lived in a shanty in it.

The garden, growing more and more open, till it became definitely a meadow, sloped down to the river, which was overgrown with green weeds and osiers. Near the milldam was the millpond, deep and full of fish; a little mill with a thatched roof was working away with a wrathful sound, and frogs croaked furiously. Circles passed from time to time over the smooth, mirror-like water, and the water-lilies trembled, stirred by the lively fish. On the further side of the river was the little village Dubetchnya. The still, blue millpond was alluring with its promise of coolness and peace. And now all this—the millpond and the mill and the snug-looking banks—belonged to the engineer!

And so my new work began. I received and forwarded telegrams, wrote various reports, and made fair copies of the notes of requirements, the complaints, and the reports sent to the office by the illiterate foremen and workmen. But for the greater part of the day I did nothing but walk about the room waiting for telegrams, or made a boy sit in the lodge while I went for a walk in the garden, until the boy ran to tell me that there was a tapping at the operating machine. I had dinner at Madame Tcheprakov's. Meat we had very rarely: our dishes were all made of milk, and Wednesdays and Fridays were fast days, and on those days we had pink plates which were called Lenten plates. Madame Tcheprakov was continually blinking—it was her invariable habit, and I always felt ill at ease in her presence.

As there was not enough work in the lodge for one, Tcheprakov did nothing, but simply dozed, or went with his gun to shoot ducks on the millpond. In the evenings he drank too much in the village or the station, and before going to bed stared in the looking-glass and said: "Hullo, Ivan Tcheprakov."

When he was drunk he was very pale, and kept rubbing his hands and laughing with a sound like a neigh: "hee-hee-hee!" By way of bravado he used to strip and run about the country naked. He used to eat flies and say they were rather sour.

IV

One day, after dinner, he ran breathless into the lodge and said: "Go along, your sister has come."

I went out, and there I found a hired brake from the town standing before the entrance of the great house. My sister had come in it with Anyuta Blagovo and a gentleman in a military tunic. Going up closer I recognized the latter: it was the brother of Anyuta Blagovo, the army doctor.

"We have come to you for a picnic," he said; "is that all right?"

My sister and Anyuta wanted to ask how I was getting on here, but both were silent, and simply gazed at me. I was silent too. They saw that I did not like the place, and tears came to my sister's eyes, while Anyuta Blagovo turned crimson.

We went into the garden. The doctor walked ahead of us all and said enthusiastically:

"What air! Holy Mother, what air!"

In appearance he was still a student. And he walked and talked like a student, and the expression of his grey eyes was as keen, honest and frank as a nice student's. Besides his tall and handsome sister he looked frail and thin; and his beard was thin too, and his voice, too, was a thin but a rather agreeable tenor. He was serving in a regiment somewhere, and had come home to his people for a holiday, and said he was going in the autumn to Petersburg for his examination as a doctor of medicine. He was already a family man, with a wife and three children, he had married very young, in his second year at the University, and now people in the town said he was unhappy in his family life and was not living with his wife.

"What time is it?" my sister asked uneasily. "We must get back in good time. Papa let me come to see my brother on condition I was back at six."

"Oh, bother your papa!" sighed the doctor.

I set the samovar. We put down a carpet before the verandah of the great house and had our tea there, and the doctor knelt down, drank out of his saucer, and declared that he now knew what bliss was.

Then Tcheprakov came with the key and opened the glass door, and we all went into the house. There it was half dark and mysterious, and smelt of mushrooms, and our footsteps had a hollow sound as though there were cellars under the floor. The doctor stopped and touched the keys of the piano, and it responded faintly with a husky, quivering, but melodious chord; he tried his voice and sang a song, frowning and tapping impatiently with his foot when some note was mute. My sister did not talk about going home, but walked about the rooms and kept saying:

"How happy I am! How happy I am!"

There was a note of astonishment in her voice, as though it seemed to her incredible that she, too, could feel light-hearted. It was the first time in my life I had seen her so happy. She actually looked prettier. In profile she did not look nice; her nose and mouth seemed to stick out and had an expression as though she were pouting, but she had beautiful dark eyes, a pale, very delicate complexion, and a touching expression of goodness and melancholy, and when she talked she seemed charming and even beautiful. We both, she and I, took after our mother, were broad shouldered, strongly built, and capable of endurance, but her pallor was a sign of ill-health; she often had a cough, and I sometimes caught in her face that look one sees in people who are seriously ill, but for some reason conceal the fact. There was something naïve and childish in her gaiety now, as though the joy that had been suppressed and smothered in our childhood by harsh education had now suddenly awakened in her soul and found a free outlet.

But when evening came on and the horses were brought round, my sister sank into silence and looked thin and shrunken, and she got into the brake as though she were going to the scaffold.

When they had all gone, and the sound had died away . . . I remembered that Anyuta Blagovo had not said a word to me all day.

"She is a wonderful girl!" I thought. "Wonderful girl!"

St. Peter's fast came, and we had nothing but Lenten dishes every day. I was weighed down by physical depression due to idleness and my unsettled position, and dissatisfied with myself. Listless and hungry, I lounged about the garden and only waited for a suitable mood to go away.

Towards evening one day, while Radish was sitting in the lodge, Dolzhikov, very sunburnt and grey with dust, walked in unexpectedly.

He had been spending three days on his land, and had come now to Dubetchnya by the steamer, and walked to us from the station. While waiting for the carriage, which was to come for him from the town, he walked round the grounds with his bailiff, giving orders in a loud voice, then sat for a whole hour in our lodge, writing letters. While he was there telegrams came for him, and he himself tapped off the answers. We three stood in silence at attention.

"What a muddle!" he said, glancing contemptuously at a record book. "In a fortnight I am transferring the office to the station, and I don't know what I am to do with you, my friends."

"I do my best, your honour," said Tcheprakov.

"To be sure, I see how you do your best. The only thing you can do is to take your salary," the engineer went on, looking at me; "you keep relying on patronage to *faire le carrière* as quickly and as easily as possible. Well, I don't care for patronage. No one took any trouble on my behalf. Before they gave me a railway contract I went about as a mechanic and worked in Belgium as an oiler. And you, Panteley, what are you doing here?" he asked, turning to Radish. "Drinking with them?"

He, for some reason, always called humble people Panteley, and such as me and Tcheprakov he despised, and called them drunkards, beasts, and rabble to their faces. Altogether he was cruel to humble subordinates, and used to fine them and turn them off coldly without explanations.

At last the horses came for him. As he said good-bye he promised to turn us all off in a fortnight; he called his bailiff a blockhead; and then, lolling at ease in his carriage, drove back to the town.

"Andrey Ivanitch," I said to Radish, "take me on as a workman."

"Oh, all right!"

And we set off together in the direction of the town. When the station and the big house with its buildings were left behind I asked: "Andrey Ivanitch, why did you come to Dubetchnya this evening?"

"In the first place my fellows are working on the line, and in the second place I came to pay the general's lady my interest. Last year I borrowed fifty roubles from her, and I pay her now a rouble a month interest."

The painter stopped and took me by the button.

"Misail Alexeyitch, our angel," he went on. "The way I look at it is that if any man, gentle or simple, takes even the smallest interest, he is doing evil. There cannot be truth and justice in such a man."

Radish, lean, pale, dreadful-looking, shut his eyes, shook his head, and, in the tone of a philosopher, pronounced:

"Lice consume the grass, rust consumes the iron, and lying the soul. Lord, have mercy upon us sinners."

V

Radish was not practical, and was not at all good at forming an estimate; he took more work than he could get through, and when calculating he was agitated, lost his head, and so was almost always out of pocket over his jobs. He undertook painting, glazing, paperhanging, and even tiling roofs, and I can remember his running about for three days to find tilers for the sake of a paltry job. He was a first-rate workman; he sometimes earned as much as ten roubles a day; and if it had not been for the desire at all costs to be a master, and to be called a contractor, he would probably have had plenty of money.

He was paid by the job, but he paid me and the other workmen by the day, from one and twopence to two shillings a day. When it was fine and dry we did all kinds of outside work, chiefly painting roofs. When I was new to the work it made my feet burn as though I were walking on hot bricks, and when I put on felt boots they were hotter than ever. But this was only at first; later on I got used to it, and everything went swimmingly. I was living now among people to whom labour was obligatory, inevitable, and who worked like cart-horses, often with no idea of the moral significance of labour, and, indeed, never using the word "labour" in conversation at all. Beside them I, too, felt like a cart-horse, growing more and more imbued with the feeling of the obligatory and inevitable character of what I was doing, and this made my life easier, setting me free frorn all doubt and uncertainty.

At first everything interested me, everything was new, as though I had been born again. I could sleep on the ground and go about barefoot, and that was extremely pleasant; I could stand in a crowd of the common people and be no constraint to anyone, and when a cab horse fell down in the street I ran to help it up without being afraid of soiling my clothes. And the best of it all was, I was living on my own account and no burden to anyone!

Painting roofs, especially with our own oil and colours, was regarded as a particularly profitable job, and so this rough, dull work was not disdained, even by such good workmen as Radish. In short breeches, and wasted, purple-looking legs, he used to go about the roofs, looking like a stork, and I used to hear him, as he plied his brush, breathing heavily and saying: "Woe, woe to us sinners!"

He walked about the roofs as freely as though he were upon the ground. In spite of his being ill and pale as a corpse, his agility was extraordinary: he used to paint the domes and cupolas of the churches without scaffolding, like a young man, with only the help of a ladder and a rope, and it was rather horrible when standing on a height far from the earth; he would draw himself up erect, and for some unknown reason pronounce:

"Lice consume grass, rust consumes iron, and lying the soul!"

Or, thinking about something, would answer his thoughts aloud:

"Anything may happen! Anything may happen!"

When I went home from my work, all the people who were sitting on benches by the gates, all the shopmen and boys and their employers, made sneering and spiteful remarks after me, and this upset me at first and seemed to be simply monstrous.

"Better-than-nothing!" I heard on all sides. "House painter! Yellow ochre!"

And none behaved so ungraciously to me as those who had only lately been humble people themselves, and had earned their bread by hard manual labour. In the streets full of shops I was once passing an ironmonger's when water was thrown over me as though by accident, and on one occasion someone darted out with a stick at me, while a fishmonger, a grey-headed old man, barred my way and said, looking at me angrily:

"I am not sorry for you, you fool! It's your father I am sorry for."

And my acquaintances were for some reason overcome with embarrassment when they met me. Some of them looked upon me as a queer fish and a comic fool; others were sorry for me; others did not know what attitude to take up to me, and it was difficult to make them out. One day I met Anyuta Blagovo in a side street near Great Dvoryansky Street. I was going to work, and was carrying two long brushes and a pail of paint. Recognizing me Anyuta flushed crimson.

"Please do not bow to me in the street," she said nervously, harshly, and in a shaking voice, without offering me her hand, and tears suddenly gleamed in her eyes. "If to your mind all this is necessary, so be it . . . so be it, but I beg you not to meet me!"

I no longer lived in Great Dvoryansky Street, but in the suburb with my old nurse Karpovna, a good-natured but gloomy old woman, who always foreboded some harm, was afraid of all dreams, and even in the bees and wasps that flew into her room saw omens of evil, and the fact that I had become a workman, to her thinking, boded nothing good.

"Your life is ruined," she would say, mournfully shaking her head, "ruined."

Her adopted son Prokofy, a huge, uncouth, red-headed fellow of thirty, with bristling moustaches, a butcher by trade, lived in the little house with her. When he met me in the passage he would make way for me in respectful silence, and if he was drunk he would salute me with all five fingers at once. He used to have supper in the evening, and through the partition wall of boards I could hear him clear his throat and sigh as he drank off glass after glass.

"Mamma," he would call in an undertone.

"Well," Karpovna, who was passionately devoted to her adopted son, would respond: "what is it, sonny?"

"I can show you a testimony of my affection, mamma. All this earthly life I will cherish you in your declining years in this vale of tears, and when you die I will bury you at my expense; I have said it, and you can believe it."

I got up every morning before sunrise, and went to bed early. We house painters ate a great deal and slept soundly; the only thing amiss was that my heart used to beat violently at night. I did not quarrel with my mates. Violent abuse, desperate oaths, and wishes such as, "Blast your eyes," or "Cholera take you," never ceased all day, but, nevertheless, we lived on very friendly terms. The other fellows suspected me of being some sort of religious sectary, and made good-natured jokes at my expense, saying that even my own father had disowned me, and thereupon would add that they rarely went into the temple of God themselves, and that many of them had not been to confession for ten years. They justified this laxity on their part by saying that a painter among men was like a jackdaw among birds.

The men had a good opinion of me, and treated me with respect;

it was evident that my not drinking, not smoking, but leading a quiet, steady life pleased them very much. It was only an unpleasant shock to them that I took no hand in stealing oil and did not go with them to ask for tips from people on whose property we were working. Stealing oil and paints from those who employed them was a house painter's custom, and was not regarded as theft, and it was remarkable that even so upright a man as Radish would always carry away a little white lead and oil as he went home from work. And even the most respectable old fellows, who owned the houses in which they lived in the suburb, were not ashamed to ask for a tip, and it made me feel vexed and ashamed to see the men go in a body to congratulate some nonentity on the commencement or the completion of the job, and thank him with degrading servility when they had received a few coppers.

With people on whose work they were engaged they behaved like wily courtiers, and almost every day I was reminded of Shakespeare's Polonius.

"I fancy it is going to rain," the man whose house was being painted would say, looking at the sky.

"It is, there is not a doubt it is," the painters would agree.

"I don't think it is a rain-cloud, though. Perhaps it won't rain after all."

"No, it won't, your honour! I am sure it won't."

But their attitude to their patrons behind their backs was usually one of irony, and when they saw, for instance, a gentleman sitting in the verandah reading a newspaper, they would observe:

"He reads the paper, but I daresay he has nothing to eat."

I never went home to see my own people. When I came back from work I often found waiting for me little notes, brief and anxious, in which my sister wrote to me about my father; that he had been particularly preoccupied at dinner and had eaten nothing, or that he had been giddy and staggering, or that he had locked himself in his room and had not come out for a long time. Such items of news troubled me; I could not sleep, and at times even walked up and down Great Dvoryansky Street at night by our house, looking in at the dark windows and trying to guess whether everything was well at home. On Sundays my sister came to see me, but came in secret, as though it were not to see me but our nurse. And if she came in to see me she was very pale, with tear-stained eyes, and she began crying at once.

"Our father will never live through this," she would say. "If anything should happen to him—God grant it may not—your conscience will torment you all your life. It's awful, Misail; for our mother's sake I beseech you: reform your ways."

"My darling sister," I would say, "how can I reform my ways if I am convinced that I am acting in accordance with my conscience? Do understand!"

"I know you are acting on your conscience, but perhaps it could be done differently, somehow, so as not to wound anybody."

"Ah, holy Saints!" the old woman sighed through the door. "Your life is ruined! There will be trouble, my dears, there will be trouble!"

VI

One Sunday Dr. Blagovo turned up unexpectedly. He was wearing a military tunic over a silk shirt and high boots of patent leather.

"I have come to see you," he began, shaking my hand heartily like a student. "I am hearing about you every day, and I have been meaning to come and have a heart-to-heart talk, as they say. The boredom in the town is awful, there is not a living soul, no one to say a word to. It's hot, Holy Mother," he went on, taking off his tunic and sitting in his silk shirt. "My dear fellow, let me talk to you."

I was dull myself, and had for a long time been craving for the society of someone not a house painter. I was genuinely glad to see him.

"I'll begin by saying," he said, sitting down on my bed, "that I sympathize with you from the bottom of my heart, and deeply respect the life you are leading. They don't understand you here in the town, and, indeed, there is no one to understand, seeing that, as you know, they are all, with very few exceptions, regular Gogolesque pig faces here. But I saw what you were at once that time at the picnic. You are a noble soul, an honest, high-minded man! I respect you, and feel it a great honour to shake hands with you !" he went on enthusiastically. "To have made such a complete and violent change of life as you have done, you must have passed through a complicated spiritual crisis, and to continue this manner of life now, and to keep up to the high standard of your convictions continually, must be a strain on your mind and heart from day to day. Now to begin our talk, tell me, don't you consider that if you had spent your strength of will, this strained activity, all these powers on something else, for instance, on gradually becoming a great scientist, or artist, your life would have been broader and deeper and would have been more productive?"

We talked, and when we got upon manual labour I expressed this idea: that what is wanted is that the strong should not enslave the weak, that the minority should not be a parasite on the majority, nor a vampire for ever sucking its vital sap; that is, all, without exception, strong and weak, rich and poor, should take part equally in the struggle for existence, each one on his own account, and that there was no better means for equalizing things in that way than manual labour, in the form of universal service, compulsory for all.

"Then do you think everyone without exception ought to engage in manual labour?" asked the doctor.

"Yes."

"And don't you think that if everyone, including the best men, the thinkers and great scientists, taking part in the struggle for existence, each on his own account, are going to waste their time breaking stones and painting roofs, may not that threaten a grave danger to progress?"

"Where is the danger?" I asked. "Why, progress is in deeds of love, in fulfilling the moral law; if you don't enslave anyone, if you don't oppress anyone, what further progress do you want?"

"But, excuse me," Blagovo suddenly fired up, rising to his feet. "But, excuse me! If a snail in its shell busies itself over perfecting its own personality and muddles about with the moral law, do you call that progress?"

"Why muddles? " I said, offended. "If you don't force your neighbour to feed and clothe you, to transport you from place to place and defend you from your enemies, surely in the midst of a life entirely resting on slavery, that is progress, isn't it? To my mind it is the most important progress, and perhaps the only one possible and necessary for man."

"The limits of universal world progress are in infinity, and to talk of some 'possible' progress limited by our needs and temporary theories is, excuse my saying so, positively strange."

"If the limits of progress are in infinity as you say, it follows that its aims are not definite," I said. " To live without knowing definitely what you are living for!"

"So be it! But that 'not knowing' is not so dull as your 'knowing.'

I am going up a ladder which is called progress, civilization, culture; I go on and up without knowing definitely where I am going, but really it is worth living for the sake of that delightful ladder; while you know what you are living for, you live for the sake of some people's not enslaving others, that the artist and the man who rubs his paints may dine equally well. But you know that's the petty, bourgeois, kitchen, grey side of life, and surely it is revolting to live for that alone? If some insects do enslave others, bother them, let them devour each other! We need not think about them. You know they will die and decay just the same, however zealously you rescue them from slavery. We must think of that great millennium which awaits humanity in the remote future."

Blagovo argued warmly with me, but at the same time one could see he was troubled by some irrelevant idea.

"I suppose your sister is not coming?" he said, looking at his watch. "She was at our house yesterday, and said she would be seeing you to-day. You keep saying slavery, slavery. . . " he went on. "But you know that is a special question, and all such questions are solved by humanity gradually."

We began talking of doing things gradually. I said that "the question of doing good or evil every one settles for himself, without waiting till humanity settles it by the way of gradual development. Moreover, this gradual process has more than one aspect. Side by side with the gradual development of human ideas the gradual growth of ideas of another order is observed. Serfdom is no more, but the capitalist system is growing. And in the very heyday of emancipating ideas, just as in the days of Baty, the majority feeds, clothes, and defends the minority while remaining hungry, inadequately clad, and defenceless. Such an order of things can be made to fit in finely with any tendencies and currents of thought you like, because the art of enslaving is also gradually being cultivated. We no longer flog our servants in the stable, but we give to slavery refined forms, at least, we succeed in finding a justification for it in each particular case. Ideas are ideas with us, but if now, at the end of the nineteenth century, it were possible to lay the burden of the most unpleasant of our physiological functions upon the working class, we should certainly do so, and afterwards, of course, justify ourselves by saying that if the best people, the thinkers and great scientists, were to waste their precious time on these functions, progress might be menaced with great danger."

But at this point my sister arrived. Seeing the doctor she was fluttered and troubled, and began saying immediately that it was time for her to go home to her father.

"Kleopatra Alexyevna," said Blagovo earnestly, pressing both hands to his heart, "what will happen to your father if you spend half an hour or so with your brother and me?"

He was frank, and knew how to communicate his liveliness to others. After a moment's though, my sister laughed, and all at once became suddenly gay as she had been at the picnic. We went out into the country, and lying in the grass went on with our talk, and looked towards the town where all the windows facing west were like glittering gold because the sun was setting.

After that, whenever my sister was coming to see me Blagovo turned up too, and they always greeted each other as though their meeting in my room was accidental. My sister listened while the doctor and I argued, and at such times her expression was joyfully enthusiastic, full of tenderness and curiosity, and it seemed to me that a new world she had never dreamed of before, and which she was now striving to fathom, was gradually opening before her eyes. When the doctor was not there she was quiet and sad, and now if she sometimes shed tears as she sat on my bed it was for reasons of which she did not speak.

In August Radish ordered us to be ready to go to the railway-line. Two days before we were "banished" from the town my father came to see me. He sat down and in a leisurely way, without looking at me, wiped his red face, then took out of his pocket our town *Messenger*, and deliberately, with emphasis on each word, read out the news that the son of the branch manager of the State Bank, a young man of my age, had been appointed head of a Department in the Exchequer.

"And now look at you," he said, folding up the newspaper, "a beggar, in rags, good for nothing! Even working-class people and peasants obtain education in order to become men, while you, a Poloznev, with ancestors of rank and distinction, aspire to the gutter! But I have not come here to talk to you; I have washed my hands of you—" he added in a stifled voice, getting up. "I have come to find out where your sister is, you worthless fellow. She left home after dinner, and here it is nearly eight and she is not back. She has taken to going out frequently without telling me; she is less dutiful—and I see in it your evil and degrading influence. Where is she?"

In his hand he had the umbrella I knew so well, and I was already flustered and drew myself up like a schoolboy, expecting my father to begin hitting me with it, but he noticed my glance at the umbrella and most likely that restrained him.

"Live as you please!" he said. "I shall not give you my blessing!"

"Holy Saints!" my nurse muttered behind the door. "You poor, unlucky child! Ah, my heart bodes ill!"

I worked on the railway-line. It rained without stopping all August; it was damp and cold; they had not carried the corn in the fields, and on big farms where the wheat had been cut by machines it lay not in sheaves but in heaps, and I remember how those luckless heaps of wheat turned blacker every day and the grain was sprouting in them. It was hard to work; the pouring rain spoiled everything we managed to do. We were not allowed to live or to sleep in the railway buildings, and we took refuge in the damp and filthy mud huts in which the navvies had lived during the summer, and I could not sleep at night for the cold and the woodlice crawling on my face and hands. And when we worked near the bridges the navvies used to come in the evenings in a gang, simply in order to beat the painters—it was a form of sport to them. They used to beat us, to steal our brushes. And to annoy us and rouse us to fight they used to spoil our work; they would, for instance, smear over the signal boxes with green paint. To complete our troubles, Radish took to paying us very irregularly. All the painting work on the line was given out to a contractor; he gave it out to another; and this subcontractor gave it to Radish after subtracting twenty per cent. for himself. The job was not a profitable one in itself, and the rain made it worse; time was wasted; we could not work while Radish was obliged to pay the fellows by the day. The hungry painters almost came to beating him, called him a cheat, a blood-sucker, a Judas, while he, poor fellow, sighed, lifted up his hand to Heaven in despair, and was continually going to Madame Tcheprakov for money.

VII

Autumn came on, rainy, dark, and muddy. The season of unemployment set in, and I used to sit at home out of work for three days at a stretch, or did various little jobs, not in the painting line. For instance, I wheeled earth, earning about fourpence a day by it. Dr. Blagovo had gone away to Petersburg. My sister had given up coming to see me. Radish was laid up at home ill, expecting death from day to day.

And my mood was autumnal too. Perhaps because, having become a workman, I saw our town life only from the seamy side, it was my lot almost every day to make discoveries which reduced me almost to despair. Those of my fellow-citizens, about whom I had no opinion before, or who had externally appeared perfectly decent, turned out now to be base, cruel people, capable of any dirty action. We common people were deceived, cheated, and kept waiting for hours together in the cold entry or the kitchen; we were insulted and treated with the utmost rudeness. In the autumn I papered the reading-room and two other rooms at the club; I was paid a penny three-farthings the piece, but had to sign a receipt at the rate of twopence halfpenny, and when I refused to do so, a gentleman of benevolent appearance in gold-rimmed spectacles, who must have been one of the club committee, said to me:

"If you say much more, you blackguard, I'll pound your face into a jelly!"

And when the flunkey whispered to him what I was, the son of Poloznev the architect, he became embarrassed, turned crimson, but immediately recovered himself and said: "Devil take him."

In the shops they palmed off on us workmen putrid meat, musty flour, and tea that had been used and dried again; the police hustled us in church, the assistants and nurses in the hospital plundered us, and if we were too poor to give them a bribe they revenged themselves by bringing us food in dirty vessels. In the post-office the pettiest official considered he had a right to treat us like animals, and to shout with coarse insolence: "You wait!" "Where are you shoving to?" Even the house-dogs were unfriendly to us, and fell upon us with peculiar viciousness. But the thing that struck me most of all in my new position was the complete lack of justice, what is defined by the peasants in the words: "They have forgotten God." Rarely did a day pass without swindling. We were swindled by the merchants who sold us oil, by the contractors and the workmen and the people who employed us. I need not say that there could never be a question of our rights, and we always had to ask for the money we earned as though it were a charity, and to stand waiting for it at the back door, cap in hand.

I was papering a room at the Club next to the reading-room; in the evening, when I was just getting ready to go, the daughter of Dolzhikov, the engineer, walked into the room with a bundle of books under her arm.

I bowed to her.

"Oh, how do you do!" she said, recognizing me at once, and holding out her hand. "I'm very glad to see you."

She smiled and looked with curiosity and wonder at my smock, my pail of paste, the paper stretched on the floor; I was embarrassed, and she, too, felt awkward.

"You must excuse my looking at you like this," she said. "I have been told so much about you. Especially by Dr. Blagovo; he is simply in love with you. And I have made the acquaintance of your sister too; a sweet, dear girl, but I can never persuade her that there is nothing awful about your adopting the simple life. On the contrary, you have become the most interesting man in the town."

She looked again at the pail of paste and the wallpaper, and went on:

"I asked Dr. Blagovo to make me better acquainted with you, but apparently he forgot, or had not time. Anyway, we are acquainted all the same, and if you would come and see me quite simply I should be extremely indebted to you. I so long to have a talk. I am a simple person," she added, holding out her hand to me, "and I hope that you will feel no constraint with me. My father is not here, he is in Petersburg."

She went off into the reading-room, rustling her skirts, while I went home, and for a long time could not get to sleep.

That cheerless autumn some kind soul, evidently wishing to alleviate my existence, sent me from time to time tea and lemons, or biscuits, or roast game. Karpovna told me that they were always brought by a soldier, and from whom they came she did not know; and the soldier used to enquire whether I was well, and whether I dined every day, and whether I had warm clothing. When the frosts began I was presented in the same way in my absence with a soft knitted scarf brought by the soldier. There was a faint elusive smell of scent about it, and I guessed who my good fairy was. The scarf smelt of lilies-of-the-valley, the favourite scent of Anyuta Blagovo.

Towards winter there was more work and it was more cheerful. Radish recovered, and we worked together in the cemetery church,

where we were putting the ground-work on the ikon-stand before gilding. It was a clean, quiet job, and, as our fellows used to say, profitable.
One could get through a lot of work in a day, and the time passed
quickly, imperceptibly. There was no swearing, no laughter, no loud
talk. The place itself compelled one to quietness and decent behaviour,
and disposed one to quiet, serious thoughts. Absorbed in our work we
stood or sat motionless like statues; there was a deathly silence in keeping with the cemetery, so that if a tool fell, or a flame spluttered in the
lamp, the noise of such sounds rang out abrupt and resonant, and made
us look round. After a long silence we would hear a buzzing like the
swarming of bees: it was the requiem of a baby being chanted slowly
in subdued voices in the porch; or an artist, painting a dove with stars
round it on a cupola would begin softly whistling, and recollecting
himself with a start would at once relapse into silence; or Radish,
answering his thoughts, would say with a sigh: "Anything is possible!
Anything is possible!" or a slow disconsolate bell would begin ringing
over our heads, and the painters would observe that it must be for the
funeral of some wealthy person. . . .

My days I spent in this stillness in the twilight of the church, and
in the long evenings I played billiards or went to the theatre in the
gallery wearing the new trousers I had bought out of my own earnings.
Concerts and performances had already begun at the Azhogins';
Radish used to paint the scenes alone now. He used to tell me the plot
of the plays and describe the *tableaux vivants* which he witnessed. I listened to him with envy. I felt greatly drawn to the rehearsals, but I
could not bring myself to go to the Azhogins'.

A week before Christmas Dr. Blagovo arrived. And again we
argued and played billiards in the evenings. When he played he used to
take off his coat and unbutton his shirt over his chest, and for some reason tried altogether to assume the air of a desperate rake. He did not
drink much, but made a great uproar about it, and had a special faculty for getting through twenty roubles in an evening at such a poor
cheap tavern as the *Volga*.

My sister began coming to see me again; they both expressed surprise every time on seeing each other, but from her joyful, guilty face it
was evident that these meetings were not accidental. One evening,
when we were playing billiards, the doctor said to me:

"I say, why don't you go and see Miss Dolzhikov? You don't know Mariya Viktorovna; she is a clever creature, a charmer, a simple, good-natured soul."

I described how her father had received me in the spring.

"Nonsense!" laughed the doctor, "the engineer's one thing and she's another. Really, my dear fellow, you mustn't be nasty to her; go and see her sometimes. For instance, let's go and see her tomorrow evening. What do you say?"

He persuaded me. The next evening I put on my new serge trousers, and in some agitation I set off to Miss Dolzhikov's. The footman did not seem so haughty and terrible, nor the furniture so gorgeous, as on that morning when I had come to ask a favour. Mariya Viktorovna was expecting me, and she received me like an old acquaintance, shaking hands with me in a friendly way. She was wearing a grey cloth dress with full sleeves, and had her hair done in the style which we used to call "dogs' ears," when it came into fashion in the town a year before. The hair was combed down over the ears, and this made Mariya Viktorovna's face look broader, and she seemed to me this time very much like her father, whose face was broad and red, with something in its expression like a sledge-driver. She was handsome and elegant, but not youthful looking; she looked thirty, though in reality she was not more than twenty-five.

"Dear Doctor, how grateful I am to you," she said, making me sit down. "If it hadn't been for him you wouldn't have come to see me. I am bored to death! My father has gone away and left me alone, and I don't know what to do with myself in this town."

Then she began asking me where I was working now, how much I earned, where I lived.

"Do you spend on yourself nothing but what you earn?" she asked.

"No."

"Happy man!" she sighed. "All the evil in life, it seems to me, comes from idleness, boredom, and spiritual emptiness, and all this is inevitable when one is accustomed to living at other people's expense. Don't think I am showing off, I tell you truthfully: it is not interesting or pleasant to be rich. 'Make to yourselves friends of the mammon of unrighteousness' is said, because there is not and cannot be a mammon that's righteous."

She looked round at the furniture with a grave, cold expression, as though she wanted to count it over, and went on:

"Comfort and luxury have a magical power; little by little they draw into their clutches even strong-willed people. At one time father and I lived simply, not in a rich style, but now you see how! It is something monstrous," she said, shrugging her shoulders; "we spend up to twenty thousand a year! In the provinces!"

"One comes to look at comfort and luxury as the invariable privilege of capital and education," I said, "and it seems to me that the comforts of life may be combined with any sort of labour, even the hardest and dirtiest. Your father is rich, and yet he says himself that it has been his lot to be a mechanic and an oiler."

She smiled and shook her head doubtfully: "My father sometimes eats bread dipped in kvass," she said. "It's a fancy, a whim!"

At that moment there was a ring and she got up.

"The rich and well-educated ought to work like everyone else," she said, "and if there is comfort it ought to be equal for all. There ought not to be any privileges. But that's enough philosophizing. Tell me something amusing. Tell me about the painters. What are they like? Funny?"

The doctor came in; I began telling them about the painters, but, being unaccustomed to talking, I was constrained, and described them like an ethnologist, gravely and tediously. The doctor, too, told us some anecdotes of working men: he staggered about, shed tears, dropped on his knees, and, even, mimicking a drunkard, lay on the floor; it was as good as a play, and Mariya Viktorovna laughed till she cried as she looked at him. Then he played on the piano and sang in his thin, pleasant tenor, while Mariya Viktorovna stood by and picked out what he was to sing, and corrected him when he made a mistake.

"I've heard that you sing, too? " I enquired.

"Sing, too!" cried the doctor in horror. "She sings exquisitely, a perfect artist, and you talk of her 'singing too'! What an idea!"

"I did study in earnest at one time," she said, answering my question, "but now I have given it up."

Sitting on a low stool she told us of her life in Petersburg, and mimicked some celebrated singers, imitating their voice and manner of singing. She made a sketch of the doctor in her album, then of me; she did not draw well, but both the portraits were like us. She laughed, and

was full of mischief and charming grimaces, and this suited her better
than talking about the mammon of unrighteousness, and it seemed to
me that she had been talking just before about wealth and luxury, not
in earnest, but in imitation of someone. She was a superb comic actress.
I mentally compared her with our young ladies, and even the handsome, dignified Anyuta Blagovo could not stand comparison with her;
the difference was immense, like the difference between a beautiful,
cultivated rose and a wild briar.

We had supper together, the three of us. The doctor and Mariya
Viktorovna drank red wine, champagne, and coffee with brandy in it;
they clinked glasses and drank to friendship, to enlightenment, to
progress, to liberty, and they did not get drunk but only flushed, and
were continually, for no reason, laughing till they cried. So as not to
be tiresome I drank claret too.

"Talented, richly endowed natures," said Miss Dolzhikov, "know
how to live, and go their own way; mediocre people, like myself for
instance, know nothing and can do nothing of themselves; there is
nothing left for them but to discern some deep social movement, and
to flow where they are carried by it."

"How can one discern what doesn't exist?" asked the doctor.

"We think so because we don't see it."

"Is that so? The social movements are the invention of the new literature. There are none among us."

An argument began.

"There are no deep social movements among us and never have
been," the doctor declared loudly. "There is no end to what the new
literature has invented! It has invented intellectual workers in the
country, and you may search through all our villages and find at the
most some lout in a reefer jacket or a black frock-coat who will make
four mistakes in spelling a word of three letters. Cultured life has not
yet begun among us. There's the same savagery, the same uniform
boorishness, the same triviality, as five hundred years ago. Movements,
currents there have been, but it has all been petty, paltry, bent upon
vulgar and mercenary interests—and one cannot see anything important in them. If you think you have discerned a deep social movement,
and in following it you devote yourself to tasks in the modern taste,
such as the emancipation of insects from slavery or abstinence from
beef rissoles, I congratulate you, Madam. We must study, and study,

and study and we must wait a bit with our deep social movements; we are not mature enough for them yet; and to tell the truth, we don't know anything about them."

"You don't know anything about them, but I do," said Mariya Viktorovna. "Goodness, how tiresome you are to-day!"

"Our duty is to study and to study, to try to accumulate as much knowledge as possible, for genuine social movements arise where there is knowledge; and the happiness of mankind in the future lies only in knowledge. I drink to science!"

"There is no doubt about one thing: one must organize one's life somehow differently," said Mariya Viktorovna, after a moment's silence and thought. "Life, such as it has been hitherto, is not worth having. Don't let us talk about it."

As we came away from her the cathedral clock struck two.

"Did you like her?" asked the doctor; "she's nice, isn't she?"

On Christmas day we dined with Mariya Viktorovna, and all through the holidays we went to see her almost every day. There was never anyone there but ourselves, and she was right when she said that she had no friends in the town but the doctor and me. We spent our time for the most part in conversation; sometimes the doctor brought some book or magazine and read aloud to us. In reality he was the first well-educated man I had met in my life: I cannot judge whether he knew a great deal, but he always displayed his knowledge as though he wanted other people to share it. When he talked about anything relating to medicine he was not like any one of the doctors in our town, but made a fresh, peculiar impression upon me, and I fancied that if he liked he might have become a real man of science. And he was perhaps the only person who had a real influence upon me at that time. Seeing him, and reading the books he gave me, I began little by little to feel a thirst for the knowledge which would have given significance to my cheerless labour. It seemed strange to me, for instance, that I had not known till then that the whole world was made up of sixty elements, I had not known what oil was, what paints were, and that I could have got on without knowing these things. My acquaintance with the doctor elevated me morally too. I was continually arguing with him and, though I usually remained of my own opinion, yet, thanks to him, I began to perceive that everything was not clear to me, and I began trying to work out as far as I could definite convictions in myself, that the dictates of conscience might be definite, and that there might be nothing vague in my mind. Yet, though he was the most cultivated and best man in the town, he was nevertheless far from perfection. In his manners, in his habit of turning every conversation into an argument, in his pleasant tenor, even in his friendliness, there was something coarse, like a divinity student, and when he took off his coat and sat in his silk shirt, or flung a tip to a waiter in the restaurant, I always fancied that culture might be all very well, but the Tatar was fermenting in him still.

At Epiphany he went back to Petersburg. He went off in the morning, and after dinner my sister came in. Without taking off her fur coat and her cap she sat down in silence, very pale, and kept her eyes fixed on the same spot. She was chilled by the frost and one could see that she was upset by it.

"You must have caught cold," I said.

Her eyes filled with tears; she got up and went out to Karpovna without saying a word to me, as though I had hurt her feelings. And a little later I heard her saying, in a tone of bitter reproach:

"Nurse, what have I been living for till now? What? Tell me, haven't I wasted my youth? All the best years of my life to know nothing but keeping accounts, pouring out tea, counting the halfpence, entertaining visitors, and thinking there was nothing better in the world! Nurse, do understand, I have the cravings of a human being, and I want to live, and they have turned me into something like a housekeeper. It's horrible, horrible!"

She flung her keys towards the door, and they fell with a jingle into my room. They were the keys of the sideboard, of the kitchen cupboard, of the cellar, and of the tea-caddy, the keys which my mother used to carry.

"Oh, merciful heavens!" cried the old woman in horror. "Holy Saints above!"

Before going home my sister came into my room to pick up the keys, and said:

"You must forgive me. Something queer has happened to me lately."

VIII

On returning home late one evening from Mariya Viktorovna's I found waiting in my room a young police inspector in a new uniform; he was sitting at my table, looking through my books.

"At last," he said, getting up and stretching himself. "This is the third time I have been to you. The Governor commands you to present yourself before him at nine o'clock in the morning. Without fail."

He took from me a signed statement that I would act upon his Excellency's command, and went away. This late visit of the police inspector and unexpected invitation to the Governor's had an overwhelmingly oppressive effect upon me. From my earliest childhood I have felt terror stricken in the presence of gendarmes, policemen, and law court officials, and now I was tormented by uneasiness, as though I were really guilty in some way. And I could not get to sleep. My nurse and Prokofy were also upset and could not sleep. My nurse had earache too; she moaned, and several times began crying with pain. Hearing that I was awake, Prokofy came into my room with a lamp and sat down at the table.

"You ought to have a drink of pepper cordial," he said, after a moment's thought. "If one does have a drink in this vale of tears it does no harm. And if Mamma were to pour a little pepper cordial in her ear it would do her a lot of good."

Between two and three he was going to the slaughter-house for the meat. I knew I should not sleep till morning now, and to get through the time till nine o'clock I went with him. We walked with a lantern, while his boy Nikolka, aged thirteen, with blue patches on his cheeks from frostbites, a regular young brigand to judge by his expression, drove after us in the sledge, urging on the horse in a husky voice.

"I suppose they will punish you at the Governor's," Prokofy said to me on the way. "There are rules of the trade for governors, and rules for the higher clergy, and rules for the officers, and rules for the doctors, and every class has its rules. But you haven't kept to your rules, and you can't be allowed."

The slaughter-house was behind the cemetery, and till then I had only seen it in the distance. It consisted of three gloomy barns, surrounded by a grey fence, and when the wind blew from that quarter on hot days in summer, it brought a stifling stench from them. Now going into the yard in the dark I did not see the barns; I kept coming across horses and sledges, some empty, some loaded up with meat. Men were walking about with lanterns, swearing in a disgusting way. Prokofy and Nikolka swore just as revoltingly, and the air was in a continual uproar with swearing, coughing, and the neighing of horses.

There was a smell of dead bodies and of dung. It was thawing, the snow was changing into mud; and in the darkness it seemed to me that I was walking through pools of blood.

Having piled up the sledges full of meat we set off to the butcher's shop in the market. It began to get light. Cooks with baskets and elderly ladies in mantles came along one after another, Prokofy, with a chopper in his hand, in a white apron spattered with blood, swore fearful oaths, crossed himself at the church, shouted aloud for the whole market to hear, that he was giving away the meat at cost price and even at a loss to himself. He gave short weight and short change, the cooks saw that, but, deafened by his shouts, did not protest, and only called him a hangman. Brandishing and bringing down his terrible chopper he threw himself into picturesque attitudes, and each time uttered the sound "Geck" with a ferocious expression, and I was afraid he really would chop off somebody's head or hand.

I spent all the morning in the butcher's shop, and when at last I went to the Governor's, my overcoat smelt of meat and blood. My state of mind was as though I were being sent spear in hand to meet a bear. I remember the tall staircase with a striped carpet on it, and the young official, with shiny buttons, who mutely motioned me to the door with both hands, and ran to announce me. I went into a hall luxuriously but frigidly and tastelessly furnished, and the high, narrow mirrors in the spaces between the walls, and the bright yellow window curtains, struck the eye particularly unpleasantly. One could see that the governors were changed, but the furniture remained the same. Again the young official motioned me with both hands to the door, and I went up to a big green table at which a military general, with the Order of Vladimir on his breast, was standing.

"Mr. Poloznev, I have asked you to come," he began, holding a letter in his hand, and opening his mouth like a round "o," "I have asked you to come here to inform you of this. Your highly respected father has appealed by letter and by word of mouth to the Marshal of the Nobility begging him to summon you, and to lay before you the inconsistency of your behaviour with the rank of the nobility to which you have the honour to belong. His Excellency Alexandr Pavlovitch, justly supposing that your conduct might serve as a bad example, and considering that mere persuasion on his part would not be sufficient, but that official intervention in earnest was essential, presents me here in this letter with his views in regard to you, which I share."

He said this, quietly, respectfully, standing erect, as though I were his superior officer and looking at me with no trace of severity. His face looked worn and wizened, and was all wrinkles; there were bags under his eyes; his hair was dyed; and it was impossible to tell from his appearance how old he was—forty or sixty.

"I trust," he went on, "that you appreciate the delicacy of our honoured Alexandr Pavlovitch, who has addressed himself to me not officially, but privately. I, too, have asked you to come here unofficially, and I am speaking to you, not as a Governor, but from a sincere regard for your father. And so I beg you either to alter your line of conduct and return to duties in keeping with your rank, or to avoid setting a bad example, remove to another district where you are not known, and where you can follow any occupation you please. In the other case, I shall be forced to take extreme measures."

He stood for half a minute in silence, looking at me with his mouth open.

"Are you a vegetarian?" he asked.

"No, your Excellency, I eat meat."

He sat down and drew some papers towards him. I bowed and went out.

It was not worth while now to go to work before dinner. I went home to sleep, but could not sleep from an unpleasant, sickly feeling, induced by the slaughter house and my conversation with the Governor, and when the evening came I went, gloomy and out of sorts, to Mariya Viktorovna. I told her how I had been at the Governor's, while she stared at me in perplexity as though she did not believe it, then suddenly began laughing gaily, loudly, irrepressibly, as only good-natured laughter-loving people can.

"If only one could tell that in Petersburg!" she brought out, almost falling over with laughter, and propping himself against the table. "If one could tell that in Petersburg!"

Now we used to see each other often, sometimes twice a day. She used to come to the cemetery almost every day after dinner, and read the epitaphs on the crosses and tombstones while she waited for me. Sometimes she would come into the church, and, standing by me, would look on while I worked. The stillness, the naïve work of the painters and gilders, Radish's sage reflections, and the fact that I did not differ externally from the other workmen, and worked just as they did in my waistcoat with no socks on, and that I was addressed familiarly by them—all this was new to her and touched her. One day a workman, who was painting a dove on the ceiling, called out to me in her presence:

"Misail, hand me up the white paint."

I took him the white paint, and afterwards, when I let myself down by the frail scaffolding, she looked at me, touched to tears and smiling.

"What a dear you are!" she said.

I remembered from my childhood how a green parrot, belonging to one of the rich men of the town, had escaped from its cage and how for quite a month afterwards the beautiful bird had haunted the town, flying from garden to garden, homeless and solitary. Mariya Viktorovna reminded me of that bird.

"There is positively nowhere for me to go now but the cemetery," she said to me with a laugh. "The town has become disgustingly dull. At the Azhogins' they are still reciting, singing, lisping. I have grown to detest them of late; your sister is an unsociable creature; Mademoiselle Blagovo hates me for some reason. I don't care for the theatre. Tell me where am I to go?"

When I went to see her I smelt of paint and turpentine, and my hands were stained—and she liked that; she wanted me to come to her in my ordinary working clothes; but in her drawing-room those clothes made me feel awkward. I felt embarrassed, as though I were in uniform, so I always put on my new serge trousers when I went to her. And she did not like that.

"You must own you are not quite at home in your new character," she said to me one day. "Your workman's dress does not feel natural to you; you are awkward in it. Tell me, isn't that because you haven't a firm conviction, and are not satisfied? The very kind of work you have chosen—your painting—surely it does not satisfy you, does it? " she asked, laughing. "I know paint makes things look nicer and last longer, but those things belong to rich people who live in towns, and after all they are luxuries. Besides, you have often said yourself that everybody ought to get his bread by the work of his own hands, yet you get money and not bread. Why shouldn't you keep to the literal sense of your words? You ought to be getting bread, that is, you ought to he plough-ing, sowing, reaping, threshing, or doing something which has a direct connection with agriculture, for instance, looking after cows, digging, building huts of logs. . . ."

She opened a pretty cupboard that stood near her writing-table, and said:

"I am saying all this to you because I want to let you into my secret. *Voilà!* This is my agricultural library. Here I have fields, kitchen garden and orchard, and cattleyard and beehives. I read them greedily, and have already learnt all the theory to the tiniest detail. My dream, my darling wish, is to go to our Dubetchnya as soon as March is here. It's marvellous there, exquisite, isn't it? The first year I shall have a look round and get into things, and the year after I shall begin to work prop-erly myself, putting my back into it as they say. My father has promised to give me Dubetchnya and I shall do exactly what I like with it."

Flushed, excited to tears, and laughing, she dreamed aloud how she would live at Dubetchnya, and what an interesting life it would be! I envied her. March was near, the days were growing longer and longer, and on bright sunny days water dripped from the roofs at midday, and there was a fragrance of spring; I, too, longed for the country.

And when she said that she should move to Dubetchnya, I real-ized vividly that I should remain in the town alone, and I felt that I envied her with her cupboard of books and her agriculture. I knew nothing of work on the land, and did not like it, and I should have liked to have told her that work on the land was slavish toil, but I remem-bered that something similar had been said more than once by my father, and held my tongue.

Lent began. Viktor Ivanitch, whose existence I had begun to for-get, arrived from Petersburg. He arrived unexpectedly, without even a telegram to say he was coming. When I went in, as usual in the evening, he was walking about the drawing-room, telling some story with his face freshly washed and shaven, looking ten years younger: his daughter was kneeling on the floor, taking out of his trunks boxes, bottles, and books, and handing them to Pavel the footman. I involuntarily drew back a step when I saw the engineer, but he held out both hands to me and said, smiling, showing his strong white teeth that looked like a sledge-driver's:

"Here he is, here he is! Very glad to see you, Mr. House-painter! Masha has told me all about it; she has been singing your praises. I quite understand and approve," he went on, taking my arm. "To be a good workman is ever so much more honest and more sensible than wasting government paper and wearing a cockade on your head. I myself worked in Belgium with these very hands and then spent two years as a mechanic. . . ."

He was wearing a short reefer jacket and indoor slippers; he walked like a man with the gout, rolling slightly from side to side and rubbing his hands. Humming something he softly purred and hugged himself with satisfaction at being at home again at last, and able to have his beloved shower bath.

"There is no disputing," he said to me at supper, "there is no disputing; you are all nice and charming people, but for some reason, as soon as you take to manual labour, or go in for saving the peasants, in the long run it all comes to no more than being a dissenter. Aren't you a dissenter? Here you don't take vodka. What's the meaning of that if it is not being a dissenter?"

To satisfy him I drank some vodka and I drank some wine, too. We tasted the cheese, the sausage, the pâtés, the pickles, and the savouries of all sorts that the engineer had brought with him, and the wine that had come in his absence from abroad. The wine was first-rate. For some reason the engineer got wine and cigars from abroad without paying duty; the caviare and the dried sturgeon someone sent him for nothing; he did not pay rent for his flat as the owner of the house provided the kerosene for the line; and altogether he and his daughter produced on me the impression that all the best in the world was at their service, and provided for them for nothing.

I went on going to see them, but not with the same eagerness. The engineer made me feel constrained, and in his presence I did not feel free. I could not face his clear, guileless eyes, his reflections wearied and sickened me; I was sickened, too, by the memory that so lately I

had been in the employment of this red-faced, well-fed man, and that
he had been brutally rude to me. It is true that he put his arm round my
waist, slapped me on the shoulder in a friendly was, approved my manner of life, but I felt that, as before, he despised my insignificance, and
only put up with me to please his daughter, and I couldn't now laugh
and talk as I liked, and I behaved unsociably and kept expecting that
in another minute he would address me as Panteley as he did his footman Pavel. How my pride as a provincial and a working man was
revolted. I, a proletarian, a house painter, went every day to rich people who were alien to me, and whom the whole town regarded as
though they were foreigners, and every day I drank costly wines with
them and ate unusual dainties—my conscience refused to be reconciled
to it! On my way to the house I sullenly avoided meeting people, and
looked at them from under my brows as though I really were a dissenter, and when I was going home from the engineer's I was ashamed
of my well-fed condition.

Above all I was afraid of being carried away. Whether I was walking along the street, or working, or talking to the other fellows, I was
all the time thinking of one thing only, of going in the evening to see
Mariya Viktorovna and was picturing her voice, her laugh, her movements. When I was getting ready to go to her I always spent a long
time before my nurse's warped looking-glass, as I fastened my tie; my
serge trousers were detestable in my eyes, and I suffered torments, and
at the same time despised myself for being so trivial. When she called
to me out of the other room that she was not dressed and asked me to
wait, I listened to her dressing; it agitated me, I felt as though the
ground were giving way under my feet. And when I saw a woman's figure in the street, even at a distance, I invariably compared it. It seemed
to me that all our girls and women were vulgar, that they were absurdly
dressed, and did not know how to hold themselves; and these compar-
isons aroused a feeling of pride in me: Mariya Viktorovna was the best
of them all! And I dreamed of her and myself at night.

One evening at supper with the engineer we ate a whole lobster. As
I was going home afterwards I remembered that the engineer twice
called me "My dear fellow" at supper, and I reflected that they treated
me very kindly in that house, as they might an unfortunate big dog who
had been kicked out by its owners, that they were amusing themselves
with me, and that when they were tired of me they would turn me out

like a dog. I felt ashamed and wounded, wounded to the point of tears as though I had been insulted, and looking up at the sky I took a vow to put an end to all this.

The next day I did not go to the Dolzhikov's. Late in the evening, when it was quite dark and raining, I walked along Great Dvoryansky Street, looking up at the windows. Everyone was asleep at the Azhogins', and the only light was in one of the furthest windows. It was Madame Azhogin in her own room, sewing by the light of three candles, imagining that she was combating superstition. Our house was in darkness, but at the Dolzhikovs', on the contrary, the windows were lighted up, but one could distinguish nothing through the flowers and the curtains. I kept walking up and down the street; the cold March rain drenched me through. I heard my father come home from the club; he stood knocking at the gate. A minute later a light appeared at the window, and I saw my sister, who was hastening down with a lamp, while with the other hand she was twisting her thick hair together as she went. Then my father walked about the drawing-room, talking and rubbing his hands, while my sister sat in a low chair, thinking and not listening to what he said.

But then they went away; the light went out. . . . I glanced round at the engineer's, and there, too, all was darkness now. In the dark and the rain I felt hopelessly alone, abandoned to the whims of destiny; I felt that all my doings, my desires, and everything I had thought and said till then were trivial in comparison with my loneliness, in comparison with my present suffering, and the suffering that lay before me in the future. Alas, the thoughts and doings of living creatures are not nearly so significant as their sufferings! And without clearly realizing what I was doing, I pulled at the bell of the Dolzhikovs' gate, broke it, and ran along the street like some naughty boy, with a feeling of terror in my heart, expecting every moment that they would come out and recognize me. When I stopped at the end of the street to take breath I could hear nothing but the sound of the rain, and somewhere in the distance a watchman striking on a sheet of iron.

For a whole week I did not go to the Dolzhikovs'. My serge trousers were sold. There was nothing doing in the painting trade. I knew the pangs of hunger again, and earned from twopence to fourpence a day, where I could, by heavy and unpleasant work. Struggling up to my knees in the cold mud, straining my chest, I tried to stifle my memories, and, as it were, to punish myself for the cheeses and preserves with which I had been regaled at the engineer's. But all the same, as soon as I lay in bed, wet and hungry, my sinful imagination immediately began to paint exquisite, seductive pictures, and with amazement I acknowledged to myself that I was in love, passionately in love, and I fell into a sound, heavy sleep, feeling that hard labour only made my body stronger and younger.

One evening snow began falling most inappropriately, and the wind blew from the north as though winter had come back again. When I returned from work that evening I found Mariya Viktorovna in my room. She was sitting in her fur coat, and had both hands in her muff.

"Why don't you come to see me?" she asked, raising her clear, clever eyes, and I was utterly confused with delight and stood stiffly upright before her, as I used to stand facing my father when he was going to beat me; she looked into my face and I could see from her eyes that she understood why I was confused.

"Why don't you come to see me?" she repeated. "If you don't want to come, you see, I have come to you."

She got up and came close to me.

"Don't desert me," she said, and her eyes filled with tears. "I am alone, utterly alone."

She began crying; and, hiding her face in her muff, articulated:

"Alone! My life is hard, very hard, and in all the world I have no one but you. Don't desert me!"

Looking for a handkerchief to wipe her tears she smiled; we were silent for some time, then I put my arms round her and kissed her, scratching my cheek till it bled with her hatpin as I did it.

And we began talking to each other as though we had been on the closest terms for ages and ages.

X

Two days later she sent me to Dubetchnya and I was unutterably delighted to go. As I walked towards the station and afterwards, as I was sitting in the train, I kept laughing from no apparent cause, and people looked at me as though I were drunk. Snow was falling, and there were still frosts in the mornings, but the roads were already dark-coloured and rooks hovered over them, cawing.

At first I had intended to fit up an abode for us two, Masha and me, in the lodge at the side opposite Madame Tcheprakov's lodge, but it appeared that the doves and the ducks had been living there for a long time, and it was impossible to clean it without destroying a great number of nests. There was nothing for it but to live in the comfortless rooms of the big house with the sunblinds. The peasants called the house the palace; there were more than twenty rooms in it, and the only furniture was a piano and a child's arm-chair lying in the attic. And if Masha had brought all her furniture from the town we should even then have been unable to get rid of the impression of immense emptiness and cold. I picked out three small rooms with windows looking into the garden, and worked from early morning till night, setting them to rights, putting in new panes, papering the walls, filling up the holes and chinks in the floors. It was easy, pleasant work. I was continually running to the river to see whether the ice were not going; I kept fancying that starlings were flying. And at night, thinking of Masha, I listened with an unutterably sweet feeling, with clutching delight to the noise of the rats and the wind droning and knocking above the ceiling. It seemed as though some old house spirit were coughing in the attic.

The snow was deep; a great deal had fallen even at the end of March, but it melted quickly, as though by magic, and the spring floods passed in a tumultuous rush, so that by the beginning of April the starlings were already noisy, and yellow butterflies were flying in the garden. It was exquisite weather. Every day, towards evening, I used to walk to the town to meet Masha, and what a delight it was to walk with bare feet along the gradually drying, still soft road. Half-way I used to sit down and look towards the town, not venturing to go near it. The sight of it troubled me. I kept wondering how the people I knew would behave to me when they heard of my love. What would my father say? What troubled me particularly was the thought that my life was more complicated, and that I had completely lost all power to set it right, and that, like a balloon, it was bearing me away, God knows whither. I no longer considered the problem how to earn my daily bread, how to live, but thought about—I really don't know what.

Masha used to come in a carriage; I used to get in with her, and we drove to Dubetchnya, feeling light-hearted and free. Or, after waiting till the sun had set, I would go back dissatisfied and dreary, won-

dering why Masha had not come; at the gate or in the garden I would
be met by a sweet, unexpected apparition—it was she! It would turn
out that she had come by rail, and had walked from the station. What
a festival it was! In a simple woollen dress with a kerchief on her head,
with a modest sunshade, but laced in, slender, in expensive foreign
boots—it was a talented actress playing the part of a little workgirl. We
looked round our domain and decided which should be her room, and
which mine, where we would have our avenue, our kitchen garden, our
beehives.

We already had hens, ducks, and geese, which we loved because
they were ours. We had, all ready for sowing, oats, clover, timothy
grass, buckwheat, and vegetable seeds, and we always looked at all
these stores and discussed at length the crop we might get; and everything Masha said to me seemed extraordinarily clever, and fine. This
was the happiest time of my life.

Soon after St. Thomas's week we were married at our parish
church in the village of Kurilovka, two miles from Dubetchnya. Masha
wanted everything to be done quietly; at her wish our "best men" were
peasant lads, the sacristan sang alone, and we came back from the
church in a small, jolting chaise which she drove herself. Our only
guest from the town was my sister Kleopatra, to whom Masha sent a
note three days before the wedding. My sister came in a white dress
and wore gloves. During the wedding she cried quietly from joy and
tenderness. Her expression was motherly and infinitely kind. She was
intoxicated with our happiness, and smiled as though she were absorbing a sweet delirium, and looking at her during our wedding, I realized that for her there was nothing in the world higher than love,
earthly love, and that she was dreaming of it secretly, timidly, but continually and passionately. She embraced and kissed Masha, and, not
knowing how to express her rapture, said to her of me: "He is good! He
is very good!"

Before she went away she changed into her ordinary dress, and
drew me into the garden to talk to me alone.

"Father is very much hurt," she said, "that you have written nothing to him. You ought to have asked for his blessing. But in reality he
is very much pleased. He says that this marriage will raise you in the
eyes of all society, and that under the influence of Mariya Viktorovna
you will begin to take a more serious view of life. We talk of nothing

but you in the evenings now, and yesterday he actually used the expression: 'Our Misail.' That pleased me. It seems as though he had some plan in his mind, and I fancy he wants to set you an example of magnanimity and be the first to speak of reconciliation. It is very possible he may come here to see you in a day or two."

She hurriedly made the sign of the cross over me several times and said:

"Well, God be with you. Be happy. Anyuta Blagovo is a very clever girl; she says about your marriage that God is sending you a fresh ordeal. To be sure—married life does not bring only joy but suffering too. That's bound to be so."

Masha and I walked a couple of miles to see her on her way; we walked back slowly and in silence, as though we were resting. Masha held my hand, my heart felt light, and I had no inclination to talk about love; we had become closer and more akin now that we were married, and we felt that nothing now could separate us.

"Your sister is a nice creature," said Masha, "but it seems as though she had been tormented for years. Your father must be a terrible man."

I began telling her how my sister and I had been brought up, and what a senseless torture our childhood had really been. When she heard how my father had so lately beaten me, she shuddered and drew closer to me.

"Don't tell me any more," she said. "It's horrible!"

Now she never left me. We lived together in the three rooms in the big house, and in the evenings we bolted the door which led to the empty part of the house, as though someone were living there whom we did not know, and were afraid of. I got up early, at dawn, and immediately set to work of some sort. I mended the carts, made paths in the garden, dug the flower beds, painted the roof of the house. When the time came to sow the oats I tried to plough the ground over again, to harrow and to sow, and I did it all conscientiously, keeping up with our labourer; I was worn out, the rain and the cold wind made my face and feet burn for hours afterwards. I dreamed of ploughed land at night. But field labour did not attract me. I did not understand farming, and I did not care for it; it was perhaps because my forefathers had not been tillers of the soil, and the very blood that flowed in my veins was purely of the city. I loved nature tenderly; I loved the fields and meadows and kitchen gardens, but the peasant who turned up the soil with his plough and urged on his pitiful horse, wet and tattered, with his craning neck, was to me the expression of coarse, savage, ugly force, and every time I looked at his uncouth movements I involuntarily began thinking of the legendary life of the remote past, before men knew the use of fire. The fierce bull that ran with the peasants' herd, and the horses, when they dashed about the village, stamping their hoofs, moved me to fear, and everything rather big, strong, and angry, whether it was the ram with its horns, the gander, or the yard-dog, seemed to me the expression of the same coarse, savage force. This mood was particularly strong in me in bad weather, when heavy clouds were hanging over the black ploughed land. Above all, when I was ploughing or sowing, and two or three people stood looking how I was doing it, I had not the feeling that this work was inevitable and obligatory, and it seemed to me that I was amusing myself. I preferred doing something in the yard, and there was nothing I liked so much as painting the roof.

I used to walk through the garden and the meadow to our mill. It was let to a peasant of Kurilovka called Stepan, a handsome, dark fellow with a thick black beard, who looked very strong. He did not like the miller's work, and looked upon it as dreary and unprofitable, and only lived at the mill in order not to live at home. He was a leather-worker, and was always surrounded by a pleasant smell of tar and leather. He was not fond of talking, he was listless and sluggish, and was always sitting in the doorway or on the river bank, humming "oo-loo-loo." His wife and mother-in-law, both white-faced, languid, and meek, used sometimes to come from Kurilovka to see him; they made low bows to him and addressed him formally, "Stepan Petrovitch," while he went on sitting on the river bank, softly humming "oo-loo-loo," without responding by word or movement to their bows. One hour and then a second would pass in silence. His mother-in-law and wife, after whispering together, would get up and gaze at him for some time, expecting him to look round; then they would make a low bow, and in sugary, chanting voices, say:

"Good-bye, Stepan Petrovitch!"

And they would go away. After that Stepan, picking up the parcel they had left, containing cracknels or a shirt, would heave a sigh and say, winking in their direction:

"The female sex!"

The mill with two sets of millstones worked day and night. I used to help Stepan; I liked the work, and when he went off I was glad to stay and take his place.

XI

After bright warm weather came a spell of wet; all May it rained and was cold. The sound of the of the millwheels and of the rain disposed one to indolence and slumber. The floor trembled, there was a smell of flour, and that, too, induced drowsiness. My wife in a short fur-lined jacket, and in men's high golosh boots, would make her appearance twice a day, and she always said the same thing:

"And this is called summer! Worse than it was in October!"

We used to have tea and make the porridge together, or we would sit for hours at a stretch without speaking, waiting for the rain to stop. Once, when Stepan had gone off to the fair, Masha stayed all night at the mill. When we got up we could not tell what time it was, as the rainclouds covered the whole sky; but sleepy cocks were crowing at Dubetchnya, and landrails were calling in the meadows; it was still very, very early. . . . My wife and I went down to the millpond and drew out the net which Stepan had thrown in over night in our presence. A big pike was struggling in it, and a cray-fish was twisting about, clawing upwards with its pincers.

"Let them go," said Masha. "Let them be happy too."

Because we got up so early and afterwards did nothing, that day seemed very long, the longest day in my life. Towards evening Stepan came back and I went home.

"Your father came to-day," said Masha.

"Where is he?" I asked.

"He has gone away. I would not see him."

Seeing that I remained standing and silent, that I was sorry for my father, she said:

"One must be consistent. I would not see him, and sent word to him not to trouble to come and see us again."

A minute later I was out at the gate and walking to the town to explain things to my father. It was muddy, slippery, cold. For the first time since my marriage I felt suddenly sad, and in my brain exhausted by that long, grey day, there was stirring the thought that perhaps I was not living as I ought. I was worn out; little by little I was overcome by despondency and indolence, I did not want to move or think, and after going on a little I gave it up with a wave of my hand and turned back.

The engineer in a leather overcoat with a hood was standing in the middle of the yard.

"Where's the furniture? There used to be lovely furniture in the Empire style: there used to be pictures, there used to be vases, while now you could play ball in it! I bought the place with the furniture. The devil take her!"

Moisey, a thin pock-marked fellow of twenty-five, with insolent little eyes, who was in the service of the general's widow, stood near him crumpling up his cap in his hands; one of his cheeks was bigger than the other, as though he had lain too long on it.

"Your honour was graciously pleased to buy the place without the furniture," he brought out irresolutely; "I remember."

"Hold your tongue!" shouted the engineer; he turned crimson and shook with anger . . . and the echo in the garden loudly repeated his shout.

XII

When I was doing anything in the garden or the yard, Moisey would stand beside me, and folding his arms behind his back he would stand lazily and impudently staring at me with his little eyes. And this irritated me to such a degree that I threw up my work and went away.

From Stepan we heard that Moisey was Madame Tcheprakov's lover. I noticed that when people came to her to borrow money they addressed themselves first to Moisey, and once I saw a peasant, black from head to foot—he must have been a coalheaver—bow down at Moisey's feet. Sometimes, after a little whispering, he gave out money himself, without consulting his mistress, from which I concluded that he did a little business on his own account.

He used to shoot in our garden under our windows, carried off victuals from our cellar, borrowed our horses without asking permission, and we were indignant and began to feel as though Dubetchnya were not ours, and Masha would say, turning pale:

"Can we really have to go on living with these reptiles another eighteen months?"

Madame Tcheprakov's son, Ivan, was serving as a guard on our railway-line. He had grown much thinner and feebler during the winter, so that a single glass was enough to make him drunk, and he shivered out of the sunshine. He wore the guard's uniform with aversion and was ashamed of it, but considered his post a good one, as he could steal the candles and sell them. My new position excited in him a mixed feeling of wonder, envy, and a vague hope that something of the same sort might happen to him. He used to watch Masha with ecstatic eyes, ask me what I had for dinner now, and his lean and ugly face wore a sad and sweetish expression, and he moved his fingers as though he were feeling my happiness with them.

"Listen, Better-than-nothing," he said fussily, relighting his cigarette at every instant; there was always a litter where he stood, for he wasted dozens of matches, lighting one cigarette. "Listen, my life now is the nastiest possible. The worst of it is any subaltern can shout: 'Hi, there, guard!' I have overheard all sorts of things in the train, my boy, and do you know, I have learned that life's a beastly thing! My mother has been the ruin of me! A doctor in the train told me that if parents are immoral, their children are drunkards or criminals. Think of that!"

Once he came into the yard, staggering; his eyes gazed about blankly, his breathing was laboured: he laughed and cried and babbled as though in a high fever, and the only worlds I could catch in his muddled talk were, "My mother! Where's my mother?" which he uttered with a wail like a child who has lost his mother in a crowd. I led him into our garden and laid him down under a tree, and Masha and I took turns to sit by him all that day and all night. He was very sick, and Masha looked with aversion at his pale, wet face, and said:

"Is it possible these reptiles will go on living another year and a half in our yard? It's awful! it's awful!"

And how many mortifications the peasants caused us! How many bitter disappointments in those early days in the spring months, when we so longed to be happy. My wife built a school. I draw a plan of a school for sixty boys, and the Zemstvo Board approved of it, but advised us to build the school at Kurilovka, the big village which was only two miles from us. Moreover, the school at Kurilovka in which children—from four villages, our Dubetchnya being one of the number—were taught, was old and too small, and the floor was scarcely safe to walk upon. At the end of March, at Masha's wish, she was appointed guardian of the Kurilovka school, and at the beginning of April we three times summoned the village assembly, and tried to persuade the peasants that their school was old and overcrowded, and that it was essential to build a new one. A member of the Zemstvo Board and the Inspector of Peasant Schools came, and they, too, tried to persuade them. After each meeting the peasants surrounded us, begging for a bucket of vodka; we were hot in the crowd; we were soon exhausted, and returned home dissatisfied and a little ill at ease. In the end the peasants set apart a plot of ground for the school, and were obliged to bring all the building material from the town with their own horses. And the very first Sunday after the spring corn was sown carts set off from Kurilovka and Dubetchnya to fetch bricks for the foundations. They set off as soon as it was light, and came back late in the evening; the peasants were drunk, and said they were worn out.

As ill-luck would have it, the rain and the cold persisted all through May. The road was in an awful state: it was deep in mud. The carts usually drove into our yard when they came back from the town—and what a horrible ordeal it was. A pot-bellied horse would appear at the gate, setting its front legs wide apart; it would stumble forward before coming into the yard; a beam, nine yards long, wet and slimy-looking, crept in on a waggon. Beside it, muffled up against the rain, strode a peasant with the skirts of his coat tucked up in his belt, not looking where he was going, but stepping through the puddles. Another cart would appear with boards, then a third with a beam, a fourth . . . and the space before our house was gradually crowded up with horses, beams, and planks. Men and women, with their heads muffled and their skirts tucked up, would stare angrily at our windows, make an uproar, and clamour for the mistress to come out to them; coarse oaths were audible. Meanwhile Moisey stood at one side, and we fancied he was enjoying our discomfiture.

"We are not going to cart any more," the peasants would shout. "We are worn out! Let her go and get the stuff herself."

Masha, pale and flustered, expecting every minute that they would break into the house, would send them out a half-pail of vodka; after that the noise would subside and the long beams, one after another, would crawl slowly out of the yard.

When I was setting off to see the building my wife was worried and said:

"The peasants are spiteful; I only hope they won't do you a mischief. Wait a minute, I'll come with you."

We drove to Kurilovka together, and there the carpenters asked us for a drink. The framework of the house was ready. It was time to lay the foundation, but the masons had not come; this caused delay, and the carpenters complained. And when at last the masons did come, it appeared that there was no sand; it had been somehow overlooked that it would be needed. Taking advantage of our helpless position, the peasants demanded thirty kopecks for each cartload, though the distance from the building to the river where they got the sand was less than a quarter of a mile, and more than five hundred cartloads were found to be necessary. There was no end to the misunderstandings, swearing, and importunity; my wife was indignant, and the foreman of the masons, Tit Petrov, an old man of seventy, took her by the arm, and said:

"You look here! You look here! You only bring me the sand; I set ten men on at once, and in two days it will be done! You look here!"

But they brought the sand and two days passed, and four, and a week, and instead of the promised foundations there was still a yawning hole.

"It's enough to drive one out of one's senses," said my wife, in distress. "What people! What people!"

In the midst of these disorderly doings the engineer arrived; he brought with him parcels of wine and savouries, and after a prolonged meal lay down for a nap in the verandah and snored so loudly that the labourers shook their heads and said: "Well!"

Masha was not pleased at his coming, she did not trust him, though at the same time she asked his advice. When, after sleeping too long after dinner, he got up in a bad humour and said unpleasant things about our management of the place, or expressed regret that he had bought Dubetchnya, which had already been a loss to him, poor Masha's face wore an expression of misery. She would complain to him, and he would yawn and say that the peasants ought to be flogged.

He called our marriage and our life a farce, and said it was a caprice, a whim.

"She has done something of the sort before," he said about Masha.

"She once fancied herself a great opera singer and left me; I was looking for her for two months, and, my dear soul, I spent a thousand roubles on telegrams alone."

He no longer called me a dissenter or Mr. Painter, and did not as in the past express approval of my living like a workman, but said:

"You are a strange person! You are not a normal person! I won't venture to prophesy, but you will come to a bad end!"

And Masha slept badly at night, and was always sitting at our bedroom window thinking. There was no laughter at supper now, no charming grimaces. I was wretched, and when it rained, every drop that fell seemed to pierce my heart, like small shot and I felt ready to fall on my knees before Masha and apologize for the weather. When the peasants made a noise in the yard I felt guilty also. For hours at a time I sat still in one place, thinking of nothing but what a splendid person Masha was, what a wonderful person. I loved her passionately, and I was fascinated by everything she did, everything she said. She had a bent for quiet, studious pursuits; she was fond of reading for hours together, of studying. Although her knowledge of farming was only from books she surprised us all by what she knew; and every piece of advice she gave was of value; not one was ever thrown away; and, with all that, what nobility, what taste, what graciousness, that graciousness which is only found in well-educated people.

To this woman, with her sound, practical intelligence, the disorderly surroundings with petty cares and sordid anxieties in which we were living now were an agony: I saw that and could not sleep at night; my brain worked feverishly and I had a lump in my throat. I rushed about not knowing what to do.

I galloped to the town and brought Masha books, newspapers, sweets, flowers; with Stepan I caught fish, wading for hours up to my neck in the cold water in the rain to catch eel-pout to vary our fare; I demeaned myself to beg the peasants not to make a noise; I plied them with vodka, bought them off, made all sorts of promises. And how many other foolish things I did!

At last the rain ceased, the earth dried. One would get up at four o'clock in the morning; one would go out into the garden—where there was dew sparkling on the flowers, the twitter of birds, the hum of insects, not one cloud in the sky; and the garden, the meadows, and the river were so lovely, yet there were memories of the peasants, of their carts, of the engineer. Masha and I drove out together in the racing droshky to the fields to look at the oats. She used to drive, I sat behind; her shoulders were raised and the wind played with her hair.

"Keep to the right!" she shouted to those she met.

"You are like a sledge-driver," I said to her one day.

"Maybe! Why, my grandfather, the engineer's father, was a sledge-driver. Didn't you know that?" she asked, turning to me, and at once she mimicked the way sledge-drivers shout and sing.

"And thank God for that," I thought as I listened to her. "Thank God."

And again memories of the peasants, of the carts, of the engineer. . . .

XIII

Dr. Blagovo arrived on his bicycle. My sister began coming often. Again there were conversations about manual labour, about progress, about a mysterious millennium awaiting mankind in the remote future. The doctor did not like our farmwork, because it interfered with arguments, and said that ploughing, reaping, grazing calves were unworthy of a free man, and all these coarse forms of the struggle for existence men would in time relegate to animals and machines, while they would devote themselves exclusively to scientific investigation. My sister kept begging them to let her go home earlier, and if she stayed on till late in the evening, or spent the night with us, there would be no end to the agitation.

"Good Heavens, what a baby you are still!" said Masha reproachfully. "It is positively absurd."

"Yes, it is absurd," my sister agreed, "I know it's absurd; but what is to be done if I haven't the strength to get over it? I keep feeling as though I were doing wrong."

At haymaking I ached all over from the unaccustomed labour; in the evening, sitting on the verandah and talking with the others, I suddenly dropped asleep, and they laughed aloud at me. They waked me up and made me sit down to supper; I was overpowered with drowsiness and I saw the lights, the faces, and the plates as it were in a dream, heard the voices, but did not understand them. And getting up early in the morning, I took up the scythe at once, or went to the building and worked hard all day.

When I remained at home on holidays I noticed that my sister and Masha were concealing something from me, and even seemed to be avoiding me. My wife was tender to me as before, but she had thoughts of her own apart, which she did not share with me. There was no doubt that her exasperation with the peasants was growing, the life was becoming more and more distasteful to her, and yet she did not complain to me. She talked to the doctor now more readily than she did to me, and I did not understand why it was so.

It was the custom in our province at haymaking and harvest time for the labourers to come to the manor house in the evening and be regaled with vodka; even young girls drank a glass. We did not keep up this practice; the mowers and the peasant women stood about in our yard till late in the evening expecting vodka, and then departed abusing us. And all the time Masha frowned grimly and said nothing, or murmured to the doctor with exasperation: "Savages! Petchenyegs!"

In the country newcomers are met ungraciously, almost with hostility, as they are at school. And we were received in this way. At first we were looked upon as stupid, silly people, who had bought an estate simply because we did not know what to do with our money. We were laughed at. The peasants grazed their cattle in our wood and even in our garden; they drove away our cows and horses to the village, and then demanded money for the damage done by them. They came in whole companies into our yard, and loudly clamoured that at the mowing we had cut some piece of land that did not belong to us; and as we did not yet know the boundaries of our estate very accurately, we took their word for it and paid damages. Afterwards it turned out that there had been no mistake at the mowing. They barked the lime-trees in our wood. One of the Dubetchnya peasants, a regular shark, who did a trade in vodka without a licence, bribed our labourers, and in collaboration with them cheated us in a most treacherous way. They took the new wheels off our carts and replaced them with old ones, stole our ploughing harness and actually sold them to us, and so on. But what was most mortifying of all was what happened at the building; the peasant women stole by night boards, bricks, tiles, pieces of iron. The village elder with witnesses made a search in their huts; the village meeting fined them two roubles each, and afterwards this money was spent on drink by the whole commune.

When Masha heard about this, she would say to the doctor or my sister indignantly:

"What beasts! It's awful! awful!"

And I heard her more than once express regret that she had ever taken it into her head to build the school.

"You must understand," the doctor tried to persuade her, "that if you build this school and do good in general, it's not for the sake of the peasants, but in the name of culture, in the name of the future; and the worse the peasants are the more reason for building the school. Understand that!"

But there was a lack of conviction in his voice, and it seemed to me that both he and Masha hated the peasants.

Masha often went to the mill, taking my sister with her, and they both said, laughing, that they went to have a look at Stepan, he was so handsome. Stepan, it appeared, was torpid and taciturn with men; in feminine society his manners were free and easy, and he talked incessantly. One day, going down to the river to bathe, I accidentally overheard a conversation. Masha and Kleopatra, both in white dresses, were sitting on the bank in the spreading shade of a willow, and Stepan was standing by them with his hands behind his back, and was saying:

"Are peasants men? They are not men, but, asking your pardon, wild beasts, impostors. What life has a peasant? Nothing but eating and drinking; all he cares for is victuals to be cheaper and swilling liquor at the tavern like a fool; and there's no conversation, no manners, no formality, nothing but ignorance! He lives in filth, his wife lives in filth, and his children live in filth. What he stands up in, he lies down to sleep in; he picks the potatoes out of the soup with his fingers; he drinks kvass with a cockroach in it, and doesn't bother to blow it away!"

"It's their poverty, of course," my sister put in.

"Poverty? There is want to be sure, there's different sorts of want, Madam. If a man is in prison, or let us say blind or crippled, that really is trouble I wouldn't wish anyone, but if a man's free and has all his senses, if he has his eyes and his hands and his strength and God, what more does he want? It's cockering themselves, and it's ignorance, Madam, it's not poverty. If you, let us suppose, good gentlefolk, by your education, wish out of kindness to help him he will drink away your money in his low way; or, what's worse, he will open a drinkshop, and with your money start robbing the people. You say poverty, but does the rich peasant live better? He, too, asking your pardon, lives like a swine: coarse, loud-mouthed, cudgel-headed, broader than he is long, fat, red-faced mug, I'd like to swing my fist and send him flying, the scoundrel. There's Larion, another rich one at Dubetchnya, and I bet he strips the bark of your trees as much as any poor one; and he is a foul-mouthed fellow; his children are the same, and when he has had a drop too much he'll topple with his nose in a puddle and sleep there. They are all a worthless lot, Madam. If you live in a village with them it is like hell. It has stuck in my teeth, that village has, and thank the Lord, the King of Heaven, I've plenty to eat and clothes to wear, I served out my time in the dragoons, I was a village elder for three years, and now I am a free Cossack, I live where I like. I don't want to live in the village, and no one has the right to force me. They say— my wife. They say you are bound to live in your cottage with your wife. But why so? I am not her hired man."

"Tell me, Stepan, did you marry for love?" asked Masha.

"Love among us in the village!" answered Stepan, and he gave a laugh. "Properly speaking, Madam, if you care to know, this is my second marriage. I am not a Kurilovka man, I am from Zalegoshtcho, but afterwards I was taken into Kurilovka when I married. You see my father did not want to divide the land among us. There were five of us brothers. I took my leave and went to another village to live with my wife's family, but my first wife died when she was young."

"What did she die of?"

"Of foolishness. She used to cry and cry and cry for no reason, and so she pined away. She was always drinking some sort of herbs to make her better looking, and I suppose she damaged her inside. And my second wife is a Kurilovka woman too, there is nothing in her. She's a village woman, a peasant woman, and nothing more. I was taken in when they plighted me to her. I thought she was young and fair-skinned, and that they lived in a clean way. Her mother was just like a Flagellant and she drank coffee, and the chief thing, to be sure, they were clean in their ways. So I married her, and next day we sat down to dinner; I bade my mother-in-law give me a spoon, and she gives me a spoon, and I see her wipe it out with her finger. So much for you, thought I; nice sort of cleanliness yours is. I lived a year with them and then I went away. I might have married a girl from the town," he went on after a pause.

"They say a wife is a helpmate to her husband. What do I want with a helpmate? I help myself; I'd rather she talked to me, and not clack, clack, clack, but circumstantially, feelingly. What is life without good conversation?"

Stepan suddenly paused, and at once there was the sound of his dreary, monotonous "oo-loo-loo-loo." This meant that he had seen me.

Masha used often to go to the mill, and evidently found pleasure in her conversations with Stepan. Stepan abused the peasants with such sincerity and conviction, and she was attracted to him. Every time she came back from the mill the feeble-minded peasant, who looked after the garden, shouted at her:

"Wench Palashka! Hulla, wench Palashka!" and he would bark like a dog: "Ga! Ga!"

And she would stop and look at him attentively, as though in that idiot's barking she found an answer to her thoughts, and probably he attracted her in the same way as Stepan's abuse. At home some piece of news would await her, such, for instance, as that the geese from the village had ruined our cabbage in the garden, or that Larion had stolen the reins; and shrugging her shoulders, she would say with a laugh:

"What do you expect of these people?"

She was indignant, and there was rancour in her heart, and meanwhile I was growing used to the peasants, and I felt more and more drawn to them. For the most part they were nervous, irritable, downtrodden people; they were people whose imagination had been stifled, ignorant, with a poor, dingy outlook on life, whose thoughts were ever the same—of the grey earth, of grey days, of black bread, people who cheated, but like birds hiding nothing but their head behind the tree—people who could not count. They would not come to mow for us for twenty roubles, but they came for half a pail of vodka, though for twenty roubles they could have bought four pails. There really was filth and drunkenness and foolishness and deceit, but with all that one yet felt that the life of the peasants rested on a firm, sound foundation. However uncouth a wild animal the peasant following the plough seemed, and however he might stupefy himself with vodka, still, looking at him more closely, one felt that there was in him what was needed, something very important, which was lacking in Masha and in the doctor, for instance, and that was that he believed the chief thing on earth was truth and justice, and that his salvation, and that of the whole people, was only to be found in truth and justice, and so more than anything in the world he loved just dealing. I told my wife she saw the spots on the glass, but not the glass itself; she said nothing in reply, or hummed like Stepan "oo-loo-loo-loo." When this good-hearted and clever woman turned pale with indignation, and with a quiver in her voice spoke to the doctor of the drunkenness and dishonesty, it perplexed me, and I was struck by the shortness of her memory. How could she forget that her father the engineer drank too, and drank heavily, and that the money with which Dubetchnya had been bought had been acquired by a whole series of shameless, impudent dishonesties? How could she forget it?

XIV

My sister, too, was leading a life of her own which she carefully hid from me. She was often whispering with Masha. When I went up to her she seemed to shrink into herself, and there was a guilty, imploring look in her eyes; evidently there was something going on in her heart of which she was afraid or ashamed. So as to avoid meeting me in the garden, or being left alone with me, she always kept close to Masha, and I rarely had an opportunity of talking to her except at dinner.

One evening I was walking quietly through the garden on my way back from the building. It was beginning to get dark. Without noticing me, or hearing my step, my sister was walking near a spreading old apple-tree, absolutely noiselessly as though she were a phantom. She was dressed in black, and was walking rapidly backwards and forwards on the same track, looking at the ground. An apple fell from the tree; she started at the sound, stood still and pressed her hands to her temples. At that moment I went up to her.

In a rush of tender affection which suddenly flooded my heart, with tears in my eyes, suddenly remembering my mother and our childhood, I put my arm round her shoulders and kissed her.

"What is the matter?" I asked her. "You are unhappy; I have seen it for a long time. Tell me what's wrong?"

"I am frightened," she said, trembling.

"What is it?" I insisted. "For God's sake, be open!"

"I will, I will be open; I will tell you the whole truth. To hide it from you is hard, so agonizing. Misail, I love . . ." she went on in a whisper, "I love him . . . I love him. . . . I am happy, but why am I so frightened?"

There was the sound of footsteps; between the trees appeared Dr. Blagovo in his silk shirt with his high top boots. Evidently they had arranged to meet near the apple-tree. Seeing him, she rushed impulsively towards him with a cry of pain as though he were being taken from her.

"Vladimir! Vladimir!"

She clung to him and looked greedily into his face, and only then I noticed how pale and thin she had become of late. It was particularly noticeable from her lace collar which I had known for so long, and which now hung more loosely than ever before about her thin, long neck. The doctor was disconcerted, but at once recovered himself, and, stroking her hair, said:

"There, there. . . . Why so nervous? You see, I'm here."

We were silent, looking with embarrassment at each other, then we walked on, the three of us together, and I heard the doctor say to me:

"Civilized life has not yet begun among us. Old men console themselves by making out that if there is nothing now, there was something in the forties or the sixties; that's the old: you and I are young; our brains have not yet been touched by *marasmus senilis;* we cannot comfort ourselves with such illusions. The beginning of Russia was in 862, but the beginning of civilized Russia has not come yet."

But I did not grasp the meaning of these reflections. It was somehow strange, I could not believe it, that my sister was in love, that she was walking and holding the arm of a stranger and looking tenderly at him. My sister, this nervous, frightened, crushed, fettered creature, loved a man who was married and had children! I felt sorry for something, but what exactly I don't know; the presence of the doctor was for some reason distasteful to me now, and I could not imagine what would come of this love of theirs.

XV

Masha and I drove to Kurilovka to the dedication of the school.

"Autumn, autumn, autumn, . . ." said Masha softly, looking away.

"Summer is over. There are no birds and nothing is green but the willows."

Yes, summer was over. There were fine, warm days, but it was fresh in the morning, and the shepherds went out in their sheepskins already; and in our garden the dew did not dry off the asters all day long. There were plaintive sounds all the time, and one could not make out whether they came from the shutters creaking on their rusty hinges, or from the flying cranes—and one's heart felt light, and one was eager for life.

"The summer is over," said Masha. "Now you and I can balance our accounts. We have done a lot of work, a lot of thinking; we are the better for it—all honour and glory to us—we have succeeded in self-improvement; but have our successes had any perceptible influence on the life around us, have they brought any benefit to anyone whatever? No. Ignorance, physical uncleanliness, drunkenness, an appallingly high infant mortality, everything remains as it was, and no one is the better for your having ploughed and sown, and my having wasted money and read books. Obviously we have been working only for ourselves and have had advanced ideas only for ourselves." Such reasonings perplexed me, and I did not know what to think.

"We have been sincere from beginning to end," said I, "and if anyone is sincere he is right."

"Who disputes it? We were right, but we haven't succeeded in properly accomplishing what we were right in. To begin with, our external methods themselves—aren't they mistaken? You want to be of use to men, but by the very fact of your buying an estate, from the very start you cut yourself off from any possibility of doing anything useful for them. Then if you work, dress, eat like a peasant you sanctify, as it were, by your authority, their heavy, clumsy dress, their horrible huts, their stupid beards. . . . On the other hand, if we suppose that you work for long, long years, your whole life, that in the end some practical results are obtained, yet what are they, your results, what can they do against such elemental forces as wholesale ignorance, hunger, cold, degeneration? A drop in the ocean! Other methods of struggle are needed, strong, bold, rapid! If one really wants to be of use one must get out of the narrow circle of ordinary social work, and try to act direct upon the mass! What is wanted, first of all, is a loud, energetic propaganda. Why is it that art—music, for instance—is so living, so popular, and in reality so powerful? Because the musician or the singer affects thousands at once. Precious, precious art!" she went on, looking dreamily at the sky. "Art gives us wings and carries us far, far away! Anyone who is sick of filth, of petty, mercenary interests, anyone who is revolted, wounded, and indignant, can find peace and satisfaction only in the beautiful."

When we drove into Kurilovka the weather was bright and joyous. Somewhere they were threshing; there was a smell of rye straw. A mountain ash was bright red behind the hurdle fences, and all the trees wherever one looked were ruddy or golden. They were ringing the bells, they were carrying the ikons to the school, and we could hear them sing: "Holy Mother, our Defender," and how limpid the air was, and how high the doves were flying.

The service was being held in the classroom. Then the peasants of Kurilovka brought Masha the ikon, and the peasants of Dubetch-nya offered her a big loaf and a gilt salt cellar. And Masha broke into sobs.

"If anything has been said that shouldn't have been or anything done not to your liking, forgive us," said an old man, and he bowed down to her and to me.

As we drove home Masha kept looking round at the school; the green roof, which I had painted, and which was glistening in the sun, remained in sight for a long while. And I felt that the look Masha turned upon it now was a one of farewell.

XVI

In the evening she got ready to go to the town. Of late she had taken to going often to the town and staying the night there. In her absence I could not work, my hands felt weak and limp; our huge courtyard seemed a deary, repulsive, empty hole. The garden was full of angry noises, and without her the house, the trees, the horses were no longer "ours."

I did not go out of the house, but went on sitting at her table beside her bookshelf with the books on land work, those old favourites no longer wanted and looking at me now so shamefacedly. For whole hours together, while it struck seven, eight, nine, while the autumn night, black as soot, came on outside, I kept examining her old glove, or the pen with which she always wrote, or her little scissors. I did nothing, and realized clearly that all I had done before, ploughing, mowing, chopping, had only been because she wished it. And if she had sent me to clean a deep well, where I had to stand up to my waist in deep water, I should have crawled into the well without considering whether it was necessary or not. And now when she was not near, Dubetchnya, with its ruins, its untidiness, its banging shutters, with its thieves by day and by night, seemed to me a chaos in which any work would be useless. Besides, what had I to work for here, why anxiety and thought about the future, if I felt that the earth was giving way under my feet, that I had played my part in Dubetchnya, and that the fate of the books on farming was awaiting me too? Oh, what misery it was at night, in hours of solitude, when I was listening every minute in alarm, as though I were expecting someone to shout that it was time for me to go away! I did not grieve for Dubetchnya. I grieved for my love which, too, was threatened with its autumn. What an immense happiness it is to love and be loved, and how awful to feel that one is slipping down from that high pinnacle!

Masha returned from the town towards the evening of the next day. She was displeased with something, but she concealed it, and only said, why was it all the window frames had been put in for the winter it was enough to suffocate one. I took out two frames. We were not hungry, but we sat down to supper.

"Go and wash your hands," said my wife; "you smell of putty."

She had brought some new illustrated papers from the town, and we looked at them together after supper. There were supplements with fashion plates and patterns. Masha looked through them casually, and was putting them aside to examine them properly later on; but one dress, with a flat skirt as full as a bell and large sleeves, interested her, and she looked at it for a minute gravely and attentively.

"That's not bad," she said.

"Yes, that dress would suit you beautifully," I said, "beautifully."

And looking with emotion at the dress, admiring that patch of grey simply because she liked it, I went on tenderly:

"A charming, exquisite dress! Splendid, glorious, Masha! My precious Masha!"

And tears dropped on the fashion plate.

"Splendid Masha . . ." I muttered; "sweet, precious Masha. . . ."

She went to bed, while I sat another hour looking at the illustrations.

"It's a pity you took out the window frames," she said from the bedroom, "I am afraid it may be cold. Oh, dear, what a draught there is!"

I read something out of the column of odds and ends, a receipt for making cheap ink, and an account of the biggest diamond in the world. I came again upon the fashion plate of the dress she liked, and I imagined her at a ball, with a fan, bare shoulders, brilliant, splendid, with a full understanding of painting, music, literature, and how small and how brief my part seemed!

Our meeting, our marriage, had been only one of the episodes of which there would be many more in the life of this vital, richly gifted woman. All the best in the world, as I have said already, was at her service, and she received it absolutely for nothing, and even ideas and the intellectual movement in vogue served simply for her recreation, giving variety to her life, and I was only the sledge-driver who drove her from one entertainment to another. Now she did not need me. She would take flight, and I should be alone.

And as though in response to my thought, there came a despairing scream from the garden.

"He-e-elp!"

It was a shrill, womanish voice, and as though to mimic it the wind whistled in the chimney on the same shrill note. Half a minute passed, and again through the noise of the wind, but coming, it seemed, from the other end of the yard:

"He-e-elp!"

"Misail, do you hear?" my wife asked me softly. "Do you hear?"

She came out from the bedroom in her nightgown, with her hair down, and listened, looking at the dark window.

"Someone is being murdered," she said. "That is the last straw."

I took my gun and went out. It was very dark outside, the wind was high, and it was difficult to stand. I went to the gate and listened, the trees roared, the wind whistled and, probably at the feeble-minded peasant's, a dog howled lazily. Outside the gates the darkness was absolute, not a light on the railway-line. And near the lodge, which a year before had been the office, suddenly sounded a smothered scream:

"He-e-elp!"

"Who's there?" I called.

There were two people struggling. One was thrusting the other out, while the other was resisting, and both were breathing heavily.

"Leave go," said one, and I recognized Ivan Tcheprakov; it was he who was shrieking in a shrill, womanish voice: "Let go, you damned brute, or I'll bite your hand off."

The other I recognized as Moisey. I separated them, and as I did so I could not resist hitting Moisey two blows in the face. He fell down, then got up again, and I hit him once more.

"He tried to kill me," he muttered. "He was trying to get at his mamma's chest. . . . I want to lock him up in the lodge for security."

Tcheprakov was drunk and did not recognize me; he kept drawing deep breaths, as though he were just going to shout "help" again.

I left them and went back to the house; my wife was lying on her bed; she had dressed. I told her what had happened in the yard, and did not conceal the fact that I had hit Moisey.

"It's terrible to live in the country," she said.

"And what a long night it is. Oh dear, if only it were over!"

"He-e-elp!" we heard again, a little later.

"I'll go and stop them," I said.

"No, let them bite each other's throats," she said with an expression of disgust.

She was looking up at the ceiling, listening, while I sat beside her, not daring to speak to her, feeling as though I were to blame for their shouting "help" in the yard and for the night's seeming so long.

We were silent, and I waited impatiently for a gleam of light at the window, and Masha looked all the time as though she had awakened from a trance and now was marvelling how she, so clever, and well-educated, so elegant, had come into this pitiful, provincial, empty hole among a crew of petty, insignificant people, and how she could have so far forgotten herself as ever to be attracted by one of these people, and for more than six months to have been his wife. It seemed to me that at that moment it did not matter to her whether it was I, or Moisey, or Tcheprakov; everything for her was merged in that savage drunken " help"—I and our marriage, and our work together, and the mud and slush of autumn, and when she sighed or moved into a more comfortable position I read in her face: "Oh, that morning would come quickly!"

In the morning she went away. I spent another three days at

Dubetchnya expecting her, then I packed all our things in one room, locked it, and walked to the town. It was already evening when I rang at the engineer's, and the street lamps were burning in Great Dvoryansky Street. Pavel told me there was no one at home; Viktor Ivanitch had gone to Petersburg, and Mariya Viktorovna was probably at the rehearsal at the Azhogins'. I remember with what emotion I went on to the Azhogins', how my heart throbbed and fluttered as I mounted the stairs, and stood waiting a long while on the landing at the top, not daring to enter that temple of the muses! In the big room there were lighted candles everywhere, on a little table, on the piano, and on the stage, everywhere in threes; and the first performance was fixed for the thirteenth, and now the first rehearsal was on a Monday, an unlucky day. All part of the war against superstition! All the devotees of the scenic art were gathered together; the eldest, the middle, and the youngest sisters were walking about the stage, reading their parts in exercise books. Apart from all the rest stood Radish, motionless, with the side of his head pressed to the wall as he gazed with adoration at the stage, waiting for the rehearsal to begin. Everything as it used to be.

I was making my way to my hostess; I had to pay my respects to her, but suddenly everyone said "Hush!" and waved me to step quietly. There was a silence. The lid of the piano was raised; a lady sat down at it screwing up her short-sighted eyes at the music, and my Masha walked up to the piano, in a low-necked dress, looking beautiful, but with a special, new sort of beauty not in the least like the Masha who used to come and meet me in the spring at the mill. She sang: "Why do I love the radiant night?"

It was the first time during our whole acquaintance that I had heard her sing. She had a fine, mellow, powerful voice, and while she sang I felt as though I were eating a ripe, sweet, fragrant melon. She ended, the audience applauded, and she smiled, very much pleased, making play with her eyes, turning over the music, smoothing her skirts, like a bird that has at last broken out of its cage and preens its wings in freedom. Her hair was arranged over her ears, and she had an unpleasant, defiant expression in her face, as though she wanted to throw down a challenge to us all, or to shout to us as she did to her horses: "Hey, there, my beauties!"

And she must at that moment have been very much like her grandfather the sledge-driver.

"You here too?" she said, giving me her hand. "Did you hear me sing? Well, what did you think of it?" and without waiting for my answer she went on: "It's a very good thing you are here. I am going to-night to Petersburg for a short time. You'll let me go, won't you?"

At midnight I went with her to the station. She embraced me affectionately, probably feeling grateful to me for not asking unnecessary questions, and she promised to write to me, and I held her hands a long time, and kissed them, hardly able to restrain my tears and not uttering a word.

And when she had gone I stood watching the retreating lights, caressing her in imagination and softly murmuring:

"My darling Masha, glorious Masha. . . ."

I spent the night at Karpovna's, and next morning I was at work with Radish, re-covering the furniture of a rich merchant who was marrying his daughter to a doctor.

XVII

My sister came after dinner on Sunday and had tea with me.

"I read a great deal now," she said, showing me the books which she had fetched from the public library on her way to me. "Thanks to your wife and to Vladimir, they have awakened me to self-realization. They have been my salvation; they have made me feel myself a human being. In old days I used to lie awake at night with worries of all sorts, thinking what a lot of sugar we had used in the week, or hoping the cucumbers would not be too salt. And now, too, I lie awake at night, but I have different thoughts. I am distressed that half my life has been passed in such a foolish, cowardly way. I despise my past; I am ashamed of it. And I look upon our father now as my enemy. Oh, how grateful I am to your wife! And Vladimir! He is such a wonderful person! They have opened my eyes!"

"That's bad that you don't sleep at night," I said.

"Do you think I am ill? Not at all. Vladimir sounded me, and said I was perfectly well. But health is not what matters, it is not so important. . . . Tell me: am I right?"

She needed moral support, that was obvious. Masha had gone away. Dr. Blagovo was in Petersburg, and there was no one left in the town but me, to tell her she was right. She looked intently into my face, trying to read my secret thoughts, and if I were absorbed or silent in her presence she thought this was on her account, and was grieved. I always had to be on my guard, and when she asked me whether she was right I hastened to assure her that she was right, and that I had a deep respect for her.

"Do you know they have given me a part at the Azhogins'?" she went on. "I want to act on the stage, I want to live—in fact, I mean to drain the full cup. I have no talent, none, and the part is only ten lines, but still this is immeasurably finer and loftier than pouring out tea five times a day, and looking to see if the cook has eaten too much. Above all, let my father see I am capable of protest."

After tea she lay down on my bed, and lay for a little while with her eyes closed, looking very pale.

"What weakness," she said, getting up. "Vladimir says all city-bred women and girls are anæmic from doing nothing. What a clever man Vladimir is! He is right, absolutely right. We must work!"

Two days later she came to the Azhogins' with her manuscript for the rehearsal. She was wearing a black dress with a string of coral round her neck, and a brooch that in the distance was like a pastry puff, and in her ears earrings sparkling with brilliants. When I looked at her I felt uncomfortable. I was struck by her lack of taste. That she had very inappropriately put on earrings and brilliants, and that she was strangely dressed, was remarked by other people too; I saw smiles on people's faces, and heard someone say with a laugh: "Kleopatra of Egypt."

She was trying to assume society manners, to be unconstrained and at her ease, and so seemed artificial and strange. She had lost simplicity and sweetness.

"I told father just now that I was going to the rehearsal," she began, coming up to me, "and he shouted that he would not give me his blessing, and actually almost struck me. Only fancy, I don't know my part," she said, looking at her manuscript. "I am sure to make a mess of it. So be it, the die is cast," she went on in intense excitement. "The die is cast. . . ."

It seemed to her that everyone was looking at her, and that all were amazed at the momentous step she had taken, that everyone was expecting something special of her, and it would have been impossible to convince her that no one was paying attention to people so petty and insignificant as she and I were.

She had nothing to do till the third act, and her part, that of a visitor, a provincial crony, consisted only in standing at the door as though listening, and then delivering a brief monologue. In the interval before her appearance, an hour and a half at least, while they were moving about on the stage reading their parts, drinking tea and arguing, she did not leave my side, and was all the time muttering her part and nervously crumpling up the manuscript. And imagining that everyone was looking at her and waiting for her appearance, with a trembling hand she smoothed back her hair and said to me:

"I shall certainly make a mess of it. . . . What a load on my heart, if only you knew! I feel frightened, as though I were just going to be led to execution."

At last her turn came.

"Kleopatra Alexyevna, it's your cue!" said the stage manager.

She came forward into the middle of the stage with an expression of horror on her face, looking ugly and angular, and for half a minute stood as though in a trance, perfectly motionless, and only her big earrings shook in her ears.

"The first time you can read it," said someone.

It was clear to me that she was trembling, and trembling so much that she could not speak, and could not unfold her manuscript, and that she was incapable of acting her part; and I was already on the point of going to her and saying something, when she suddenly dropped on her knees in the middle of the stage and broke into loud sobs.

All was commotion and hubbub. I alone stood still, leaning against the side scene, overwhelmed by what had happened, not understanding and not knowing what to do. I saw them lift her up and lead her away. I saw Anyuta Blagovo come up to me; I had not seen her in the room before, and she seemed to have sprung out of the earth. She was wearing her hat and veil, and, as always, had an air of having come only for a moment.

"I told her not to take a part," she said angrily, jerking out each word abruptly and turning crimson. "It's insanity! You ought to have prevented her!"

Madame Azhogin, in a short jacket with short sleeves, with cigarette ash on her breast, looking thin and flat, came rapidly towards me.

"My dear, this is terrible," she brought out, wringing her hands, and, as her habit was, looking intently into my face. "This is terrible!

Your sister is in a condition. . . . She is with child. Take her away, I implore you. . . ."

She was breathless with agitation, while on one side stood her three daughters, exactly like her, thin and flat, huddling together in a scared way. They were alarmed, overwhelmed, as though a convict had been caught in their house. What a disgrace, how dreadful! And yet this estimable family had spent its life waging war on superstition; evidently they imagined that all the superstition and error of humanity was limited to the three candles, the thirteenth of the month, and to the unluckiness of Monday!

"I beg you . . . I beg," repeated Madame Azhogin, pursing up her lips in the shape of a heart on the syllable "you." "I beg you to take her home."

XVIII

A little later my sister and I were walking along the street. I covered her with the skirts of my coat; we hastened, choosing back streets where there were no street lamps, avoiding passers-by; it was as though we were running away. She was no longer crying, but looked at me with dry eyes. To Karpovna's, where I took her, it was only twenty minutes' walk, and, strange to say, in that short time we succeeded in thinking of our whole life; we talked over everything, considered our position, reflected. . . .

We decided we could not go on living in this town, and that when I had earned a little money we would move to some other place. In some houses everyone was asleep, in others they were playing cards; we hated these houses; we were afraid of them. We talked of the fanaticism, the coarseness of feeling, the insignificance of these respectable families, these amateurs of dramatic art whom we had so alarmed, and I kept asking in what way these stupid, cruel, lazy, and dishonest people were superior to the drunken and superstitious peasants of Kurilovka, or in what way they were better than animals, who in the same way are thrown into a panic when some incident disturbs the monotony of their life limited by their instincts. What would have happened to my sister now if she had been left to live at home?

What moral agonies would she have experienced, talking with my father, meeting every day with acquaintances? I imagined this to myself, and at once there came into my mind people, all people I knew, who had been slowly done to death by their nearest relations. I remembered the tortured dogs, driven mad, the live sparrows plucked naked by boys and flung into the water, and a long, long series of obscure lingering miseries which I had looked on continually from early childhood in that town; and I could not understand what these sixty thousand people lived for, what they read the gospel for, why they prayed, why they read books and magazines. What good had they gained from all that had been said and written hitherto if they were still possessed by the same spiritual darkness and hatred of liberty, as they were a hundred and three hundred years ago? A master carpenter spends his whole life building houses in the town, and always, to the day of his death, calls a "gallery" a "galdery." So these sixty thousand people have been reading and hearing of truth, of justice, of mercy, of freedom for generations, and yet from morning till night, till the day of their death, they are lying, and tormenting each other, and they fear liberty and hate it as a deadly foe.

"And so my fate is decided," said my sister, as we arrived home. "After what has happened I cannot go back *there*. Heavens, how good that is! My heart feels lighter."

She went to bed at once. Tears were glittering on her eyelashes, but her expression was happy; she fell into a sound sweet sleep, and one could see that her heart was lighter and that she was resting. It was a long, long time since she had slept like that.

And so we began our life together. She was always singing and saying that her life was very happy, and the books I brought her from the public library I took back unread, as now she could not read; she wanted to do nothing but dream and talk of the future, mending my linen, or helping Karpovna near the stove; she was always singing, or talking of her Vladimir, of his cleverness, of his charming manners, of his kindness, of his extraordinary learning, and I assented to all she said, though by now I disliked her doctor. She wanted to work, to lead an independent life on her own account, and she used to say that she would become a school-teacher or a doctor's assistant as soon as her health would permit her, and would herself do the scrubbing and the washing. Already she was passionately devoted to her child; he was not yet born, but she knew already the colour of his eyes, what his hands would be like, and how he would laugh. She was fond of talking about education, and as her Vladimir was the best man in the world, all her discussion of education could be summed up in the question how to make the boy as fascinating as his father. There was no end to her talk, and everything she said made her intensely joyful. Sometimes I was delighted, too, though I could not have said why.

I suppose her dreaminess infected me. I, too, gave up reading, and did nothing but dream. In the evenings, in spite of my fatigue, I walked up and down the room, with my hands in my pockets, talking of Masha.

"What do you think?" I would ask of my sister. "When will she come back? I think she'll come back at Christmas, not later; what has she to do there?"

"As she doesn't write to you, it's evident she will come back very soon."

"That's true," I assented, though I knew perfectly well that Masha would not return to our town.

I missed her fearfully, and could no longer deceive myself, and tried to get other people to deceive me. My sister was expecting her doctor, and I— Masha; and both of us talked incessantly, laughed, and did not notice that we were preventing Karpovna from sleeping. She lay on the stove and kept muttering:

"The samovar hummed this morning, it did hum! Oh, it bodes no good, my dears, it bodes no good!"

No one ever came to see us but the postman, who brought my sister letters from the doctor, and Prokofy, who sometimes came in to see us in the evening, and after looking at my sister without speaking went away, and when he was in the kitchen said:

"Every class ought to remember its rules, and anyone, who is so proud that he won't understand that, will find it a vale of tears."

He was very fond of the phrase "a vale of tears." One day—it was in Christmas week, when I was walking by the bazaar—he called me into the butcher's shop, and not shaking hands with me, announced that he had to speak to me about something very important. His face was red from the frost and vodka; near him, behind the counter, stood Nikolka, with the expression of a brigand, holding a bloodstained knife in his hand.

"I desire to express my word to you," Prokofy began. "This incident cannot continue, because, as you understand yourself that for such a vale, people will say nothing good of you or of us. Mamma, through pity, cannot say something unpleasant to you, that your sister should move into another lodging on account of her condition, but I won't have it any more, because I can't approve of her behaviour."

I understood him, and I went out of the shop. The same day my sister and I moved to Radish's. We had no money for a cab, and we walked on foot; I carried a parcel of our belongings on my back; my sister had nothing in her hands, but she gasped for breath and coughed, and kept asking whether we should get there soon.

<h2 style="text-align:center">XIX</h2>

At last a letter came from Masha.

"Dear, good M. A." (she wrote), "our kind, gentle 'angel' as the old painter calls you, farewell; I am going with my father to America for the exhibition. In a few days I shall see the ocean—so far from Dubetchnya, it's dreadful to think! It's far and unfathomable as the sky, and I long to be there in freedom. I am triumphant, I am mad, and you see how incoherent my letter is. Dear, good one, give me my freedom, make haste to break the thread, which still holds, binding you and me together. My meeting and knowing you was a ray from heaven that lighted up my existence; but my becoming your wife was a mistake, you understand that, and I am oppressed now by the consciousness of the mistake, and I beseech you, on my knees, my generous friend, quickly, quickly, before I start for the ocean, telegraph that you consent to correct our common mistake, to remove the solitary stone from my wings, and my father, who will undertake all the arrangements, promised me not to burden you too much with formalities. And so I am free to fly whither I will? Yes?

"Be happy, and God bless you; forgive me, a sinner.

"I am well, I am wasting money, doing all sorts of silly things, and I thank God every minute that such a bad woman as I has no children. I sing and have success, but it's not an infatuation; no, it's my haven, my cell to which I go for peace. King David had a ring with an inscription on it: 'All things pass.' When one is sad those words make one cheerful, and when one is cheerful it makes one sad. I have got myself a ring like that with Hebrew letters on it, and this talisman keeps me from infatuations. All things pass, life will pass, one wants nothing. Or at least one wants nothing but the sense of freedom, for when anyone is free, he wants nothing, nothing, nothing. Break the thread. A warm hug to you and your sister. Forgive and forget your M."

My sister used to lie down in one room, and Radish, who had been ill again and was now better, in another. Just at the moment when I received this letter my sister went softly into the painter's room, sat down beside him and began reading aloud. She read to him every day, Ostrovsky or Gogol, and he listened, staring at one point, not laughing, but shaking his head and muttering to himself from time to time:

"Anything may happen! Anything may happen!"

If anything ugly or unseemly were depicted in the play he would say as though vindictively, thrusting his finger into the book:

"There it is, lying! That's what it does, lying does."

The plays fascinated him, both from their subjects and their moral, and from their skilful, complex construction, and he marvelled at "him," never calling the author by his name. How neatly *he* has put it all together.

This time my sister read softly only one page, and could read no more: her voice would not last out. Radish took her hand and, moving his parched lips, said, hardly audibly, in a husky voice:

"The soul of a righteous man is white and smooth as chalk, but the soul of a sinful man is like pumice stone. The soul of a righteous man is like clear oil, but the soul of a sinful man is gas tar. We must labour, we must sorrow, we must suffer sickness," he went on, "and he who does not labour and sorrow will not gain the Kingdom of Heaven. Woe, woe to them that are well fed, woe to the mighty, woe to the rich, woe to the moneylenders! Not for them is the Kingdom of Heaven. Lice eat grass, rust eats iron . . ."

"And lying the soul," my sister added laughing.

I read the letter through once more. At that moment there walked into the kitchen a soldier who had been bringing us twice a week parcels of tea, French bread and game, which smelt of scent, from some unknown giver. I had no work. I had had to sit at home idle for whole days together, and probably whoever sent us the French bread knew that we were in want.

I heard my sister talking to the soldier and laughing gaily. Then, lying down, she ate some French bread and said to me:

"When you wouldn't go into the service, but became a house

painter, Anyuta Blagovo and I knew from the beginning that you were right, but we were frightened to say so aloud. Tell me what force is it that hinders us from saying what one thinks? Take Anyuta Blagovo now, for instance. She loves you, she adores you, she knows you are right, she loves me too, like a sister, and knows that I am right, and I daresay in her soul envies me, but some force prevents her from coming to see us, she shuns us, she is afraid."

My sister crossed her arms over her breast, and said passionately:

"How she loves you, if only you knew! She has confessed her love to no one but me, and then very secretly in the dark. She led me into a dark avenue in the garden, and began whispering how precious you were to her. You will see, she'll never marry, because she loves you. Are you sorry for her?"

"Yes."

"It's she who has sent the bread. She is absurd really, what is the use of being so secret? I used to be absurd and foolish, but now I have got away from that and am afraid of nobody. I think and say aloud what I like, and am happy. When I lived at home I hadn't a conception of happiness, and now I wouldn't change with a queen."

Dr. Blagovo arrived. He had taken his doctor's degree, and was now staying in our town with his father; he was taking a rest, and said that he would soon go back to Petersburg again. He wanted to study anti-toxins against typhus, and, I believe, cholera; he wanted to go abroad to perfect his training, and then to be appointed a professor. He had already left the army service, and wore a roomy serge reefer jacket, very full trousers, and magnificent neckties. My sister was in ecstasies over his scarf-pin, his studs, and the red silk handkerchief which he wore, I suppose from foppishness, sticking out of the breast pocket of his jacket. One day, having nothing to do, she and I counted up all the suits we remembered him wearing, and came to the conclusion that he had at least ten. It was clear that he still loved my sister as before, but he never once even in jest spoke of taking her with him to Petersburg or abroad, and I could not picture to myself clearly what would become of her if she remained alive and what would become of her child. She did nothing but dream endlessly, and never thought seriously of the future; she said he might go where he liked, and might abandon her even, so long as he was happy himself; that what had been was enough for her.

As a rule he used to sound her very carefully on his arrival, and used to insist on her taking milk and drops in his presence. It was the same on this occasion. He sounded her and made her drink a glass of milk, and there was a smell of creosote in our room afterwards.

"That's a good girl," he said, taking the glass from her. "You mustn't talk too much now; you've taken to chattering like a magpie of late. Please hold your tongue."

She laughed. Then he came into Radish's room where I was sitting and affectionately slapped me on the shoulder.

"Well, how goes it, old man?" he said, bending down to the invalid.

"Your honour," said Radish, moving his lips slowly, "your honour, I venture to submit. . . . We all walk in the fear of God, we all have to die. . . . Permit me to tell you the truth. . . . Your honour, the King-dom of Heaven will not be for you!"

"There's no help for it," the doctor said jestingly; "there must be somebody in hell, you know."

And all at once something happened with my consciousness; as though I were in a dream, as though I were standing on a winter night in the slaughterhouse yard, and Prokofy beside me, smelling of pep-per cordial; I made an effort to control myself, and rubbed my eyes, and at once it seemed to me that I was going along the road to the interview with the Governor. Nothing of the sort had happened to me before, or has happened to me since, and these strange memories that were like dreams, I ascribed to over-exhaustion of my nerves. I lived through the scene at the slaughterhouse, and the interview with the Governor, and at the same time was dimly aware that it was not real.

When I came to myself I saw that I was no longer in the house, but in the street, and was standing with the doctor near a lamp-post.

"It's sad, it's sad," he was saying, and tears were trickling down his cheeks. "She is in good spirits, she's always laughing and hopeful, but her position's hopeless, dear boy. Your Radish hates me, and is always trying to make me feel that I have treated her badly. He is right from his standpoint, but I have my point of view too; and I shall never regret all that has happened. One must love; we ought all to love—oughtn't we? There would be no life without love; anyone who fears and avoids love is not free."

Little by little he passed to other subjects, began talking of science, of his dissertation which had been liked in Petersburg. He was carried away by his subject, and no longer thought of my sister, nor of his grief, nor of me. Life was of absorbing interest to him. She has America and her ring with the inscription on it, I thought, while this fellow has his doctor's degree and a professor's chair to look forward to, and only my sister and I are left with the old things.

When I said good-bye to him, I went up to the lamp-post and read the letter once more. And I remembered, I remembered vividly how that spring morning she had come to me at the mill, lain down and covered herself with her jacket—she wanted to be like a simple peasant woman. And how, another time—it was in the morning also—we drew the net out of the water, and heavy drops of rain fell upon us from the riverside willows, and we laughed. . . .

It was dark in our house in Great Dvoryansky Street. I got over the fence and, as I used to do in the old days, went by the back way to the kitchen to borrow a lantern. There was no one in the kitchen. The samovar hissed near the stove, waiting for my father. "Who pours out my father's tea now?" I thought. Taking the lantern I went out to the shed, built myself up a bed of old newspapers and lay down. The hooks on the walls looked forbidding, as they used to of old, and their shadows flickered. It was cold. I felt that my sister would come in in a minute, and bring me supper, but at once I remembered that she was ill and was lying at Radish's, and it seemed to me strange that I should have climbed over the fence and be lying here in this unheated shed. My mind was in a maze, and I saw all sorts of absurd things.

There was a ring. A ring familiar from childhood: first the wire rustled against the wall, then a short plaintive ring in the kitchen. It was my father come back from the club. I got up and went into the kitchen. Axinya the cook clasped her hands on seeing me, and for some reason burst into tears.

"My own !" she said softly. "My precious! O Lord!"

And she began crumpling up her apron in her agitation. In the window there were standing jars of berries in vodka. I poured myself out a teacupful and greedily drank it off, for I was intensely thirsty. Axinya had quite recently scrubbed the table and benches, and there was that smell in the kitchen which is found in bright, snug kitchens kept by tidy cooks. And that smell and the chirp of the cricket used to lure us as children into the kitchen, and put us in the mood for hearing fairy tales and playing at "Kings." . . .

"Where's Kleopatra?" Axinya asked softly, in a fluster, holding her breath; "and where is your cap, my dear? Your wife, you say, has gone to Petersburg?"

She had been our servant in our mother's time, and used once to give Kleopatra and me our baths, and to her we were still children who had to be talked to for their good. For a quarter of an hour or so she laid before me all the reflections which she had with the sagacity of an old servant been accumulating in the stillness of that kitchen, all the time since we had seen each other. She said that the doctor could be forced to marry Kleopatra; he only needed to be thoroughly frightened; and that if an appeal were promptly written the bishop would annul the first marriage; that it would be a good thing for me to sell Dubetchnya without my wife's knowledge, and put the money in the bank in my own name; that if my sister and I were to bow down at my father's feet and ask him properly, he might perhaps forgive us; that we ought to have a service sung to the Queen of Heaven. . . .

"Come, go along, my dear, and speak to him," she said, when she heard my father's cough. "Go along, speak to him; bow down, your head won't drop off."

I went in. My father was sitting at the table sketching a plan of a summer villa, with Gothic windows, and with a fat turret like a fireman's watch tower—something peculiarly stiff and tasteless. Going into the study I stood still where I could see this drawing. I did not know why I had gone in to my father, but I remember that when I saw his lean face, his red neck, and his shadow on the wall, I wanted to throw myself on his neck, and as Axinya had told me, bow down at his feet; but the sight of the summer villa with the Gothic windows, and the fat turret, restrained me.

"Good evening," I said.

He glanced at me, and at once dropped his eyes on his drawing.

"What do you want?" he asked, after waiting a little.

"I have come to tell you my sister's very ill. She can't live very long," I added in a hollow voice.

"Well," sighed my father, taking off his spectacles, and laying them on the table. "What thou sowest that shalt thou reap. What thou sowest," he repeated, getting up from the table. "that shalt thou reap. I ask you to remember how you came to me two years ago, and on this very spot I begged you, I besought you to give up your errors; I reminded you of your duty, of your honour, of what you owed to your forefathers whose traditions we ought to preserve as sacred. Did you obey me? You scorned my counsels, and obstinately persisted in clinging to your false ideals; worse still you drew your sister into the path of error with you, and led her to lose her moral principles and sense of shame. Now you are both in a bad way. Well, as thou sowest, so shalt thou reap!"

As he said this he walked up and down the room. He probably imagined that I had come to him to confess my wrong doings, and he probably expected that I should begin begging him to forgive my sister and me. I was cold, I was shivering as though I were in a fever, and spoke with difficulty in a husky voice.

"And I beg you, too, to remember," I said, "on this very spot I besought you to understand me, to reflect, to decide with me how and for what we should live, and in answer you began talking about our forefathers, about my grandfather who wrote poems. One tells you now that your only daughter is hopelessly ill, and you go on again about your forefathers, your traditions. . . . And such frivolity in your old age, when death is close at hand, and you haven't more than five or ten years left!"

"What have you come here for?" my father asked sternly, evidently offended at my reproaching him for his frivolity.

"I don't know. I love you, I am unutterably sorry that we are so far apart—so you see I have come. I love you still, but my sister has broken with you completely. She does not forgive you, and will never forgive you now. Your very name arouses her aversion for the past, for life."

"And who is to blame for it?" cried my father. "It's your fault, you scoundrel!"

"Well, suppose it is my fault?" I said. "I admit I have been to blame in many things, but why is it that this life of yours, which you think binding upon us, too—why is it so dreary, so barren? How is it that in not one of these houses you have been building for the last thirty years has there been anyone from whom I might have learnt how to live, so as not to be to blame? There is not one honest man in the whole town! These houses of yours are nests of damnation, where mothers and daughters are made away with, where children are tortured. . . . My poor mother!" I went on in despair. "My poor sister! One has to stupefy oneself with vodka, with cards, with scandal; one must become a scoundrel, a hypocrite, or go on drawing plans for years and years, so as not to notice all the horrors that lie hidden in these houses. Our town has existed for hundreds of years, and all that time it has not produced one man of service to our country—not one. You have stifled in the germ everything in the least living and bright. It's a town of shop-keepers, publicans, counting-house clerks, canting hypocrites; it's a useless, unnecessary town, which not one soul would regret if it suddenly sank through the earth."

"I don't want to listen to you, you scoundrel!" said my father, and he took up his ruler from the table. "You are drunk. Don't dare come and see your father in such a state! I tell you for the last time, and you can repeat it to your depraved sister, that you'll get nothing from me, either of you. I have torn my disobedient children out of my heart, and if they suffer for their disobedience and obstinacy I do not pity them. You can go whence you came. It has pleased God to chastise me with you, but I will bear the trial with resignation, and, like Job, I will find consolation in my sufferings and in unremitting labour. You must not cross my threshold till you have mended your ways. I am a just man, all I tell you is for your benefit, and if you desire your own good you ought to remember all your life what I say and have said to you. . . ."

I waved my hand in despair and went away. I don't remember what happened afterwards, that night and next day.

I am told that I walked about the streets bareheaded, staggering, and singing aloud, while a crowd of boys ran after me, shouting:

"Better-than-nothing!"

XX

If I wanted to order a ring for myself, the inscription I should choose would be: "Nothing passes away." I believe that nothing passes away without leaving a trace, and that every step we take, however small, has significance for our present and our future existence.

What I have been through has not been for nothing. My great troubles, my patience, have touched people's hearts, and now they don't call me "Better-than-nothing," they don't laugh at me, and when I walk by the shops they don't throw water over me. They have grown used to my being a workman, and see nothing strange in my carrying a pail of paint and putting in windows, though I am of noble rank; on the contrary, people are glad to give me orders, and I am now considered a first-rate workman, and the best foreman after Radish, who, though he has regained his health, and though, as before, he paints the cupola on the belfry without scaffolding, has no longer the force to control the workmen; instead of him I now run about the town looking for work, I engage the workmen and pay them, borrow money at a high rate of interest, and now that I myself am a contractor, I understand how it is that one may have to waste three days racing about the town in search of tilers on account of some twopenny-halfpenny job. People are civil to me, they address me politely, and in the houses where I work, they offer me tea, and send to enquire whether I wouldn't like dinner. Children and young girls often come and look at me with curiosity and compassion.

One day I was working in the Governor's garden, painting an arbour there to look like marble. The Governor, walking in the garden, came up to the arbour and, having nothing to do, entered into conversation with me, and I reminded him how he had once summoned me to an interview with him. He looked into my face intently for a minute, then made his mouth like a round "O," flung up his hands, and said: "I don't remember!"

I have grown older, have become silent, stern, and austere, I rarely laugh, and I am told that I have grown like Radish, and that like him I bore the workmen by my useless exhortations.

Mariya Viktorovna, my former wife, is living now abroad, while her father is constructing a railway somewhere in the eastern provinces, and is buying estates there. Dr. Blagovo is also abroad. Dubetchnya has passed again into the possession of Madame Tcheprakov, who has bought it after forcing the engineer to knock the price down twenty per cent. Moisey goes about now in a bowler hat; he often drives into the town in a racing droshky on business of some sort, and stops near the bank. They say he has already bought up a mortgaged estate, and is constantly making enquiries at the bank about Dubetchnya, which he means to buy too. Poor Ivan Tcheprakov was for a long while out of work, staggering about the town and drinking. I tried to get him into our work, and for a time he painted roofs and put in window-panes in our company, and even got to like it, and stole oil, asked for tips, and drank like a regular painter. But he soon got sick of the work, and went back to Dubetchnya, and afterwards the workmen confessed to me that he had tried to persuade them to join him one night and murder Moisey and rob Madame Tcheprakov.

My father has greatly aged; he is very bent, and in the evenings walks up and down near his house. I never go to see him.

During an epidemic of cholera Prokofy doctored some of the shopkeepers with pepper cordial and pitch, and took money for doing so, and, as I learned from the newspapers, was flogged for abusing the doctors as he sat in his shop. His shop boy Nikolka died of cholera. Karpovna is still alive and, as always, she loves and fears her Prokofy. When she sees me, she always shakes her head mournfully, and says with a sigh: "Your life is ruined."

On working days I am busy from morning till night. On holidays, in fine weather, I take my tiny niece (my sister reckoned on a boy, but the child is a girl) and walk in a leisurely way to the cemetery. There I stand or sit down, and stay a long time gazing at the grave that is so dear to me, and tell the child that her mother lies here.

Sometimes, by the graveside, I find Anyuta Blagovo. We greet each other and stand in silence, or talk of Kleopatra, of her child, of how sad life is in this world; then, going out of the cemetery we walk along in silence and she slackens her pace on purpose to walk beside me a little longer. The little girl, joyous and happy, pulls at her hand, laughing and screwing up her eyes in the bright sunlight, and we stand still and join in caressing the dear child.

When we reach the town Anyuta Blagovo, agitated and flushing crimson, says good-bye to me and walks on alone, austere and respectable. . . . And no one who met her could, looking at her, imagine that she had just been walking beside me and even caressing the child.

1896

Peasants

I

Nikolay Tchikildyeev, a waiter in the Moscow hotel, Slavyansky Bazaar, was taken ill. His legs went numb and his gait was affected, so that on one occasion, as he was going along the corridor, he tumbled and fell down with a tray full of ham and peas. He had to leave his job. All his own savings and his wife's were spent on doctors and medicines; they had nothing left to live upon. He felt dull with no work to do, and he made up his mind he must go home to the village. It is better to be ill at home, and living there is cheaper; and it is a true saying that the walls of home are a help.

He reached Zhukovo towards evening. In his memories of childhood he had pictured his home as bright, snug, comfortable. Now, going into the hut, he was positively frightened; it was so dark, so crowded, so unclean. His wife Olga and his daughter Sasha, who had come with him, kept looking in bewilderment at the big untidy stove, which filled up almost half the hut and was black with soot and flies. What lots of flies! The stove was on one side, the beams lay slanting on the walls, and it looked as though the hut were just going to fall to pieces. In the corner, facing the door, under the holy images, bottle labels and newspaper cuttings were stuck on the walls instead of pictures. The poverty, the poverty! Of the grown-up people there were none at home; all were at work at the harvest. On the stove was sitting a white-headed girl of eight, unwashed and apathetic; she did not even glance at them as they came in. On the floor a white cat was rubbing itself against the oven fork.

"Puss, puss!" Sasha called to her. "Puss!"

"She can't hear," said the little girl; "she has gone deaf."

"How is that?"

"Oh, she was beaten."

Nikolay and Olga realized from the first glance what life was like here, but said nothing to one another; in silence they put down their bundles, and went out into the village street. Their hut was the third from the end, and seemed the very poorest and oldest-looking; the second was not much better; but the last one had an iron roof, and curtains in the windows. That hut stood apart, not enclosed; it was a tavern. The huts were in a single row, and the whole of the little village—quiet and dreamy, with willows, elders, and mountain-ash trees peeping out from the yards—had an attractive look.

Beyond the peasants' homesteads there was a slope down to the river, so steep and precipitous that huge stones jutted out bare here and there through the clay. Down the slope, among the stones and holes dug by the potters, ran winding paths; bits of broken pottery, some brown, some red, lay piled up in heaps, and below there stretched a broad, level, bright green meadow, from which the hay had been already carried, and in which the peasants' cattle were wandering. The river, three-quarters of a mile from the village, ran twisting and turning, with beautiful leafy banks; beyond it was again a broad meadow, a herd of cattle, long strings of white geese; then, just as on the near side, a steep ascent uphill, and on the top of the hill a hamlet, and a church with five domes, and at a little distance the manor-house.

"It's lovely here in your parts!" said Olga, crossing herself at the sight of the church. "What space, oh Lord!"

Just at that moment the bell began ringing for service (it was Saturday evening). Two little girls, down below, who were dragging up a pail of water, looked round at the church to listen to the bell.

"At this time they are serving the dinners at the Slavyansky Bazaar," said Nikolay dreamily.

Sitting on the edge of the slope, Nikolay and Olga watched the sun setting, watched the gold and crimson sky reflected in the river, in the church windows, and in the whole air—which was soft and still and unutterably pure as it never was in Moscow. And when the sun had set the flocks and herds passed, bleating and lowing; geese flew across from the further side of the river, and all sank into silence; the soft light died away in the air, and the dusk of evening began quickly moving down upon them.

Meanwhile Nikolay's father and mother, two gaunt, bent, toothless old people, just of the same height, came back. The women—the sisters-in-law Marya and Fyokla—who had been working on the landowner's estate beyond the river, arrived home, too. Marya, the wife of Nikolay's brother Kiryak, had six children, and Fyokla, the wife of Nikolay's brother Denis—who had gone for a soldier—had two; and when Nikolay, going into the hut, saw all the family, all those bodies big and little moving about on the lockers, in the hanging cradles and in all the corners, and when he saw the greed with which the old father and the women ate the black bread, dipping it in water, he realized he had made a mistake in coming here, sick, penniless, and with a family, too— a great mistake!

"And where is Kiryak?" he asked after they had exchanged greetings.

"He is in service at the merchant's," answered his father; "a keeper in the woods. He is not a bad peasant, but too fond of his glass."

"He is no great help!" said the old woman tearfully. "Our men are a grievous lot; they bring nothing into the house, but take plenty out. Kiryak drinks, and so does the old man; it is no use hiding a sin; he knows his way to the tavern. The Heavenly Mother is wroth."

In honour of the visitors they brought out the samovar. The tea smelt of fish; the sugar was grey and looked as though it had been nibbled; cockroaches ran to and fro over the bread and among the crockery. It was disgusting to drink, and the conversation was disgusting, too—about nothing but poverty and illnesses. But before they had time to empty their first cups there came a loud, prolonged, drunken shout from the yard:

"Ma-arya!"

"It looks as though Kiryak were coming," said the old man. "Speak of the devil."

All were hushed. And again, soon afterwards, the same shout, coarse and drawn-out as though it came out of the earth:

"Ma-arya!"

Marya, the elder sister-in-law, turned pale and huddled against the stove, and it was strange to see the look of terror on the face of the strong, broad-shouldered, ugly woman. Her daughter, the child who had been sitting on the stove and looked so apathetic, suddenly broke into loud weeping.

"What are you howling for, you plague?" Fyokla, a handsome

woman, also strong and broad-shouldered, shouted to her. "He won't kill you, no fear!"

From his old father Nikolay learned that Marya was afraid to live in the forest with Kiryak, and that when he was drunk he always came for her, made a row, and beat her mercilessly.

"Ma-arya!" the shout sounded close to the door.

"Protect me, for Christ's sake, good people!" faltered Marya, breathing as though she had been plunged into very cold water. "Protect me, kind people. . . ."

All the children in the hut began crying, and looking at them, Sasha, too, began to cry. They heard a drunken cough, and a tall, black-bearded peasant wearing a winter cap came into the hut, and was the more terrible because his face could not be seen in the dim light of the little lamp. It was Kiryak. Going up to his wife, he swung his arm and punched her in the face with his fist. Stunned by the blow, she did not utter a sound, but sat down, and her nose instantly began bleeding.

"What a disgrace! What a disgrace!" muttered the old man, clambering up on to the stove. "Before visitors, too! It's a sin!"

The old mother sat silent, bowed, lost in thought; Fyokla rocked the cradle.

Evidently conscious of inspiring fear, and pleased at doing so, Kiryak seized Marya by the arm, dragged her towards the door, and bellowed like an animal in order to seem still more terrible; but at that moment he suddenly caught sight of the visitors and stopped.

"Oh, they have come, . . ." he said, letting his wife go; "my own brother and his family. . . ."

Staggering and opening wide his red, drunken eyes, he said his prayer before the image and went on:

"My brother and his family have come to the parental home . . . from Moscow, I suppose. The great capital Moscow, to be sure, the mother of cities. . . . Excuse me."

He sank down on the bench near the samovar and began drinking tea, sipping it loudly from the saucer in the midst of general silence. . . . He drank off a dozen cups, then reclined on the bench and began snoring.

They began going to bed. Nikolay, as an invalid, was put on the stove with his old father; Sasha lay down on the floor, while Olga went with the other women into the barn.

"Aye, aye, dearie," she said, lying down on the hay beside Marya; "you won't mend your trouble with tears. Bear it in patience, that is all. It is written in the Scriptures: 'If anyone smite thee on the right cheek, offer him the left one also.' . . . Aye, aye, dearie."

Then in a low singsong murmur she told them about Moscow, about her own life, how she had been a servant in furnished lodgings.

"And in Moscow the houses are big, built of brick," she said; "and there are ever so many churches, forty times forty, dearie; and they are all gentry in the houses, so handsome and so proper!"

Marya told her that she had not only never been in Moscow, but had not even been in their own district town; she could not read or write, and knew no prayers, not even "Our Father." Both she and Fyokla, the other sister-in-law, who was sitting a little way off listening, were extremely ignorant and could understand nothing. They both disliked their husbands; Marya was afraid of Kiryak, and whenever he stayed with her she was shaking with fear, and always got a headache from the fumes of vodka and tobacco with which he reeked. And in answer to the question whether she did not miss her husband, Fyokla answered with vexation:

"Miss him!"

They talked a little and sank into silence.

It was cool and a cock crowed at the top of his voice near the barn, preventing them from sleeping. When the bluish morning light was already peeping through all the crevices, Fyokla got up stealthily and went out, and then they heard the sound of her bare feet running off somewhere.

II

Olga went to church, and took Marya with her. As they went down the path towards the meadow both were in good spirits. Olga liked the wide view, and Marya felt that in her sister-in-law she had someone near and akin to her. The sun was rising. Low down over the meadow floated a drowsy hawk. The river looked gloomy; there was a haze hovering over it here and there, but on the further bank a streak of light already stretched across the hill. The church was gleaming, and in the manor garden the rooks were cawing furiously.

"The old man is all right," Marya told her, "but Granny is strict; she is continually nagging. Our own grain lasted till Carnival. We buy flour now at the tavern. She is angry about it; she says we eat too much."

"Aye, aye, dearie! Bear it in patience, that is all. It is written: 'Come unto Me, all ye that labour and are heavy laden.' "

Olga spoke sedately, rhythmically, and she walked like a pilgrim woman, with a rapid, anxious step. Every day she read the gospel, read it aloud like a deacon; a great deal of it she did not understand but the words of the gospel moved her to tears, and words like "forasmuch as" and "verily" she pronounced with a sweet flutter at her heart. She believed in God, in the Holy Mother, in the Saints; she believed one must not offend anyone in the world—not simple folks, nor Germans, nor gypsies, nor Jews—and woe even to those who have no compassion on the beasts. She believed this was written in the Holy Scriptures; and so, when she pronounced phrases from Holy Writ, even though she did not understand them, her face grew softened, compassionate, and radiant.

"What part do you come from?" Marya asked her.

"I am from Vladimir. Only I was taken to Moscow long ago, when I was eight years old."

They reached the river. On the further side a woman was standing at the water's edge, undressing.

"It's our Fyokla," said Marya, recognizing her. "She has been over the river to the manor yard. To the stewards. She is a shameless hussy and foul-mouthed—fearfully!"

Fyokla, young and vigorous as a girl, with her black eyebrows and her loose hair, jumped off the bank and began splashing the water with her feet, and waves ran in all directions from her.

"Shameless—dreadfully!" repeated Marya.

The river was crossed by a rickety little bridge of logs, and exactly below it in the clear, limpid water was a shoal of broad-headed mullets. The dew was glistening on the green bushes that looked into the water. There was a feeling of warmth; it was comforting! What a lovely morning! And how lovely life would have been in this world, in all likelihood, if it were not for poverty, horrible, hopeless poverty, from which one can find no refuge! One had only to look round at the village to remember vividly all that had happened the day before, and the illusion of happiness which seemed to surround them vanished instantly.

They reached the church. Marya stood at the entrance, and did not dare to go farther. She did not dare to sit down either. Though they only began ringing for mass between eight and nine, she remained standing the whole time.

While the gospel was being read the crowd suddenly parted to make way for the family from the great house. Two young girls in white frocks and wide-brimmed hats walked in; with them a chubby, rosy boy in a sailor suit. Their appearance touched Olga; she made up her mind from the first glance that they were refined, well-educated, handsome people. Marya looked at them from under her brows, sullenly, dejectedly, as though they were not human beings coming in, but monsters who might crush her if she did not make way for them.

And every time the deacon boomed out something in his bass voice she fancied she heard "Ma-arya!" and she shuddered.

III

The arrival of the visitors was already known in the village, and directly after mass a number of people gathered together in the hut. The Leonytchevs and Matvyeitchevs and the Ilyitchovs came to inquire about their relations who were in service in Moscow. All the lads of Zhukovo who could read and write were packed off to Moscow and hired out as butlers or waiters (while from the village on the other side of the river the boys all became bakers), and that had been the custom from the days of serfdom long ago when a certain Luka Ivanitch, a peasant from Zhukovo, now a legendary figure, who had been a waiter in one of the Moscow clubs, would take none but his fellow-villagers into his service, and found jobs for them in taverns and restaurants; and from that time the village of Zhukovo was always called among the inhabitants of the surrounding districts Slaveytown. Nikolay had been taken to Moscow when he was eleven, and Ivan Makaritch, one of the Matvyeitchevs, at that time a head-waiter in the "Hermitage" garden, had put him into a situation. And now, addressing the Matvyeitchevs, Nikolay said emphatically:

"Ivan Makaritch was my benefactor, and I am bound to pray for him day and night, as it is owing to him I have become a good man."

"My good soul!" a tall old woman, the sister of Ivan Makaritch, said tearfully, "and not a word have we heard about him, poor dear."

"In the winter he was in service at Omon's, and this season there was a rumour he was somewhere out of town, in gardens. . . . He has aged! In old days he would bring home as much as ten roubles a day in the summer-time, but now things are very quiet everywhere. The old man frets."

The women looked at Nikolay's feet, shod in felt boots, and at his pale face, and said mournfully:

"You are not one to get on, Nikolay Osipitch; you are not one to get on! No, indeed!"

And they all made much of Sasha. She was ten years old, but she was little and very thin, and might have been taken for no more than seven. Among the other little girls, with their sunburnt faces and roughly cropped hair, dressed in long faded smocks, she with her white little face, with her big dark eyes, with a red ribbon in her hair, looked funny, as though she were some little wild creature that had been caught and brought into the hut.

"She can read, too," Olga said in her praise, looking tenderly at her daughter. "Read a little, child!" she said, taking the gospel from the corner. You read, and the good Christian people will listen."

The testament was an old and heavy one in leather binding, with dog's-eared edges, and it exhaled a smell as though monks had come into the hut. Sasha raised her eyebrows and began in a loud rhythmic chant:

" 'And the angel of the Lord . . . appeared unto Joseph, saying unto him: Rise up, and take the Babe and His mother.' "

"The Babe and His mother," Olga repeated, and flushed all over with emotion.

" 'And flee into Egypt, . . . and tarry there until such time as . . .' "

At the word "tarry" Olga could not refrain from tears. Looking at her, Marya began to whimper, and after her Ivan Makaritch's sister. The old father cleared his throat, and bustled about to find something to give his grand-daughter, but, finding nothing, gave it up with a wave of his hand. And when the reading was over the neighbours dispersed to their homes, feeling touched and very much pleased with Olga and Sasha.

As it was a holiday, the family spent the whole day at home. The old woman, whom her husband, her daughters-in-law, her grandchildren all alike called Granny, tried to do everything herself; she heated the stove and set the samovar with her own hands, even waited at the midday meal, and then complained that she was worn out with work. And all the time she was uneasy for fear someone should eat a piece too much, or that her husband and daughters-in-law would sit idle. At one time she would hear the tavern-keeper's geese going at the back of the huts to her kitchen-garden, and she would run out of the hut with a long stick and spend half an hour screaming shrilly by her cabbages, which were as gaunt and scraggy as herself; at another time she fancied that a crow had designs on her chickens, and she rushed to attack it with loud words of abuse. She was cross and grumbling from morning till night. And often she raised such an outcry that passers-by stopped in the street.

She was not affectionate towards the old man, reviling him as a lazy-bones and a plague. He was not a responsible, reliable peasant, and perhaps if she had not been continually nagging at him he would not have worked at all, but would have simply sat on the stove and talked. He talked to his son at great length about certain enemies of his, complained of the insults he said he had to put up with every day from the neighbours, and it was tedious to listen to him.

"Yes," he would say, standing with his arms akimbo, "yes. . . . A week after the Exaltation of the Cross I sold my hay willingly at thirty kopecks a pood. . . . Well and good. . . . So you see I was taking the hay in the morning with a good will; I was interfering with no one. In an unlucky hour I see the village elder, Antip Syedelnikov, coming out of the tavern. 'Where are you taking it, you ruffian?' says he, and takes me by the ear."

Kiryak had a fearful headache after his drinking bout, and was ashamed to face his brother.

"What vodka does! Ah, my God!" he muttered, shaking his aching head. "For Christ's sake, forgive me, brother and sister; I'm not happy myself."

As it was a holiday, they bought a herring at the tavern and made a soup of the herring's head. At midday they all sat down to drink tea, and went on drinking it for a long time, till they were all perspiring; they looked positively swollen from the tea-drinking, and after it began sipping the broth from the herring's head, all helping themselves out of one bowl. But the herring itself Granny had hidden.

In the evening a potter began firing pots on the ravine. In the meadow below the girls got up a choral dance and sang songs. They played the concertina. And on the other side of the river a kiln for baking pots was lighted, too, and the girls sang songs, and in the distance the singing sounded soft and musical. The peasants were noisy in and about the tavern. They were singing with drunken voices, each on his own account, and swearing at one another, so that Olga could only shudder and say:

"Oh, holy Saints!"

She was amazed that the abuse was incessant, and those who were loudest and most persistent in this foul language were the old men who were so near their end. And the girls and children heard the swearing, and were not in the least disturbed by it, and it was evident that they were used to it from their cradles.

It was past midnight, the kilns on both sides of the river were put out, but in the meadow below and in the tavern the merrymaking still went on. The old father and Kiryak, both drunk, walking arm-in-arm and jostling against each other's shoulders, went to the barn where Olga and Marya were lying.

"Let her alone," the old man persuaded him; "let her alone. . . . She is a harmless woman. . . . It's a sin . . ."

"Ma-arya!" shouted Kiryak.

"Let her be. . . . It's a sin. . . . She is not a bad woman."

Both stopped by the barn and went on.

"I lo-ove the flowers of the fi-ield," the old man began singing suddenly in a high, piercing tenor. "I lo-ove to gather them in the meadows!"

Then he spat, and with a filthy oath went into the hut.

IV

Granny put Sasha by her kitchen-garden and told her to keep watch that the geese did not go in. It was a hot August day. The tavern-keeper's geese could make their way into the kitchen-garden by the backs of the huts, but now they were busily engaged picking up oats by the tavern, peacefully conversing together, and only the gander craned his head high as though trying to see whether the old woman were coming with her stick. The other geese might come up from below, but they were now grazing far away the other side of the river, stretched out in a long white garland about the meadow. Sasha stood about a little, grew weary, and, seeing that the geese were not coming, went away to the ravine.

There she saw Marya's eldest daughter Motka, who was standing motionless on a big stone, staring at the church. Marya had given birth to thirteen children, but she only had six living, all girls, not one boy, and the eldest was eight. Motka, in a long smock, was standing barefooted in the full sunshine; the sun was blazing down right on her head, but she did not notice that, and seemed as though turned to stone. Sasha stood beside her and said, looking at the church:

"God lives in the church. Men have lamps and candles, but God has little green and red and blue lamps like little eyes. At night God walks about the church, and with Him the Holy Mother of God and Saint Nikolay, thud, thud, thud! . . . And the watchman is terrified, terrified! Aye, aye, dearie," she added, imitating her mother. "And when the end of the world comes all the churches will be carried up to heaven."

"With the-ir be-ells?" Motka asked in her deep voice, drawling every syllable.

"With their bells. And when the end of the world comes the good will go to Paradise, but the angry will burn in fire eternal and unquenchable, dearie. To my mother as well as to Marya God will say: 'You never offended anyone, and for that go to the right to Paradise'; but to Kiryak and Granny He will say: 'You go to the left into the fire.' And anyone who has eaten meat in Lent will go into the fire, too."

She looked upwards at the sky, opening wide her eyes, and said:

"Look at the sky without winking, you will see angels."

Motka began looking at the sky, too, and a minute passed in silence.

"Do you see them?" asked Sasha.

"I don't," said Motka in her deep voice.

"But I do. Little angels are flying about the sky and flap, flap with their little wings as though they were gnats."

Motka thought for a little, with her eyes on the ground, and asked:

"Will Granny burn?"

"She will, dearie."

From the stone an even gentle slope ran down to the bottom, covered with soft green grass, which one longed to lie down on or to touch with one's hands. . . . Sasha lay down and rolled to the bottom. Motka with a grave, severe face, taking a deep breath, lay down, too, and rolled to the bottom, and in doing so tore her smock from the hem to the shoulder.

"What fun it is!" said Sasha, delighted.

They walked up to the top to roll down again, but at that moment they heard a shrill, familiar voice. Oh, how awful it was! Granny, a toothless, bony, hunchbacked figure, with short grey hair which was fluttering in the wind, was driving the geese out of the kitchen-garden with a long stick, shouting.

"They have trampled all the cabbages, the damned brutes! I'll cut your throats, thrice accursed plagues! Bad luck to you!"

She saw the little girls, flung down the stick and picked up a switch, and, seizing Sasha by the neck with her fingers, thin and hard as the gnarled branches of a tree, began whipping her. Sasha cried with pain and terror, while the gander, waddling and stretching his neck, went up to the old woman and hissed at her, and when he went back to his flock all the geese greeted him approvingly with "Ga-ga-ga!" Then Granny proceeded to whip Motka, and in this Motka's smock was torn again. Feeling in despair, and crying loudly, Sasha went to the hut to complain. Motka followed her; she, too, was crying on a deeper note, without wiping her tears, and her face was as wet as though it had been dipped in water.

"Holy Saints!" cried Olga, aghast, as the two came into the hut. "Queen of Heaven!"

Sasha began telling her story, while at the same time Granny walked in with a storm of shrill cries and abuse; then Fyokla flew into a rage, and there was an uproar in the hut.

"Never mind, never mind!" Olga, pale and upset, tried to comfort them, stroking Sasha's head. "She is your grandmother; it's a sin to be angry with her. Never mind, my child."

Nikolay, who was worn out already by the everlasting hubbub, hunger, stifling fumes, filth, who hated and despised the poverty, who was ashamed for his wife and daughter to see his father and mother, swung his legs off the stove and said in an irritable, tearful voice, addressing his mother:

"You must not beat her! You have no right to beat her!"

"You lie rotting on the stove, you wretched creature!" Fyokla shouted at him spitefully. "The devil brought you all on us, eating us out of house and home."

Sasha and Motka and all the little girls in the hut huddled on the stove in the corner behind Nikolay's back, and from that refuge listened in silent terror, and the beating of their little hearts could be distinctly heard. Whenever there is someone in a family who has long been ill, and hopelessly ill, there come painful moments when all timidly, secretly, at the bottom of their hearts long for his death; and only the children fear the death of someone near them, and always feel horrified at the thought of it. And now the children, with bated breath, with a mournful look on their faces, gazed at Nikolay and thought that he was soon to die; and they wanted to cry and to say something friendly and compassionate to him.

He pressed close to Olga, as though seeking protection, and said to her softly in a quavering voice:

"Olya darling, I can't stay here longer. It's more than I can bear. For God's sake, for Christ's sake, write to your sister Klavdia Abramovna. Let her sell and pawn everything she has; let her send us the money. We will go away from here. Oh, Lord," he went on miserably, "to have one peep at Moscow! If I could see it in my dreams, the dear place!"

And when the evening came on, and it was dark in the hut, it was so dismal that it was hard to utter a word. Granny, very ill-tempered, soaked some crusts of rye bread in a cup, and was a long time, a whole hour, sucking at them. Marya, after milking the cow, brought in a pail of milk and set it on a bench; then Granny poured it from the pail into a jug just as slowly and deliberately, evidently pleased that it was now the Fast of the Assumption, so that no one would drink milk and it would be left untouched. And she only poured out a very little in a saucer for Fyokla's baby. When Marya and she carried the jug down to the cellar Motka suddenly stirred, clambered down from the stove, and going to the bench where stood the wooden cup full of crusts, sprinkled into it some milk from the saucer.

Granny, coming back into the hut, sat down to her soaked crusts again, while Sasha and Motka, sitting on the stove, gazed at her, and they were glad that she had broken her fast and now would go to hell. They were comforted and lay down to sleep, and Sasha as she dozed off to sleep imagined the Day of Judgment: a huge fire was burning, somewhat like a potter's kiln, and the Evil One, with horns like a cow's, and black all over, was driving Granny into the fire with a long stick, just as Granny herself had been driving the geese.

V

On the day of the Feast of the Assumption, between ten and eleven in the evening, the girls and lads who were merrymaking in the meadow suddenly raised a clamour and outcry, and ran in the direction of the village; and those who were above on the edge of the ravine could not for the first moment make out what was the matter.

"Fire! Fire!" they heard desperate shouts from below. "The village is on fire!"

Those who were sitting above looked round, and a terrible and extraordinary spectacle met their eyes. On the thatched roof of one of the end cottages stood a column of flame, seven feet high, which curled round and scattered sparks in all directions as though it were a fountain. And all at once the whole roof burst into bright flame, and the crackling of the fire was audible.

The light of the moon was dimmed, and the whole village was by now bathed in a red quivering glow: black shadows moved over the ground, there was a smell of burning, and those who ran up from below were all gasping and could not speak for trembling; they jostled against each other, fell down, and they could hardly see in the unaccustomed light, and did not recognize each other. It was terrible. What seemed particularly dreadful was that doves were flying over the fire in the smoke; and in the tavern, where they did not yet know of the fire, they were still singing and playing the concertina as though there were nothing the matter.

"Uncle Semyon's on fire," shouted a loud, coarse voice.

Marya was fussing about round her hut, weeping and wringing her hands, while her teeth chattered, though the fire was a long way off at the other end of the village. Nikolay came out in high felt boots, the children ran out in their little smocks. Near the village constable's hut an iron sheet was struck. Boom, boom, boom! . . . floated through the air, and this repeated, persistent sound sent a pang to the heart and turned one cold. The old women stood with the holy ikons. Sheep, calves, cows were driven out of the back-yards into the street; boxes, sheepskins, tubs were carried out. A black stallion, who was kept apart from the drove of horses because he kicked and injured them, on being set free ran once or twice up and down the village, neighing and paw-ing the ground; then suddenly stopped short near a cart and began kicking it with his hind-legs.

They began ringing the bells in the church on the other side of the river.

Near the burning hut it was hot and so light that one could distinctly see every blade of grass. Semyon, a red-haired peasant with a long nose, wearing a reefer-jacket and a cap pulled down right over his ears, sat on one of the boxes which they had succeeded in bringing out: his wife was lying on her face, moaning and unconscious. A little old man of eighty, with a big beard, who looked like a gnome—not one of the villagers, though obviously connected in some way with the fire—walked about bareheaded, with a white bundle in his arms. The glare was reflected on his bald head. The village elder, Antip Syedelnikov, as swarthy and black-haired as a gypsy, went up to the hut with an axe, and hacked out the windows one after another—no one knew why—then began chopping up the roof.

"Women, water!" he shouted. "Bring the engine! Look sharp!"

The peasants, who had been drinking in the tavern just before, dragged the engine up. They were all drunk; they kept stumbling and falling down, and all had a helpless expression and tears in their eyes.

"Wenches, water!" shouted the elder, who was drunk, too. "Look sharp, wenches!"

The women and the girls ran downhill to where there was a spring, and kept hauling pails and buckets of water up the hill, and, pouring it into the engine, ran down again. Olga and Marya and Sasha and Motka all brought water. The women and the boys pumped the water; the pipe hissed, and the elder, directing it now at the door, now at the windows, held back the stream with his finger, which made it hiss more sharply still.

"Bravo, Antip!" voices shouted approvingly. "Do your best."

Antip went inside the hut into the fire and shouted from within.

"Pump! Bestir yourselves, good Christian folk, in such a terrible mischance!"

The peasants stood round in a crowd, doing nothing but staring at the fire. No one knew what to do, no one had the sense to do anything, though there were stacks of wheat, hay, barns, and piles of faggots standing all round. Kiryak and old Osip, his father, both tipsy, were standing there, too. And as though to justify his doing nothing, old Osip said, addressing the woman who lay on the ground:

"What is there to trouble about, old girl! The hut is insured—why are you taking on?"

Semyon, addressing himself first to one person and then to another, kept describing how the fire had started.

"That old man, the one with the bundle, a house-serf of General Zhukov's. . . . He was cook at our general's, God rest his soul! He came over this evening: 'Let me stay the night,' says he. . . . Well, we had a glass, to be sure. . . . The wife got the samovar—she was going to give the old fellow a cup of tea, and in an unlucky hour she set the samovar in the entrance. The sparks from the chimney must have blown straight up to the thatch; that's how it was. We were almost burnt ourselves. And the old fellow's cap has been burnt; what a shame!"

And the sheet of iron was struck indefatigably, and the bells kept ringing in the church the other side of the river. In the glow of the fire Olga, breathless, looking with horror at the red sheep and the pink doves flying in the smoke, kept running down the hill and up again. It seemed to her that the ringing went to her heart with a sharp stab, that the fire would never be over, that Sasha was lost. . . . And when the ceiling of the hut fell in with a crash, the thought that now the whole village would be burnt made her weak and faint, and she could not go on fetching water, but sat down on the ravine, setting the pail down near her; beside her and below her, the peasant women sat wailing as though at a funeral.

Then the stewards and watchmen from the estate the other side of the river arrived in two carts, bringing with them a fire-engine. A very young student in an unbuttoned white tunic rode up on horseback. There was the thud of axes. They put a ladder to the burning framework of the house, and five men ran up it at once. Foremost of them all was the student, who was red in the face and shouting in a harsh hoarse voice, and in a tone as though putting out fires was a thing he was used to. They pulled the house to pieces, a beam at a time; they dragged away the corn, the hurdles, and the stacks that were near.

"Don't let them break it up!" cried stern voices in the crowd. "Don't let them."

Kiryak made his way up to the hut with a resolute air, as though he meant to prevent the newcomers from breaking up the hut, but one of the workmen turned him back with a blow in his neck. There was the sound of laughter, the workman dealt him another blow, Kiryak fell down, and crawled back into the crowd on his hands and knees.

Two handsome girls in hats, probably the student's sisters, came from the other side of the river. They stood a little way off, looking at the fire. The beams that had been dragged apart were no longer burning, but were smoking vigorously; the student, who was working the hose, turned the water, first on the beams, then on the peasants, then on the women who were bringing the water.

"George!" the girls called to him reproachfully in anxiety, "George!"

The fire was over. And only when they began to disperse they noticed that the day was breaking, that everyone was pale and rather dark in the face, as it always seems in the early morning when the last stars are going out. As they separated, the peasants laughed and made jokes about General Zhukov's cook and his cap which had been burnt; they already wanted to turn the fire into a joke, and even seemed sorry that it had so soon been put out.

"How well you extinguished the fire, sir!" said Olga to the student. "You ought to come to us in Moscow: there we have a fire every day."

"Why, do you come from Moscow?" asked one of the young ladies.

"Yes, miss. My husband was a waiter at the Slavyansky Bazaar. And this is my daughter," she said, indicating Sasha, who was cold and huddling up to her. "She is a Moscow girl, too."

The two young ladies said something in French to the student, and he gave Sasha a twenty-kopeck piece.

Old Father Osip saw this, and there was a gleam of hope in his face.

"We must thank God, your honour, there was no wind," he said, addressing the student, "or else we should have been all burnt up together. Your honour, kind gentlefolks," he added in embarrassment in a lower tone, "the morning's chilly . . . something to warm one . . . half a bottle to your honour's health."

Nothing was given him, and clearing his throat he slouched home. Olga stood afterwards at the end of the street and watched the two carts crossing the river by the ford and the gentlefolks walking across the meadow; a carriage was waiting for them the other side of the river. Going into the hut, she described to her husband with enthusiasm:

"Such good people! And so beautiful! The young ladies were like cherubim."

"Plague take them!" Fyokla, sleepy, said spitefully.

VI

Marya thought herself unhappy, and said that she would be very glad to die; Fyokla, on the other hand, found all this life to her taste: the poverty, the uncleanliness, and the incessant quarrelling. She ate what was given her without discrimination; slept anywhere, on whatever came to hand. She would empty the slops just at the porch, would splash them out from the doorway, and then walk barefoot through the puddle. And from the very first day she took a dislike to Olga and Nikolay just because they did not like this life.

"We shall see what you'll find to eat here, you Moscow gentry!" she said malignantly. "We shall see!"

One morning, it was at the beginning of September, Fyokla, vigorous, good-looking, and rosy from the cold, brought up two pails of water; Marya and Olga were sitting meanwhile at the table drinking tea.

"Tea and sugar," said Fyokla sarcastically. "The fine ladies!" she added, setting down the pails. "You have taken to the fashion of tea every day. You better look out that you don't burst with your tea-drinking," she went on, looking with hatred at Olga. "That's how you have come by your fat mug, having a good time in Moscow, you lump of flesh!" She swung the yoke and hit Olga such a blow on the shoulder that the two sisters-in-law could only clasp their hands and say:

"Oh, holy Saints!"

Then Fyokla went down to the river to wash the clothes, swearing all the time so loudly that she could be heard in the hut.

The day passed and was followed by the long autumn evening. They wound silk in the hut; everyone did it except Fyokla; she had gone over the river. They got the silk from a factory close by, and the whole family working together earned next to nothing, twenty kopecks a week.

"Things were better in the old days under the gentry," said the old father as he wound silk. "You worked and ate and slept, everything in its turn. At dinner you had cabbage-soup and boiled grain, and at supper the same again. Cucumbers and cabbage in plenty: you could eat to your heart's content, as much as you wanted. And there was more strictness. Everyone minded what he was about."

The hut was lighted by a single little lamp, which burned dimly and smoked. When someone screened the lamp and a big shadow fell across the window, the bright moonlight could be seen. Old Osip, speaking slowly, told them how they used to live before the emancipation; how in those very parts, where life was now so poor and so dreary, they used to hunt with harriers, greyhounds, retrievers, and when they went out as beaters the peasants were given vodka; how whole waggonloads of game used to be sent to Moscow for the young masters; how the bad were beaten with rods or sent away to the Tver estate, while the good were rewarded. And Granny told them something, too. She remembered everything, positively everything. She described her mistress, a kind, God-fearing woman, whose husband was a profligate and a rake, and all of whose daughters made unlucky marriages: one married a drunkard, another married a workman, the other eloped secretly (Granny herself, at that time a young girl, helped in the elopement), and they had all three as well as their mother died early from grief. And remembering all this, Granny positively began to shed tears.

All at once someone knocked at the door, and they all started.

"Uncle Osip, give me a night's lodging."

The little bald old man, General Zhukov's cook, the one whose cap had been burnt, walked in. He sat down and listened, then he, too, began telling stories of all sorts. Nikolay, sitting on the stove with his legs hanging down, listened and asked questions about the dishes that were prepared in the old days for the gentry. They talked of rissoles, cutlets, various soups and sauces, and the cook, who remembered everything very well, mentioned dishes that are no longer served. There was one, for instance—a dish made of bulls' eyes, which was called "waking up in the morning."

"And used you to do cutlets *à la maréchal*?" asked Nikolay.

"No."

Nikolay shook his head reproachfully and said:

"Tut, tut! You were not much of a cook!"

The little girls sitting and lying on the stove stared down without blinking; it seemed as though there were a great many of them, like cherubim in the clouds. They liked the stories: they were breathless;

they shuddered and turned pale with alternate rapture and terror, and they listened breathlessly, afraid to stir, to Granny, whose stories were the most interesting of all.

They lay down to sleep in silence; and the old people, troubled and excited by their reminiscences, thought how precious was youth, of which, whatever it might have been like, nothing was left in the memory but what was living, joyful, touching, and how terribly cold was death, which was not far off, better not think of it! The lamp died down. And the dusk, and the two little windows sharply defined by the moonlight, and the stillness and the creak of the cradle, reminded them for some reason that life was over, that nothing one could do would bring it back. . . . You doze off, you forget yourself, and suddenly someone touches your shoulder or breathes on your cheek—and sleep is gone; your body feels cramped, and thoughts of death keep creeping into your mind. You turn on the other side: death is forgotten, but old dreary, sickening thoughts of poverty, of food, of how dear flour is getting, stray through the mind, and a little later again you remember that life is over and you cannot bring it back. . . .

"Oh, Lord!" sighed the cook.

Someone gave a soft, soft tap at the window. It must be Fyokla come back. Olga got up, and yawning and whispering a prayer, opened the door, then drew the bolt in the outer room, but no one came in; only from the street came a cold draught and a sudden brightness from the moonlight. The street, still and deserted, and the moon itself floating across the sky, could be seen at the open door.

"Who is there?" called Olga.

"I," she heard the answer—"it is I."

Near the door, crouching against the wall, stood Fyokla, absolutely naked. She was shivering with cold, her teeth were chattering, and in the bright moonlight she looked very pale, strange, and beautiful. The shadows on her, and the bright moonlight on her skin, stood out vividly, and her dark eyebrows and firm, youthful bosom were defined with peculiar distinctness.

"The ruffians over there undressed me and turned me out like this," she said. "I've come home without my clothes . . . naked as my mother bore me. Bring me something to put on."

"But go inside!" Olga said softly, beginning to shiver, too.

"I don't want the old folks to see." Granny was, in fact, already stirring and muttering, and the old father asked: "Who is there?" Olga brought her own smock and skirt, dressed Fyokla, and then both went softly into the inner room, trying not to make a noise with the door.

"Is that you, you sleek one?" Granny grumbled angrily, guessing who it was. "Fie upon you, nightwalker! . . . Bad luck to you!"

"It's all right, it's all right," whispered Olga, wrapping Fyokla up; "it's all right, dearie."

All was stillness again. They always slept badly; everyone was kept awake by something worrying and persistent: the old man by the pain in his back, Granny by anxiety and anger, Marya by terror, the children by itch and hunger. Now, too, their sleep was troubled; they kept turning over from one side to the other, talking in their sleep, getting up for a drink.

Fyokla suddenly broke into a loud, coarse howl, but immediately checked herself, and only uttered sobs from time to time, growing softer and on a lower note, until she relapsed into silence. From time to time from the other side of the river there floated the sound of the beating of the hours; but the time seemed somehow strange—five was struck and then three.

"Oh Lord!" sighed the cook.

Looking at the windows, it was difficult to tell whether it was still moonlight or whether the dawn had begun. Marya got up and went out, and she could be heard milking the cows and saying, "Stea-dy!" Granny went out, too. It was still dark in the hut, but all the objects in it could be discerned.

Nikolay, who had not slept all night, got down from the stove. He took his dress-coat out of a green box, put it on, and going to the window, stroked the sleeves and took hold of the coat-tails—and smiled. Then he carefully took off the coat, put it away in his box, and lay down again.

Marya came in again and began lighting the stove. She was evidently hardly awake, and seemed dropping asleep as she walked. Probably she had had some dream, or the stories of the night before came into her mind as, stretching luxuriously before the stove, she said:

"No, freedom is better."

The master arrived—that was what they called the police inspector. When he would come and what he was coming for had been known for the last week. There were only forty households in Zhukovo, but more than two thousand roubles of arrears of rates and taxes had accumulated.

The police inspector stopped at the tavern. He drank there two glasses of tea, and then went on foot to the village elder's hut, near which a crowd of those who were in debt stood waiting. The elder, Antip Syedelnikov, was, in spite of his youth—he was only a little over thirty—strict and always on the side of the authorities, though he himself was poor and did not pay his taxes regularly. Evidently he enjoyed being elder, and liked the sense of authority, which he could only display by strictness. In the village council the peasants were afraid of him and obeyed him. It would sometimes happen that he would pounce on a drunken man in the street or near the tavern, tie his hands behind him, and put him in the lock-up. On one occasion he even put Granny in the lock-up because she went to the village council instead of Osip, and began swearing, and he kept her there for a whole day and night. He had never lived in a town or read a book, but somewhere or other had picked up various learned expressions, and loved to make use of them in conversation, and he was respected for this though he was not always understood.

When Osip came into the village elder's hut with his tax book, the police inspector, a lean old man with a long grey beard, in a grey tunic, was sitting at a table in the passage, writing something. It was clean in the hut; all the walls were dotted with pictures cut out of the illustrated papers, and in the most conspicuous place near the ikon there was a portrait of the Battenburg who was the Prince of Bulgaria. By the table stood Antip Syedelnikov with his arms folded.

"There is one hundred and nineteen roubles standing against him," he said when it came to Osip's turn. "Before Easter he paid a rouble, and he has not paid a kopeck since."

The police inspector raised his eyes to Osip and asked:

"Why is this, brother?"

"Show Divine mercy, your honour," Osip began, growing agitated. "Allow me to say last year the gentleman at Lutorydsky said to me,

'Osip,' he said, 'sell your hay . . . you sell it,' he said. Well, I had a hundred poods for sale; the women mowed it on the water-meadow. Well, we struck a bargain all right, willingly. . . ."

He complained of the elder, and kept turning round to the peasants as though inviting them to bear witness; his face flushed red and perspired, and his eyes grew sharp and angry.

"I don't know why you are saying all this," said the police inspector. "I am asking you . . . I am asking you why you don't pay your arrears. You don't pay, any of you, and am I to be responsible for you?"

"I can't do it."

"His words have no sequel, your honour," said the elder. "The Tchikildyeevs certainly are of a defective class, but if you will just ask the others, the root of it all is vodka, and they are a very bad lot. With no sort of understanding."

The police inspector wrote something down, and said to Osip quietly, in an even tone, as though he were asking him for water:

"Be off."

Soon he went away; and when he got into his cheap chaise and cleared his throat, it could be seen from the very expression of his long thin back that he was no longer thinking of Osip or of the village elder, nor the Zhukovo arrears, but was thinking of his own affairs. Before he had gone three-quarters of a mile Antip was already carrying off the samovar from the Tchikildyeevs' cottage, followed by Granny, screaming shrilly and straining her throat:

"I won't let you have it, I won't let you have it, damn you!"

He walked rapidly with long steps, and she pursued him panting, almost falling over, a bent, ferocious figure; her kerchief slipped on to her shoulders, her grey hair with greenish lights on it was blown about in the wind. She suddenly stopped short, and like a genuine rebel, fell to beating her breast with her fists and shouting louder than ever in a sing-song voice, as though she were sobbing:

"Good Christians and believers in God! Neighbours, they have ill-treated me! Kind friends, they have oppressed me! Oh, oh! dear people, take my part."

"Granny, Granny!" said the village elder sternly, "have some sense in your head!"

It was hopelessly dreary in the Tchikildyeevs' hut without the samovar; there was something humiliating in this loss, insulting, as though the honour of the hut had been outraged. Better if the elder had carried off the table, all the benches, all the pots—it would not have seemed so empty. Granny screamed, Marya cried, and the little girls, looking at her, cried, too. The old father, feeling guilty, sat in the corner with bowed head and said nothing. And Nikolay, too, was silent. Granny loved him and was sorry for him, but now, forgetting her pity, she fell upon him with abuse, with reproaches, shaking her fist right in his face. She shouted that it was all his fault; why had he sent them so little when he boasted in his letters that he was getting fifty roubles a month at the Slavyansky Bazaar ? Why had he come, and with his family, too? If he died, where was the money to come from for his funeral . . . ? And it was pitiful to look at Nikolay, Olga, and Sasha.

The old father cleared his throat, took his cap, and went off to the village elder. Antip was soldering something by the stove, puffing out his cheeks; there was a smell of burning. His children, emaciated and unwashed, no better than the Tchikildyeevs, were scrambling about the floor; his wife, an ugly, freckled woman with a prominent stomach, was winding silk. They were a poor, unlucky family, and Antip was the only one who looked vigorous and handsome. On a bench there were five samovars standing in a row. The old man said his prayer to Battenburg and said:

"Antip, show the Divine mercy. Give me back the samovar, for Christ's sake!"

"Bring three roubles, then you shall have it."

"I can't do it!"

Antip puffed out his cheeks, the fire roared and hissed, and the glow was reflected in the samovar. The old man crumpled up his cap and said after a moment's thought:

"You give it me back."

The swarthy elder looked quite black, and was like a magician; he turned round to Osip and said sternly and rapidly:

"It all depends on the rural captain. On the twenty-sixth instant you can state the grounds for your dissatisfaction before the administrative session, verbally or in writing."

Osip did not understand a word, but he was satisfied with that and went home.

Ten days later the police inspector came again, stayed an hour and went away. During those days the weather had changed to cold and windy; the river had been frozen for some time past, but still there was no snow, and people found it difficult to get about. On the eve of a holiday some of the neighbours came in to Osip's to sit and have a talk. They did not light the lamp, as it would have been a sin to work, but talked in the darkness. There were some items of news, all rather unpleasant. In two or three households hens had been taken for the arrears, and had been sent to the district police station, and there they had died because no one had fed them; they had taken sheep, and while they were being driven away tied to one another, shifted into another cart at each village, one of them had died. And now they were discussing the question, who was to blame?

"The Zemstvo," said Osip. "Who else?"

"Of course it is the Zemstvo."

The Zemstvo was blamed for everything—for the arrears, and for the oppressions, and for the failure of the crops, though no one of them knew what was meant by the Zemstvo. And this dated from the time when well-to-do peasants who had factories, shops, and inns of their own were members of the Zemstvos, were dissatisfied with them, and took to swearing at the Zemstvos in their factories and inns.

They talked of God's not sending the snow; they had to bring in wood for fuel, and there was no driving nor walking in the frozen ruts. In old days fifteen to twenty years ago conversation was much more interesting in Zhukovo. In those days every old man looked as though he were treasuring some secret; as though he knew something and was expecting something. They used to talk about an edict in golden letters, about the division of lands, about new land, about treasures; they hinted at something. Now the people of Zhukovo had no mystery at all; their whole life was bare and open in the sight of all, and they could talk of nothing but poverty, food, there being no snow yet. . . .

There was a pause. Then they thought again of the hens, of the sheep, and began discussing whose fault it was.

"The Zemstvo," said Osip wearily. "Who else?"

VIII

The parish church was nearly five miles away at Kosogorovo, and the peasants only attended it when they had to do so for baptisms, weddings, or funerals; they went to the services at the church across the river. On holidays in fine weather the girls dressed up in their best and went in a crowd together to church, and it was a cheering sight to see them in their red, yellow, and green dresses cross the meadow; in bad weather they all stayed at home. They went for the sacrament to the parish church. From each of those who did not manage in Lent to go to confession in readiness for the sacrament the parish priest, going the round of the huts with the cross at Easter, took fifteen kopecks.

The old father did not believe in God, for he hardly ever thought about Him; he recognized the supernatural, but considered it was entirely the women's concern, and when religion or miracles were discussed before him, or a question were put to him, he would say reluctantly, scratching himself:

"Who can tell!"

Granny believed, but her faith was somewhat hazy; everything was mixed up in her memory, and she could scarcely begin to think of sins, of death, of the salvation of the soul, before poverty and her daily cares took possession of her mind, and she instantly forgot what she was thinking about. She did not remember the prayers, and usually in the evenings, before lying down to sleep, she would stand before the ikons and whisper:

"Holy Mother of Kazan, Holy Mother of Smolensk, Holy Mother of Troerutchitsy. . . ."

Marya and Fyokla crossed themselves, fasted and took the sacrament every year, but understood nothing. The children were not taught their prayers, nothing was told them about God, and no moral principles were instilled into them; they were only forbidden to eat meat or milk in Lent. In the other families it was much the same: there were few who believed, few who understood. At the same time everyone loved the Holy Scripture, loved it with a tender, reverent love; but they had no Bible, there was no one to read it and explain it, and because Olga sometimes read them the gospel, they respected her, and they all addressed her and Sasha as though they were superior to themselves.

For church holidays and services Olga often went to neighboring villages, and to the district town, in which there were two monasteries and twenty-seven churches. She was dreamy, and when she was on these pilgrimages she quite forgot her family, and only when she got home again suddenly made the joyful discovery that she had a husband and daughter, and then would say, smiling and radiant:

"God has sent me blessings!"

What went on in the village worried her and seemed to her revolting. On Elijah's Day they drank, at the Assumption they drank, at the Ascension they drank. The Feast of the Intercession was the parish holiday for Zhukovo, and the peasants used to drink then for three days; they squandered on drink fifty roubles of money belonging to the Mir, and then collected more for vodka from all the households. On the first day of the feast the Tchikildyeevs killed a sheep and ate of it in the morning, at dinner-time, and in the evening; they ate it ravenously, and the children got up at night to eat more. Kiryak was fearfully drunk for three whole days; he drank up everything, even his boots and cap, and beat Marya so terribly that they had to pour water over her. And then they were all ashamed and sick.

However, even in Zhukovo, in this "Slaveytown," there was once an outburst of genuine religious enthusiasm. It was in August, when throughout the district they carried from village to village the Holy Mother, the giver of life. It was still and overcast on the day when they expected *Her* at Zhukovo. The girls set off in the morning to meet the ikon, in their bright holiday dresses, and brought Her towards the evening, in procession with the cross and with singing, while the bells pealed in the church across the river. An immense crowd of villagers and strangers flooded the street; there was noise, dust, a great crush. . . . And the old father and Granny and Kiryak—all stretched out their hands to the ikon, looked eagerly at it and said, weeping:

"Defender! Mother! Defender!"

All seemed suddenly to realize that there was not an empty void between earth and heaven, that the rich and the powerful had not taken possession of everything, that there was still a refuge from injury, from slavish bondage, from crushing, unendurable poverty, from the terrible vodka.

"Defender! Mother!" sobbed Marya. "Mother!"

But the thanksgiving service ended and the ikon was carried away, and everything went on as before; and again there was a sound of coarse drunken oaths from the tavern.

Only the well-to-do peasants were afraid of death; the richer they were the less they believed in God, and in the salvation of souls, and only through fear of the end of the world put up candles and had services said for them, to be on the safe side. The peasants who were rather poorer were not afraid of death. The old father and Granny were told to their faces that they had lived too long, that it was time they were dead, and they did not mind. They did not hinder Fyokla from saying in Nikolay's presence that when Nikolay died her husband Denis would get exemption to return home from the army. And Marya, far from fearing death, regretted that it was so slow in coming, and was glad when her children died.

Death they did not fear, but of every disease they had an exaggerated terror. The merest trifle was enough—a stomach upset, a slight chill, and Granny would be wrapped up on the stove, and would begin moaning loudly and incessantly:

"I am dy-ing!"

The old father hurried off for the priest, and Granny received the sacrament and extreme unction. They often talked of colds, of worms, of tumours which move in the stomach and coil round to the heart. Above all, they were afraid of catching cold, and so put on thick clothes even in the summer and warmed themselves at the stove. Granny was fond of being doctored, and often went to the hospital, where she used to say she was not seventy, but fifty-eight; she supposed that if the doctor knew her real age he would not treat her, but would say it was time she died instead of taking medicine. She usually went to the hospital early in the morning, taking with her two or three of the little girls, and came back in the evening, hungry and ill-tempered—with drops for herself and ointments for the little girls, Once she took Nikolay, who swallowed drops for a fortnight afterwards, and said he felt better.

Granny knew all the doctors and their assistants and the wise men for twenty miles round, and not one of them she liked. At the Intercession, when the priest made the round of the huts with the cross, the deacon told her that in the town near the prison lived an old man who had been a medical orderly in the army, and who made wonderful cures, and advised her to try him. Granny took his advice. When the first snow fell she drove to the town and fetched an old man with a big beard, a converted Jew, in a long gown, whose face was covered with blue veins. There were outsiders at work in the hut at the time: an old tailor, in terrible spectacles, was cutting a waistcoat out of some rags, and two young men were making felt boots out of wool; Kiryak, who had been dismissed from his place for drunkenness, and now lived at home, was sitting beside the tailor mending a bridle. And it was crowded, stifling, and noisome in the hut. The converted Jew examined Nikolay and said that it was necessary to try cupping.

He put on the cups, and the old tailor, Kiryak, and the little girls stood round and looked on, and it seemed to them that they saw the disease being drawn out of Nikolay; and Nikolay, too, watched how the cups suckling at his breast gradually filled with dark blood, and felt as though there really were something coming out of him, and smiled with pleasure.

"It's a good thing," said the tailor. "Please God, it will do you good."

The Jew put on twelve cups and then another twelve, drank some tea, and went away. Nikolay began shivering; his face looked drawn, and, as the women expressed it, shrank up like a fist; his fingers turned blue. He wrapped himself up in a quilt and in a sheepskin, but got colder and colder. Towards the evening he began to be in great distress; asked to be laid on the ground, asked the tailor not to smoke; then he subsided under the sheepskin and towards morning he died.

IX

Oh, what a grim, what a long winter!

Their own grain did not last beyond Christmas, and they had to buy flour. Kiryak, who lived at home now, was noisy in the evenings, inspiring terror in everyone, and in the mornings he suffered from headache and was ashamed; and he was a pitiful sight. In the stall the starved cows bellowed day and night—a heart-rending sound to Granny and Marya. And as ill-luck would have it, there was a sharp frost all the winter, the snow drifted in high heaps, and the winter dragged on. At Annunciation there was a regular blizzard, and there was a fall of snow at Easter.

But in spite of it all the winter did end. At the beginning of April there came warm days and frosty nights. Winter would not give way, but one warm day overpowered it at last, and the streams began to flow and the birds began to sing. The whole meadow and the bushes near the river were drowned in the spring floods, and all the space between Zhukovo and the further side was filled up with a vast sheet of water, from which wild ducks rose up in flocks here and there. The spring sunset, flaming among gorgeous clouds, gave every evening something new, extraordinary, incredible—just what one does not believe in afterwards, when one sees those very colours and those very clouds in a picture.

The cranes flew swiftly, swiftly, with mournful cries, as though they were calling themselves. Standing on the edge of the ravine, Olga looked a long time at the flooded meadow, at the sunshine, at the bright church, that looked as though it had grown younger; and her tears flowed and her breath came in gasps from her passionate longing to go away, to go far away to the end of the world. It was already settled that she should go back to Moscow to be a servant, and that Kiryak should set off with her to get a job as a porter or something. Oh, to get away quickly!

As soon as it dried up and grew warm they got ready to set off. Olga and Sasha, with wallets on their backs and shoes of plaited bark on their feet, came out before daybreak: Marya came out, too, to see them on their way. Kiryak was not well, and was kept at home for another week. For the last time Olga prayed at the church and thought of her husband, and though she did not shed tears, her face puckered up and looked ugly like an old woman's. During the winter she had grown thinner and plainer, and her hair had gone a little grey, and instead of the old look of sweetness and the pleasant smile on her face, she had the resigned, mournful expression left by the sorrows she had been through, and there was something blank and irresponsive in her eyes, as though she did not hear what was said. She was sorry to part from the village and the peasants. She remembered how they had carried out Nikolay, and how a requiem had been ordered for him at almost every hut, and all had shed tears in sympathy with her grief. In the course of the summer and the winter there had been hours and days when it seemed as though these people lived worse than the beasts, and to live with them was terrible; they were coarse, dishonest, filthy, and drunken; they did not live in harmony, but quarrelled continually, because they distrusted and feared and did not respect one another. Who keeps the tavern and makes the people drunken? A peasant. Who wastes and spends on drink the funds of the commune, of the schools, of the church? A peasant. Who stole from his neighbours, set fire to their property, gave false witness at the court for a bottle of vodka? At the meetings of the Zemstvo and other local bodies, who was the first to fall foul of the peasants? A peasant. Yes, to live with them was terrible; but yet, they were human beings, they suffered and wept like human beings, and there was nothing in their lives for which one could not find excuse. Hard labour that made the whole body ache at night, the cruel winters, the scanty harvests, the over-crowding; and they had no help and none to whom they could look for help. Those of them who were a little stronger and better off could be no help, as they were themselves coarse, dishonest, drunken, and abused one another just as revoltingly; the paltriest little clerk or offi-cial treated the peasants as though they were tramps, and addressed even the village elders and church wardens as inferiors, and consid-ered they had a right to do so. And, indeed, can any sort of help or good example be given by mercenary, greedy, depraved, and idle per-sons who only visit the village in order to insult, to despoil, and to ter-rorize? Olga remembered the pitiful, humiliated look of the old people when in the winter Kiryak had been taken to be flogged. . . . And now she felt sorry for all these people, painfully so, and as she walked on she kept looking back at the huts.

After walking two miles with them Marya said good-bye, then kneeling, and falling forward with her face on the earth, she began wailing:

"Again I am left alone. Alas, for poor me! poor, unhappy! . . ."

And she wailed like this for a long time, and for a long way Olga and Sasha could still see her on her knees, bowing down to someone at the side and clutching her head in her hands, while the rooks flew over her head.

The sun rose high; it began to get hot. Zhukovo was left far behind. Walking was pleasant. Olga and Sasha soon forgot both the village and Marya; they were gay and everything entertained them. Now they came upon an ancient barrow, now upon a row of telegraph posts running one after another into the distance and disappearing into the horizon, and the wires hummed mysteriously. Then they saw a homestead, all wreathed in green foliage; there came a scent from it of dampness, of hemp, and it seemed for some reason that happy peo-ple lived there. Then they came upon a horse's skeleton whitening in solitude in the open fields. And the larks trilled unceasingly, the corn-crakes called to one another, and the landrail cried as though some-one were really scraping at an old iron rail.

At midday Olga and Sasha reached a big village. There in the broad street they met the little old man who was General Zhukov's cook. He was hot, and his red, perspiring bald head shone in the sunshine. Olga and he did not recognize each other, then looked round at the same moment, recognized each other, and went their separate ways without saying a word. Stopping near the hut which looked newest and most prosperous, Olga bowed down before the open windows, and said in a loud, thin chanting voice:

"Good Christian folk, give alms, for Christ's sake, that God's blessing may be upon you, and that your parents may be in the Kingdom of Heaven in peace eternal."

"Good Christian folk," Sasha began chanting, "give, for Christ's sake, that God's blessing, the Heavenly Kingdom . . ."

1897

In the Ravine

I

The village of Ukleevo lay in a ravine so that only the belfry and the chimneys of the printed cottons factories could be seen from the high road and the railway-station. When visitors asked what village this was, they were told:

"That's the village where the deacon ate all the caviare at the funeral."

It had happened at the dinner at the funeral of Kostukov that the old deacon saw among the savouries some large-grained caviare and began eating it greedily; people nudged him, tugged at his arm, but he seemed petrified with enjoyment: felt nothing, and only went on eating. He ate up all the caviare, and there were four pounds in the jar. And years had passed since then, the deacon had long been dead, but the caviare was still remembered. Whether life was so poor here or people had not been clever enough to notice anything but that unimportant incident that had occurred ten years before, anyway the people had nothing else to tell about the village Ukleevo.

The village was never free from fever, and there was boggy mud there even in the summer, especially under the fences over which hung old willow-trees that gave deep shade. Here there was always a smell from the factory refuse and the acetic acid which was used in the finishing of the cotton print.

The three cotton factories and the tanyard were not in the village itself, but a little way off. They were small factories, and not more than four hundred workmen were employed in all of them. The tanyard often made the water in the little river stink; the refuse contaminated the meadows, the peasants' cattle suffered from Siberian plague, and orders were given that the factory should be closed. It was considered

573

to be closed, but went on working in secret with the connivance of the local police officer and the district doctor, who was paid ten roubles a month by the owner. In the whole village there were only two decent houses built of brick with iron roofs; one of them was the local court, in the other, a two-storeyed house just opposite the church, there lived a shopkeeper from Epifan called Grigory Petrovitch Tsybukin.

Grigory kept a grocer's shop, but that was only for appearance' sake: in reality he sold vodka, cattle, hides, grain, and pigs; he traded in anything that came to hand, and when, for instance, magpies were wanted abroad for ladies' hats, he made some thirty kopecks on every pair of birds; he bought timber for felling, lent money at interest, and altogether was a sharp old man, full of resources.

He had two sons. The elder, Anisim, was in the police in the detective department and was rarely at home. The younger, Stepan, had gone in for trade and helped his father: but no great help was expected from him as he was weak in health and deaf; his wife Aksinya, a handsome woman with a good figure, who wore a hat and carried a parasol on holidays, got up early and went to bed late, and ran about all day long, picking up her skirts and jingling her keys, going from the granary to the cellar and from there to the shop, and old Tsybukin looked at her good-humouredly while his eyes glowed, and at such moments he regretted she had not been married to his elder son instead of to the younger one, who was deaf, and who evidently knew very little about female beauty.

The old man had always an inclination for family life, and he loved his family more than anything on earth, especially his elder son, the detective, and his daughter-in-law. Aksinya had no sooner married the deaf son than she began to display an extraordinary gift for business, and knew who could be allowed to run up a bill and who could not: she kept the keys and would not trust them even to her husband; she kept the accounts by means of the reckoning beads, looked at the horses' teeth like a peasant, and was always laughing or shouting; and whatever she did or said the old man was simply delighted and muttered:

"Well done, daughter-in-law! You are a smart wench!"

He was a widower, but a year after his son's marriage he could not resist getting married himself. A girl was found for him, living twenty miles from Ukleevo, called Varvara Nikolaevna, no longer quite young, but good-looking, comely, and belonging to a decent family. As soon as she was installed into the upper-storey room everything in the house seemed to brighten up as though new glass had been put into all the windows. The lamps gleamed before the ikons, the tables were covered with snow-white cloths, flowers with red buds made their appearance in the windows and in the front garden, and at dinner, instead of eating from a single bowl, each person had a separate plate set for him. Varvara Nikolaevna had a pleasant, friendly smile, and it seemed as though the whole house were smiling, too. Beggars and pilgrims, male and female, began to come into the yard, a thing which had never happened in the past; the plaintive sing-song voices of the Ukleevo peasant women and the apologetic coughs of weak, seedy-looking men, who had been dismissed from the factory for drunkenness were heard under the windows. Varvara helped them with money, with bread, with old clothes, and afterwards, when she felt more at home, began taking things out of the shop. One day the deaf man saw her take four ounces of tea and that disturbed him.

"Here, mother's taken four ounces of tea," he informed his father afterwards; "where is that to be entered?"

The old man made no reply but stood still and thought a moment, moving his eyebrows, and then went upstairs to his wife.

"Varvarushka, if you want anything out of the shop," he said affectionately, "take it, my dear. Take it and welcome; don't hesitate."

And the next day the deaf man, running across the yard, called to her:

"If there is anything you want, mother, take it."

There was something new, something gay and light-hearted in her giving of alms, just as there was in the lamps before the ikons and in the red flowers. When at Carnival or at the church festival, which lasted for three days, they sold the peasants tainted salt meat, smelling so strong it was hard to stand near the tub of it, and took scythes, caps, and their wives' kerchiefs in pledge from the drunken men; when the factory hands stupefied with bad vodka lay rolling in the mud, and sin seemed to hover thick like a fog in the air, then it was a relief to think that up there in the house there was a gentle, neatly dressed woman who had nothing to do with salt meat or vodka; her charity had in those burdensome, murky days the effect of a safety valve in a machine.

The days in Tsybukin's house were spent in business cares. Before the sun had risen in the morning Aksinya was panting and puffing as she washed in the outer room, and the samovar was boiling in the kitchen with a hum that boded no good. Old Grigory Petrovitch, dressed in a long black coat, cotton breeches and shiny top boots, looking a dapper little figure, walked about the rooms, tapping with his little heels like the father-in-law in a well-known song. The shop was opened. When it was daylight a racing droshky was brought up to the front door and the old man got jauntily on to it, pulling his big cap down to his ears; and, looking at him, no one would have said he was fifty-six. His wife and daughter-in-law saw him off, and at such times when he had on a good, clean coat, and had in the droshky a huge black horse that had cost three hundred roubles, the old man did not like the peasants to come up to him with their complaints and petitions; he hated the peasants and disdained them, and if he saw some peasants waiting at the gate, he would shout angrily:

"Why are you standing there? Go further off."

Or if it were a beggar, he would say:

"God will provide!"

He used to drive off on business; his wife, in a dark dress and a black apron, tidied the rooms or helped in the kitchen. Aksinya attended to the shop, and from the yard could be heard the clink of bottles and of money, her laughter and loud talk, and the anger of customers whom she had offended; and at the same time it could be seen that the secret sale of vodka was already going on in the shop. The deaf man sat in the shop, too, or walked about the street bare-headed, with his hands in his pockets looking absent-mindedly now at the huts, now at the sky overhead. Six times a day they had tea; four times a day they sat down to meals; and in the evening they counted over their takings, put them down, went to bed, and slept soundly.

All the three cotton factories in Ukleevo and the houses of the factory owners—Hrymin Seniors, Hrymin Juniors, and Kostukov—were on a telephone. The telephone was laid on in the local court, too, but it soon ceased to work as bugs and beetles bred there. The elder of the rural district had had little education and wrote every word in the official documents in capitals. But when the telephone was spoiled he said:

"Yes, now we shall be badly off without a telephone."

The Hrymin Seniors were continually at law with the Juniors, and sometimes the Juniors quarrelled among themselves and began going to law, and their factory did not work for a month or two till they were reconciled again, and this was an entertainment for the people of Ukleevo, as there was a great deal of talk and gossip on the occasion of each quarrel. On holidays Kostukov and the Juniors used to get up races, used to dash about Ukleevo and run over calves. Aksinya, rustling her starched petticoats, used to promenade in a low-necked dress up and down the street near her shop; the Juniors used to snatch her up and carry her off as though by force. Then old Tsybukin would drive out to show his new horse and take Varvara with him.

In the evening, after the races, when people were going to bed, an expensive concertina was played in the Juniors' yard and, if it were a moonlight night, those sounds sent a thrill of delight to the heart, and Ukleevo no longer seemed a wretched hole.

II

The elder son Anisim came home very rarely, only on great holidays, but he often sent by a returning villager presents and letters written in very good writing by some other hand, always on a sheet of foolscap in the form of a petition. The letters were full of expressions that Anisim never made use of in conversation: "Dear papa and mamma, I send you a pound of flower tea for the satisfaction of your physical needs."

At the bottom of every letter was scratched, as though with a broken pen: "Anisim Tsybukin," and again in the same excellent hand: "Agent."

The letters were read aloud several times, and the old father, touched, red with emotion, would say:

"Here he did not care to stay at home, he has gone in for an intellectual line. Well, let him! Every man to his own job!"

It happened just before Carnival there was a heavy storm of rain mixed with hail; the old man and Varvara went to the window to look at it, and lo and behold! Anisim drove up in a sledge from the station. He was quite unexpected. He came indoors, looking anxious and troubled about something, and he remained the same all the time; there was something free and easy in his manner. He was in no haste to go away, it seemed, as though he had been dismissed from the service.

Varvara was pleased at his arrival; she looked at him with a sly expression, sighed, and shook her head.

"How is this, my friends?" she said. "Tut, tut, the lad's in his twenty-eighth year, and he is still leading a gay bachelor life; tut, tut, tut. . . ."

From the other room her soft, even speech sounded like tut, tut, tut. She began whispering with her husband and Aksinya, and their faces wore the same sly and mysterious expression as though they were conspirators.

It was decided to marry Anisim.

"Oh, tut, tut . . . the younger brother has been married long ago," said Varvara, "and you are still without a helpmate like a cock at a fair. What is the meaning of it? Tut, tut, you will be married, please God, then as you choose—you will go into the service and your wife will remain here at home to help us. There is no order in your life, young man, and I see you have forgotten how to live properly. Tut, tut, it's the same trouble with all you townspeople."

When the Tsybukins married, the most handsome girls were chosen as brides for them as rich men. For Anisim, too, they found a handsome one. He was himself of an uninteresting and inconspicuous appearance; of a feeble, sickly build and short stature; he had full, puffy cheeks which looked as though he were blowing them out; his eyes looked with a keen, unblinking stare; his beard was red and scanty, and when he was thinking he always put it into his mouth and bit it; moreover he often drank too much, and that was noticeable from his face and his walk. But when he was informed that they had found a very beautiful bride for him, he said:

"Oh well, I am not a fright myself. All of us Tsybukins are handsome, I may say."

The village of Torguevo was near the town. Half of it had lately been incorporated into the town, the other half remained a village. In the first—the town half—there was a widow living her own little house; she had a sister living with her who was quite poor and went out to work by the day, and this sister had a daughter called Lipa, a girl who went out to work, too. People in Torguevo were already talking about Lipa's good looks, but her terrible poverty put everyone off; people opined that some widower or elderly man would marry her regardless of her poverty, or would perhaps take her to himself without marriage, and that her mother would get enough to eat living with her. Varvara heard about Lipa from the matchmakers, and she drove over to Torguevo.

Then a visit of inspection was arranged at the aunt's, with lunch and wine all in due order, and Lipa wore a new pink dress made on purpose for this occasion, and a crimson ribbon like a flame gleamed in her hair. She was pale-faced, thin, and frail, with soft, delicate features sunburnt from working in the open air; a shy, mournful smile always hovered about her face, and there was a childlike look in her eyes, trustful and curious.

She was young, quite a little girl, her bosom still scarcely perceptible, but she could be married because she had reached the legal age. She really was beautiful, and the only thing that might be thought unattractive was her big masculine hands which hung idle now like two big claws.

"There is no dowry—and we don't think much of that," said Tsybukin to the aunt. "We took a wife from a poor family for our son Stepan, too, and now we can't say too much for her. In house and in business alike she has hands of gold."

Lipa stood in the doorway and looked as though she would say: "Do with me as you will, I trust you," while her mother Praskovya the work-woman hid herself in the kitchen numb with shyness. At one time in her youth a merchant whose floors she was scrubbing stamped at her in a rage; she went chill with terror and there always was a feeling of fear at the bottom of her heart. When she was frightened her arms and legs trembled and her cheeks twitched. Sitting in the kitchen she tried to hear what the visitors were saying, and she kept crossing herself, pressing her fingers to her forehead, and gazing at the ikons. Anisim, slightly drunk, opened the door into the kitchen and said in a free-and-easy way:

"Why are you sitting in here, precious mamma? We are dull without you."

And Praskovya, overcome with timidity, pressing her hands to her lean, wasted bosom, said:

"Oh, not at all. . . . It's very kind of you."

After the visit of inspection the wedding day was fixed. Then Anisim walked about the rooms at home whistling, or suddenly thinking of something, would fall to brooding and would look at the floor fixedly, silently, as though he would probe to the depths of the earth. He expressed neither pleasure that he was to be married, married so soon, on Low Sunday, nor a desire to see his bride, but simply went on whistling. And it was evident he was only getting married because his father and stepmother wished him to, and because it was the custom in the village to marry the son in order to have a woman to help in the house. When he went away he seemed in no haste, and behaved altogether not as he had done on previous visits—was particularly free and easy, and talked inappropriately.

III

In the village Shikalovo lived two dressmakers, sisters, belonging to the Flagellant sect. The new clothes for the wedding were ordered from them, and they often came to try them on, and stayed a long while drinking tea. They were making Varvara a brown dress with black lace and bugles on it, and Aksinya a light green dress with a yellow front, with a train. When the dressmakers had finished their work Tsybukin paid them not in money but in goods from the shop, and they went away depressed, carrying parcels of tallow candles and tins of sardines which they did not in the least need, and when they got out of the village into the open country they sat down on a hillock and cried.

Anisim arrived three days before the wedding, rigged out in new clothes from top to toe. He had dazzling india-rubber goloshes, and instead of a cravat wore a red cord with little balls on it, and over his shoulder he had hung an overcoat, also new, without putting his arms into the sleeves.

After crossing himself sedately before the ikon, he greeted his father and gave him ten silver roubles and ten half-roubles; to Varvara he gave as much, and to Aksinya twenty quarter-roubles. The chief charm of the present lay in the fact that all the coins, as though carefully matched, were new and glittered in the sun. Trying to seem grave and sedate he pursed up his face and puffed out his cheeks, and he smelt of spirits. Probably he had visited the refreshment bar at every station. And again there was a free-and-easiness about the man—something superfluous and out of place. Then Anisim had lunch and drank tea with the old man, and Varvara turned the new coins over in her hand and inquired about villagers who had gone to live in the town.

"They are all right, thank God, they get on quite well," said Anisim. "Only something has happened to Ivan Yegorov: his old wife Sofya Nikiforovna is dead. From consumption. They ordered the memorial dinner for the peace of her soul at the confectioner's at two and a half roubles a head. And there was real wine. Those who were peasants from our village—they paid two and a half roubles for them, too. They ate nothing, as though a peasant would understand sauce!"

"Two and a half," said his father, shaking his head.

"Well, it's not like the country there, you go into a restaurant to have a snack of something, you ask for one thing and another, others join till there is a party of us, one has a drink—and before you know where you are it is daylight and you've three or four roubles each to pay. And when one is with Samorodov he likes to have coffee with brandy in it after everything, and brandy is sixty kopecks for a little glass."

"And he is making it all up," said the old man enthusiastically; "he is making it all up, lying!"

"I am always with Samorodov now. It is Samorodov who writes my letters to you. He writes splendidly. And if I were to tell you, mamma," Anisim went on gaily, addressing Varvara, "the sort of fellow that Samorodov is, you would not believe me. We call him Muhtar, because he is black like an Armenian. I can see through him, I know all his affairs like the five fingers of my hand, and he feels that, and he always follows me about, we are regular inseparables. He seems not to like it in a way, but he can't get on without me. Where I go he goes. I have a correct, trustworthy eye, mamma. One sees a peasant selling a shirt in the market place. 'Stay, that shirt's stolen.' And really it turns out it is so: the shirt was a stolen one."

"What do you tell from?" asked Varvara.

"Not from anything, I have just an eye for it. I know nothing about the shirt, only for some reason I seem drawn to it: it's stolen, and that's all I can say. Among us detectives it's come to their saying, 'Oh, Anisim has gone to shoot snipe!' That means looking for stolen goods. Yes. . . . Anybody can steal, but it is another thing to keep! The earth is wide, but there is nowhere to hide stolen goods."

"In our village a ram and two ewes were carried off last week," said Varvara, and she heaved a sigh, "and there is no one to try and find them. . . . Oh, tut, tut. . . ."

"Well, I might have a try. I don't mind."

The day of the wedding arrived. It was a cool but bright, cheerful April day. People were driving about Ukleevo from early morning with pairs or teams of three horses decked with many-coloured ribbons on their yokes and manes, with a jingle of bells. The rooks, disturbed by this activity, were cawing noisily in the willows, and the starlings sang their loudest unceasingly as though rejoicing that there was a wedding at the Tsybukins'.

Indoors the tables were already covered with long fish, smoked hams, stuffed fowls, boxes of sprats, pickled savouries of various sorts, and a number of bottles of vodka and wine; there was a smell of smoked sausage and of sour tinned lobster. Old Tsybukin walked about near the tables, tapping with his heels and sharpening the knives against each other. They kept calling Varvara and asking for things, and she was constantly with a distracted face running breathlessly into the kitchen, where the man cook from Kostukov's and the woman cook from Hrymin Juniors' had been at work since early morning. Aksinya, with her hair curled, in her stays without her dress on, in new creaky boots, flew about the yard like a whirlwind showing glimpses of her bare knees and bosom.

It was noisy, there was a sound of scolding and oaths; passers-by stopped at the wide-open gates, and in everything there was a feeling that something extraordinary was happening.

"They have gone for the bride!"

The bells began jingling and died away far beyond the village. . . . Between two and three o'clock people ran up: again there was a jingling of bells: they were bringing the bride! The church was full, the candelabra were lighted, the choir were singing from music books as old Tsybukin had wished it. The glare of the lights and the bright coloured dresses dazzled Lipa; she felt as though the singers with their loud voices were hitting her on the head with a hammer. Her boots and the stays, which she had put on for the first time in her life, pinched her, and her face looked as though she had only just come to herself after fainting; she gazed about without understanding. Anisim, in his black coat with a red cord instead of a tie, stared at the same spot lost in thought, and when the singers shouted loudly he hurriedly crossed himself. He felt touched and disposed to weep. This church was familiar to him from earliest childhood; at one time his dead mother used to bring him here to take the sacrament; at one time he used to sing in the choir; every ikon he remembered so well, every corner. Here he was being married, he had to take a wife for the sake of doing the proper thing, but he was not thinking of that now, he had forgotten his wedding completely. Tears dimmed his eyes so that he could not see the ikons, he felt heavy at heart; he prayed and besought God that the misfortunes that threatened him, that were ready to burst upon him to-morrow, if not to-day, might somehow pass him by as storm-clouds in time of drought pass over the village without yielding one drop of rain. And so many sins were heaped up in the past, so many sins, all getting away from them or setting them right was so beyond hope that it seemed incongruous even to ask forgiveness. But he did ask forgiveness, and even gave a loud sob, but no one took any notice of that, since they all supposed he had had a drop too much.

There was a sound of a fretful childish wail:

"Take me away, mamma darling!"

"Quiet there!" cried the priest.

When they returned from the church people ran after them; there were crowds, too, round the shop, round the gates, and in the yard under the windows. The peasant women came in to sing songs of congratulation to them. The young couple had scarcely crossed the threshold when the singers, who were already standing in the outer room with their music books, broke into a loud chant at the top of their voices; a band ordered expressly from the town began playing. Foaming Don wine was brought in tall wine-glasses, and Elizarov, a carpenter who did jobs by contract, a tall, gaunt old man with eyebrows so bushy that his eyes could scarcely be seen, said, addressing the happy pair:

"Anisim and you, my child, love one another, live in God's way, little children, and the Heavenly Mother will not abandon you."

He leaned his face on the old father's shoulder and gave a sob.

"Grigory Petrovitch, let us weep, let us weep with joy!" he said in a thin voice, and then at once burst out laughing in a loud bass guffaw. "Ho-ho-ho! This is a fine daughter-in-law for you too! Everything is in its place in her; all runs smoothly, no creaking, the mechanism works well, lots of screws in it."

He was a native of the Yegoryevsky district, but had worked in the factories in Ukleevo and the neighborhood from his youth up, and had made it his home. He had been a familiar figure for years as old and gaunt and lanky as now, and for years he had been nicknamed "Crutch." Perhaps because he had been for forty years occupied in repairing the factory machinery he judged everybody and everything by its soundness or its need of repair. And before sitting down to the table he tried several chairs to see whether they were solid, and he touched the smoked fish also.

After the Don wine, they all sat down to the table. The visitors talked, moving their chairs. The singers were singing in the outer room. The band was playing, and at the same time the peasant women in the yard were singing their songs all in chorus—and there was an awful, wild medley of sounds which made one giddy.

Crutch turned round in his chair and prodded his neighbours with his elbows, prevented people from talking, and laughed and cried alternately.

"Little children, little children, little children," he muttered rapidly. "Aksinya my dear, Varvara darling, we will live all in peace and harmony, my dear little axes. . . ."

He drank little and was now only drunk from one glass of English bitters. The revolting bitters, made from nobody knows what, intoxicated everyone who drank it as though it had stunned them. Their tongues began to falter.

The local clergy, the clerks from the factories with their wives, the tradesmen and tavern-keepers from the other villages were present. The clerk and the elder of the rural district who had served together for fourteen years, and who had during all that time never signed a single document for anybody nor let a single person out of the local court without deceiving or insulting him, were sitting now side by side, both fat and well-fed, and it seemed as though they were so saturated in injustice and falsehood that even the skin of their faces was somehow peculiar, fraudulent. The clerk's wife, a thin woman with a squint, had brought all her children with her, and like a bird of prey looked aslant at the plates and snatched anything she could get hold of to put in her own or her children's pockets.

Lipa sat as though turned to stone, still with the same expression as in church. Anisim had not said a single word to her since he had made her acquaintance, so that he did not yet know the sound of her voice; and now, sitting beside her, he remained mute and went on drinking bitters, and when he got drunk he began talking to the aunt who was sitting opposite:

"I have a friend called Samorodov. A peculiar man. He is by rank an honorary citizen, and he can talk. But I know him through and through, auntie, and he feels it. Pray join me in drinking to the health of Samorodov, auntie!"

Varvara, worn out and distracted, walked round the table pressing the guests to eat, and was evidently pleased that there were so many dishes and that everything was so lavish—no one could disparage them now. The sun set, but the dinner went on: the guests were beyond knowing what they were eating or drinking, it was impossible to distinguish what was said, and only from time to time when the band subsided some peasant woman could be heard shouting:

"They have sucked the blood out of us, the Herods; a pest on them!"

In the evening they danced to the band. The Hrymin Juniors came, bringing their wine, and one of them, when dancing a quadrille, held a bottle in each hand and a wineglass in his mouth, and that made everyone laugh. In the middle of the quadrille they suddenly crooked their knees and danced in a squatting position; Aksinya in green flew by like a flash, stirring up a wind with her train. Someone trod on her flounce and Crutch shouted:

"Aie, they have torn off the panel! Children!"

Aksinya had naïve grey eyes which rarely blinked, and a naïve smile played continually on her face. And in those unblinking eyes, and in that little head on the long neck, and in her slenderness there was something snake-like; all in green but for the yellow on her bosom, she looked with a smile on her face as a viper looks out of the young rye in the spring at the passers-by, stretching itself and lifting its head. The Hrymins were free in their behaviour to her, and it was very noticeable that she was on intimate terms with the elder of them. But her deaf husband saw nothing, he did not look at her; he sat with his legs crossed and ate nuts, cracking them so loudly that it sounded like pistol shots.

But, behold, old Tsybukin himself walked into the middle of the room and waved his handkerchief as a sign that he, too, wanted to dance the Russian dance, and all over the house and from the crowd in the yard rose a roar of approbation:

"*He's* going to dance! *He* himself!"

Varvara danced, but the old man only waved his handkerchief and kicked up his heels, but the people in the yard, propped against one another, peeping in at the windows, were in raptures, and for the moment forgave him everything—his wealth and the wrongs he had done them.

"Well done, Grigory Petrovitch!" was heard in the crowd. "That's right, do your best! You can still play your part! Ha-ha!"

It was kept up till late, till two o'clock in the morning. Anisim, staggering, went to take leave of the singers and bandsmen, and gave each of them a new half-rouble. His father, who was not staggering but still seemed to be standing on one leg, saw his guests off, and said to each of them:

"The wedding has cost two thousand."

As the party was breaking up, someone took the Shikalovo innkeeper's good coat instead of his own old one, and Anisim suddenly flew into a rage and began shouting:

"Stop, I'll find it at once; I know who stole it, stop."

He ran out into the street and pursued someone. He was caught, brought back home and shoved, drunken, red with anger, and wet, into the room where the aunt was undressing Lipa, and was locked in.

IV

Five days had passed. Anisim, who was preparing to go, went upstairs to say good-bye to Varvara. All the lamps were burning before the ikons, there was a smell of incense, while she sat at the window knitting a stocking of red wool.

"You have not stayed with us long," she said. "You've been dull, I dare say. Oh, tut, tut. . . . We live comfortably; we have plenty of everything. We celebrated your wedding properly, in good style; your father says it came to two thousand. In fact we live like merchants, only it's dreary. We treat the people very badly. My heart aches, my dear; how we treat them, my goodness! Whether we exchange a horse or buy something or hire a labourer—it's cheating in everything. Cheating and cheating. The Lenten oil in the shop is bitter, rancid, the people have pitch that is better. But surely, tell me pray, couldn't we sell good oil?"

"Every man to his job, mamma."

"But you know we all have to die? Oy, oy, really you ought to talk to your father . . . !"

"Why, you should talk to him yourself."

"Well, well, I did put in my word, but he said just what you do: 'Every man to his own job.' Do you suppose in the next world they'll consider what job you have been put to? God's judgment is just."

"Of course no one will consider," said Anisim, and he heaved a sigh. "There is no God, anyway, you know, mamma, so what considering can there be?"

Varvara looked at him with surprise, burst out laughing, and clasped her hands. Perhaps because she was so genuinely surprised at his words and looked at him as though he were a queer person, he was confused.

"Perhaps there is a God, only there is no faith. When I was being married I was not myself. Just as you may take an egg from under a hen and there is a chicken chirping in it, so my conscience was beginning to chirp in me, and while I was being married I thought all the time there was a God! But when I left the church it was nothing. And indeed, how can I tell whether there is a God or not? We are not taught right from childhood, and while the babe is still at his mother's breast he is only taught 'every man to his own job.' Father does not believe in God, either. You were saying that Guntorev had some sheep stolen. . . . I have found them; it was a peasant at Shikalovo stole them; he stole them, but father's got the fleeces . . . so that's all his faith amounts to."

Anisim winked and wagged his head.

"The elder does not believe in God, either," he went on. "And the clerk and the deacon, too. And as for their going to church and keeping the fasts, that is simply to prevent people talking ill of them, and in case it really may be true that there will be a Day of Judgment. Nowadays people say that the end of the world has come because people have grown weaker, do not honour their parents, and so on. All that is nonsense. My idea, mamma, is that all our trouble is because there is so little conscience in people. I see through things, mamma, and I understand. If a man has a stolen shirt I see it. A man sits in a tavern and you fancy he is drinking tea and no more, but to me the tea is neither here nor there; I see further, he has no conscience. You can go about the whole day and not meet one man with a conscience. And the whole reason is that they don't know whether there is a God or not. . . . Well, good-bye, mamma, keep alive and well, don't remember evil against me."

Anisim bowed down at Varvara's feet.

"I thank you for everything, mamma," he said. "You are a great gain to our family. You are a very ladylike woman, and I am very pleased with you."

Much moved, Anisim went out, but returned again and said:

"Samorodov has got me mixed up in something: I shall either make my fortune or come to grief. If anything happens, then you must comfort my father, mamma."

"Oh, nonsense, don't you worry, tut, tut, tut . . . God is merciful. And, Anisim, you should be affectionate to your wife, instead of giving each other sulky looks as you do; you might smile at least."

"Yes, she is rather a queer one," said Anisim, and he gave a sigh. "She does not understand anything, she never speaks. She is very young, let her grow up."

A tall, sleek white stallion was already standing at the front door, harnessed to the chaise.

Old Tsybukin jumped in jauntily with a run and took the reins. Anisim kissed Varvara, Aksinya, and his brother. On the steps Lipa, too, was standing; she was standing motionless, looking away, and it seemed as though she had not come to see him off but just by chance for some unknown reason. Anisim went up to her and just touched her cheek with his lips.

"Good-bye," he said.

And without looking at him she gave a strange smile; her face began to quiver, and everyone for some reason felt sorry for her. Anisim, too, leaped into the chaise with a bound and put his arms jauntily akimbo, for he considered himself a good-looking fellow.

When they drove up out of the ravine Anisim kept looking back towards the village. It was a warm, bright day. The cattle were being driven out for the first time, and the peasant girls and women were walking by the herd in their holiday dresses. The dun-coloured bull bellowed, glad to be free, and pawed the ground with his forefeet. On all sides, above and below, the larks were singing. Anisim looked round at the elegant white church—it had only lately been whitewashed—and he thought how he had been praying in it five days before; he looked round at the school with its green roof, at the little river in which he used once to bathe and catch fish, and there was a stir of joy in his heart, and he wished that walls might rise up from the ground and prevent him from going further, and that he might be left with nothing but the past.

At the station they went to the refreshment room and drank a glass of sherry each. His father felt in his pocket for his purse to pay.

"I will stand treat," said Anisim. The old man, touched and delighted, slapped him on the shoulder, and winked to the waiter as much as to say, "See what a fine son I have got."

"You ought to stay at home in the business, Anisim," he said; "you would be worth any price to me! I would shower gold on you from head to foot, my son."

"It can't be done, papa."

The sherry was sour and smelt of sealing-wax, but they had another glass.

When old Tsybukin returned home from the station, for the first moment he did not recognize his younger daughter-in-law. As soon as her husband had driven out of the yard, Lipa was transformed and suddenly brightened up. Wearing a threadbare old petticoat, with her feet bare and her sleeves tucked up to the shoulders, she was scrubbing the stairs in the entry and singing in a silvery little voice, and when she brought out a big tub of dirty water and looked up at the sun with her childlike smile it seemed as though she, too, were a lark.

An old labourer who was passing by the door shook his head and cleared his throat.

"Yes, indeed, your daughters-in-law, Grigory Petrovitch, are a blessing from God," he said. "Not women, but treasures!"

V

On Friday the 8th of July, Elizarov, nicknamed Crutch, and Lipa were returning from the village of Kazanskoe, where they had been to a service on the occasion of a church holiday in the honour of the Holy Mother of Kazan. A good distance after them walked Lipa's mother Praskovya, who always fell behind, as she was ill and short of breath. It was drawing towards evening.

"A-a-a . . ." said Crutch, wondering as he listened to Lipa. "A-a! . . . We-ell!"

"I am very fond of jam, Ilya Makaritch," said Lipa. "I sit down in my little corner and drink tea and eat jam. Or I drink it with Varvara Nikolaevna, and she tells some story full of feeling. We have a lot of jam—four jars. 'Have some, Lipa; eat as much as you like.'"

"A-a-a, four jars!"

"They live very well. We have white bread with our tea; and meat, too, as much as one wants. They live very well, only I am frightened with them, Ilya Makaritch. Oh, oh, how frightened I am!"

"Why are you frightened, child?" asked Crutch, and he looked back to see how far Praskovya was behind.

"To begin with, when the wedding had been celebrated I was afraid of Anisim Grigoritch. Anisim Grigoritch did nothing, he didn't ill-treat me, only when he comes near me a cold shiver runs all over me, through all my bones. And I did not sleep one night, I trembled all over and kept praying to God. And now I am afraid of Aksinya, Ilya Makaritch. It's not that she does anything, she is always laughing, but sometimes she glances at the window, and her eyes are so fierce and there is a gleam of green in them—like the eyes of the sheep in the shed. The Hrymin Juniors are leading her astray: 'Your old man,' they tell her, 'has a bit of land at Butyokino, a hundred and twenty acres,' they say, 'and there is sand and water there, so you, Aksinya,' they say, 'build a brickyard there and we will go shares in it.' Bricks now are twenty roubles the thousand, it's a profitable business. Yesterday at dinner Aksinya said to my father-in-law: 'I want to build a brickyard at Butyokino; I'm going into business on my own account.' She laughed as she said it. And Grigory Petrovitch's face darkened, one could see he did not like it. 'As long as I live,' he said, 'the family must not break up, we must go on altogether.' She gave a look and gritted her teeth. . . . Fritters were served, she would not eat them."

"A-a-a! . . ." Crutch was surprised.

"And tell me, if you please, when does she sleep?" said Lipa. "She sleeps for half an hour, then jumps up and keeps walking and walking about to see whether the peasants have not set fire to something, have not stolen something. . . . I am frightened with her, Ilya Makaritch. And the Hrymin Juniors did not go to bed after the wedding, but drove to the town to go to law with each other; and folks do say it is all on account of Aksinya. Two of the brothers have promised to build her a brickyard, but the third is offended, and the factory has been at a standstill for a month, and my uncle Prohor is without work and goes about from house to house getting crusts. 'Hadn't you better go working on the land or sawing up wood, meanwhile, uncle?' I tell him; 'why disgrace yourself?' 'I've got out of the way of it.' he says: 'I don't know how to do any sort of peasant's work now, Lipinka.' . . ."

They stopped to rest and wait for Praskovya near a copse of young aspen-trees. Elizarov had long been a contractor in a small way, but he kept no horses, going on foot all over the district with nothing but a little bag in which there was bread and onions, and stalking along with big strides, swinging his arms. And it was difficult to walk with him.

At the entrance to the copse stood a milestone. Elizarov touched it; read it. Praskovya reached them out of breath. Her wrinkled and always scared-looking face was beaming with happiness; she had been at church to-day like anyone else, then she had been to the fair and there had drunk pear cider. For her this was unusual, and it even seemed to her now that she had lived for her own pleasure that day for the first time in her life. After resting they all three walked on side by side. The sun had already set, and its beams filtered through the copse, casting a light on the trunks of the trees. There was a faint sound of voices ahead. The Ukleevo girls had long before pushed on ahead but had lingered in the copse, probably gathering mushrooms.

"Hey, wenches!" cried Elizarov. "Hey, my beauties!"

There was a sound of laughter in response.

"Crutch is coming! Crutch! The old horseradish."

And the echo laughed, too. And then the copse was left behind. The tops of the factory chimneys came into view. The cross on the belfry glittered: this was the village: "the one at which the deacon ate all the caviare at the funeral." Now they were almost home; they only had to go down into the big ravine. Lipa and Praskovya, who had been walking barefooted, sat down on the grass to put on their boots; Elizar sat down with them. If they looked down from above Ukleevo looked beautiful and peaceful with its willow-trees, its white church, and its little river, and the only blot on the picture was the roof of the factories, painted for the sake of cheapness a gloomy ashen grey. On the slope on the further side they could see the rye—some in stacks and sheaves here and there as though strewn about by the storm, and some freshly cut lying in swathes; the oats, too, were ripe and glistened now in the sun like mother-of-pearl. It was harvest-time. To-day was a holiday, to-morrow they would harvest the rye and carry the hay, and then Sunday a holiday again; every day there were mutterings of distant thunder. It was misty and looked like rain, and, gazing now at the fields, everyone thought, God grant we get the harvest in in time; and everyone felt gay and joyful and anxious at heart.

"Mowers ask a high price nowadays," said Praskovya. "One rouble and forty kopecks a day."

People kept coming and coming from the fair at Kazanskoe: peasant women, factory workers in new caps, beggars, children. . . . Here a cart would drive by stirring up the dust and behind it would run an unsold horse, and it seemed glad it had not been sold; then a cow was led along by the horns, resisting stubbornly; then a cart again, and in it drunken peasants swinging their legs. An old woman led a little boy in a big cap and big boots; the boy was tired out with the heat and the heavy boots which prevented his bending his legs at the knees, but yet blew unceasingly with all his might at a tin trumpet. They had gone down the slope and turned into the street, but the trumpet could still be heard.

"Our factory owners don't seem quite themselves . . ." said Elizarov. "There's trouble. Kostukov is angry with me. 'Too many boards have gone on the cornices.' 'Too many? As many have gone on it as were needed, Vassily Danilitch; I don't eat them with my porridge.' 'How can you speak to me like that?' said he, 'you good-for-nothing blockhead! Don't forget yourself! It was I made you a contractor.' 'That's nothing so wonderful,' said I. 'Even before I was a contractor I used to have tea every day.' 'You are a rascal . . .' he said. I said nothing. 'We are rascals in this world,' thought I, 'and you will be rascals in the next. . . .' Ha-ha-ha! The next day he was softer. 'Don't you bear malice against me for my words, Makaritch,' he said. 'If I said too much,' says he, 'what of it? I am a merchant of the first guild, your superior—you ought to hold your tongue.' 'You,' said I, 'are a merchant of the first guild and I am a carpenter, that's correct. And Saint Joseph was a carpenter, too. Ours is a righteous calling and pleasing to God, and if you are pleased to be my superior you are very welcome to it, Vassily Danilitch.' And later on, after that conversation I mean, I thought: 'Which was the superior? A merchant of the first guild or a carpenter?' The carpenter must be, my child!"

Crutch thought a minute and added:

"Yes, that's how it is, child. He who works, he who is patient is the superior."

By now the sun had set and a thick mist as white as milk was rising over the river, in the church enclosure, and in the open spaces round the factories. Now when the darkness was coming on rapidly, when lights were twinkling below, and when it seemed as though the mists were hiding a fathomless abyss, Lipa and her mother who were born in poverty and prepared to live so till the end, giving up to others everything except their frightened, gentle souls, may have fancied for a minute perhaps that in the vast, mysterious world, among the endless series of lives, they, too, counted for something, and they, too, were superior to someone; they liked sitting here at the top, they smiled happily and forgot that they must go down below again all the same.

At last they went home again. The mowers were sitting on the ground at the gates near the shop. As a rule the Ukleevo peasants did not go to Tsybukin's to work, and they had to hire strangers, and now in the darkness it seemed as though there were men sitting there with long black beards. The shop was open, and through the doorway they could see the deaf man playing draughts with a boy. The mowers were singing softly, scarcely audibly, or loudly demanding their wages for the previous day, but they were not paid for fear they should go away before to-morrow. Old Tsybukin, with his coat off, was sitting in his waistcoat with Aksinya under the birch-tree, drinking tea; a lamp was burning on the table.

"I say, grandfather," a mower called from outside the gates, as though taunting him, "pay us half anyway! Hey, grandfather."

And at once there was the sound of laughter, and then again they sang hardly audibly. . . . Crutch, too, sat down to have some tea.

"We have been at the fair, you know," he began telling them. "We have had a walk, a very nice walk, my children, praise the Lord. But an unfortunate thing happened: Sashka the blacksmith bought some tobacco and gave the shopman half a rouble to be sure. And the half rouble was a false one"—Crutch went on, and he meant to speak in a whisper, but he spoke in a smothered husky voice which was audible to everyone. "The half-rouble turned out to be a bad one. He was asked where he got it. 'Anisim Tsybukin gave it me,' he said. 'When I went to his wedding,' he said. They called the police inspector, took the man away. . . . Look out, Grigory Petrovitch, that nothing comes of it, no talk. . . ."

"Gra-andfather!" the same voice called tauntingly outside the gates. "Gra-andfather!"

A silence followed.

"Ah, little children, little children, little children . . ." Crutch muttered rapidly, and he got up. He was overcome with drowsiness. "Well, thank you for the tea, for the sugar, little children. It is time to sleep. I am like a bit of rotten timber nowadays, my beams are crumbling under me. Ho-ho-ho! I suppose it's time I was dead."

And he gave a gulp. Old Tsybukin did not finish his tea but sat on a little, pondering; and his face looked as though he were listening to the footsteps of Crutch, who was far away down the street.

"Sashka the blacksmith told a lie, I expect," said Aksinya, guessing his thoughts.

He went into the house and came back a little later with a parcel; he opened it, and there was the gleam of roubles—perfectly new coins. He took one, tried it with his teeth, flung it on the tray; then flung down another.

"The roubles really are false . . ." he said, looking at Aksinya and seeming perplexed. "These are those Anisim brought, his present. Take them, daughter," he whispered, and thrust the parcel into her hands. "Take them and throw them into the well . . . confound them! And mind there is no talk about it. Harm might come of it. . . . Take away the samovar, put out the light."

Lipa and her mother sitting in the barn saw the lights go out one after the other; only overhead in Varvara's room there were blue and red lamps gleaming, and a feeling of peace, content, and happy ignorance seemed to float down from there. Praskovya could never get used to her daughter's being married to a rich man, and when she came she huddled timidly in the outer room with a deprecating smile on her face, and tea and sugar were sent out to her. And Lipa, too, could not get used to it either, and after her husband had gone away she did not sleep in her bed, but lay down anywhere to sleep, in the kitchen or the barn, and every day she scrubbed the floor or washed the clothes, and felt as though she were hired by the day. And now, on coming back from the service, they drank tea in the kitchen with the cook, then they went into the barn and lay down on the ground between the sledge and the wall. It was dark here and smelt of harness. The lights went out about the house, then they could hear the deaf man shutting up the shop, the mowers settling themselves about the yard to sleep. In the distance at the Hrymin Juniors' they were playing on the expensive concertina. . . . Praskovya and Lipa began to go to sleep.

And when they were awakened by somebody's steps it was bright moonlight; at the entrance of the barn stood Aksinya with her bedding in her arms.

"Maybe it's a bit cooler here," she said; then she came in and lay down almost in the doorway so that the moonlight fell full upon her.

She did not sleep, but breathed heavily, tossing from side to side with the heat, throwing off almost all the bedclothes. And in the magic moonlight what a beautiful, what a proud animal she was! A little time passed, and then steps were heard again: the old father, white all over, appeared in the doorway

Aksinya," he called, "are you here?"

"Well?" she responded angrily.

"I told you just now to throw the money into the well, have you done so?"

"What next, throwing property into the water! I gave them to the mowers. . . ."

"Oh my God! "cried the old man, dumbfounded and alarmed. "Oh my God! you wicked woman. . . ."

He flung up his hands and went out, and he kept saying something as he went away. And a little later Aksinya sat up and sighed heavily with annoyance, then got up and, gathering up her bedclothes in her arms, went out.

"Why did you marry me into this family, mother?" said Lipa.

"One has to be married, daughter. It was not us who ordained it."

And a feeling of inconsolable woe was ready to take possession of them. But it seemed to them that someone was looking down from the height of the heavens, out of the blue from where the stars were seeing everything that was going on in Ukleevo, watching over them. And however great was wickedness, still the night was calm and beautiful, and still in God's world there is and will be truth and justice as calm and beautiful, and everything on earth is only waiting to be made one with truth and justice, even as the moonlight is blended with the night.

And both, huddling close to one another, fell asleep comforted.

VI

News had come long before that Anisim had been put in prison for coining and passing bad money. Months passed, more than half a year passed, the long winter was over, spring had begun, and everyone in the house and the village had grown used to the fact that Anisim was in prison. And when anyone passed by the house or the shop at night he would remember that Anisim was in prison; and when they rang at the churchyard for some reason, that, too, reminded them that he was in prison awaiting trial.

It seemed as though a shadow had fallen upon the house. The house looked darker, the roof was rustier, the heavy, iron-bound door into the shop, which was painted green, was covered with cracks, or, as the deaf man expressed it, "blisters"; and old Tsybukin seemed to have grown dingy, too. He had given up cutting his hair and beard, and looked shaggy. He no longer sprang jauntily into his chaise, nor shouted to beggars: "God will provide!" His strength was on the wane, and that was evident in everything. People were less afraid of him now, and the police officer drew up a formal charge against him in the shop though he received his regular bribe as before; and three times the old man was called up to the town to be tried for illicit dealing in spirits, and the case was continually adjourned owing to the non-appearance of witnesses, and old Tsybukin was worn out with worry.

He often went to see his son, hired somebody, handed in a petition to somebody else, presented a holy banner to some church. He presented the governor of the prison in which Anisim was confined with a silver glass stand with a long spoon and the inscription: "The soul knows its right measure."

"There is no one to look after things for us," said Varvara. "Tut, tut. . . . You ought to ask someone of the gentlefolks, they would write to the head officials. . . . At least they might let him out on bail! Why wear the poor fellow out?"

She, too, was grieved, but had grown stouter and whiter; she lighted the lamps before the ikons as before, and saw that everything in the house was clean, and regaled the guests with jam and apple cheese. The deaf man and Aksinya looked after the shop. A new project was in progress—a brickyard in Butyokino—and Aksinya went there almost every day in the chaise. She drove herself, and when she met acquaintances she stretched out her neck like a snake out of the young rye, and smiled naïvely and enigmatically. Lipa spent her time playing with the baby which had been born to her before Lent. It was a tiny, thin, pitiful little baby, and it was strange that it should cry and gaze about and be considered a human being, and even be called Nikifor. He lay in his swinging cradle, and Lipa would walk away towards the door and say, bowing to him:

"Good-day, Nikifor Anisimitch!"

And she would rush at him and kiss him. Then she would walk away to the door, bow again, and say:

"Good-day, Nikifor Anisimitch!"

And he kicked up his little red legs, and his crying was mixed with laughter like the carpenter Elizarov's.

At last the day of the trial was fixed. Tsybukin went away five days before. Then they heard that the peasants called as witnesses had been fetched; their old workman who had received a notice to appear went too.

The trial was on a Thursday. But Sunday had passed, and Tsybukin was still not back, and there was no news. Towards the evening on Tuesday Varvara was sitting at the open window, listening for her husband to come. In the next room Lipa was playing with her baby. She was tossing him up in her arms and saying enthusiastically:

"You will grow up ever so big, ever so big. You will be a peasant, we shall go out to work together! We shall go out to work together!"

"Come, come," said Varvara, offended. "Go out to work, what an idea, you silly girl! He will be a merchant . . . !"

Lipa sang softly, but a minute later she forgot and again:

"You will grow ever so big, ever so big. You will be a peasant, we'll go out to work together."

"There she is at it again!"

Lipa, with Nikifor in her arms, stood still in the doorway and asked:

"Why do I love him so much, mamma? Why do I feel so sorry for him?" she went on in a quivering voice, and her eyes glistened with tears. "Who is he? What is he like? As light as a little feather, as a little crumb, but I love him; I love him like a real person. Here he can do nothing, he can't talk, and yet I know what he wants with his little eyes."

Varvara was listening; the sound of the evening train coming in to the station reached her. Had her husband come? She did not hear and she did not heed what Lipa was saying, she had no idea how the time passed, but only trembled all over—not from dread, but intense curiosity. She saw a cart full of peasants roll quickly by with a rattle. It was the witnesses coming back from the station. When the cart passed the shop the old workman jumped out and walked into the yard. She could hear him being greeted in the yard and being asked some questions. . . .

"Deprivation of rights and all his property," he said loudly, "and six years' penal servitude in Siberia."

She could see Aksinya come out of the shop by the back way; she had just been selling kerosene, and in one hand held a bottle and in the other a can, and in her mouth she had some silver coins.

"Where is father?" she asked, lisping.

"At the station," answered the labourer. " 'When it gets a little darker,' he said, 'then I shall come.' "

And when it became known all through the household that Anisim was sentenced to penal servitude, the cook in the kitchen suddenly broke into a wail as though at a funeral, imagining that this was demanded by the proprieties:

"There is no one to care for us now you have gone, Anisim Grigoritch, our bright falcon. . . ."

The dogs began barking in alarm. Varvara ran to the window, and rushing about in distress, shouted to the cook with all her might, straining her voice:

"Sto-op, Stepanida, sto-op! Don't harrow us, for Christ's sake!"

They forgot to set the samovar, they could think of nothing. Only Lipa could not make out what it was all about and went on playing with her baby.

When the old father arrived from the station they asked him no questions. He greeted them and walked through all the rooms in silence; he had no supper.

"There was no one to see about things . . ." Varvara began when they were alone. "I said you should have asked some of the gentry, you would not heed me at the time. . . . A petition would . . ."

"I saw to things," said her husband with a wave of his hand. "When Anisim was condemned I went to the gentleman who was defending him. 'It's no use now,' he said, 'it's too late'; and Anisim said the same; it's too late. But all the same as I came out of the court I made an agreement with a lawyer, I paid him something in advance. I'll wait a week and then I will go again. It is as God wills."

Again the old man walked through all the rooms, and when he went back to Varvara he said:

"I must be ill. My head's in a sort of . . . fog. My thoughts are in a maze."

He closed the door that Lipa might not hear, and went on softly:

"I am unhappy about my money. Do you remember on Low Sunday before his wedding Anisim's bringing me some new roubles and half-roubles? One parcel I put away at the time, but the others I mixed with my own money. When my uncle Dmitri Filatitch—the kingdom of heaven be his—was alive, he used constantly to go journeys to Moscow and to the Crimea to buy goods. He had a wife, and this same wife, when he was away buying goods, used to take up with other men. She had half a dozen children. And when uncle was in his cups he would laugh and say: 'I never can make out,' he used to say, 'which are my children and which are other people's.' An easy-going disposition, to be sure; and so I now can't distinguish which are genuine roubles and which are false ones. And it seems to me that they are all false."

"Nonsense, God bless you."

"I take a ticket at the station, I give the man three roubles, and I keep fancying they are false. And I am frightened. I must be ill."

"I here's no denying it, we are all in God's hands. . . . Oh dear, dear . . ." said Varvara, and she shook her head. "You ought to think about this, Grigory Petrovitch: you never know, anything may happen, you are not a young man. See they don't wrong your grandchild when you are dead and gone. Oy, I am afraid they will be unfair to Nikifor! He has as good as no father, his mother's young and foolish . . . you ought to secure something for him, poor little boy, at least the land, Butyokino, Grigory Petrovitch, really! Think it over!" Varvara went on persuading him. "The pretty boy, one is sorry for him! You go to-morrow and make out a deed; why put it off?"

"I'd forgotten about my grandson," said Tsybukin. "I must go and have a look at him. So you say the boy is all right? Well, let him grow up, please God."

He opened the door and, crooking his finger, beckoned to Lipa. She went up to him with the baby in her arms.

"If there is anything you want, Lipinka, you ask for it," he said.

"And eat anything you like, we don't grudge it, so long as it does you good. . . ." He made the sign of the cross over the baby. "And take care of my grandchild. My son is gone, but my grandson is left."

Tears rolled down his cheeks; he gave a sob and went away. Soon afterwards he went to bed and slept soundly after seven sleepless nights.

VII

Old Tsybukin went to the town for a short time. Someone told Aksinya that he had gone to the notary to make his will and that he was leaving Butyokino, the very place where she had set up a brickyard, to Nikifor, his grandson. She was informed of this in the morning when old Tsybukin and Varvara were sitting near the steps under the birch-tree, drinking their tea. She closed the shop in the front and at the back, gathered together all the keys she had, and flung them at her father-in-law's feet

"I am not going on working for you," she began in a loud voice, and suddenly broke into sobs. "It seems I am not your daughter-in-law, but a servant! Everybody's jeering and saying, 'See what a servant the Tsybukins have got hold of!' I did not come to you for wages! I am not a beggar, I am not a slave, I have a father and mother."

She did not wipe away her tears, she fixed upon her father-in-law eyes full of tears, vindictive, squinting with wrath; her face and neck were red and tense, and she was shouting at the top of her voice.

"I don't mean to go on being a slave!" she went on. "I am worn out. When it is work, when it is sitting in the shop day in and day out, scurrying out at night for vodka—then it is my share, but when it is giving away the land then it is for that convict's wife and her imp. She is mistress here, and I am her servant. Give her everything, the convict's wife, and may it choke her! I am going home! Find yourselves some other fool, you damned Herods!"

Tsybukin had never in his life scolded or punished his children, and had never dreamed that one of his family could speak to him rudely or behave disrespectfully; and now he was very much frightened; he ran into the house and there hid behind the cupboard. And Varvara was so much flustered that she could not get up from her seat, and only waved her hands before her as though she were warding off a bee.

"Oh, Holy Saints! what's the meaning of it?" she muttered in horror. "What is she shouting? Oh, dear, dear! . . . People will hear! Hush. Oh, hush!"

"He has given Butyokino to the convict's wife," Aksinya went on bawling. "Give her everything now, I don't want anything from you! Let me alone! You are all a gang of thieves here! I have seen my fill of it, I have had enough! You have robbed folks coming in and going out; you have robbed old and young alike, you brigands! And who has been selling vodka without a licence? And false money? You've filled boxes full of false coins, and now I am no more use!"

A crowd had by now collected at the open gate and was staring into the yard.

"Let the people look," bawled Aksinya. "I will shame you all! You shall burn with shame! You shall grovel at my feet. Hey! Stepan," she called to the deaf man, "let us go home this minute! Let us go to my father and mother; I don't want to live with convicts. Get ready!"

Clothes were hanging on lines stretched across the yard; she snatched off her petticoats and blouses still wet and flung them into the deaf man's arms. Then in her fury she dashed about the yard by the linen, tore down all of it, and what was not hers she threw on the ground and trampled upon.

"Holy Saints, take her away," moaned Varvara. "What a woman! Give her Butyokino! Give it her, for the Lord's sake!"

"Well! Wha-at a woman!" people were saying at the gate. "She's a wo-oman! She's going it—something like!"

Aksinya ran into the kitchen where washing was going on. Lipa was washing alone, the cook had gone to the river to rinse the clothes. Steam was rising from the trough and from the caldron on the side of the stove, and the kitchen was thick and stifling from the steam. On the floor was a heap of unwashed clothes, and Nikifor, kicking up his little red legs, had been put down on a bench near them, so that if he fell he should not hurt himself. Just as Aksinya went in Lipa took the former's chemise out of the heap and put it in the trough, and was just stretching out her hand to a big ladle of boiling water which was standing on the table.

"Give it here," said Aksinya, looking at her with hatred, and snatching the chemise out of the trough; "it is not your business to touch my linen! You are a convict's wife, and ought to know your place and who you are."

Lipa gazed at her, taken aback, and did not understand, but suddenly she caught the look Aksinya turned upon the child, and at once she understood and went numb all over.

"You've taken my land, so here you are!" Saying this Aksinya snatched up the ladle with the boiling water and flung it over Nikifor.

After this there was heard a scream such as had never been heard before in Ukleevo, and no one would have believed that a little weak creature like Lipa could scream like that. And it was suddenly silent in the yard.

Aksinya walked into the house with her old naïve smile. . . . The deaf man kept moving about the yard with his arms full of linen, then he began hanging it up again, in silence, without haste. And until the cook came back from the river no one ventured to go into the kitchen and see what was there.

VIII

Nikifor was taken to the district hospital, and towards evening he died there. Lipa did not wait for them to come for her, but wrapped the dead baby in its little quilt and carried it home.

The hospital, a new one recently built, with big windows, stood high up on a hill; it was glittering from the setting sun and looked as though it were on fire from inside. There was a little village below. Lipa went down along the road, and before reaching the village sat down by a pond. A woman brought a horse down to drink and the horse did not drink.

"What more do you want?" said the woman to it softly. "What do you want?"

A boy in a red shirt, sitting at the water's edge, was washing his father's boots. And not another soul was in sight either in the village or on the hill.

"It's not drinking," said Lipa, looking at the horse.

Then the woman with the horse and the boy with the boots walked away, and there was no one left at all. The sun went to bed wrapped in cloth of gold and purple, and long clouds, red and lilac, stretched across the sky, guarded its slumbers. Somewhere far away a bittern cried, a hollow, melancholy sound like a cow shut up in a barn. The cry of that mysterious bird was heard every spring, but no one knew what it was like or where it lived. At the top of the hill by the hospital, in the bushes close to the pond, and in the fields the nightingales were trilling. The cuckoo kept reckoning someone's years and losing count and beginning again. In the pond the frogs called angrily to one another, straining themselves to bursting, and one could even make out the words: "That's what you are! That's what you are!" What a noise there was! It seemed as though all these creatures were singing and shouting so that no one might sleep on that spring night, so that all, even the angry frogs, might appreciate and enjoy every minute: life is given only once.

A silver half-moon was shining in the sky; there were many stars. Lipa had no idea how long she sat by the pond, but when she got up and walked on everybody was asleep in the little village, and there was not a single light. It was probably about nine miles' walk home, but she had not the strength, she had not the power to think how to go: the moon gleamed now in front, now on the right, and the same cuckoo kept calling in a voice grown husky, with a chuckle as though gibing at her: "Oy, look out, you'll lose your way!" Lipa walked rapidly; she lost the kerchief from her head . . . she looked at the sky and wondered where her baby's soul was now: was it following her, or floating aloft yonder among the stars and thinking nothing now of his mother? Oh, how lonely it was in the open country at night, in the midst of that singing when one cannot sing oneself; in the midst of the incessant cries of joy when one cannot oneself be joyful, when the moon, which cares not whether it is spring or winter, whether men are alive or dead, looks down as lonely, too. . . . When there is grief in the heart it is hard to be without people. If only her mother, Praskovya, had been with her, or Crutch, or the cook, or some peasant!

"Boo-oo!" cried the bittern. "Boo-oo!"

And suddenly she heard clearly the sound of human speech:

"Put the horses in, Vavila!"

By the wayside a camp fire was burning ahead of her: the flames had died down, there were only red embers. She could hear the horses munching. In the darkness she could see the outlines of two carts, one with a barrel, the other, a lower one with sacks in it, and the figures of two men; one was leading a horse to put it into the shafts, the other was standing motionless by the fire with his hands behind his back. A dog growled by the carts. The one who was leading the horse stopped and said:

"It seems as though someone were coming along the road."

"Sharik, be quiet!" the other called to the dog.

And from the voice one could tell that the second was an old man. Lipa stopped and said:

"God help you."

The old man went up to her and answered not immediately:

"Good-evening!"

"Your dog does not bite, grandfather?"

"No, come along, he won't touch you."

"I have been at the hospital," said Lipa after a pause. "My little son died there. Here I am carrying him home."

It must have been unpleasant for the old man to hear this, for he moved away and said hurriedly:

"Never mind, my dear. It's God's will. You are very slow, lad," he added, addressing his companion; "look alive!"

"Your yoke's nowhere," said the young man; "it is not to be seen."

"You are a regular Vavila."

The old man picked up an ember, blew on it—only his eyes and nose were lighted up—then, when they had found the yoke, he went with the light to Lipa and looked at her, and his look expressed compassion and tenderness.

"You are a mother," he said; "every mother grieves for her child."

And he sighed and shook his head as he said it. Vavila threw something on the fire, stamped on it— and at once it was very dark; the vision vanished, and as before there were only the fields, the sky with the stars, and the noise of the birds hindering each other from sleep. And the landrail called, it seemed, in the very place where the fire had been.

But a minute passed, and again she could see the two carts and the old man and lanky Vavila. The carts creaked as they went out on the road.

"Are you holy men?" Lipa asked the old man.

"No. We are from Firsanovo."

"You looked at me just now and my heart was softened. And the young man is so gentle. I thought you must be holy men."

"Are you going far?"

"To Ukleevo."

"Get in, we will give you a lift as far as Kuzmenki, then you go straight on and we turn off to the left."

Vavila got into the cart with the barrel and the old man and Lipa got into the other. They moved at a walking pace, Vavila in front.

"My boy was in torment all day," said Lipa. "He looked at me with his little eyes and said nothing; he wanted to speak and could not. Holy Father, Queen of Heaven! In my grief I kept falling down on the floor. I stood up and fell down by the bedside. And tell me, grandfather, why a little thing should be tormented before his death? When a grown-up person, a man or woman, are in torment their sins are forgiven, but why a little thing, when he has no sins? Why?"

"Who can tell?" answered the old man.

They drove on for half an hour in silence.

"We can't know everything, how and wherefore," said the old man. "It is ordained for the bird to have not four wings but two because it is able to fly with two; and so it is ordained for man not to know everything but only a half or a quarter. As much as he needs to know so as to live, so much he knows."

"It is better for me to go on foot, grandfather. Now my heart is all of a tremble."

"Never mind, sit still."

The old man yawned and made the sign of the cross over his mouth.

"Never mind," he repeated. "Yours is not the worst of sorrows. Life is long, there will be good and bad to come, there will be everything. Great is mother Russia," he said, and looked round on each side of him. "I have been all over Russia, and I have seen everything in her, and you may believe my words, my dear. There will be good and there will be bad. I went as a delegate from my village to Siberia, and I have been to the Amur River and the Altai Mountains and I settled in Siberia; I worked the land there, then I was homesick for mother Russia and I came back to my native village. We came back to Russia on foot; and I remember we went on a steamer, and I was thin as thin, all in rags, barefoot, freezing with cold, and gnawing a crust, and a gentleman who was on the steamer—the kingdom of heaven be his if he is dead—looked at me pitifully, and the tears came into his eyes. 'Ah,' he said, 'your bread is black, your days are black. . . .' And when

I got home, as the saying is, there was neither stick nor stall; I had a wife, but I left her behind in Siberia, she was buried there. So I am living as a day labourer. And yet I tell you: since then I have had good as well as bad. Here I do not want to die, my dear, I would be glad to live another twenty years; so there has been more of the good. And great is our mother Russia!" and again he gazed to each side and looked round.

"Grandfather," Lipa asked, "when anyone dies, how many days does his soul walk the earth?"

"Who can tell! Ask Vavila here, he has been to school. Now they teach them everything. Vavila!" the old man called to him.

"Yes!"

"Vavila, when anyone dies how long does his soul walk the earth?"

Vavila stopped the horse and only then answered:

"Nine days. My uncle Kirilla died and his soul lived in our hut thirteen days after."

"How do you know?"

"For thirteen days there was a knocking in the stove."

"Well, that's all right. Go on," said the old man, and it could be seen that he did not believe a word of all that.

Near Kuzmenki the cart turned into the high road while Lipa went straight on. It was by now getting light. As she went down into the ravine the Ukleevo huts and the church were hidden in fog. It was cold, and it seemed to her that the same cuckoo was calling still.

When Lipa reached home the cattle had not yet been driven out; everyone was asleep. She sat down on the steps and waited. The old man was the first to come out; he understood all that had happened from the first glance at her, and for a long time he could not articulate a word, but only moved his lips without a sound.

"Ech, Lipa," he said, "you did not take care of my grandchild. . . ."

Varvara was awakened. She clasped her hands and broke into sobs, and immediately began laying out the baby.

"And he was a pretty child . . ." she said. "Oh, dear, dear. . . . You only had the one child, and you did not take care enough of him, you silly girl. . . ."

There was a requiem service in the morning and the evening. The funeral took place the next day, and after it the guests and the priests ate a great deal, and with such greed that one might have thought that they had not tasted food for a long time. Lipa waited at table, and the priest, lifting his fork on which there was a salted mushroom, said to her:

"Don't grieve for the babe. For of such is the kingdom of heaven."

And only when they had all separated Lipa realized fully that there was no Nikifor and never would be, she realized it and broke into sobs. And she did not know what room to go into to sob, for she felt that now that her child was dead there was no place for her in the house, that she had no reason to be here, that she was in the way; and the others felt it, too.

"Now what are you bellowing for?" Aksinya shouted, suddenly appearing in the doorway; in honour of the funeral she was dressed all in new clothes and had powdered her face. "Shut up!"

Lipa tried to stop but could not, and sobbed louder than ever.

"Do you hear?" shouted Aksinya, and she stamped her foot in violent anger. "Who is it I am speaking to? Go out of the yard and don't set foot here again, you convict's wife. Get away."

"There, there, there," the old man put in fussily. "Aksinya, don't make such an outcry, my girl. . . . She is crying, it is only natural . . . her child is dead. . . ."

" 'It's only natural,' " Aksinya mimicked him. "Let her stay the night here, and don't let me see a trace of her here to-morrow! 'It's only natural!'. . ." she mimicked him again, and, laughing, she went into the shop.

Early the next morning Lipa went off to her mother at Torguevo.

IX

At the present time the steps and the front door of the shop have been repainted and are as bright as though they were new, there are gay geraniums in the windows as of old, and what happened in Tsybukin's house and yard three years ago is almost forgotten.

Grigory Petrovitch is looked upon as the master as he was in old days, but in reality everything has passed into Aksinya's hands; she buys and sells, and nothing can be done without her consent. The brickyard is working well; and as bricks are wanted for the railway the price has gone up to twenty-four roubles a thousand; peasant women and girls cart the bricks to the station and load them up in the trucks and earn a quarter-rouble a day for the work.

Aksinya has gone into partnership with the Hrymin Juniors, and their factory is now called Hrymin Juniors and Co. They have opened a tavern near the station, and now the expensive concertina is played not at the factory but at the tavern, and the head of the post office often goes there, and he, too, is engaged in some sort of traffic, and the stationmaster, too. Hrymin Juniors have presented the deaf man Stepan with a gold watch, and he is constantly taking it out of his pocket and putting it to his ear.

People say of Aksinya that she has become a person of power; and it is true that when she drives in the morning to her brickyard, handsome and happy, with the naïve smile on her face, and afterwards when she is giving orders there, one is aware of great power in her. Everyone is afraid of her in the house and in the village and in the brickyard. When she goes to the post the head of the postal department jumps up and says to her:

"I humbly beg you to be seated, Aksinya Abramovna!"

A certain landowner, middle-aged but foppish, in a tunic of fine cloth and patent leather high boots, sold her a horse, and was so carried away by talking to her that he knocked down the price to meet her wishes. He held her hand a long time and, looking into her merry, sly, naïve eyes, said:

"For a woman like you, Aksinya Abramovna, I should be ready to do anything you please. Only say when we can meet where no one will interfere with us!"

"Why, when you please."

And since then the elderly fop drives up to the shop almost every day to drink beer. And the beer is horrid, bitter as wormwood. The landowner shakes his head, but he drinks it.

Old Tsybukin does not have anything to do with the business now at all. He does not keep any money because he cannot distinguish between the good and the false, but he is silent, he says nothing of this weakness. He has become forgetful, and if they don't give him food he does not ask for it. They have grown used to having dinner without him, and Varvara often says:

"He went to bed again yesterday without any supper."

And she says it unconcernedly because she is used to it. For some reason, summer and winter alike, he wears a fur coat, and only in very hot weather he does not go out but sits at home. As a rule putting on his fur coat, wrapping it round him and turning up his collar, he walks about the village, along the road to the station, or sits from morning till night on the seat near the church gates. He sits there without stirring. Passers-by bow to him, but he does not respond, for as of old he dislikes the peasants. If he is asked a question he answers quite rationally and politely, but briefly.

There is a rumour going about in the village that his daughter-in-law turns him out of the house and gives him nothing to eat, and that he is fed by charity; some are glad, others are sorry for him.

Varvara has grown even fatter and whiter, and as before she is active in good works, and Aksinya does not interfere with her.

There is so much jam now that they have not time to eat it before the fresh fruit comes in; it goes sugary, and Varvara almost sheds tears, not knowing what to do with it.

They have begun to forget about Anisim. A letter has come from him written in verse on a big sheet of paper as though it were a petition, all in the same splendid handwriting. Evidently his friend Samorodov was sharing his punishment. Under the verses in an ugly, scarcely legible handwriting there was a single line: "I am ill here all the time; I am wretched, for Christ's sake help me!"

Towards evening—it was a fine autumn day—old Tsybukin was sitting near the church gates, with the collar of his fur coat turned up and nothing of him could be seen but his nose and the peak of his cap. At the other end of the long seat was sitting Elizarov the contractor, and beside him Yakov the school watchman, a toothless old man of seventy. Crutch and the watchman were talking.

"Children ought to give food and drink to the old. . . . Honour thy father and mother . . ." Yakov was saying with irritation, "while she, this daughter-in-law, has turned her father-in-law out of his own house; the old man has neither food nor drink, where is he to go? He has not had a morsel for these three days."

"Three days!" said Crutch, amazed.

"Here he sits and does not say a word. He has grown feeble. And why be silent? He ought to prosecute her, they wouldn't flatter her in the police court."

"Wouldn't flatter whom?" asked Crutch, not hearing.

"What?"

"The woman's all right, she does her best. In their line of business they can't get on without that . . . without sin, I mean. . . ."

"From his own house," Yakov went on with irritation. "Save up and buy your own house, then turn people out of it! She is a nice one, to be sure! A pla-ague!"

Tsybukin listened and did not stir.

"Whether it is your own house or others' it makes no difference so long as it is warm and the women don't scold . . ." said Crutch, and he laughed. "When I was young I was very fond of my Nastasya. She was a quiet woman. And she used to be always at it: 'Buy a house, Makaritch! Buy a house, Makaritch! Buy a house, Makaritch!' She was dying and yet she kept on saying, 'Buy yourself a racing droshky, Makaritch, that you may not have to walk.' And I bought her nothing but gingerbread."

"Her husband's deaf and stupid," Yakov went on, not hearing Crutch; "a regular fool, just like a goose. He can't understand anything. Hit a goose on the head with a stick and even then it does not understand."

Crutch got up to go home to the factory. Yakov also got up, and both of them went off together, still talking. When they had gone fifty paces old Tsybukin got up, too, and walked after them, stepping uncertainly as though on slippery ice.

The village was already plunged in the dusk of evening and the sun only gleamed on the upper part of the road which ran wriggling like a snake up the slope. Old women were coming back from the woods and children with them; they were bringing baskets of mushrooms. Peasant women and girls came in a crowd from the station where they had been loading the trucks with bricks, and their noses and their cheeks under their eyes were covered with red brick-dust. They were singing. Ahead of them all was Lipa singing in a high voice, with her eyes turned upwards to the sky, breaking into trills as though triumphant and ecstatic that at last the day was over and she could rest. In the crowd was her mother Praskovya, who was walking with a bundle in her arms and breathless as usual.

"Good-evening, Makaritch!" cried Lipa, seeing Crutch. "Good-evening, darling!"

"Good-evening, Lipinka," cried Crutch delighted. "Dear girls and women, love the rich carpenter! Ho-ho! My little children, my little children. (Crutch gave a gulp.) My dear little axes!"

Crutch and Yakov went on further and could still be heard talking. Then after them the crowd was met by old Tsybukin and there was a sudden hush. Lipa and Praskovya had dropped a little behind, and when the old man was on a level with them Lipa bowed down low and said:

"Good-evening, Grigory Petrovitch."

Her mother, too, bowed down. The old man stopped and, saying nothing, looked at the two in silence; his lips were quivering and his eyes full of tears. Lipa took out of her mother's bundle a piece of savoury turnover and gave it him. He took it and began eating.

The sun had by now set: its glow died away on the road above. It grew dark and cool. Lipa and Praskovya walked on and for some time they kept crossing themselves.

1900

A NOTE ON THE TYPE

The principal text of this Modern Library edition
was set in a digitized version of Janson,
a typeface that dates from about 1690 and was cut by Nicholas Kis,
a Hungarian working in Amsterdam. The original matrices have
survived and are held by the Stempel foundry in Germany.
Hermann Zapf redesigned some of the weights and sizes for Stempel,
basing his revisions on the original design.